W9-AUZ-719

SECOND EDITION

Applying Career Development Theory to Counseling

Richard S. Sharf
University of Delaware

Brooks/Cole Publishing Company
I(T)P® An International Thomson Publishing Company

Pacific Grove • Albany • Belmont • Bonn • Boston • Cincinnati • Detroit
Johannesburg • London • Madrid • Melbourne • Mexico City
New York • Paris • Singapore • Tokyo • Toronto • Washington

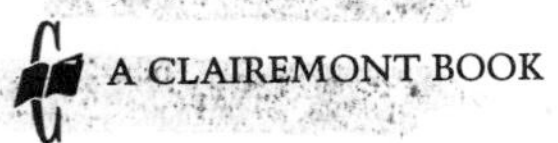

Sponsoring Editor: *Eileen Murphy*
Marketing Team: *Jean Thompson, Margaret Parks*
Editorial Assistant: *Lisa Blanton*
Production Editor: *Keith Faivre*
Permissions Editor: *Mary Kay Hancharick*
Interior and Cover Design: *Roy R. Neuhaus*
Art Editor and Interior Illustration: *Kathy Joneson*
Typesetting: *Bookends Typesetting*
Cover Printing: *Phoenix Color Corporation*
Printing and Binding: *Quebecor Printing–Fairfield*

For more information, contact:

BROOKS/COLE PUBLISHING COMPANY
511 Forest Lodge Road
Pacific Grove, CA 93950
USA

International Thomson Publishing Europe
Berkshire House 168-173
High Holborn
London WC1V 7AA
England

Thomas Nelson Australia
102 Dodds Street
South Melbourne, 3205
Victoria, Australia

Nelson Canada
1120 Birchmount Road
Scarborough, Ontario
Canada M1K 5G4

International Thomson Editores
Seneca 53
Col. Polanco 11560
México D.F. México

International Thomson Publishing GmbH
Königswinterer Strasse 418
53227 Bonn
Germany

International Thomson Publishing Asia
221 Henderson Road
#05-10 Henderson Building
Singapore 0315

International Thomson Publishing Japan
Hirakawacho Kyowa Building, 3F
2-2-1 Hirakawacho
Chiyoda-ku, Tokyo 102
Japan

Printed in the United States of America

10 9 8 7 6 5 4 3

Library of Congress Cataloging-in-Publication Data

Sharf, Richard S.
Applying career development theory to counseling / Richard S. Sharf.—2nd ed.
Includes bibliographical references and index.
ISBN 0-534-34503-4
1. Vocational guidance. 2. Career development. I. Title.
HF5381.S515 1996
158.6—dc20 96-18526
CIP

In loving memory of my mother, Edith Sycle Sharf
In loving appreciation of my father, Nathaniel Sharf

Brooks/Cole Titles of Related Interest

Taking Charge of Your Career Direction, Third Edition
by Robert D. Lock (1996)

Job Search, Third Edition
by Robert D. Lock (1996)

Student Activities for *Taking Charge of Your Career Direction,* Third Edition, and *Job Search,* Third Edition
by Robert D. Lock (1996)

Discover the Career Within You, Fourth Edition
by Clark G. Carney and Cinda Field Wells (1995)

Career Guide: Road Maps to Meaning in the World of Work
by Gary Lynn Harr (1995)

Changing Careers: Steps to Success
by Lola Sikula (1994)

Career Counseling: Applied Concepts of Life Planning, Fourth Edition
by Vernon G. Zunker (1994)

Using Assessment Results for Career Development, Fourth Edition
by Vernon G. Zunker (1994)

Occupational Information Overview
by Richard S. Sharf (1993)

Career Development and Services: A Cognitive Approach
by Gary W. Peterson, James P. Sampson, Jr.,
and Robert C. Reardon (1991)

Preface

Students taking a beginning graduate course in career guidance, career theory, or career counseling want to know how to assist clients with career concerns. This book will help them relate career theory and research to the practice of counseling, aiding them in their practicum, their internship, and their jobs as counselors. In this second edition of *Applying Career Development Theory to Counseling,* I show how each career development theory can be used in counseling. Each theory gives special insight into various perspectives on career development as it affects career counseling. Furthermore, the theories organize facts into a comprehensible system for students to understand and use, rather than overwhelm them with unrelated lists of information.

Case examples are a special feature of this book. For each theory and its significant constructs, one or more cases are used to illustrate the conceptual approach of the theory. The examples are given in a dialogue between counselor and client. In the dialogue, the counselor's conceptualization follows most counselor statements and is indicated by brackets. This approach provides a direct application of the theory to counseling practice, making the book useful to both students and practicing counselors. In a few places, narrative descriptions of cases are used to illustrate theories.

New to the second edition are several significant additions. The introduction (Chapter 1) has been expanded to emphasize personal factors in career counseling, so that students can see how personal problems and career problems are intertwined. Also, counseling skills that are particularly important in applying career development theory to counseling and that are used in the case examples are explained in Chapter 1. Since the early 1990s, there has been considerable research on the career development concerns of women and people of color. In almost every chapter, I have been able to expand the section on women and people of color as a result of these new investigations. Added to Chapter 13, "Social Learning Theory," is a section on career self-efficacy theory, which has been the subject of much recent research and has significant implications for counseling women and people of color. Chapter 12, "Parental Influence Theories," has been broadened to include ideas from attachment theory and family therapy, as well as the ideas of Anne Roe. More information on occupational classification systems has been added to Chapter 2, "Trait and Factor Theory," and material describing the role of education and the impact of gender and race on the labor force has been added to Chapter 15, "The Labor Market: Sociological and Economic Perspectives." Some instructors may choose to assign Chapter 15 to follow Chapter 2, so that students may focus on occupational information in one section of the course. Other instructors may decide to assign Chapter 15 near the end of the course to emphasize the contrast between psychological approaches to career development and sociological or economic approaches. Each chapter in this second edition has been revised to reflect the results of new research and changes in the theory, where there have been changes.

SPECIAL CONSIDERATIONS IN EACH CHAPTER

Each career development theory is discussed in terms of its implication for using occupational information, for using tests, and for special issues that may affect the application of the theory. Some theories use an occupational classification system; others specify how occupational information can be used in counseling. Yet other theories have relatively little to say about the use of occupational information. Since occupational information (and educational information) is such an important part of career counseling, special efforts are made to link theory and career information. Many theories use tests and inventories both as a means of researching career development theory and as tools for the counselor to use in helping clients assess themselves. This book focuses on tests as they relate to theories and does not assume knowledge of testing issues, such as reliability and validity. Also, career development theories provide insight into possible conflicts between counselor values and client values, which will present problems to the counselor. Further, the application of some career development theories presents other difficulties. Considering the problems in applying theory, occupational information, and testing can help students select the career development theories that will help them most in their work as counselors.

In each chapter, a section addresses the application of theories of career development to women and to people of color. Theories vary greatly in how they address the issues of women. For example, Gottfredson's career development theory deals very specifically with the career issues of women. Other theories deal only tangentially with women's career choice issues. Many career development theories were originally created for white males and were later expanded to include women and people of color. Some research that has studied the career development issues of people of color can be related to a variety of career theories. This is a particularly difficult issue to address because of the wide variety of cultural groups and the differences within cultural groups. For example, there are many significant cultural differences between Native American tribal groups. Also, some career development issues may be different for African Americans and for black people in other countries. For individuals with disabilities or same-sex sexual preferences, the application of the theories in this book should be considered appropriate.

CONTENTS OF THIS BOOK

This book is divided into an introduction and four parts: "Trait and Type Theories," "Life-Span Theory," "Special Focus Theories," and "Theoretical Integration." Trait and type theories emphasize the assessment of interests, abilities, achievements, personality, and values, along with the acquisition of occupational information. Life-span theory follows a chronological approach, studying people across four broad stages in the life span. Special focus theories include the application to career development issues of research in psychology, such as psychodynamic theory and learning theory. Part Three also includes contributions from sociology and economics. Part Four deals with how these theories can be combined for effective career counseling. The last chapter also discusses the relevance of career development theories to special issues such as noncounseling interventions, group counseling, job placement, and other concerns. Each chapter is briefly described in Chapter 1 on page 19–20.

COURSE APPLICATION

This book is intended for a beginning graduate course of which career issues are a major component. The book can be used differently, depending on whether the emphasis of the course is on career counseling, career testing, career guidance, or career theory.

Whereas most books that describe career counseling describe one method or many components of methods, this book presents a number of different theoretical and conceptual approaches to career counseling. After studying these various approaches to career counseling, the student can decide which theories will be most helpful to him or her in counseling work. In general, the chapters are independent of each other, and not all chapters need be assigned. Since trait and factor theory represents a straightforward approach to career choice and adjustment, it is often an appropriate starting place.

The assignment of career tests and inventories, along with their manuals, can be combined with the use of this book. Table 16-1 on pages 436–437 lists the tests that this book refers to and the theory with which they are associated. Trait and factor theories make the most use of tests and inventories, and life-span theory, decision-making theory, social learning theory, and psychodynamic approaches make less direct use of them. Many tests and inventories may be assigned along with Part One and before any of the appropriate chapters.

The focus of this book is on career counseling, not on instructional guidance programs for the classroom. One reason is that, when counselors are first employed, they are likely to be assigned counseling functions rather than responsibilities for guidance programs. When they work on guidance programs, they are usually supervised by someone who has established a system for introducing career materials into the classroom. Although classroom activities and career education are mentioned in Part Two, their discussion is limited. However, this book will provide a background for designing guidance activities and programs.

This text combines career development theory with suggestions for using and understanding theory in counseling. Instructors may use the material in the order that suits them. Some may prefer to assign Chapter 11 ("Psychodynamic Approaches to Career Development") and Chapter 12 ("Parental Influence Theories") before discussing life-span theory, because these chapters emphasize the importance of early child development in career development. The assignment of chapters is likely to depend on the emphasis preferred by the instructor.

SUPPLEMENTS

To provide instructors with materials that they may use in the classroom and to assist in preparation of lectures and examinations, I have greatly expanded the instructor's manual. I have included numerous discussion questions for each chapter as well as suggestions for role playing of counseling in class. For examinations, I have prepared 440 multiple choice questions (not available in the previous edition of the manual). Also, I have expanded the number of essay questions that instructors may draw from. Included also are 94 transparency masters that instructors may use in their classroom presentations. I believe that all of these materials will help instructors use *Applying Career Development Theory to Counseling,* Second Edition, in teaching career development and career counseling courses. Some instructors may find that the materials I have provided will suggest other classroom exercises, transparencies, or examination questions that they may wish to develop for their own purposes.

ACKNOWLEDGMENTS

Many people have been extremely helpful in reading one or more chapters of the book. I would like to thank the following people who have read and commented on the second edition of this book: LeeAnn Eschbach of the

University of Scranton, Greg Jackson of California State University–Northridge, Cindy Juntunen of the University of North Dakota, Lewis Patterson of Cleveland State University, Margaret Pinder of Amber University, Paul Salomone of Syracuse University, and Mitchell Young of Northeast Louisiana University. I would also like to thank David A. Jepsen of the University of Iowa, Michelle M. Simko, and Jane L. Winer of Texas Tech University, who read the entire first edition. Karen J. Forbes of Lafayette College and Matthew R. Elliott of Holy Cross College read several early chapters, making suggestions for the ultimate form that the book would take. The following people read, commented on, or supplied materials for chapters in this book: Kimberly M. Ewing, James E. Hoffman, Lawrence Hotchkiss, Janice Jordan, Charles Link, Mary C. Miller, and Steven M. Sciscione, of the University of Delaware; Gail Hackett of the University of Arizona; John L. Holland; and John D. Krumboltz of Stanford University. The comments of the following reviewers of the first edition were also helpful: Edward S. Bordin of the University of Michigan, Thomas G. Carskadon of Mississippi State University, Rene V. Dawis of the University of Minnesota, Helen Farmer of the University of Illinois, Milton M. Foreman of the University of Cincinnati, Jerald Forster of the University of Washington, Robert Hill of the University of Utah, Patricia W. Lunneborg, Mark L Savickas of Northeastern Ohio Universities College of Medicine, and Michael Smith of McGill University. I would also like to thank Florence Baron for typing the first edition of the book and Lisa Sweder for typing the second edition. Both Cindy Carroll and Elizabeth Parisan provided additional secretarial support. Finally, I would like to thank my wife, Jane, and my children, Jennie and Alex, for their patience and understanding when this book was being prepared.

Richard S. Sharf

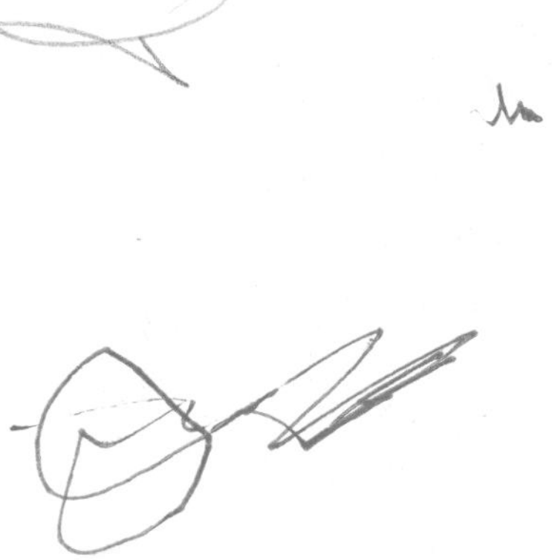

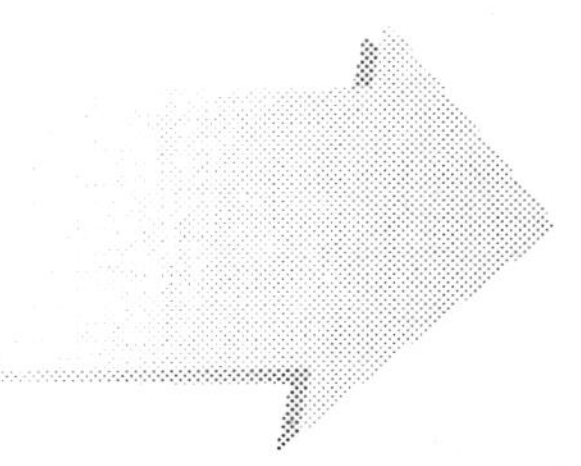

Brief Contents

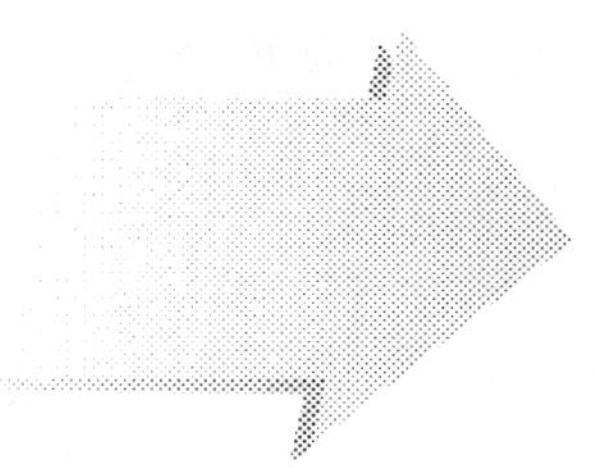

Contents

CHAPTER 8 Adolescent Career Development 177

CHAPTER 9 Late Adolescent and Adult Career Development 207

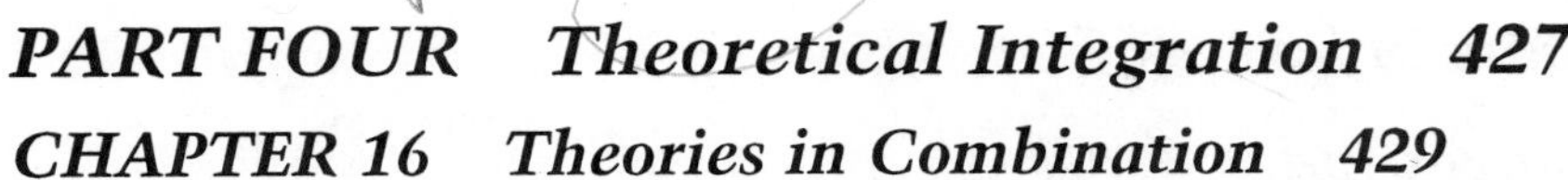

1

Introduction

Being satisfied with one's career is one of the most important aspects of an individual's personal happiness. Career concerns occur throughout one's lifetime. As young children are exposed to their parents' occupations, television programs, and the people around them, they become aware of career opportunities and choices. This exposure becomes broader and deeper throughout elementary school, junior high school, and high school. It is difficult for students not to be overwhelmed by the many occupations and choices around them. After high school, temporary and transitional occupations are often chosen, with continued adjustment throughout one's life span to increase career satisfaction. During retirement, questions of career satisfaction continue to be important. Since approximately one-half of a person's waking hours are spent working, dissatisfaction with career demands can spread into other parts of one's life. It is not uncommon for job dissatisfaction to affect relationships with one's family and friends. People who are dissatisfied with their work or find it boring or monotonous must look for satisfaction to other areas of their lives, such as leisure and family. For many people, however, these other satisfactions do not compensate for frustrations at work. The opportunity to help someone adjust to a selected career is an opportunity to affect a person's life positively, in meaningful and significant ways.

The knowledge that several hours spent in counseling can greatly influence the outcome of an individual's life is an exciting challenge to the counselor. Individuals unfamiliar with career counseling have sometimes compartmentalized counseling by saying there is personal counseling, and then there is career counseling. In editing a special section of *The Career Development Quarterly* (Volume 42, No. 2, 1993), Linda Subich (1993) asked the question "How personal is career counseling?" She received 32 submissions, of which 10 were published. The clear, virtually unanimous answer was "Very personal."

These respondents recognized that personal issues pervade career counseling, and that career issues are often prominent in personal counseling, thus making the distinction between the two moot. For example, Krumboltz (1993) showed that career and personal concerns are intertwined, in many cases, and that there are strong emotional components within career counseling that counselors should address. Also, Davidson and Gilbert (1993) stated that personal identity is a part of an individual's career development and that personal issues affect career development and vice versa. Croteau and Thiel (1993) also addressed the personal aspects of career counseling by giving examples of how sexual orientation affects career development. With exemplary insight, Lucas (1993) showed how family and development issues affected her career counseling of three clients. In a study comparing the level of psychological distress of clients who presented career concerns and of clients who presented noncareer concerns, Gold and Scanlon (1993) found that the level of psychological distress was equivalent, but that those who reported career concerns received fewer sessions of counseling. Another way of seeing the relationship between personal and career counseling is to examine Spokane's (1991) three-phase model of career intervention, which is drawn from the literature on psychotherapy. These experienced counselors and therapists pointed out the personal nature of career counseling from many different vantage points. Because career issues do not always have the immediate impact on counselors that negative or stressful events or feelings may have, career issues may be neglected or dismissed if they are not examined thoroughly.

In this text, numerous case examples are used to illustrate the application of career development theory to counseling. Most of the examples have personal as well as career components. Winifred, in Chapter 3, is a 45-year-old farmer who is faced with the difficulty of changing jobs after experiencing chronic back pain. Chester (Chapter 4), is a high school dropout whose boredom and frustration with his life and work are affecting his personal life. George (Chapter 5) is tense and anxious at work and has difficulty dealing with his supervisees. Arthur (Chapter 7), a fourth-grader, is starting to fall behind in school, is withdrawing from his peers, and is frustrated by reading. Personal issues confront Harold (Chapter 8) as he decides between selling drugs and staying in school to prepare for a career. Matthew (Chapter 9) is 64 and confused and afraid as he faces retirement. Having been laid off from a job that he has had for 23 years, John, who is 55, is angry and depressed (Chapter 10). The trauma of sexual harassment and racial discrimination forces Roberta (Chapter 10) to deal with her anger and the perpetrators. Carlotta (Chapter 12), 26, is facing career crises as she makes decisions about graduate school. Her reactions are affected by her early parental relationships and her sense of responsibility for her family. A senior in high school, Susan is trying to make plans about what to do after graduation as she deals with her mother's terminal cancer (Chapter 14). This is a sampling of some of the cases that appear in this book, many concerned with both personal and career issues.

Life issues and problems occur at many different times. The developmental nature of career concerns can be seen in the case of Lucy, who is discussed in Chapters 7, 8, and 9. As a fifth-grader, she is upset about her mother's forcing her father out of the house, and her reaction affects her interactions at school and in the family. At 15, the pressures on Lucy from her father and a boyfriend to go to nursing school rather than to medical school are affecting her self-confidence and causing confusion. At 28, Lucy is hurting from the breakup of a three-year relationship and is deciding whether to return to school to become a physician. These personal and career issues are intertwined, as they are for many clients.

The term *career* refers to how individuals see themselves in relationship to what they do. The case studies presented offer snapshots of a person's career or an aspect of a person's working and leisure behavior. The National Career Development Association (Sears, 1982) defines the term *career* as the individual's work and leisure that take place over her or his life span. In this text, *career choice* applies to decisions that individuals make at any point in their career about particular work or leisure activities that they choose to pursue at that time. The focus is on the individual, in contrast to the terms *job* and *occupation.* In this text, jobs refers to positions requiring similar skills within one organization. *Occupation* refers to similar jobs found in many organizations. Occupations exist regardless of whether individuals are employed in them. *Career* refers to the lifetime pursuits of the individual.

Career development theory can serve as a guide for career counseling, and for problems similar to those previously described. By tying together research about career choice and adjustment with ideas about these issues, career development theorists have provided a conceptual framework within which to view the types of career problems that emerge during a person's lifetime. To understand these theories, it is first important to understand the role of theory in psychology.

THE ROLE OF THEORY IN PSYCHOLOGY

In reviewing the role of theory in psychology, Heinen (1985) describes theory as "a group of logically organized laws or relationships that constitute explanation in a discipline" (p. 414). Theory has been particularly important in the development of physical and biological science. Within psychology, theory has made a distinct impact in the area of learning. When applied to career development, theory becomes more crude and less precise. Career development theory attempts to explain behavior that occurs over many years and is made up of reactions to thousands of experiences and situations such as school, hobbies, and parents.

Regardless of the type of theory, there are certain general principles for judging the appropriateness of a theory. The following are criteria by which career development theories can be evaluated (Fawcett & Downs, 1986; Marx, 1951; Snow, 1973).

1. *Theories should be explicit about their rules and theorems. Terms that are used in describing these rules should be clear.* Theories that attempt to explain how people make career choices often have difficulty in defining terms such as *growth, development,* and *self-concept.* Theorems about career selection are also difficult to make. In general, the broader the theory, the more difficult it is to be specific about the terms that are used.

2. *Theories should be precise about the limitations of their predictions. Theories differ in the breadth of behavior that they attempt to predict.* For example, some theories attempt to explain career development for women, some for both men and women, and some for people of different age groups. Some theories attempt to explain vocational choice, while others try to explain how people adjust to this choice; still others explain both. It is important to understand what the subject of the theory is. It is unfair to criticize a theory for failing to do something that it does not set out to do.

3. *When theories are developed, they need to be tested. This is accomplished by doing research that can be expressed in terms of quantitative relationships. By doing research studies that use clear and measurable terms, investigators can best determine if data are in agreement with the theory.* Within the field of career development, it is sometimes difficult to determine whether or not research supports a theory. The reason may be that an investigator has defined terms in a different way from the theorist or has used an unrepresentative sample to make predictions or generalizations. For example, if a theorist attempts to explain how all people make choices, the research samples should include both men and women, regardless of race, education, and income. Sometimes evidence from a research study is unclear, supporting some propositions of a theory but not others, or supporting the theory for some populations but not others. A helpful method for confirming theoretical constructs is the development of inventories that define constructs and relate them to other constructs within the theory as well as to other theories and instruments. By the accumulation of such information, construct validity is established for the theory and the instrument.

4. *A theory needs to be consistent and clear.* A theory should provide constructs that have a logical relationship to each other. To be clear, the theory should not be too complex. It should provide the simplest way to explain propositions. On the other hand, there is the danger of oversimplification. Essential components should not be left out of a theory. Because vocational theorists attempt to explain exceedingly complex behavior, it is only natural that they may oversimplify their theories. In doing so, they may provide a useful and understandable guide for the counselor.

In summary, a theory needs to be explicit about its theorems and terms. Further, it needs to be clear about what it is theorizing and the breadth of its propositions. In addition, research should be able to provide positive or negative support for the theory. Sometimes research findings add to and develop a theory, showing that it is open to change. Also, a theory, while being neither too simple nor too complex, must provide a useful way of explaining and understanding career development.

Judgments about the soundness and relative utility of theories are difficult for the counselor to make. Authors such as Osipow and Fitzgerald (1995), and Brown and Brooks (1996) attempt to evaluate how well career development theories meet criteria similar to those described above. While research will receive comment, the primary focus of this book is on the application of the theory by the counselor. All theories that have been included were determined by me to meet, at least minimally, the four criteria just listed.

COUNSELORS' USE OF CAREER DEVELOPMENT THEORY

To select a theory of career development, counselors must not only have confidence in the theory as described in the previous section but also make judgments about the advisability of using that theory with their clients. Further, counselors need to consider their own view and style of counseling or psychotherapy. Their theory of counseling is likely to influence their selection of a theory of career development. Still further, the counselor needs to select a theory of career development that is manageable and relatively easy to draw upon in a counseling session. These three concepts are discussed in more detail in the following paragraphs.

Client Population

Counselors work in a wide variety of settings and are likely to encounter a preponderance of one or another type of career problem. For example, elementary and junior high school counselors work with students who are at the very beginning of the career information and selection process. High school and college counselors tend to help their clients with vocational choice, development of alternatives, and job placement. Employment counselors, although they deal with some of the same issues as high school and college counselors, may encounter more issues related to satisfaction with and adjustment to a job. Some counselors work in business and industry with a limited number of professions, such as accounting and engineering. These counselors are likely to be involved in issues of work satisfaction, adjustment, and promotion. Vocational rehabilitation counselors and other counselors who work with clients with physical and mental disabilities deal not only with the issues mentioned previously but must also judge the applicability of the theory to the disabilities of their clientele. Moreover, retirement issues have become a greater concern of counselors in recent years. Choosing new, part-time, or volunteer work and scaling down the demands of current work are issues that retirement counselors must consider. Pastoral counselors, physicians, clinical psychologists, and psychiatrists work in settings where their clients may have career choice or adjustment issues that are related to other problems. Although career concerns may not be the presenting problem of the client for these and other mental health workers, they may still be significant issues. Further, the gender of the client can be an important variable in theory selection. Counselors must ask themselves if a theory is as appropriate for females as males. Since career development theories differ in the populations that they choose to explain, it is for the counselor to decide whether a particular career development theory is appropriate for the population with which he or she works.

Theories of Counseling and Theories of Career Development

Like counseling theories, many theories of career development are derived from theories of personality. Often it is difficult to distinguish theories of counseling and theories of career development clearly from theories of personality. In general, counseling and psychotherapy theories tend to be a subset of personality theory used to bring about a desired change in feeling, thinking, or behavior. Similarly, many theories of career development tend to be a subset of personality theories, which include how people relate to work and career issues. Therefore, since personality, counseling, and career development theory are highly interrelated, it is natural for counselors who prefer a certain personality theory or theory of counseling to be drawn to a similar career development theory.

Because theories of personality and counseling form the core of a counselor's training, they tend to influence the counselor's selection of a theory of career development. Rarely would the selection of a theory of career development determine a counselor's theory of personality or career counseling. For example, counselors who are influenced by psychoanalytic theory or developmental theory are apt to find psychodynamic career development theories particularly appropriate. Those attracted to Jungian theory may wish to use the Myers-Briggs theory of types. Those counselors who employ rational emotive behavior therapy, behavioral therapy, or cognitive therapy may find trait and factor theory, Holland's theory of types, and social learning approaches to be particularly helpful. Many counselors are eclectic in their practical orientation; that is, they may draw from many theories. Although it is helpful to be open to the value of all theories of career development, it is important to remember the connection between career development theory and counseling theory. The theories presented in this book differ in terms of how similar they are to theories of personality, a few being quite different.

Chunking

The concept of chunking is important for counselors to consider when selecting a theory of career development. Unlike computers, counselors have a limited ability to store information. Psychologists have studied the limited capacity of both short-term and long-term memory. In studying short-term memory, Miller (1956) suggested that people can process five to nine concepts, ideas, numbers, words, or sentences at a time. This processing is done by grouping concepts or ideas and is called *chunking*. In reviewing the literature, Simon (1974) examined a number of different verbal learning areas, basically supporting the findings of Miller. Challenging Miller's findings, Broadbent (1975) suggested that the number 3 was the basic unit of memory. Trying to reconcile the views of Miller and Broadbent, MacGregor (1987) suggested individuals sometimes chunk or group information into three items and other times chunk into seven items.

The concept of chunking has been extended beyond the field of human learning. Swann, Pelham, and Roberts (1987) applied the concept to remembering the offensive and defensive social behavior of another person. Hackman (1983) gave examples of the presentation of institutional research in chunks to make data more meaningful to decision makers. Ye and Salvendy (1994) find subtle differences between the chunking of novice and experienced computer programmers. Age differences do not appear to be a factor in chunking activity (Allen & Crozier, 1992). Investigators in several fields of psychology have found the concept of chunking useful in demonstrating the capacity of human memory (Baddeley, 1994).

There is value in applying the concept of chunking to the use of career development theory in career counseling. Theories that have three or four basic constructs are likely to be learned relatively easily. Theories with up to eight or nine concepts may be remembered and used with some difficulty, depending on how often the concepts are reused in counseling. Theories with more than eight or nine concepts are likely to present a retention problem for the counselor when he or she is starting to put a theory into practice. One solution is to divide the theory into several chunks. In discussing theories that have a large number of constructs, I will attempt to suggest meaningful subdivisions or chunks of concepts. It is important to do this, as counselors need to learn information about a number of subjects, such as helping skills, career testing, and occupational information, when assisting clients in career decision making.

COUNSELOR SKILLS

The primary purpose of this book is to describe the usefulness of career development theory in counseling people with problems of career selection and adjustment. Information about theories can be combined with helping skills, which are based primarily on the early work of Carl Rogers (1951). Further, the use of occupational information as found in pamphlets and books and on computers is a necessary component of career counseling. Since the 1940s, career testing has also been an integral part of this type of counseling. These three areas of knowledge—helping skills, occupational information, and testing—are described in the following paragraphs in terms of their relationship to career development theory.

Helping Skills

Since the early 1980s, a number of books have described helping skills. The authors of these books appear to agree generally on the helping skills necessary for change in most counseling situations, including career counseling. Their work is based on the precepts of Carl Rogers (1958), which specify four basic conditions necessary for counseling change: unconditional positive regard, genuineness, congruence, and empathy. Unconditional positive regard can be described as the acceptance of a person as being worthwhile and valuable, regardless of age, sex, race, or what he or she has done. Genuineness refers to sincerity—the need for the counselor to be honest with the client. Congruence requires that the counselor's voice tone, body language, and verbal statements be consistent with one another. Finally, empathy refers to the ability to communicate to the client that the counselor understands the client's concerns and feelings from the point of view of the client. These four basic conditions have become the cornerstone of research involving over 260 studies.

Truax and Carkhuff (1967) and Carkhuff and Berenson (1967) have done considerable research to further define and develop Rogers's work. Recently, authors such as Brammer (1993), Egan (1994), Gazda et al. (1995), Ivey (1994), Martin and Moore (1995), and Okun (1992) have provided methods for learning the basic or core helping skills. In addition, these writers have emphasized (to varying degrees) other important skills such as asking open-ended and nonbiased questions. Besides discussing, paraphrasing and reflecting feelings (basic empathic listening skills), these writers explain important issues of confrontation and the need for concreteness and specificity. The authors just listed provide texts for courses in basic counseling skills or helping relationships. A detailed explanation of these skills goes beyond the scope of this book. However, I describe the most common interventions and counseling techniques that are likely to be used in career counseling. Many of these interventions are used in the case examples that are found throughout this book.

Attending Skills A basic counseling skill is the counselor's nonverbal presence in the counseling situation. In an attending position, counselors face their clients squarely, adopting an open posture (legs and arms not crossed) and leaning slightly toward the other person. Maintaining good eye contact, not staring, is natural for people who are having a deep conversation. Counselors also maintain a relaxed, rather than tense or fidgety, presence. These skills are used primarily in North America when addressing clients. In other cultures, people may show attentiveness in other ways (Egan, 1994).

Questions Questions are used to get specific information or to help clients describe or elaborate on certain subjects, feelings, or events. Closed-ended questions request specific information, and the answers are often of the "yes" or "no" variety. Open-ended questions encourage a broader response, asking the client to explain more fully the what, how, when, or where of a situation, feeling, or event. Both are illustrated in this dialogue:

CO: What grade did you get in English last year? [Closed-ended question]
CL: I got an "A."
CO: Did you like the class? [Closed-ended question]
CL: Yes. It was OK.
CO: What did you learn about in class? [Open-ended question]
CL: We studied modern writers, and I learned how to critique short stories. I was surprised that my ability to develop a good paragraph really changed during the course. My teacher was very helpful and complimented me about my progress.
CO: How does that affect your thoughts about college? [Open-ended question]
CL: It really gets me thinking. I hadn't known that I could write that well. The short reviews we did in class really made me more comfortable with writing and made me think, "Hey, I can do more of this." I could even do it in college.

As shown here, open-ended questions usually elicit a much broader explanation from the client than do closed-ended questions. Questions, in general, and especially closed-ended questions tend to place the burden of the interview on the counselor. In a sense, if questions are used frequently, clients develop an expectation that if they answer the questions the counselor will provide a solution to the problem. In this book, questions are used very sparingly in the case examples, in which the counselors are much more apt to use reflections of client statements.

Statements and Reflections By rephrasing what the client has said, counselors focus on the cognitive or emotional content of a client's statement. When a client makes a statement, restating it directs attention to the situation, the person, or the general idea. The client is thus encouraged to add or to develop his or her statement. Restatements may reflect not only the words of the client, but also the voice tone, gestures, and facial expression. Because information and affect are attached to career issues, it is often helpful to make content and feeling reflections. Feeling reflections contain an emotional word or phrase (or imply it). Content reflections focus on the information that the client provides.

CL: My work is so boring. All I do is wait on one customer after another. I ring up the sale. Give the customer the receipt. Ring up the sale. Give the customer the receipt. And on and on.

Content reflection: Each day you perform the same actions over and over again.

Feeling reflection: Waiting on customers is really boring you and annoying you. You can't wait till the day is over.

In this situation, the content reflection tells only a small part of the story. The feeling reflection provides a fuller expression of the client's experience. In the cases in this book, when feeling or emotional content is provided in the client's response, the counselor response usually reflects the affective component. Content reflections tend to be used mainly when the counselor perceives little affect.

Continuation Responses Often, in career counseling (and other counseling), it is helpful to request more information. A nonverbal gesture such as nodding or using a hand movement invites a client to continue. Verbal comments include "Tell me more," "Can you say more about that?" "Go on," "Hmm," "And then?" and "And what happened then?" A brief example will clarify:

CO: What are your plans for next year? [Open-ended question]

CL: I think that I'm going to work in the department store's hardware department. I've done it for three years, and it's easy to continue to do so. Besides, I really think I need to get more money before I can continue college.

CO: Say more about that, if you would. [Continuation]

CL: It's easy to stay in the hardware department. I know it really well, but I'm not getting very far with it. Sometimes, I think I should go back to school anyway, even though I don't have the money, and just hope things will work out.

CO: Hmm. Tell me more. [Continuation]

CL: I don't think that I have the money, but maybe I can get my father to take out a loan. He really doesn't want to, but if I'm really persuasive, maybe he can help me. It sure would be better than having to be back in that old job.

When discussing career issues, continuation techniques bring out more information than the client may volunteer at first. The career development theories in this book focus on the client as an important informational resource about himself or herself. Thus, continuation responses are frequently seen in the examples.

Giving Information, Not Opinion Often, counselors give clients information about educational or occupational opportunities. It is important that this information be accurate, up to date, and clear. Biased information can be destructive and confusing to the client. Opinions that are given by the counselor represent only one person's view. However, because clients are likely to view counselors as experts, the counselors' opinions may be perceived as being information or *the truth.* Counselors who give opinions risk discouraging or encouraging a client inappropriately.

CL: Now, after I've completed my first year of college, I have a "C" average. I'm not sure whether I should revise my plans to go to medical school.

Opinion 1: I think that you should revise your plans. Students with a "C" average have little chance of getting into medical school.

Opinion 2: Things are likely to get better. You still have a chance to pull your grades up and probably get into medical school.

Information: What do you think about your chances of getting into medical school? [The counselor wants to know what is the basis of the client's information.]

CL: I realize that most students have to have an "A–" average to go to medical school, but I think I can raise my grades.

Information: You may find it helpful to go to the premed adviser to get more information about how students have done here in getting into medical school. [The counselor does not have the specific information that the client needs at hand but directs the client to a source.]

Although individuals with a "C" average in their freshman year in college may find it difficult to be admitted to medical school, there are some exceptions. The counselor assumes a powerful role if she or he gives Opinions 1 or 2. The theories that are covered in this book assume that the client, rather than the counselor, is the decision maker, thus providing guidance for career decision making.

Reinforcement A behavioral technique, verbal reinforcement of the client's behavior is often used in career counseling. This technique is particularly featured in Chapter 13, where social learning theory is described. In verbal reinforcement, it is the client's behavior that is reinforced, rather than the client.

CL: I've been wanting to tell my boss that he's been giving me too many assignments lately. I've really been afraid to do so, and I've been really anxious. I'm afraid that he will be really mad at me and tell me I'll have to leave my job. This is something I don't want to do. It's a great job otherwise. This has bugged me so much that I've been losing sleep over it and I'm really starting to feel depressed. Finally, I got up the courage and talked to my boss and told him exactly what it was that was bothering me. He was understanding, and I was really relieved.

CO: That's terrific. You did something that you have wanted to do for quite a while. You explained the problem, explained the difficulties, and you got satisfaction. That's wonderful.

If the client had said, "I told my boss all these things, and he got really angry." The counselor might have replied, "You did what you wanted to do.

You explained the problem to him specifically, and told him how it was bothering you. It's great that you were able to do so. It's too bad that he didn't respond the way you wanted him to." In both cases, the counselor is reinforcing the client's behavior. A common behavior that counselors reinforce is information seeking. For example, when a client has read about or talked to people in a particular profession, counselors may say, "That's terrific that you spent so much time in finding out about that. Great!"

Family Background Exploration The chapters on psychodynamic approaches to career development (11) and parental influence theories (12) discuss ways of exploring the role of parenting in career decision making. For example, the genogram—a method of diagramming family relationships—is a tool for discussing the relationship of clients' career plans to those of their families.

Test and Inventory Interpretation An important career-counseling intervention is test interpretation. Discussed particularly in the theories that are explained in Part One, test interpretation provides information about the client to the client. In interpreting tests or inventories for clients, counselors use many of the skills that have just been described. Throughout the book, examples of test interpretation are given for interest, ability, value, and personality tests and inventories. Some of the specific knowledge that is needed to make accurate test interpretations is discussed briefly in the next section of this chapter. Test interpretation, like many of the techniques described here, is helpful in career counseling. Other techniques, such as confrontation, self-disclosure, and counselor interpretations, can also be helpful and are described in some of the texts mentioned previously.

Career development theories, for the most part, do not specify counseling techniques. Rather, they provide a way of comprehending and organizing the information that is contained in counseling sessions. The tools that produce this information are the content and feeling reflections, open-ended questions, and other techniques mentioned previously. Career development theory, which only indirectly affects the technique used, aids the counselor in understanding the client. It is likely that the counselors using trait and factor theory will ask more questions and will use fewer feeling reflections than those who employ Super's life-span theory. However, this does not have to be the case. The focus of this book is making use of career development theory in conceptualizing career counseling when assisting a client.

Testing

The term *test* refers generally to ability and achievement tests on which there are correct answers, and on which individuals perform as well as possible ("maximum performance"). The term *inventory* refers to instruments that solicit a preference or viewpoint from the counselee and have no "right" or "wrong" answers; individuals perform at typical levels. Common inventories used in counseling measure interests, values, and personality. Career development theories differ on the weight they give to the importance of tests and inventories in the career development process. Tests and inventories have been in wide use for career counseling since the 1930s and 1940s. Extensive test development took place during World War II because of the need to assign men and women to the military tasks for which they were best suited. Although originally designed for the selection of employees, tests and inventories have been particularly useful in counseling. To be competent in test selection, counselors need to understand measurement and concepts such as validity, reliability, and normative information. Because these concepts are so important in understanding testing, they will be described briefly here. However, this description does not take the place of a course or text on psychological measurement.

Norms It is useful to compare a client's score on a test with a normative sample (norms) that is used in developing a standard for scoring. Such a sample should be normal scores, those that are typical of a population. Sometimes, norms are based on a general population and, at other times, on specific groups, such as high school students, accountants, or former drug abusers. In some cases, norms are listed separately for males and females; in other cases, they are combined. Norms are also sometimes separated for people of different races or ages. Good norms are helpful in providing counselors a full understanding of the basis of the comparisons that they will make. For example, a counselor would not want to compare a 12th-grade client's biology achievement score with the scores of 9th-graders. Although national norms are frequently used, it is sometimes helpful to have local norms, so as to compare students within a school system or a state. Norms are typically presented in percentile scores, which are easy to understand because counselors can see the percentage of individuals above or below a particular score. Often, standard scores are used because, unlike percentile scores, they provide for a uniform difference between each score. Thus, the difference between 50 and 55 is the same as the difference between 70 and 75, which is not true of percentages. Reading a test manual to learn about norms and to decide, where appropriate, which norms to use is important for counselors who wish to use the tests or inventories that are described in this book.

Reliability To be used, a test must be dependable and consistent. If a student takes a test one time, the score that he or she receives a second time should be similar. A test that has perfect reliability would be one on which everyone's scores were in the same relative position on every additional administration of the test. There are two major sources of unreliability:

variation in human performance and variation in the technical aspects of measurement. For example, a measurement of math ability should be more stable than a measure of depression, which varies according to mood. Error may be due to the testing conditions, such as lighting, heat or cold, and poor instructions. On many tests, the reliability coefficients usually exceed .80, but there are some situations in which an acceptable reliability may be less. Reliability may be measured by administering the same test on two different occasions or two different forms of the same test on different occasions. Split-half reliability is obtained by dividing a single test into two comparable halves and comparing the results from the two halves. Yet another measure is interitem consistency, which is arrived at by examining the average intercorrelations among the items on a test. Knowledge of the reliability of an instrument is important in deciding whether to use it with clients.

Validity Does a test measure what it is supposed to measure? Does a measure of English skills really measure skills in English? How well a test measures what is requested of it is referred to as *validity.* For a test to be valid, it must first be reliable; that is, it must be a consistent measure of a trait or other variable. Different types of scales require different types of validity. *Content validity* refers to the actual content of the items. Do the items reflect the area, such as knowledge of algebra, that the test is attempting to measure. *Concurrent validity* is a measure against a specific criterion. For example, scores on a test of clerical ability can be compared to the performance of secretaries who have established clerical abilities. *Predictive validity* also refers to a criterion, but in the future. For example, does a test of clerical aptitude predict how well applicants for secretarial positions will perform on clerical aspects of their positions in a year? *Construct validity* is more complex, referring to whether or not the scales make psychological sense and are related to the variables that they should be related to. A test of depression should be related to other tests of depression or psychiatric ratings of depressed people on specific symptoms of depression. Test manuals provide the counselor with information on these types of validity. A test that is not valid has little value for the counselor. In this book, many tests are mentioned, and all have at least moderate validity in some, but not all, of the four types of validity described here.

Testing plays two major roles in career development theory. First, tests can be used to develop and verify a theory. Second, tests can provide the counselor with information that can then be used as a means of understanding the client from the point of view of career development theory. For example, John Holland developed and used the Self-Directed Search and the Vocational Preference Inventory as a way to test the constructs of his theory. Another example is Super's career development theory. Donald Super developed the Values Scale and the Career Development Inventory, among many other inventories; other investigators have developed career maturity scales, all of which can be used to test various aspects of Super's theory. Counselors can use these instruments to develop knowledge about the client that they can then relate directly to a theoretical context.

For the counselor, tests and inventories have three major features: selection, administration, and interpretation. Norms, reliability and validity are important considerations in deciding which tests to select. Test selection may also be based on theoretical concepts that are relevant to the counselees, which will be discussed further in this text. Administration is described in detail in each test manual, and different considerations apply to individual and group test-taking procedures. Interpreting a test requires a knowledge of both the client and the test or inventory. In this text, examples of test interpretation are given to show how a counselor might discuss portions of test results with a client.

Providing Occupational Information

Career counseling differs from other types of counseling in its reliance on occupational and educational information. Hoppock (1976) describes in detail the information that counselors should know about occupations and the importance of occupational information in counseling. Hoppock believes that counselors should

- Know where their clients get their first jobs or where their clients go to work after they've completed counseling.
- Determine the principal employment opportunities in their local area. The geographic area within which college students search for jobs is likely to be much larger than for high school students, who are more likely to look for work close to home.
- Learn about occupations that are being considered by their clients, so they can provide information appropriate for their clients.
- Learn about at least one occupation that is central to each of three of the most important and largest local employers. This will entail visiting and developing contacts with these employers.
- Know how to obtain information and to evaluate it for accuracy and usefulness.

Essentially, counselors need to know certain types of information and specific sources of career information. The types of information that are perhaps most important (Sharf, 1984) include descriptions of the occupation, working conditions, qualifications required by the job duties, beginning and average salaries, the employment outlook, the education (courses, majors, or degree) required by the job, and where one can get more information about the occupation. Answers to these questions are provided in publications such as the *Occupational Outlook Handbook* (1996) and the *Encyclopedia of Careers and Vocational Guidance* (Hopke, 1993). These publications offer occupational information about a broad and representative sample of occupations. In addition, pamphlets produced by publishers specializing in occupation information and by trade organizations describe hundreds of occupations that are available. Textbooks and courses on occupational information deal fully with these topics and are helpful for effective career counseling. Furthermore, a number of computerized guidance products such as DISCOVER and SIGI PLUS provide occupational information along with career assessment.

Career development theories vary widely in the attention that they pay to occupational information. For example, Holland's theory provides a system for classifying all occupational information through the use of six categories. Holland provides an identifiable code for each occupation that has clear meaning according to his theory. On the other hand, the Myers-Briggs theoretical formulation focuses almost entirely on the person's type and not on occupational information. Super and his colleagues (Starishevsky & Matlin, 1963) used the term *occtalk* to describe occupational information that clients learn; they used the term *psychtalk* to delineate the views that clients have of themselves. For instance, "It is helpful for musicians to know a number of instruments" is an example of occtalk; "I enjoy learning music theory" is an example of psychtalk. This example illustrates how theorists built a bridge between occupational information and information about the client from a counseling interview. Although occupational information is described in this chapter, it is explained in detail in Chapter 2 as a means of classifying careers, and in Chapter 15 as a way of viewing the labor market. Classifying occupations and learning about the labor market are two important aspects of occupational information.

How Career Development Theory Relates

Just as counseling theories provide a framework for the conceptualization of client problems, career development theory provides a framework for helping with a client's career problems. Career development theory can be considered the part of the process of career counseling that offers a means of conceptualizing career concerns. Basic helping skills are the essential ingredient in bringing about change and progress in career issues. Tests and inventories, as well as occupational information, can be seen as additional information that aids in the conceptualization process. Counseling skills are used to provide feedback about tests and inventories or to give information about occupations. Overall, it is career development theory that can give counselors an idea of how they are going to help their clients and what the eventual outcome of counseling may be. The goal-directedness that career development theory can provide gives counselors, particularly beginning counselors, a sense of confidence.

GOALS OF CAREER COUNSELING

The two most common goals of career counseling are the selection of an occupation and the adjustment to an occupation. Normally, career selection takes place anytime after the age of 14, but most commonly during high school and/or college. When helping a client in the process of choosing occupations, counselors often use information about the client's satisfaction with any previous work. When adults are trying to find more satisfaction in an occupation, they often question their current career choice and review their reasons for seeking that occupation. This may happen at any time during a person's working life. Some theorists, such as Dawis and Lofquist (1984), focus on vocational adjustment as well as vocational selection. Implicit in all career development theories is the notion that the client, rather than the counselor, makes the final choice.

Goals, whether explicit or implicit, are essential to counseling. Goals serve as a guide for the work that is done in the counseling session. An example of making goals explicit is when the counselor and the client agree that the purpose of counseling is to select from appropriate career alternatives. An example of making goals implicit is when the counselor assumes that the client wishes to select appropriate career alternatives. Whether the goals are explicit or implicit, the use of career development theories can make goals clear and specific for the counselor.

For each theory in this book, methods of conceptualizing theoretical constructs in terms of counseling goals will be described to the extent that the theory permits. A counselor using theoretical constructs in conceptualizing client goals should have a sense of how well the counseling is progressing, what (in general) should happen next in the counseling, and what needs to take place for the counseling to be completed. These goals and their implementation may not be identical for all people. Research on the career development of women and people of color has provided information that has changed the way many of the theories can be conceptualized for these groups.

CAREER DEVELOPMENT OF WOMEN

Some career development theories were created before 1960 and were based solely on research on white males from middle-class or upper-middle-class families. Although most of these theories have since incorporated women into their sampling and theoretical statements, career development theorists have been criticized for their neglect of women's career development issues. The role of women in work has changed greatly since the early 1960s. Because women represent over half the population of the United

States and of the world, it is particularly important to illustrate the application of career development theories to women.

In this book, each chapter has a section dealing with applications of theory to career counseling issues for women. In some cases, this section is quite brief, as the theory may not be sufficiently detailed and researched to include information about women. In other cases, especially life-span and career self-efficacy theory, much space is devoted to career development issues for women, as well as to examples of counselor conceptualizations of client concerns. Theories of women's life-span career development are incorporated into Part Two. There is approximately equal representation of men and women in the case examples illustrating career development theory.

CAREER DEVELOPMENT OF PEOPLE OF COLOR

While there are only two sexes, there are many cultures. No theories of career development have been formulated to apply specifically to one race or another. However, research has been done on the applicability of particular career development theories to specific cultural groups. When this research will help in understanding the context of the theory for a particular group, it is presented.

Within the field of career development, more research has been done on African Americans than on other people of color. Some research has also studied the career development of Hispanics, Asians, and Native Americans, but even these groups do not represent uniform cultural backgrounds. For example, Asians include Japanese, Chinese, Vietnamese, Cambodians, and East Indians, as well as many other nationalities. Within each of these nationalities, there are groups that may have little in common with each other. For example, there are many regions in India that do not share a common language, religion, or social customs. Immigrants to the United States may come as refugees from wars. Many Vietnamese people have come to the United States seeking employment. Discussion of these different cultures is beyond the scope of this book and can be found in other sources (for example, Atkinson, Morten, & Sue, 1989; Sue, 1981), although their emphasis is not on career or employment issues. This book gives some examples of the conceptualization of career development issues when counseling people from some of these cultures, but it is not possible to include examples from all cultures.

In this book, the term *people of color* is used to designate non-Caucasian people. The term *minority* is reserved for people who represent a minority of a given population. Worldwide, people of color are a majority, and Caucasians are a minority.

WHAT'S AHEAD

The theories described in this book are grouped into four parts: type and trait theories, life-span theory, special focus theories, and theoretical integration. Part One deals with characteristics or types of people, focusing on the behavior and concerns of a person at the present moment. Chapter 2 discusses the earliest formal theory of career development: trait and factor theory. This theory deals with the study of interests, values, aptitudes, and other traits that are used in assisting clients with career decisions. In Chapter 3, Lofquist and Dawis's theory focusing on adult adjustment to work is detailed. The fourth chapter describes John Holland's typology of people and environments, including an explanation of the six Holland types and their application to career counseling. Another typology, based on Carl Jung's approach to personality theory, is the focus of Chapter 5, featuring the Myers-Briggs view of personality types as it affects career development.

Part Two includes life-span theories, introduced in Chapter 6. Unlike Parts One and Three, in which each chapter describes a specific theory, Part Two focuses on four aspects of life-span development: childhood (Chapter 7), early adolescence (Chapter 8), late adolescence and adulthood (Chapter 9), and adult career crises and career transitions (Chapter 10). This format is followed for several reasons. Super's life-span theory is more developed than other life-span theories, having produced much more research and instrumentation. Most other life-span theories do not cover the entire life span. Further, the conceptualization of career counseling is similar among all life-span theories. In Chapters 7, 8, and 9, Super's theory is used as the basis for explaining career development concepts. Other theories are used to add to Super's work, particularly as it relates to the career development of women and people of color. In Chapter 10, Hopson and Adams's theory of adult transitions is used to discuss career crises. It is placed within the context of Super's life-span theory.

In Part Three, additional theories emphasize various aspects of career development. Chapter 11 describes Bordin's psychodynamic concept of play and work, Erikson's concept of identity issues in adolescence, and Adler's view of early childhood experience and society as they affect later choice and adjustment. Parental influence on career choice, along with Roe's classification of occupations, is explained in Chapter 12. Krumboltz's behavioral approach to career decision making, along with career self-efficacy theory, both based on social learning theory, is described in Chapter 13. How one makes career decisions and styles of career decision making are examined by contrasting the work of Tiedeman and Miller-Tiedeman with that of Gati in Chapter 14. As described in Chapter 15, sociologists and economists have developed broad views of career development. These views focus on the effect of societal expectations of individuals, as well as stereotypes of women and minorities and their impact on employment. This research examines the importance of family, school, and the work setting in the career decision-making process.

The final part (Chapter 16) shows counselors how to integrate several theories in their counseling conceptualization. Examples of how this integration can take place, depending on the work setting and the counselor's theoretical preferences, are given. Also, special issues, such as the use of computer guidance programs, career group counseling, and job placement counseling, are discussed.

Each chapter follows the same format. The first part of the chapter describes a specific theory and its important constructs. Integrated into the description of the theories is information about counseling strategies, with examples of how to conceptualize client concerns by using theoretical constructs. Brief dialogues between counselor and client, which include counselor conceptualizations, illustrate the application of each career development theory. The use of dialogue enables readers to learn about the thought process a counselor goes through to conceptualize a client problem. Occasionally, case studies are also used. Included in each chapter is a discussion of how the theory incorporates testing and occupational information. Applicability to women and people of color is also described, with reference to reviews of the literature and to general research findings. Another section of each chapter deals with counselor problems in applying the theory, including feelings and thoughts that counselors may have that interfere in applying a particular theoretical approach. After reading each chapter, readers should have a clear idea of how to think about client problems by using a particular theory.

There are several ways readers can apply the information in this book to make it more meaningful for them. Readers who counsel clients can try to picture a client and think about his or her presenting concerns in terms of a particular theory. Another approach is to think of one's own life or that of friends or family in terms of the theory. For students, an effective way of integrating career development theory into counseling is to role-play counseling situations with other students, using a particular theoretical orientation. All of these approaches are likely to make the material seem more helpful and exciting.

References

Allen, P. A., & Crozier, L. C. (1992). Age and ideal chunk size. *Journals of Gerontology, 47,* 47–51.

Atkinson, D. R., Morten, G., & Sue, D. W. (1989) *Counseling American minorities: A cross-cultural perspective* (3rd ed.). Dubuque, IA: William C. Brown.

Baddeley, A. (1994). The magical number seven: Still magic after all these years? *Psychological Review, 101,* 353–356.

Brammer, L. M. (1993). *The helping relationship: Process and skills* (5th ed.). Boston: Allyn & Bacon.

Broadbent, D. E. (1975). The magic number seven after fifteen years. In A. Kennedy & A. Wilkes (Eds.), *Studies in long term memory* (pp. 3–18). London: Wiley.

Brown, D., & Brooks, L. (Eds.). (1990). *Career choice and development* (2nd ed.). San Francisco: Jossey-Bass.

Carkhuff, R., & Berenson, B. (1967). *Beyond counseling and therapy.* New York: Holt, Rinehart & Winston.

Croteau, J. M., & Thiel, M. J. (1993). Integrating sexual orientation in career counseling: Acting to end a form of the personal-career dichotomy. *The Career Development Quarterly, 42,* 174–179.

Davidson, S. L., & Gilbert, L. A. (1993). Career counseling is a personal matter. *The Career Development Quarterly, 42,* 149–153.

Dawis, R. V., & Lofquist, L. H. (1984). *A psychological theory of work adjustment.* Minneapolis: University of Minnesota Press.

Egan, G. (1994). *The skilled helper* (5th ed.). Pacific Grove, CA: Brooks/Cole.

Fawcett, J., & Downs, F. S. (1986). *The relationship of theory and research.* Norwalk, CT: Appleton-Century-Crofts.

Gazda, G. M., Asbury, F. S., Balzer, F. J., Childers, W. C., Phelps, R. E., & Walters, R. P. (1995). *Human relationship development: A manual for educators* (5th ed.). Boston: Allyn & Bacon.

Gold, J. M., & Scanlon, C. R. (1993). Psychological distress and counseling duration of career and noncareer clients. *The Career Development Quarterly, 42,* 186–191.

Hackman, J. D. (1983). Seven maxims for institutional researchers: Applying cognitive theory and research. *Research in Higher Education, 18,* 195–208.

Heinen, J. R. (1985). A primer on psychological theory. *Journal of Psychology, 119,* 413–421.

Hopke, W. E. (Ed.). (1993). *Encyclopedia of careers and vocational guidance* (9th ed.). Chicago: J. G. Ferguson.

Hoppock, R. (1976). *Occupational information.* New York: McGraw-Hill.

Ivey, A. E. (1994). *Intentional interviewing and counseling: Facilitating client development in a multicultural society* (3rd ed.). Pacific Grove, CA: Brooks/Cole.

Krumboltz, J. D. (1993). Integrating career and personal counseling. *The Career Development Quarterly, 42,* 161–166.

Lucas, M. S. (1993). Personal aspects of career counseling: Three examples. *The Career Development Quarterly, 42,* 161–166.

MacGregor, J. N. (1987). Short-term memory capacity: Limitation or optimization? *Psychological Review, 94,* 107–108.

Martin, D. G., & Moore, A. D. (1995). *First steps in the art of interviewing.* Pacific Grove, CA: Brooks/Cole.

Marx, M. H. (1951). The general nature of theory construction. In M. H. Marx (Ed.), *Psychological theory* (pp. 4–19). New York: Macmillan.

Miller, G. A. (1956). The magical number seven, plus or minus two: Some limits on our capacity to process information. *Psychological Review, 63,* 81–97.

Occupational outlook handbook. (1996). Washington, DC: U.S. Department of Labor.

Okun, B. F. (1992). *Effective helping: Interviewing and counseling techniques* (4th ed.). Pacific Grove, CA: Brooks/Cole.

Osipow, S. H., & Fitzgerald, L. F. (1995). *Theories of career development* (4th ed.). Boston: Allyn & Bacon.

Rogers, C. (1951). *Client-centered therapy.* Boston: Houghton Mifflin.

Rogers, C. (1958). The characteristics of a helping relationship. *Personnel and Guidance Journal, 37,* 6–16.

Sears, S. (1982). A definition of career guidance terms: A National Vocational Guidance Association perspective. *Vocational Guidance Quarterly, 31,* 137–143.

Sharf, R. S. (1984). Vocational information-seeking behavior: Another view. *Vocational Guidance Quarterly, 33,* 120–129.

Simon, H. A. (1974). How big is a chunk? *Science, 183,* 482–488.

Snow, R. E. (1973). Theory construction for research and testing. In R. W. Travers (Ed.), *Second handbook of research on teaching* (pp. 77–112). Chicago: Rand McNally.

Spokane, A. R. (1991). *Career interventions.* Englewood Cliffs, NJ: Prentice-Hall.

Starishevsky, R., & Matlin, N. A. (1963). A model for the translation of self-concept into vocational terms. In D. E. Super, R. Starishevsky, N. A. Matlin, & J. P. Jordaan (Eds.), *Career development: Self-concept theory* (Research Monograph No. 4, pp. 33–41). New York: College Entrance Examination Board.

Subich, L. M. (1993). How personal is career counseling? *The Career Development Quarterly, 42,* 129–131.

Sue, D. W. (1981). *Counseling the culturally different: Theory and practice.* New York: Wiley.

Swann, W., Pelham, B., & Roberts, D. (1987). Causal chunking: Memory and inference in ongoing interaction. *Journal of Personality and Social Psychology, 53,* 858–865.

Truax, C. B., & Carkhuff, R. R. (1967). *Toward effective counseling and psychotherapy: Training and practice.* Chicago: Aldine.

Ye, N., & Salvendy, G. (1994). Quantitative and qualitative differences between experts and novices in chunking computer software knowledge. *International Journal of Human Computer Interaction, 6,* 105–118.

PART ONE

Trait and Type Theories

Trait and type theories were the first career development theories to be described. In general, they were developed to analyze traits or characteristics of individuals so these traits could be matched with qualifications required by jobs. Groups of traits or characteristics could be combined so that types of individuals could be identified. Likewise, qualifications of jobs and work requirements could be combined to describe types of work.

In this part, four trait or type theories are presented. Trait and factor theory, described in Chapter 2, assesses characteristics of people and characteristics of jobs, which are then matched to help an individual select an occupation. As described in Chapter 3, work adjustment theory provides a framework for assessing an individual's needs and skills so that they can be matched with similar needs and skills required by a small group of different occupations. Holland's typological theory, the focus of Chapter 4, describes six types of people and six types of environments. The counselor assists in career selection by matching the person with the environment. The Myers-Briggs type theory, introduced in Chapter 5, describes ways of perceiving and judging the world. Matching an individual's style of judging and perceiving with the styles of judging and perceiving used by people employed in certain careers can assist an individual in finding an appropriate work environment. Each of these theories shares the goal of attempting to measure characteristics or types of individuals so that they can be matched with characteristics or types of work to provide assistance in career selection.

2

Trait and Factor Theory

In 1909, Frank Parsons described his concept of vocational guidance in his book *Choosing a Vocation.* These views and his contribution to career development have been described in a special issue (Volume 20, Number 4, 1994) of the *Journal of Career Development.* His views became the foundation for what later evolved into trait and factor theory. The term *trait* refers to a characteristic of an individual that can be measured through testing. *Factor* refers to a characteristic required for successful job performance. It also refers to a statistical approach used to differentiate important characteristics of a group of people. Thus, the terms *trait* and *factor* refer to the assessment of characteristics of the person and the job.

Assessment of traits is referred to in the first and most crucial of the steps Parsons identified that describe his approach to occupational selection. Parsons (1909) proposed that, to select an occupation, an individual should ideally have

1. A clear understanding of yourself, your attitudes, abilities, interests, ambitions, resource limitations, and their causes;
2. A knowledge of the requirements and conditions of success, advantages and disadvantages, compensation, opportunities, and prospects in different lines of work;
3. True reasoning on the relations of these two groups of facts. (p. 5)

Frank Parsons's book, derived from his work in career counseling with adolescents in the Boston area, was not the only contribution to trait and factor theory. At about the same time, Elton Mayo at Harvard and Frederick Taylor working in business were doing early industrial psychological work that involved the study of worker conditions such as fatigue and boredom. They developed various ways to study how an individual reacts to his or her work environment. It was natural that their objective measurements would fit into the discipline of trait and factor psychology. In the 1930s and 1940s, particularly during World War II, much work was done on assessing abilities of personnel. It was necessary for the U.S. Employment Service and the War Manpower Commission to develop a research testing and placement program so that Americans would be better able to serve the war effort. One of the most important tests that grew out of that program was the Army General Classification Test. It set new standards for test development and was used to select recruits for a wide variety of tasks. Many other tests were also developed through federal funding. This gave a boost to the assessment techniques that were needed for the development of trait and factor theory. After World War II, research continued in the area of assessment, much of it taking place at the University of Minnesota. In fact, trait and factor theory has also been called the *Minnesota point of view* and *actuarial counseling.*

The most well-known contributor to "the Minnesota point of view" was Edmund G. Williamson, dean of students at the University of Minnesota between 1941 and 1969. His writings epitomize the trait and factor approach (Williamson, 1939, 1965). Although Williamson, like Carl Rogers, was concerned with the whole person, his approach was entirely different from Rogers's and was labeled *directive* in contrast to the nondirective approach of Carl Rogers. Among Williamson's methods were information giving and direct suggestion. It was his view that the counselor should share his or her wisdom with the client in guiding the client to a correct decision. In contrast, Rogers emphasized reflection of the client's feelings rather than imparting information. Williamson's approach has been criticized by a number of writers; its criticism is documented by Aubrey (1977). Stephenson (1963) discusses interpreting test results to clients and focusing on assisting the client in making a decision about his or her career choice rather than on information-seeking strategies. Such approaches are more similar to that of Carl Rogers and are in contrast to the directive approach of Williamson.

There is little research supporting or refuting trait and factor theory itself as a viable theory of career development. Rather, the research that has been done, of which there is a large amount, has related traits and factors to one another or has established the validity and reliability of measurements of traits and factors. Aptitudes, achievements, interests, values, and personality have been correlated with each other by developers of tests and inventories. When validating and developing tests, it is necessary to relate the scales of one test to the scales of very similar tests. For example, Schmidt (1988) and Gottfredson (1988) reviewed studies that use, with moderate success, a general ability to predict job performance.

In this chapter, a broad view of trait and factor theory will be taken to show how it can be used to conceptualize career development. Parsons's (1909) concepts of more than 80 years ago have been embellished by integrating tests and occupational information with his precepts. Parsons characterized the first step of career choice as gaining "a clear understanding of yourself, your attitudes, abilities, interests, ambitions, resource limitations, and their causes." We will look at this step in terms of aptitudes, achievements, interests, values, and personality to reflect five types of assessment that have emerged as important to career counseling. Parsons's second step is obtaining "a knowledge of the requirements and conditions of success, advantages and disadvantages, compensation, opportunities, and prospects in different lines of work." We will discuss how the counselor can assist the client in gaining a knowledge of occupations. Third, Parsons said that a wise choice is made by "true reasoning of the relations of these two groups of facts." We will consider integration of information about oneself and the world of work, giving a focus that is not limited to the use of cognitive skills but that also includes reflecting and questioning skills. Information regarding various traits and factors in women and people of color will also be given. This will be followed by a discussion of potential counseling difficulties in using trait and factor theory.

STEP 1: GAINING SELF-UNDERSTANDING

When Parsons and early career counselors started to help young people choose a career, they had few resources available to them (such as tests, inventories, and occupational information). They relied primarily on interviews and discussions with clients. Asking a client what she enjoyed doing (interests) and how well she did it (aptitude and achievement) was an important method of helping the client gain self-understanding. As a client talked about aspects of her life that were important to her (her values), the counselor was able to make a further assessment. As the counselor observed the client and listened to her comments about herself and others, the counselor could make observations about the client's personality. The counseling interview continues to be an important part of the trait and factor assessment process. However, the development of tests and inventories has given counselors additional useful tools.

Since the beginning of the twentieth century, psychologists have been very productive in the development of psychometric measures. These are reviewed in the *Eleventh Mental Measurements Yearbook* (Kramer & Conoley, 1993) and in *Tests in Print IV* (Murphy, Conoley, & Impara, 1994), which lists 3,009 tests, of which 91 are achievement batteries, 233 are intelligence and academic aptitude tests, 568 are vocational tests, and 669 are personality inventories. For the counselor to become familiar with each of these is, of course, practically impossible. Here we will describe only a few well-accepted tests that counselors are likely to use in the trait and factor approach and that are frequently used by counseling psychologists (Watkins, Campbell, & Nieberding, 1994). This does not necessarily mean that these are the best tests, but they are ones in wide usage that are different enough from each other so that their main features can be contrasted. *A Counselor's Guide to Career Assessment* (Kapes, Mastie, & Whitfield, 1994) presents test reviews of most of the instruments described in this text. When a counselor chooses a test to use with clients, the counselor may incorporate the concepts of the tests into his or her thinking about the client. For example, a counselor wishing to conceptualize a client's sociability may use the definition of *sociability* on the Sociability scale of the California Psychological Inventory rather than invent a new definition of *sociability.* It is the purpose of this chapter not to evaluate these tests and inventories, but to show how tests can be used in conceptualizing clients' career concerns.

The five basic traits and factors that can be assessed by testing and interviewing are aptitudes, achievements, interests, values, and personality. We will consider each of these areas in turn.

Aptitudes

The terms *aptitude, ability,* and *achievement* are easily confused, as are the tests that measure these traits. It is helpful to make these distinctions: An achievement test is designed to reveal how much an individual has learned; an ability test measures maximum performance and reveals the level of a person's present ability to perform a task; and an aptitude test reveals a person's probable future level of ability to perform a task (Goldenson, 1984). In other words, these tests measure past achievement, present ability and future aptitude. Often the line between them is not very clear. For example, the assessment of past achievement may provide a measure of possible aptitude. Aptitude tests have been particularly attractive to clients who believe that, if they can find the occupations in which they have aptitude, they can predict their future success in a specific occupation. Unfortunately, aptitude tests measure a number of general aptitudes, and there are no aptitude tests precise enough to predict with certainty the eventual success of an individual.

Aptitude tests have been used to predict future success in either further educational endeavors or occupational training. Table 2-1 lists a sample of well-known aptitude tests, along with their subtests. The first two tests listed—the College Board Scholastic Assessment Test (SAT), and the American College Testing Assessment Program: Academic Test (ACT)—are used for predicting college success. The Differential Aptitude Tests (DAT) are used to assist people in selecting a career. The U.S. Employment Service General Aptitude Test Battery (GATB) and the Armed Services Vocational Aptitude Battery (ASVAB) are used by the U.S. Employment Service and Armed Services, respectively, for counseling and selection by these two agencies and by educational and other institutions. Note that all five of the tests measure verbal and quantitative (mathematical or numerical) aptitudes. These two, verbal and mathematical aptitude, are common to almost all academic aptitude tests. Note also that fewer subtests are used for measuring college aptitude than are used for predicting aptitude for occupations not requiring college skills, such as secretary, mechanic, and electronics technician. Further, the DAT, GATB, and ASVAB give occupational profiles that match high scores on various aptitudes. Thus, one can

Table 2-1 *Five Aptitude Tests and Their Subtests*

College Board Scholastic Assessment Test (SAT)	*ACT Assessment Program: Academic Tests (ACT)*	*Differential Aptitude Tests (DAT)*	*U.S. Employment Service General Aptitude Test Battery (GATB)*	*Armed Services Vocational Aptitude Battery (ASVAB)*
Verbal	English usage	General learning	General learning	Coding speed
Mathematical	Mathematics usage	Verbal reasoning	Verbal	Word knowledge
Standard written English	Social studies reading	Numerical ability	Numerical	Arithmetic reasoning
	Natural sciences reading	Abstract reasoning	Spatial	Tool knowlegdge
		Clerical speed and accuracy	Form perception	Space perception
		Mechanical reasoning	Clerical perception	Mechanical comprehension
		Space relations	Eye-hand coordination	Shop information
		Spelling	Finger dexterity	Automotive information
		Language usage	Manual dexterity	Electronics information

look up an occupation in one of the test manuals and find the scores that are needed on various subtests for suggested entry into that specific occupation. These scores should be considered guidelines rather than requirements. Research on the validity of these instruments continues to be important. For example, the U.S. Department of Labor has critically reviewed the GATB because of questions about validity and fairness to minority and majority test takers (Adler, 1991).

More than most other types of tests, the aptitude test that a counselor uses depends upon his or her setting. For example, high school and college counselors in the East and on the West Coast tend to use the SAT, whereas their colleagues in the Midwest tend to use the ACT. Counselors working at a federal employment service are likely to use the GATB, whereas those working with the military or prospective applicants to the military will use the ASVAB. The selection of appropriate norms is necessary, so that clients' aptitudes are compared to an appropriate comparison group. Clients' self-estimates of their own aptitudes can be useful, so that comparisons can be made with measured aptitudes, allowing the client to develop a fuller understanding of his or her aptitudes.

Although discussion with a client may produce information to make an objective judgment about aptitude and abilities, counselors should be wary of making *predictions* about a client's success based on aptitude test scores. It is one thing for employers to make selections based on aptitude; it is another for a counselor to say to a client, "You could not become a physician because your scores are not high enough." There are examples in our society of how the client proved the counselor wrong by doing much better than was predicted. Clients are in a better position than the counselor to determine the risk they are willing to take in trying to enter an occupation in which they would appear to have little chance for success. Clients must live with the effects of their decisions. For example, a client with mediocre grades who has always wanted to be a doctor but who does not apply to medical school may regret that decision for many years.

Achievements

Achievement refers to a broad range of events that individuals participate in and accomplish during their lifetime. These can be separated into three types of achievements. The first is academic accomplishment, measured most often by grades, but also by honors and specific test scores. The second is accomplishments in work, such as tasks completed and supervisor ratings. The third, and the one that most easily fits with the trait and factor approach, pertains to tests of achievement for certification or entry into an occupation.

Over the years, research studies have shown that the best single predictor of academic performance is previous academic performance (Ramist et al., 1984). In other words, one can predict performance in college better from high school grades than from aptitude test scores. In fact, high school grades can be given twice the weight of scholastic aptitude tests when predicting college grades (Astin, 1993). Although not strictly traits or factors, accomplishments that can be attained at work, through hobbies, or through extracurricular activity can be very useful in determining the nature of an individual's abilities and achievements. These accomplishments can be very diverse and include such activities as athletic honors, ability to help a sick person, ability to type a paper quickly, ability to tally numbers with speed and accuracy, and ability to give a speech in front of an audience. Although such activities are important, many may be very difficult to measure quantitatively.

Achievement *can* be measured quantitatively through tests that are used for licensure, certification, or entry into a particular field or profession. For example, doctors, nurses, and lawyers must all pass the board examinations of a particular state prior to becoming licensed to do their specific work. Similarly, plumbers, police officers, and many other professionals must take tests before advancing from one level to another. The wide range of achievement tests available at present includes tests pertaining to the following kinds of work:

Accountant	Electrician
Actuary	Funeral director
Artist	Life insurance agent
Cosmetologist	Mechanic
Musician	Psychologist
Nurse	Real estate agent
Physician	Teacher
Plumber	Typist
Police officer	X-ray technician

What characterizes all of these tests is that they are very specific to a given task or profession. For example, the best test of typing ability is to obtain a typing sample from an individual. A written or multiple-choice test about typing would not be adequate. Likewise, the best test of artistic or musical ability is to look at a portfolio of artwork or listen to a musical audition.

One of the problems in using client self-report of accomplishments, such as helping someone in distress, is that in the United States people are often taught to be modest about their achievements. Encouragement is often needed for people to accurately present their successes. Emphasizing these accomplishments can be useful as they may serve as building blocks for further accomplishments. For example, if a student has successfully presented a project at a science fair, that becomes a starting place to discuss other types of projects and science interests that the person may have.

Interests

Over the years, interests have become the most important trait used in occupational selection. The reason is that occupational entry can be predicted better from interests than from aptitude for individuals with many abilities who are able to choose from a wide range of occupations. (See Herr & Cramer, 1984, p. 94, for a brief discussion of evidence for the primacy of interests.) Reviews of the relationship between interests and abilities have shown a small but significant correlation between the two (r = .20) (Lent, Brown, & Hackett, 1994). Thus, some individuals may like some things that they don't do well, and some may be good at activities they don't like. Unlike aptitude tests, interest inventories have scales for specific occupations. Two particularly well-known interest inventories that use occupational scales are the Kuder DD and the Strong Interest Inventory. By measuring the interests of successful and satisfied people in an occupation, the authors of these instruments were able to develop a scale that compares the interests of these individuals to the interests of those who are unsure of their career choice. Such scales tend to predict occupational success and satisfaction decades after the test was taken.

Besides occupational interests, general areas of interest have been measured. Whereas occupational interest scales describe interests of people in a specific occupation, such as secretary, basic interest scales measure interests in activities, such as office practices. An office practice interest scale may include tasks such as typing, taking dictation, and answering the phone. To use another example, a mathematics scale may measure interests in abstract math and computation, whereas a mathematician scale measures the similarity of the interests of the test taker to the interests of those who are employed as mathematicians. Several inventories measure a broad spectrum of general interests. Three of them are listed in Table 2-2: The Kuder preference Record—Vocational Form C (KPRC); the Basic Interest Scales of the Strong Interest Inventory (SII); and the California Occupational Preference Survey (COPS). Note that the California Occupational Preference Survey has separate professional and skilled interest scales for five different interest areas. In general, the basic interest scales are quite similar for all three of the inventories. Any one of these inventories can provide a framework for categorizing interests in counseling.

By using a particular structure to evaluate a client's interests, the counselor can more easily understand the client's experience. For example, if a counselor uses the ten interest scales of the KPRC as a framework, he or she can categorize the client's discussion of preferences during an interview. If a client talks of enjoying painting and drawing throughout his school experience as well as writing for high school and college publications, the counselor can conceptualize and categorize these interests as artistic and literary. Later, when the client talks about enjoying going to art museums and discussing art with friends, this same conceptualization of artistic interests can be made. Having this frame of reference allows the

Table 2-2 *Three Interest Inventories and Their Scales*

Kuder Preference Record—Form C (KPRC)	*Strong Interest Inventory (SII) Basic Interest Scales*	*California Occupational Preference Survey (COPS)*
Outdoor	Agriculture	Consumer economics
Mechanical	Applied arts	Outdoor
Computational	Art	Clerical
Scientific	Athletics	Communication
Persuasive	Computer activities	Science—professional
Artistic	Law/politics	Science—skilled
Literary	Mathematics	Technology—professional
Musical	Mechanical activities	Technology—skilled
Social service	Medical science	Business—professional
Clerical	Medical service	Business—skilled
	Merchandising	Arts—professional
	Military activities	Arts—skilled
	Music/dramatics	Service—professional
	Nature	Service—skilled
	Office services	
	Organizational management	
	Public speaking	
	Religious activities	
	Sales	
	Science	
	Social service	
	Teaching	
	Writing	

counselor to group concepts and ideas that come from the counseling interview. If the counselor then administers the KPRC to the student, the counselor can get further validation of the client's interest in art if the score is high. If the score is low, the counselor can discuss the discrepancy between the client's expressed interest in art and low inventoried interest in art. When selecting inventories to use with clients, it is helpful to use those that make conceptual sense to the counselor. For example, it is possible but more difficult to use the Strong Interest Inventory Basic Interest Scales as a conceptual base when using the KPRC. Trying to conceptualize or chunk 10 scales (KPRC), 14 scales (COPS), or 23 scales (SII) can be very difficult. Holland's theory, which is described in Chapter 4, uses only 6 scales or constructs. When discussing the interests of clients in one trait, it is often helpful to discuss abilities and achievements in that trait at the same time. This helps the counselor to better organize the client's previous experiences and to use fewer chunks of material.

Table 2-3 *Two Values Inventories and Their Scales*

Study of Values (SV)	*Values Scale (VS)*
Theoretical	Ability utilization
Economic	Achievement
Aesthetic	Advancement
Social	Aesthetics
Political	Altruism
Religious	Authority
	Autonomy
	Creativity
	Economic rewards
	Life style
	Personal development
	Physical activity
	Prestige
	Risk
	Social interaction
	Social relations
	Variety
	Working conditions
	Cultural identity
	Physical prowess
	Economic security

Values

Neglected by many trait and factor counselors, values represent an important but difficult concept to measure. For career counseling, two types of values are considered important: general values and work-related values. Table 2-3 lists the 6 general values that are found in the Study of Values (SV) and the 21 work values listed in the Values Scale (VS). Inspection of Table 2-3 shows the contrast between the general values of the SV and the more specific work-related values of the VS. However, counselors may not make use of any value inventories, preferring to conceptualize work values or general values rather than to measure them. One reason is that it is very difficult to develop a reliable and valid value inventory, as these concepts are often elusive and not ones that can be predicted easily.

Values, as difficult to assess as they may be, are often helpful to clients who are deciding upon a career direction. For example, the client who wishes to help others may feel that this desire is more important than any of his or her other traits or factors, such as interests or abilities. In such a case, the counselor helps the client find an interesting way to satisfy his or her values. For example, a client who wishes to help the homeless may pursue social work or business management, depending on the direction of the

Table 2-4 *Two Personality Inventories and Their Scales*

California Psychological Inventory (CPI)	*Sixteen Personality Factor Questionnaire (16 PF)*
Dominance	Cool vs. warm
Capacity for status	Concrete thinking vs. abstract thinking
Sociability	Affected by feelings vs. emotionally stable
Social presence	Submissive vs. dominant
Self-acceptance	Sober vs. enthusiastic
Independence	Expedient vs. conscientious
Empathy	Shy vs. bold
Sense of well-being	Tough-minded vs. tender-minded
Responsibility	Trusting vs. suspicious
Socialization	Practical vs. imaginative
Self-control	Forthright vs. shrewd
Tolerance	Self-assured vs. apprehensive
Good impression	Conservative vs. experimenting
Communality	Group-oriented vs. self-sufficient
Achievement via independence	Undisciplined self-conflict vs. following self-image
Achievement via conformance	Relaxed vs. tense
Intellectual efficiency	
Psychological-mindedness	
Flexibility	
Femininity/masculinity	

client's interests. The value of helping others is called *altruism* on the VS. Being able to label a value and compare it to other values can be very useful for the counselor. Although the list of 21 work values in the VS is long, it does give the counselor a framework to assess the values important to a client. Some counselors may wish to use a shortened version of such a list of values, while others may be satisfied using the 6 values of the SV.

Personality

The measurement of personality has been an important area of study for the last 80 years. Although much of the work has centered on abnormal personality, with the development of the Minnesota Multiphasic Personality Inventory (MMPI), the Rorschach, and the Thematic Apperception Test (TAT), work has also been done in the area of normal personality. For purposes of illustration, two different measures of personality are listed in Table 2-4 that give insight into the conceptualization of personality for vocational selection. The two tests that will be described here are the California Psychological Inventory (CPI) and the Sixteen Personality Factor

Questionnaire (16 PF). The CPI represents a commonsense or folk approach to personality, and the 16 PF represents a statistical approach.

The CPI, developed by Harrison Gough (1987), uses 20 scales to measure different aspects of personality. The terms are inoffensive ones to which clients might not object (Table 2-4). Gough used many items from the MMPI to develop this inventory; however, the two inventories are very different in that the MMPI uses pathological terminology and the CPI does not. For example, the MMPI uses scale names such as "schizophrenia" and "hypochondriasis," whereas the CPI uses names such as "self-control" and "flexibility." People who score high on flexibility are likely to be rated by others as flexible. Such comparisons between scores on a scale and ratings by experts or peers were widely used in developing the CPI. The scale names represent terms that counselors can use when trying to assess the characteristics of individual clients.

The 16 PF lists 16 primary personality factors. These are presented using a bipolar method, indicating the two extremes of each trait. Examples are cool versus warm, submissive versus dominant, and shy versus bold. These factors are similar in may ways to the 20 scales of the CPI; the difference is in their development. A statistical technique, factor analysis, was used to try to make the scales as different from each other as possible. These factors can be useful in conceptualizing a client who is trying to make occupational selection decisions.

Personality profiles have been developed using the CPI and the 16 PF for individuals in a variety of occupations. Therefore, a counselor is able to match the profile of a client with an appropriate occupational pattern. Personality inventories are more difficult to learn to use than are ability, achievement, interest, or values tests because of the complexity of the variables involved and their abstraction. In fact, many counselors who use the trait and factor approach may not use personality tests at all. Although personality is related to occupational selection, the strength of the relationship is not as strong as the relationship between occupational success and measured interest (Herr & Cramer, 1984). For example, an accountant may have needs for order and deference, but these are not likely to be as important in occupational selection as an interest in business, accounting principles, and math. Further, intelligence and mathematical ability are likely to be more important factors in the choice of accounting than a need for order or deference. Still, being able to integrate the concepts of order and deference with interests, abilities, achievements, and values is very helpful.

Example of Step 1

Jack, a white freshman at a large university, is undecided about his career choice. He has already met with the counselor for one session and has gone over his results on the KPRC, the VS, and the CPI (Table 2-5). The counselor now has the results of his SAT. This dialogue might occur in the

Table 2-5 *Jack's High and Low Scores on Selected Tests and Inventories*

	SAT	*KPRC*	*VS*	*CPI*
High	Verbal	Artistic Persuasive	Creativity Ability utilization	Social presence Socialization
Low	Math	Outdoor Computational Clerical	Economic security Altruism	Independence

second session as the counselor attempts to integrate the test results. Other sources (Goldman, 1971) go into detail about test interpretation, whereas this dialogue focuses on conceptualizing the client's use of information about his traits and factors taken from assessment instruments:

CL: Some of my courses this semester are really boring. I wish I didn't have so many course requirements.

CO: I'd like to hear more about them [Detail is needed to evaluate the client's experience in terms of his various traits and factors.]

CL: Calculus is a nuisance. It takes a lot of time, there doesn't seem to be any use for it, and I just feel so bored after the class. My history course isn't much better—medieval civilization is not exactly earthshaking to me. I knew I had to take a history course, but maybe I should have taken something else.

CO: Having to fulfill requirements is really quite difficult for you. [It is not surprising that Jack is having difficulty with math and does not like it—low SAT and KPRC scores. The counselor lets Jack determine what he wants to talk about next by using a feeling reflection.]

CL: Fortunately, not all my courses are so bad. My speech course is easy and kind of fun. I've enjoyed standing up in front of class and trying to capture the attention of the other students, which really is a challenge, as many of them like the class as much as I like math. That class reminds me a bit of when I worked at carnival concessions two summers ago and I had to give a spiel to people about why they should play a game.

CO: It sounds like fun, trying to present yourself in an impressive way to others. It reminds me of what we were talking about last time when we were going over the California Psychological Inventory. [The counselor makes a direct connection between the client's high score on the social presence scale of the CPI and his desire to present his work in the speech class and be involved in the carnival situation.]

CL: Yes, I sure enjoy the attention I get. It's kind of fun. I remember when I first came to visit this campus, I was impressed with the guy who showed us around. In fact, even though I'm just a freshman, I think I want to try to see if I can give campus tours, too.

CO: You really are enjoying doing a lot of things that get you out in front of others. [Jack seems quite aware and accepting of his own enjoyment of getting the attention of others.]

CL: I guess so. I'm all over the place. I've got our whole dorm working on this massive homecoming float. It really looks good. I think we're going to win first prize.

CO: You really seem to enjoy designing and developing new things. [The counselor is aware of the client's high score on Creativity on the Values Scale and chooses to comment on this trait of the client without mentioning the test score itself.]

CL: Yes, I don't know how to find time to study sometimes, but I also seem to manage. There's so much to learn here and so much to do. I need some 48-hour days.

CO: It really is hard to decide what to do sometimes. [The counselor is aware of Jack's interest in socializing and communicating with others from the CPI, as well as his desire to use his skills, indicated by his ability-utilization score on the VS. The counselor is also aware that this may create some problems for Jack in deciding what to do. Note that the counselor combines traditional nondirective responses with trait and factor conceptualization.]

STEP 2: OBTAINING KNOWLEDGE ABOUT THE WORLD OF WORK

Occupational information is the second ingredient of trait and factor theory. It is the counselor's role to help the client gather occupational information. To do this, it is not necessary to rely solely on the counselor's knowledge of occupations, but to use many resources to supplement this knowledge. There are three aspects of occupational information to consider. The first is the type of information; for example, a description of the occupation, the working conditions, or the salary. The second important aspect is classification. There are several classification systems that enable the client and the counselor to put 20,000 occupations into some meaningful order. Third, it is helpful to know the trait and factor requirements for each occupation that one is seriously considering. For example, if a client is thinking about becoming a veterinarian, it is helpful to know which aptitudes, achievements, interests, values, and personality traits predict success and satisfaction in veterinary medicine.

Types of Occupational Information

Occupational information is available from a variety of different sources. These include booklets made available by professional trade associations, pamphlets available through publishers that specialize in producing occupational information, and lengthier books or encyclopedias. Furthermore, occupational information is available on audio and video cassettes, as well as on microfiche and in computer-based information systems. At its most basic, almost all occupational information includes a description of the occupation, the qualifications required for entry, the necessary education, the working conditions, the salary, and the employment outlook. Many publications go beyond this by giving information about career ladders, similar occupations, examples of people working in the profession, and special information for women and minorities. A more detailed explanation of types of occupational information is given in the next section (Sharf, 1993, pp. 303–305).

It is impossible for counselors to remember all of this information about many occupations. Perhaps the most important type of information for counselors to know is the description of an occupation. Beyond that, it is helpful to have books such as the *Occupational Outlook Handbook* (1996), which is issued every two years and is available to answer questions about occupations. To make matters more difficult, occupational information changes from year to year. Specifically, the salary and employment outlook is apt to vary. Further, these two variables are apt to differ depending on what section of the country one lives in. For example, plumbers make a higher salary in New York City then they do in Des Moines, Iowa, or Augusta, Maine. When evaluating occupational information, it is useful to examine language, content, and pictures for race or gender bias. *The Career Development Quarterly* evaluates occupational material according to guidelines established by the National Vocational Guidance Association (1980).

The National Vocational Guidance Association (1980), now the National Career Development Association, has published guidelines that address the quality and content of occupational information. Regarding quality, questions such as the following are asked: Are the written information and pictures accurate and nonbiased with regard to gender and race? Is the information clear and interesting, and is it appropriate for the intended audience? Is the material updated frequently? Regarding content, the following areas are covered: the duties and nature of the work, the physical activities required, social and psychological satisfactions and dissatisfactions, the type of preparation required, earnings and benefits, advancement possibilities, the employment outlook, part-time and volunteer opportunities for exploring the occupation, related occupations, sources of training, and sources of additional information. By examining a description of one occupation in the *Occupational Outlook Handbook* (1996), readers can see how these topics are covered.

Classification Systems

Because it is easy to be overwhelmed by the volume of information available to counselors and clients, it is essential to have a way to organize occupational information. Classification systems have been developed to fill this need. Three different government classification systems that have evolved over the years are particularly important. In addition, Holland's classification of occupations (see Chapter 4) has been found helpful by a number of counselors. The most comprehensive listing of occupations is the *Dictionary of Occupational Titles* (DOT), which is in its fourth edition (1991). It classifies about 20,000 occupations that exist in the United States. To organize these occupations, it uses a nine-digit code. The first three numbers designate an occupational group. The first digit identifies one of nine broad categories. The second digit breaks up the occupations into 82 divisions (Table 2-6) and the third digit divides the occupations into 559 groups. For example, the occupation of counselor has the first three digits *045*. The *0* refers to professional, technical, and managerial occupations. The *04* makes reference to occupations in the life sciences. Within that division, *045* designates occupations in psychology. The next three digits relate to three ways of doing tasks. The fourth digit describes how the individual deals with data (Table 2-7); the fifth, how a person deals with people (Table 2-8); and the sixth, how a person uses things (Table 2-9). Tables 2-7, 2-8, and 2-9 are based on information in Volume 2 of the DOT (1991, pp. 1005–1007). This assignment is based on an analysis of the tasks done by people in the occupation. The last three digits indicate the alphabetical order of the occupational titles that have the same six-digit code. Many other sources give further details of this system, for example, *Improved Career Decision Making through the Use of Labor Market Information* (1991), a U.S. Department of Labor publication. Also, the DOT continues to be updated.

Another government classification system, the *Enhanced Guide for Occupational Exploration* (GOE; 1991), uses a three-digit code somewhat similar to the first three digits of the DOT code. The difference is that the codes are more related to the interest requirements of occupations than are the DOT codes. The 12 basic interest areas are listed in Table 2-10. The GOE lists occupations in 348 subgroups, with the DOT code given for each code or occupation in the subgroup. Because the GOE makes more intuitive sense to the client, using the GOE requires less help from the counselor than using the DOT.

A more complex system is the *Standard Occupational Classification Manual* (SOC; 1980). It has four levels: division, major group, minor group, and unit group. The SOC code clusters jobs by similar work function, rather than by interests as in the GOE. The 22 broad occupational divisions that make up this classification system are listed in Table 2-11 along with the 64 major groups. The SOC was developed to bridge the DOT and a classification system used by the U.S. Census Bureau. Because the National Occupational Information Coordinating Committee (NOICC) has adopted this system for its work, many career centers have also used it. Since these three classification systems (DOT, GOE, and SOC) all attempt to classify about 20,000 occupations, they are a helpful tool for the counselor in organizing a large amount of material.

Table 2-6 *Dictionary of Occupational Titles: Two-Digit Occupational Divisions*

Code	Division
0/1	*Professional, Technical, and Managerial Occupations*
00/01	Occupations in architecture, engineering, and surveying
02	Occupations in mathematics and physical sciences
03	Computer-related occupations
04	Occupations in life sciences
05	Occupations in social sciences
07	Occupations in medicine and health
09	Occupations in education
10	Occupations in museum, library, and archival sciences
11	Occupations in law and jurisprudence
12	Occupations in religion and theology
13	Occupations in writing
14	Occupations in art
15	Occupations in entertainment and recreation
16	Occupations in administrative specializations
18	Managers and officials, n.e.c.*
19	Miscellaneous professional, technical, and managerial occupations
2	*Clerical and Sales Occupations*
20	Stenography, typing, filing, and related occupations
21	Computing and account-recording occupations
22	Production and stock clerks and related occupations
23	Information and message distribution occupations
24	Miscellaneous clerical occupations
25	Sales occupations, services
26	Sales occupations, consumable commodities
27	Sales occupations, commodities, n.e.c.
29	Miscellaneous sales occupations
3	*Service Occupations*
30	Domestic service occupations
31	Food and beverage preparation and service occupations
32	Lodging and related service occupations
33	Barbering, cosmetology, and related service occupations
34	Amusement and recreation service occupations
35	Miscellaneous personal service occupations
36	Apparel and furnishing service occupations
37	Protective service occupations
38	Building and related service occupations
4	*Agricultural, Fishery, Forestry, and Related Occupations*
40	Plant farming occupations
41	Animal farming occupations
42	Miscellaneous agricultural and related occupations
44	Fishery and related occupations
45	Forestry occupations
46	Hunting, trapping, and related occupations
5	*Processing Occupations*
50	Occupations in processing of metal
51	Ore refining and foundry occupations
52	Occupations in processing of food, tobacco, and related products

(continued)

*n.e.c. is an abbreviation for "not elsewhere classified." Based on *Dictionary of Occupational Titles* (Vol. 1, 4th ed., rev.). Washington, DC: U.S. Department of Labor, Employment and Training Administration, 1991.

Table 2-6 *(continued)*

53	Occupations in processing of paper and related materials
54	Occupations in processing of petroleum, coal, natural and manufactured gas, and related products
55	Occupations in processing of chemicals, plastics, synthetics, rubber, paint, and related products
56	Occupations in processing of wood and wood products
57	Occupations in processing of stone, clay, glass, and related products
58	Occupations in processing of leather, textiles, and related products
59	Processing occupations, n.e.c.
6	*Machine Trades Occupations*
60	Metal machining occupations
61	Metalworking occupations, n.e.c.
62/63	Mechanics and machinery repairers
64	Paperworking occupations
65	Printing occupations
66	Wood machining occupations
67	Occupations in machining stone, clay, glass, and related materials
68	Textile occupations
69	Machine trades occupations, n.e.c.
7	*Benchwork Occupations*
70	Occupations in fabrication, assembly, and repair of metal products, n.e.c.
71	Occupations in fabrication and repair of scientific, medical, photographic, optical, horological, and related products
72	Occupations in assembly and repair of electrical equipment
73	Occupations in fabrication and repair of products made from assorted materials
74	Painting, decorating, and related occupations
75	Occupations in fabrication and repair of plastics, synthetics, rubber, and related products
76	Occupations in fabrication and repair of wood products
77	Occupations in fabrication and repair of sand, stone, clay, and glass products
78	Occupations in fabrication and repair of textile, leather, and related products
79	Benchwork occupations, n.e.c.
8	*Structural Work Occupations*
80	Occupations in metal fabricating, n.e.c.
81	Welders, cutters, and related occupations
82	Electrical assembling, installing, and repairing occupations
84	Painting, plastering, waterproofing, cementing, and related occupations
85	Excavating, grading, paving, and related occupations
86	Construction occupations, n.e.c.
89	Structural work occupations, n.e.c.
9	*Miscellaneous Occupations*
90	Motor freight occupations
91	Transportation occupations, n.e.c.
92	Packaging and materials handling occupations
93	Occupations in extraction of minerals
95	Occupations in production and distribution of utilities
96	Amusement, recreation, motion picture, radio and television occupations, n.e.c.
97	Occupations in graphic art work

Table 2-7 *Working with Data*

The fourth digit refers to the level at which workers must deal with data, including numbers, words, symbols, ideas, and concepts. *Data,* as used here, refers to information and knowledge obtained by observing, investigating, or creating. The seven levels of working with data are described below, starting with the most complex.

0 Synthesizing: Data are analyzed and integrated to discover facts and/or develop knowledge.
1 Coordinating: Data are analyzed to determine the time, place, and sequence of actions. Also included are planning actions and reporting on them.
2 Analyzing: Data are examined and evaluated, and alternative actions are prescribed, depending on the evaluation of the data.
3 Compiling: Individuals collate, classify, or gather information and may follow through with an action.
4 Computing: Individuals perform arithmetic operations, which may be followed by some action.
5 Copying: Data are entered into a computer, posted into a billing machine, or in some other way transcribed.
6 Comparing: Data, people, or things are observed, and judgments are made.

Tables 2-7, 2-8, and 2-9 are based on *Dictionary of Occupational Titles* (Vol. 2, 4th ed., rev.). Washington, DC: U.S. Department of Labor, Employment and Training Administration, 1991.

Table 2-8 *Working with People*

The fifth digit, *people,* refers to dealing with human beings. On occasion, it may also refer to dealing with animals as if they were human.

0 Mentoring: Advising, counseling, or guiding people with regard to problems that may be resolved by means of legal, scientific, clinical, spiritual, or other professional principles.
1 Negotiating: Exchanging ideas, information, and opinions with others to make policies or to arrive at decisions, conclusions, or solutions.
2 Instructing: Teaching subject matter to others or training others (including animals) through explanation, demonstration, and supervised practice.
3 Supervising: Assigning specific duties to workers, maintaining good relations among them, and promoting efficiency. Determining what others are to do and helping them interpret work procedures.
4 Diverting: Amusing others, generally through stage, screen, television, or radio.
5 Persuading: Influencing others to buy a product, service, or point of view.
6 Speaking/Signaling: Talking with or signaling to others to convey or exchange information. This may include giving assignments or directions to assistants.
7 Serving: Attending to the needs or requests of people or animals. Immediate responses are required.
8 Taking Instructions/Helping: Following through on work assignment instructions or orders from a supervisor.

Table 2-9 *Working with Things*

The sixth digit refers to dealing with *things*—substances, materials, machines, tools, equipment, and products—as opposed to human beings or ideas.

0 Setting Up: Preparing machines for operation by planning the order of the operations that will be undertaken; installing and adjusting tools and other machine components; using tools, equipment, and work aids such as gauges and measuring instruments. Setting up machines for others to operate would be included here.
1 Precision Working: Moving or guiding objects or materials into place and adjusting tools for tasks that require considerable judgment; involves precise accuracy and responsibility for attainment of standards as well as selection of tools.
2 Operating/Controlling: Operating machines involves setting up and adjusting the machine and materials as the work progresses. Controlling refers to observing gauges and dials, turning valves to regulate temperature, pressure flow, speed of pumps, and the like. The machine may have to be started, stopped, or otherwise adjusted.
3 Driving/Operating: Observing gauges and dials, estimating distances, determining speed, turning cranks and wheels. The machines must be started, stopped, controlled, or adjusted. Machines include cranes, conveyor systems, tractors, paving machines, and hoisting machines.
4 Manipulating: Selecting and moving or guiding tools, objects, or materials. Some judgment is required to attain precision, but not as much as in Number 1, Precision Working.
5 Tending: Adjusting materials or controls of machines; starting, stopping, and observing the machine or equipment. Little judgment is involved in making these adjustments.
6 Feeding/Offbearing: Throwing, dumping, or placing materials in machines that are automatic or operated by others; removing materials from such machines.
7 Handling: Moving or carrying objects or materials. If done with tools or other materials, these are usually selected by others.

Trait and Factor Requirements

Occupational information can be related directly to the client's traits and factors. Information about required aptitudes, achievements, interests, values, and personality is contained in occupational pamphlets and books. For example, when reading that a lawyer must learn the law, must write arguments, and so forth, a client can ask himself or herself if he or she has interest in doing those activities. When the qualifications and the educational requirements of an occupation are explained in occupational resources, clients can determine whether they have the necessary ability to proceed into that occupation. With regard to working conditions, a client can decide whether or not he or she has the appropriate personality and abilities to find the working conditions satisfying. For example, a person with a need for organization and cleanliness may find work in factories with dirt and

Table 2-10 *Guide for Occupational Exploration System: Interest Areas, Work Groups, and Subgroups*

Code	Area / Work Group
01	*Artistic*
01.01	Literary arts
01.02	Visual arts
01.03	Performing arts: Drama
01.04	Performing arts: Music
01.05	Performing arts: Dance
01.06	Craft arts
01.07	Elemental arts
01.08	Modeling
02	*Scientific*
02.01	Physical sciences
02.02	Life sciences
02.03	Medical sciences
02.04	Laboratory technology
03	*Plants and Animals*
03.01	Managerial work: Plants and animals
03.02	General supervision: Plants and animals
03.03	Animal training and service
03.04	Elemental work: Plants and animals
04	*Protective*
04.01	Safety and law enforcement
04.02	Security services
05	*Mechanical*
05.01	Engineering
05.02	Managerial work: Mechanical
05.03	Engineering technology
05.04	Air and water vehicle operation
05.05	Craft technology
05.06	Systems operation
05.07	Quality control
05.08	Land and water vehicle operation
05.09	Materials control
05.10	Crafts
05.11	Equipment operation
05.12	Elemental work: Mechanical
06	*Industrial*
06.01	Production technology
06.02	Production work
06.03	Quality control
06.04	Elemental work: Industrial
07	*Business Detail*
07.01	Administrative detail
07.02	Mathematical detail
07.03	Financial detail
07.04	Oral communications
07.05	Records processing
07.06	Clerical machine operation
07.07	Clerical handling
08	*Selling*
08.01	Sales technology
08.02	General sales
08.03	Vending
09	*Accommodating*
09.01	Hospitality services
09.02	Barber and beauty services
09.03	Passenger services
09.04	Customer services
09.05	Attendant services
10	*Humanitarian*
10.01	Social services
10.02	Nursing, therapy, and specialized teaching services
10.03	Child and adult care
11	*Leading-Influencing*
11.01	Mathematics and statistics
11.02	Educational and library services
11.03	Social research
11.04	Law
11.05	Business administration
11.06	Finance
11.07	Services administration
11.08	Communications
11.09	Promotion
11.10	Regulations enforcement
11.11	Business management
11.12	Contracts and claims
12	*Physical Performing*
12.01	Sports
12.02	Physical feats

Based on *Guide for Occupational Exploration.* Washington, DC: U.S. Department of Labor, 1979.

Table 2-11 *Standard Occupational Classification System: 22 Divisions and 64 Major Groups*

Code	Group
Executive, Administrative, and Managerial Occupations	
11	Officials and administrators, public administration
12–13	Officials and administrators, other
14	Management-related occupations
Engineers, Surveyors, and Architects	
16	Engineers, surveyors, and architects
Natural Scientists and Mathematicians	
17	Computer, mathematical, and operations research occupations
18	Natural scientists
Social Scientists, Social Workers, Religious Workers, and Lawyers	
19	Social scientists and urban planners
20	Social, recreation, and religious workers
21	Lawyers and judges
Teachers, Librarians, and Counselors	
22	Teachers, college, university, and other postsecondary institutions
23	Teachers, except postsecondary institutions
24	Vocational and educational counselors
25	Librarians, archivists, and curators
Health Diagnosing and Treating Practitioners	
26	Physicians and dentists
27	Veterinarians
28	Other health diagnosing and treating practitioners
Registered Nurses, Pharmacists, Dietitians, Therapists, and Physician's Assistants	
29	Registered nurses
30	Pharmacists, dietitians, therapists, and physician's assisants
Writers, Artists, Entertainers, and Athletes	
32	Writers, artists, performers, and related workers
33	Editors, reporters, public relations specialists, and announcers
34	Athletes and related workers
Health Technologists and Technicians	
36	Health technologists and technicians
Technologists and Technicians, except Health	
37	Engineering and related technologists and technicians
38	Science technologists and technicians
39	Technicians, except health, engineering, and science
Marketing and Sales Occupations	
40	Supervisors, marketing and sales occupations
41	Insurance, securities, real estate, and business service sales occupations
42	Sales occupations, commodities, except retail
43	Sales occupations, retail
44	Sales-related occupations
Administrative Support Occupations, Including Clerical	
45	Supervisors, administrative support occupations, including clerical
46–47	Administrative support occupations, including clerical
Service Occupations	
50	Private household occupations
51	Protective service occupations
52	Service occupations, except private household and protective

Table 2-11 *(continued)*

Code	Occupation
Agricultural, Forestry, and Fishing Occupations	
55	Farm operators and managers
56	Other agricultural and related occupations
57	Forestry and logging occupations
58	Fishers, hunters, and trappers
Mechanics and Repairers	
60	Supervisors, mechanics and repairers
61	Mechanics and repairers
Construction and Extractive Occupations	
63	Supervisors, construction and extractive occupations
64	Construction trades
65	Extractive occupations
Precision Production Occupations	
67	Supervisors, precision production occupations
68	Precision production occupations
69	Plant and systems operators
Production Working Occupations	
71	Supervisors, production occupations
73–74	Machine setup operators
75–76	Machine operators and tenders
77	Fabricators, assemblers, and hand-working occupations
78	Production inspectors, testers, samplers, and weighers
Transportation and Material-Moving Occupations	
81	Supervisors, transportation and material-moving occupations
82	Transportation occupations
83	Material-moving occupations, except transportation
Handlers, Equipment Cleaners, Helpers, and Laborers	
85	Supervisors, handlers, equipment cleaners, helpers, and laborers
86	Helpers
87	Handlers, equipment cleaners, and laborers
Military Occupations	
91	Military occupations
Miscellaneous Occupations	
99	Miscellaneous occupations

Based on *Standard Occupational Classification Manual.* Washington, DC: U.S. Department of Commerce, 1980.

scrap parts objectionable. A client's values are tested when the client must consider if the salary is sufficient or if the employment outlook is too risky. Occupational literature contains information that allows a client to assess the fit between his or her aptitudes, achievements, interests, values, and personality and the occupation being described.

What the Counselor Needs to Know

Since there are thousands of occupations open to clients, it is helpful for the counselor to be able to decide what he or she must know about occupations. For example, if a counselor uses the Strong Interest Inventory (SII), it is helpful to know the description of all occupations listed, as clients are likely to ask about them. If a counselor uses a personality inventory or an aptitude test such as the GATB or ASVAB, it is beneficial to have at hand a list of occupations that match scores on those inventories or tests. Often the classification system that the counselor uses is determined by the classification system used by the occupational library in his or her setting. By making use of an organized library, the counselor can direct the client to appropriate occupational information. Then the client can read information not only about a specific occupation, but also about occupations with similar codes. For example, by looking under the DOT code with the first three digits of *045,* the client will find information about several different kinds of counseling and psychology occupations.

Example of Step 2

As Jack and the counselor discuss Jack's experience and test scores (Table 2-5), they arrive at several occupations that Jack may want to examine. They've chosen these occupational titles because these are occupations that seem to fit some of Jack's interests, aptitudes, values, and personality.

CL: Although I had thought of sales before, I had never given it much thought because my knowledge of sales was limited to door-to-door or telephone sales, and I never really liked that.

CO: There is a wide variety of sales occupations, and I can help you learn about them by showing you information about some of the job descriptions that we have in our career library. [The counselor is aware that books such as the *Occupational Outlook Handbook* and other pamphlets on occupations may be a good start in broadening Jack's knowledge about sales. The counselor does not need to know all of the sales occupations that exist. If he or she wishes to find as large a number of sales occupations as possible, then the *Dictionary of Occupational Titles* will provide that information.]

CL: Although sales seems OK, I'm still interested in doing artwork. But on the other hand, I don't want to be a starving artist. There must be some ways to use art and still make a living.

CO: There are. Although some artistic occupations are extremely competitive, there are some that are not as competitive. It is really worth looking into some of these, such as graphic arts. [Even though painting for a living is very competitive, it is not appropriate to discourage the client from learning more about this occupation or others like it. The counselor wishes to encourage the client to read about a wide variety of artistic occupations that may include the use of drawing, painting, or sculpting.]

CL: I haven't taken any art courses in college, but in high school last year, I worked closely with my art teacher. Perhaps that's something that I should look into.

CO: Maybe you will be able to talk to your teacher during your vacation. [Jack is being encouraged to get occupational information. Even though the test and inventory scores may not fit with art teaching as much as they may with other occupations, it is helpful to encourage Jack to make this decision himself. This decision is best made after getting more information about being an art teacher.]

CL: When I think of it, there are a lot of people I know in careers that I'm considering. And some in careers I'm really not considering. My uncle sells Cadillacs in Philadelphia.

CO: Even though you're not considering selling cars, you're interested in sales. Perhaps you could talk to him about sales. [Getting information from all sources, both direct and indirect, is helpful.]

CL: Yes, but my uncle's like me. He'll probably try to sell me on selling.

CO: But you're able to separate the good information from opinion. Further, you can compare what he says to information that you learn when you read about sales occupations. [Being aware of the subjectivity of one person's impressions of an occupation, the counselor encourages Jack to consult other sources of more objective information, such as books or pamphlets.]

STEP 3: INTEGRATING INFORMATION ABOUT ONESELF AND THE WORLD OF WORK

According to trait and factor theory, this third step, integrating information about oneself and about occupations, is the major goal of career counseling. As mentioned previously, the manuals that accompany many tests and inventories indicate which occupations match specific patterns of scores. Further, occupational information has within it material indicating the aptitudes, achievements, interests, values, and personality characteristics required for each occupation. In a sense, the matching is built into the first two steps of trait and factor theory. However, this all sounds neater in theory than it is in practice. It is possible for a person's abilities as measured on the GATB to suggest one set of occupations, interests as measured on the SII to suggest another group of occupations, and personality as measured on the 16PF to suggest yet a third group of occupations. There may also be disagreement among tests that measure the same trait, emphasizing the fallibility of testing and the need for care in test interpretation. In addition to the fallibility of tests is the notion that much information that is useful in making career decisions may come not necessarily from tests, but from the counseling interview.

Tests are not the only methods for measuring and assessing traits and factors. Computer guidance systems tend to fit neatly into trait and factor theory. They often combine tests and occupational information in such a way that clients can meet their own individual needs for self-assessment and occupational information. Two of the more comprehensive systems are SIGI PLUS (1985) and DISCOVER (1984). Both systems allow an opportunity to measure interests, values, and self-reported competencies. These systems do not measure personality, but they do provide assessment of work values. Occupational information is then matched with the student's competencies, values, and interests so that the student can examine information about occupations that match his or her self-assessment. Both instruments provide an opportunity to help with the decision-making process by reducing a list of occupational alternatives. In fact, DISCOVER allows the opportunity to put into the system test scores from a number of instruments such as those that have been discussed previously. One advantage that both SIGI PLUS and DISCOVER have over the tests and inventories previously described is that the computer programs are interactive. In other words, as a student answers some questions and receives information, he or she can choose to move to any one of several sections. There is an interplay of information between the client and the computer, resulting in immediate feedback to the client. Computers can be used instead of or with other tests or inventories. However, neither tests nor computers can help clients in working out difficult and unusual concerns such as parental pressure to enter an unwanted occupation.

How the Counselor Can Help

The process of counseling by using trait and factor theory requires moving between the assessment of oneself and occupational information. Since much occupational information can be obtained outside the counseling session, most of the focus within the session is on self-assessment.

Counselors have available to them a full range of helping skills as described in Chapter 1. In using trait and factor theory, a counselor need not be limited to making suggestions and giving information. Both reasoning and feelings are important in making a career decision. When a client expresses a feeling, it is often helpful to find the reason behind it. For example, if a client says, "I wouldn't like to be a nurse," the counselor can respond in a number of ways: "What is it about nursing that you don't like?" or "Nursing doesn't feel right to you." By doing this, the counselor is likely to find out what lies behind the feelings. If the client replies, "I don't have what it takes to get into a nursing school," the counselor can reply, "You feel a nursing school wouldn't accept you" (content reflection) or "You don't feel smart enough to enter a nursing school" (feeling reflection) or "What makes you think you couldn't enter a nursing school?" (open question). These are examples of helping skills that would assist the student in exploring his or her interest or abilities in nursing. Counseling can proceed by going repeatedly over a client's aptitudes, achievements, interests, abilities, and values so that understanding is reached.

As counseling progresses, it may be important to get more specific occupational information as well as more specific information about interests, aptitudes, achievements, values, and personality. An excellent way to do this is for the client to talk with people in a specific job. He or she can obtain even more detailed information by trying out an activity as a volunteer or part-time worker. For example, if a student is trying to choose between becoming an occupational therapist and a salesperson, it may be helpful to get a summer job as a salesperson in a retail store and volunteer to work in a hospital doing occupational therapy. A potential problem is that occasionally one may work in a setting that is unrepresentative because of low morale, inadequate administrative structure, or unhelpful colleagues. Counselors can help the client separate the setting from the idiosyncrasies of the people in the work setting. As occupational experience and exploration in the counseling session help the client define his or her interests and ability more clearly, the client moves toward a career decision. Although a career decision has been reached, it may be only temporary. Career counseling can be repeated at various times in the client's lifetime. Traits and factors can be reassessed as clients have new experiences that affect their assessment of their aptitudes, achievements, interests, values, and personality.

Example of Step 3

The following illustration is from a session that occurs after Jack has talked to others and read about occupations of interest to him:

CL: Some of the information that I read was really helpful. I hadn't realized that there were so many different types of sales occupations and so many different places where you could work.

CO: That's great. It sounds as if you've done a lot of work. [The counselor chooses to reinforce the client's information seeking. Without occupational information, career counseling will be unsuccessful.]

CL: I think I would really like to take more art courses, perhaps in graphic arts. I know that graphic arts is a competitive field; at least that's what the material said. But I still think it would be good for me.

CO: Tell me a little more about what you like about it. [The counselor is aware of Jack's low score on economic security on the VS. His lack of concern about the competitiveness of graphic arts seems consistent with this.]

CL: Well, there is really an opportunity to draw, to be precise, to create new things. I could see myself doing advertising work.

CO: The artistic work really seems to fit for you. [Jack's high score on artistic on the KPRC and creativity on the VS are consistent with this statement.]

CL: When I was looking in the career library, I found information about public relations. That got me thinking, too, because you can use all kinds of methods to try to persuade people to a certain point of view. I guess I hadn't realized that there are a lot of ways of doing this. I suppose you can do this artistically as well as by talking to people.

CO: That's a clever way of looking at that. You can combine several interests of yours, perhaps. [Reinforcing the client's insight into how to combine artistic and persuasive interests, as indicated on the KPRC, furthers the client in his decision making.]

CL: I wonder if you can really do this in public relations or maybe advertising.

CO: Perhaps we can find some people for you to talk to about this idea. [The counselor realizes that written occupational information may not suffice to answer the client's question. The counselor is prepared to provide other resources to help Jack clarify his career decision making. Note how the counselor moves back and forth between self-assessment and occupational information, gradually moving the client closer to a career decision.]

APPLYING THE THEORY TO WOMEN

Differences in the abilities, achievements, values, personality, and interests of men and women have been a frequent source of study. Betz and Fitzgerald (1987) bring together a number of disparate studies that identify traits and factors that differentiate women from men. Much research has focused on the differences between men and women in their real and perceived mathematical and verbal ability, resulting in differential educational and occupational achievements by men and women. Although the values and interests of men and women are becoming more similar, there are some significant variations. These issues are the focus of this section.

Perhaps more important than the minor differences that exist between males and females in terms of verbal and mathematical ability are the factors that bring about or affect these differences. Although Maccoby and Jacklin (1974) and Hyde (1981) show that men tend to score higher than women on math aptitude tests and women tend to score higher than men on verbal tests, they caution about drawing generalizations from these observations. As Betz and Fitzgerald (1987) point out, the differences may be cultural. Asian women and Finnish women tend to do as well as, if not better than, men on measures of math ability. In the United States, Fennema and Sherman (1977) have reported that there are no sex differences in mathematical ability of high school girls when the number of high school courses that emphasize spatial ability, such as drafting courses, are the same for both men and women. The relationship between math ability and later career achievement has been the focus of several informative investigations.

As Betz and Fitzgerald (1987) and Fitzgerald and Betz (1994) observe, women's own achievements have not always been considered important. In earlier times, women were recognized for being wives, mistresses, or mothers of famous men, rather than for their own accomplishments. Recent research focuses on the comparative achievement of men and women. In a study of 440,000 high school students, Card, Steel, and Abeles (1980) found that, although women had higher high school grades than men, 5 and 11 years later men had obtained more education and were being paid more for their work than women. An earlier study by Terman and Oden (1959) showed that many highly talented women (with extremely high IQs) were working as homemakers or office workers. Betz and Fitzgerald (1987) point out that those women who continue to study math have a much broader range of career options than those who do not. Campbell (1976) observed that IQ scores for girls decrease between the 7th and 12th grades, whereas those for boys increase. The greatest decline is for women who have stereotypically feminine interests. Thus, conversely, one would expect that those women who are least willing to conform to traditional feminine sex roles are more likely to have higher educational and occupational achievements. Related to the differing achievements of women in school and in careers is their attitude toward their ability to be successful. Kerr and Maresh (1994) find that gifted women do not use their intellectual abilities as fully as possible in achieving occupational success.

Personality factors such as confidence and self-esteem have been a focus of research that attempts to explain the different levels of accomplishment and ability of women when compared to men. Ernest (1976) reported that women often decide not to take math as soon as it is an elective course in high school or college, and Chipman, Krantz, and Silver (1992) reported that math anxiety negatively affected interest in science careers. Related to this is the concept of self-efficacy, which is discussed in more detail in Chapter 13, "Social Learning Theory." The research on math self-efficacy, as reviewed by Lent and Hackett (1987), shows that women are often less confident and more anxious about their math ability than are men. Girls aged 7–10 are also less confident about math than boys (Eccles, Wigfield, Harold, & Blumenfeld, 1993) but are more confident about reading and music activities.

Lack of self-confidence about career-related activities is not confined to math. For example, Swanson and Lease (1990) found that women rated the general abilities of peers higher than their own abilities, while men rated the abilities of peers lower than their own abilities. Read (1994) found that women in nontraditional training programs had greater confidence in being able to succeed in school and on the job than did women in traditional and gender-balanced programs. Furthermore, Betz and Fitzgerald (1987) reported several studies of women in male-dominated occupations, such as physician, attorney, writer, and scientist, that show that these women have relatively high levels of self-esteem. However, they also observed that women, in general, are more likely to underestimate their own abilities and probable levels of future performance than are men. Clearly, the lack of self-esteem and confidence of many women has kept them from greater educational and occupational accomplishments.

In a very broad sense, the interests of men and women have been shown to be different (Hansen, Collins, Swanson, and Fouad, 1993). Interest inventories have revealed that, in general, women have more interest in artistic, clerical, and social occupations than men. Conversely, they have less interest in scientific and technical occupations (Betz & Fitzgerald, 1987). One of the problems in measuring interests has been that early forms of interest inventories were often sex-biased. For example, separate forms were used for men and women, and occupational titles were often male-oriented, such as *mailman,* rather than *mail carrier* (Diamond, 1975). Although interest inventories have been improved to measure interests more accurately, without sex bias contaminating the assessment, interest inventories still reflect social values about occupations. Social values that women should enter occupations such as teaching, nursing, and social work continue. For counselors, the challenge is to help women develop occupational interests in areas such as science and math.

Some research has focused on the different values that men and women have regarding work. Studying medical students, Kutner and Brogan (1980) found that the men's and women's work values were somewhat similar, but the men rated income and prestige as more important than the women did. In terms of commitment to work, Luzzo (1994) found that college women had a stronger commitment to work than did college men. Lips (1992) found that college women rated people-related values and intrinsic values higher than did college men. Although there are differences in the values of men and women within various professions and occupations, Betz and Fitzgerald (1987) conclude that differences in the career values of men and women are decreasing, with both males and females valuing accomplishment, salary, security, and so on.

Although differences in abilities, achievements, personality, interests, and values between men and women do exist, they are often rather small. The differences between workers within occupational groups are often much greater than those between men and women in general. Being aware of how men and women differ on various traits and factors may help counselors attend to societal pressures on their female clients, while attempting to maximize their educational and occupational opportunities.

APPLYING THE THEORY TO PEOPLE OF COLOR

Regarding the traits and factors of people of color, perhaps the most research has focused on the interests and work values of different cultural groups. For the purposes of this section, the interests and work values of Asian Americans, African Americans, Hispanics, and Native Americans will be discussed. Related to the formation of work values is the availability of occupational information. It is not valid to assume that occupational information is equally available to all Americans.

Research on the interests of people of color has focused mainly on measures of interests. For example, Sewell and Martin (1976) found, in general, that African American high school students tended to have fewer interests than white students and scored higher than white students in artistic interests and lower in scientific, technical, mechanical, and outdoor interests. However, Helms and Piper (1994) cite studies to show that the interests of black and white Americans are more similar to each other than prior research would suggest. Much of the research has used Holland's inventories, discussed in Chapter 4. There is not sufficient information to reveal how accurately interest inventories measure the likes and dislikes of people of color. A study done by Chu (1975) comparing freshman college students in the United States with Chinese college students suggested that the Strong-Campbell Interest Inventory is not effective in identifying the interests of Chinese students. Leung, Ivey, and Suzuki (1994) found that Asian American college students had interests in social as well as scientific and technical occupations, in contrast to the traditional view that Asian American interests are primarily scientific.

In her discussion of the work values of different cultural groups, Smith (1983) described studies that emphasize the various characteristics of cultural groups but cautioned against generalizing about the behavior of individuals in a particular cultural group. Observing that Asian Americans are often willing to adopt the work values of a new culture and to assimilate into it, Sue (1975) states that this is due in part to the development of independent work behavior in their native country. Leong (1991) found that Asian Americans placed a greater emphasis on making money and on security than did white Americans. Studying the values of adolescents in Hong Kong, Lau and Wong (1992) found that they valued personal and competency factors, enjoyment, and security in contrast to independence and obedience. This finding contradicts traditional views of the values of Chinese adolescents. More research has been done on the values of African Americans (Smith, 1977, 1980) than on those of other people of color. For example, Weathers, Thompson, Robert, and Rodriguez (1994) found that, when making career decisions, African American college women valued flexibility in pursuing career and family concerns as most important.

Studying Mexican Americans, Chandler (1974) found that family values took precedence over work values. More specifically, younger and higher-status Mexican Americans tended to value occupational success more than older and less-educated Mexican Americans. In a study of Latina undergraduates, Gomez and Fassinger (1994) found that women who were more bicultural in their value system tended to show a wider array of achievement behaviors than those who were less acculturated.

Regarding Native Americans, Richardson (1981) pointed out that the values of Native Americans are very different from those of white Americans. Native Americans tend to work for a specific purpose and stop when they have enough money to enjoy life. They may value working with their hands rather than doing mental work or paperwork. Native American students who valued working with their hands were more likely to drop out of high school than those who had other values (Gade, Hurlburt, & Fuqua, 1992). These studies are examples of the findings on different cultural values among people of color. Such generalizations help us to recognize the variety of work values that exist in society.

To choose an occupation, one must have, according to trait and factor theory, information not only about oneself, but also about occupations. Limited occupational information has been a problem for Native American youth (Spencer, Windham, & Peterson, 1975) and for Mexican American adolescents (Kuvlesky & Juarez, 1975). Furthermore, Davidson (1980) and Gottfredson (1978) note that African American teenagers have less occupational information than white teenagers and are thus hampered in career decision making. A possible solution to the problem of inadequate occupational information for people of color is to make available biographical information about specific workers, including discussions of how they overcame discrimination or financial hardship (Rodriguez, 1994). A question-and-answer format in printed materials, as well as pictures of people of color working in the profession, can also help to make occupational literature more attractive.

Differences in work values and interests combined with limited access to occupational information make the career choice process difficult for nonwhite Americans. Being aware of such information can help counselors avoid making assumptions about the occupational knowledge and values of their clients.

COUNSELOR ISSUES

One concern about trait and factor theory is its emphasis on testing. One hopes that a client will not leave the final counseling session saying "The test told me I should be a . . ." Although tests and inventories are used in trait and factor counseling, they are not necessarily the determinant of a final career choice. Since many clients are often looking for a quick solution, it is easy to allow the client to avoid the responsibility of making a career decision. Beginning counselors may find themselves giving test information rather than using more difficult counseling skills such as content and feeling reflections.

Trait and factor theory is deceptively simple. It is easy for the beginning counselor to develop a style in which he or she asks questions and the client gives the answers. Because tests seem so authoritative to the client, they can prevent an easy interaction and rapport between the client and the counselor. However, by taking ample time to leave the test information and discuss relevant personal experience, the counselor can help the client accept responsibility for career decision making.

Another reason that trait and factor theory is so deceptively simple is that the three basic tenets of trait and factor theory provide an overview but do not provide much detail. Trait and factor theory does not provide a guide to which traits or factors the counselor will include in his or her repertoire. It is up to the counselor to choose from hundreds of tests and inventories and to choose which traits and factors are most important. Conceptually, the theory provides less guidance for the counselor than do most of the other theories discussed in this book.

Trait and factor theory is a static rather than a developmental theory. It does not focus on how achievements, aptitudes, interests, values, and personalities grow and change; rather, it focuses on identifying traits and factors. This does not mean that this information cannot be useful in counseling. The counselor needs to help the client assess his or her interests and abilities. One way to do this is to discuss how these interests or aptitudes have changed over a period of years. This is certainly permissible within the guidelines of trait and factor theory; however, it is not emphasized. Often, the discussion of previous choices will be helpful in making a present choice. Thus, past traits and factors and their evolution may be useful in assessing current traits and factors.

Another problem that counselors may encounter is the difference between their own aptitudes, achievements, interests, values, and personality and those of the client. In particular, if the counselor has work values that are very different from those of the client, the counselor should recognize this and be tolerant. Counselors often value altruism and good working relationships with their associates. They need to be careful to understand those who do not value these factors and prefer prestige or management, which counselors might not value. This and the other problems mentioned make trait and factor theory one of the more difficult theories for a counselor to implement.

SUMMARY

Being the oldest, and arguably the most widely used, of all career development theories, trait and factor theory focuses on the match between an individual's aptitudes, achievements, interests, values, and personality and the requirements and conditions of occupations. Having obtained relevant information, the counselor and client work to bring about a match between the individual and the world of work. This approach relies heavily on the use of tests and inventories to measure aptitudes, achievements, interests, values, and personality. In test selection, the theory is vague, allowing the counselor to select those instruments that seem most appropriate to the counselor and the client. Selection of tests and inventories will usually determine the occupational classification system that the counselor will use. Such a system is helpful to the client in organizing information about occupations. The research focus in trait and factor theory has been on the traits and factors themselves rather than on the applicability of trait and factor theory as a career counseling approach. Additional research has been done delineating the aptitudes, achievements, interests, values, and personality of women and people of color. However, there is a vast need for more research, particularly on the latter group. The general trait and factor theory described in this chapter can be seen as a precursor to the more highly defined trait and factor theories of Holland (Chapter 4) and Lofquist and Dawis (Chapter 3).

References

Adler, T. (1991). Tug of war develops over use of GATB. *American Psychological Association Monitor, 22*(5), 14.

Astin, A. W. (1993). *What matters in college? Four critical years revisited.* San Francisco: Jossey-Bass.

Aubrey, R. F. (1977). Historical development of guidance and counseling and implications for the future. *Personnel and Guidance Journal, 55,* 288–295.

Betz, N. E., & Fitzgerald, L. F. (1987). *The career psychology of women.* Orlando, FL: Academic Press.

Campbell, P. B. (1976). Adolescent intellectual decline. *Adolescence, 11,* 631–635.

Card, J. J., Steel, L., & Abeles, R. P. (1980). Sex differences in realization of individual potential for achievement. *Journal of Vocational Behavior, 17,* 1–21.

Chandler, C. R. (1974). Value orientations among Mexican Americans in a southwestern city. *Sociology and Social Research, 58,* 262–271.

Chipman, S. F., Krantz, D. H., & Silver, A. (1992). Mathematics anxiety and science careers among able college women. *Psychological Science, 3,* 292–295.

Chu, P. H. (1975). Cross-cultural study of vocational interests measured by the Strong-Campbell Interest Inventory. *ACTa Psychological Taiwanica, 17,* 69–84.

Davidson, J. P. (1980). Urban black youth and career development. *Journal of Non-White Concerns in Personnel and Guidance, 8,* 119–142.

Diamond, E. E. (1975). Guidelines for the assessment of sex bias and sex fairness in career interest inventories. *Measurement and Evaluation in Guidance, 8,* 7–11.

Dictionary of occupational titles (4th ed.). (1991). Washington, DC: U.S. Department of Labor, Employment and Training Administration.

DISCOVER: A computer-based career development and counselor support system. (1984). Iowa City, IA: American College Testing Foundation.

Eccles, J., Wigfield, A., Harold, R. D., & Blumenfeld, P. (1993). Age and gender differences in children's self and task perceptions during elementary school. *Child Development, 64,* 830–847.

Enhanced guide for occupational exploration. (1991). Indianapolis, IN: JIST Works.

Ernest, J. (1976). Mathematics and sex. *American Mathematical Monthly, 83,* 595–614.

Fennema, E., & Sherman, J. A. (1977). Sex-related differences in mathematics achievement, spatial visualization, and affective factors. *American Educational Research Association Journal, 14,* 51–71.

Fitzgerald, L. F., & Betz, N. E. (1994). Career development in cultural context: The role of gender, race, class, and sexual orientation. In M. L. Savickas & R. W. Lent (Eds.). *Convergence in career development theories* (pp. 103–118). Palo Alto, CA: CPP Books.

Gade, E.M., Hurlburt, G., & Fuqua, D. (1992). The use of the Self-Directed Search to identify American Indian high school dropouts. *School Counselor, 39,* 311–315.

Goldenson, R. M. (Ed.). (1984). *Longman dictionary of psychology and psychiatry.* New York: Longman.

Goldman, L. (1971). *Using tests in counseling* (2nd ed.). New York: Appleton-Century-Crofts.

Gomez, M. J., & Fassinger, R. E. (1994). An initial model of Latina achievement: Acculturation, biculturalism, and achieving styles. *Journal of Counseling Psychology, 41,* 205–215.

Gottfredson, L. S. (1978). *Race and sex differences in occupational aspirations: Their development and consequences for occupational segregation.* (Grant No. NIE-G-78-0210). Washington, DC: National Institute of Education.

Gottfredson, L. S. (1988). Reconsidering fairness: A matter of social and ethical priorities. *Journal of Vocational Behavior, 33,* 293–319.

Gough, H. G. (1987). *California Psychological Inventory: Administrator's guide.* Palo Alto, CA: Consulting Psychologists Press.

Hansen, J. C., Collins, R. C., Swanson, J. L., & Fouad, N. A. (1993). Gender differences in the structure of interests. *Journal of Vocational Behavior, 42,* 200–211.

Helms, J. E., & Piper, R. E. (1994). Implications of racial identity theory for vocational psychology. *Journal of Vocational Behavior, 44,* 124–138.

Herr, E. L., & Cramer, S. H. (1984). *Career guidance and counseling through the life span* (2nd ed.). Boston: Little, Brown.

Hyde, J. S. (1981). How large are cognitive gender differences? *American Psychologist, 36,* 892–901.

Improved career decision making through the use of labor market information. (1991). Garrett Park, MD: Garrett Park Press.

Kapes, J. T., Mastie, M. M., & Whitfield, E. A. (Eds.). (1994). *A counselor's guide to career assessment instruments* (3rd ed.). Alexandria, VA: National Career Development Association.

Kerr, B., & Maresh, S. (1994). Career counseling for gifted women. In W. B. Walsh & S. H. Osipew (Eds.), *Career counseling for women* (pp. 197–235). Hillsdale, NJ: Erlbaum.

Kramer, J. J., & Conoley, J. C. (1993). *The eleventh mental measurements year book.* Lincoln, NE: University of Nebraska Press.

Kutner, N. G., & Brogan, D. R. (1980). The decision to enter medicine: Motivation, social support, and encouragements for women. *Psychology of Women Quarterly, 5,* 321–340.

Kuvlesky, W. P., & Juarez, R. (1975). Mexican American youth and the American dream. In J. S. Picou & R. E. Campbell (Eds.), *Career behavior of special groups: Theory, research, and practice* (pp. 241–296). Columbus, OH: Merrill.

Lau, S., & Wong, A. K. (1992). Value and sex-role orientation of Chinese adolescents. *International Journal of Psychology, 27,* 3–17.

Lent, R. W., Brown, S. D., & Hackett, G. (1994). Toward a unifying social cognitive theory of career and academic interest, choice and performance. *Journal of Vocational Behavior, 45,* 79–122.

Lent, R. W., & Hackett, G. (1987). Career self-efficacy: Empirical status and future directions. *Journal of Vocational Behavior, 30,* 347–382.

Leong, F. T. L. (1991). Career development attributes and occupational values of Asian American and white American college students. *The Career Development Quarterly, 39,* 221–230.

Leung, S. A., Ivey, D., & Suzuki, L. (1994). Factors affecting the career aspirations of Asian Americans. *Journal of Counseling & Development, 72,* 404–410.

Lips, H. M. (1992). Gender and science-related attitudes as predictors of college students' academic choices. *Journal of Vocational Behavior, 40,* 62–81.

Luzzo, D. A. (1994). An analysis of gender and ethnic differences in college students' commitment to work. *Journal of Employment Counseling, 31,* 38–45.

Maccoby, E. E., & Jacklin, C. N. (1974). *The psychology of sex differences.* Stanford, CA: Stanford University Press.

Murphy, L. L., Conoley, J. C., & Impara, J. C. (1994). *Tests in print IV.* Lincoln, NE: University of Nebraska Press.

National Vocational Guidance Association (1980). Guidelines for the preparation and evaluation of career information literature. *The Vocational Guidance Quarterly, 28,* 291–296.

Occupational outlook handbook. (1996). Washington, DC: U.S. Department of Labor.

Parsons, F. (1909). *Choosing a vocation.* Boston: Houghton Mifflin.

Ramist, L., Angoff, W. H., Broudy, I. L., Burton, T. W., Donlon, T. F., Stern, J., & Thorne, P. A. (1984). The predictive validity of the A & P tests. In T. F. Donlon (Ed.), *The College Board technical handbook for the Scholastic Aptitude Tests and Achievement Tests* (pp. 141–207). New York: College Entrance Examination Board.

Read, B. K. (1994). Motivational factors in technical college women's selection of nontraditional careers. *Journal of Career Development, 20,* 239–258.

Richardson, E. H. (1981). Cultural and historical perspectives in counseling American Indians. In D. W. Sue (Ed.), *Counseling the culturally different* (pp. 216–255). New York: Wiley.

Rodriguez, M. A. (1994). Preparing an effective occupational information brochure for ethnic minorities. *The Career Development Quarterly, 43,* 178–184.

Schmidt, F. L. (1988). The problem of group differences in ability test scores in employment selection. *Journal of Vocational Behavior, 33,* 272–292.

Sewell, T. E., & Martin, R. P. (1976). Racial differences in patterns of occupational choice in adolescents. *Psychology in the Schools, 13,* 326–333.

Sharf, R. S. (1993). *Occupational information overview.* Pacific Grove, CA: Brooks/Cole.

SIGI PLUS: Counselor's manual. (1985). Princeton, NJ: Educational Testing Service.

Smith, E. J. (1977). Work attitudes and job satisfactions of black workers. *Vocational Guidance Quarterly, 25,* 252–263.

Smith, E. J. (1980). Career development of minorities in nontraditional fields. *Journal of Non-White Concerns in Personnel and Guidance, 8,* 141–156.

Smith, E. J., (1983). Issues in racial minorities' career behavior. In W. B. Walsh & S. H. Osipow (Eds.), *Handbook of vocational psychology* (Vol. 1, pp. 101–122). Hillsdale, NJ: Erlbaum.

Spencer, B. F., Windham, G. O., & Peterson, J. H., Jr. (1975). Occupational orientations of an American group. In J. S. Picou & R. E. Campbell (Eds.), *Career behavior of special groups: Theory research, and practice* (pp. 199–223). Columbus, OH: Merrill.

Standard occupational classification manual. (1980). Washington, DC: U.S. Department of Commerce.

Stephenson, R. R. (1963). Client interpretation of tests. *Vocational Guidance Quarterly, 12,* 51–56.

Sue, D. W. (1975). Asian-Americans: Social-psychological forces affecting their life styles. In J. S. Picou & R. E. Campbell (Eds.), *Career behavior of special groups: Theory, research, and practice* (pp. 97–121). Columbus, OH: Merrill.

Swanson, J. L., & Lease, S. H. (1990). Gender differences in self-ratings of abilities and skills. *Career Development Quarterly, 38,* 347–359.

Terman, L. M., & Oden, M. H. (1959). *Genetic studies of genius: V. The gifted group at midlife.* Stanford, CA: Stanford University Press.

Watkins, C. E., Jr., Campbell, V. L., & Nieberding, R. (1994). The practice of vocational assessment by counseling psychologists. *The Counseling Psychologist, 22,* 115–128.

Weathers, P. L., Thompson, C. E., Robert, S., & Rodriguez, J., Jr. (1994). Black college women's career values: A preliminary investigation. *Journal of Multicultural Counseling and Development, 22,* 96–105.

Williamson, E. G. (1939) *How to counsel students.* New York: McGraw-Hill.

Williamson, E. G. (1965) *Vocational counseling.* New York: McGraw-Hill.

3

Work Adjustment Theory

Work adjustment theory is the outgrowth of more than 35 years of research by René Dawis and Lloyd Lofquist and their colleagues. Their work, which reflects the trait and factor tradition of the University of Minnesota, evolved into a growing body of research that led to several revisions and refinements of their theory. In the process of this development, the Work Adjustment Project was designed to provide improved rehabilitation services for vocationally disabled clients. At the University of Minnesota, an adult Vocational Assessment Clinic treated clients and a Vocational psychology Research unit was designed to develop and score the tests that are part of work adjustment theory. Originally designed to meet the needs of vocational rehabilitation clients, the theory is now applicable to adults who wish to make career choices or are experiencing work adjustment problems.

Work adjustment theory (Dawis & Lofquist, 1984) consists of 18 propositions and corollaries. The current theory is based on research that has modified earlier work (Dawis, England, & Lofquist, 1964; Dawis, Lofquist, & Weiss, 1968; Lofquist & Dawis, 1969). Each of these statements of theory has had as a goal the prediction of work adjustment. Dawis and Lofquist (1984) define work adjustment as a "continuous and dynamic process by which a worker seeks to achieve and maintain correspondence with a work environment" (p. 237). Put another way, work adjustment is indicated by the length of time, or tenure, on the job. This concern with job tenure and a similar concept, job performance, distinguishes work adjustment theory from most other theories described in this book, which are concerned with career selection or work adjustment but not actual performance on the job.

There are two major components to the prediction of work adjustment (and therefore tenure): satisfaction and satisfactoriness. *Satisfaction* refers to being satisfied with the work that one does. In contrast, *satisfactoriness* refers to the employer's satisfaction with the individual's performance. Or to rephrase, satisfaction refers to the extent to which an individual's needs and requirements are fulfilled by the work that he or she does. Satisfactoriness concerns the appraisal of others, usually supervisors, of the extent to which an individual adequately completes the work that is assigned to him or her, and it is of interest to industrial and organizational psychologists.

"Satisfaction is a key indicator of work adjustment," state Lofquist and Dawis (1984, p. 217). Satisfaction is important because the individual must be satisfied with many aspects of the work, such as salary and type of work task. This chapter will focus primarily on the individual's satisfaction with work. However, work adjustment theory is also concerned with other indicators of satisfaction and satisfactoriness, including the amount of turnover, absenteeism, and tardiness on the job; devotion to a job; job morale; and productivity on a job. These aspects of job performance are all indicators of work adjustment. The work environment must satisfy the individual's needs, and he or she must have the requisite skills to meet the job's needs.

Skills and needs are observable entities that are the essence of work personality. However, hundreds of skills may be required in different types of jobs, as well as many needs, so that measurement of them is awkward and difficult. Dawis and Lofquist (1984) propose the concept of abilities, which combines the common elements of skills required in many jobs. In a similar vein, values serve to group needs together in a meaningful way. Much of these researchers' theoretical work concerns the discussion and measurement of abilities and values. They also discuss personality style and interests. Their experimental work on personality styles and adjustment styles is not as highly developed as is their work on needs and values. They view interests as a derived construct, being a reflection of ability-value relationships.

In describing work adjustment theory, a specific application of trait and factor theory, an approach similar to that employed in Chapter 2—Trait and Factor Theory—will be used. Work adjustment theory differs from general trait and factor theory in that it makes use of clearly defined concepts and follows an articulated theoretical model. The first section of this chapter will be concerned with assessing abilities, values, personality, and interests (similar to Parsons's first step). Since abilities and values are the major emphasis of Lofquist and Dawis's (1984) work, they will receive the most attention. The second section, also similar to Parsons's second step, will be concerned with knowledge of the requirements and conditions of occupations. In this section, abilities required by work and reinforcement of individual needs will be discussed. The third section, similar to Parsons's third step, will outline the matching of the abilities and values of an individual with the abilities required by the job and the reinforcers provided by the job.

Work adjustment theory also has implications for helping clients with adjustment problems, such as problems with co-workers and superiors, boredom, inability to meet job demands, and retirement, as well as many other issues. In addition, work adjustment theory provides some psychometric data on the ability and values differences of women and people of color. This is not a major focus of the theory, as it is concerned with differences among individuals, not group differences.

ASSESSING ABILITIES, VALUES, PERSONALITY, AND INTERESTS

Consistent with trait and factor theory, measurement of values and abilities is crucial to the understanding of work adjustment theory. To assess abilities, Dawis and Lofquist (1984) make use of the General Aptitude Test Battery (GATB) developed by the U.S. Department of Labor (1979). As a measure of values and needs, they have developed the Minnesota Importance Questionnaire (Rounds, Henly, Dawis, Lofquist, & Weiss, 1981), which is critical to the use and understanding of work adjustment theory. They are also in the process of developing measures of personality style and adjustment style as they relate to work adjustment (Lawson, 1993). Because Dawis and Lofquist (1984) see interests as an expression of abilities and values, their focus is on ability and value assessment. Each of these components of work adjustment theory will be discussed and illustrated.

Abilities

Dawis and Lofquist (1984) define abilities as "reference dimensions for skills" (p. 233). Abilities are viewed as encompassing aptitudes, which are predicted skills as contrasted to acquired skills. For Lofquist and Dawis, the notion of abilities is needed in order to conceptualize a vast array of work skills. The latter can include typing, waiting on tables, fixing teeth or engines, planing wood, plastering walls, selling insurance policies, and so forth. There are hundreds, perhaps thousands, of such skills. Ability tests measure factors common to many skills. Many ability tests measure between 8 and 15 ability dimensions. Dawis and Lofquist (1984) describe the General Aptitude Test Battery (U.S. Department of Labor, 1982) as an example of a measure of ability. The GATB is used widely by employment counseling agencies and measures 9 specific abilities:

G—General learning ability: Overall ability to learn as well as general knowledge

V—Verbal ability: Understanding of words and paragraphs

N—Numerical ability: Ability to perform arithmetic quickly

S—Spatial ability: Ability to see objects in space and understand relationships between two-dimensional and three-dimensional objects

P—Form perception: Ability to see details in two- or three-dimensional drawings and to make discriminations in shapes and shadings

Q—Clerical ability: Ability to see differences in tables and lists that include both words and numbers

K—Eye-hand coordination: Ability to coordinate hand movements with visual perception
F—Finger dexterity: Ability to move small objects quickly and with precision
M—Manual dexterity: Ability to use hands and arms in manipulating objects quickly and skillfully

Although other abilities could be used in addition to those listed, these nine abilities are used by Dawis and Lofquist in their application of work adjustment theory. Other ability tests could be used that would be consistent with work adjustment theory, but the GATB is most practical because of the information it provides for counselors to use in matching jobs with individuals' abilities and values. In general, the GATB incorporates abilities required for many jobs and measures a broader base of abilities than many academic aptitude tests. For example, one would expect an electrician to have, among other abilities, numerical ability, form perception, and eye-hand coordination. The GATB manual (U.S. Department of Labor, 1982) provides a list of abilities that are needed in a vast variety of jobs.

Values

Just as abilities represent a distillation of many work skills, so values represent a grouping of needs. Unlike the hundreds of work skills that may exist, the number of needs is fewer. The Minnesota Importance Questionnaire (MIQ) (Rounds, Henley, Dawis, Lofquist, & Weiss, 1981) is a measure of needs. Although not encompassing all needs, the 20 need scales of the Minnesota Importance Questionnaire characterize important work-related concepts. The 20 need scales are listed in Table 3-1 along with the statement that represents each scale. In the questionnaire each statement is paired in a comparison with every other statement, to constitute 190 items. For example, an individual is asked whether he or she would rather "be busy all the time" (activity) or "do things for other people" (social service). By comparing the relative importance of each need, scores on each scale are determined. The disadvantage of this method is that it represents a narrower definition of the need than if several items were used for a particular scale. Choosing this method to define needs reflects Dawis and Lofquist's emphasis on the importance of rigorous measurement in their theory.

Using the statistical technique of factor analysis, Dawis and Lofquist (1984) have derived six values from the 20 needs, also listed in Table 3-1. Values are clustered with their opposites: achievement is negatively related to comfort, status is very different from altruism, and safety is negatively related to autonomy. The relationship of the needs to the values and the values to each other provides a way for a counselor to chunk and derive meaning from the need scales of the MIQ. The values are described as follows:

Table 3-1 *Values, Need Scales, and Statements from the Minnesota Importance Questionnaire*

Value	*Need Scale*	*Statement*
Achievement	Ability utilization	I could do something that makes use of my abilities.
	Achievement	The job could give me a feeling of accomplishment.
Comfort	Activity	I could be busy all the time.
	Independence	I could work alone on the job.
	Variety	I could do something different every day.
	Compensation	My pay would compare well with that of other workers.
	Security	The job would provide for steady employment.
	Working conditions	The job would have good working conditions.
Status	Advancement	The job would provide an opportunity for advancement.
	Recognition	I could get recognition for the work I do.
	Authority	I could tell people what to do.
	Social status	I could be "somebody" in the community.
Altruism	Co-workers	My co-workers would be easy to make friends with.
	Moral values	I could do the work without feeling it is morally wrong.
	Social service	I could do things for other people.
Safety	Company policies and practices	The company would administer its policies fairly.
	Supervision-human relations	My boss would back up the workers (with top management).
	Supervision-technical	My boss would train the workers well.
Autonomy	Creativity	I could try out some of my ideas.
	Responsibility	I could make decisions on my own.

From *A Psychological Theory of Work Adjustment*, by R. V. Dawis and L. H. Lofquist.

Achievement: This value is reflected in the need to make use of one's abilities and to do things that give one a sense of accomplishment. For example, a carpenter who is proud of her abilities and the products she makes is likely to value achievement.

Comfort: Included in this value are a variety of needs dealing with specific aspects of work that make the job less stressful for the worker. These are quite diverse, including being busy all the time (activity), working alone (independence), doing different things (variety), and being paid well (compensation). Other aspects of comfort can be long range, for example, a desire for steady employment (security). Also, specific working conditions can be important. These might include lighting, heating and amount of space. All of these have in common an emphasis on a nonstressful work environment, one that will yield benefits to the employee, such as security and compensation.

Status: How one is perceived by others and the recognition one gets are the emphasis of this value. Status can be attained by an opportunity for advancement, recognition for the work that one does, or, more generally, prestige (social status) that comes from being important in the community. In addition, telling people what to do (authority) is another way of achieving status. Recognizing that status needs are important to some individuals can be particularly helpful both in career choice and in recognizing a problem with work dissatisfaction. For example, some people who have initially enjoyed a particular job may lose interest in it when they find that they are not advancing and are not being recognized for what they do.

Altruism: Altruism is quite the opposite of status because it is concerned not with how one is perceived by others but with how one can help or work with others. Doing things for other people (social service) and, more specifically, getting along with colleagues at work (co-workers) can be a very important aspect of work. In particular, being able to do work that feels morally correct (moral values) can be a need that is directly tied to work satisfaction. For example, persons who are required to sell products that they feel are harmful or worthless may find that they must terminate their jobs because their moral values are being violated.

Safety: Rather than being seen in the narrow sense of avoiding hazardous conditions, this value is broader in that it reflects the importance of orderliness and predictability. It includes the enforcement of policies in a fair manner (company policies and practices) as well as support from supervisors (supervision-human relations). Also, safety includes how co-workers are trained (supervision-technical) as it can affect how a person does his or her job. For example, an automobile assembly worker who could not count on co-workers to do their jobs well and who felt that management was lax in providing workers with training and materials would not have his or her safety needs met.

Autonomy: Some people are not concerned with how they are treated by their bosses (safety) but want the opportunity to work on their own.

This might include trying out some of their own ideas (creativity) or making decisions on their own (responsibility). For example, an auto assembly worker who wants to try out new ideas to make her work easier or more efficient is concerned with autonomy rather than safety.

These values and needs provide a way for the counselor to understand a person's work experience. Without such a guideline, work experience can appear to be a series of unrelated events. The MIQ is a method of measuring the importance of needs that emerge from experience. For example, individuals who want to accomplish a lot in their work, help others, and make decisions on their own (achievement, altruism, and autonomy) will find satisfaction in very different occupations from persons who are concerned with pay and steady employment, getting recognition for the work they do, and being in a company with fair policies (comfort, status, and safety).

Personality Styles

According to Dawis and Lofquist (1984), personality style is concerned with how an individual with particular abilities and values interacts with his or her work situation. They have identified four characteristics of personality style: celerity, pace, rhythm, and endurance. These describe ways in which people respond to their environment: how quickly, with how much intensity, in what particular pattern, and for how long. Celerity is concerned with the speed with which one approaches tasks; pace is concerned with the effort one spends in working; rhythm is the pattern of one's effort or pace; and endurance concerns how long one is likely to continue working at a task. Thus, someone who is high on celerity, pace, rhythm, and endurance works quickly, is involved in a large number of activities, is consistent in his or her work, and can be relied on to complete projects. These work personality styles are an interesting addition to the ability and values concepts of Lofquist and Dawis. However, scales for the assessment of celerity, pace, rhythm, and endurance are still in the developmental stage (Lawson, 1993). Questions such as "Do individuals maintain the same work personality style (celerity, pace, rhythm, and endurance) in one work environment that they do in another?" remain to be answered.

Interests

As stated earlier, interests are seen by Dawis and Lofquist (1984) as derived from values and abilities in that they are an expression of ability-value relationships. For these researchers, an interest in being an engineer or a bricklayer is derived from the abilities and values that one has. They believe that  interest inventories can be helpful in counseling but do not feature them in their approach to work adjustment counseling. Rounds (1990) analyzed data that assessed the relative contribution of work values and vocational interests. His conclusion was that both are important, but that work values appear to be a slightly better predictor of job satisfaction than interests. Differences were found also for females and males. This study lends support to the weight that Dawis and Lofquist put on values as an important aspect of prediction of job satisfaction.

A Counseling Example

In the following example, the GATB and MIQ are used to assist a client with self-assessment. Later in this chapter, after a description of the work adjustment theory approach to occupational information, a continuing discussion with the client will show how work adjustment theory matches information about values and abilities with occupational information.

Winifred is a 45-year-old white farmer living with her husband in rural Missouri. Her husband is an auto mechanic in the local village, and Winifred runs the family farm. They have no children but cared for foster children until about 10 years ago. Winifred has been the principal farm manager and farm laborer for 20 years, raising feed corn and hogs. Winifred has been primarily responsible for planting, fertilizing, and harvesting the corn. She also takes the major responsibility for the constant activity of feeding the hogs. Winifred had no formal training in farming and learned most of it from her parents and from attending special agricultural extension programs. Recently, she sprained her back badly while harvesting. This came as an addition to chronic back pain that she had experienced over the last 3 years. After consulting with her physician, who has made several X-rays of her spine, Winifred has come to the realization that she can no longer handle the heavy task of farming. Furthermore, she has become dissatisfied and bored with the work. Because Winifred is self-employed, she is both employee and employer. One measure of her satisfactoriness as a farmer is the productivity of the farm. Winifred has made the farm financially productive in good weather conditions and has been able to maintain the farm's solvency in times of drought.

When discussing her concerns with her physician, Winifred was referred to a local career counselor. He asked her to complete the GATB and the MIQ after talking with her briefly. Winifred's scores are summarized in Table 3-2. Her scores are highest in numerical ability, spatial ability, form perception, eye-hand coordination, and finger dexterity. Her highest needs as registered on the MIQ are for ability utilization and achievement.

CL: It was strange taking those tests. When I was in high school, I remember tests like that aptitude test I took. [The GATB.] It's been 25 years. I never thought I'd see one of those again. But I was surprised to be playing with blocks and washers and things. [Winifred is referring to the finger and manual dexterity tests.]

Table 3-2 *Test Scores for Winifred*

	High	*Moderate*	*Low*
GATB	Numerical ability Spatial ability Form perception Eye-hand coordination Finger dexterity		Verbal ability Clerical ability
MIQ	Ability utilization Achievement	Creativity Responsibility Activity Independence Compensation	

CO: Well, you seemed to do fine. There's a lot of information for us to look at. [The counselor wants to explore Winifred's abilities, and the GATB seems to be a good place to start.]

CL: My husband always says that I can fix the tractor faster than he can. He says that my hands really whiz around when I get going.

CO: Well, you also have the abilities to visualize objects and to understand relationships of objects on paper. [The counselor wants to talk to Winifred about her spatial ability and her form perception.]

CL: When I was a girl in school 25 years ago, I couldn't take courses that I wanted to. Shop courses were for boys; home economics and business education were for girls. I know my mom wanted me to be a secretary. What a mess I would have been! I know that I don't have those kinds of skills. It drives me nuts even when I have to do some of that at the farm. I can't type lists, and I don't like it.

CO: Tell me more about what you're good at and not so good at on the farm. [So far, it seems as if Winifred's perception of her own abilities matches that of the GATB. The counselor wants to check further.]

CL: Well, I'm good at fixing things. My husband has taught me a lot of mechanical stuff that he learned when he took courses in high school. I seem to pick it up real well. Later, I learned about electrical things. That's probably the most fun for me. My husband keeps telling me how good I am at it. I guess I am. That's the good part. The bad part is moving around and lifting. It really hurts. I used to do a lot more heavy work. Now I look for ways I can get other people to do it or get some machine to do it. You should see the way I use a tractor. I practically try to wash dishes with it. We've got all kinds of additions for the tractor, but sometimes it's real hard to hook them up.

CO: Seems like working on the farm has really given you a chance to see what you can do and what you can't do. [Winifred's own perception of her abilities seems to check out with her scores on the GATB.]

Winifred and the counselor continue to discuss the GATB and then move to a discussion of her work values, needs, and the MIQ. Even from the discussion so far, the counselor senses that achievement is important to Winifred. She seems proud of her abilities and of what she has done.

CL: I like what I've done on the farm. A lot of my friends sit around and make pies. That's not me. At first, that bothered my husband. Now, he's OK with it. We figure it's OK to buy frozen foods, desserts, and such. He doesn't seem to mind that I don't cook. He doesn't want to, either.

CO: You've done a lot with the farm. What else have you done? [The counselor hears the achievement value and wants to inquire further.]

CL: I've done a lot of different things. I do so much on my own, particularly the last few years. My husband seems to have lost some interest in the farm, too. I wish he hadn't. I kind of like it, but it gets to be a burden sometimes. I don't mind deciding what to do, but I guess I get tired of having to be there all the time. We can never leave the farm, it seems. A few times we have; my folks come in. It's hard. You know pigs. You can't leave them for long.

CO: I would like to talk to you about the Minnesota Importance Questionnaire. Some of the scores fit in with what you're saying about what's important to you. You really do seem to like to be active and to work on your own. [Finding that Winifred's expressed values seem to fit with the MIQ makes things go smoothly.]

CL: I wondered how I did with the MIQ. That was easy. Not like the GATB.

CO: Well, your high scores show that you like to use your abilities and want to be able to get a sense of accomplishment in what you do.

CL: That's for sure. I can't imagine doing something that didn't matter. To do the same thing time after time that didn't matter would be awful. I want to feel like I'm getting somewhere, making progress.

CO: Well, we will consider that when we start to look at things that you might want to do. [The counselor makes a mental note that achievement is, again, important to Winifred. Its opposite, comfort, is not. Work conditions do not seem to be important to her.]

The counselor and Winifred continue to talk about Winifred's abilities, values, and interests. Later they will discuss possible occupations and matching occupations that fit the GATB.

MEASURING THE REQUIREMENTS AND CONDITIONS OF OCCUPATIONS

Just as there are methods to measure individuals' values and abilities, there are methods to measure the abilities and values needed for many occupations. In brief, this is done by averaging scores for people in various occupations on the GATB and the MIQ. Such information is not available for the work personality styles of celerity, pace, rhythm, and endurance. Also, information about interest patterns of people in various occupations has not been used by Dawis and Lofquist in their psychometric application of work adjustment theory. This is because Lofquist and Dawis believe that interest is a secondary concept, as mentioned earlier, and that the information provided by the occupational patterns of abilities and values is sufficient. These two will be discussed in more detail here.

Ability Patterns

Occupational Ability Patterns have been developed by the U.S. Department of Labor to describe the important abilities that are required for a great variety of jobs. To do this, job analysts assessed an occupation at various sites. Furthermore, individuals employed in occupations were administered the GATB. From these two methods, a set of GATB ability requirements (three or four) was developed for each occupation. Furthermore, cutoff scores were selected. Those scoring above the cutoff point were people who had done their jobs successfully as determined by supervisor ratings or other means. This information enables an individual to assess whether he or she has abilities similar to those of successful people in a given occupation. However, in determining cutoff scores for occupations, it is important not to set the scores too high and possibly exclude adequate potential candidates.

Value Patterns

Work environments differ in the degree to which they meet the needs and values of an individual. Lofquist and Dawis have developed a list of Occupational Reinforcer Patterns to assess how much an occupation reinforces the values of individuals. To do that, they developed the Minnesota Job Description Questionnaire (MJDQ; Borgen, Weiss, Tinsley, Dawis, & Lofquist, 1968a), which assesses how well an occupation reinforces or meets each of 20 needs. The MJDQ uses the same needs as the Minnesota Importance Questionnaire. Table 3-3 shows the wording of the items on the MJDQ. Comparing the items in Table 3-1 with those in Table 3-3 will illustrate the similarity. For example, on the MIQ the need for activity is assessed by the item "I would be busy all the time." Activity as a reinforcer is assessed through this MJDQ item: "Workers on this job are busy all the time." Thus, the needs of an individual are matched with the reinforcers provided by the job. Many occupations were assessed with the MJDQ so that reinforcer patterns could be established (Borgen et al., 1968b). Recently, Dawis, Dohm, and Jackson (1993) have described occupations as reinforcer systems, which can offer predictable versus unpredictable reinforcements, self-reinforcements versus non-self-reinforcements, and social versus nonsocial reinforcement. These ratings of reinforcement schedules are related to, but different from, occupational reinforcement patterns. Using information about value patterns helps counselors to see how the values of their clients match the values that are met or reinforced by a large number of occupations.

Table 3-3 *Need Scales and Statements from the Minnesota Job Description Questionnaire*

Need Scale	*Statement (Workers on this job . . .)*
Ability utilization	Make use of their individual abilities
Achievement	Get a feeling of accomplishment
Activity	Are busy all the time
Advancement	Have opportunities for advancement
Authority	Tell other workers what to do
Company policies and practices	Have a company that administers its policies fairly
Compensation	Are paid well in comparison with other workers
Co-workers	Have co-workers who are easy to make friends with
Creativity	Try out their own ideas
Independence	Do their work alone
Moral values	Do work without feeling that it is morally wrong
Recognition	Receive recognition for the work they do
Responsibility	Make decisions on their own
Security	Have steady employment
Social service	Have work where they do things for other people
Social status	Have a position of "somebody" in the community
Supervision—human relations	Have bosses who back up their workers (with top management)
Supervision—technical	Have bosses who train the workers well
Variety	Have something different to do every day
Working conditions	Have good working conditions

From *Minnesota Job Description Questionnaire,* by Borgen, Weiss, Tinsley, Dawis, and Lofquist. Copyright © 1968, Vocational Psychology Research, Department of Psychology, University of Minnesota. Reprinted by permission.

Table 3-4 *Instruments Used in Work Adjustment Theory*

Assessment of Individuals	*Assessment of Occupations*
Abilities	Ability Patterns
General Aptitude Test Battery (GATB)	Occupational Ability Patterns
Values	Value Patterns
Minnesota Importance Questionnaire (MIQ)	Minnesota Job Description Questionnaire (MJDQ)
Personality Styles	Personality Styles
Instruments are being developed	Instruments are being developed
Matching Assessment of Individual and Occupation	
Minnesota Occupational Classification System (MOCS)	
Adjustment Styles (Instruments are being developed)	

Combining Ability and Value Patterns

Important information about occupations can be provided by combining information about Occupational Ability Patterns and Occupational Reinforcer Patterns. The combined data were used to create the Minnesota Occupational Classification System (MOCS). The original MOCS had 337 occupations. The third revision of the MOCS has 1,769 occupations. The relationship of instruments used to assess individual abilities and values and those found in occupations is shown in Table 3-4. The individual and occupational patterns are matched by using the MOCS, which is described in the next section.

MATCHING ABILITIES, VALUES, AND REINFORCERS

When matching values and abilities with the Occupational Ability Patterns and Occupational Reinforcer Patterns, the counselor has three tools available: the Minnesota Importance Questionnaire report form, the GATB manual (U.S. Department of Labor, 1982), and the Minnesota Occupational Classification System (MOCS). All can be helpful in identifying occupations for clients to explore further. In addition, a relatively new but useful concept is adjustment style. This concept concerns the degree of fit between the person and the environment. Four qualities describe this fit: flexibility, activeness, reactiveness, and perseverance. All of these tools can help the client and the counselor make use of a wealth of information and narrow the number of occupational alternatives so that the client has a manageable number of choices.

When clients take the Minnesota Importance Questionnaire, they receive scores on the six values and 20 needs described earlier and on 90 occupations. Table 3-5 shows an example of a report. It lists occupations whose reinforcer patterns match the client's identified needs. The strength of the correspondence (or relationship) between the individual's rating of the importance of a need on the MIQ and the importance attached to that need by a sample of people in an occupation is indicated by the C Index. By using this, a counselor can help the client locate occupations for future consideration. If the sample of 90 occupations is not sufficient, the counselor can request an extended report, which lists the scores of more than 183 occupations.

The client and counselor can also match the client's ability scores and need patterns to occupations by using the Minnesota Occupational Classification System. Since the MOCS lists both Occupational Ability Patterns and Occupational Reinforcer Patterns for more than 1,700 occupations, it can be a particularly helpful resource. The counselor and client can examine occupations, perhaps taken from the Minnesota Importance Questionnaire report (Table 3-5), and ascertain the match between the client and the occupational group, a very thorough matching process. However, this is not the only way of looking at the correspondence between the individual and the working environment.

Although still in an experimental stage, the notion of adjustment style can be useful to the counselor. *Adjustment style* refers to how an individual relates to the occupational environment (Dawis & Lofquist, 1984). The concepts of flexibility, activeness, reactiveness, and perseverance all concern the relationship of the individual to the occupation. *Flexibility* refers to the ability of an individual to tolerate unpleasant or difficult aspects of the job. For example, individuals differ in terms of their flexibility in working in a cramped working environment or with an unpleasant superior. When individuals are faced with unpleasant or difficult work situations, they may try to change the environment (activeness) or make a change in themselves (reactiveness). For example, a person who must deal with an unpleasant superior may choose to confront the superior and try to resolve the discomfort (activeness). On the other hand, an individual may demonstrate reactiveness by trying to ignore the superior and by paying attention to other colleagues or the job itself. Perseverance refers to how long an individual can tolerate adverse conditions before changing jobs. For example, some people can persevere longer than others in cramped quarters or with an unpleasant superior. These concepts show how individuals deal with a conflict between themselves and their job. These dimensions may be helpful in conceptualizing different solutions to irritating job circumstances. Lawson (1993) has had success in measuring three of these dimensions. She has developed an Inflexibility Scale, which measures the low end of the flexibility dimension, an Achievement Scale, which measures the high end of the activeness continuum, and a Reactiveness Scale, which measures some components of poor mental health.

By matching the individual's abilities and values with Occupational Ability Patterns and Occupational Reinforcer Patterns, the counselor atempts to increase the likelihood of the client's future job satisfaction and satisfactoriness. This is a major focus of work adjustment theory. Thus, the

Table 3-5 *Minnesota Importance Questionnaire Sample Report Form (Winifred's Scores)*

MIQ profile is compared with Occupational Reinforcer Patterns for 90 representative occupations. Correspondence is indicated by the C Index. A prediction of Satisfied (S) results from C values greater than .50, Likely Satisfied (L) for C values between .10 and .49, and Not Satisfied (N) for C values less than .10. Occupations are clustered by similarity of Occupational Reinforcer Pattern. Abbreviations after each cluster refer to the primary values (all capitals) and secondary values: For example, Achievement (ACH) is a primary value, and Comfort (Com) is secondary value.

	C Index	*Prediction Satisfied*		*C Index*	*Prediction Satisfied*
Cluster A (ACH-AUT-Alt)	.30	L	Cluster B (ACH-Com)	.15	L
Architect	.25	L	Bricklayer	–.07	N
Dentist	.21	L	Carpenter	.24	L
Family practitioner	.21	L	Cement mason	–.16	N
Interior designer-decorator	.43	L	Elevator repairer	.48	L
Lawyer	.35	L	Heavy equipment operator	.30	L
Minister	.13	L	Landscape gardener	–.11	N
Nurse, occupational health	.12	L	Lather	–.05	N
Occupational therapist	.33	L	Millwright	.10	L
Optometrist	.39	L	Painter-paperhanger	.11	L
Psychologist, counseling	.21	L	Patternmaker, metal	.28	L
Recreation leader	.15	L	Pipefitter	.34	L
Speech pathologist	.28	L	Plasterer	–.13	N
Teacher, elementary school	.23	L	Plumber	.37	L
Teacher, secondary school	.28	L	Roofer	–.04	N
Vocational evaluator	.36	L	Salesperson, automobile	.43	L
Cluster C (ACH-Aut-Com)	.44	L	Cluster D (ACH-STA-Com)	.57	S
Alteration tailor	.27	L	Accountant, certified public	.43	L
Automobile mechanic	.25	L	Airplane copilot, commercial	.25	L
Barber	.46	L	Cook (hotel-restaurant)	.48	L

	C Index	*Prediction Satisfied*		*C Index*	*Prediction Satisfied*
Beauty operator	.44	L	Department head, supermarket	.39	L
Caseworker	.28	L	Drafter, architectural	.41	L
Claim adjuster	.51	S	Electrician	.44	L
Commercial artist, illustrator	.56	S	Engineer, civil	.45	L
Electronics mechanic	.39	L	Engineer, time study	.59	S
Locksmith	.28	L	Farm equipment mechanic I	.52	S
Maintenance repairer, factory	.41	L	Line-installer-repairer (tel)	.13	L
Mechanical-engineering tech	.40	L	Machinist	.54	S
Office-machine servicer	.53	S	Programmer (bus., eng., sci.)	.65	S
Photoengraver (stripper)	.54	S	Sheet metal worker	.50	S
Sales agent, real estate	.32	L	Statistical-machine servicer	.56	S
Salesperson, general hardware	.15	L	Writer, technical publications	.61	S
Cluster E (COM)	.19	L	Cluster F (Alt-Com)	.21	L
Assembler, production	.05	N	Airplane-flight attendant	.02	N
Baker	.16	L	Clerk (gen. ofc., civil svc.)	.03	N
Bookbinder	.28	L	Dietitian	.56	S
Bookkeeper I	.31	L	Fire fighter	.16	L
Bus driver	.17	L	Librarian	.28	L
Key-punch operator	.10	L	Medical technologist	.21	L
Meat cutter	.16	L	Nurse, professional	.15	L
Post-office clerk	.13	L	Orderly	–.08	N
Production helper (food)	.24	L	Physical therapist	.34	L
Punch press operator	.11	L	Police officer	.13	L
Sales, general (department store)	.20	L	Receptionist, civil service	.29	L
Sewing-machine operator, auto	.03	N	Secretary (general office)	.26	L
Solderer (production line)	.16	L	Taxi driver	.12	L
Telephone operator	.17	L	Telephone installer	.42	L
Teller (banking)	.18	L	Waiter-waitress	.18	L

counselor is trying to find not just an occupation that will be appealing to the client at the moment, but one that will lead to long-term satisfaction or job tenure.

By returning to our example of Winifred, we can illustrate this concept further:

> *CL:* I'm wondering what other careers I can consider now that farming looks like it's going to be difficult for me.
>
> *CO:* Let's look at your Minnesota Importance Questionnaire [Winifred's scores are those reported in Table 3-5.] Note that it lists some occupations that it predicts would satisfy you (S) or are likely to satisfy you (L). Let's take a look at some of the S occupations. [The counselor wants to work with matches between the client's values as measured by the Minnesota Importance Questionnaire and the Occupational Reinforcer Patterns.]
>
> *CL:* Oh, this is interesting. I don't think that I would want to be a claim adjuster. There isn't much call for that around here. Commercial artist—that's interesting. I guess that's a dream occupation. I don't think I have the ability to do that, however. Oh, look, farm equipment mechanic. I am doing that now, sort of. I know there is a demand for that around here. If I could do some light work, maybe that would work out for me.
>
> *CO:* Well, that is one that we can look into. We may need to find out about some specific employers and the kind of work they do. [The counselor's concern is that the client's physical condition will preclude being a farm equipment mechanic. However, some employers may have opportunities for work that requires little lifting or standing.]
>
> *CL:* I see time study engineer on there, too. I don't know what that is.
>
> *CO:* We can find out more about it. We can use the *Dictionary of Occupational Titles* to tell us more about it.
>
> *CL:* Wow! Programmer—I think that I would like that. I just don't think that I could go back to school. Also, I'm not sure whether I have the mathematical ability that would be necessary.
>
> *CO:* Well, let's look into that. Let us see how your GATB scores compare to those of programmers. [The counselor then consults the Minnesota Occupational Classification System.]
>
> *CL:* But what kind of schooling would I need?
>
> *CO:* Let's look in the *Occupational Outlook Handbook.* [The client and the counselor look at it together. They see that there are several ways of entering the occupation of programmer.]

The client and counselor continue in this manner to investigate possible occupations that the client may consider. The counselor will ask the client to do more reading to find out more about occupations that seem initially attractive. While using a method of matching the client with potential occupations, the counselor has narrowed the number of potential occupations to be considered to about 15. The client and counselor not only will explore occupational information but will also examine educational opportunities, physical limitations, salary, and other issues that will affect the client's eventual choice.

Work adjustment theory has produced over 250 studies that lend support to its validity as an effective method of helping individuals with career choice and work adjustment problems. Research such as that done by Breeden (1993), which followed up 436 adults who had received career counseling, found that, after two years, those who had changed jobs and occupations were more satisfied after counseling than before counseling. Following up high school seniors eight years after graduation, Bizot and Goldman (1993) found that the match between the aptitude of the individual and the aptitude required by the job were good predictors of satisfactoriness and, to a somewhat smaller extent, job satisfaction. Bretz and Judge (1994) support work adjustment theory as useful in describing the fit between individuals and organizations, as well as between individuals and jobs. Such studies are examples of those that support the value of work adjustment theory in career counseling.

JOB ADJUSTMENT COUNSELING

Work adjustment theory can also be used to conceptualize the types of problems that an individual may have in adjusting to the job. An individual's skills may not yet have been developed sufficiently to meet the skill requirements of the job. Furthermore, the job may require skills that the individual is unable to develop because of lack of education or ability. A frequent problem is that an individual's values and needs are not met by the work environment. Another concern could be that the individual does not understand the reinforcer patterns of the work involved. Sometimes, dissatisfaction with the job is due not to the job itself but to problems outside work. For example, a person who is having difficulty at home may carry these problems into the workplace and become dissatisfied with the job as well.

When a client complains of problems at work, the basic approach is to make an assessment of the client's work personality and the working environment. Assessing the work values and needs of a client can be done by using the MIQ or, if this is not possible, by using the conceptual schema of the MIQ. Thus, a counselor can determine the significance of each of the six values (achievement, comfort, status, altruism, safety, and autonomy) during the counseling session. Furthermore, the counselor can determine which of the 20 needs that make up the six values are most relevant for the client, discussing the work environment in terms of the reinforcers offered. The counselor need not ask about each reinforcer specifically, but using the 20 reinforcers as a conceptual system can determine the correspondence between the individual's most important needs and the reinforcers offered by the job.

Similarly, using the nine abilities described by the GATB as a guide, the counselor can assess, in a general sense, the abilities that the client has and the occupational ability patterns of the job itself. Correspondence between the abilities of the client and the abilities required by the job can then be assessed. Although it is possible to use tests such as the GATB, the counselor may not choose to do so, as they take several hours to complete.

Possible solutions for problems can come by assessing the discrepancies between the individual's values and abilities and the ability patterns and reinforcer patterns of the job. By further understanding the reinforcer patterns of work, the client may be able to improve his or her satisfaction level. Another possibility is to make changes in the work itself so that the reinforcer patterns are altered. For example, a person who values independence may discuss with her supervisor ways in which she can work alone on the job. When these solutions fail, individuals can look for reinforcers outside the work environment. These might include hobbies and part-time or volunteer work. If none of these suggestions are appropriate, then an individual may consider changing jobs.

The next example shows how a counselor can use work adjustment theory to assist a client with job adjustment counseling. Nick is a 37-year-old Russian American construction worker who is experiencing increasing job dissatisfaction. He works for a construction firm that builds new houses. Doing a variety of construction tasks, especially carpentry, he has worked with the same crew of construction workers for the last five years. However, there have been some changes as the crew has grown or shrunk in size and workers have left for other jobs. Recently, a new supervisor has been assigned to the crew. Nick is finding that he dislikes the new supervisor and is considering quitting his job. He returns to talk to a Veterans Administration counselor whom he had talked to four years ago when he was having problems in his marriage. The following is an excerpt from their first session.

CL: My new supervisor, Wally, drives me nuts. I can't stand working with him. I never know where I stand. He never says anything. Other supervisors would give me direction. This guy just stand around like a two-by-four. I always knew where I stood with the other supervisors. With Wally I have no idea. I even ask him questions, and he doesn't give me much of an answer.

CO: Nick, tell me more about what you're doing at work. [The counselor hears that Nick values safety. He seems to feel that supervision, both human relations and technical, is lacking. The counselor wants to hear more before jumping to conclusions.]

CL: Well, we're building some real fancy homes now. We have to follow blueprints and make sure that everybody's doing what they're supposed to—that people aren't knocking into each other, getting in the way. It seems to be the same whether we're framing the house, putting up drywall, or whatever. All Wally does is stand around. Since I've been there a long time, some of the guys look to me for help. That is not my job.

CO: You don't want to be a supervisor? [Nick doesn't seem to want responsibility; he seems to place little value on autonomy, the opposite of safety.

On the other hand, his supervisor seems to be reinforcing responsibility and not providing much supervision.]

CL: No, I just want to do my job. I want to get paid. I don't want to do the same thing all the time. I don't mind keeping busy, but I'd just as soon do what I'm told.

CO: Sounds as if before, you knew what to expect. You knew what to do and what you were going to do. Now you don't, and it's real frustrating. [Nick needs to be active, to do a variety of work, and to receive compensation. These indicate that Nick values comfort as opposed to achievement. A sense of achievement does not seem to be important to him.]

CL: I want to figure out some way to be more comfortable. It's terrible not knowing what to do.

Nick and the counselor will explore how Nick's values of safety and comfort can be met on the job. One solution that may emerge from counseling is discussing strategies of receiving more direction from Wally. Another possibility would be to determine if Nick can transfer to a different construction crew. The counselor may also wish to consider Nick's adjustment style. Nick does not appear to be flexible. He does not seem to be able to tolerate much discomfort in the work environment. The counselor, along with Nick, may try to decide whether Nick is likely to be able to actively change his environment by talking to his supervisor or to react to the problem by focusing on out-of-job activities and his relationship with his co-workers. In this way, work adjustment theory provides a conceptualization system for the counselor to use to help Nick improve his current work adjustment.

ADJUSTMENT TO RETIREMENT

When individuals face retirement, they may encounter some problems that have components of both job adjustment and career selection. Often, individuals have maintained a satisfactory correspondence with the work environment. In other words, their work satisfaction is usually good, and their abilities and values match the abilities and reinforcers required and offered by the job. Now, the task is to find work in a "nonwork environment." If the individual has found the reinforcers offered by his or her current work to be satisfactory, then the counselor should help the individual find similar reinforcers in a nonwork environment.

To help the client, the counselor will need to make some assessment of skills and ability, as well as needs and values. This can be done by discussing in some detail the aspects of the current work that the individual finds particularly valuable. Then, the counselor and client will try to identify environments that will match the individual's needs and abilities. One difficulty for the counselor is that there is relatively little organized information about retirement activities. There are many books and pamphlets on career options and there are several occupational classification systems. However, no comparable system exists for retirement activities. Ideally, a counselor could assess the abilities and needs of a client who was about to retire and match them by using a system similar to the Minnesota Occupational Classification System. However, there is no Minnesota Retirement Classification System.

An addition to this concern is the changing nature of the retiree in his or her situation. As people age, their physical abilities change. Assessing these changes is an important aspect of helping the retiring worker. In addition, the financial needs of an individual must be assessed, as the need for earning income may continue. Furthermore, retirees may not be able to move from their current location to take advantage of a variety of community activities, hobbies, and part-time or volunteer work. Thus, there are more constraining factors in retirement counseling than in career decision-making or job adjustment counseling. A case study will help to illustrate some of the factors involved in using work adjustment theory to counsel people on retirement issues.

Henrietta is a 64-year-old African American first-grade teacher living in New Orleans. She is widowed and living alone. Her two children are married and living out of state. Henrietta has been depressed for several months and has sought counseling because of the depression. As the counselor and Henrietta have talked, it has become clear that her impending retirement is disturbing her very much.

Henrietta has always enjoyed working with small children. Helping others is very important to her. One reason that she has enjoyed teaching so much is that most of her colleagues share her views. When her husband died 12 years ago, she became very active in her church. This activity helped her deal with her husband's death. Henrietta's religious values are strong. She not only is involved in attending services weekly but also participates in social service projects that her church undertakes. Henrietta wants to be busy. She has enjoyed teaching so much because it has given her an extraordinary sense of accomplishment. She has never felt that her aging has distanced her from her young students. Each year, she has looked forward to a new class.

The counselor recognizes how much Henrietta values altruism. She sees that the reinforcers offered by teaching first-grade children clearly match Henrietta's moral values and social service needs. Further, the counselor assesses how important achievement is to Henrietta. Their task is to discuss alternatives to teaching that will provide similar reinforcers. Because of the retirement plan of her school district, it is economically appropriate for Henrietta to retire at the age of 65. However, she feels a need to continue some work to supplement her income. Furthermore, she has many friends in her neighborhood and has strong ties with her church. She has no desire to move.

Many of the options that Henrietta and the counselor discuss have to do with part-time and volunteer activities that would satisfy her values of altruism and achievement. Some of these are working at, or possibly supervising, day-care activities at a nearby church that is larger than her own. Other alternatives are to assist at a senior center in the neighborhood. Henrietta also considers work with the homeless but is concerned about transportation and safety. After talking with Henrietta for a little while, it is evident to the counselor that Henrietta has been rewarded by the school district for her teaching skills and her human relationship abilities. By concentrating on activities that would reinforce Henrietta's values of altruism and achievement, the counselor gets a sense of which activities would be appropriate to consider and which are likely to be unattractive. Henrietta feels helped by the counselor, because the suggested alternatives appear to meet her social service and achievement needs.

THE ROLE OF TESTING

Although the preceding examples show that work adjustment theory can be used in counseling without testing, tests are an extremely important component of work adjustment theory. Particularly with regard to career selection, testing is essential. Furthermore, the development of psychometric instruments has gone hand in hand with the development of work adjustment theory. Of all the instruments developed by the Work Adjustment Project, the Minnesota Importance Questionnaire is the one most likely to be used by counselors. Other instruments have been developed to test the theory: the Minnesota Job Description Questionnaire, the Minnesota Satisfaction Questionnaire, the Minnesota Satisfactoriness Scales, and a biographical information form. Described briefly by Dawis and Lofquist (1984), these instruments, as well as other research, are the subject of 30 monographs published by the University of Minnesota over a period of more than 35 years. This emphasis on the importance of testing in theory development carries over to Dawis and Lofquist's (1984) approach to counseling. More than other theorists, even other trait and factor theorists, Dawis and Lofquist emphasize the importance of measuring an individual's traits and matching them with information about occupations. Unlike most tests and inventories, their materials are not published commercially, but they can be purchased from Vocational Psychology Research, Department of Psychology, University of Minnesota.

These instruments can be used in combination with each other. For example, Thompson and Blain (1992) describe how a grid can be used to present information from the Minnesota Importance Questionnaire (MIQ). They suggest using a 3 × 3 grid that combines MIQ and MSQ data in low, moderate, and high categories. In this way, counselors can group the importance of the 20 client needs and the degree to which they are being satisfied into nine areas.

The use of this grid can be illustrated by applying it to Winifred, discussed earlier. Winifred has studied computer programming and has

Importance \ *Satisfaction*	Low	Moderate	High
Low			
Moderate		Creativity Responsibility Independence Compensation	Activity
High	Ability utilization Achievement		

Figure 3-1 The importance × satisfaction grid, including Winifred's data for seven vocational needs. (Adapted from Thompson and Blain, 1992.)

worked at a grain company as a programmer for five months. She tells the counselor that she has enjoyed learning programming but does not find her current job fulfilling. The counselor asks her to take the MSQ and then writes in her seven highest MIQ needs (see Table 3-2, p. 70) in a 3 × 3 grid, placing them in boxes depending on Winifred's MSQ scores (Figure 3-1). Winifred discusses these scores with her counselor. Her frustration with the lack of challenge in her current job becomes clearer. Although she enjoys keeping busy (activity), she feels she is basically rewriting programs used in the first few months of her job. She does not feel that she is accomplishing very much (achievement) or using her new skills (ability utilization), needs that are very important to her. Going over the grid helps Winifred decide that it is important that she get her supervisor to assign her more varied and challenging tasks.

THE ROLE OF OCCUPATIONAL INFORMATION

Occupational information presents a particular challenge for the counselor using work adjustment theory. Normally, a counselor using this theory would make use of the MIQ and the GATB. As shown earlier, each of these instruments provides a list of occupations that fit occupational patterns. In addition, the Minnesota Occupational Classification System lists Occupational Ability Patterns and Occupational Reinforcer Patterns for more than 1,700 occupations. Therefore, if the counselor is to use this system, it is important to have information available that explains these occupations. Perhaps the most essential reference is the *Dictionary of Occupational Titles,* which lists definitions of 12,000 occupations. Furthermore, pamphlets and books that more fully explain occupations are necessary so that the client can learn more about any occupation that is suggested by the results of the MIQ and the GATB. Although it is not necessary for counselors to memorize the description of each of the 1,769 occupations in the Minnesota Occupational Classification System, the system is so specific in its recommendations of occupations for individual clients that a wide knowledge of occupational information is extremely helpful to the counselor.

APPLYING THE THEORY TO WOMEN AND PEOPLE OF COLOR

Group differences have not been a focus of work adjustment theory. Dawis and Lofquist (1984) have focused on the large differences *within* groups, rather than the small differences that may exist *between* groups. For example, there is a very wide range of scores on the achievement scale for men and for women (*within* groups), but there are very small differences between men and women on the achievement scale. Although Rounds, Dawis, and Lofquist (1979) found some differences *between* males and females on various MIQ needs, Flint (1980) and Borgen et al. (1968b) found few differences. Gay, Weiss, Hendel, Dawis, and Lofquist (1971) found that women scored higher than males on the following needs: achievement, activity, company policies and practices, co-workers, independence, and working conditions. Men scored higher than women on advancement, authority, creativity, responsibility, security, social status, and supervision. Fitzgerald and Rounds (1993) conclude that few sex differences are found in variables related to work adjustment theory.

The GATB manual (U.S. Department of Labor, 1982) shows that boys score higher than girls on spatial ability, but lower than girls on form perception, clerical ability, eye-hand coordination, and finger dexterity. A review of other research shows very minor differences in the cognitive abilities of men and of women (Fitzgerald & Rounds, 1993). Although there are some differences between men and women in their abilities and preferences for needs, the implications for counseling are negligible. The information available for women and men from the Minnesota Occupational Classification System is identical.

Fitzgerald and Rounds (1993) suggest how work adjustment theory can be expanded to encompass two issues related to women: integrating work and family and sexual harassment. For example, they suggest that "variables such as convenient and flexible hours of work, or benefits (e.g., leave for a sick child) (p. 343) could be added to the theory's list of needs. Further needs such as "compensation" could be broadened to include benefits such as parental leave for a sick child or child care at the workplace. Regarding sexual harassment, they suggest that the need "company policies and practices" could include how clear organizations make guidelines on sexual harassment and how well they are implemented. Furthermore, measures of satisfaction that include questions about sexual harassment or measures of sexual harassment could be included to broaden the theory. Another suggestion, focusing on the environment rather than the person, is to study how sexual harassment affects the workplace.

Dawis (1992) is clear in stating that work adjustment focuses on individual differences in needs, values, abilities, and skills. More specifically, Dawis (1994) says that "gender, ethnicity, national origin, religion, age, sexual orientation, and disability status are seen as inaccurate and unreliable bases for estimating the skills, abilities, needs, values, personality styles, and adjustment style of a particular person" (p. 41). Adding to this view, Rounds and Hesketh (1994) suggest ways in which work adjustment theory could address discrimination based on race or sex. They say that work needs and values could be broadened to include statements that address fairness issues, such as "supervisors create an environment of mutual respect," "my supervisors and co-workers treat me fairly," "promotions are based on merit," and "company policies concerning discriminatory pracices are enforced" (p. 184). Such statements give counselors ideas on how work adjustment issues can be conceptualized when clients discuss problems at work related to discrimination by co-workers, supervisors, or customers.

COUNSELOR ISSUES

Lofquist and Dawis have applied work adjustment theory to nonwork areas of life—called person-environment-correspondence theory—in their book *Essentials of Person-Environment-Correspondence Counseling* (1991). Dawis and Lofquist (1993) and Lofquist and Dawis (1991) show the value of expanding work adjustment theory in a broader approach to counseling. Lofquist and Dawis (undated) suggest that it is helpful for counselors to see themselves as well as their clients, as environments. Both the client and the counselor can serve as reinforcers for each other, just as a job environment can serve as a reinforcer for a worker. Furthermore, both the client and the counselor have needs that are met by the other. Lofquist and Dawis suggest that, in the course of training, counselors should identify their own needs and values. Awareness of their needs and values can help counselors understand the effect that they can have on a client. In a counseling session, a counselor should be able to identify the needs of a client. For example, if a counselor has a high need for social service (doing things for others) and the client has a high need for responsibility (deciding on one's own), the altruistic counselor may be frustrated. Realization that there are differences between the values of the counselor (altruism) and the reinforcement pattern of the client (responsibility) will help the counselor be less frustrated and more effective. Examining another example, a client who has a strong safety value may be frustrated by a counselor who uses an unstructured style. Lofquist and Dawis (undated) believe that it is necessary for the counselor to identify basic abilities and reinforcers within himself or herself and the client so that effective counseling can take place. A key characteristic for a counselor is flexibility. It is important for the counselor to be able to adapt to the environment of the client so that the client's needs can be met. This can be done best when a counselor has knowledge about his or her needs and response requirements so that the counselor can suspend, when necessary, his or her own needs, to meet those of the client.

SUMMARY

The work adjustment theory of Lofquist and Dawis is notable because of its emphasis on specifying the traits and factors of an individual and matching them with job requirements and reinforcers. Work adjustment theory is made up of 18 theoretical propositions that have been supported by research (Dawis and Lofquist, 1984; Lofquist & Dawis, 1991). The focus of the theory is the prediction of adjustment to work. For Dawis and Lofquist, an individual's abilities and values can be predictive of work adjustment and length of time on a particular job, if the ability requirements and reinforcer pattern of the job are known. A major contribution of work adjustment theory is the development of the Minnesota Importance Questionnaire, which measures an individual's work needs. Combined with information about abilities, scores on the MIQ can be matched with Occupational Ability Patterns and Occupational Reinforcer Patterns. This matching yields specific occupations for an individual to consider in making a job choice. Broader than many career development theories, work adjustment theory has implications not only for career selection, but also for a great variety of other counseling situations. Two that were discussed in this chapter were job adjustment counseling and retirement counseling. More than any other theory, work adjustment theory represents a clear application of trait and factor theory.

References

Bizot, E. B., & Goldman, S. H. (1993). Prediction of satisfactoriness and satisfaction: An 8 year follow-up. *Journal of Vocational Behavior, 43,* 19–29.

Borgen, F. H., Weiss, D. J., Tinsley, H. E. A., Dawis, R. V., & Lofquist, L. H. (1968a). *Minnesota Job Description Questionnaire.* Minneapolis: University of Minnesota, Psychology Department, Vocational Psychology Research.

Borgen, F. H., Weiss, D. J., Tinsley, H. E. A., Dawis, R. V., & Lofquist, L. H. (1968b). Occupational reinforcer patterns. *Minnesota Studies in Vocational Rehabilitation, 24.*

Breeden, S. A. (1993). Job and occupational change as a function of occupational correspondence and job satisfaction. *Journal of Vocational Behavior, 43,* 30–45.

Bretz, R. D., Jr. & Judge, T. A. (1994). Person-organizations fit and the theory of work adjustment. Implications for satisfaction, tenure, and career success. *Journal of Vocational Behavior, 44,* 32–54.

Dawis, R. V. (1992). Individual differences tradition in counseling psychology. *Journal of Counseling Psychology, 39,* 7–19.

Dawis, R. V. (1994). The theory of work adjustment as convergent theory. In M. L. Savickas & R. W. Lent (Eds.), *Convergence in career development theories* (pp. 33–44). Palo Alto, CA: Consulting Psychologists Press.

Dawis, R. V., Dohm, T. E., & Jackson, C. R. S. (1993). Describing work environments as reinforcer systems: Reinforcement schedules versus reinforcer classes. *Journal of Vocational Behavior, 43,* 5–18.

Dawis, R. V., England, G. W., & Lofquist, L. H. (1964). A theory of work adjustment. *Minnesota Studies in Vocational Rehabilitation, 15.*

Dawis, R. V., & Lofquist, L. H. (1984). *A psychological theory of work adjustment.* Minneapolis: University of Minnesota Press.

Dawis, R. V., & Lofquist, L. H. (1993). From TWA to PEC. *Journal of Vocational Behavior, 43,* 113–121.

Dawis, R. V., Lofquist, L. H., & Weiss, D. J. (1968). A theory of work adjustment (a revision). *Minnesota Studies in Vocational Rehabilitation, 23.*

Fitzgerald, L, & Rounds, J. (1993). Women and work: theory encounters reality. In W. Walsh & S. Osipow (Eds.), *Career counseling for women* (pp. 327–354). Hillsdale, NJ: Erlbaum.

Flint, P. L. (1980). *Sex differences in perceptions of occupational reinforcers.* Unpublished doctoral dissertation, University of Minnesota.

Gay, E. G., Weiss, D. J., Hendel, D. D., Dawis, R. V., & Lofquist, L. H. (1971). Manual for the Minnesota Importance Questionnaire. *Minnesota Studies in Vocational Rehabilitation, 28.*

Lawson, L. (1993). Theory of work adjustment personality constructs. *Journal of Vocational Behavior, 43,* 46–57.

Lofquist, L. H., & Dawis, R. V. (undated). *Client and counselor as environments: Implications for counseling.* Unpublished manuscript, University of Minnesota, Psychology Department.

Lofquist, L. H., & Dawis, R. V. (1969). *Adjustment to work.* New York: Appleton-Century-Crofts.

Lofquist, L. H., & Dawis, R. V. (1984). Research on work adjustment and satisfaction: Implications for career counseling. In S. Brown and & R. Lent (Eds.), *Handbook of counseling psychology* (pp. 216–237). New York: Wiley.

Lofquist, L. H., & Dawis, R. V. (1991). *Essentials of person-environment correspondence counseling.* Minneapolis: University of Minnesota.

Rounds, J. B. (1990). The comparative and combined utility of work value and interest data in career counseling with adults. *Journal of Vocational Behavior, 37,* 32–45.

Rounds, J. B., Dawis, R. V. & Lofquist, L. H. (1979). Life history correlates of vocational needs for a female adult sample. *Journal of Counseling Psychology, 26,* 487–496.

Rounds, J. B., Henley, G. A., Dawis, R. V., Lofquist, L. H., & Weiss, D. J. (1981). *Manual for the Minnesota Importance Questionnaire.* Minneapolis: University of Minnesota, Psychology Department, Work Adjustment Project.

Rounds, J. B., & Hesketh, B. (1994). Emerging directions of person-environment fit. In M. L. Savickas & R. W. Lent (Eds.), *Convergence in career development theories* (pp. 177–186). Palo Alto, CA: Consulting Psychologists Press.

Thompson, J. M., & Blain, M. D. (1992). Presenting feedback on the Minnesota Importance Questionnaire and the Minnesota Satisfaction Questionnaire. *The Career Development Quarterly, 41,* 62–66.

U.S. Department of Labor. (1982). *Manual for the USES General Aptitude Test Battery, Section II: Occupational aptitude pattern structure.* Washington, DC: U.S. Government Printing Office.

4

Holland's Theory of Types

It is John Holland's view that career choice and career adjustment represent an extension of a person's personality. People express themselves, their interests and values, through their work choices and experience. In his theory, Holland assumes that people's impressions and generalizations about work, which he refers to as *stereotypes,* are generally accurate. By studying and refining these stereotypes, Holland assigns both people and work environments to specific categories.

Holland (1966, 1973, 1985a, 1992) has published four books that explain his typological theory. Each book represents an update and a further-refined version of earlier work in the development of his theory. Two psychological inventories were important in the development of his theory: the Vocational Preference Inventory (1985b) and the Self-Directed Search (1994). These instruments, in different ways, measure self-perceived competencies and interests, which are an assessment of an individual's personality. Holland (1992) recognizes that his theory can account for only a portion of the variables that underlie career selection. He is clear in stating that his theoretical model can be affected by age, gender, social class, intelligence, and education. With that understood, he goes on to specify how the individual and the environment interact with each other through the development of six types: Realistic, Investigative, Artistic, Social, Enterprising, and Conventional. Both individuals and environment consist of a combination of types.

THE SIX TYPES

In the following pages, each of the six work environments is described, followed by a description of the personality type of the person who matches that environment. Next, behavior that can be expected from each type in the context of counseling is discussed. Other important concepts, such as congruence and differentiation, to be discussed later, describe the interaction between the person and the environment. When describing real people and work environments, which are never purely of one type,

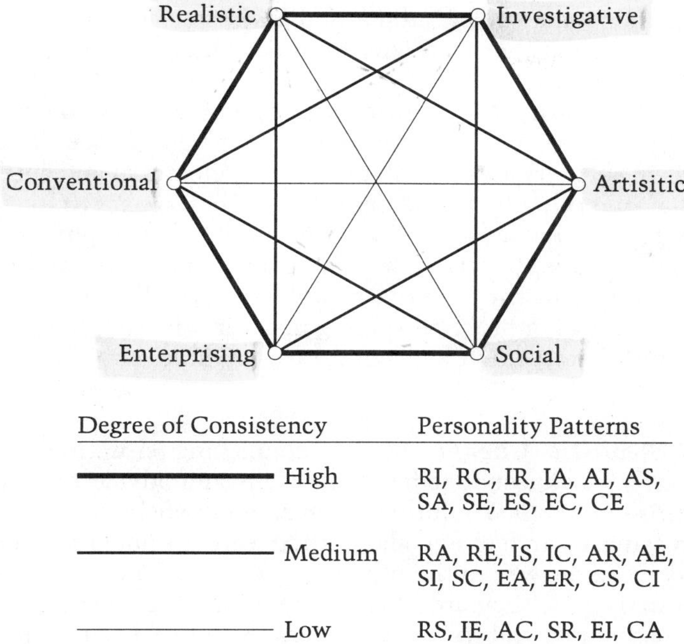

Figure 4-1 The relationships among Holland types. (Adapted from *Holland's Hexagon, ACT Research Report No. 29,* by J. L. Holland, D. R. Whitney, N. S. Cole, and J. M. Richards, Jr. Copyright © 1969 The American College Testing Program. Reprinted by permission.)

Holland uses a combination of three types, also discussed later. The relationships among the six types are illustrated in Figure 4-1. The placement of the types on the hexagon is purposeful; the arrangement is explained later when the concept of consistency is described.

Realistic

The Realistic Environment The Realistic (R) environment makes physical demands on the person. Such work settings have tools, machines, or animals that the individual manipulates. In such a setting, individuals are required to have technical competencies that will allow them to do such things as fix machines, repair electronic equipment, drive cars or trucks, herd animals, or deal with other physical aspects of their environment. The ability to work with things is more important than the ability to interact with other people. Construction sites, factories, and auto garages are examples of environments that provide machinery or other things for Realistic people to master. Some Realistic environments require a great deal of physical agility or strength, such as roofing, outdoor painting, and pipe fitting.

These environments may be hazardous and may produce more physical illness or accidents than other work environments.

The Realistic Personality Type Realistic people are likely to enjoy using tools or machines in their hobbies or work. They tend to seek to develop competencies in such areas as plumbing, roofing, electrical and automotive repair, farming, and other technical disciplines. They are apt to like courses that are very practical and teach the use of mechanical or physical skills. Realistic people are likely to have little tolerance of abstract and theoretical descriptions. Often, they approach problems, whether mechanical or personal, in a practical or problem-solving manner. They are likely to value money, power, and status, while placing a lesser value on human relationships.

Behavior of Realistic Clients In the counseling situation, Realistic clients are likely to expect specific suggestions and advice to solve their career problems—a practical solution. Such clients may be somewhat resistant to expressing their feelings about their career choice and prefer to move directly to an answer to the problem of choosing a career. When discussing their activities, they are likely to enjoy talking about such activities as hunting, fishing, and fixing cars. They are apt to discuss things they have done that show an expertise in using tools. They may also talk about specific possessions, such as cars, radios, or other machinery, with which they like to tinker.

Women may encounter more resistance and harassment from males in a Realistic environment than in any other of the six types. Since many of the activities and participants in the Realistic environment tend to be traditionally masculine, Realistic women may encounter a considerable amount of sexism in trying to enter a Realistic occupation such as auto mechanics, coal mining, or roofing. Women who have received encouragement from their fathers and brothers in the development of Realistic competencies may become hurt and angry when they encounter resistance from men in a Realistic working environment. Dealing with such issues requires that the counselor be sensitive to and support women who have Realistic interests and competencies. Still, not all Realistic occupations present such problems. Many occupations have significant Realistic components, yet are not traditionally masculine. Examples include silversmith, dressmaker, floral designer, and inventory clerk.

Investigative

The Investigative Environment The Investigative (I) environment is one in which people search for solutions to problems through mathematical and scientific interests and competencies. In such a situation, people are encouraged to use complex and abstract thinking to solve problems creatively. Examples of occupations that offer the opportunity to use analytical thinking skills are computer programmer, physician, mathematician, biologist, science teacher, veterinarian, and research-and-development manager. In each of these environments, cautious and critical thinking is valued. Individuals are likely to need to use logic and precise methodical thinking in order to find solutions to problems in these fields. These jobs require that people use their intellect to work independently to solve problems. They are not required or encouraged to use human relations skills to solve problems, nor are they likely to need to use machines. For example, a computer programmer uses logic to figure out solutions to problems (an Investigative environment), whereas the computer operator works with machinery and may operate it or fix it (a Realistic environment).

The Investigative Personality Type The Investigative person is likely to enjoy puzzles and challenges that require the use of intellect. Such a person is apt to enjoy learning and to feel confident about his or her ability to solve mathematical and scientific problems. Such people often enjoy reading about science and discussing scientific issues. They seek to work independently to solve problems such as mathematical or scientific questions. They are likely to enjoy courses in math, physics, chemistry, biology, geology, and other physical or biological sciences. They are not likely to enjoy supervising other people or dealing directly with personal problems, but they may enjoy analyzing or searching for solutions to psychological problems.

Behavior of Investigative Clients Clients who are primarily Investigative in their personality tend to enjoy the challenge of an unanswered question. They are often excited by a problem and want to work hard to find a solution even though there may be relatively little financial or other reward. When it comes to solving a career problem, they may wish to solve it themselves and to approach it from a rational rather than emotional point of view. When the career problem itself is seen as a challenge, they may feel better if they view the counselor as a fellow investigator rather than as an expert who is telling them what to do.

Artistic

The Artistic Environment The Artistic (A) environment is one that is free and open, encouraging creativity and personal expression. Such an environment offers much freedom in developing products and answers. Examples of occupations in which people can use creative and unconventional ways to express themselves are musician, fine artist, and freelance writer. Such settings allow people to dress the way they wish, keep few appointments, and structure their own time. These work environments encourage personal and emotional expression rather than logical expression. If tools are used, they are used to express oneself (for example, a clarinet or a paintbrush) rather than as a means to complete a task (for example, an electric drill or a wrench).

The Artistic Personality Type The Artistic person likes the opportunity to express himself or herself in a free and unsystematic way, creating music, art, or writing. Such people may use instruments to do this, such as a violin, the voice, sculpting tools, or a word processor. They are likely to want to improve their ability in language, art, music, or writing. Originality and creativity are particularly important in expression. To use a paint-by-numbers kit would be deeply offensive to an Artistic type, who needs and desires the opportunity to express herself or himself in a free and open manner. A pure Artistic type would dislike technical writing and would prefer writing fiction or poetry.

Behavior of Artistic Clients In a counseling session, Artistic clients often make clear how important art, music, or writing is in their lives. They may prefer a nonstructured counseling approach to one that uses worksheets and written materials. They may enjoy discussing the expression and development of an Artistic product. They may also like to comment on or criticize the products of others. When talking to Artistic people, it becomes clear that their excitement centers on their creative activity. They may enjoy using humor or other methods of expression to show that they are unique and not like other clients. Their expression may be unclear or may appear disordered. Often, they discuss their own thinking and creative process. More than any other type, Artistic people are likely to rely on emotions in their discussion of career issues and to see the choice process as an affective rather than a logical one.

Social

The Social Environment The Social (S) environment is one that encourages people to be flexible and understanding of each other, where people can work with others through helping with personal or career problems, teaching others, affecting others spiritually, and being socially responsible. The Social environment emphasizes human values such as being idealistic, kind, friendly, and generous. These ideals most commonly exist in the education, social service, and mental health professions. Examples of these occupations are elementary school teacher, special-education teacher, high school teacher, marriage counselor, counseling psychologist, speech therapist, school superintendent, and psychiatrist.

The Social Personality Type The Social person is interested in helping people through teaching, helping with personal or vocational problems, or providing personal services. Social people enjoy solving problems through discussion and teamwork rather than through delegation. Preferring to talk and resolve complex problems that may be ethical or idealistic in nature, they often choose to avoid working with machines. They seek out environments where they can use verbal skills and social skills, such as in education, welfare, and mental health.

Behavior of Social Clients In a counseling situation, Social people express their idealism, wanting to help others through religion, politics, or social service. Often altruistic, they are more concerned with contributing to a better world than with economic achievement for themselves. They are likely to value informal activities that they have done such as teaching young children and helping friends with personal problems. When talking with a counselor, they may be interested in the counselor's profession (a Social environment) and may be appreciative of the counselor's help. Because it is in their nature to be helpful, they may wish to cooperate with their counselor's plans to assist them. Also, their Social nature may make them good candidates for career group counseling, where they may enjoy the opportunity to help others. On the other hand, they may be too verbal, since they value talking, making it difficult for the counselor to assist them and other career group members in dealing with questions of career planning.

Enterprising

The Enterprising Environment The Enterprising (E) environment is one where people manage and persuade others in order to attain organizational or personal goals. These are situations where finance and economic issues are of prime importance and risks may be taken to achieve rewards. In such an environment, people tend to be self-confident, sociable, and assertive. It's an environment where promotion and power are important, and persuasion and selling take place. Examples of Enterprising environments are sales work, buying, business management, restaurant management, politics, real estate, the stock market, insurance, and lobbying. All of these environments provide the opportunity for power, status, and wealth.

The Enterprising Personality Type The acquisition of wealth is particularly important for Enterprising people. They enjoy being with others and like to use verbal skills in order to sell, persuade, or lead. They tend to be assertive and popular, trying to take on leadership positions. They enjoy working with people but prefer to persuade and manage rather than to help.

Behavior of Enterprising Clients Enterprising people may present themselves in a self-assured manner. They may appear to be more self-confident than they feel. Some Enterprising people may be quite open about their goal to accomplish wealth, whereas others may be very reluctant to admit to a goal that they see as socially inappropriate. Like Social types, they may be very verbal with a counselor and willing to talk about past accomplishments. Unlike Social types, they will value convincing and persuading others rather than helping others. In part, because of their self-confidence, Enterprising types may have difficulty seeing their competencies accurately and may overestimate their abilities. Enterprising types may be impatient with entry-level positions or occupations that don't lead quickly to the accumulation of wealth or power. They are also likely to experience conflict with other Enterprising types who are competing for both power and money.

Conventional

The Conventional Environment Organization and planning best describe the Conventional (C) environment. Much of the Conventional environment is an office environment, where one needs to keep records, file papers, copy materials, and organize reports. In addition to written material, the Conventional environment includes mathematical materials, such as bookkeeping and accounting records. Word-processing, calculating, and copy machines are the type of equipment that is found in a Conventional environment. Competencies that are needed to work well in a Conventional environment are clerical skills, an ability to organize, dependability, and an ability to follow directions.

The Conventional Personality Type The Conventional person is one who values money, being dependable, and the ability to follow rules and orders. These people prefer being in control of situations and not dealing with ambiguous requests. They enjoy an office environment where their values of earning money and following rules, regulations, and guidelines can be met. Their strengths are their clerical and numerical ability, which they use to solve straightforward problems in their environment. Their relationships with people tend to be directed toward accomplishing tasks and establishing an organized approach to problems.

Behavior of Conventional Clients In a counseling situation, Conventional people are likely to present themselves as organized, yet dependent on others for direction. They may have difficulty being open to examining new occupations or career paths on their own initiative. However, they are often proud of their organizational ability in high school extracurricular activities and in business activities. If they have had work experience, they are likely to have had the opportunity to work in an office and to have enjoyed that. If they have worked in environments that are not Conventional, they are likely to have been frustrated by the lack of organization in these environments and will have tried to bring some type of order into their working world. When they explore occupational possibilities, they are most likely to be excited and interested in jobs in financial institutions such as banks, or in occupations where they can use counting skills, such as tax expert, inventory controller, and data processor. They are also likely to be interested in financial and accounting analysis. Other personality types are likely to see these jobs as routine or boring. Conventional types appreciate the opportunity to organize and regulate.

COMBINATIONS OF TYPES

Clearly, no real work environment is purely of one type. Rather, most working situations involve a combination of types. When describing occupational environments in *The Occupations Finder* (Holland, 1994) and training environments in *The Educational Opportunities Finder* (Rosen, Holmberg, & Holland, 1994), which accompanies his Self-Directed Search (Holland, Powell, & Fritzsche, 1994), Holland uses a three-letter code to describe each of these environments. Holland's *Occupations Finder* lists three-letter codes for 1,156 occupations, and *The Educational Opportunities Finder* lists over 750 programs of study. For example, a bookkeeping environment is not one that is strictly Conventional. It is primarily Conventional, secondly Investigative, and thirdly Social, summarized as CIS. Environments differ in terms of how much they are dominated by one or two types. For example, the bookkeeper may work in a primarily Conventional environment, but a detective may work in an environment that is Social, Realistic, and Enterprising. It would be Social because of the need to help other people; Realistic because of the importance of driving cars, using guns and fingerprint material, and so forth; and Enterprising because of the persuasiveness and assertiveness that are required. Another book, the *Dictionary of Holland Occupational Codes* (Gottfredson & Holland, 1989), lists more than 12,000 occupations that have been coded by translating the U.S. Department of labor system of DOT codes into Holland codes. Thus, it is possible to look up any occupation and determine its three-letter code.

Just as no single environment can be described by one code, it is rare for a person to fit only one Holland psychological type. Through their experiences in school, with hobbies, and with parents, people are exposed to a large number of situations that help them become familiar with certain types of environments. For example, repairing a car exposes one to a Realistic environment, being involved in clubs at school is likely to involve one in a Social environment, and drawing and painting are examples of an Artistic environment. As people are exposed to these activities, they become more interested in certain environments and develop many specific abilities. They become more able to be successful in some environments than in others. As they do this, certain of the Holland types become stronger than others, and their personality type becomes more definite.

These types can be measured by instruments Holland has developed such as the Vocational Preference Inventory (VPI) or the Self-Directed Search (SDS). In addition, other inventories, such as the Strong Interest Inventory (SII), use Holland's types and can be used to code the interests of individuals according to a three-letter Holland code.

When listening to a client describe his or her career history, it is helpful to think in terms of Holland's six types of people and environments. As a client describes a particular experience, a fit between personality type and interest and experience is likely to become apparent. As the client moves on to another topic, another type is likely to emerge. In this way, the counselor can keep a rough count or impression of the dominant personality types. For example, as a client describes her interest in military activities and parachuting, the counselor conceptualizes these activities in terms of Holland's Realistic type. When she talks about her interest in biology class in high school and her desire to take an advanced course in biology, the notion of interests and abilities in Investigative activities arises. As counselors become more familiar with Holland's theory, it is possible that the mention of activities will "ring a bell" and they will recall the appropriate type that the person is fitting at the moment. For the beginning counselor, it is often necessary to consciously memorize the Holland types and bring them into active memory to compare the type with the activity being discussed by the client. Sometimes, it is helpful to explain Holland's system to clients, providing them with an opportunity to organize their thoughts about themselves and the world of work.

EXPLANATORY CONSTRUCTS

Three important constructs for conceptualizing and using Holland's types in counseling are congruence, differentiation, and consistency. These refer to the relationship between the personality and the environment (congruence), the relationship between and the relative importance of types (differentiation), and the relationship of the types to each other (consistency). In addition, the concept of identity, which is less directly tied to types, is important for counselors to be familiar with.

Congruence

The term *congruence* refers to the relationship of the personality to the environment. The more similar the personality is to the environment, the more congruent the relationship. Social types tend to enjoy working in a Social environment; Investigative types prefer the Investigative environment. Thus, a Social type working in a sales environment (Enterprising) might find the environment incongruent. An Investigative type working in an Artistic environment might also find that incongruent and would be frustrated by the ambiguity and flexibility that are required in the production of artistic or musical products. Using Holland's three-letter code, an SRA personality would be most congruent with an SRA environment and slightly less congruent with an SRC environment. Likewise, an SIC environment would be more incongruent, and an ICR environment would be quite incongruent with an SRA type of person. Thus, congruence decreases as the similarity of the three-letter code of the person and of the environment decreases.

Counseling Implications The concept of congruence is essential in counseling, where it can provide an important goal. A client wishing to make a career choice will want to find an environment that is congruent with his or her personality. It is the counselor's job to assess the client's personality and assist in finding environments that will fit the counselee according to the Holland type. Working toward the discovery of congruent occupations becomes the major purpose of career-counseling sessions. The counselor thinks about the client and possible career choices in terms of the six Holland types and the degree to which they match.

Example of Congruence Jane, a white high school sophomore, has a counseling session with her guidance counselor that includes this dialogue:

CL: Recently, I was working with a friend who was making a project for her high school science fair. It got kind of messy—we spent a lot of time sorting ants into different piles and developing different terrains—but it was a lot of fun. I was surprised how the time just went by so quickly. In fact, I got in trouble for getting home late. We worked on it Thursday night and then most of last Saturday.

CO: Sounds like you really got intrigued with all of the different things that you could do. [The counselor encourages the client to keep talking about her interest in the science project to see if her interest in Investigative activities will sustain itself.]

CL: It was a lot of fun. I never knew that observing ants could be so interesting. It really got me thinking about what I might do. I wish that I had thought about doing a science project. But it's too late now.

CO: It you were to do a science project now, what do you think it might be? [The exploration of Investigative activities continues.]

CL: I'm not sure, really. But I think it might have something to do with mice and how they act. I'm taking biology now, and I really like it. I wish that I had room in my schedule next year for another biology course.

CO: You seem surprised that you have so much interest in biology. [The counselor tries to understand how important Investigative activities are to the client and if this is a recent awareness for the client.]

CL: I am surprised. I never thought I would like science so much. I've known all along that I enjoy art. My art teachers really like my work, and I enjoy painting. Last summer, I won first place in a contest with my paintings.

CO: That sounds exciting. It's great to have things that seem different from each other but are so enjoyable. [While reinforcing the client's enjoyment, the counselor acknowledges the existence of both Investigative and Artistic interests.]

CL: I've thought that it would be neat to do something with these after college. I've thought of doing something with biology, becoming a biologist or geneticist or something like that. But I'm not sure what I'd do with art. Sometimes, I think that I might like to be an artist or an architect.

CO: These are occupations worth looking into. They certainly fit with the things that you've been telling me so far about yourself. [Without knowing exact Holland codes for the occupations that the student mentions, the counselor can still tell that the occupations that have been described are congruent with the client's emerging personality type. The counselor is then in a position to find other occupations that may be congruent with the AI type. Further, the counselor will have the opportunity to see if there are other Holland types that reflect the individual's personality. If so, this may help the counselor in finding other occupations to suggest that will be congruent with her type.]

Differentiation

Both people and environments may differ in terms of how clearly they belong to one or two types. Some people may predominantly resemble one Holland type, whereas others may be quite undifferentiated and have interests and competencies across all six types. Most people are likely to have one, two, or three dominant types. For example, some people enjoy painting, writing, helping others, leading youth groups, and doing volunteer work in a hospital. They may dislike working with machinery, office work, science, and business. Such people would be readily identified as differentiated, as their interests (Social and Artistic) are clearly different from their dislikes (Investigative, Realistic, Conventional, and Enterprising). On the other hand, some people enjoy doing all kinds of activities and do them well. These people are undifferentiated according to Holland's system. Holland determines differentiation by subtracting the lowest score of any type from the highest score of any type. Any inventory that measures his six types can be used. A high result indicates a differentiated profile and a low result an undifferentiated profile.

Just as people vary in terms of differentiation, so do environments. Some environments allow for more freedom of movement to various Holland environments than do others. For example, assembly line work usually allows an individual only the opportunity to do Realistic work—a differentiated environment. On the other hand, a teacher working in a university may have the opportunity to do research in his or her field (Investigative), teach students and help them select courses (Social), and possibly consult with industry (Enterprising)—an undifferentiated environment. Sometimes, environments are varied enough so that people who at first find that their personality and environment are not congruent can find a way to work within the environment that provides eventual congruence.

For example, a physician who is predominantly Enterprising rather than Investigative (the predominant type of physician) may find enough diversity in a hospital environment to work as a hospital administrator or fund-raiser, thus meeting his or her Enterprising needs. To use another example, a secretary working in an office that requires typing, filing, and reception work will find an opportunity to meet both Conventional and Social needs, whereas a secretary in a typing pool will be able to meet only Conventional needs. Thus, environments differ in the degree to which they are differentiated.

Counseling Implications Undifferentiated people are likely to have difficulty in making career decisions and may seek career counseling. One goal of counseling is to help clients to differentiate and broaden their knowledge of their interests, abilities, and values within each of the six types. Some clients who are trying to find a new career goal will find that they have interests and abilities in many different areas (undifferentiated). It is then the counselor's role to discuss more deeply their interests, values, and experiences, and to make explicit the differing values of each of the six types for the client. Other clients may find that they have few interests and low self-estimates of their abilities across all types. Such clients may need to address issues of depression or low self-esteem. The typology serves as a frame of reference for exploring areas of interest of which the client may not be aware. A discussion of a client's experiences with hobbies, part-time work, volunteer work, full-time work, extracurricular activities, and leisure time is apt to give the counselor an opportunity to conceptualize the client according to all six of Holland's personality types. Sometimes, it is not possible to provide further differentiation for a client without more work experience—whether part time, volunteer, or full time. The pursuit of differentiation can be a means of finding a congruent occupation for a client.

Example of Differentiation The client, Chester, is a young Chinese American man who dropped out of high school at the end of the 11th grade. For the past three years, he has been employed on an automobile assembly line. He has taken the Self-Directed Search (SDS) at a guidance program offered in the evening at his local high school. His highest score on the SDS was E, considerably higher than R and I, the next highest scores. His counselor uses this information along with Chester's description of career-related experiences to help Chester in career selection:

CL: When I was in school, there just wasn't very much that interested me. Now I have a job that gets more and more boring. When I first worked in autobody assembly, I didn't mind it. Things were kind of fun then. Now I've done most of the jobs on the line, and there's never a challenge. It's the same thing all over again.

CO: The assembly work really sounds as if it is bothering you and making you rethink what you want to do. [Perhaps Realistic activities are not for this client. Do the client's R interests match his SDS scores?]

CL: Yes. There are a lot of things that I enjoy doing much more.

CO: Can you tell me about them? [More information about the client's personality, according to the six Holland personality types, is needed to compare with his scores on the SDS.]

CL: Well, on weekends my friend and I work on cars to resell. It's fun and interesting, and I'm making a lot of extra cash.

CO: Sounds good; I'd like to hear more.

CL: Well, we get old cars from people who are about ready to junk them. We fix the mechanical problems, touch them up with paint, and list them in the newspaper.

CO: Which aspect of this work do you do most? [Realistic interests, in terms of working on cars, and Enterprising interests, selling the cars, sound like possibilities. The counselor revises the original view that Realistic activities are not of interest to this client.]

CL: My friend really knows cars. I help him in some of the simple work. As I've worked with him, I've been able to help him when he takes an engine apart. But I couldn't do that myself. When it comes to people buying the car, I'm the one who sells it. It really is a challenge for me to take something that we've worked on and get someone to buy it. I feel as if we've got a good product, and I want them to know about it.

CO: Is selling something new for you? [The counselor is differentiating between the Realistic and Enterprising interests of the client, choosing to follow up and get more detail on the Enterprising aspect, Chester's highest score on the SDS.]

CL: No, I've sold before. When I was in high school I used to work in a tire store. I sold truck tires and auto tires, then put them on. Although I didn't mind putting on new tires, it was more interesting to me to help the customer select tires and buy a real good set. I'd get a commission on what I sold, not a big one, but I liked it.

CO: That sounds as if there were a lot of things that you could take advantage of on that job. [The counselor continues to differentiate the interests in Realistic and Enterprising activities from each other, exploring the differentiation suggested by the difference between the E and R scores on the SDS. This content reflection asks for further differentiation.]

Consistency

Consistency refers to the similarity or dissimilarity of types. Certain types, whether environment or personality, have more in common with some types than with others. For example, as shown in Figure 4-1 (page 91), Social and Artistic types are similar (close together). On the other hand, Social types and Realistic types are quite different from each other, as are Enterprising types and Investigative types. The closer the types are to each other on the chart, the more consistent they are. For example, Social people tend to like to help others, work as a team, and value their interactions with people; Realistic types prefer not to work with people, but to work with machines in technical challenges. Social people may often have an aversion to machines, or put another way, Social people tend to have more in common with Artistic and Enterprising types than they do with Realistic individuals. Likewise, Realistic people are apt to have more in common with Investigative and Conventional individuals than with Social people.

Consistency also applies to environments. Some environments require skills and interests that are generally inconsistent. One example is athletic trainer (SRE). The Social and Realistic environments are inconsistent, yet athletic trainers must help injured athletes who may be under emotional and physical stress. Further, they use a variety of sophisticated medical equipment to remedy injuries. In general, there are very few occupations that have codes that are inconsistent. For example, there are no occupations that could be labeled CA. When applied to a working environment, the term *inconsistent* means that the environment requires types of interests and abilities that rarely are required in the same job. Creative and artistic production (A) is seldom seen in conjunction with demands for numerical skill (C) in any occupation. On the other hand, individuals with inconsistent types may be able to identify a special niche for themselves. For example, an individual with a CA personality may enjoy organizing a music library for a symphony orchestra.

Consistency is not a goal of counseling, whereas differentiation and congruence can both be goals. Consistency is a more subtle concept than the others. Lack of consistency does not mean that a choice is poor. For example, a person who has an inconsistent type (SIC) has not made a poorer career choice than a person who has a more consistent type (SAI). Perhaps the notion of consistency can best be used in counseling by making the counselor aware that it may be difficult to find an environment that will fit two or three inconsistent Holland codes. Often, the client may have to choose an occupation that fits one of the two inconsistent types, but not both. For example, a client with strong Artistic and Conventional interests and skills may choose to do accounting during the day and then moonlight as a musician. It would not be possible to find occupations that would easily incorporate both of these personality types.

Identity

Identity refers to the clarity and stability of a person's current and future goals. It also refers to the stability of the working environment. If an organization has identity, the tasks and goals of an occupation or employer do not vary widely. Identity is different from any of the other concepts relevant to Holland's system because it does not relate directly to his typology. It is measured not by the VPI or the SDS, but through a third instrument entitled My Vocational Situation (MVS).

Although the inventory My Vocational Situation will measure the concept of identity, the counselor's assessment of identity in a counseling interview can also prove to be helpful. A question for the counselor to consider is: Now that we are completing career counseling, does this client have a clear idea of career plans and contingency plans, as well as knowledge of how to implement the plans? For example, a man who decides to pursue acting should not only be aware of his interest in this profession but also be able to assess feedback he has received from directors and acting teachers. This man should be aware of the risks in obtaining work, alternative careers when unemployed, contacts for employment, and so on. To start looking for work without planning would be to have a diffuse sense of identity. To use another example, a young woman who wants to be a lawyer because lawyers make good salaries and work on exciting cases has not yet formed a sense of identity. When she has information about how to become a lawyer and whether she would like the duties of a lawyer, then her sense of identity will become clearer.

Identity can be an important goal of career counseling. Achievement of identity may occur when the goal of congruence has been accomplished. If a woman decides on the occupation of roofer, feeling that laying new roofs would be something that she is able to do and would enjoy (congruence between person and environment), a sense of identity will develop. As she moves from one job site to another, her goals may stabilize, and she may grow more certain of her interests and abilities.

RESEARCH ON HOLLAND'S CONSTRUCTS

Holland's theory has produced over 500 studies, more research than any other career development theory. Holland himself has been very influential in the production of research and the compilation of it. His four books (1966, 1973, 1985a, 1992) are indications of his continuing work to refine existing and develop additional theoretical constructs. Research on career development is reviewed periodically in the *Journal of Vocational Behavior* (for example, Walsh & Srsic, 1995; Fouad, 1994), the *Career Development Quarterly* (Subich, 1994), and the *Journal of Career Assessment* (Spokane & Jacob, 1995). These reviews devote a section to discussions of current research on Holland's theory.

Congruence is the most important of Holland's concepts and the one that is most widely researched. What seems like a straightforward concept is actually quite complex. For example, Brown and Gore (1994) evaluated 10 different methods of measuring congruence between personality type and employment, and Camp and Chartrand (1992) examined 13 methods. Many studies have related congruence to other important variables such as stress, job satisfaction, and personality variables. Spokane (1985) reviewed 63 studies showing a small relationship between congruence and job satisfaction. A meta-analysis of studies measuring congruence and satisfaction reached similar conclusions (Assouline & Meir, 1987). More recently Tranberg, Slane, and Ekeberg (1993) showed a weak relationship between congruence and satisfaction, stating, "Interest congruence alone does not predict satisfaction" (p. 261). They concluded that congruence is most important for job satisfaction in Social environments and least important in Realistic and Conventional environments. Studying the relationship between stress and congruence, Sutherland, Fogarty, and Pithers (1995) found a small correlation between congruence and lack of stress. Because of the different ways that congruence can be measured and the different variables, such as personality and achievement, that it can be related to, congruence is likely to be an important focus of research for some time.

Another area of research involves studying the relationship of Holland's personality types to various personality characteristics. For example, Tokar and Swanson (1995) found that Holland's six personality types fit with those of the NEO Five-Factor Inventory. This inventory measures five broad factors known as the big five: Extraversion, Neuroticism, Agreeableness, Conscientiousness, and Openness to Experience. The big five supported Holland's characterization of six personality types, and the Openness and Extraversion factors were particularly relevant to Holland's typology. Using SDS scores of adult participants in career workshops, Holland, Johnston, and Asama (1994) also found these two factors to be particularly related to Holland's typology. Other instruments, such as the *Personality Adjective Check List* (Strack, 1994), have been compared to Holland's vocational typology, and orientation to achievement has been related to congruence (Schwartz, 1991). Others of Holland's concepts have been studied, but to a lesser degree than congruence.

Although some studies have focused on redefining and developing consistency (Latona, 1989; Pazy & Zin, 1987) and differentiation (Monahan, 1987), vocational identity has received the most recent attention. Studying 211 male and 353 female academically superior high school juniors, Leung, Conoley, Scheel, and Sonnenberg (1992) found no relationship between scores on the Vocational Identity scale of My Vocational Situation and consistency and differentiation. Holland, Gottfredson, and Baker (1990) found no relationship between vocational identity and the degree of similarity (coherence) among three career choices that individuals aspired to. Also, Gehlert, Timberlake, and Wagner (1992) found no relationship between vocational identity and academic achievement. However, Conneran and Hartman (1993) found that chronically career-undecided high school students showed lower levels of congruence and vocational identity than those students who were not chronically undecided. On a theoretical level, Vondracek (1991, 1992) has criticized Holland's definition of identity as being oversimplified and less complex than "identity" as originally described by Erik Erikson.

Holland's theory has attracted researchers for several reasons. Holland defines his terms clearly and simply. His theory is directly related to the practice of vocational counseling. Most studies on Holland's concepts do not require longitudinal research or extensive follow-up studies. Also, John Holland has been very involved in research on his theory and helpful to those who wish to engage in research related to his work. In general, the research on Holland's theory offers counselors confidence that Holland's concepts have merit and can be used for counseling conceptualization.

THE ROLE OF OCCUPATIONAL INFORMATION

Holland's typological system is particularly useful to clients because it helps to integrate occupational information into the counseling process. By dividing all occupations (or environments) into six types, Holland gives the client an easy framework to use for conceptualizing all occupations. With this system, clients are less likely to ask, "Are there some occupations that I have never considered?" Using this system, counselors have a clear approach to explaining the world of work. Both client and counselor can use *The Occupations Finder* (Holland, 1994) to identify a thousand of the more common occupations and *The Educational Opportunities Finder* (Rosen, et al., 1994) to identify over 750 programs of study. If more detail is wanted, Holland's *Dictionary of Holland Occupational Codes* (Gottfredson & Holland, 1989) lists 12,099 occupations sorted by Holland code.

For the counselor, Holland's typological system is a helpful way to group occupational information. Not only can Holland's system be used to classify items in an occupational library, but it can also be used by a counselor to classify the client's experiences with environments. For example, as a counselor talks to employers about their needs for employees, the environment that the employers describe can be classified mentally by the counselor. In a similar way, as a client describes work experience that he or she has enjoyed or disliked, the environment can also be classified according to Holland type. The knowledge gained from experiences such as visiting plants, reading occupational information, and talking to other counselors about work can be used to help in coding occupations according to Holland type. By practicing with the Holland system, whether formally or informally, the counselor becomes increasingly familiar with it.

THE ROLE OF TESTING

Testing has had two purposes in Holland's system. The first is in the development of the theory. For example, the Vocational Preference Inventory was initiated prior to Holland's theory and was partly responsible for the definition of his six types of people and environments. The VPI and the SDS then became research instruments to verify and validate Holland's theory. The second use of tests is for individuals in need of career assistance. By using the SDS or the VPI or another inventory that yields Holland types, the counselor can get an objectively determined personality type for the client. By comparing the counselor's assessment of the client's Holland type with that of an objective inventory, the counselor can get confirmation or try to determine why there is a discrepancy, if one exists. By doing so, the counselor is likely to gain further insight into the client's interests, abilities, and values. Testing is an important part of the development of Holland's theory. Making use of validated and reliable information can be a great help to counselors in working with clients.

APPLYING THE THEORY TO WOMEN

Because Holland's system has six clearly defined types supplemented by explanatory constructs such as congruence, consistency, and differentiation, it has been the subject of a great deal of research. Much of the research has used both males and females, thus providing data on the appropriateness of Holland's theory for women. Holland (1985a) has shown that men are more likely to score high on the Realistic, Investigative, or Enterprising scales, whereas women may score higher on the Social, Artistic, and Conventional scales. Holland's conclusion about summary codes is somewhat similar to that of Arbona (1989), who used an analysis of 1980 census data that reflected the occupational choices of 97 million Americans. Men predominated in the Realistic and Enterprising categories, whereas women were found more often in Social and Conventional careers. Investigative and artistic occupations made up a small proportion of workers. Some critics of Holland's theory have taken these differential preferences to mean that Holland's theory is biased against women. Holland points out that his system is a reflection of society and cultural expectations; it does not determine them.

Regarding Holland's concept of congruence, his review (1985a) shows that the SDS or the VPI can predict occupational choice or entry about equally well for men and women. In general, Holland, Powell, and Fritzsche (1994) conclude that the predicted validities of aspirations and assessment tend to be higher for women than for men. Although there is less research on consistency and differentiation, there seems to be little difference in these two concepts when the gender variable is examined. In concluding their discussion of sex differences, Holland, Powell, and Fritzsche (1994) state that "women are most likely to have low scores on R and high scores on S" (p. 37). Thus, Holland points out those types that have been most influenced by cultural stereotyping.

Research on Holland's typology and theoretical constructs usually contains information that addresses the issue of male-female differences on relevant variables. Two recent studies illustrate attention to gender differences. Hansen, Collins, Swanson, and Fouad (1993) found that Holland's hexagon generally represented the interests of men quite accurately, but that there was little discrimination between women's Realistic and Investigative interests. Social interests stood out as being particularly important in the structure of women's interests. Relating Millon's personality styles to Holland's typology, Strack (1994) found that males and females of a specific Holland type shared similar Millon personality characteristics. However, Millon's introverted and extraverted styles were related to Holland types for women, but not men. Millon's neurotic styles were linked to Holland types for men, but not for women. Studies such as these two help to show how Holland's theory applies differently to men and women.

APPLYING THE THEORY TO PEOPLE OF COLOR

Holland's theory and instruments have been used internationally as well as with people of color in the United States. Research (Holland, Powell, & Fritzsche, 1994) in Israel, France, Nigeria, New Zealand, and Australia gives some support to the use of Holland's six categories and the constructs of congruence, consistency, and differentiation (although there has been less work on the latter two concepts).

Recent studies have examined how well Holland's hexagon fits people from a variety of backgrounds and cultures. Swanson (1992) found that, in general, Holland's typology fit African American female college students somewhat better than African American males. Contrasting white American college students with Asian Americans, Havercamp, Collins, and Hansen (1994) supported the similarity of interest for these two groups. Also, comparing Asian American and white American college students, Leung, Ivey, and Suzuki (1994) found that Asian Americans were more likely to have considered Investigative occupations and less likely to have considered Enterprising and Conventional occupations than white college students. However, Asian Americans showed interests in both Investigative and Social occupations. Studying male engineers in Mexico, Fouad and Dancer (1992) found that Holland types fit well for this group, but there were differences in distance between types on Holland's hexagon. In a study of Pakistani men and women, Khan and Alvi (1991) found that men fit Holland's hexagonal model better than women. Other studies, such as Day and Bedeian's (1995) research on the fit of person-environment models (including Holland's) with African American nursing-service employees, extend the information available about the applicability of Holland's model to individuals from diverse cultures and employment settings. However, information about the appropriateness of Holland's topological system for specific cultural groups is neither sufficient nor consistent enough to allow generalizations about its usefulness for specific groups.

Information about the distribution of the Holland types of different cultural groups working in the United States provides a useful perspective on the employment of people of color. In her study of the distribution of workers by ethnic group, Arbona (1989) reported that more Hispanic men (71%) and African American men (68%) than white men (54%) were in Realistic types of work. Furthermore, fewer African American men (10%) and Hispanic men (6%) than white men (23%) were in Enterprising occupations. With regard to women, more African American women (37%) and Hispanic women (41%) than white women (24%) were in Realistic jobs. More white women (15%) than African American women (7%) and Hispanic women (10%) were in Enterprising occupations. In a further analysis of this data, Arbona found that African American and Hispanic men were found more often in low-level Realistic jobs. Arbona (1989) suggests that African American and Hispanic students may be exposed to role models working in relatively low-level jobs. Such data are not a critique of Holland's theory but show its utility in identifying social inequities.

COUNSELOR ISSUES

Research on providing appropriate counseling techniques and approaches for different Holland types yields insights into how best to meet the career counseling needs of individuals who are predominantly of one Holland type. Boyd and Cramer (1995) found that Social and Enterprising college students preferred counseling with unlimited sessions, with little structure in the sessions, with a focus on self-awareness, and with the opportunity for follow-up counseling. They preferred a less concrete focus than did Realistic or Conventional college students. Using a description of six counseling approaches that corresponded to each of Holland's six environments, Niles (1993) found that students identified as a specific Holland type tended (but not strongly) to select a counseling approach similar to their type. This was particularly true of Realistic and Enterprising males and was less true of Investigative, Artistic, and Conventional males, and of females, in general. Speculating from their research on Holland's types and personality variables, Holland, Johnston, Hughey, and Asama (1991) concluded that Realistic and Conventional individuals would be poor candidates for traditional psychotherapy because they are not very open to feelings or new ideas. Consistent with the findings described here, Lenz, Reardon, and Sampson (1993) found that individuals scoring high on Social and Enterprising scales rated a computer system (SIGI PLUS) lower in its ability to help them acquire occupational knowledge and self-knowledge than did college students scoring high on other types. Issues that face counselors in using Holland's theory with clients of different Holland types are discussed next.

Although there are a number of counselor aids built into the Holland system, such as methods for conceptualizing client problems, classifying occupational information, and incorporating inventories, there are some problems that counselors are likely to encounter. By using the concepts of congruence and differentiation, a few potential problem issues can be described.

In this chapter, discussion has focused on the congruence between the client's personality and his or her working environment. Often, the client's personality type and the counselor's personality type are incongruent. For counselors, the most common types are SE, SI, or SA. Most counselors are predominantly Social; many are secondarily Enterprising, Investigative, or Artistic. When counselors with these Holland codes encounter clients who are primarily Realistic and/or Conventional, they are dealing with a type quite opposite to and incongruent with their own. The danger is that the values of the counselor, in terms of valuing personal interaction and helping, are likely to be very different from those of the client. Being aware of this divergence of values can help counselors be more open toward and understanding of interests, abilities, and values that are very different from theirs. Many counselors may not respect hunting, fishing, being outdoors, fixing cars, and such, but their Realistic clients will. Appreciating the differences among incongruent types can be very helpful in counseling.

Another problem concerns Holland's concept of differentiation. Counselors are likely to be differentiated according to their preference for types of environments. Because they have made a career choice, they are likely to have preferences for two or three types and lack interest in three or four types. For clients of any age who are having difficulty with career selection, there may be little differentiation among four, five, or all six types. For example, a client may enjoy and have abilities in Social, Realistic, Enterprising, Conventional, and Artistic activities. It then becomes the counselor's role to help further differentiate the client's experiences and desires, perhaps ascertaining that Realistic and Conventional activities are most satisfying. Counselors may become frustrated with the client's difficulty in differentiating, when the counselor is not having that difficulty. Being aware of this divergence often helps the counselor become more patient.

There are times when Holland's personality theory will not suffice. For example, there are 53 RIE, 30 REI, and 17 SEA occupations listed in Holland's *Occupations Finder* (1994). Holland's theory does not provide enough information for the client to choose within a specific three-letter category, such as RIE. Other factors such as location or non-Holland personality factors may also need to be considered. Arriving at a code for a client is a help in counseling, not the end of the counseling process. For some clients, Holland's theory will provide a start for differentiating interests and talents or for developing a sense of identity. Other factors such as education, ability, location, and/or personal responsibilities to family may be equally important, if not more so, than personality types. Holland's theory is a useful way of conceptualizing client concerns, but it does not provide a conceptualization system that will work with all clients, all problems, all of the time.

SUMMARY

John Holland's typological theory has been accepted widely by counselors and psychologists, for several reasons. Conceptually, it is easy to use because the six personality types (Realistic, Investigative, Artistic, Social, Enterprising, and Conventional) can be matched with a corresponding environment. Usually, an individual and an environment are described by the most important, second in importance, and third in importance of the six categories. When the three letters of the code describing the person and the environment match or approximate a match, then congruence results. Congruence, the most important of Holland's constructs, is sought by assessing the type of the client and trying to match it with appropriate occupations. Other constructs, such as consistency, differentiation, and identity are also valuable in using Holland's theory conceptually. Because Holland's theoretical constructs are clearly defined, they have generated much research relevant to the applicability of his theory to all individuals, including women and people of color. The occupational classification system that has been developed using the three-letter code is another practical aid for counselors. Several inventories besides Holland's Self-Directed Search and Vocational Preference Inventory are useful in identifying the client's type. Because of its wide acceptance by counselors and the abundance of supportive research, Holland's theory is likely to be used widely in the future.

References

Arbona, C. (1989). Hispanic employment and the Holland typology of work. *Career Development Quarterly, 37,* 257–268.

Assouline, M., & Meir, E. I. (1987). Metaanalysis of the relationship between congruence and well-being measures. *Journal of Vocational Behavior, 31,* 319–332.

Boyd, C. U., & Cramer, S. H. (1995). Relationship between Holland high-point code and client preference for selected vocational counseling strategies. *Journal of Career Development, 21,* 213–221.

Brown, S. D., & Gore, P. A., Jr. (1994). An evaluation of interest congruence indices: Distribution, characteristics and measurement properties. *Journal of Vocational Behavior, 45,* 310–327.

Camp, C. C., & Chartrand, J. M. (1992). A comparison and evaluation of interest congruence indices. *Journal of Vocational Behavior, 41,* 162–182.

Conneran, J. M., & Hartman, B. W. (1993). The concurrent validity of the Self-Directed Search in identifying chronic career indecision among vocational education students. *Journal of Career Development, 19,* 197–208.

Day, D. V., & Bedeian, A. G. (1995). Personality similarity and work-related outcomes among African-American nursing personnel: A test of the supplementary model of person-environment congruence. *Journal of Vocational Behavior, 46,* 55–70.

Fouad, N. A. (1994). Annual review 1991–1993: Vocational choice decision making, assessment, and intervention. *Journal of Vocational Behavior, 45,* 125–176.

Fouad, N. A., & Dancer, L. S. (1992). Cross-cultural structure of interests: Mexico and the United States (Special Issue: Holland's theory). *Journal of Vocational Behavior, 40,* 129–143.

Gehlert, K., Timberlake, D., & Wagner, B. (1992). The relation between vocational identity and academic achievement. *Journal of College Student Development, 33,* 143–148.

Gottfredson, G. D., & Holland, J. L. (1989). *Dictionary of Holland Occupational Codes* (2nd ed.). Odessa, FL: Psychological Assessment Resources.

Hansen, J. C., Collins, R. C., Swanson, J. L., & Fouad, N. A. (1993). Gender differences in the structure of interests. *Journal of Vocational Behavior, 42,* 200–211.

Haverkamp, B. E., Collins, R. C., & Hansen, J. C. (1994). Structure of interests of Asian-American college students. *Journal of Counseling Psychology, 41,* 256–264.

Holland, J. L. (1966). *The psychology of vocational choice.* Waltham, MA: Blaisdell.

Holland, J. L. (1973). *Making vocational choices: A theory of careers.* Englewood Cliffs, NJ: Prentice-Hall.

Holland, J. L. (1985a). *Making vocational choices: A theory of personalities and work environments* (2nd ed.). Englewood Cliffs, NJ: Prentice-Hall.

Holland, J. L. (1985b). *Manual for the Vocational Preference Inventory.* Odessa, FL: Psychological Assessment Resources.

Holland, J. L. (1992). *Making vocational choices: A theory of vocational personalities and work environments.* Odessa, FL: Psychological Assessment Resources.

Holland, J. L. (1994). *The Occupations Finder.* Odessa, FL: Psychological Assessment Resources.

Holland, J. L., Gottfredson, G. D., & Baker, H. G. (1990). Validity of vocational aspirations and interest inventories: Extended, replicated, and reinterpreted. *Journal of Counseling Psychology, 37,* 337–342.

Holland, J. L., Johnston, J. A., & Asama, N. F. (1994). More evidence for the relationship between Holland's personality types and personality variables. *Journal of Career Assessment, 2,* 331–340.

Holland, J. L., Johnston, J. A., Hughey, K. F., & Asama, N. F. (1991). Some explorations of a theory of careers: VII. A replication and some possible exceptions. *Journal of Career Development, 18,* 91–100.

Holland, J. L., Powell, A. B., & Fritzsche, B. A. (1994). *The Self-Directed Search professional user's guide.* Odessa, FL: Psychological Assessment Resources.

Khan, S. B., & Alvi, S. A. (1991). The structure of Holland's typology: A study in a non-Western culture. *Journal of Cross Cultural Psychology, 22*(2), 283–292.

Latona, J. R. (1989). Consistency of Holland code and its relation to persistence in a college major. *Journal of Vocational Behavior, 34,* 253–265.

Lenz, J. G., Reardon, R. C., & Sampson, J. P. (1993). Holland's theory and effective use of computer-assisted career guidance systems. *Journal of Career Development, 19,* 245–253.

Leung, S. A., Conoley, C. W., Scheel, M. J., & Sonnenberg, R. T. (1992). An examination of the relation between vocational identity, consistency, and differentiation, *Journal of Vocational Behavior, 40,* 95–107.

Leung, S. A., Ivey, D., & Suzuki, L. (1994). Factors affecting the career aspirations of Asian Americans. *Journal of Counseling and Development, 72,* 404–410.

Monahan, C. J. (1987). Construct validation of a modified differential index. *Journal of Vocational Behavior, 30,* 217–226.

Niles, S. G. (1993). The relationship between Holland types preferences for career counseling. *Journal of Career Development, 19,* 209–220.

Pazy, A., & Zin, R. (1987). A contingency approach to consistency: A challenge to prevalent views. *Journal of Vocational Behavior, 30,* 84–101.

Rosen, D., Holmberg, K., & Holland, J. L. (1994). *The educational opportunities finder.* Odessa, FL: Psychological Assessment Resources.

Schwartz, R. H. (1991). Achievement-Orientation of Personality Type: A variable to consider in tests of Holland's congruence-achievement and other hypotheses. *Journal of Vocational Behavior, 38,* 225–235.

Spokane, A. R. (1985). A review of research on person-environment congruence in Holland's theory of careers. *Journal of Vocational Behavior, 26,* 300–343.

Spokane, A. R., & Jacob, E. J. (1995). *Career and vocational assessment 1993–1994: A biannual review. Journal of Career Assessment, 4,* 1–32.

Strack, S. (1994). Relating Millon's basic personality styles and Holland's occupational types. *Journal of Vocational Behavior, 45,* 41-54.

Subich, L. M. (1994). Annual review: Practice and research in career counseling and development—1993. *Career Development Quarterly, 43,* 114–151.

Sutherland, L. F., Fogarty, G. J., & Pithers, R. T. (1995). Congruence as a predictor of occupational stress. *Journal of Vocational Behavior, 46,* 292–309.

Swanson, J. L. (1992). The structure of vocational interests for African-American college students. *Journal of Vocational Behavior, 40,* 144-157.

Tokar, D. M., & Swanson, J. L. (1995). Evaluation of the correspondence between Holland's vocational personality typology and the five-factor model of personality. *Journal of Vocational Behavior, 46,* 89–108.

Tranberg, M., Slane, S., & Ekeberg, S. E. (1993). The relation between interest congruence and satisfaction: A metaanalysis. *Journal of Vocational Behavior, 42,* 253–264.

Vondracek, F. W. (1991). Current status of the concept of vocational identity. *Man and Work, 3,* 291–301.

Vondracek, F. W. (1992). The construct of vocational identity and its use in career theory and research. *Career Development Quarterly, 41,* 130–144.

Walsh, W. B., & Srsic, C. (1995). Vocational behavior and career development, 1994: A review. *Career Development Quarterly, 44,* 98–145.

5

Myers-Briggs Type Theory

Unlike most other theories in this book, the Myers-Briggs type theory was not designed to be a theory of career development. Why then is it included? The Myers-Briggs type theory has become very popular with career counselors, as many find that it is applicable to their work with clients. The Myers-Briggs type theory is a psychological theory based on the work of Carl Gustav Jung and adapted by Katharine Briggs in the 1920s.

Because the development of the Myers-Briggs typology is unusual, it would be helpful to describe its origins briefly. Katharine Briggs was not a psychologist but was an acute observer of people. Prior to reading Jung's (1921/1971) book *Psychological Types,* she had developed her own categories of people's behavior. Becoming intrigued with Jung's work, she studied it extensively. During the next 20 years, she continued to observe people and to try to classify them into Jungian types. In the 1940s, she was joined by her only child, Isabel Myers, in the development of the Myers-Briggs Type Indicator (MBTI). They worked together sorting and analyzing responses to the MBTI. In 1956, she was able to persuade the Educational Testing Service to publish the MBTI. In 1962, a manual for the MBTI was published, and Isabel Myers spoke at the American Psychological Association meeting. Gradually, the MBTI attracted the attention of psychologists. In 1969, Isabel started to work with Mary McCaulley and began a typology laboratory at the University of Florida in Gainesville. In 1972, this laboratory became the Center for the Application of Psychological Type, sponsoring research on the MBTI and coordinating research efforts in the development of the Myers-Briggs typology. Sponsored by the Association for Psychological Type are a research journal, *Journal of Psychological Type,* and a newsletter, *Bulletin of Psychological Type* (Kroeger & Thuesen, 1988). Although the Myers-Briggs typology has increased in popularity among psychologists and counselors over the years, it is not without its critics. Some psychologists have questioned both the theory and the methodology of the MBTI. This criticism is discussed in more detail in a later section of this chapter.

In his book *Psychological Types* (1921/1971), Jung wrote about different ways that individuals use perception and judgment. He was concerned both with what people pay attention to and how they make decisions about what they see. Further, he viewed some people as being more concerned about what is happening in the world outside themselves and others as being more concerned with their own views and ideas. This is a very brief synopsis of the groundwork on which the Myers-Briggs typology is based. To put Jung's typology into perspective, it is only one of the many aspects of his theory of personality. Many Jungian psychotherapists are concerned with analysis of dreams and other concepts besides those of personality type. However, many psychologists and counselors who use Jungian theory do so only within the limited confines of the Myers-Briggs typological system.

To put the Myers-Briggs type system within the context of career development, it is helpful to think of it as a trait and factor theory. In Chapter 2, the first step in selecting a career, according to trait and factor theory, was listed as gaining "a clear understanding of your aptitudes, achievements, interests, values, and personality." Within that context, the Myers-Briggs typology can be seen as a theory of personality. Those counselors who use Myers-Briggs theory in helping clients with career choices use the Myers-Briggs theory as a personality theory. Rarely, if ever, would the Myers-Briggs theory be used without an assessment of aptitudes, achievements, or interests as well. Certainly, the Myers-Briggs theory can be used with other theories besides trait and factor theory. However, it fits rather neatly into that model. Available in the MBTI manual (Myers & McCaulley, 1985) are listings of environments (or occupations) in which various types of people work. This information, along with knowledge of a person's type, enables a counselor to help a client with the third step of trait and factor career selection: "integrating information about self and the world of work." In addition, the Myers-Briggs typology can be used in assisting a client with career adjustment, applying type concepts to both individuals and their current working conditions.

In this chapter, the four bipolar dimensions basic to Myers-Briggs theory will be explained: extraversion-introversion, sensing-intuition, thinking-feeling, and judgment-perception. Although the number of concepts in the Myers-Briggs typology is not great, the interrelationships among the types make for a complex and sometimes difficult theory to "chunk," or learn. Thus, to understand the theory, it is necessary to understand the four bipolar categories and how they work in conjunction with each other. Examples of counseling for career decision making and for work adjustment will illustrate the interrelationships among the constructs. Because the MBTI is such an important part of the use of the Myers-Briggs type theory, it will receive considerable attention. The interaction between the counselor's MBTI type and the client's MBTI type also has interesting ramifications. Because of its complexity, readers will find that the information in this chapter is insufficient to enable them to use the Myers-Briggs type theory in counseling without formal coursework or attendance at workshops, as well as further reading.

Within the Myers-Briggs typology, the two most basic concepts are perception-judgment and extraversion-introversion. The next section deals with how individuals perceive their surroundings and then make judgments or decisions about their observations. This then can be related to an individual's view of the world, that is, focus on the outer world (extraversion) or on the inner world (introversion). These can be seen as "preference patterns," or different ways that individuals prefer to make decisions and choices.

PERCEIVING AND JUDGING

Myers-Briggs theory pertains to the way that individuals observe their world and make decisions based on their perceptions (Myers, 1993). In dealing with the world, the first step is perception. Becoming aware of events, people, objects, or ideas, the individual perceives this information. Then, the individual must decide or make conclusions about the observed events, people, objects, or ideas. In doing so, the individual is judging the events and ideas that have been perceived. According to Myers, much of an individual's mental activity is devoted to *perceiving* and/or *judging*. For example, when an adolescent watches a movie, he or she takes in information (perceives) and then makes decisions about the movie: whether it was liked, appreciated, informative, and so on (judges). Throughout school and work activities, individuals are constantly perceiving and judging. There are two modes of perceiving and two modes of judging.

The Two Ways of Perceiving

The two contrasting ways of perceiving are *sensing* and *intuition.* Sensing is taking in information by using visual and auditory processes along with smell, taste, and touch. In contrast, intuition concerns the use of the unconscious, a concept of great importance in Jungian theory. Rather than direct perception, as in sensing, intuition is indirect and adds ideas to external perceptions. It was the belief of Jung, incorporated into the Myers-Briggs theory, that a preference for perception (and other Myers-Briggs concepts) was innate and not learned through interaction with the environment.

People who prefer sensing prefer to observe, primarily through hearing, vision, and touch. Their focus is on events that happen immediately around them. People who prefer sensing often have a good memory for details and are able to make clear observations. An adolescent who visits the dentist and makes use of the sensing perception may well be aware of the tools the dentist uses, the mannerisms of the dentist, and the location of the dental tools in the mouth. This common experience may eventually have some effect on occupational choice at a later time. At this point, the detailed information about the dental experience is stored in memory. This is in marked contrast to the opposite mode of perceiving: intuition.

By use of insight, an individual may perceive meanings and relationships in events. This insight into observations and ideas can be called *intuition*. Intuition takes visible and auditory (and other) information as a base and goes beyond it. Often the individual using intuition is focused not on the current event, but on a future event. Rather than being concrete, intuition is abstract, imaginative, and often creative. An adolescent who uses intuition while at the dentist's is likely to imagine what the next dental appointment may be like (that it may be much worse than the current one) or may imagine himself or herself as a dentist (filling cavities and doing other dental work). This response to the dentist is in marked contrast to the practical, present-oriented sensing response described in the previous paragraph. After an idea is perceived, whether sensed or intuited, a judgment is often made about it.

The Two Ways of Judging

Just as there are two kinds of perception (sensing and intuition), there are two types of judgment: *thinking* and *feeling*. After perceiving an event, an individual is likely to act primarily in one way, thinking or feeling. Thinking refers to analyzing and being objective about an observed idea or event. Feeling is a subjective reaction, often related to one's own values.

When using thinking judgment, an individual may be concerned with logic or analysis. The person tries to be objective in making a judgment about a perceived event. He or she may be concerned with judging the event or idea fairly and in the process may use objective criticism to analyze his or her perception. Returning to the adolescent in the dentist's chair, the individual may judge whether the experience will be similar next time, whether he or she would like to be a dentist and could perform dental functions, or what the dentist will do next.

A feeling judgment is deciding based on the values applied to observations or ideas. In making a feeling judgment, an individual is concerned with the impact of the judgment. Such individuals are more likely to be interested in human as opposed to technical problems. Again returning to the dentist's chair as an example, a feeling judgment may be concerned with wondering what it would be like to be a dentist who helps someone but creates physical pain in the process. This concern for others is in marked contrast to the previous example, which uses thinking judgment.

Combinations of Perceiving and Judging

Since perceiving precedes judging, these two functions are combined in individuals. Myers (1980) describes the four combinations of perceiving and judging that can occur:

Sensing and Thinking
Sensing and Feeling
Intuition and Feeling
Intuition and Thinking

According to Myers (1993), individuals prefer one of these four categories. How people perceive and judge has an impact not only on their own way of life, but also on how they interact with others. People who use sensing and thinking abilities to perceive events and make judgments about events are very different from those who use primarily intuition and feeling. Some examples will help to illustrate.

Sensing and Thinking People who rely on sensing for perceiving and on thinking for judging are likely to focus on collecting facts that can be verified by their observations. They may want to see or hear what has happened. They may want to count the profits or assess the output of a machine. Such people are quite practical and pragmatic. They are likely to choose occupations that demand analysis of facts. Examples of such occupations are law, business management, accounting and auditing, and production and purchasing. When making a career decision for themselves, they are likely to use a rational decision-making process based on information they have acquired through occupational literature and talking with others.

Sensing and Feeling Although relying on vision, hearing, and other senses, these people make decisions based on feeling. They are aware of the importance of feelings to themselves and others when making a decision. Because of their emphasis on others, they are more likely to be interested in observations about people than about objects. Examples of occupations that they are likely to seek out are the medical profession, social work, teaching children, and providing customer services. In making a career decision, they will focus on information about people and occupations, being aware of how they will feel doing a certain kind of work on a day-to-day basis.

Intuition and Feeling Rather than focus on current observations or happenings, people who intuit are likely to be concerned about future possibilities. Their feeling involvement is likely to be personal, warm, and inspired. They are apt to take a creative approach to meeting human needs and to be less concerned about objects. Examples of occupations would include clergy, teaching at the college or high school level, advertising, and social service occupations. When making a career decision, they are likely to use hunches based on what is best for them. Their emphasis in on feelings about observations rather than weighing the observations themselves.

Intuition and Thinking Those who use intuition and thinking are likely to make decisions based on analysis that uses hunches and projections about the future. They tend to enjoy solving problems, particularly those of a theoretical nature. Occupations that they tend to seek out include scientific research, computing, business (particularly financial) decision making, and development of new projects. In making their own career decisions, people using intuition and thinking are likely to project themselves into the future, thinking about what types of work would offer particular opportunities. Although based on projections about the future, their decision making would be logical and clear to them.

Two Counseling Examples

Two brief counseling dialogues will illustrate two different combinations of perception and judgment. The first will illustrate a counselor's assessment of sensing and thinking, and the second will illustrate intuition and feeling.

Sharon is a college sophomore who has sought career counseling because she is thinking of entering a business occupation but is not sure which one.

CL: Since we talked last week, I've been looking into a number of occupations. I went to the career library and started to read about careers such as stockbroker and banker. I only had time to read about six, but I intend to come back.

CO: It's good to hear that you got off to a quick start. [The concrete approach of the client sounds as if she is perceiving by using her sensing abilities.]

CL: There are several brochures on stockbroker and banker, not to mention other careers. I want to make sure that I have time to read them and weigh the information. Do you think it would be helpful for me to take notes?

CO: You seem to have a systematic way of doing things; notes seem to fit for you. [The counselor wants to reinforce the logical method that the client uses, which fits with people who use sensing and thinking.]

CL: I know that the occupational scales that I scored high on on that interest inventory fit with these careers. But I do want to find out more about them. Maybe I'll talk with my father about it.

CO: That sounds like a good idea. You're really getting a lot of information to make a decision. [Getting and collecting information about occupations and then analyzing it seems to be the style of this client, which fits in well with the sensing, thinking modes of perceiving and judging.]

Harvey uses a very different approach to career decision making. Also a sophomore in college, Harvey is exploring occupations in the social sciences and uses an approach that combines intuition with feeling.

CL: I'm so bored with school. I want to get out and do something, something that is going to mean something. I feel as if I'm just marking time. I'm not doing anything that's meaningful.

CO: You'd feel happier if you were doing something now that would make you feel worthwhile. [The client's feeling of frustration is strong and there is an absence of observations about events in his statements.]

CL: Yes, I feel that I'd like to make a difference. I am working on an adult literacy project at the Literacy Center at school. That's probably the thing I get the most out of, even more than my courses. Helping an adult, like this man I'm working with, to learn to read really makes me feel good. I just wish that I could do more of it.

CO: You really want to have an impact on others. [Harvey's perceptions of what goes on at the Literacy Center are intuitive. The counselor hears how important feeling is to Harvey in making judgments about his work with the literacy project.]

CL: I know that I want to help people; that's why I've tried to keep my grades up. I figure I have to in order to get into clinical psychology or psychiatry.

CO: It sounds as if it's difficult, but you really seem to be putting a lot of effort into what you eventually might do, even though you're not sure. [Being aware of Harvey's commitment, the counselor wants to reinforce it, even though Harvey's exact choice about the future is not yet determined.]

Note the contrast between Harvey and Sharon. Sharon's approach is very practical and systematic. On the other hand, Harvey has a mission, which he is enthusiastic about. He just hasn't defined it very clearly at this point. This contrast between a sensing, thinking, and an intuitive, feeling, approach is an illustration of how Myers-Briggs theory can aid in understanding career decision making.

The Preference for Perception or Judgment

When using the Myers-Briggs typology, it is important not only to understand how a client perceives and judges, but also to know which process is more important. People differ as to how important they consider perceiving objects and people around them in contrast to making judgments or decisions. Some people prefer to make decisions based on relatively few facts (*judgment*), while others prefer to weigh many facts before reaching a judgment (*perception*). In order to make a decision, people must stop perceiving and then judge. People who have a perceiving attitude continue to take information in and do not decide. Those who have a judging attitude are apt to stop perceiving and make a judgment without including any more evidence. People who use judgment are apt to have a sense of order in their lives, whereas people who use perception just live their lives.

EXTRAVERSION AND INTROVERSION

Another factor that adds to the understanding of how individuals use perception and judgment is introversion versus extraversion. The common meanings of *introvert* and *extravert* are different from those used by Jung and Myers. In common terminology, *introversion* is generally associated with being shy and quiet while *extraversion* refers to being louder and more outgoing. For Jung and Myers, the terms *introversion* and *extraversion* refer to how one sees the world. *Introversion* refers to making perceptions and judgments based on one's interests in his or her inner world. In contrast, *extraversion* refers to using perceptions and judgments in the outer world. For the introvert, the inner world, consisting of concepts and ideas, is important. For the extravert, the outer world, concern with other people and objects, is important. Obviously, both introverts and extraverts live in the inner and outer world. The difference is that introverts prefer the inner world, whereas extraverts prefer the outer world.

Extraverts often like to take action. They want to work with people or things by talking and interacting. They prefer to speak directly to an individual rather than to write a memo. Being verbally and physically active is important to them.

In contrast, introverts enjoy thinking. They may like to work out problems or think for a long time before acting on an experience. They may be more quiet than extraverts, not due to shyness, but due to the need for time to think.

Introversion and extraversion are used in combination with judgment and perception in the Myers-Briggs system. Some people prefer to use judgment and perception in the outer world, others in the inner world. Each of the four perceiving and judging types described earlier will have a preference for either the inner world (introvert) or the outer world (extravert).

Regarding preference for work, extraverts tend to like activity that provides contact with people, whereas introverts are likely to prefer activity where there is time for concentration. Thus, extraverts may prefer sales and business management occupations as well as social service occupations. On the other hand, introverts may prefer occupations such as science and accounting, where they spend time solving problems on their own. When they do this, they are likely to be more careful in dealing with details than extraverts, being more patient in that they can work on one project for a long time. Introverts do not need to work as part of a team; rather, they prefer to work alone without interruptions.

THE SIXTEEN TYPE COMBINATIONS

In the Myers-Briggs typology, the different ways of judging and perceiving, the preference for judgment or perception, and the preference for introversion or extraversion act in concert with each other to yield 16 different types. Type tables, such as Table 5-1 (pp. 124–127), are often used to describe the relationships among types. In order to examine the interrelationships of the four basic bipolar dimensions, it is helpful to use abbreviations. The following abbreviations will be used throughout the rest of the chapter:

ISTJ	ISFJ	INFJ	INTJ
ISTP	ISFP	INFP	INTP
ESTP	ESFP	ENFP	ENTP
ESTJ	ESFJ	ENFJ	ENTJ

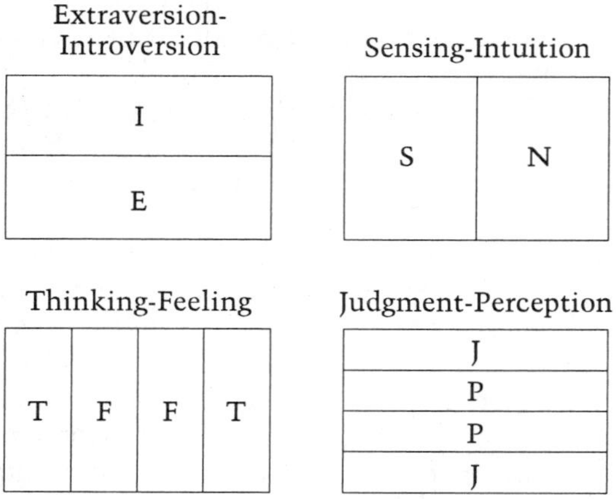

Extraversion-Introversion

I
E

Sensing-Intuition

S	N

Thinking-Feeling

T	F	F	T

Judgment-Perception

J
P
P
J

Figure 5-1 Format of type of tables. (Modified and reproduced by special permission of the Publisher, Consulting Psychologists Press, Inc., Palo Alto, CA 94303, from *Manual: A Guide to the Development and Use of the Myers-Briggs Type Indicator* by Isabel Briggs Myers and Mary H. McCaulley. Copyright 1985 by Peter Briggs Myers and Katherine D. Myers. All rights reserved. Further reproduction is prohibited without the Publisher's written consent.)

extravert = E; introvert = I
sensing = S; intuition = N
thinking = T; feeling = F
judgment = J; perception = P

Figure 5-1 illustrates the format of the type tables in terms of the four bipolar dimensions. At the top of the figure are the 16 combinations of four dimensions. By examining the diagrams directly below the 16 combinations, you can see the relationships of the dimensions more clearly. Note that introversion appears in the top half and extraversion in the bottom half of the 16 combinations. Sensing functions appear on the left side of the table and intuition on the right side. Likewise, thinking and feeling dimensions as well as judgment and perception dimensions are distributed in a systematic manner. Figure 5-1 serves as an outline for the descriptions found in Table 5-1. These descriptions give a brief overview of the characteristics of people who fall into each of the 16 categories. In their extensive manual, Myers and McCaulley (1985) caution that type definitions are not to be taken literally; they describe general characteristics of individuals falling into 16 types. They see these types as gifts or attributes that people make use of. They discourage the notion that there are only 16 types of people in the world and that all people within a category are similar to each other. These types are described in far greater detail in the manual, along with the various letter combinations. The Myers-Briggs Type Indicator yields scores on each of the four dimensions that point in the direction of sensing or intuiting, thinking or feeling, judging or perceiving, and extraversion or introversion. The MBTI, an important component when using the Myers-Briggs theory, will be discussed in more detail in a later section. When using the Myers-Briggs typology, it is helpful to be aware that either the judging or the perceiving process may be more significant, an important consideration in how the categorization by type is to be interpreted.

DOMINANT AND AUXILIARY PROCESSES

Probably the most complex and confusing concept to those who are beginning to learn the Myers-Briggs type theory is dominant and auxiliary processes. Perhaps the easiest way to understand this concept is to think of the last letter of the type code as determining the dominant or auxiliary process. If the last letter is P, then the style of perceiving (either intuitive or sensing) is the key process. If the last letter is J, then the way of judging (either thinking or feeling) is the key process.

The dominant process is the guiding one. It is the general, and the auxiliary process is the lieutenant. What makes this particularly complex is that for extraverts, the last letter of the code (J or P) indicates the dominant process; for introverts, the last letter indicates the auxiliary function. The reason is that since introverts function in the inner world, the dominant function is an inner-world function rather than an outer-world function. For extraverts, the dominant process is in the outer world of people and things. For introverts, the dominant process is in ideas and thoughts.

Another way of describing why the introvert's dominant process is the opposite of that indicated by the last letter of the Myers-Briggs code (J or P, judging or perceiving) is that introverts use their dominant process for the inner world and their auxiliary process for the outer world, whereas extraverts use their auxiliary process for the inner world and their dominant process for the outer world. The last letter of the code (J or P) thus refers to a preference for perceiving or judging in the outer world. Introverts whose dominant process is a judging process (thinking or feeling) show perceptiveness of their auxiliary process in dealing with the outer world and live their outer lives in this perceptive framework. The inner judgingness

Table 5-1 *Effects of the Combinations of All Four Preferences in Young People*

		Sensing Types	
		With Thinking	*With Feeling*
Introverts	*Judging*	ISTJ Serious, quiet, earn success by concentration and thoroughness. Practical, orderly, matter-of-fact, logical, realistic, and dependable. See to it that everything is well organized. Take responsibility. Make up their own minds as to what should be accomplished and work toward it steadily, regardless of protests or distractions.	ISFJ Quiet, friendly, responsible, and conscientious. Work devotedly to meet their obligations. Lend stability to any project or group. Thorough, painstaking, accurate. Their interests are usually not technical. Can be patient with necessary details. Loyal, considerate, perceptive, concerned with how other people feel.
	Perceptive	ISTP Cool onlookers—quiet, reserved, observing and analyzing life with detached curiosity and unexpected flashes of original humor. Usually interested in cause and effect, how and why mechanical things work, and in organizing facts using logical principles. Excel at getting to the core of a practical problem and finding the solution.	ISFP Retiring, quietly friendly, sensitive, kind, modest about their abilities. Shun disagreements, do not force their opinions or values on others. Usually do not care to lead but are often loyal followers. Often relaxed about getting things done because they enjoy the present moment and do not want to spoil it by undue haste or exertion.

		Sensing Types	
		With Thinking	*With Feeling*
Extraverts	*Perceptive*	**ESTP** Good at on-the-spot problem solving. Like action, enjoy whatever comes along. Tend to like mechanical things and sports, with friends on the side. Adaptable, tolerant, pragmatic; focused on getting results. Dislike long explanations. Are best with real things that can be worked, handled, taken apart or put together.	**ESFP** Outgoing, accepting, friendly, enjoy everything and make things more fun for others by their enjoyment. Like action and making things happen. Know what's going on and join in eagerly. Find remembering facts easier than mastering theories. Are best in situations that need sound common sense and practical ability with people.
	Judging	**ESTJ** Practical, realistic, matter-of-fact, with a natural head for business or mechanics. Not interested in abstract theories; want learning to have direct and immediate application. Like to organize and run activities. Often make good administrators; are decisive, quickly move to implement decisions; take care of routine details.	**ESFJ** Warm-hearted, talkative, popular, conscientious, born cooperators, active committee members. Need harmony and may be good at creating it. Always doing something nice for someone. Work best with encouragement and praise. Main interest is in things that directly and visibly affect people's lives.

(continued)

Table 5-1 *Effects of the Combinations of All Four Preferences in Young People (continued)*

		Intuitive Types	
		With Feeling	*With Thinking*
Introverts	*Judging*	INFJ Succeed by perseverance, originality, and desire to do whatever is needed or wanted. Put their best efforts into their work. Quietly forceful, conscientious, concerned for others. Respected for their firm principles. Likely to be honored and followed for their clear convictions as to how best to serve the common good.	INTJ Have original minds and great drive for their own ideas and purposes. Have long-range vision and quickly find meaningful patterns in external events. In fields that appeal to them, they have a fine power to organize a job and carry it through. Skeptical, critical, independent, determined, have high standards of competence and performance.
	Perceptive	INFP Quiet observers, idealistic, loyal. Important that outer life be congruent with inner values. Curious, quick to see possibilities, often serve as catalysts to implement ideas. Adaptable, flexible, and accepting unless a value is threatened. Want to understand people and ways of fulfilling human potential. Little concern with possessions or surroundings.	INTP Quiet and reserved. Especially enjoy theoretical or scientific pursuits. Like solving problems with logic and analysis. Interested mainly in ideas, with little liking for parties or small talk. Tend to have sharply defined interests. Need careers where some strong interest can be used and useful.

		Intuitive Types	
		With Feeling	*With Thinking*
Extraverts	*Perceptive*	ENFP Warmly enthusiastic, high-spirited, ingenious, imaginative. Able to do almost anything that interests them. Quick with a solution for any difficulty and ready to help anyone with a problem. Often rely on their ability to improvise instead of preparing in advance. Can always find compelling reasons for whatever they want.	ENTP Quick, ingenious, good at many things. Stimulating company, alert and outspoken. May argue for fun on either side of a question. Resourceful in solving new and challenging problems, but may neglect routine assignments. Apt to turn to one new interest after another. Skillful in finding logical reasons for whatever they want.
	Judging	ENFJ Responsive and responsible. Feel real concern for what others think or want, and try to handle things with due regard for other's feelings. Can present a proposal or lead a group discussion with ease and tact. Sociable, popular, sympathetic. Responsive to praise and criticism. Like to facilitate others and enable people to achieve their potential.	ENTJ Frank, decisive, leaders in activities. Develop and implement comprehensive systems to solve organizational problems. Good in anything that requires reasoning and intelligent talk, such as public speaking. Are usually well informed and enjoy adding to their fund of knowledge.

is not apparent to others. Also, introverts whose dominant process is perceptive (sensing or intuition) do not outwardly behave as if they were perceptive people. Rather, they show the judgingness of the auxiliary process. Others would see them as leading their outer lives in the judging attitude.

The preceding discussion is complex. Describing the auxiliary and dominant processes requires thorough familiarity with the Myers-Briggs typology. Critics of the Myers-Briggs theory may point to the dominant and auxiliary processes as having little research support (Healy, 1989). On the other hand, some who find the Myers-Briggs theory to be useful in their counseling claim that the concept of dominant and auxiliary processes is essential. Because not all counselors apply the concepts of dominant and auxiliary, the examples that will be used to illustrate Myers-Briggs conceptualization in counseling will focus on the types themselves rather than on the dominant and auxiliary processes.

USING THE MYERS-BRIGGS TYPOLOGY IN COUNSELING

This section will focus on examples that illustrate two major career issues: career decision making and career adjustment. Over a period of many years, researchers have accumulated a considerable amount of data that relate Myers-Briggs type to occupational choice. In Appendix D of their manual, Myers and McCaulley (1985) list a summary of the types of over 250,000 people in hundreds of different occupations. These are listed both by four-letter codes and by two-letter codes. More data are available in the *Atlas of Type Tables* (1987), which includes more information about occupational groups and their codes. To summarize this information, Table 5-2 lists examples of frequent occupational choices that are made by people of each type. Some occupations occur in more than one category. Still, this table gives an idea of those occupations that are most commonly associated with certain Myers-Briggs types. This information that categorizes occupations by type can be useful in both career decision making and work adjustment counseling.

Table 5-3 can also be useful in that it lists the effects of each of the eight poles (extravert-introvert, sensing-intuition, thinking-feeling, and judgment-perception) on individuals' preferences for work situations. For example, extraverts tend to prefer variety and action, whereas introverts prefer quiet and working alone. Sensing types like established ways of doing things, whereas intuitive types dislike doing the same thing repeatedly. Thinking types tend to respond to people's ideas rather than their feelings, whereas feeling types respond more to people's values than their thoughts. Judging types work best when they can follow a plan, while perceptive types do not mind last-minute changes. In the examples that follow, some reference will be made to these tables.

Table 5-2 *Examples of Frequent Occupational Choices Made by Each Type*

ISTJ	*ISFJ*	*INFJ*	*INTJ*
Accountants Auditors Engineers Financial managers Police officers Steelworkers Technicians	Health workers Librarians Service workers Teachers	Artists Clergy Musicians Psychiatrists Social workers Teachers Writers	Computer analysts Engineers Judges Lawyers Operations researchers Scientists Social scientists
ISTP	*ISFP*	*INFP*	*INTP*
Crafts workers Construction workers Mechanics Protective service workers Statisticians	Clerical workers Construction workers Musicians Outdoor workers Painters Stock clerks	Artists and entertainers Editors Psychiatrists Psychologists Social workers Writers	Artists Computer analysts Engineers Scientists Writers
ESTP	*ESFP*	*ENFP*	*ENTP*
Auditors Carpenters Marketing personnel Police officers Sales clerks Service workers	Child care workers Mining engineers Secretaries Supervisors	Actors Clergy Counselors Journalists Musicians Public relations workers	Actors Journalists Marketing personnel Photographers Sales agents
ESTJ	*ESFJ*	*ENFJ*	*ENTJ*
Administrators Financial managers Managers Salespeople Supervisors	Beauticians Health workers Office managers Secretaries Teachers	Actors Clergy Consultants Counselors Home economists Musicians Teachers	Administrators Credit managers Lawyers Managers Marketing personnel Operations researcher

Table 5-3 *Effects of Each Preference in Work Situations*

Extraversion	*Introversion*
Like variety and action	Like quiet for concentration
Often impatient with long, slow jobs	Tend not to mind working on one project for a long time uninterruptedly
Are interested in the activities of their work and in how other people do it	Are interested in the facts/ideas behind their work
Often act quickly, sometimes without thinking	Like to think a lot before they act, sometimes without acting
Develop ideas by discussion	Develop ideas by reflection
Like having people around	Like working alone with no interruptions
Learn new tasks by talking and doing	Learn new tasks by reading and reflecting

Sensing	*Intuition*
Like using experience and standard ways to solve problems	Like solving new complex problems
Enjoy applying what they have already learned	Enjoy learning a new skill more than using it
May distrust and ignore their inspirations	Will follow their inspirations
Seldom make errors of fact	May ignore or overlook facts
Like to do things with a practical bent	Like to do things with an innovate bent
Like to present the details of their work first	Like to present an overview of their work first
Prefer continuation of what is, with fine tuning	Prefer change, sometimes radical, to continuation of what is
Usually proceed step-by-step	Usually proceed in bursts of energy

Thinking	*Feeling*
Use logical analysis to reach conclusions	Use values to reach conclusions
Want mutual respect among colleagues	Want harmony and support among colleagues
May hurt people's feelings without knowing it	Enjoy pleasing people, even in unimportant things
Tend to decide impersonally, sometimes paying insufficient attention to people's wishes	Often let decisions be influenced by their own and other people's likes and dislikes
Tend to be firm-minded and can give criticism when appropriate	Tend to be sympathetic and dislike, even avoid, telling people unpleasant things
Look at the principles involved in the situation	Look at the underlying values in the situation
Feel rewarded when job is done well	Feel rewarded when people's needs are met

Judging	*Perceiving*
Work best when they can plan their work and follow their plan	Enjoy flexibility in their work
Like to get things settled and finished	Like to leave things open for last-minute changes
May not notice new things that need to be done	May postpone unpleasant tasks that need to be done
Tend to be satisfied once they reach a decision on a thing, situation, or person	Tend to be curious and welcome a new light on a thing, situation, or person
Reach closure by deciding quickly	Postpone decisions while searching for options
Feel supported by structure and schedule	Adapt well to changing situations and feel restricted without variety
Focus on completion of a project	Focus on the process of a project

Example of Career Decision-Making Counseling

Edna is a 25-year-old African American female who has just been discharged from the U.S. Army after spending three years of active duty on a large military base. Much of her work entailed keeping records of supplies and office management. Although she liked her military experience, enjoying the colleagues whom she worked with, she did not want to reenlist. Rather, she decided to take advantage of the GI Bill, which would finance much of her future education. Prior to entering the military, she had been a waitress. This is not an occupation that she wishes to return to. She is living in a small apartment with her sister and her sister's husband in Pittsburgh. Now she has decided to seek counseling to help her decide on future plans.

The following segment is part of the second interview. During the first appointment with the counselor, Edna went over her work experience, discussing activities that she had enjoyed. Immediately after finishing the session, she completed the Myers-Briggs Type Indicator as well as the Strong Interest Inventory. On the Myers-Briggs Type Indicator, she scored ESFJ, or extraverted feeling with sensing. The last letter, J, means that her dominant process is feeling, which is a judging process; therefore, her auxiliary process is one of perception, which is sensing. Thus, she uses her favorite process, feeling, in dealing with others, and the auxiliary function, sensing, in her inner world. The counselor has just gone over this information with Edna and has reviewed the results of her Strong Interest Inventory. Her high scores were on the occupational theme S, Social, and on the basic interest scales for teaching and social service; she received many high scores on S and E (Enterprising) occupational scales. Examples of these include human resources director, public administrator, social worker, and elementary school teacher.

Edna is a soft-spoken young woman with a pleasant smile and a very friendly presentation. This portion of the dialogue will focus on the counselor's use of the Myers-Briggs typology in conceptualizing Edna's career decision-making concerns.

CL: It's helpful to look at these tests. I knew that I didn't like the work in the army. It really was boring for me to monitor inventory records and to keep track of purchase requisitions and things like that. It was funny: People thought I liked my work, I guess because I got along so well with the others. The other women that I worked with were real nice. Sure, there was turnover, but I seemed to be able to get along with everyone.

CO: Sounds as if getting along with others is very important to you in your work. [Feeling is an important process for Edna. It is not surprising that she emphasizes her feelings about others and wants to get along well with others.]

CL: Oh, yes, it is. I know some friends who worked in offices that were unfriendly, and I would have hated that. It seemed to me that the more my work had to do with people, the more I liked it. When I would have to fill in for the receptionist sometimes, I liked that more than my usual work, even though my usual work required more training. Often, when people would come into my office, they were looking for help, trying to find the right person, or trying to find a requisition. When I could help them, I really felt good, but I sometimes think I want to help in a different way.

CO: What kind of helping gives you a really good feeling? [The counselor speaks to Edna's emphasis on feeling. He wants to know what things are important to her. He suspects that it will be more difficult to get at her auxiliary process, sensing, which deals with her inner world, than to talk with her about her outer world, the dominant process of feeling.]

CL: I think I feel best when I'm helping children. It seems when I'm at home, not when I'm with my sister, I am always helping kids. I help them read; I help them when they're crying. All my mother's friends know I'm a soft touch. They can rely on me to help out.

CO: Yet you don't mind being a soft touch. [Again, the focus is on Edna's feeling type.]

CL: No, I don't. When we looked at the Strong Interest Inventory, I was glad to see teaching show up. I was afraid that maybe it would, and maybe it wouldn't.

CO: Can you tell me what you mean by would and wouldn't? [Because this is confusing, the counselor wants to hear what Edna seems to have mixed feelings about.]

CL: Well, sometimes I think deep down I've wanted to be a teacher.

CO: Tell me your thoughts about teaching. [Teaching is an occupation that ESFJ people often enter—see Table 5-2.]

CL: My father wanted me to work right away. We really didn't have any money. There were four children. Four of us girls. I was the second youngest, and my oldest sister had gone to college. My father was pretty strict with me, and he didn't really let me do what I wanted. But I really admired him. He worked very hard, and I wanted to please him very much.

CO: But it seems as if now you want to please yourself. [Being compliant and wanting to be loyal to people they respect can be characteristic of ESFJ people.]

CL: My father died two years ago, and I hate to say this, but somehow I feel relieved a little bit. Like now there are no blockades in my way.

CO: It's hard to be critical of your father now. [The counselor wants to be gentle with Edna, because her father is an important part of her.]

CL: I want to do something that I will enjoy. Now with money available, I think that I could go to school. It really seems like that would be a wonderful thing to do. Even my father wouldn't have objected if I had support from the government like I do.

CO: It really is nice to be able to be concerned about a decision that can be helpful for you. [The counselor is aware that Edna is starting to appreciate his confidence in her. Knowing that people who are ESFJ often appreciate support, he starts to offer more. He knows that Edna was disappointed by her father's lack of support.]

CL: I guess sometimes down inside I feel that teaching small children would be marvelous for me. I guess it scares me sometimes to think that. I used to hear that there weren't many jobs in teaching and things like that. I don't hear that much anymore. But I guess I never really had much confidence that I could do it.

CO: You seem to be excited when you think of it now, though. [Again, the counselor wants to reinforce feelings that Edna has inside that this is right. Her judgment about career choice is based on feeling. The fact that her Myers-Briggs type code and her Strong Interest Inventory results are in agreement with her preference relates to the thinking aspect of judging, which Edna does not use much.]

In this example, the Myers-Briggs Type Indicator serves as a source for guiding the counselor in conceptualizing Edna's issues about her future career choices. He chooses not to introduce the terminology to her, but to use the conceptual framework of the Myers-Briggs theory as a basis for his own work. If it seems helpful to him to explain the concepts to Edna again, or to use them with her, then he will.

Example of Career Adjustment Counseling

Often, in counseling, a counselor finds it helpful to develop weaker components of an individual's perception and judgment. For example, a person whose Myers-Briggs type is INTP uses sensing and feeling less frequently than intuition and thinking. Myers and McCaulley (1985, p. 65) suggest that a counselor should work on one process at a time, for example, should work on judgment but not perception and judgment at the same time. Further, the work should be conscious and purposeful, and the counselor should not let other processes interfere. When working with people who are having difficulty on their job, counselors often find it helpful to make use of functions that are not a strong part of the individual's personality. These weaker functions are called *tertiary* and *inferior functions*. They are described in more detail in other publications, such as Myers and McCaulley (1985) and Schemel and Borbely (1982). An example of making use of weaker functions follows.

George is a 45-year-old Native American raised in New Mexico. He is married, with two teenage children. He has a doctorate in biology and has been employed at a large cancer research hospital to do basic research for the past 12 years. Two years ago, he was put in charge of a research team. Research progress has been frustrating. As a result, his team of five people have become upset with each other. Two of the team members don't talk to each other any longer. George's supervisor has been concerned about this lack of progress. Members of George's team have talked to the supervisor about the fact that there is much tension among members of the group.

George recently complained of chest pain. After being checked thoroughly by a physician, George was referred to a counselor for help with work-related issues. The physician felt, after talking with George, that tension experienced at work might be the cause of the pain. Although somewhat reluctant to seek counseling, feeling that he should be able to handle the problems himself, George has come back for his second meeting with the counselor. After their first meeting, he completed the Myers-Briggs Type Indicator. His scores are summarized as INTP.

CL: I've been having much trouble at work. I find myself distracted constantly. We're involved in much important research, and the people who work with me seem to spend more time bickering with each other and less time researching. I can't concentrate, and I don't like it. I find that I'm upset at the end of the day. I keep hoping things will work out, but they do not.

CO: This sounds very disturbing for you. You can't get your work done, and other people aren't getting their work done. [The counselor is aware that George's dominant process is thinking. He is thinking a lot about his research and the problems at work without the input of others. This process is an introverted one; thus it stays in his mind.]

CL: Yes. I am working often in my own head. I'm thinking constantly. I think at work; I can't stop thinking at home. I find that I'm distracted. My children notice this, too.

CO: What seems to be bothering you the most? [The counselor wishes to focus on a problem that she may be able to help with.]

CL: Part of it is we have some new doctoral-level people who have done good work before but haven't worked under my supervision. They don't say much to me, and I don't say much to them. I know I need to do something about it. Sometimes I can feel the tension; sometimes I can feel it in my chest.

CO: Tell me more about that feeling in the chest. [The counselor seizes the opportunity to talk about the least well-developed function, the inferior function, feeling, which is the opposite of George's dominant function, thinking.]

CL: I guess I feel tight. I usually feel upset, and I don't want to say anything.

CO: That's important information. [The counselor wants to deal with the feeling process, the least well developed of George's perception and judgment functions.]

CL: I guess it is important. It's hard for me sometimes to focus on things other than my research. These personal matters seem so trivial to me. But I'm starting to find that they are not. I remember what you said earlier when we were talking about the Myers-Briggs Type Indicator. You spoke of how important thinking is to me. It really is.

CO: I know, George. One of the things that we can work on is developing that other side of thinking, feeling. [The counselor avoids a long technical discussion of the Myers-Briggs Type Indicator and is eager to follow the lead-in that George has provided.]

CL: I know what happens at work is important. Sometimes I will tell myself it's not.

CO: It's good that you recognize that, George. Perhaps we can work more on that—recognizing not only your own feelings, but the feelings of others also.

CL: It is just uncomfortable for me. Sometimes I find myself almost rushing to get through the laboratory into my own little office, where I can work alone. I need to do more.

CO: What is it that you need to do more of, George?

CL: I need to talk to the people working at their desks and tables in the lab.

CO: That sounds good, George. How might you do it? [The counselor is pleased that George recognizes the need to develop his feeling side. She wants to see what he can do to develop his feeling function.]

CL: I think I need to stop and talk with them, see how things are going, maybe relax. I have some idea that my tension may be communicated to them.

CO: That sounds good, George. That could be happening. [George may be taking advantage of his intuitive process at this point. The counselor is pleased to hear that and yet can return to working on the feelings that are being discussed.]

CL: I know I need to slow down; I need to relax when I'm talking with someone in the lab and not pull away as quickly as I do. How can I do that?

CO: Being in a comfortable position, slowing your breathing, relaxing your hands. Anything to slow yourself down might help. [The counselor responds to this specific request for information, knowing that problem solving is something that is likely to appeal to George because of his emphasis on thinking.]

CL: It sounds simple.

CO: It's not so simple. Maybe we can work on some relaxation techniques later today. There are different ways of slowing down. [The counselor does not want to let relaxation be the only answer to dealing with the feeling function. She wants to return to ways that George can feel more and understand the feelings of others at his work site.]

In this example, the counselor tries to strengthen and develop George's weakest function, the judging function of feeling. For her, the Myers-Briggs Type Indicator provides a way of conceptualizing George's work adjustment problem. Being well versed in the Myers-Briggs theory, she can think about George in terms of the concepts themselves. She can then relate George's type to her knowledge of the concepts, integrating this relationship into her counseling conceptualization. The counselor recognizes that the problem is a difficult one. Developing one's inferior function is not easy. In her continuing work with George, she may look at ways in which he can change his work environment to alleviate the situation, believing (Myers & McCaulley, 1985) that it is easier for George to change his work environment to match his type than to change his type to match his work environment. Some examples of such changes would be getting others to assist him in supervision or changing his assignment to return to more research and less supervision. Certainly, George's choice of work, science, is a frequent choice of INTP individuals (Table 5-2). His difficulty with supervision is consistent with the description of thinking in Table 5-3. It is for the counselor and George to decide how much George can change and how much the environment can change.

The counseling dialogues used in this chapter give a small sample of the use of Myers-Briggs typological theory in counseling on career issues. Several books have been written that describe the 16 types in detail and include case studies that emphasize the conceptualization of the Myers-Briggs Indicator. Keirsey and Bates (1978) describe both temperaments and types in detail. Another book that gives many examples of understanding types in a variety of work and relationship situations is by Kroeger and Thuesen (1988). Specifically focusing on career counseling is *Do What You Are: Discover the Perfect Career for You through the Secrets of Personality Type* (Tieger & Barron-Tieger, 1992). An approach to group counseling focusing on type, including numerous discussion topics and exercises for counselors to use, has been designed by Hartzler (1990). A casebook approach, such as the one by Provost (1984), which has a case illustration for each of the 16 types, can be particularly helpful to counselors learning the Myers-Briggs typology. Possibly, the single best overview of the Myers-Briggs typological theory is *Gifts Differing* (1993) by Isabel Myers. These books use numerous examples and cases to explore and explain the intricacies of the Myers-Briggs system of types.

THE ROLE OF OCCUPATIONAL INFORMATION

From a career development point of view, Myers-Briggs type theory can be conceived of as a matching kind of trait and factor theory. Using the Myers-Briggs Type Indicator (or its conceptual system), the counselor can match the client's Myers-Briggs type with the Myers-Briggs types of occupations. By using information such as that in Table 5-3 and in *Introduction to Type and Careers* (Hammer, 1993), the counselor can gain an idea of the preferred work setting of different Myers-Briggs types. Knowledge of an individual's type can be matched with knowledge of which types select which work settings most frequently (Table 5-2 and Appendix D of *Manual: A Guide to the Development and Use of the Myers-Briggs Type Indicator* by Myers and McCaulley, 1985). In their manual, Myers and McCaulley give an example of a counselor giving occupational information to a client based on information known about various types. An excerpt from their example will help illustrate this*:

Q. I am an ISTJ and want to enter psychology. Where would I fit?

A. You are more likely to like the work of an experimental psychologist. In one study, more than twice the expected number of ISTJs chose experimental

*Modified and reproduced by special permission of the Publisher, Consulting Psychologists Press, Inc., Palo Alto, CA 94303 from *Manual: A Guide to the Development and Use of the Myers-Briggs Type Indicator* by Isabel Briggs Myers and Mary H. McCaulley.

(I ratio 2.4, $p < .01$). In fact, all the ISTJs in that study chose one of the experimental fields. Remember that most of your colleagues are likely to prefer intuition, but you will probably find more people who share your interest in the experimental fields.

Q. I know I want psychology, but I'm not sure which field to choose. What is the difference between clinical and experimental psychology?

A. Clinical psychology attracts more psychologists who are concerned with possibilities (N-intuition) for people (F-feeling) (NF 72%; ratio 1.6; $p < .01$). Experimental psychology attracts more people interested in theory (N) and logical analysis (T-thinking), but there is also a sizable number of more practical people in experimental psychology (S ratio 1.8, $p<.001$). You will find all types in each area, but these facts may help you think about how your interests relate to the psychological specialties. (pp. 83, 84).

This example shows how a counselor who is extremely knowledgeable about Myers-Briggs type theory can extrapolate knowledge from the *Atlas of Type Tables* (1987) and Appendix D of the *Manual* (1985) to give information to clients. There is no single source of occupational information that describes occupations solely in terms of Myers-Briggs types. Because many Myers-Briggs types can exist within a given occupation, counselors need to be careful not to give the impression that only certain Myers-Briggs types can work in specified occupations. People with different Myers-Briggs types who enjoy the same occupations are likely to approach their work in a way that allows them to express their type. In their manual, Myers and McCaulley are careful to describe the advantages of different points of view of various Myers-Briggs types within any given occupation.

THE ROLE OF TESTING

The Myers-Briggs Type Indicator and the Myers-Briggs typological theory are very closely wedded. Even counselors who are very familiar with the Myers-Briggs theory rarely use the theory with a client without administering the Myers-Briggs Type Indicator. More than for any other theory discussed in this book, the inventory is closely tied to the conceptualization process that a counselor uses with a client. The 309-page manual is extensive in its description of research that supports the use of the four Myers-Briggs dimensions. Furthermore, Thorne and Gough (1991) have summarized 30 years of research on types done at the Institute of Personality and Social Research at the University of California at Berkeley.

The manual describes the construction of the Myers-Briggs Type Indicator as well as the construction of the earlier forms of the MBTI. Tischler (1994) and Karesh, Pieper, and Holland (1994) found support for the bipolar scales of the MBTI. In a study of 348 successful chief executive officers, Rytting, Ware, and Prince (1994) found a bimodal distribution of scores supporting the polarity of the four scales of the MBTI. Using a

Norwegian translation of the MBTI, Nordvik (1994) found relationships between MBTI scores and occupational groupings supporting the validity of the MMPI. Further, Nordvik reported a greater similarity of types when work tasks were similar than when they were diverse. For example, the type scores of pilots and industrial workers were more similar to each other than were those of social service workers and health service workers. Some attempts have been made to develop short forms of the MBTI. Harvey, Murry, and Markham (1994) tested three different short forms and found that they provided less information than the long form and that there were unacceptably high disagreement rates between the short forms and the long form. Other studies have looked at the relationship between interest inventories and the Myers-Briggs Type Indicator (Dillon & Weissman, 1987) as well as personality inventories such as the NEO Personality Inventory (MacDonald, Anderson, Tsagarakis, & Holland, 1994). Thus, those who find the Myers-Briggs Type Indicator valuable have expended much effort to provide supportive evidence for it, as Carlson's (1985, 1989) thorough reviews show.

However, the Myers-Briggs Type Indicator is not above question, and several writers have challenged the findings presented previously. Pittenger (1993) provides evidence that the MBTI has limited counseling utility, reliability, and validity. Using a sample of men, Lorr (1991) was critical of the factor structure of the MBTI. Also, Healy (1989) argues against using the MBTI in counseling. He believes that there is limited evidence that classifying people into 16 types will enhance counseling, a view challenged by Murray (1990) and Tischler (1994). Further, Healy questions whether the Myers-Briggs Type Indicator measures the constructs defined by Jung. He also finds that there is no evidence that using the MBTI in counseling will help clients with their concerns. In general, the research on the MBTI tends to focus on the four dimensions and not on the complex concepts that are used in counseling, such as the dominant and auxiliary processes. Another criticism is that the manual provides combined norms for men and women, rather than separate norms. Despite these criticisms, researchers continue to develop and study the Myers-Briggs Type Indicator.

Several report forms and scoring systems are available for the MBTI. For the regular form of the MBTI, a special report is available called the *MBTI Career Report* (Hammer & MacDaid, 1994), which lists work behaviors and preferences that match the clients' type. Two instruments are available that provide more information, through more scales, for the four basic Myers-Briggs dimensions. The *MBTI Expanded Analysis* (Saunders, Myers, & Briggs, 1989a) offers 5 subscales for each of the four dimensions. Also, the *Type Differentiation Indicator* (Saunders, Myers, & Briggs, 1989b) includes the same 20 subscales for the four dimensions as the MBTI Expanded Analysis, as well as 7 other subscales. These instruments are relatively recent and have not been available long enough to generate validating research. However, they would appear to be useful to counselors as they help individuals explore MBTI concepts in depth and make a bridge to occupational choices that could be considered.

APPLYING THE THEORY TO WOMEN AND PEOPLE OF COLOR

In general, cultural and gender differences have not been a major focus of research in the study of the Myers-Briggs typology. The manual (Myers & McCaulley, 1985, p. 59) does report the percentage of males and females at four levels of preference (slight, moderate, clear, or very clear) for each of the eight types. The sample sizes ranged between 15,000 and 25,000 for two different forms of the Myers-Briggs Type Indicator. By way of summary, Myers (1962) estimated that about 65% of women in the United States prefer feeling to thinking, and about 60% of men in the United States prefer thinking to feeling. Another view into this difference is provided by Laribee (1994), who studied accounting students, who would be expected to have a preference for thinking over feeling. The male preference for thinking was 83% to 85%, and the female preference ranged from 44% to 63%. With regard to the sex distribution of type for the other scales, it appears that about half the men and half the women fall on either side of the other bipolar dimensions. Stokes (1987a, 1987b) has provided more information on gender differences on the MBTI.

Studies of Myers-Briggs type for people of color are infrequent. Levy and Ostrowski (1983) found that Hawaiians of Japanese descent tended to score more frequently than whites in the I (introvert) and J (judging) as well as the SJ (sensing and judging) categories. Sim and Kim (1993) found similar patterns in a sample of 774 Korean students and adults. In characterizing the values of Native Americans, Little Soldier (1989) stressed the importance of cooperation, sharing, and the extended family. In a study of 210 nonreservation Native American college freshmen, Simmons and Barrineau (1994) found that sensing for males and sensing and feeling for females were overrepresented among Native Americans compared to other freshmen, preferences that fit with the values described by Little Soldier. It is likely that in the future more studies such as these will be reported.

An interesting concept of the Myers-Briggs typology that may be particularly appropriate to understanding populations that may be oppressed, such as women and people of color, is *falsification* of type. Since the development of type is assumed to be inborn, environmental influences can distort or falsify it. Individuals who are taught to respond in a certain way may learn and outwardly behave as one type, while inwardly their true type is being frustrated. This interesting clinical concept presents a difficult research problem: How can one separate the real type from the falsified type? Those who counsel using Myers-Briggs typology may find that they are able to do this. Whether some women and some people of color have felt trained or expected by society to behave in a certain way that does not fit their true type remains to be proved.

COUNSELOR ISSUES

Some of the research on how counselors communicate with their clients suggests that counselors need to adjust their style of communication for different Myers-Briggs types. In exploratory research, Yeakley (1982, 1983) suggested that it may be helpful for two people to be using the same communication style at the same time, whether it is in a business, a marriage, or a counseling relationship. For Yeakley, listening to sensing types means listening at a pragmatic and literal level. On the other hand, listening to an intuitive type requires listening to the underlying meaning. What does the speaker really mean, and what are the implications? When listening to a thinking type of person, the counselor should focus on the organization of the individual's comments, as in reading an essay: What are the main points, the less important points, and the overall concept? In contrast, listening to a feeling type would mean being aware of feelings about the client and the values or feelings projected by the client in the message.

The implication is that counselors whose types are very different from those of their clients will have to expend considerable effort to alter their style of interaction to fit with that of their clients. For example, a counselor whose perceiving style is sensing and whose judging style is feeling may have to adjust to a client whose perceiving style is intuitive and whose judging style is thinking. Erickson (1993) found that, among 23 counselors, thinking types tended to choose to use behavioral, cognitive, rational-emotive, and reality therapies, whereas feeling types preferred Gestalt and person-centered approaches. Thus, counselors may perceive treatment methods for similar problems differently, depending on their type.

SUMMARY

Although not generally considered a theory of career development, the Myers-Briggs type theory has been used as such by many counselors. Its broad focus is on how people perceive and judge the world. There are two different ways of perceiving (sensing and intuition), as well as two different ways of judging (thinking and feeling). Individuals must use the perceiving and judging functions many times during the course of a day. In addition, they deal with their inner world of ideas (introversion) and with the outer world of people and objects (extraversion). In this chapter, the focus has been on relating these styles to career decision making and work adjustment. The complex interactions between the eight Myers-Briggs types, which represent four bipolar dimensions, have been illustrated in several counseling situations. Because the Myers-Briggs Type Indicator is an essential part of the Myers-Briggs theory of types, a discussion of research on the Myers-Briggs Type Indicator, as well as criticism of it, was presented. Readers will find that the presentation in this chapter is insufficient to enable them to use the Myers-Briggs Type Indicator in career counseling. Attendance at workshops that teach the use of the Myers-Briggs Type Indicator, as well as a thorough study of the manual (Myers & McCaulley, 1985), is strongly recommended.

References

Atlas of type tables. (1987). Gainesville, FL: Center for the Application of Psychological Type.

Carlson, J. G. (1985). Recent assessments of the Myers-Briggs Type Indicator. *Journal of Personality Assessment, 49,* 356–365.

Carlson, J. G. (1989). Affirmative: In support of researching the Myers-Briggs Type Indicator. *Journal of Counseling and Development, 67,* 484–486.

Dillon, M., & Weissman, S. (1987). Relationships between the Strong-Campbell and Myers-Briggs instruments. *Measurement and Evaluation in Counseling and Development, 20,* 68–80.

Erickson, D. B. (1993). The relationship between personality type and preferred counseling model. *Journal of Psychological Type, 27,* 39–41.

Hammer, A. L. (1993). *Introduction to type and careers.* Palo Alto, CA: Consulting Psychologists Press.

Hammer, A. L., & MacDaid, G. P. (1994). *MBTI Career Report.* Palo Alto, CA: Consulting Psychologists Press.

Hartzler, M. (1990). *Using type theory in counseling.* Gaithersburg, MD: Type Resources.

Harvey, R. J., Murry, W. D., & Markham, S. E. (1994). Evaluation of three short-form versions of the Myers-Briggs Type Indicator. *Journal of Personality Assessment, 63,* 181–184.

Healy, C. C. (1989). Negative: The MBTI: Not ready for routine use in counseling. *Journal of Counseling and Development, 67,* 487–488.

Jung, C. G. (1971). *Psychological types* (H. B. Baynes, Trans., rev. by R. F. C. Hull). *The collected works of C. G. Jung* (Vol. 6). Princeton, NJ: Princeton University Press. (Original work published 1921)

Karesh, D., Pieper, W. A., & Holland, C. L. (1994). Comparing the *MBTI,* the Jungian Type Survey, and the Singer-Loomis Inventory of Personality. *Journal of Psychological Type, 30,* 30–38.

Keirsey, D., & Bates, M. (1978). *Please understand me* (3rd ed.). Del Mar, CA: Prometheus Nemesis Books.

Kroeger, O., & Thuesen, J. M. (1988). *Type talk.* New York: Delacorte Press.

Laribee, S. F. (1994). The psychological types of college accounting students. *Journal of Psychological Type, 28,* 37–38.

Levy, N., & Ostrowski, B. (1983). A comparison of the distributions of Jungian personality types among Hawaiians of Japanese and Caucasian ancestry. *Research in Psychological Types, 6,* 54–57.

Little Soldier, L. (1989). Cooperative learning and the Native American student. *Phi Delta Kappa, 71,* 161–163.

Lorr, M. (1991). An empirical evaluation of the *MBTI* typology. *Personality and Individual Differences, 12,* 1141–1145.

MacDonald, D. A., Anderson, P. E., Tsagarakis, C. I., & Holland, C. J. (1994). Examination of the relationship between the Myers-Briggs Type Indicator and the NEO Personality Inventory. *Psychological Reports, 74,* 339–344.

Murray, J. B. (1990). Review of research on the Myers-Briggs Type Indicator. *Perceptual and Motor Skills, 70,* 1187–1202.

Myers, I. B. (1962). *Manual: The Myers-Briggs Type Indicator.* Princeton, NJ: Educational Testing Service.

Myers, I. B. (1987). *Introduction to type* (3rd ed.). Palo Alto, CA: Consulting Psychologists Press.

Myers, I. B. (1993). *Gifts differing.* Palo Alto, CA: Consulting Psychologists Press.

Myers, I. B., & McCaulley, M. H. (1985). *Manual: A guide to the development and use of the Myers-Briggs Type Indicator.* Palo Alto, CA: Consulting Psychologists Press.

Nordvik, H. (1994). Type, vocation, and self-report personality variables: A validity study of a Norwegian Translation of the MBTI, Form G. *Journal of Psychological Type, 29,* 32–37.

Pittenger, D. J. (1993). The utility of the Myers-Briggs Type Indicator. *Review of Educational Research, 63,* 467–488.

Provost, J. A. (1984). *Casebook: Applications of the Myers-Briggs Type Indicator in counseling.* Gainesville, FL: Center for the Application of the Psychological Type.

Rytting, M., Ware, R., & Prince, R. A. (1994). Bimodal distributions in a sample of CEOs: Validating evidence for the *MBTI. Journal of Psychological Type, 31,* 16–23.

Saunders, D., Myers, I. B., & Briggs, K. C. (1989a). *MBTI expanded analysis.* Palo Alto, CA: Consulting Psychologists Press.

Saunders, D., Myers, I. B., & Briggs, K. C. (1989b). *Type differentiation indicator.* Palo Alto, CA: Consulting Psychologists Press.

Schemel, G. J., & Borbely, J. A. (1982). *Facing your type.* Wernersville, PA: Typrofile Press.

Sim, H. S., & Kim, J. T. (1993). The development and validation of the Korean version of the *MBTI. Journal of Psychological Type, 26,* 18–27.

Simmons, G., & Barrineau, P. (1994). Learning style and the Native American. *Journal of Psychological Type, 28,* 3–10.

Stokes, J. (1987a). Exploring the relationship of type and gender. Part I: Anecdotal experiences of MBTI users. *Journal of Psychological Type, 13,* 34–43.

Stokes, J. (1987b). Exploring the relationship of type and gender. Part 2: A review and critique of empirical research and other data. *Journal of Psychological Type, 13,* 44–51.

Thorne, A., & Gough, H. (1991). *Portraits of type: An MBTI research compendium.* Palo Alto, CA: Consulting Psychologists Press.

Tieger, P. D., & Barron-Tieger, B. (1992). *Do what you are: Discover the perfect career for you through the secrets of personality type.* Boston: Little, Brown.

Tischler, L. (1994). The MBTI factor structure. *Journal of Psychological Type, 31,* 24–31.

Yeakley, F. R. (1982). Communication style preferences and adjustments as an approach to studying effects of similarity in psychological type. *Research in Psychological Type, 5,* 30–48.

Yeakley, F. R. (1983). Implications of communication style research for psychological type theory. *Research in Psychological Type, 6,* 5–23.

PART TWO

Life-Span Theory

Life-span theory, as it applies to career development, concerns the growing and changing ways that an individual deals with career issues over the entire life span. This approach is in marked contrast to that of the theories in Part One, which dealt with career issues at one point in time. Because life-span theory covers a long period of time, it tends to be more complex, in terms of the number of constructs that are used, than typological or trait and factor theories. Therefore, four chapters are needed to cover the entire life span. Chapter 7 discusses the development of career decision making in childhood. Included is the development of curiosity and exploration, which leads to obtaining information from role models and observed events. This approach leads to the development of interests and a self-concept, resulting in the ability to plan and problem-solve. Chapter 8 covers the development of interests, capacities, and values in adolescence. Related is the development of career maturity, which includes knowledge about decision making and occupational information. Chapter 9 is a discussion of career issues in late adolescence and adulthood. It focuses on life roles as well as developmental stages. In Chapter 10, the emphasis is on the career transitions and crises that often occur in adulthood. Each chapter treats special problems related to women and people of color that occur during each aspect of the life span. Theoretical concepts are used to provide a conceptual framework for dealing with counseling issues that occur in childhood, adolescence, and adulthood.

The theoretical approach used in Part Two is based on the work of Donald Super and his colleagues, although other theories are used to augment their life-span concepts. The theory, which is introduced in Chapter 6, will be referred to as *Super's theory,* even though it represents the work of many researchers throughout the world who have collaborated with

Super in developing his theory. There are several reasons for selecting Super's theory as the basis for the chapters on life-span theory. First, Super's developmental theory is one of the few to cover the entire life span. Second, more than any other life-span theorist, Super has developed inventories to validate the constructs of his theory and thus has provided instruments to be used in counseling. Third, much more research has been done in conjunction with the concepts of Super's developmental theory than with others. Fourth, unlike trait and factor and other career development theories, life-span theories are rather similar to each other. Discussing each life-span theory separately in terms of its implication for counseling would tend to produce similar suggestions for each theory. Therefore, other developmental theories are integrated into Part Two to supplement Super's life-span theory.

Several theorists have contributed to an understanding of career issues at various points during the life span. Gottfredson's developmental theory of occupational aspirations has much to say about the development of sex-role stereotyping in childhood. Her theory, discussed in Chapter 7, provides an understanding of the development of women's career choices. A theory that had a significant and early impact on career development theory is that of Ginzberg, Ginsburg, Axelrad, and Herma. Their focus is the stages of development that young people go through in choosing an occupation. These stages are quite similar to those formulated by Super and are presented in Chapter 8, along with a discussion of the differences between the two theories. The work of Vondracek and his colleagues is referred to in discussing adolescent development in Chapter 8. This recent approach is likely to have a great impact on life-span theory. However, relatively little research has been done, and instrumentation does not yet exist. In terms of implications for conceptualizing counseling issues, its impact is rather limited. The model of minority identity development proposed by Atkinson, Morton, and Sue, although not a career development theory, helps in conceptualizing life-span issues that affect the career development of minorities and/or people of color. Discussed in Chapter 9, the theory focuses on the development of adults but is applicable to adolescents as well. Another theory that is not a career development theory is used as the basis for a discussion of adult career crises and transitions in Chapter 10. Hopson and Adams's theory for understanding adult transitions is integrated into the developmental stages of Super's theory. By combining these theories with work done by Super and his colleagues, we can arrive at a conceptual framework for counseling clients of all ages.

6

Introduction to Super's Life-Span Theory

An overview of Super's theory will be given in this brief chapter. The details of Super's theory are provided in the next three chapters. Underlying Super's theory of career development are assumptions about individuals and the world they live in. Super (1990) considers individual roles that include study, community service, leisure, work, and family to be important when studying career development across the life span. Developmental tasks and stages are an important aspect of Super's (1990) theory. Life roles within developmental tasks may vary for individuals at different points during their life. The assumptions of Super's theory, roles, and developmental stages are discussed further in the following pages.

BASIC ASSUMPTIONS OF SUPER'S THEORY

Super (1990, p. 205) described his theory as a segmental theory, one that includes the work of many other theories: Thorndike, Hull, Bandura, Freud, Jung, Adler, Rank, Murray, Maslow, Allport, Rogers, and others. From the work of these theorists, he derived basic assumptions that allowed him to develop his own theory. Perhaps most basic is the assumption that physiological aspects, such as genetic predisposition, along with geographic aspects (country of origin) have an impact on other aspects of career development. These aspects include the development of psychological characteristics and the social-economic structure of the environment, which are all incorporated into the self-concept. Psychological characteristics include the development of needs, values, interests, intelligence, ability, and special aptitudes. These lead to the development of the personality of an individual and to his or her accomplishments. The social-economic factors include one's community, school, family, and peer groups, along with the state of the economy and the labor market. These influence the job structure and employment practices—the conditions outside the individual with which he or she must interact. Psychological and social-economic factors combine in the development of the self. As individuals learn about themselves and their environment, they go through developmental stages in which they evolve a concept of themselves. This model is discussed more fully in Super (1990) and is illustrated by the diagram of an archway. It is presented here (Figure 6-1) because it is the basis of the research and writing by Super and his colleagues on life roles and developmental stages. A brief critique of Super's contribution to vocational development is provided by Salomone (1995).

SELF-CONCEPT

Self-concept has been at the core of Super's developmental theory. Super (1953) described vocational development as the process of developing and implementing a self-concept. He saw self-concept as a combination of biological characteristics, the social roles individuals play, and evaluations of the reactions other individuals have to the person. *Self-concept* refers to how individuals view themselves and their situation. Figure 6-1 shows Super's arch, which illustrates his segmental theory, which is the subject of the next three chapters. Note that the self is at the top of the arch. How individuals perceive themselves and interact is a reflection of personality, needs, values, and interests (the left-hand column). These perceptions change over the life span. Discussed in *Career Development: Self-Concept Theory* (Super, Starishevsky, Matlin, & Jordaan, 1963), the developing nature of the self-concept is of particular importance. Super et al. described processes such as self-differentiation, role playing, exploration, and reality testing, which led to the development of the self-concept. Interaction with society (the right-hand column) brings about the development of the self-concept as the individual interacts with family, school, peers, and co-workers. The self-concept refers to individuals' views of themselves and society and is subjective. This is in contrast to trait and factor theory, which emphasizes objective or outside measures of the self, for example, interest inventories and aptitude tests. Super's emphasis on the self-concept can be seen in his development of inventories that focus on evaluating roles and values that are important in the different stages of life.

As Betz (1994) and Bejian and Salomone (1995) show, defining *self-concept* is a very difficult task. Super (1990) wrote of constellations or systems of self-concepts. In developing his theory, Super was influenced by Kelly's (1955) personal construct theory, which examined bipolar constructs, such as smart-stupid and kind-mean that could be differentially important to various individuals. Self-efficacy theory (Betz, 1994), described in Chapter 13, has had a long and active history (Bandura, 1977) as a means of defining the self-concept. Basically, *self-efficacy* refers to the "expectations or beliefs concerning one's ability to perform successfully a given behavior" (Betz, 1994, p. 35). A somewhat similar term, but less precise, is self-esteem, which refers to how good one feels about oneself, or to

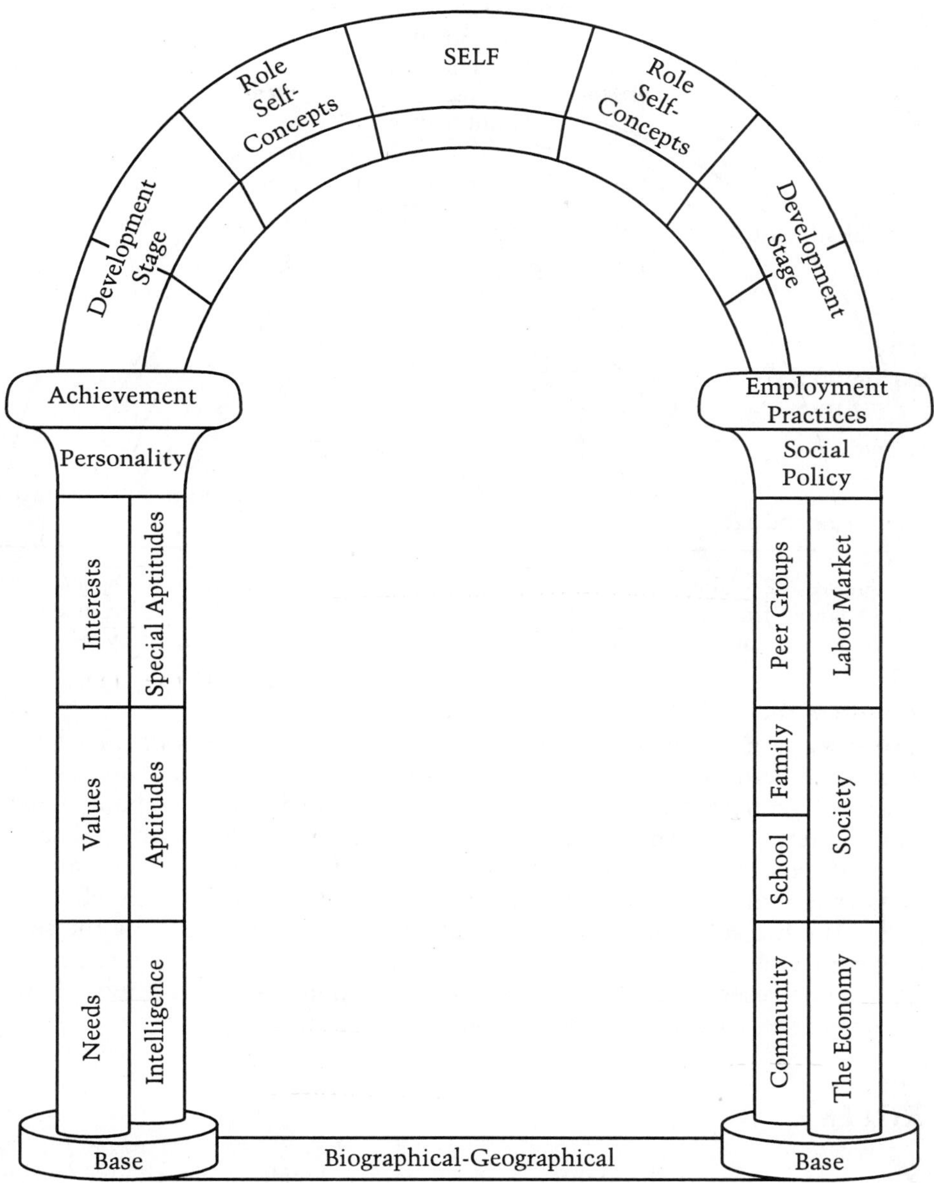

Figure 6-1 The archway of career determinants. (From "A Life-Span, Life-Space Approach to Career Development" by Donald E. Super (1990). In D. Brown, L. Brooks, and Associates, *Career Choice and Development: Applying Contemporary Theories to Practice,* 2nd ed., p. 200. Copyright 1990 by Jossey-Bass. Reprinted by permission.)

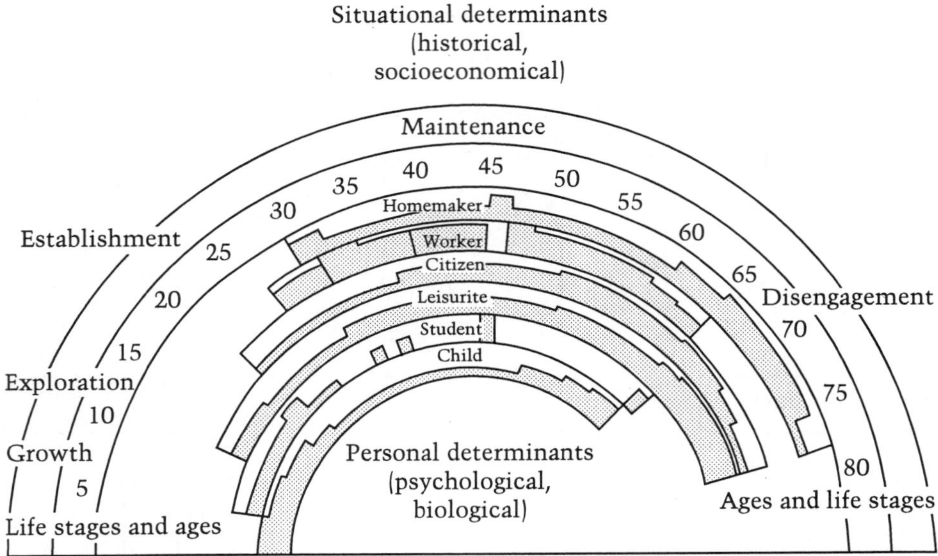

Figure 6-2 The life-career rainbow: Six life roles in schematic life space. (Adapted from *Career Choice and Development,* by D. Brown, L. Brooks, and Associates. Copyright © 1984 by Jossey-Bass, Inc. Reprinted by permission.

how certain or confident one is about aspects of one's life, such as school, work, and being liked. In Chapter 7, Gottfredson's theory examines children's self-concepts as they encounter societal expectations about men's and women's roles, the values of being in a specific occupation, and their societal expectations. For Super, self-concept served to organize varying roles that individuals played and their view of the roles as they changed across the life span. Increasingly, Super became interested in how the self-concept developed differently for women and people of color. An examination of his research shows a cross-cultural emphasis in his study of the roles that individuals value as they grow.

ROLES

A constant concept throughout Super's career development theory is the concept of role. Super describes six major roles: homemaker, worker, citizen, leisurite, student, and child. His Salience Inventory (Nevill & Super, 1986) measures the importance of all the roles, except that of child. In childhood, the roles of leisurite, student, and child are particularly important. The roles of worker, citizen, and homemaker (in the sense of responsibility for these roles) are minimal. In adolescence, citizen and worker may become more important roles, but they are generally limited. In adolescence, work is not often directly related to one's eventual career. It is in adulthood that one has more choice in life roles. Therefore, a full discussion of these roles is given in Chapter 9, "Late Adolescent and Adult Career Development."

Super's rainbow (Figure 6-2) shows how the roles may vary within the lifetime of one person. In this figure, each arc represents a role in life. The thicker the shaded area in each arc, the more important the role. As Super and Nevill (1986) explain, "The person portrayed in this rainbow finished college at the age of 22, went at once to work, married at age 26, became a parent at age 27, intermittently attended school part-time until returning full-time at age 47, suffered the loss of parents at age 57, retired at 67, was widowed at 78, and died at age 81 (p. 3)." The rainbow has been used in several different ways to illustrate the value of life role concepts (Bowlsbey, 1984; Super & Bowlsbey, 1979). In conjunction with developmental stages, the concept of life roles may be useful in many career-counseling situations.

Developmental Stages

The notion of stages and substages is essential to Super's life-span theory. Figure 6-3 depicts the stages and substages associated with various ages. Chapter 7, "Career Development in Childhood," describes those tasks that take place during the growth stage. Chapter 8, "Adolescent Career Development," focuses on the development of interests, capacities, and values that takes place during the exploration stage. How and when interests and capacities emerge in career decision making is an aspect of career maturity that is a central part of Super's theory. Further exploration that may occur during late adolescence or early adulthood is described in Chapter 9, "Late Adolescent and Adult Career Development." The exploration stage includes crystallizing: making an occupational choice, becoming more specific in the choice, and implementing it by finding and choosing a job. The other stages encompassed in Chapter 9 are establishing oneself in one's career, maintaining one's position, and disengaging from the world of work. A concept essential to the understanding of Super's theory is recycling. One may recycle through various stages at any time. For example, if someone at midlife desires to change his or her job, the individual is likely to reenter the exploration stage. Implied in the developmental stages is the interaction of the individual with the world of work.

THE ROLE OF OCCUPATIONAL INFORMATION AND TESTING

The use of occupational information and testing is an integral part of Super's theory. Emphasized particularly in Chapter 8, "Adolescent Career Development," and Chapter 9, "Late Adolescent and Adult Career

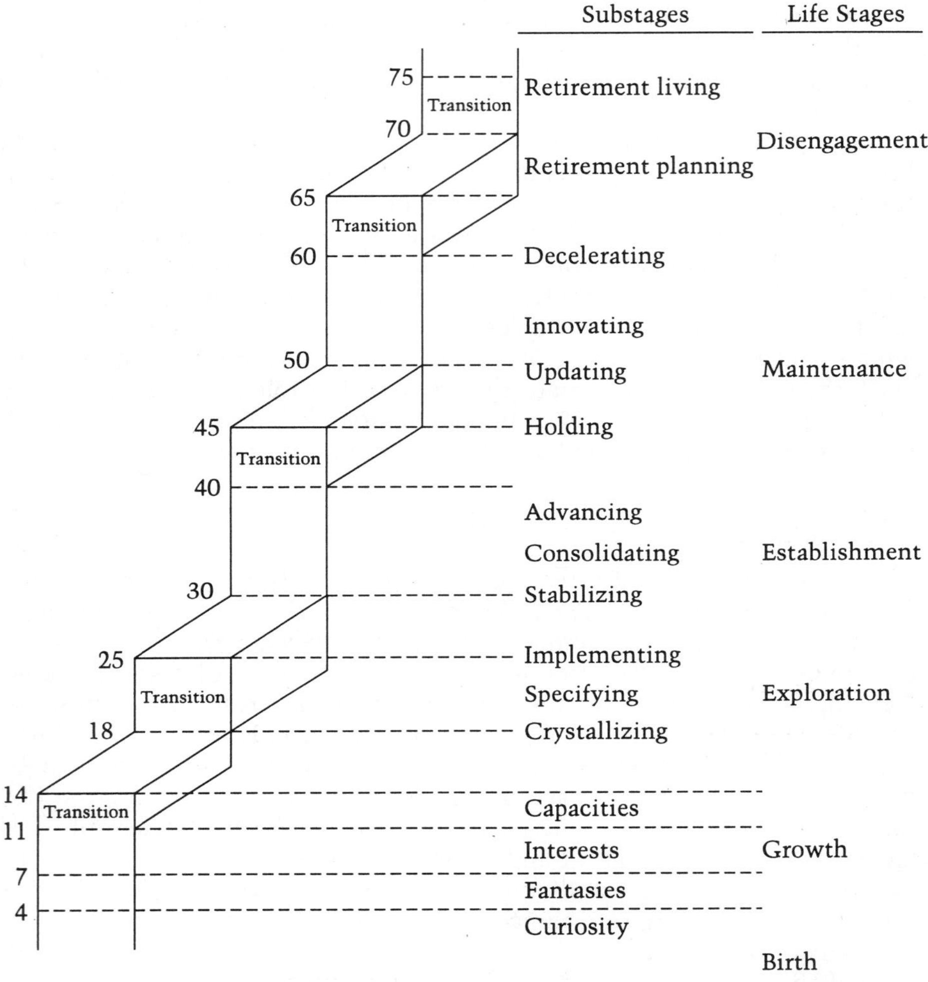

Figure 6-3 Life stages and substages based on the typical development tasks. (From *Career Choice and Development,* by D. Brown, L. Brooks, and Associates. Copyright © 1984 by Jossey-Bass, Inc. Reprinted by permission.)

Development," occupational information and testing are a focus of counseling. Further, the acquisition of occupational information plays a predominant role in career maturity, an important concept in adolescence. Super has developed more inventories to test his theories than any other career development theorist. By doing so, he has not only supported constructs of his own theory but has also provided useful instruments for counselors to use in their work.

APPLYING THE THEORY TO WOMEN AND PEOPLE OF COLOR

While Super (1957) was concerned about the career development of women, other theorists have focused more specifically on gender issues in career development. Gottfredson (1981; 1996) has dealt with the effect of sex-role stereotyping on career choice, which can occur early in the elementary school years. Her work, along with that of other researchers, is described more specifically in Chapter 7, "Career Development in Childhood." Many researchers have documented the impact of sex-role stereotyping on the career choices of adolescent men and women. Chapter 8, "Adolescent Career Development," describes how sex-role stereotyping affects the career choices of adolescents. Adult women (Chapter 10), because of choices about marriage and children, often have more varied career concerns than men. Because they are more likely to reenter and leave the work force at different points in their lives, these factors are taken into consideration in a discussion of the applicability of Super's career development theory to women. During the course of their working lives, women may experience career crises not experienced as often by men: discrimination, disruption due to child raising, and sexual harassment. Methods for conceptualizing these issues are discussed in Chapter 10, "Adult Career Crises and Transitions."

Super (1957, 1990) was also concerned about the career issues facing people of color. Because people of color make up a wide range of cultural groups, each with different experiences, it is difficult to present unified explanatory information for childhood, adolescent, and adult career development. However, information about career concerns of people of color is discussed as it relates to Super's life-span theory. In Chapter 10, Atkinson, Morten, and Sue's (1989) model of minority identity development is presented to augment Super's life-span model. In discussing career crises that people of color may encounter in their adult lives, Hopson and Adams's (1977) theory of adult transitions is applied to the discrimination issues that people of color may experience in their careers.

SUMMARY

This introduction to developmental career concerns at varying times in the life span describes issues that will be explained in the next four chapters. Super's life-span theory will be used to show how life roles and developmental stages can assist the counselor to understand career development for individuals at all ages. Each of the following four chapters incorporates developmental stage issues for women and people of color. Examples of approaches to counseling individuals at different life stages and crises will be given.

References

Atkinson, D. R., Morten, G., & Sue, D. W. (1989). *Counseling American minorities: A cross-cultural perspective* (3rd ed.). Dubuque, IA: William C. Brown.

Bandura, A. (1977). Self-efficacy: Toward a unifying theory of behavioral change. *Psychology Review, 84,* 191–215.

Bejian, D. V., & Salomone, P. R. (1995). Understanding midlife career renewal: Implications for counseling. *The Career Development Quarterly, 44,* 52–63.

Betz, N. E. (1994). Self concept theory in career development and counseling. *The Career Development Quarterly, 43,* 32–42.

Bowlsbey, J. H. (1984). The computer as a tool in career guidance programs. In N. C. Gysbers & Assoc. (Eds.), *Designing careers* (pp. 362–383). San Francisco: Jossey-Bass.

Gottfredson, L. S. (1981). Circumscription and compromise: A developmental theory of occupational aspirations. *Journal of Counseling Psychology, 28,* 545–579.

Gottfredson, L. S. (1996). A theory of circumscription and compromise. In D. Brown & L. Brooks (Eds.), *Career choice and development: Applying contemporary theories to practice* (3rd ed., pp. 179–232). San Francisco: Jossey-Bass.

Hopson, B., & Adams, J. (1977). Towards an understanding of transition. In J. Adams & B. Hopson (Eds.), *Transitions: Understanding and managing personal change* (pp. 1–19). Montclair, NJ: Allenheld & Osmund.

Kelly, G. A. (1955). *A theory of personality: The psychology of personal constructs.* New York: Norton.

Nevill, D. D., & Super, D. E. (1986). *Manual for the Salience Inventory: Theory, application, and research.* Palo Alto, CA: Consulting Psychologists Press.

Salomone, P. (1995). Tracing Super's theory of vocational development: A 40 year retrospective. *Journal of Career Development, 22,* 167–173.

Super, D. E. (1953). A theory of vocational development. *American Psychologist, 8,* 185–190.

Super, D. E. (1957). *The psychology of careers.* New York: Harper & Row.

Super, D. E. (1990). A life-span, life-space approach to career development. In D. Brown, L. Brooks, & Assoc. (Eds.), *Career choice and development: Applying contemporary theories to practice* (2nd ed, pp. 197–261). San Francisco: Jossey-Bass.

Super, D. E., & Bowlsbey, J. H. (1979). *Guided career exploration.* New York: Psychological Corporation.

Super, D. E., & Nevill, D. D. (1986). *The Salience Inventory.* Palo Alto, CA: Consulting Psychologists Press.

Super, D. E., Starishevsky, R., Matlin, N., & Jordaan, J. P. (1963). *Career development: Self-concept theory.* New York: College Entrance Examination Board.

7

Career Development in Childhood

This chapter covers career-related issues that affect the child until the age of 12. The primary emphases of the chapter are the maturational activities in elementary school and Super's (1990) model of the bases of career maturity. This chapter also covers the development of sex role, the career development of children of color, and presentation of occupational information to children. Super's model of childhood career development deals only in general ways with gender issues. Gottfredson's (1981, 1996) theory is concerned with the development of sex-role stereotyping during childhood, making hypotheses about the relationship of sex-role stereotyping to career choice. Research on children of color is more limited than is research on gender issues and children, but there is information to assist the counselor in conceptualizing career issues for children of color.

When counselors work with vocational issues with young children, it is usually as a secondary issue in counseling or in organizing an occupational information program. In either event, occupational information is an essential aspect of career interventions. Counselors have an opportunity to influence the later career development of children in significant ways. However, the impact of counselors' interventions may not be recognizable until many years later. Implications of Super's career development theory for the communication of vocational information to children are discussed with suggestions. Super's theory also has implications for ways in which counselors can look developmentally at themselves in relationship to their clients. By using a developmental approach to occupations, testing, and counselor issues, counselors can establish a consistent framework within which to view their young clients.

SUPER'S MODEL OF THE CAREER DEVELOPMENT OF CHILDREN

In general, this chapter describes Super's (1990, 1994) model of childhood career development as illustrated in Figure 7-1. A very basic drive in children is curiosity. Curiosity is often satisfied through exploration, an

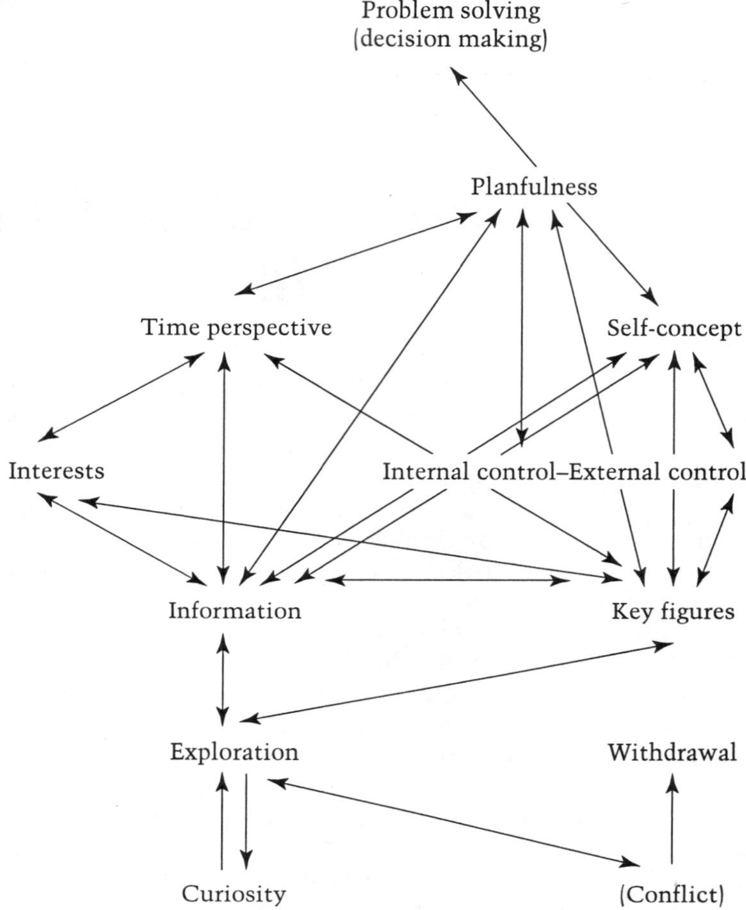

Figure 7-1 A person-environment interactive model of the bases of career maturity. (From *Career Development in Britain,* by A. G. Watts, D. E. Super, and J. M. Kidd, Eds. Copyright © 1981 by Hobson's Press. Reprinted by permission.)

important career development activity that may never cease. This exploratory activity leads to the acquisition of information. Several views of how children process information are given. One important source of information is the key figure—a person whom a child may choose to imitate. Using information derived from exploratory activities and impressions of role models, interests are developed. During the maturational process, children develop ways to control their own behavior by listening to themselves and others. To make career decisions, children need to develop a time perspective, a sense of the future. This along with the development of a self-concept will eventually lead to planful career decision making. The development of a self-concept is an exceedingly important part of Super's life-span theory. The self-concept derives from the child's exploratory behavior, which leads to acquiring occupational information, imitating key figures, and developing interests. Each of these concepts is illustrated through counseling examples.

Curiosity

Curiosity is among the most basic of all needs or drives, being observed in animals as well as infants. Using Berlyne's (1960) work as a starting point for his discussion of exploratory behavior, Jordaan (1963) provides a useful approach to the understanding of exploration and curiosity in children. According to Jordaan (1963), curiosity may develop when there are changes in an individual's physical or social needs. For a child, curiosity may be prompted by hunger, thirst, loneliness, and a variety of other stimuli. When a child is uncertain or confused, the child may decide to resolve his or her perplexity. Also, boredom, a wish for excitement, or a desire for stimulation may produce curiosity. In relating curiosity to vocational development, Jordaan emphasizes more complex stimuli than did Berlyne (1960) in his study of animal and infant behavior. Curiosity may be observed in very young children with new objects, new people, and new concepts. Being exposed to puzzling new stimuli, the child must try to understand them or try out new behaviors. For example, a child seeing a toy horse in a playpen may try to ride it, fantasizing that he is riding a real horse. Another child may pick up a stick, pretending that it is a baseball bat and that she is a professional baseball player. Through curiosity, fantasized thinking may develop. Fantasy is the first stage of Ginzberg, Ginsburg, Axelrad, and Herma's (1951) theory of career development. Both Jordaan and Ginzberg et al. agree that curiosity and fantasy in the young child are important and should be encouraged, particularly in the early years of elementary school.

Although it is appropriate for elementary school guidance counselors to encourage curiosity as an acceptable goal of career development for young children, doing so is often not simple. Guidance counselors often see children because they are not doing what they are told to do by their teacher. A child who draws when he or she is expected to be reading or talks to another child when the teacher is talking may be expressing curiosity. In other words, being curious may often be disruptive. Reinforcing curiosity while discouraging disruptive behavior can be difficult. Encouraging the child to find ways to express curiosity in a positive sense may be one alternative to punishment as a means of dealing with disruptive behavior. Curiosity may lead to vocational exploration in later years; it is not important that curiosity have a career component at an early age.

Exploration

Being curious can lead to children's exploring their environment, home, school, and peer and parental relationships. Curiosity refers to the desire for knowledge or for something new or unusual, whereas exploration is the act of searching or examining. Curiosity is a need; exploration, a behavior. For children, play and playful activities are an expression of exploratory behavior and help to meet curiosity needs. Jordaan (1963) lists ten dimensions of exploratory behavior. These are combined here to give examples of important activities that make up exploration. The behavior may be intentional and systematic, or it may be accidental. For example, children may want to find out how a clock works by carefully disassembling the pieces and putting them back together (intentional), or they may find a broken clock and just start to play with it (accidental). Exploratory behavior can occur because others ask a child to do it or because a child seeks it out. Sometimes, a teacher requests that a child put a puzzle together, or the child may take the initiative to do it. In exploring, a child can use either current or past experience. Having played with a puzzle three weeks ago, a child may decide to play with a similar one now. Some exploratory behavior may benefit a child and help the child learn. Other behavior may just be for the enjoyment of the activity, such as writing one's name backward. Some exploratory behavior that is required can later turn out to be enjoyable. For example, being required to read does not mean that reading will always be a chore. Once the skill is partially mastered, children are likely to read on their own initiative. All these play behaviors are vocationally relevant only in an indirect sense. However, as the behaviors become more complex, they are likely to be more related to tasks required by various jobs.

When exploration is thwarted, the child may experience conflict and have less to do with peers, adults, and school subjects. (Note the arrow leading away from exploratory and planful behavior at the bottom of Figure 7-1.) When exploration is stifled, a child is likely to lose the motivation to study. His or her work may become less imaginative. The child is less likely to respond to teachers' questions or to initiate activities in the classroom, obtaining information only because of external factors. A truly withdrawn child will have difficulty developing vocational maturity, because interests and information about career-related activities will be missing. Naturally, most children are not at one end or the other of the exploration-withdrawal continuum. Rather, they choose to explore some activities and not others.

Exploratory behavior builds on other exploratory behavior. To encourage exploratory behavior of any type (that is not damaging to oneself or others) can have eventual positive consequences in terms of career development. Trusting the exploration process without forcing it can be a useful goal for counselors and teachers. For example, a third-grader may learn, in very general terms, how a phone works. Such learning will develop in sophistication, both at a teacher's request and also perhaps on the child's own initiative in later years. As a fifth-grader, the child may draw on past experience with the phone, as he or she learns more about the details of its operation. When counselors are talking to children about problems at school or at home, exploratory activity may play a minor role. However, there are times when reinforcement of this activity is helpful. For example, a young girl who is complaining about her unmarried mother's new boyfriend may feel some satisfaction and control in her life when she can talk about the new things she has learned while reading stories at home. Exploratory behavior is not a panacea for family or school problems. Rather, it is an activity that is likely to produce more exploratory behavior, leading eventually to an increased likelihood of successful vocational planning. In the process of exploratory activity, the child obtains much information about the environment. How this information is learned and processed is the subject of the next section.

Information

Clearly, the learning of information is essential to a child's development and success as an adolescent and an adult. The focus in this section is on how theories of learning can be applied to occupational information for elementary school children. A point that is repeatedly stressed in the work of Jean Piaget is that children are not merely uninformed adults; rather, there are differences in how children process information throughout their development. Only a brief synopsis of the work of Piaget, Vygotsky, and Erikson will be given here so that different theoretical approaches to the acquisition of knowledge by elementary school children can be compared.

Piaget (1977) describes four major periods of cognitive development: sensorimotor, preoperational, concrete operational, and formal operational. The sensorimotor stage occurs from birth to age 2, when infants attend to objects and events around them and then respond to these objects or events. *Attending* refers to the sensory acts of touching, seeing, smelling, and so on. *Responding* refers to such motor acts as biting, hitting, and screaming.

The preoperational thought period occurs from approximately ages 2 to 7. In this period, the child can learn to add and subtract and perform similar operations. Children before the age of 7 are characterized as being egocentric. If a teacher announces that one child in a classroom will be selected to do a highly regarded task, each child is apt to think that he or she will be chosen. Further, it is difficult for young children to tell fantasy from reality. When war scenes are shown on the evening news, it may be hard for young children to have an idea of how far this occurrence is from their house. Another example of the egocentricity of the young child is the "internalization of action" that occurs when young children describe what they are doing out loud, apparently talking to no one.

The third stage, and the one of most interest here, is concrete operations. In this stage, occurring between about the ages of 7 and 11, children think in concrete terms. They do not have to see an object to imagine manipulating it, but they must be aware that it exists. They can imagine adding three elephants to five elephants, but they cannot add 3*y* to 5*y*. This ability to think abstractly takes place in the final period, called *formal operations,* beginning about the age of 12. It is easier for children between the ages of 7 and 11 to learn what a dentist does—how he or she uses equipment, examines teeth, and so forth—than it is for them to sense how long eight years of post–high school training really is or what a $75,000 income means. It is hard, for example, for an 8-year-old to grasp what it means to "help others feel better about themselves," as a social worker does. This idea is more likely to be understood by adolescents.

Although somewhat critical of Piaget's approach, Vygotsky (1986), a Russian psychologist, has described a system similar to that of Piaget. He describes three stages, each characterized by a "leading activity" that is the main feature in the child's psychological development and the foundation for the next major feature. Further, in a "leading activity," particular mental functions emerge for the first time. For ages 1 through 3, the leading activity is object manipulation. During the preschool years, up to the age of 7, the leading activity is playing games. And for ages 7 through 11, it is learning. At the age of 7, children are ready to learn about the world of things and objective laws of reality. This system, although it differs from Piaget's, also emphasizes the importance of learning activities in the acquisition of occupational information for elementary-school-aged children.

A very different view, but one with somewhat similar conclusions, is that of Erik Erikson (1963). In his eight stages of psychosocial development, he lists as the fourth stage that of industry versus inferiority. This occurs between the ages of 6 and 11. Children at this age have the freedom to make things and to organize them. This can give them a sense of industriousness if they are successful and inferiority if they are unsuccessful. In this stage, children develop a sense of achievement by organizing, developing, and applying information, or they have a sense of failure if they do not master these skills. From an occupational information perspective, if elementary school students have an opportunity to make signs or drawings for an occupation, or to use tools, such as an electrician's pliers, they may be able to experience a sense of success. The concrete completion of an activity will be appreciated. The emphasis on the concrete is not unlike that of Piaget's third stage of learning. As will be shown in the next section, having role models to imitate and observe is consistent with the emphasis on concrete thinking and industriousness.

Key Figures

Adults are important role models for children in learning about the world of work and the development of their own self-concept. Key figures for children are parents, teachers, public figures such as athletes and television personalities, and people with whom they come in contact in their own community, such as police officers or mail carriers. Thelen, Frautsh, Roberts, Kirkland, and Dollinger (1981) have found that children are likely to copy the behavior of others. Parents' impact on children's view of occupations is illustrated by Trice and Tillapaugh's (1991) finding that children's aspirations to their parents' occupations are influenced by their perception of how satisfied their parents are with their own work. This is consistent with Bandura's (1977) finding that a significant method of learning for children is imitation. Rich's (1979) study shows that children know best those occupations that are in their own communities. Support for this conclusion was found by Trice, Hughes, Odom, Woods, and McClennan (1995), who reported that, among boys, 42% of kindergartners, 40% of second-graders, 47% of fourth-graders, and 36% of sixth-graders knew someone holding a job similar to their career choice. Because of population density, rural children may be exposed to fewer occupations than urban children. People who work in occupations that children can observe have the potential of becoming key figures. As children imitate the behavior of important others, they may choose to adopt or discard those aspects of the individual that seem to fit themselves. This process is one aspect of the development of the child's self-concept.

Super's emphasis on key figures in the development of children's self-concept can be a useful reminder to the counselor to listen carefully to what a child learns from his or her observation of role models. For example, a child whose father is a long-distance truck driver may be impressed by the father's mastery of such a huge vehicle, entranced by the father's visiting distant places, or impressed by the father's ability to lift heavy objects. Depending on the parent-child interaction, any one of these impressions may have an impact on the child. If the person modeling truck driving is not the father, but an uncle or neighbor, the impact of the role model is likely to be different. Sometimes children's observation of role models are inaccurate. If there is an occasion to correct the misinformation, counselors can take advantage of that opportunity by describing the behavior of other key figures or different behaviors of the misperceived key figure. Key figures are likely to make a greater impact on children as they are more able to observe others, thus developing a greater amount of control over their own behavior.

Internal versus External Control

Gradually, children begin to experience a feeling of control over their own surroundings. In a study of 28,000 nine-year-olds, Miller (1977) found that most of the children did not see themselves as responsible for their own behavior. Children are often used to doing what they are told to do by their teachers and parents. Rules are to be followed. Even in games that elementary school children devise, the following of rules is often quite important.

As children are successful in completing tasks and projects, they develop a feeling of autonomy and of being in control of future events. For counselors, children's "out-of-control" behavior is a frequent source of concern. The notion that self-control can have a direct impact on one's concept of oneself and also on one's ability to make career decisions (as shown in Figure 7-1) is an interesting one. Often, the counselor who is dealing with a child who has hit another child in the classroom or talked back to a teacher is concerned with controlling the situation. Helping to develop a balance between self-control and external control may be a counseling goal. Relating this goal to career maturity may never be in the counselor's thoughts. The notion that self-control has an eventual impact on career planning, however, is an important one, whether or not it is a conscious element of the counselor's thinking when working with a child. Being able to control their behavior can help children become more aware of their likes and dislikes.

Development of Interests

In time, children's fantasies of occupations are affected by information about the world, and they become interests. The child who wants to become a professional athlete may enjoy the activity, playing ball or gymnastics, and not just imagine himself or herself receiving the adulation of an audience. In the development of interests, the capacity of a child to actually become an athlete is immaterial. Young children often do not see any barriers to what they may want to do in their future. In Miller's (1977) study of 28,000 nine-year-olds, most of the children were able to state strong and weak interests (although fewer were able to state weak interests than strong interests). Nelson (1963) showed that third-grade children are often able to discard some occupations because they do not interest them. The development of interests is clearly an outgrowth of exploration. As the child tries new behaviors, some become attractive and some do not. The development of interests in activities in school and outside school becomes an important facet of decision making in adolescence.

Encouraging children's emerging interests is helpful in the development of their career maturity. Talking about those aspects of their life that are exciting can eventually be helpful in career planning. Because counselors of elementary school children are rarely concerned with career issues, it may seem unimportant to focus on interests. Further, the impact that counselors and other significant role models have may not be seen for many years. Talking to a child about an interest in baseball, an excitement about helping an injured animal, or the pleasure of a recent trip to a zoo may help the child to feel more important. This feeling of importance can contribute to the child's ability to develop a sense of what he or she is like, and of how he or she is different from others. This development of self-concept is essential to the later career selection process.

Time Perspective

To develop a time perspective is to develop a sense of the future, to have a real appreciation that six months is different from six years. For children under the age of 9, this is very difficult, if not impossible. For example, the child who says, "I want to be a boat captain so I can steer a boat now," has a sense only of the present. The notion of how long "later" is develops over time (Ginzberg et al., 1951). The implication of time perspective for counseling is that it is unrealistic to expect young children, particularly those below fourth grade, to think about planning future vocational or higher education. Rather, it is more important to examine jobs and job tasks now, to start to develop interests, and to reinforce exploratory behavior. As a future orientation develops, children are able to construct a sense of planfulness that will allow them to start to make educational choices in junior high school that will have an impact on their eventual career choices.

Self-Concept and Planfulness

A sense of self begins to emerge in late childhood or early adolescence. By following through on the need to discover more about the environment and to explore objects and people in the environment, the child learns information that will be one basis for the development of a self-concept. The child learns how he or she is different from or similar to other people. Further, by observing important people in their lives, children learn occupational and other roles. Also, exploratory behavior leads to information and experience with key figures that will eventually help the child develop interests in some activities and a lack of interest in others. The child starts to have a clear profile in terms of interest and experience that separates him or her from others. As a sense of self develops, the drama and excitement of activity becomes less important, and the accomplishment of goals becomes more so. Children now are in a position where they can plan and make decisions. Naturally, not all children have the same experience, and not all are able to develop a strong sense of self and an ability to plan. Differences in career maturity between individuals and the elements of career maturity are the focus of Chapter 8, "Adolescent Career Development."

The point of the preceding discussion is to emphasize the importance of those concepts that lead to a sense of self and a feeling of planfulness. To plan, children must have sufficient information, motivation in terms of interests and activities, a sense of control over their own future, and an idea of what that future will be (a time perspective). Although the development of interests, the acquisition of information, and the development of a time perspective are goals that can be achieved in counseling, they are not ends in themselves. They are important because they lead to the development of planfulness and a sense of self. As these important concepts are developing, it is not possible for children to make career choices that are planful. Rather, they may express an interest in an occupation because of information they may have or because of their experience with role models. Therefore, career counseling as it is done with adolescents and adults is inappropriate for children. An awareness of Super's model of the bases of career maturity can be helpful when discussing other issues with children in counseling.

USING SUPER'S MODEL IN COUNSELING CHILDREN

Common topics in counseling young children deal with school and family. Thomas (1989) describes the following as typical elementary-school guidance problems: lack of academic progress; dyslexia; lack of reading achievement; problems having to do with intellectual ability, sight, or hearing; and disruptive behavior. Typical family problems that Thomas (1989) cites are child abuse, child neglect, and issues arising from single-parent families, divorce, unwed parents, stepfamilies, and working parents. Occasionally, in dealing with these issues, counselors have the opportunity to make comments that fit with Super's model of childhood career development. This might mean a discussion of the child's exploratory behavior, the reaction the child is having to experiences with school, or a positive or negative reaction to key figures. An awareness of a limited time perspective in children can help the counselor in not expecting planful behavior from them. Another area where Super's view can be useful is in the attention that the counselor pays to the development of interests. The following example shows how a counselor can incorporate a knowledge of Super's concepts while working with a child on a topic seemingly not related to career choice.

Arthur is a white fourth-grade student in a predominantly wealthy suburban school system. Both parents were raised in Toronto, Canada. A student who has received "C"s in his previous classes, Arthur is starting to fall behind the other children in his class in reading, and he senses it. He seems to have few social contacts with his peers and cries rather easily when frustrated by reading assignments. His teacher has referred Arthur to the counselor because the teacher is concerned about his behavior and suspects that Arthur may have a learning disability. This dialogue between Arthur and the counselor occurs rather late in their discussion:

CL: I hate reading! It's too hard.

CO: What do you like to do? [The counselor very much feels Arthur's frustration with reading and wishes to move to a topic where Arthur does not have a sense of failure. Later, they will return to the topic of reading.]

CL: I like baseball. My friends and I play after school. We trade cards, too.

CO: What teams do you collect? [The counselor, almost randomly, chooses to follow up on collecting baseball cards rather than playing baseball.

Mainly, the counselor wants to follow up on an area of interest that Arthur has.]

CL: All kinds. I like the American League. I like new players and pitchers' stats.

CO: You really seem to enjoy collecting cards. [The counselor notes that Arthur is starting to relax and sound more enthusiastic. Further, the counselor notes that Arthur is interested in an activity that requires reading but chooses not to comment about it; rather, the counselor follows Arthur's exploratory behavior.]

CL: Oh, yes. It's really great. I buy cards when my parents will give me money, and I trade with whatever kids I can find. People know I am a good trader and sometimes it's hard to find kids to trade with. I've got a box full of cards.

CO: Seems like that's something that you do well. [The counselor is concerned about Arthur's sense of failure, coming from his difficulty with reading, and wishes to reinforce his area of interests and strength. Arthur's self-concept is important. The collecting of baseball cards itself does not need to have direct occupational relevance.]

CL: Yeah. I know the cards, and I know the players. I like to watch them on TV. It's fun to see a player whose card I have. Sometimes, when I'm playing baseball, I pretend that I'm a player.

CO: Who would you like to be like? [In his fantasy, Arthur is influenced by a key figure. The counselor wants to hear more about it.]

CL: The center fielder for the Red Sox. He can really hit. I like to watch him. I want to hit just like him. I want to be a ballplayer like him. I want to hit home runs and have a high batting average. I want to play for the Boston Red Sox. I love to hit the baseball hard. I love to catch the balls.

CO: Sound like great things to do. [The counselor is aware that Arthur's time perspective is vague. Arthur seems to see himself in a short time being a professional baseball player. Not wanting to push Arthur into developing a time perspective when he is not able to, the counselor reinforces Arthur's interest in and exploration of baseball. The counselor is aware that they are moving away from the reading issue, but the counselor feels it is important to spend some time on areas that will strengthen Arthur's concept of himself.]

In this example, the counselor has used Super's concepts to encourage exploratory behavior in Arthur and to help him feel better about himself. Although the goal of counseling is to help Arthur with his reading problem, and this discourse seems unrelated, it is likely that helping Arthur have a sense of success will make him feel less frustrated in general. At a later point in the interview, the counselor may be able to draw a parallel between reading baseball cards and reading schoolwork. The counselor does not introduce career issues in a forced sense but uses knowledge of Super's theory to respond helpfully in the context of the situation. This example uses a sex-stereotyped situation. It is one in which a boy is choosing a traditionally masculine activity. The issue of sex-role stereotyping is an important one in the development of occupational selection. It is dealt with extensively in the next section.

SEX-ROLE STEREOTYPING

Super (1957), having long been concerned about career development issues as they apply to women, identified seven career patterns of women. The major factors determining these patterns are the ways in which women deal with marriage and homemaking. His theory does not speak directly to gender issues related to the career development of boys and girls, whereas Gottfredson's theory does.

Gottfredson's Theory of Career Development

Gottfredson (1981, 1996) has articulated a life-stage theory of career development in childhood and adolescence that emphasizes the important part that sex roles and prestige play in making choices. This focus on gender and social class background is generally not an active part of other career development theories. Like other career development theorists, Gottfredson includes intelligence, vocational interest, competencies, and values in her theory. Essential to her theory are four stages of cognitive development that provide a way to view oneself in the world. The first stage, occurring between the ages of 3 and 5, is the orientation to size and power. In this stage, children grasp the idea of becoming an adult, by orienting themselves to the size differences between themselves and adults. In the second stage, ages 6 to 8, they develop an orientation to sex roles, becoming aware of the different sex roles of men and women. Their career choices are influenced by their view of sex roles. In the third stage, approximately 9 to 13, they are affected by the abstract ideas of social class. At this point, prestige becomes an important factor in career choice. In the fourth stage, occurring after the age of 14, adolescents become more introspective and develop greater self-awareness and perceptiveness toward others. Adolescents develop a more insightful view of vocational aspirations as they are affected by their view of themselves, sex roles, and prestige. This section will focus particularly on the second stage, and on the role of sex stereotyping in young children.

Gottfredson (1996) cites many studies that support her proposition that sex-role stereotyping occurs during the ages of 6 to 8, when children develop *tolerable sex-type boundaries,* beliefs about which occupations are appropriate for their own sex and for the opposite sex. For example, a girl may see police officers on the street and on television and conclude that police officers are men, and that she could not become a police officer. Looft (1971) asked second-grade boys and girls what they wanted to be when they grew up. For boys, the most frequent choices were football player and police officer, with doctor, dentist, priest, and pilot being less frequent. For girls, nurse and teacher were most frequently mentioned, followed by mother and flight attendant. In a study including first- to sixth-grade children done about eight years later, Biehler (1979) found that teacher and nurse were still important, but girls had included some nontraditional occupations in their choices as well. Professional athlete was still an important occupational choice for boys. Studies by MacKay and Miller (1982) and Umstot (1980) generally confirmed these findings. In most of these studies, boys showed a narrower range of traditionally stereotyped occupations than did girls. In another study, Frost and Diamond (1978) found that fourth-, fifth-, and sixth-graders who stereotyped children's jobs, such as baby-sitting and delivering newspapers, also stereotyped adult jobs. Trice et al. (1995) reported that fourth-grade girls were less likely than boys to make career choices based on money/status or danger/excitement. Girls were more likely than boys to base their career choices on specific abilities, parental influence, and helping others. These studies tend to support Gottfredson's (1981, 1996) proposition that sex-role stereotyping is an important factor in career choice in 6- to 8-year-olds.

Insight into why sex-role stereotyping is so strong is provided by Betz and Fitzgerald (1987) in their review of sex bias in education. They cite many studies that show how pervasive sex stereotyping is in schools. For example, Nilsen's (1971) term "apron syndrome" refers to pictures in children's reading books and textbooks of women in aprons. Scott (1981) reports that boys and girls are pictured in stereotyped roles: girls are depicted as passive and dull, whereas boys are shown as problem solvers. Examining changes in pictures in children's literature over a 50-year period, Kortenhaus and Demarest (1993) report that girls are pictured and described more frequently than in earlier years, but they are still shown in more passive activities than boys. For example, girls may be shown caring for a pet, while boys may be shown participating in sports. Another aspect of sex-role stereotyping in the schools is the key figures themselves. According to Betz and Fitzgerald (1987), teachers tend to be women, whereas principals tend to be men. This pattern further reinforces children's view of sex-role stereotypes. In the early 1970s, most schools had sex tracking systems. That is, girls tended to go into typing and home economics, whereas boys took courses in science. Although major changes have occurred in the participation rate of boys and girls in various classes since then, there is both direct and indirect support for Gottfredson's emphasis on sex-role stereotyping in the career development of children.

Two significant aspects of Gottfredson's (1981, 1996) theory are circumscription and compromise. In general, *circumscription* concerns the idea that various factors limit career choices at different ages; it is "the progressive elimination of unacceptable alternatives" (Gottfredson, 1996, p. 187), leaving acceptable alternatives. More specifically, *circumscription* refers to the prediction that gender will influence occupational preferences from the age of 6 up, and that social background, or prestige level, will influence preferences at 9 years and beyond. In this way, choices are circumscribed or limited. Henderson, Hesketh, and Tuffin (1988) found that sex type had more of an effect at ages 6 to 8 than did prestige when career choices were examined. After the age of 8, prestige had more of an effect on occupational choice than did gender. Leung and Harmon (1990) and Lapan and Jingeleski (1992) support the importance of sex typing and prestige as issues that adolescents consider in career exploration. Also, Lapan and Jingeleski (1992) showed how self-efficacy, assertiveness, and emotional expressiveness can affect the circumscribing of career choices for eighth-graders.

Compromise refers to the necessity for an individual to modify her or his career choices because of the reality of limiting environmental factors such as a competitive job market. This means that they may have to accept less attractive career alternatives. To be more precise, the compromise portion of Gottfredson's (1981) theory concerns the prediction that the earlier a stage occurs, the more resistant it will be to change and the less willing an individual will be to compromise on issues related to that stage. Thus, Gottfredson hypothesizes that sex type, prestige, and interest will be compromised (or sacrificed) in such a way that, when making a change in career choice, individuals will give up their interests first, then prestige, and finally sex type. The hypothesis deals directly with why it seems so difficult to encourage girls and women to consider nontraditional careers. Hesketh and colleagues (Hesketh, Durant, & Pryor, 1990; Hesketh, Elmslie, & Kaldor, 1990) have found that interests are most important in career decision making, followed by prestige, and then by sex type. Studying 14- and 15-year-old Spanish students, Sastre and Mullet (1992) found that gender was the best predictor of occupational choice for girls, and that prestige and free time were the best predictors for boys. Hall, Kelly, and Van Buren (1995) reported that the degree to which 8th- and 11th-graders' interests were compromised, if any, depended on the area of interest, for example, scientific or business-oriented. Asian American college students were more likely to compromise sex type for prestige than prestige for sex type as hypothesized by Gottfredson (1996).

Gottfredson (1996) comments that the reasons for the variation in support for the compromise aspect of her theory may be explained, in part, by whether the compromises under investigation are major or minor, or are real or artificial. As a way of making the issue of compromise less artificial and more practical, a workbook has been designed to help middle school students understand factors that can limit (compromise) their career options (Lapan, Loehr-Lapan, & Tupper, 1993).

Implications of Gottfredson's Theory for Super's Theory

Super's (1990) model of early career development, as shown in Figure 7-1, does not deal with sex bias. Gottfredson's (1981, 1996) theory is relevant to several of Super's important concepts. Consistent with both theories is the importance of career exploration unrestricted by sex-role stereotyping. Thus, children of both sexes should be able to explore activities such as knitting, sewing, sports, and science. Further, information made available in the schools should not reinforce sex-role stereotypes. In general, publishers of textbooks have made strides in showing adults and children in pictures that do not reinforce traditional sex-role models. By providing information free of sex-role bias, educational systems are more likely to provide an atmosphere in which wide varieties of interests can develop, regardless of sex. If exploration and information are not gender-biased, the selection of key figures by children is also more likely to be unbiased. These concepts will ultimately affect the child's self-concept and ability to make career decisions.

Use of Gottfredson's and Super's Concepts in Counseling

When counseling children, counselors may introduce alternative information about occupational sex roles when discussing exploration, key figures, information, and interest. If a young girl enjoys studying and watching insects and has been told by someone that little girls don't do that kind of thing, the counselor can indicate that this may be a view of one individual and emphasize the young girl's pleasure in learning about insects. By doing this, the counselor is providing alternative information to the young girl about those activities that may lead to an interest in biology. Dealing with key figures, particularly parents, who provide sex-stereotyped examples or information is more difficult. In a direct challenge to an important key figure, the counselor is likely to lose, and the child is likely to believe or identify with the key figure. In the following example, a counselor deals with this issue.

Lucy is a white fifth-grader in a small city in Texas. She has recently turned 11 and has done well in her schoolwork. She has been referred to the counselor by one of her teachers, who talked briefly with Lucy about why she seemed to be less interested in her English, history, and science work. Lucy just shrugged and said that things weren't fun anymore. In talking with Lucy, the counselor learns that Lucy's mother, a practical nurse at a local hospital, has asked Lucy's father to move out of the house. Lucy's father is a self-employed electrician. Lucy describes him as yelling a lot at her mother and as throwing things around the room. In talking with Lucy, the counselor is trying to decide how best to intervene to help Lucy: whether to talk to one or both parents, to make suggestions to Lucy, and/or to help Lucy express her feelings about the events at home. The following dialogue takes place in the middle of the initial counseling session:

CL: My mom usually gets home right after I do because she works from seven in the morning 'til three. She doesn't talk to me the way she used to. I usually go to the refrigerator, and she may go to her room. It's not like it used to be.

CO: How did it used to be? [The counselor wants to learn more about what is happening to Lucy and how things have changed in the family.]

CL: She used to come home and talk with me. Sometimes she'd ask me about school, and sometimes she'd talk about her work.

CO: That felt good, to talk with her. [The counselor, in an attempt to learn more about the situation, is encouraging Lucy to talk about her relationship with her mother.]

CL: Yeah! Like sometimes she'd tell me funny things that happened at work. She doesn't like being a nurse. She tells me it's awful being told what to do all the time and taking care of sick people who yell at her. I wouldn't want to do that.

CO: What seems so bad about that? [Not wanting to reinforce nursing as an occupation for women and not wanting to reinforce Lucy's biased view of nursing, the counselor feels caught. Further, Lucy's mother is an obvious key figure. Challenging her is not likely to work. Thus, the counselor asks for Lucy's view.]

CL: I don't know. I like doing things for other people. I like to baby-sit my little sister. She's only 3 and kind of fun sometimes—a brat at other times—and likes to play with me, too.

CO: What do you like to do with her? [Wanting to follow Lucy's lead, the counselor asks Lucy about her work.]

CL: I like to pretend that I'm her mother, and I make her do things, like behave right or read her a story. I'd like to be a mother sometime. Mom says that's what she wishes she could be all the time and not have to work. I don't want to work.

CO: Why not? [The counselor is concerned about Lucy's attitude toward work, which is learned from a key figure, her mother, as well as the sex-role stereotyping Lucy may be learning that suggests the woman's place is in the home.]

CL: You have to do what everybody tells you to, and you get tired.

CO: Baby-sitting is work, and you seem to like that. [Hearing Lucy voice some of her mother's objections to work, the counselor gently confronts Lucy with her own positive experience of work, which is different from her mother's experience. The counselor wants Lucy to learn from her own exploratory behavior. Although baby-sitting is something that Lucy is required to do, the ways in which she does it are of her own choosing, and she seems to like them. To reply, "Not everyone has to take orders in their work. Some people enjoy helping and taking care of others" might work, but the counselor is afraid that it would be challenging Lucy's mother's view, and that Lucy would reject it.]

CL: Yes, it's fun to do different things with my baby sister. Sometimes we try to fix things like my father. We broke a lamp that way. I was in lots of trouble for a while.

CO: What do you like to fix? [Seizing the opportunity to move away from traditional female occupational roles, the counselor is pleased that Lucy brings up a more traditionally male activity, fixing things, so that the counselor can explore this.]

Clearly, the career issue is secondary to the more pressing problem of helping Lucy with the crisis that has happened in her home. However, though the career issue may be subtle, it is far-reaching. This brief career intervention may have an impact on Lucy, allowing her to broaden her occupational possibilities, have a more positive attitude toward work, and continue in exploratory activities. Hopefully, when she enters high school, she will conceive of herself as someone who can listen to the input of others and will also be able to start to make her own decisions. It should be noted that the counselor was aware of Lucy's developmental stage in terms of processing information. Thus, the conversation stayed on a concrete level and did not deal with abstract concepts. When she enters high school, Lucy will be more able to deal with intangible issues.

CAREER DEVELOPMENT OF CHILDREN OF COLOR

Within the study of the career development of children, very little research has been done on issues that confront children of color in their career development. Miller (1977) found that more 9-year-old white children than 9-year-old African American children were able to list both strengths and weaknesses. African Americans had fewer out-of-school learning experiences such as piano and dancing lessons than did whites. Nine-year-old African American students were less likely than white children to see their career decisions as their own. Further, the 9-year-old African American children had less occupational knowledge. As Slaney (1980) points out, it is difficult to separate social class and racial effects when studying factors influencing career development. Vondracek and Kirchner (1974) studied urban African American children under the age of 11 in 51 day-care centers. They found that these children were less able than urban white children to see themselves in a future career. Further, the African American children had a more limited view than white children of what types of work adults did. Very little research has been done on children in other racial groups. Frost and Diamond (1978) studied fourth-, fifth-, and sixth-grade children who were Hispanic, African American, and white. They found that Hispanic and white girls chose more nontraditional and higher-status occupations than did African American girls. Further, Hispanic and white girls had a more open and less stereotyped view of career behavior than did African American girls. These studies are typical of the few studies investigating differences between white children and children of color.

This research suggests that children of color may be impeded in their exposure to exploratory activities in finding information that would enhance their development. This conclusion is similar to that arrived at by Osipow (1975), who notes how people of color have been oppressed, in part by being denied access to opportunities available to whites. The implication for counselors is that it is particularly important to try to provide the same opportunities for all children. This platitude can become a possibility when counselors have an opportunity to work individually with children of color. Counselors can help children of color develop effective role models so that they may learn more information about occupations and educational opportunities. Counselors can do this by talking with the child about parents and relatives and the work they do. Research suggests that people of color are being denied this opportunity (see Chapter 15). In the following section, suggestions are made about how occupational information can be used with children of all racial and ethnic groups to put them in a better position to make career decisions when they reach adolescence.

THE ROLE OF OCCUPATIONAL INFORMATION

Both Super's and Gottfredson's theories have implications for the delivery of occupational information to elementary school children. Most occupational information is provided not in the counseling office, but in the classroom. The provision of occupational information through the educational system is called *career education.* Rather than review the many programs for educating students about the world of work, this section will deal with theoretical implications for the use of occupational information in elementary school counseling and career education.

Occupational Information in Counseling

Suggestions for giving information to children about occupations can be taken from developmental theorists. Piaget's view of learning suggests that information given to children under the age of 12 should be concrete and clear. Erikson focuses on the importance of success and achievement for the young child. Learning about an occupation should not be overwhelming but can be done in small pieces. Because of the limited time perspective that younger children have, counselors should focus on what adults do now rather than on future occupational entry. Research such as that done by Miller (1977) suggests that children have vocational choices and are able to learn about these choices, but that planning ahead is more difficult. Gottfredson's theory is useful in reminding the counselor that information about occupations should be without gender bias. The actual discussion of occupational information between guidance counselor and child may be infrequent. However, when such a dialogue occurs, these suggestions may be helpful. More common is the provision of occupational information in classroom activities.

Career Education in the Classroom

Because career education is a curricular rather than an individual or group counseling function, full treatment is beyond the scope of this book. However, one activity of counselors is the development of or consultation on career education systems. Because career education is such an important part of the pre-career-decision-making process, discussion is warranted. According to Hoyt, Evans, Mackin, and Mangum (1972), *career education* refers to helping others learn about values of a work-oriented society and important values in their lives (p. 1). A similar definition, but with a different perspective, is that of Evans (in Hoyt et al., 1972), who feels that career education emphasizes an effort to develop a personally satisfying succession of opportunities for service through work (p. 1). Hoyt and Shylo (1989) show how career education is evolving and suggest future directions, including how industry can become further involved in education. Clements (1977) sees as the major task of career education for elementary school children the development of an awareness of self, occupational roles, the role of work in society, social behavior, and responsible actions. How this can be done is illustrated by three basic types of career education in elementary school (Herr & Cramer, 1996). The first type is the infusion of occupational information into the classroom in the form of films, oral reports on occupations, or the development of interest centers in the classroom. A second and less formal approach in the classroom involves group activities such as writing a skit using terms from the world of work; crossword puzzles using occupational terms; and comparing lists of interests, abilities, and achievements with requirements of occupations. The third type is community involvement, which can mean taking students out of the classroom or bringing the community into the classroom. Examples include going to a factory and observing each aspect of a manufacturing process or having students follow workers on the job as they go through their daily activities. Herr and Cramer (1996) list 69 of these activities that can be helpful to counselors in designing programs in collaboration with teachers.

These exercises can be structured in such a way that they are consistent with the learning stage of children and with their ability to process information. In general, the successful activities focus on concrete functions, not abstract ones. They are often visual, for example, using films of an occupation or using tools brought into class. Exposure to people in occupations gives an increased opportunity for modeling behavior, as well as an opportunity for the child to have more exposure to key figures. Being able to explore equipment in a factory or to explore dental tools can be very helpful to a child in acquiring information about the world of work. Having a veterinarian show animals and how he or she helps them is more useful and concrete than just talking about his or her daily work. Gottfredson's theory suggests the importance of being careful to avoid sex-role stereotyping in factory visits or choice of outside speakers. This is often difficult, as the counselor or teacher may have less control over these activities than over ones that they direct in the classroom.

THE ROLE OF TESTING

Because interests, capacities, and values are not sufficiently developed in elementary school children, assessment of them is premature. Rather, the emphasis is on acquiring information about oneself, others, and occupations and the development of a self-concept. Children need to be able to see a future and to have a sense of how far away college or work is in time. The appropriate timing of career testing is a difficult issue and is discussed in Chapter 8, "Adolescent Career Development." Various tests of career maturity serve as a means of assessing this readiness.

COUNSELOR ISSUES

Career counseling with young children can be challenging because children are at the very beginning of the career choice process, and counselors are usually in an establishment or maintenance phase. Counselors have gone through the process of making career decisions; assessing their abilities, capacities, and values; and acting on them. Children are far from this. They need to experience and acquire information long before they are able to make decisions. This gap in developmental stage makes patience on the part of the counselor particularly important. Piaget's (1977) reminder that children are not adults without information is quite helpful. Being aware of Super's explanation of the career development of children can aid the counselor in dealing with them.

SUMMARY

Counseling children on career issues is rarely thought of as a duty of counselors. The purpose of this chapter has not been to show that it should be an important activity, but that, when it does occur, there are effective ways of talking about career development with children. Super's model of the bases of career maturity is helpful in stressing how curiosity leads to exploration, which can lead to the acquisition of information and the development of interests. Further, Super emphasizes the importance of key figures in the development of the self-concept, along with the development of a sense of internal control and with a respect for parental and educational authorities. As the young child develops a sense of the future and a sense of self, he or she becomes ready to plan and decide. This complex topic is dealt with in detail in the next chapter, on adolescence.

References

Bandura, A. (1977). *Social learning theory.* Englewood Cliffs, NJ: Prentice-Hall.

Berlyne, D. E. (1960). *Conflict, arousal, and curiosity.* New York: McGraw-Hill.

Betz, E. L., & Fitzgerald, L. F. (1987). *The career psychology of women.* Orlando, FL: Academic Press.

Biehler, R. F. (1979). Unpublished study, California State University at Chico.

Clements, I. (1977). *Career education and vocational education.* Washington, DC: National Education Association.

Erikson, E. H. (1963). *Childhood and society* (2nd ed.). New York: Norton.

Frost, F., & Diamond, E. E. (1978). Ethnic and sex differences in occupational stereotyping for elementary school children. *Journal of Vocational Behavior, 15,* 43–54.

Ginzberg, E., Ginsburg, S. W., Axelrad, S., & Herma, J. (1951). *Occupational choice: An approach to a general theory.* New York: Columbia University Press.

Gottfredson, L. S. (1981). Circumscription and compromise: A developmental theory of occupational aspirations. *Journal of Counseling Psychology, 28,* 545–579.

Gottfredson, L. S. (1996). A theory of circumscription and compromise. In D. Brown and L. Brooks (Eds.), *Career choice and development: Applying contemporary theories to practice* (3rd ed., pp. 179–232). San Francisco: Jossey-Bass.

Hall, A. S., Kelly, K. R., & Van Buren, J. B. (1995). Effects of grade level, community of residence, and sex on adolescent career interests in the zone of acceptable alternatives. *Journal of Career Development, 21,* 223–232.

Henderson, S., Hesketh, B., & Tuffin, K. (1988). A test of Gottfredson's theory of circumscription. *Journal of Vocational Behavior, 32,* 37–48.

Herr, E. L., & Cramer, S. H. (1996). *Career guidance and counseling through the life span* (5th ed.). New York: Harper Collins.

Hesketh, B., Durant, C., & Pryor, R. (1990). Career compromise: A test of Gottfredson's (1981) theory using a policy capturing procedure. *Journal of Vocational Behavior, 36,* 97–108.

Hesketh, B., Elmslie, S., & Kaldor, W. (1990). Career compromise: Alternative account to Gottfredson's theory. *Journal of Counseling Psychology, 37,* 49–56.

Hoyt, K. B., Evans, R. N., Mackin, E. F., & Mangum, G. L. (1972). Career education: What it is and how to do it. Sale Lake City: Olympus.

Hoyt, K. B., & Shylo, K. R. (1989). *Career education in transition: trends and implications for the future.* Columbus, OH: National Center for Research in Vocational Education.

Jordaan, J. P. (1963). Exploratory behavior: The formation of self and occupational concepts. In D. Super, R. Starishevsky, N. Matlin, & J. P. Jordaan (Eds.), *Career development: Self-concept theory* (pp. 42–78). New York: College Entrance Examination Board.

Kortenhaus, C. M., & Demarest, J. (1993). Gender role stereotyping in children's literature: An update. *Sex Roles, 28,* 219–232.

Lapan, R. T., & Jingeleski, J. (1992). Circumscribing vocational aspirations in junior high school. *Journal of Counseling Psychology, 39,* 81–90.

Lapan, R. T., Loehr-Lapan, S. J., & Tupper, T. W. (1993). *Tech-prep careers workbook: Counselor's manual.* Columbia, MO: Department of Educational and Counseling Psychology, University of Missouri-Columbia.

Leung, S. A., & Harmon, L. W. (1990). Individual and sex differences in the zone of acceptable alternatives. *Journal of Counseling Psychology, 37,* 153–159.

Looft, W. R. (1971). Sex differences in the expression of vocational aspirations by elementary school children. *Developmental Psychology, 5,* 366.

MacKay, W. R., & Miller, C. A. (1982). Relations of socioeconomic status and sex variables to the complexity of worker functions in the occupational choices of elementary school children. *Journal of Vocational Behavior, 20,* 31–37.

Miller, J. (1977). *Career development needs of 9-year-olds: How to improve career development programs.* Washington, DC: National Advisory Council for Career Education.

Nelson, R. C. (1963). Knowledge and interest concerning 16 occupations among elementary and secondary students. *Educational and Psychological Measurement, 27,* 741–754.

Nilsen, A. P. (1971). Women in children's literature. *College English,* 32, 918–926.

Osipow, S. H. (1975). The relevance of theories of career development to special groups: Problems, needed data, and implications. In J. S. Picou & R. E. Campbell (Eds.), *Career behavior of special groups* (pp. 9–22). Columbus, OH: Merrill.

Piaget, J. (1977). *The development of thought: Equilibration of cognitive structures.* New York: Viking Press.

Rich, N. S. (1979). Occupational knowledge: To what extent is rural youth handicapped? *Vocational Guidance Quarterly, 27,* 320–325.

Sastre, M. T. M., & Mullet, E. (1992). Occupational preferences of Spanish adolescents in relation to Gottfredson's theory. *Journal of Vocational Behavior, 40,* 306–317.

Scott, K. P. (1981). Whatever happened to Jane and Dick? Sexism in tests reexamined. *Peabody Journal of Education, 58,* 135–140.

Slaney, R. B. (1980). An investigation of racial differences in vocational values among college women. *Journal of Vocational Behavior, 16,* 197–207.

Super, D. E. (1957). The psychology of careers. New York: Harper & Row.

Super, D. E. (1990). A life-span, life-space approach to career development. In D. Brown, L. Brooks, & Assoc. (Eds.), *Career choice and development: Applying contemporary theories to practice* (2nd ed, pp. 197–261). San Francisco: Jossey-Bass.

Super, D. E. (1994). A life-span, life-space perspective on convergence. In M. L. Savickas & R. W. Lend (Eds.), *Convergence in career development theories* (pp. 63–74). Palo Alto, CA: Consulting Psychologists Press.

Thelen, M., Frautsh, N., Roberts, M., Kirkland, K., & Dollinger, S. (1981). Being imitated, conformity, and social influence: An integrative review. *Journal of Research in Personality, 15,* 403–426.

Thomas, R. M. (1989). *Counseling and life-span development.* Newbury Park, CA: Sage.

Trice, A. D., Hughes, M. A., Odom, K. W., Woods, K., & McClellan, N. C. (1995). The origins of children's career aspirations: IV. Testing hypotheses from four theories. *The Career Development Quarterly, 43,* 307–322.

Trice, A. D., & Tillapaugh, P. (1991). Children's estimates of their parents' job satisfaction. *Psychological Reports, 69,* 63–66.

Umstot, M. E. (1980). Occupational sex-role liberality of third-, fifth-, and seventh-grade females. *Sex Roles, 6,* 611–618.

Vondracek, S. J., & Kirchner, E. P. (1974). Vocational development in early childhood: An examination of young children's expressions of vocational aspirations. *Journal of Vocational Behavior, 5,* 251–260.

Vygotsky, L. S. (1986). *Thought and language.* Cambridge: MIT Press.

8

Adolescent Career Development

Many career development theorists have focused their attention on adolescence, as it is the time when educational commitment to career choices is made. Life-stage theorists have been helpful in identifying developmental tasks that are important for individuals in the career selection process. This chapter first describes cognitive and emotional factors that bear on career decision making. Then, the emergence of interests, capacities, and values will be discussed in terms of Ginzberg, Ginsburg, Axelrad, and Herma's (1951) theory of the stages of adolescent career development. These theorists also explain the transition that takes place around the 12th grade to a realistic phase of decision making. Their stages are compared to those proposed by Super, who is more concerned with the development of self-concept than with the actual timing of stages. Research is cited that disputes some of the timing of the stages postulated by Ginzberg and his colleagues. More important, examples are given of how counselors can recognize the emergence of interests, capacities, and values. Perhaps the single most important contribution to adolescent career development has been the research on career maturity. In this chapter, Super's research on the Career Development Inventory (Super, Bohn, Forrest, Jordaan, Lindeman, & Thompson, 1971; Thompson & Lindeman, 1981) is used as a formulation for a conceptual understanding of career maturity. Although there are no theories that specifically address the career development of adolescent girls or adolescents of color, there are some theories, as well as a wide body of research, that bear indirectly on this topic. As in other areas of career life-span theory, there has been much more research on the career development of white adolescent boys and girls than on adolescents of color. Counseling examples will demonstrate how Super's theory can be used with different groups.

FACTORS INFLUENCING ADOLESCENT CAREER DEVELOPMENT

Abstract thinking is a process that greatly facilitates career planning. According to Piaget (1977), adolescents start a gradual process of developing their ability to solve problems and to plan. With age, planning becomes more ordered, permitting adolescents to introspect and think about themselves in a variety of situations. At this point, adolescents can more accurately picture themselves working in occupations than they could a few years earlier. This ability, which occurs in the last of Piaget's (1977) four stages of cognitive development, is called *formal thought.* There are individual differences in when an adolescent develops the ability to think abstractly. Furthermore, there are differences across courses in the requirement to think abstractly. For example, a high school sophomore may be able to think abstractly in algebra class but not in biology. Ability to use logic develops gradually. As formal thought emerges, the egocentrism of the concrete operational thinking of childhood does not disappear quickly. Because adolescents have developed the ability to think logically, they are apt to be quite idealistic, expecting their world to be logical when it is not. The process of job entry and job selection can help young people become more realistic in their thinking (Inhelder & Piaget, 1958). Cognitively, the period of formal thought is likely to bring the adolescent into conflict with parents and teachers, as students are likely to think that they are right and others are wrong. Although overstated, this suggests that adolescent thinking is a more tumultuous process than the thinking that takes place in elementary school children.

Just as Piaget has identified adolescence as a time of mild turmoil, so Erikson (1963) has posited that, in terms of psychosocial development, adolescence is a time of identity and role confusion. No longer concerned with following rules and being productive as in Erikson's (1963) earlier stage focusing on industry and accomplishment, adolescents question their world. Along with their physical development and their exposure to difficult sexual decisions (premarital sex, pregnancy, AIDS) come career decisions that may affect the rest of their lives. As early as junior high school, adolescents need to decide whether they want a "vocational track," a "college track," or something else. Ability to deal with these decisions varies greatly among adolescents. Career theorists have studied those aspects of adolescent development that are pertinent to the career choice process, such as interests, capacities, and values.

GINZBERG'S TENTATIVE STAGE OF ADOLESCENT CAREER DEVELOPMENT

Ginzberg, Ginsburg, Axelrad, and Herma's book *Occupational Choice: An Approach to a General Theory* (1951) was one of the earliest significant contributions to life-span theory. Their approach was a multidisciplinary one. Eli Ginzberg was an economist, Sol Ginsburg was a psychiatrist, Sidney Axelrad was a sociologist, and John Herma was a psychologist. In their work, they intensively studied the career choice process (mainly of upper-middle-class white adolescents). Their research consisted of interviews with students and reviews of the existing literature. As they interviewed adolescents and children, they distinguished three periods in the choice process. The fantasy stage (up to age 12) involves play and imagination in thinking about future work. The tentative stage, described in detail in this chapter, concerns a recognition of one's interests, abilities, and values, as well as one's knowledge of work. The realistic stage, occurring after age 17, includes specifying and crystallizing occupational choice. Within the tentative stage, four periods have been identified: the development of interests, the development of capacities, the development of values, and the transition period. Following the progress of adolescents through these periods can help the counselor appreciate the readiness of an adolescent to make career decisions.

Ginzberg (1970, 1972, 1984) has reformulated his theory, making several changes in the model proposed by Ginzberg et al. (1951). Although only his views of childhood and adolescent development are discussed here, Ginzberg acknowledged that vocational choice making continues throughout life. Earlier, Ginzberg had argued that vocational choices were irreversible. He modified this view to include aspects of reversibility or changing one's mind, but he still kept the idea that, when choices are made, such as choosing to study printing rather than welding, this choice, while reversible, may have many implications, including impediments in the person's career development (Ginzberg, 1984). In general, Ginzberg (1984) saw the process of choosing an occupation as one of optimization, weighing one's needs and desires against the constraints and opportunities occurring in the work environment. These views show the breadth of his model, although our discussion will focus on the development of interests, capacities, and values.

Development of Interests

Ginzberg et al. (1951) felt that, at about the age of 11, children cease to make fantasy choices and instead tend to base their choices on interests. In particular, Ginzberg et al. found that many choices of young boys were related in some way to their fathers' careers. Based on their current interests, 11-year-old boys would comment about whether they would like to be in an occupation like their father's or not. The children were quite aware that their interests might change and that they might make different choices. However, they were very vague about alternative choices and not concerned, because they knew that there was much time to make choices. At this time, the ability to judge their competencies was limited and relatively unimportant to them. Using a sample of 478 elementary school boys and 471 girls, Trice, Hughes, Odom, Woods, and McClellan (1995) found support for Ginzberg's idea that interests are the major factor in the selection and rejection of career choices during childhood. Kelso (1977) and others support these and Ginzberg's findings.

When talking to students who are ready to enter junior high school, counselors may notice that the students can speak more clearly about what they like than about what they are able to do. Children may have some exposure through their community to a number of occupations. They may be interested in being a detective or a doctor after seeing these occupations portrayed on television. They may observe the roles of their parents and of the parents of friends. They are able to ask themselves: Is this something I may like to do? Participating in sports and childhood jobs such as lawn mowing and baby-sitting also permits them to test their interests. Children who have not yet developed the ability to judge their capacities may want to be, for example, professional athletes and are not able to consider the quality of their performance.

Development of Capacities

According to Ginzberg et al. (1951), the capacity period covers the ages of 13 and 14 (junior high school). In their discussions with counselors, adolescents are more likely to assess their own abilities than they would have been two years before. They may be able to say, "Two years ago, I wanted to be a basketball player, but now I realize I will never be good enough." Or, "I'm not sure that I could ever be an engineer like my father; you have to know so much difficult math." For 13- and 14-year-olds, the educational process becomes more important in their preparation for work. Two years before, they may have been less concerned about that process. It is at this point that their time perspective improves and they are able to have a more realistic view of themselves and their future (adapted from Ginzberg et al., 1951).

Recognizing an adolescent's ability to assess his or her own capacities can be useful to the counselor. It is difficult for children to make decisions about curricular choice in eighth grade if they are not able to assess their capacities. Their choices at this point are likely to be based on interests or what their parents have told them. Often, parents make decisions for their junior high school children, partially because the children have not yet developed the ability to assess their own capacities.

Development of Values

At the ages of 15 and 16, adolescents are able to take their goals and values into consideration when making a career decision. They may not know how to weigh their interests, capacities, and values, but they have the necessary building blocks for choice. They are becoming aware that they must make choices so that they can fit into a very complex world. With their developed cognitive abilities, they may start to consider such abstract questions as: Is it better to make money or to help others? Weighing the satisfaction of helping others or contributing to environmental protection may be issues they had not thought about two years before. Making a contribution to the world and being a credit to society are factors that may now be considered. The issue of marriage and life plans may emerge, even though there is no marriage partner in mind. Such abstract conceptualization allows adolescents to continue to the next period.

Transition period

At this point, reality conditions start to play an important role in career choice. This period usually occurs in the last year of high school, at age 17 or 18. Decisions about whether to go to college and, if college is the choice, what to major in—these are real, immediate questions. Adolescents are aware that they need to pay attention to issues such as job availability. They know that they may not be able to get into the college or the field of their choice. Often, adolescents at 17 or 18 are aware that they may not have to make a decision, such as one about medical school, for a few years, but they are aware of the imminence of the decision. They know that they can determine their own future and must take action to do so, even if they cannot do it immediately. Considering salary, the education required, and work conditions becomes more important in this period than it was two years before. This period directly precedes the realistic stage, which includes exploration, crystallization, and specification. The realistic stage is very similar to Super's exploration stage, which is discussed in Chapter 9.

Career guidance for 17- and 18-year-olds usually includes an assessment of their interests, capacities, and values. When hearing a student discussing the world of work and her or his own abilities and desires, counselors can feel that testing and in-depth counseling may be helpful. This topic is dealt with in great detail by Super and his colleagues in their discussion of career maturity. The previous discussion provides a starting place for a critique of Ginzberg's work, which will lead to an understanding of some of the factors that make up career maturity.

Comparison of Super's and Ginzberg's Stages

In general, the adolescent life stages of Super are very similar to those of Ginzberg. We can see this similarity by comparing the stages of each theorist and the ages at which adolescents are supposed to enter those stages. However, there are also important differences of emphasis between Super and Ginzberg et al. Also, since the time that Ginzberg and his colleagues developed their theory, there has been research that questions the timing of their stages.

By comparing Ginzberg's stages to those of Super in Figure 6-2, small differences can be ascertained. Inspection of Super's diagram shows that, in his formulation, interests are followed by capacities, which are followed by a transition to the exploration stage. Super does not include values in his overview. Perhaps the reason is that the issue of values is quite complex. According to Super (Super, Thompson, & Lindeman, 1988), different values may emerge and become more important at various times in the life span. Except for omission of the values stage, the two theories are similar in that they both place interests before capacities.

A number of important differences also exist. Because Super emphasizes recycling of stages, time guidelines are not important in the same sense that they are in Ginzberg's work. To Super, it is the adolescent's attitude toward careers and his or her knowledge of careers that are important. In general, Super believes adolescents enter these stages about two or three years earlier than the ages proposed by Ginzberg. This difference is not an important one from the point of view of the counselor, as a client may enter a stage at a different time than the guidelines described by Super or Ginzberg. Of interest is the research that describes when adolescents and children pursue the tasks of developing interests, capacities, and values.

In a study of 9-year-olds, Miller (1977) found that many were able to state interests in activities and occupations. Aubrey (1977) found that many children were able to say what they could and could not do, although girls were better able to do this than boys. The difficulty in making accurate self-estimates is raised by Tierney and Herman (1973). This is consistent with O'Hara and Tiedeman (1959), who observed that, during the high school years, adolescents had difficulty in accurately seeing their capacities. Westbrook, Buck, Wynne, and Sanford (1994) found that adolescents were most accurate in rating their scholastic aptitude and least accurate in rating specific or special aptitudes, which they tended to overrate. Regarding values, Kapes and Strickler (1975) found little consistency in the work values of high school students. They suggested that different high school curricula may bring about different changes in work values. In a contrasting study, Hales and Fenner (1972, 1973) found that attitudes toward work were present in 11-year-olds and continued through 11th grade. Even though their sample was a homogeneous one in terms of socioeconomic and geographic characteristics, they did find a wide variety in the value profiles of students. These studies do not support the use of age guidelines in expecting consistent patterns in development of interests, capacities, and values in adolescents. Rather, they reaffirm the importance of assessing the individual student. The theorists and the research, however, are consistent in predicting that, in most adolescents, the development of interests precedes that of capacities.

A Counseling Example

To show the usefulness of assessing the relative development of interests, capacities, and values, an example of a 14-year-old ninth-grade student will be used. She is an African American girl from an affluent Chicago suburb.

Both parents work in the advertising field. Her father is an account executive with a Chicago firm, and her mother is a market researcher in another firm. Although Joan's grades through her first two quarters of school have been "A"s and "B"s, her parents are concerned by her lack of motivation for college and have asked that she talk with her guidance counselor. This section of the interview takes place toward the beginning of the hour with her counselor:

CO: Do you have any idea what you want to do when you finish high school? [This question is designed to get Joan started talking about her plans.]

CL: Well, I'm not sure, but I have some ideas.

CO: Go ahead. I'd like to hear them.

CL: Well, I think I'd like to go into advertising like my parents. They seem to know lots of people and have fun with the products. Sometimes they talk about the products on TV that they've worked with. Sometimes my father will show me a magazine ad that he worked on. But sometimes I think I might like to be an actress or a model, or an aeronautical engineer, like my friend's mother. Sometimes, I think I would like to be a teacher like Mrs. Morgan. I have her for English now, and she's great. Then, I've thought of writing, too. It would be fun to write for a magazine.

CO: Can you tell me more of what appeals to you about advertising? [Feeling bombarded, the counselor decides to concentrate on depth rather than on breadth. Returning to the first topic, because it was talked about in detail, the counselor inquires about advertising, wanting to hear more about Joan's interest.]

CL: I think that I'd like to write ads. It would be fun to do. Sometimes my dad talks about them at dinner. I'm not sure I'd like to do research on toilet paper, the way my mother does.

CO: You seem to enjoy English. [Wanting to follow up on Joan's interest in advertising, the counselor explores further.]

CL: Writing seems so much fun, especially with Mrs. Morgan. She's given us great assignments to do. For her, I like to do my homework.

CO: How is your work going? [This question may get at Joan's perception of her performance in English.]

CL: Oh, I'm doing OK; Mrs. Morgan likes me and my work, I think. But I don't know how I'm *really* doing.

CO: I'm not quite sure what you mean. [The counselor has an idea that Joan is making some distinction between school and occupational ability but is not sure.]

CL: Maybe I could do schoolwork OK, but doing what my father does seems really hard. You really have to be smart to get people to work with your company and give them good ads.

CO: It seems difficult for you to make plans about what you want to do. [Joan seems able to differentiate between ability needed at school and in an occupation. She seems to be aware that she doesn't know yet whether she has the ability needed in advertising.]

CL: Sometimes it seems too hard. I wish I were a psychiatrist.

CO: Tell me more about that, please. [Where did this come from? the counselor wonders. Joan's interests are varied and seem to have no end.]

CL: I really like to help people. I have seen psychiatrists on television programs and how they do it. It seems great.

CO: To help people? [Wanting to learn more about Joan's motivation, the counselor inquires further.]

CL: Yes, it's just so easy to sit there and talk and make a lot of money.

CO: Seems like fun to you. [What had started out as a possible value for Joan has turned into a rather naive interest.]

Joan's difficulty in establishing her capacities and values suggests that career counseling using tests may be premature. Although the use of a career maturity instrument (to be described in the next section) may be helpful, the counselor wishes to continue discussing Joan's interests, as they are varied and confused. This may lead to more suggestions as to how to proceed. Currently, the counselor's goal for counseling is to assess career maturity rather than to work on career selection, and to continue to conceptualize Joan's interests, capacities, and values.

CAREER MATURITY

Vocational maturity was described by Super (1955) as having the following five major components:

1. Orientation to vocational choice, which deals with concern about career choice and using occupational information
2. Information and planning about a preferred occupation, that is, the specific information that the individual has about the occupation he or she intends to enter
3. Consistency of vocational preference, concerned not only with stability of an occupational choice over time, but also with its consistency within occupational fields and levels
4. Crystallization of traits, including seven indexes of attitudes toward work
5. The wisdom of vocational preference, which refers to the relationship between choice and abilities, activities, and interests

This work of Super's was a major focus of the early monographs published by the Career Pattern Study, an in-depth study of a sample of adolescents followed into adulthood. Super and his colleagues further refined the concept of vocational maturity (Super et al., 1957; Super & Overstreet, 1960). This extensive work led to the development of the original Career Development Inventory (Super et al., 1971) and culminated in a revised edition of the Career Development Inventory (Thompson & Lindeman, 1981). The concepts that make up Super's definition of career maturity have been arrived at by studying the responses of boys and girls, and men and women, to various versions of the Career Development Inventory. These concepts are described in detail later. First, however, we will examine the definition of career maturity proposed by Crites.

Crites's Career Maturity Inventory

Perhaps the most widely used measure of career maturity is the Career Maturity Inventory (Crites, 1965, 1973, 1978). Crites, a colleague of Super's, made use of the Career Pattern Study to develop this measure of vocational maturity, consisting of the Attitude Scale and the Competency Test. From a conceptual point of view, they are quite similar to Super's Career Development Inventory. So that a comparison can be made with Super's concepts of vocational maturity, the concepts are listed here briefly. The five subtests of the 75-item Attitude Scale include the following:

Decisiveness: This subtest measures the degree to which an individual is sure of his or her career choice.

Involvement: This assesses the degree to which an individual is active in making his or her own career choice.

Independence: This measures the degree to which a person depends on another in choosing an occupation.

Orientation: This ascertains attitudes toward work, whether oriented to work as pleasure or work as drudgery.

Compromise: This assesses the extent to which a person will compromise between the reality of the job market and his or her own needs and desires.

The other major portion of the Career Maturity Inventory is the Competence Test. In general, the Competence Test is a measure of knowledge. Its five scales are as follows:

Self-appraisal: The student reads a description of an individual and then chooses the item that represents the most accurate appraisal of the person.

Occupational information: Job duties are listed along with occupational titles; the test taker must identify the correct occupational title for each description.

Goal selection: In this subtest, the student is given the background of an individual and is asked to identify which jobs would be most appropriate for the individual.

Planning: In this section, the test taker must place in order three steps that a fictitious person must follow to plan his or her career appropriately.

Problem solving: A brief case study is given, and the test taker is asked to identify the best solution to the problem given.

Crites has created a measure of career maturity that has been validated over a period of years. It is in general agreement, with some minor differences, with Super's conception of vocational maturity. Westbrook (1983) has critiqued Crites's, Super's and several other tests of vocational maturity. He has compared the reliability, validity, and factor structure of these instruments. Some of the other instruments that he reviews are the Gribbons and Lohnes Readiness for Vocational Planning Questionnaire (Gribbons & Lohnes, 1968); his own Vocational Maturity Project, which has produced the Cognitive Vocational Maturity Test (Westbrook, 1970); Healy and Klein's (1973) New Mexico Career Education Test Series; and several others. More than any other area of life-span theory, vocational maturity has been the focus of measurement and test development. Super's Career Development Inventory is another example of a measure of vocational maturity that has been the subject of study over a long period of years.

Super's Conception of Career Maturity

Throughout the extensive research that Super and his colleagues have done with adolescents, they have been concerned with readiness of individuals to make good choices. They do not assume that, just because a student reaches ninth grade, he or she is ready to plan his or her future career. Not only do they see differences in career maturity among individuals, but they are also able to identify different components of career maturity, just as Crites has done. To understand Super's model, it is helpful to use the structure of the Career Development Inventory (Thompson & Lindeman, 1981). With Figure 8-1 as a guide, the five subscales that make up the Career Development Inventory will be explained: Career Planning, Career Exploration, Decision Making, World-of-Work Information, and Knowledge of the Preferred Occupational Group. Also, the Career Orientation Total, which is a combination of subscales, will be described. Another concept that is part of Super's definition of career maturity but that is not tested by the Career Development Inventory is realism. The concepts described in the following paragraphs can by used to guide client discussion, with or without the use of the Career Development Inventory.

Career Planning This scale (and therefore the concept of planning) measures how much thought individuals have given to a variety of information-seeking activities and how much they feel they know about various aspects of work. The amount of planning that an individual has done is critical to this concept. Some of the activities that are included are learning about occupational information, talking with adults about plans, taking courses that would help one make career decisions, participating in extracurricular activities or part-time or summer jobs, and obtaining training or education for a job. In addition, this concept deals with knowledge of working conditions, education required, job outlook, different approaches to job entry, and chances of advancement. *Career planning* refers to how much a student *feels* that he or she knows about these activities, not how much he or she actually knows. The latter is covered by the World-of-Work Information and the Knowledge of the Preferred Occupational Group scales.

When talking with a student about career planning activities, it is helpful to know not only what the student has done, but also what the student *thinks* he or she has done. Discussion of future plans, including courses to be taken the following year, college selection, or ideas about a potential col-

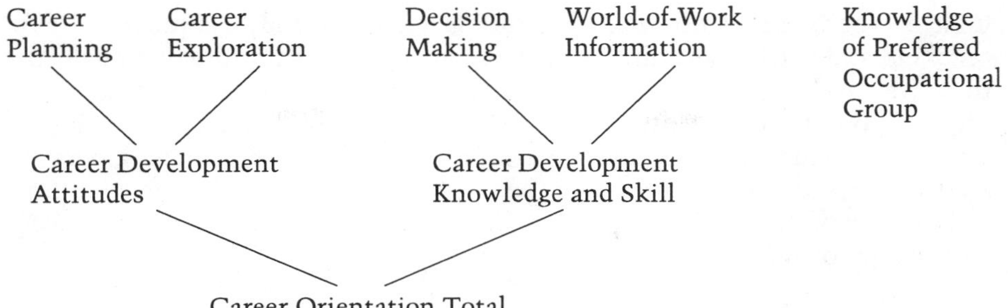

Figure 8-1 Relationship of the Career Development Inventory scales. (Reproduced by special permission of the Publisher, Consulting Psychologists Press, Inc., Palo Alto, CA 94303, from *Career Development Inventory: User's Manual,* by Albert S. Thompson and Richard H. Lindeman, with Donald E. Super, Jean Pierre Jordaan, and Roger A. Myers. Copyright 1981 by Consulting Psychologists Press, Inc. All rights reserved. Further reproduction is prohibited without the Publisher's consent.)

lege major or postsecondary education, all contribute to career planning. Either a low score on the Career Planning scale of the Career Development Inventory or, in lieu of this, the counselor's assessment that the student has not given much thought to career plans suggests the next step in counseling. This step is to give more thought to experiences that may provide more information to serve as a basis for planning.

Career Exploration Willingness to explore or look for information is the concept basic to the Career Exploration scale. In this subscale (and concept), students' willingness to use resources such as parents, other relatives, friends, teachers, counselors, books, and movies is investigated. Besides willingness, career exploration also deals with how much information the student has already acquired from the source. Career exploration differs from career planning in that the latter concerns thinking and planning about the future, whereas the former deals with use of resources, but both focus on attitudes toward work. Combined, they are referred to by Super as career development attitudes, and a score for this concept is given on the Career Development Inventory.

Counselors may often find that students are reluctant, for various reasons, to use resources to get occupational information, sometimes because of a student's attitude that he or she does not need information. In such a case, the counselor can explore reasons for this thinking. Sometimes, students are hostile to authority figures and rule out certain valuable resources such as parents, teachers, or coaches. Other students may be afraid to use resources because they are apprehensive that teachers or relatives will not take them seriously. Encouraging career exploration can be an important activity prior to assisting a student with career selection. Giving the student a week, three months, or some specified period of time to talk to teachers and use books containing occupational information, or some other resource, and then to return for counseling, is often a useful strategy. By focusing on attitudes toward work, the counselor can determine the next step in assisting the student with career development. However, a positive attitude toward work may not be sufficient to start career planning. Knowledge of how to make a career decision and some knowledge of occupational information is also important.

Decision Making The idea that a student must know how to make career decisions is an important one in Super's concept of vocational maturity. This concept concerns the ability to use knowledge and thought to make career plans. In the Decision Making scale, students are given situations in which others must make career decisions and are asked to decide which decision would be best. An assumption is that, if students know how others should make career decisions, they will be able to make good career decisions for themselves.

Asking students how they plan to go about making a career decision can be useful. Some students will be unable to answer the question, or to say anything more than "I don't know; it will come to me." This is an opportunity for the counselor to explain portions of the career decision process. The counselor can focus on what the next steps may be for career decision making. If the counselor uses the Career Development Inventory, it would be helpful to go over that section of the test with the student, explaining why some of the student's answers were correct and others were wrong.

World-of-Work Information This concept has two basic components. The first deals with knowledge of important developmental tasks, such as when others should explore their interests and abilities; how others learn about their jobs; and why people change jobs. The other portion of this concept (and subscale) covers knowledge of job duties in a few selected occupations, as well as job application behaviors. Super believes that it is important for individuals to have some knowledge about the world of work before effective career decision-making counseling can be done.

For the counselor, knowledge of the accuracy of the information that students have about work is helpful. Some students have misinformation about how to obtain a job and how to behave when they get a job. Others have little idea of the work that people such as doctors, lawyers, stockbrokers, and secretaries do. Often, some information is inaccurately gathered from television or films. Correcting students' inaccurate perceptions of the world of work may be a part of pre-decision-making counseling.

Knowledge of the Preferred Occupational Group In the Career Development Inventory, students are asked to choose which of 20 occupational groups they prefer. Then, they are asked questions about their preferred occupational group. They are asked about duties of the job, tools and equipment, and physical requirements of the job. In addition, they are asked to judge their own ability (or capacities) in nine different areas: verbal ability, nonverbal reasoning, numerical ability, clerical ability, mechanical ability, spatial ability, motor coordination, English skills, and reading ability. They are also asked to identify the interests of the people in the preferred occupation. The interest categories that they choose from are verbal, numerical, clerical, mechanical, scientific, artistic/musical, promotional, social, and outdoor. This, then, constitutes a very thorough inquiry into students' knowledge of their preferred occupational group.

Information about students' knowledge of the occupation that they want to enter can be extremely helpful in determining what type of counseling should be offered. In talking to students about their knowledge of occupations, counselors can learn about their progress in career planning. For example, some students may have misinformation about their career choice. Some students may be quite naive, thinking that to be a veterinarian does not require more than an associate's degree. Others may believe that, to enter a business career, one needs a bachelor's degree in business. The assessment of knowledge of a preferred occupation is often a key aspect of counseling. If a counselor is not aware of a student's assumptions about his or her preferred occupation, the counselor may assume the student has made a good decision, when in fact that is not true. Assessing good decision making is related to another of Super's concepts: realism.

Realism A concept that is part of Super's view of career maturity (Super, 1990), realism is not tested in the Career Development Inventory. Rather, Super describes it as a "mixed affective and cognitive entity best assessed by combining personal, self-report, and objective data as in comparing the aptitudes of the individual with the aptitudes typical of people in the occupation" (p. 213). Thus, to measure whether a choice of an individual is realistic, a counselor would need knowledge of the ability required in the occupation along with aptitude or grade information about the student.

The use of realism in career counseling has some dangers. It requires that the counselor be a very accurate judge of the student's aptitudes and the aptitudes required by the job. Inappropriate use of judging realistic choices can lead to the following: "My high school guidance counselor told me I could never make it to medical school, but I am in medical school now"; "My high school guidance counselor said I could never make it through college, and I graduated last year"; "My high school guidance counselor said I don't have the ability to go to college, so I guess I won't." Because students can misinterpret or misuse aptitude information, it has to be used quite carefully. Inaccurate predictions can have an effect on an individual's later choice of occupation.

Career Orientation *Career orientation* is a general term encompassing the concepts described previously. The Career Orientation Total score gives a single summary of the following scales: Career Planning, Career

Exploration, Career Decision Making, and World-of-Work Information. It does not include the Knowledge of the Preferred Occupational Group score or the unmeasured concept, realism. Having a general sense of students' career maturity may be useful for the counselor before looking at the specific subscales. It may provide a summary of what to expect from the student in terms of orientation toward careers. However, the five subscales are likely to have more relevance for the counselor in deciding which areas of career maturity to explore with a student. Probably, the counselor will want to talk most about those in which the student scores low. The following is an example of how a counselor used both career maturity concepts derived from the Career Development Inventory and the inventory itself.

Using the Concept of Career Maturity in Counseling

Ralph is a white tenth-grade student in a Providence, Rhode Island, high school. His parents are second-generation Italian Americans. His father is a mail carrier, and his mother is a waitress. Ralph has taken the Career Development Inventory along with the rest of his tenth-grade class in the early fall. He is talking about his schedule with his career guidance counselor in trying to decide what courses to take next year. Ralph has had "C"s in science and math and "A"s in English and social studies. He works after school in a fast-food restaurant and spends much of his weekends working with his older brother on his brother's car. Compared to other tenth-graders, Ralph's Career Planning and Career Exploration scores are at about the 15th percentile. His Decision Making score on the Career Development Inventory is at the 50th percentile, and his World-of-Work Information score is at about the 45th percentile. His scores on Knowledge of the Preferred Occupational Group and the Career Orientation Total are at about the 25th percentile. The transcript begins after the counselor and client have exchanged some introductory remarks:

CL: I know I need to think about next year and beyond, but I just haven't had time.

CO: Been very busy? [The counselor wants to know what life roles are important to Ralph. This is related to Super's concepts of work salience, which were described in Chapter 6 and will be described in more detail in Chapter 9.]

CL: After school, I work at that fast-food place down the street, and then at night, I go out with my friends.

CO: Does it give you any time to think about what you want to do? [The counselor wants to inquire again about career planning that Ralph may have done. The counselor has Ralph's Career Development Inventory results. He has not shared these directly with Ralph at this point.]

CL: I really haven't thought about it much. It doesn't sound like fun. After work, I'm kind of tired, and I like to go home, have dinner. Then I like to go out. Sometimes I do some homework, but not too much.

CO: Have you had a chance to talk to anyone about what you might do? [The counselor, aware of Ralph's low scores on Career Planning and Career Exploration, wants to see if there is a possibility for Ralph to make progress in this area.]

CL: Not really. My parents don't seem to know much about what is available. They just think I should work hard and get a good, secure job that pays well. My friends don't seem to know anything serious anyway.

CO: Would you like to know more about what's available? [Possibly, Ralph's friends and relatives are limited sources of information. Maybe there are other sources that can help Ralph.]

CL: Yes, I know I should do more than I am doing. Where can I learn?

CO: Your teachers, the Career Center here at school, maybe friends of your parents.

CL: I know that our math teacher brought in an accountant, and I learned a little bit that way. But I certainly don't want to be an accountant.

CO: Sounds as if you've given some thought to possible occupations. [The counselor wants to reinforce the little career exploration that Ralph has done.]

CL: Actually, what seems more interesting to me—and it suprises me—is doing what my social studies teacher does.

CO: Surprises you? [Ralph is starting to think a bit about world-of-work information and is using a key figure—the importance of which is described in the previous chapter—in that exploration.]

CL: Yes. I never thought about doing anything like teaching. I always just thought that work was work, a real pain.

CO: Now it seems maybe work could be fun. You seem to be interested in teaching. [Wanting to note this change in attitude, the counselor emphasizes it.]

CL: Yes, I think I would like to help people learn things. My social studies teacher seems to really like what he's doing, and that's great. All I ever do at home is hear my parents complain about their work.

CO: You seem to be picking up some ideas about what teachers do, more than you have in past years. [Perhaps Ralph is starting to learn more world-of-work information because of a growing maturity. Even though he has been exposed to teachers for the last 11 years, he is just now starting to think about teaching as an occupation.]

By exploring ideas about career choice, the counselor is helping Ralph become more vocationally mature. As their counseling progresses, the counselor will make some decisions, as will Ralph. The counselor will decide when to share the Career Development Inventory scores with Ralph and how to help him learn from them. Further, the counselor will decide whether to do interest, aptitude, or values testing with Ralph. For Ralph, decisions about whether to continue thinking about career planning and the world of work will have to be made. By making use of Super's career maturity concepts, the counselor is able to make some assessment of Ralph's readiness for career decision making. When to introduce occupational information and more testing is a future consideration. Occupational information and testing, as used in Super's theory, are the subject of the next sections.

THE ROLE OF OCCUPATIONAL INFORMATION

As may be apparent from the description of the Career Development Inventory, occupational information is critical to Super's theory. The Career Planning subtest asks students how much thinking and planning they have done about various educational and occupational opportunities. The Career Exploration scale asks students whom they have gone to, or whom they would go to, for occupational information. Implicit in the Decision Making scale is the integration of occupational information with career decision making. The World-of-Work Information and the Knowledge of the Preferred Occupational Group scales are measures of occupational knowledge. Clearly, Super's theory depends on the integration of self-concept and information about the world of work.

A concept described by two of Super's colleagues (Starishevsky & Matlin, 1963) provides another view of the relationship between self-concept and the world of work. Concepts of psychtalk and occtalk emphasize the relationship between occupation and self. *Psychtalk* refers to statements used to describe aptitudes, interests, and other characteristics of oneself. *Occtalk* refers to statements about occupations. Starishevsky and Matlin (1963) believe that occtalk and psychtalk statements can be translated from one to the other. For example, they state (p. 34) that wanting to be a lawyer may translate as being socially minded or being aggressive. A person who says that she will be a physician may also be saying, "I am intelligent, healthy, and concerned about others." Likewise, a person may say, "I am intelligent, healthy, and concerned about others (psychtalk); I could be a physician (occtalk)." The notion that discussion about occupations implies beliefs about self, and that beliefs about self can have implications for occupations, can be useful for counselors. The concepts of occtalk and psychtalk provide a convenient bridge in Super's theory between what could appear to be two very different concepts.

THE ROLE OF TESTING

Testing and assessment are a very important part of Super's developmental model. Testing of career maturity has been discussed in detail in this chapter. Inventories measuring the importance of the work roles, as well as the stages of late adolescent and adult development, are discussed in the next chapter. These stem directly from Super's life-span theory. In addition to these inventories, Super also advocates the use of inventories and tests that measure interests, capacities or abilities, and values. His Values Scale

(Nevill & Super, 1989) is an example of the latter. Super (1990; Super, Osborne, Walsh, Brown, & Niles, 1992) provides a very detailed and extensive model for career assessment, making use of many measures of career-related concepts. Clients are not always ready for or open to an in-depth assessment, and counselors often do not have the time necessary. Sometimes, assessment in counseling can be done in groups; sometimes, it can occur over a period of months or even years. Super has developed a multitude of assessment techniques, and he advocates the use of many others. It is up to the counselor to decide how best to use these tests and inventories. Additional information about male and female adolescents and adolescents of color can influence the use of assessment and Super's theoretical concepts.

GENDER ISSUES IN ADOLESCENCE

Just as sex-role stereotyping has a limiting effect on the selection of occupations by children, so it does also for adolescents. Research studies are cited here to give some idea of the effect that sex-role stereotyping has on occupational choice and aspirations for occupational success. In a study of 2,000 Alabama seniors, Fottler and Bain (1980) found females tending to aspire slightly more than males to professional and technical occupations and aspiring slightly less than males to managerial occupations. Among lower levels of occupations, Fottler and Bain observed traditional patterns of females choosing clerical and service positions, and of males choosing craft and labor positions. In reviewing studies by Lunneborg and Gerry (1977) and Osipow and Gold (1968), Osipow (1983) suggests that males are somewhat more free to behave in a less stereotypical male way than formerly. In a similar vein, Rosen and Aneshensel (1978) and Aneshensel and Rosen (1980) found that adolescent females saw sex roles in stereotypical ways and believed that men and women should have different occupational roles. When McKenna and Ferrero (1991) compared 9th-grade boys and girls on how traditional their career choices were, they found that 77% of the boys and 45% of the girls said their choice was traditional. Additionally, they found that 52% of the boys and 85% of the girls thought it was acceptable to work in nontraditional occupations. For about a third of the 10th- and 12th-grade girls whom they studied, Davey and Stoppard (1993) found that desired occupations were significantly less traditional than the occupations the girls actually expected to enter. As these studies show, stereotyping occupations according to gender continues to be an issue for adolescents.

Some studies have used less direct approaches to examine the effect of sex-role stereotyping on adolescents. In a study of high school juniors, Hurwitz and White (1977) found that women saw females in lower-paying and lower-status jobs than males. If high school girls were led to believe that the sex ratios in certain occupations would be balanced in the future, they expressed more interest in traditionally male occupations (Heilman, 1979). However, high school boys expressed less interest when they were told that the sex ratio would be more balanced in the future. These findings suggest that males preferred the dominant sex ratio and females were put off by occupations if they felt that other women were not going to be in them. Studying 7th-grade adolescents, Robison-Awana, Kehle, and Jenson (1986) asked their subjects to take a self-esteem inventory, both as themselves and as someone of the opposite sex. They found that both boys and girls believed that girls had lower self-esteem. To educate 8th- and 11th-graders about choosing nontraditional occupations, Van Buren, Kelly, and Hall (1993) used videotape to model various occupations. They found that the boys' interest in social occupations increased. Van Buren et al.'s work represents an effort to make career information free of sex bias, a need that has been emphasized by Betz and Fitzgerald (1987).

The career self-efficacy theory described by Hackett and Betz (1981) suggests that, in certain situations, adolescent women, particularly college women, have less confidence in their abilities than do men. This theory, although not a developmental theory but a theory of social learning, has implications for the career development of adolescent women (see Chapter 13). Hackett and Betz believe that women lack strong expectations of their own personal efficacy in a number of occupational areas. They find that women often do not live up to their capabilities. Further, women have fewer opportunities for successful career behaviors, and they receive less encouragement than men in this process. These observations are confirmed in reviews by Lent and Hackett (1987) and Lent, Brown, and Hackett (1994).

Related to the finding that women often feel less competent than men in a number of career-related behaviors is the research on women's participation in math. Fennema and Sherman (1977) and Pedro, Wolleat, Fennema, and Becker (1981) document that girls take fewer math courses than boys throughout high school and college. Studying this issue further, Chipman and Wilson (1985) and Wise (1985) found that sex differences in math achievement do not start until ninth or tenth grade. During those years, girls tend to take less math, and therefore, their math achievement test scores are lower than those of boys. When girls do continue the study of math, their work is on a par with that of boys (Chipman & Wilson, 1985). Betz and Fitzgerald (1987) believe that girls stop taking math because of female socialization patterns that suggest that math is for men, and that women do not need to study math. Research suggests that math confidence is a better predictor of taking more math courses than are grades in math (Chipman & Wilson, 1985). In another study Chipman, Krantz, and Silver (1992) found that math anxiety interfered with being interested in careers in science. In a report related to these findings, Monaco and Gaier (1992) found that adolescent females are less confident than males in a coeducational setting but perform better academically. Studying mathematics self-efficacy (a concept similar to career self-efficacy), Betz and Hackett (1983) found that college men had more confidence in their math ability than did college women. This study was one of the first of many studies to emphasize how women's beliefs, ("Can I do math?") negatively effect women's interest in math, their intentions to enroll in math courses, and their performance in math courses (Lent, Lopez, & Bieschke, 1991, 1993; Multon, Brown & Lent, 1991). A different model (Fassinger, 1990) also emphasizes the importance of math self-efficacy in career choices for women. O'Brien and Fassinger (1993) found that women's valuing careers and work was related to liberal sex-role values, high math self-efficacy, and moderate attachment to and separation from their mothers.

Implications of Gender Research for Super's Theory

The research just cited has implications for how adolescent women deal with Super's career maturity concepts. In reviewing sex differences on both the Career Development Inventory and Crites's Career Maturity Inventory, Super (1990) and Westbrook (1983) state that girls tend to score slightly higher than boys on measures of career maturity. Although this is true, the research cited earlier suggests that adolescent girls may have difficulty using occupational information about traditionally male-dominated occupations. Further, they may have less confidence in their ability to make certain career-related decisions. These are not factors that are directly measured by any of Super's career decision-making scales. Rather than refute Super's concepts of vocational maturity, the research seems to suggest additional constructs to be considered.

Implications for Counseling

It is important for the counselor to provide as many avenues as possible for girls in making career choices. With regard to career planning, it is helpful to encourage women to explore many sources of career information, such as books and working in a field of interest. The counselor may find it necessary to encourage and support girls in taking math and to help them reduce their math anxiety. With regard to career exploration, counselors may find it helpful to discuss information obtained from various resources. Sometimes, teachers, parents, relatives, and especially friends are the sources of sex-biased information about occupations. Magazines, movies, and TV shows sometimes perpetuate these stereotypes. The research cited earlier and Lent, Brown, and Hackett's (1994) self-efficacy theory suggest that, although adolescent girls may know how to make career decisions, they may lack self-confidence in decision making. Regarding Super's World-of-Work Information scale, the impact of sex-role stereotyping is such that it may be helpful, if the Career Development Inventory is not used, to inquire about the accuracy of the information that girls have acquired. The same can be said about the Knowledge of Preferred Occuations scale. Thus, awareness of the difficulties posed by sex-role stereotyping for adolescents can help the counselor use Super's life-span theory incisively. Following is an example of how a counselor can use Super's life-span theory while being sensitive to sex-role stereotyping in adolescent career development.

A Counseling Example

The following dialogue takes place between Lucy, a high school sophomore, and her guidance counselor. Lucy is the same student who appeared as an example in the last chapter. In the previous example, she was 11 years old and talking to a counselor about problems at home that were having an effect on her schoolwork. Now she is 15. Her current counselor does not have the benefit of information from the Career Development Inventory but is able to use Super's concepts of career development.

CL: I wanted to talk to you because I'm not sure what to do next year. I'm thinking of applying to a bunch of different schools in two years. Maybe I can get a scholarship. I'm not sure.

CO: What have you been thinking about?

CL: Well, I really would like to go to medical school, but I'm not sure I can afford it, and I'm not sure I can get into it.

CO: What makes you hesitant? [The counselor wants to know more about Lucy's uncertainty in questioning her career plans.]

CL: Well, my father would like me to go to work soon. He says to me that he doesn't want to support me forever. And my boyfriend says if I go to med school we'll never get married until we're 55.

CO: It's hard to separate out what you might want from what others want for you. [The counselor wants to relieve Lucy of some of the burdens put on her by others.]

CL: I know. I've given a lot of thought to this. Most people might think it's only a dream, but I've got "A"s and "B"s in my courses. I think I might be able to do it. I know you need "B"s in sciences, at least, and "A"s, too, to get into medical school. I know that it takes a lot of training. There are scholarships in college, and it is possible to get money for medical school. I could work for a while to earn money to go to medical school.

CO: You seem to have found out a lot about college. [Lucy certainly seems to have some knowledge of her preferred occupation and some information about the abilities required. Further, she seems to have some world-of-work information.]

CL: Yes, I've talked to my family doctor about medicine, and my cousin works for another doctor. He was really nice and took some time to talk to me. I think it seems fine, but I'm not sure. There are other medical occupations that don't take so long to get into and are easier to get into. Maybe I should just go into nursing like my mother. I know there's a nursing shortage. It would be easier.

CO: You seem to be questioning yourself. [The counselor is impressed again that Lucy has done considerable initial career exploration and has some knowledge of decision making. Noticing that Lucy's confidence is beginning to wane, the counselor focuses on her self-efficacy beliefs.]

CL: It seems that I am in this all alone. [Lucy starts to cry.] Nobody seems to think I know what I'm doing. Sometimes, I think others want me to do things their way.

CO: You seem scared about doing it your way. [Lucy's lack of self-confidence seems to be getting stronger.]

CL: I am scared. Do you think I'm making the right decision?

CO: It's hard to know what the right decision is. I really am impressed that you've talked to so many people and seem to have such good information about your future. It is just hard to do things when there's not a lot of support. [The counselor doesn't know the "right" decision for Lucy but does want to support her career exploration and information seeking, and to support her growing feelings of self-efficacy.]

Being knowledgeable about the career maturity concepts of Super and being aware of gender biases in the culture, the counselor is able to understand Lucy's struggle with her career choice. Even though Lucy is asking for limited help in career selection (not being sure about the right area of health science), counseling serves a valuable purpose. Lucy's decision making is being supported in part by the knowledge the counselor has of the important components of career maturity. The goal of counseling in this particular portion of the interview is to help Lucy regain her confidence in her career decision-making ability. This goal certainly is consistent with Super's theoretical propositions regarding career maturity and the concept of reinforcing beliefs of self-efficacy.

CAREER DEVELOPMENT OF ADOLESCENTS OF COLOR

One area of research with adolescents of color has been the study of the applicability of the concept of career maturity. Studying the career maturity of 90 economically disadvantaged rural youth, Rojewski (1994) found that career-immature students were more likely to be African American, educationally disadvantaged, male, and indecisive about their career choice. More vocationally mature students (scoring high on Crites's Career Maturity Inventory), were more likely to be white, not educationally disadvantaged, female, and decisive about their career choice. McNair and Brown (1983) reported that white youths scored higher on measures of career development than did African Americans. In another study, Westbrook and Sanford (1991) found that white students scored higher on career maturity (on the attitude scale of the Career Maturity Inventory) than did African American students, but that the scores were not related to the appropriateness of the career choices of the African American students. Fouad and Kelly (1992) studied African American high school students and reported similar results. Compared to white students, Asian students scored lower in career maturity and indicated a stronger preference for a dependent style of decision making than did white students (Leong, 1991). Discussing the career maturity of Asian students, Leong and Serifica (1995) questioned the applicability of Super's concept to Asian Americans, pointing out the effect of differing cultural values on developmental tasks. These studies suggest the need for more research on the use of Super's concept of career maturity with adolescents of color.

Another focus of research has been the vocational aspirations of adolescents from different cultural backgrounds. Arbona (1990) and Kuvlesky and Juarez (1975) have pointed out that Hispanic/Latino and African American students often have aspirations that are more prestigious or desirable than the occupations that they actually enter. It may be that this gap results from expectations that do not match the availability of jobs, especially gender-stereotyped jobs (Arbona & Novy, 1991). For Hispanic/Latina women, aspirations to attend and stay in college were more likely to be achieved when the mother had more education and the student did not stereotype jobs by gender (Cardoza, 1991). Studying the career aspirations of 11th- and 12th-grade African American inner-city males, Parmer (1993) found that 32% thought they were likely or very likely to become professional athletes in ten years. The chances of becoming a professional athlete are about 1 in 50,000 (Parmer, 1993). These studies provide detailed information for counselors to consider when discussing vocational aspirations with adolescents of color.

Information about occupational opportunities and job duties is an important aspect of Super's life-span theory, making up much of the content of the Career Development Inventory. In her review, Smith (1983) reports many studies that suggest that African Americans, Hispanics, and Native Americans have less information about occupations than do white Americans. Not only is the lack of occupational information a barrier, but the attitude of employers who are biased against adolescents of color (Smith, 1983) is a very real concern.

Osipow (1975) questions whether Super's career development theory can be applied to poor African American males, because many must leave school early to take a variety of jobs that may be quite unrelated and unrewarding. They may not have the opportunity to explore occupations and learn decision-making skills, as do more affluent adolescents. Further, poor African American adolescent males, who make up a disproportionate number of unemployed young people, are apt to develop low self-esteem because of their perceptions of their lack of accomplishment. Such discouragement is apt to dissuade these adolescents from career exploration and planning. Such pessimism, however, does not mean that Super's theory has no value for adolescents of color. Rather, the counselor should be cautious in its application.

The theoretical work of Vondracek and his colleagues (Vondracek & Fouad, 1994; Vondracek, Lerner, & Schulenberg, 1983; Vondracek & Schulenberg, 1986), while being rather broad, has implications for use of

Super's theory with adolescents of color. Their theory focuses not only on individual development, but also on development within the context of the individual's historical and social situation. They highlight the importance of factors external to individuals that influence them: changes in the economy, local and federal social and educational policy, advances in technology affecting job performance and job availability, and a variety of other factors. Keeping in mind these environmental factors, the counselor can with more confidence use Super's developmental concepts regarding interests, capacities, values, and career maturity. The following example will help to clarify.

Harold is a 15-year-old African American student who lives in Detroit's inner city with his mother, two younger brothers, and an older and a younger sister. His mother is currently unemployed and is receiving welfare payments. Harold has been sent to talk to the counselor because he has been absent from school sporadically throughout the year and has recently missed a week of school. As Harold enters the counselor's office, she sees an attractive, average-size young man wearing jeans, a black T-shirt, a gold chain, and expensive sneakers. The counselor, to use the terms of Vondracek and his colleagues, is well aware of the context of the situation. The counselor has walked by Harold's building several times and has worked with many of the children of the neighborhood. The major employment of adolescents on Harold's street is in food service, drug sales, and prostitution—the latter two providing a far greater financial reward than the first. The counselor resists making hypotheses based only on Harold's appearance and address and wants to listen to him:

CL: [smiling] Sorry, I haven't been in school as much as I should. I've been sick a lot.

CO: What's happening with you, Harold? [The counselor does not want to get into an argument with Harold, but neither does she want to show that she will take his story at face value.]

CL: Times are tough.

CO: Yes, can you tell me what's been happening?

CL: I've needed to make some extra money. My mother just doesn't have enough money for the kids.

CO: It's been hard for you. [The counselor doesn't want to challenge Harold immediately. Rather, she prefers to take his side.]

CL: Yes. My little brother broke his leg, and my mother doesn't get much money anyway. I've had to pick some up on the side.

CO: Selling drugs? [The counselor decides to get to the point. She believes that Harold knows that she can guess this anyway.]

CL: Yes. [Defensively] Not too much—just enough.

CO: What are you going to do? [The counselor asks a very broad, open question about Harold's future to see in what direction he will take it.]

CL: I don't know. Maybe get a job. I'm not sure.

CO: Some thoughts about what you'd like to do? [The counselor wants to know how developed Harold's interests are.]

CL: I like cars—fixing them, riding in them, racing them, anything to do with them. And I like TV and movies.

CO: Have you thought about doing more with working on cars? [The counselor picks the activity that has the most vocational relevance and asks about it.]

CL: I've thought about the vo-tech school, but I don't know. I don't think that mechanics make enough money.

CO: Do you know how much they make? [Not having access to the Career Development Inventory or other maturity inventories, the counselor asks about Super's concept of world-of-work information.]

CL: No.

CO: Let's find out.

As the counselor goes with Harold to look at information about auto mechanics, she has several thoughts running through her mind. Super's life-span rainbow flashes through her head for a moment. But it is not the rainbow in Figure 6-2; rather, it is a truncated rainbow, as shown in Figure 8-2. The thicker the shaded area, the more important the role. Harold's role as child is most important (the role with the greatest shaded area). His role as worker has barely begun. Although she has not stated it at this point, the counselor believes that she is working with a life-or-death issue. If Harold continues to sell drugs, there is a chance that he may be killed or may kill someone. To Harold, being an auto mechanic may not be as attractive as selling drugs because of the excitement and the income. The counselor does not want to argue directly with Harold, feeling that she will lose. She is desperately trying to find a way for Harold to look into his future, so that his life will not end, as shown in Figure 8-2. Harold is not able (using Super's concept of decision making) to make appropriate decisions. The counselor hopes that she will be able to develop a relationship with Harold so that he will return, and so that she will gradually be able to make an impact. Harold's self-awareness and occupational awareness are limited. The counselor can look to the future, and she is scared. A number of the hundreds of students that she has talked with have died or are in jail.

Super's theory of life-span development for adolescents is not a panacea. It does provide guidelines for what to look for in career decision making. Sometimes, the context of a situation is so overwhelming that a theoretical conceptualization makes very little difference. It is possible in the case of Harold that the application of Super's concepts of career decision making will be just enough to keep Harold looking into a legitimate form of work. If the counselor is able to help Harold develop his interests in auto mechanics, find an auto mechanics program that he likes, and support his efforts, there may be a chance of his success. Or possibly, Harold and the counselor will arrive at some entirely different vocational goal. If Harold believes that the counselor is just some other adult who has a good income and for whom life is wonderful, then the counselor is likely to be discounted.

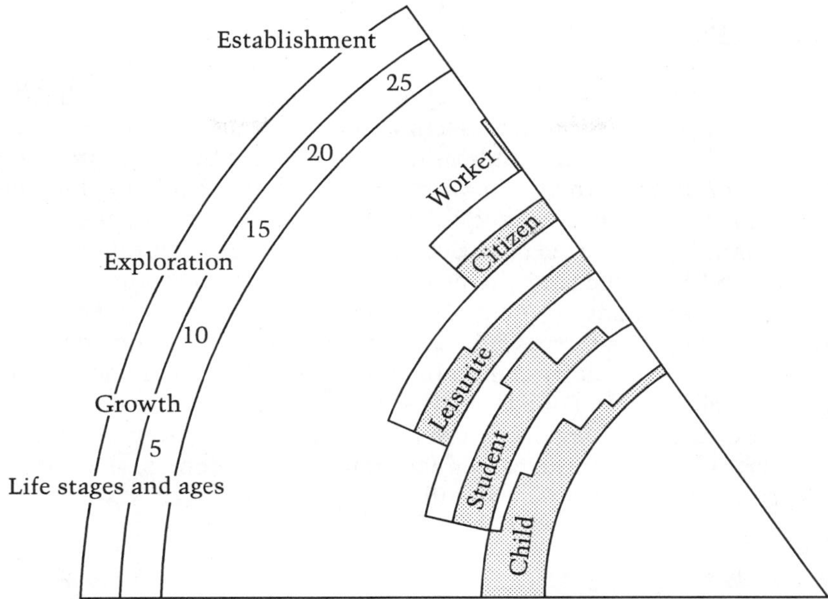

Figure 8-2 A truncated life-career rainbow. (Adapted from *Career Choice and Development,* by D. Brown, L. Brooks, and Associates. Copyright © 1984 by Jossey-Bass, Inc. Reprinted by permission.)

COUNSELOR ISSUES

A number of issues make counseling adolescents difficult. Earlier in the chapter, the notion (Piaget, 1977) that formal thinking brings with it a certain amount of egocentrism suggested that the client may think that he or she is right and the counselor is wrong. Further, Erikson's point that adolescents may be in an uncomfortable search for identity suggested that they need to separate themselves from adults and may be less likely to listen to them. In contrast, the counselor may be in a stage, according to Super's theory, of establishment or maintenance. Because the counselor has decided on a career, and has much information about that occupation and other occupations as well, the counselor's life situation is in marked contrast to that of the adolescent. These factors make it very important for the counselor to be empathic toward the client's decision-making issues. One of the frustrations of a counselor is that he or she can look ahead in terms of a client's occupational direction. Often, adolescents still have a limited time perspective and find it very difficult to see themselves in five or ten years. Super's life-stage theory makes it possible to see how vastly different the goals of the counselor can be from those of the client. This knowledge enables the counselor to structure limited goals consistent with the student's vocational maturity.

SUMMARY

Super and his colleagues offer concepts and inventories that can assist the counselor in working with adolescents. Being able to assess the development of interests, capacities, and values in a teenage client is quite helpful. Super's theory and the theory of Ginzberg, Ginsburg, Axelrad, and Herma are useful in this regard. Also helpful to the counselor are Super's concepts of career planning, career exploration, decision making, world-of-work information, and knowledge of the preferred occupational group. These concepts, used in combination, help the counselor assess the student's career orientation. Sex-role stereotyping and the obstacles confronting adolescents of color present additional problems. Knowledge of the context of the situation (Vondracek & Fouad, 1994) serves as a useful adjunct to Super's theory as it deals with barriers external to the individual. Since adolescence is such a critical time in the career decision-making process, the impact of Super's life-span theory can be significant.

References

Aneshensel, C. S., & Rosen, B. C. (1980). Domestic roles and sex differences in occupational expectations. *Journal of Marriage and the Family, 42,* 121–131.

Arbona, C. (1990). Career counseling research with Hispanics: A review of the literature. *The Counseling Psychologist, 18,* 300–323.

Arbona, C., & Novy, D. M. (1991). Career aspirations and expectations among Black, Mexican American, and White college students. *Career Development Quarterly, 39,* 231–239.

Aubrey, R. G. (1977). *Career development needs of thirteen-year-olds: How to improve career development programs.* Washington, DC: National Advisory Council for Career Education.

Betz, N. E., & Fitzgerald, L. F. (1987). *The career psychology of women.* Orlando, FL: Academic Press.

Betz, N. E., & Hackett, G. (1983). The relationship of mathematics self-efficacy expectations to the selection of science-based majors. *Journal of Vocational Behavior, 23,* 329–345.

Cardoza, D. (1991). College attendance and persistence among Hispanic women: An examination of some contributing factors. *Sex Roles, 24,* 133–147.

Chipman, S. F., Krantz, D. H., & Silver, R. (1992). Mathematics anxiety and science careers among able college women. *Psychological Science, 3,* 292–295.

Chipman, S. F., & Wilson, D. M. (1985). Understanding mathematics course enrollment and mathematics achievement: A synthesis of the research. In S. F. Chipman, L. R. Brush, & D. M. Wilson (Eds.), *Women and mathematics* (pp. 275–328). Hillsdale, NJ: Erlbaum.

Crites, J. O. (1965). Measurement of vocational maturity in adolescence: Attitude test of the Vocational Development Inventory. *Psychological Monographs, 79,* (1, Whole No. 595).

Crites, J. O. (1973). *Career Maturity Inventory.* Monterey, CA: California Test Bureau/McGraw-Hill.

Crites, J. O. (1978). *Theory and research handbook for the Career Maturity Inventory*. Monterey, CA: California Test Bureau/McGraw-Hill.

Davey, F. H., & Stoppard, J. M. (1993). Some factors affecting the occupational expectations of female adolescents. *Journal of Vocational Behavior, 43,* 235–330.

Erikson, E. H. (1963). *Childhood and society*. New York: Norton.

Fassinger, R. E. (1990). Causal models of career choice in two samples of college women. *Journal of Vocational Behavior, 36,* 225–248.

Fennema, E. & Sherman, J. A. (1977). Sex-related differences in mathematics achievement, spatial visualization, and affective factors. *American Educational Research Association Journal, 14,* 51–71.

Fottler, M. D., & Bain, T. (1980). Sex differences in occupational aspirations. *Academy of Management Journal, 23,* 144–149.

Fouad, N. A., & Kelly, T. J. (1992). The relation between attitudinal and behavioral aspects of career maturity. *Career Development Quarterly, 40,* 257–271.

Ginzberg, E. (1970). The development of a developmental theory of occupational choice. In W. H. Van Hoose & J. J. Pietrofesa (Eds.), *Counseling and guidance in the twentieth century* (pp. 58–67). Boston: Houghton Mifflin.

Ginzberg, E. (1972). Restatement of the theory of occupational choice. *Vocational Guidance Quarterly, 20,* 169–176.

Ginzberg, E. (1984). Career development. In D. Brown & L. Brooks (Eds.), *Career choice and development: Applying contemporary theories to practice* (pp. 169–191). San Francisco: Jossey-Bass.

Ginzberg, E., Ginsburg, S. W., Axelrad, S., & Herma, J. (1951). *Occupational choice: An approach to a general theory.* New York: Columbia University Press.

Gribbons, W. D., & Lohnes, P. R. (1968). *Emerging careers.* New York: Teachers College Press, Columbia University.

Hackett, G., & Betz, N. E. (1981). A self-efficacy approach to the career development of women. *Journal of Vocational Behavior, 18,* 326–329.

Hales, L. W., & Fenner, B. (1972). Work values of 5th, 8th, and 11th grade students. *Vocational Guidance Quarterly, 20,*199–203.

Hales, L. W., & Fenner, B. (1973). Sex and social class differences in work values. *Elementary School Guidance and Counseling, 8,* 26–32.

Healy, C. C., & Klein, S. P. (1973). *Manual for the New Mexico Career Education Test Series.* Hollywood, CA: Monitor.

Heilman, M. E. (1979). Perception of male models of femininity related to career choice. *Journal of Counseling Psychology, 19,* 308–313.

Hurwitz, R. E., & White, M. A. (1977). Effect of sex-linked vocational information on reported occupational choices of high school juniors. *Psychology of Women Quarterly, 2,* 149–156.

Inhelder, B., & Piaget, J. (1958). *The growth of logical thinking from childhood to adolescence.* New York: Basic Books.

Kapes, J. T., & Strickler, R. T. (1975). A longitudinal study of change in work values between ninth and twelfth grade as related to high school curriculums. *Journal of Vocational Behavior, 6,* 81–93.

Kelso, G. I. (1977). The relation of school grade to ages and stages in vocational development. *Journal of Vocational Behavior, 10,* 287–301.

Kuvlesky, W. P., & Juarez, R. (1975). Mexican American youth and the American dream. In J. S. Picou & R. E. Campbell (Eds.), *Career behavior of special groups: Theory, research, and practice* (pp. 241–296). Columbus, OH: Merrill.

Lent, R. W., Brown, S. D., & Hackett, G. (1994). Toward a unified social cognitive theory of career and academic interest, choice, and performance. *Journal of Vocational Behavior, 45,* 79–122.

Lent, R. W., & Hackett, G. (1987). Career self-efficacy: Empirical status and future directions. *Journal of Vocational Behavior, 30,* 347–382.

Lent, R. W., Lopez, F. G., & Bieschke, K. J. (1991). Mathematics self-efficacy: Sources and relations to science-based career choice. *Journal of Counseling Psychology, 38,* 424–430.

Lent, R. W., Lopez, F. G., & Bieschke, K. J. (1993). Predicting mathematics-related choice and success behaviors: Test of an expanded social cognitive model. *Journal of Vocational Behavior, 42,* 223–236.

Leong, F. T. L. (1991). Career development attributes and occupational values of Asian American and White American college students. *Career Development Quarterly, 39,* 221–230.

Leong, F. T. L., & Serifica, F. C. (1995). Career development of Asian Americans: A research area in need of a good theory. In F. T. L. Leong (Ed.), *Career development and vocational behavior of racial and ethnic minorities* (pp. 67–102). Mahwah, NJ: Erlbaum.

Lunneborg, P. W., & Gerry M. H. (1977). Sex differences in changing sex stereotyped vocational interests. *Journal of Counseling Psychology, 24,* 247–250.

McKenna, A. E., & Ferrero, G. W. (1991). Ninth-grade students' attitudes toward non-traditional occupations. *Career Development Quarterly, 40,* 168–181.

McNair, D., & Brown, D. (1983). Predicting the occupational aspirations, occupational expectations and career maturity of black and white male and female 10th graders. *Vocational Guidance Quarterly, 32,* 29–36.

Miller, J. (1977). *Career development needs of 9-year-olds: How to improve career development programs.* Washington, DC: National Advisory Council for Career Education.

Monaco, N. M., & Gaier, E. L. (1992). Single sex versus coeducational environment and achievement in adolescent females. *Adolescence, 27,* 579–594.

Multon, K. D., Brown, S. D. & Lent, R. W. (1991). Relation of self-efficacy beliefs to academic outcomes: A meta-analytic investigation. *Journal of Counseling Psychology, 38,* 30–38.

Nevill, D. D., & Super, D. E. (1989). *The Values Scale: Theory, application, and research* (2nd. Ed.). Palo Alto, CA: Consulting Psychologists Press.

O'Brien, K. M., & Fassinger, R. E. (1993). A causal model of the career orientation and career choice of adolescent women. *Journal of Counseling Psychology, 40,* 456–569.

O'Hara, R. P., & Tiedeman, D. V. (1959). Vocational self-concept in adolescence. *Journal of Counseling Psychology, 6,* 292–301.

Osipow, S. H. (1975). The relevance of theories of career development to special groups: Problems, needed data, and implications. In J. S. Picou & R. E. Campbell (Eds.), *Career behavior of special groups* (pp. 9–22). Columbus, OH: Merrill.

Osipow, S. H. (1983). *Theories of career development* (3rd. ed.). Englewood Cliffs, NJ: Prentice-Hall.

Osipow, S. H., & Gold, J. A. (1968). Personal adjustment and career development. *Journal of Counseling Psychology, 15,* 439–443.

Parmer, T. (1993). The athletic dream—but what are the career dreams of other African American urban high school students? *Journal of Career Development, 20,* 131–145.

Pedro, J. D., Wolleat, P., Fennema, E., & Becker, A. D. (1981). Election of high school mathematics by females and males: Attributions and attitudes. *American Educational Research Journal, 18,* 207–218.

Piaget, J. (1977). *The development of thought: Equilibration of cognitive structure.* New York: Viking Press.

Robison-Awana, P., Kehle, T. J., & Jenson, W. R. (1986). But what about smart girls? Adolescent self-esteem and sex role perceptions as a function of academic achievement. *Journal of Educational Psychology, 78,* 179–183.

Rojewski, J. W. (1994). Career indecision types for rural adolescents from disadvantaged and nondisadvantaged backgrounds. *Journal of Counseling Psychology, 41,* 356–363.

Rosen, B. C., & Aneshensel, C. S. (1978). Sex differences in the educational-occupational expectation process. *Social Forces, 57,* 164–185.

Smith, E. J. (1983). Issues in racial minorities' career behavior. In W. B. Walsh & S. H. Osipow (Eds.), *Handbook of vocational psychology* (Vol. 1, pp. 161–222). Hillsdale, NJ: Erlbaum.

Starishevsky, R., & Matlin, N. A. (1963). A model for the translation of self-concept into vocational terms. In D. E. Super, R. Starishevsky, N. Matlin, & J. P. Jordaan (Eds.), *Career development: Self-concept theory* (pp. 33–41.) (Research Monograph No. 4). New York: College Entrance Examination Board.

Super, D. E. (1955). Personality integration through vocational counseling. *Journal of Counseling Psychology, 2,* 217–226.

Super, D. E. (1990). A life-span, life-space approach to career development. In D. Brown, L. Brooks, & Assoc. (Eds.), *Career choice and development: Applying contemporary theories to practice* (2nd. ed., pp. 197–261). San Francisco: Jossey-Bass.

Super, D. E., Bohn, M. J., Forrest, D. J., Jordaan, J. P., Lindeman, R. H., & Thompson, A. S. (1971). *Career Development Inventory.* New York: Teachers College Press, Columbia University.

Super, D. E., Crites, J. O., Hummel, R. C., Moser, H. P., Overstreet, P. L., & Warnath, C. F. (1957). *Vocational development: A framework for research.* New York: Teachers College Press, Columbia University.

Super, D. E., Osborne, W. L., Walsh, D. J., Brown, S. D., & Niles, S. G., (1992). Developmental career assessment and counseling: The C-DAC model. *Journal of Counseling and Development, 71,* 74–80.

Super, D. E., & Overstreet, P. L. (1960). *The vocational maturity of ninth-grade boys.* New York: Teachers College Press, Columbia University.

Super, D. E., Thompson, A. S., & Lindeman, R. H. (1988). *Adult Career Concerns Inventory.* Palo Alto, CA: Consulting Psychologists Press.

Thompson, A. S., & Lindeman, R. H. (1981). *Career Development Inventory: Vol. 1. User's manual.* Palo Alto, CA: Consulting Psychologists Press.

Tierney, R. J., & Herman, A. (1973). Self-estimates of ability in adolescence. *Journal of Counseling Psychology, 20,* 298–302.

Trice, A. D., Hughes, M. A., Odom, C., Woods, K., & McClellan, N. C. (1995). The origins of children's career aspirations: IV. Testing hypothesis from four theories. *The Career Development Quarterly, 45,* 307–322.

Van Buren, J. B., Kelly, K. R., & Hall, A. S. (1993). Modeling nontraditional career choices: Effects of gender and school location on response to a brief videotape. *Journal of Counseling Psychology, 20,* 298–302.

Vondracek, F. W., & Fouad, N. A. (1994). Developmental contextualism: An integrative framework for theory and practice. In M. L. Savickas & R. W. Lent, *Convergence in career development theories* (pp. 207–213.). Palo Alto, CA: Consulting Psychologists Press.

Vondracek, F. W., Lerner, R. W., & Schulenberg, J. E. (1983). The concept of development in vocational theory and intervention. *Journal of Vocational Behavior, 23,* 179–202.

Vondracek, F. W., & Schulenberg, J. E. (1986). Career development in adolescence: Some conceptual and intervention issues. *Vocational Guidance Quarterly, 34,* 247–254.

Westbrook, B. W. (Ed.). (1970). *The Cognitive Vocational Maturity Test.* Unpublished test, North Carolina State University, Department of Psychology, Raleigh.

Westbrook, B. W. (1983). Career maturity: The concept, the instrument, and the research. In W. B. Walsh & S. H. Osipow (Eds.), *Handbook of vocational psychology* (Vol. 1, pp. 263–304). Hillsdale, NJ: Erlbaum.

Westbrook, B. W., Buck, R. W., Jr., Wynne, D, C., & Sanford, E. (1994). Career maturity in adolescence: Reliability and validity of self-ratings of ability by gender and ethnicity. *Journal of Career Assessment, 2,* 125–161.

Westbrook, B. W., & Sanford, E. E. (1991). The validity of career maturity attitude measures among Black and White high school students. *The Career Development Quarterly, 40,* 198–208.

Wise, L. L. (1985). Project TALENT: Mathematics course participation in the 1960s and its career consequences. In S. F. Chipman, L. R. Brush, & D. M. Wilson (Eds.), *Women and mathematics* (pp. 25–58). Hillsdale, NJ: Erlbaum.

9

Late Adolescent and Adult Career Development

Super's life-span theory of late adolescent and adult career development makes use of two major concepts: life role and life stage. For Super, important roles for an individual are studying, working, community service, home and family, and leisure activities, as illustrated earlier in Figure 6-2. The importance, or salience, of these roles can be seen by a person's participation in an activity, commitment to the activity, or how much that activity is valued. Values are also significant in Super's theory, as can be seen by the development of several values inventories (Super, 1970; Super & Nevill, 1986, 1989).

In Super's theory, roles form the context within which to view the basic stages of career development: exploration, establishment, maintenance, and disengagement. The exploration stage includes the substages of crystallization, specification, and implementation. Next follows the establishment stage, which includes the tasks of stabilizing, consolidating, and advancing. The substages of holding, updating, and innovating make up the maintenance stage. Finally, the disengagement stage includes deceleration, retirement planning, and retirement living. A key aspect of Super's theory is that these stages are not entirely age-related. Individuals may recycle, or go through these stages, at many different times in life. Explanations and examples of counseling conceptualizations that can be useful in these stages are given in this chapter. Theorists and researchers have questioned whether these stages apply to women and people of color. Research on women suggests several factors to be considered. Atkinson, Morten, and Sue (1989) offer a series of developmental stages that people of color may experience. This provides another dimension to Super's view of the life span. Developmental issues that arise for the counselor in dealing with people in various life stages will help to elucidate some of the issues that counselors face in counseling adults.

ROLE SALIENCE

Super (1990) believes that people differ in terms of the importance they assign to work in their lives. As shown by the research of Kanungo (1982), not everyone wants to work. Work can vary in importance to an individual at different points in that person's life. In fact, the normative data provided by Nevill and Super (1986) for the Salience Inventory show that people at different ages, across different cultures, value work differentially. For example, high school students in the United States tend to value work, home, and leisure more than study and community service. In general, this is also true for college students. However, adults in the United States tend to value work and family life more than study, community service, or leisure. Not surprisingly, there are great individual differences across all age ranges.

In the Salience Inventory, Nevill and Super (1986) measure three aspects of life roles: commitment, participation, and value expectations. Another important aspect of work salience, but one not measured by the Salience Inventory, is knowledge of roles. The following pages describe first the life roles measured by the Salience Inventory (studying, working, community service, home and family, and leisure activities) and then different indicators of the salience of these life roles.

Life Roles

Studying Studying includes a number of activities that may take place throughout the life span. During the school years, these include taking courses, going to school, and studying in a library or at home. We know that people may choose to continue education at any time during their lifetime. Newspapers show pictures of 80-year-old men and women receiving their high school diplomas or college degrees. Many people continue their education on a part-time basis at some stage during their lives for pleasure or to enhance their job advancement or success.

Working Working may start in childhood, when children help their parents around the home, mow the lawn, or take jobs such as baby-sitting and delivering newspapers. It is common for adolescents to take a part-time job after school or during the summer. Many adults work at one or more jobs at various times during their lives. During retirement, jobs for pay or profit may be for fewer hours than they were during a person's younger years.

Community Service Community service includes a broad range of voluntary service groups that may be social, political, or religious. Young people often participate in Boy or Girl Scouts, Indian Guides, or boys' or girls' clubs, which have as a part of their purpose either direct service to others or indirect service through the collection of money or goods. These groups, along with service fraternities and sororities, are available in various forms to adolescents. Activities may include literacy projects, environmental cleanup, or assistance in hospitals. Activity in these service groups, along with participation in political parties and trade unions, is available to adults throughout the entire life span.

Home and Family This role can vary greatly depending on the age of the individual. A child may help out at home by taking care of his or her room or by doing the dishes or mowing the lawn. Adolescents may take on more responsibility by doing more complex tasks and ones with more responsibility, such as baby-sitting. For adults, responsibility for children and a home becomes much more important than it was in earlier years. Adults may have to take care not only of their own children but also of their aging parents. As adults enter their later years, their responsibility for home and family may increase or markedly decrease. For example, grandparents may live with their children and/or grandchildren, live in adult communities, or live alone.

Leisure Activities The nature and importance of leisure are likely to vary considerably throughout the lifetime. Leisure is a particularly important and valued activity of children and adolescents. Often, this includes active participation in sports as well as more sedentary activities such as watching television and reading. The term *lifetime sports* refers to sports that are less physically demanding and require fewer participants, so are easier for adults to participate in at various points in their lifetime. Contrast football and basketball with golf, tennis, and bowling. For adults, leisure activities may become more sophisticated and intellectual, such as attending the theater and museums or joining groups that discuss books, stocks and bonds, or religious issues.

Indicators of the Salience of Life Roles

Not only does the importance of the roles change during a person's lifetime, but the nature of the involvement also changes. This involvement can be measured in terms of participation, commitment, knowledge, and value expectations.

Participation Participation in a role can take a number of different forms. It can include spending time on something, improving a performance, accomplishing something, being active in an organization concerned with an activity, or just being active. A slightly less direct way of participating is through talking to people or reading about an activity. The concept of participation is particularly useful because it measures the actual behavior of an individual, not just what he or she says is important. For example, a person may say that he is committed to his religion but may never pray or go to church (participate).

Commitment Commitment often concerns future plans. It may deal with a desire to be involved or be active. It also concerns the present: feeling proud of doing well or being personally committed. A less direct way of being committed is to admire people who are good at something.

Knowledge Acquiring information about a role by experiencing the role either directly or by observing it brings about knowledge, a cognitive aspect of role importance. A child's knowledge may be limited to leisure and study. Knowledge of parental roles is gained by observation; only much later will the experience be direct. Knowledge of the worker role may be very different for a food service worker in high school and for that same individual employed as an engineer or physician 15 years later. The Salience Inventory does not measure knowledge. A measurement of knowledge is available only for the worker role in the Career Development Inventory, in the Decision Making, World-of-Work Information, and Knowledge of the Preferred Occupational Group subscales (see Chapter 8). However, when talking with clients about their study, leisure, or community service roles, the counselor may find assessing the client's knowledge to be helpful. For example, new college students often have little knowledge of the changing studying role that they will soon encounter. However, they are likely to be committed to the role and soon will participate in it. Knowledge, commitment, and participation, along with value expectations, are components of role salience.

Value Expectations Similar theoretically to the concept of commitment, value expectations concern the opportunity for various roles to meet a variety of value needs. There are many values related to career issues. Values are measured by two of Super's instruments: the Values Scale (Super & Nevill, 1989) and the Salience Inventory (Nevill & Super, 1986). The Values Scale lists 21 different values; 14 of these are used in the Value Expectation scale of the Salience Inventory. These 14 value expectations are described in the following paragraphs in terms of how they can be met in the five life roles. Reading through this list of values, the counselor can determine the relevance of the values for his or her clientele and thus decide which of the many values to focus on when conceptualizing client issues.

Ability utilization: For some, an important value, regardless of the role performed, is using one's skills and knowledge. This may mean doing work or studying to develop one's ability. It also refers to applying one's skills in community service or being a good parent.

Achievement: Regardless of role, *achievement* refers to the feeling that one has produced good results. Individuals with this value set high standards for their work or study. If the role is leisure, achievement may mean a feeling of accomplishing something significant in sports or music.

Aesthetics: This value deals with finding beauty in the role that one chooses. It is often associated with artistic values, which are satisfied by creating a picture, a musical composition, or a poem.

Altruism: Referring to helping others with problems, the need for altruism can clearly be met in several roles. One can help people with personal problems in one's family and in one's career (social work). Also, there are many community organizations, such as the Red Cross, that are devoted to helping others. Athletic coaching is a way of helping others in the pursuit of leisure.

Autonomy: Some individuals value the opportunity to be independent and work on their own. They may want to make their own decisions about studying, about sports, about how to run their family.

Creativity: To be able to discover or design new things can be important in a variety of situations. Being able to try out new ideas in a hobby or in a community organization can be as important to some people as creating a new product at work.

Economic rewards: To have a high standard of living and the material things that one desires requires income derived from the working role. Although study may eventually lead to high income, and a wealthy family serves as a source of high income for a few people, the primary role for obtaining economic rewards is as a worker.

Lifestyle: To plan one's own activities, to live the way one wants to, can be an overriding issue for some people. Since studying is a solitary activity, studying the way one wants can sometimes be done rather easily. Some leisure activities can be chosen without regard to other people's needs. However, working is most often a role done with others, and certainly community service and family life make it difficult to live life the way one wants, unless individuals can find people who feel the same way they do.

Physical activity: Although being physically active in studying is quite difficult, the other roles allow opportunity for physical activity. One can do community service by helping repair church or community center buildings. With one's family, one can choose to be active in taking trips, boating, or making things.

Prestige: Many roles provide the opportunity for individuals to be acknowledged for what they accomplish. Although prestige is ordinarily associated with the work role, teachers recognize good students, and local communities recognize the contributions that citizens have made to them. A wife, husband, or children can acknowledge the contributions of a parent or a spouse.

Risk: Some people like to have dangerous or exciting challenges in their lives. Leisure can provide that opportunity. Activities such as mountain climbing, wind surfing, and parachute jumping provide such an occasion. In work, logging, high-rise steel construction, and race car driving may provide another outlet. Risks taken in community service, studying, or home and family may be more psychological and less physical. In studying, taking risks could include trying a very challenging course, procrastinating until the night before an examination to study, or waiting until the last minute to write a paper. For home and family, taking risks may mean surprising someone with a gift or, to be more negative, having an affair.

Social interaction: Being with other people and working in a group can be accomplished in all roles. Some people prefer to study in a group, and some enjoy working as part of a team on a project. Certainly, community service provides that opportunity. Working with one's children and spouse to have a pleasant vacation or to paint a room can be enjoyable to some people. Leisure activity provides the opportunity for many types of social interaction, for example, parties, sports, and visiting friends.

Variety: Being able to change work activities is very pleasing to some people. Variety in other roles may mean changing the subject that one is studying or moving from one type of task at work to another. Being involved in many different sports or community organizations can also meet these needs. At home, one can spend time with children or various relatives, cook, clean, and socialize.

Working conditions: Having the proper light to study, a pleasing home, or the right equipment for sports activities can be necessary for some people. Also, working conditions, which would include lighting, pleasant temperature, and good equipment, can be important in work with community organizations or in the workplace itself.

When counseling using Super's theory, counselors will sometimes have the Salience Inventory available to them; at other times, they will not. Assessing which roles are important to a client and which value expectations are met by the roles can be extremely helpful. To do this, the counselor may want to make use of the Values Scale. Although the Minneosota Importance Questionnaire (see Chapter 3) could be used, Hackbarth and Mathay (1991) found only low to moderate correlations between similar scales of the two inventories. In addition to the concepts just listed, which are contained in but not measured by the Salience Inventory, the Values Scale includes the following: authority (telling others what to do); personal development (developing as a person); social relations (being with friends); cultural identity (being with people of the same race and religion); physical prowess (working hard physically); and economic security (having secure and regular employment). A counselor working with Super's concepts for the first time may wish to become comfortable with the five roles measured in the Salience Inventory. Also, incorporating values into the career stages described in the next section may be useful. Later, the counselor can memorize the values in the Values Scale for use in counseling sessions. To help the reader understand how the Salience Inventory's and the Values Scale's constructs can be useful, they will be integrated into examples demonstrating counseling issues in each of the four major adult life stages described in the next section.

ADULT LIFE STAGES

Super's (1990) concepts of life stages and substages can be confusing because they are both age-related and not age-related. They are age-related in the sense that there are typical times when people go through stages of exploration, establishment, maintenance, and decline or disengagement. However, it is also possible for an individual to experience a stage at almost any time during his or her lifetime. Further, one can be involved in several stages at one time. Super (1990) used the term *maxicycle* to describe the five major lifestages. *Minicycle* is a term used to describe the growth, exploration, establishment, maintenance, and disengagement that can occur within any of the stages in the maxicycle. For example, a 42-year-old dentist could be in the establishment stage. She may become less concerned with stabilizing and advancing in her practice, explore ways to maintain herself in her practice, gradually disengage from the establishment stage, and grow into the maintenance stage. Or more dramatically, she could start to explore other career options and discover that she wants to become an artist and disengage from dentistry. Each of these is an example of a minicycle within a maxicycle. The concept of the minicycle highlights the dynamic nature of Super's theory. Throughout their lives, individuals are constantly trying out new ideas and activities as they make transitions to a new stage. For consistency and clarity, the stages and substages of the maxicycle will first be presented in the typical order in which the average person encounters them. Then, the concept of *recycling,* which refers to going through aspects of the stages at various times in one's life, will be discussed.

Super's life-stage theory has a long history. Beginning in 1951 with the Career Pattern Study (Super et al., 1957), the study of life-stage theory has continued ever since. Super's book *The Psychology of Careers* (1957) presented a more general exposition of his ideas. The work of Gribbons and Lohnes (1968), Crites (1979), and Super (Thompson & Lindeman, 1981) presents a vast array of studies on vocational maturity and measures that were developed to describe the concepts of maturity and life stages. After studying adolescents, Super paid considerable attention to developing instruments with which to measure and define adult development (Super & Kidd, 1979; Super & Knasel, 1979). From this work, Super, Thompson, and Lindeman (1988) developed the Adult Career Concerns Inventory (ACCI). This instrument, like others that Super has developed, is useful in counseling. It also assists in the conceptualization of life stages. Confirmation of the validity of these stages can be seen in studies such as that of Smart and Peterson (1994), who found that 219 male and 238 female Australian adults could be classified accurately using the ACCI. Additional support was found for 881 Portuguese employed men on the ACCI (Duarte, 1995). These stages and their substages are described in more detail in the following pages.

Exploration

According to Super (1957), the exploration stage ranges from about 15 to 25 years of age. This stage includes the efforts that individuals make to get a better idea of occupational information, choose career alternatives, decide on occupations, and start to work. This stage includes three substages: crystallizing, specifying, and implementing.

Crystallizing This is the stage in which people clarify what they want to do. They learn about entry-level jobs that may be appropriate for them, and they learn what skills are required by the jobs that interest them. Many high school students go through this stage. Much of what was described in the previous chapter in terms of the realization of abilities, interests, and values is applicable to this stage. Work experience and work knowledge help the person narrow his or her choices. When a person changes fields, as an adult may do at any time, he or she is likely to recycle through this stage to reexamine interests, abilities, and values.

Specifying For college graduates, this stage occurs in the early 20s. For those who seek employment directly after high school graduation, specification occurs earlier. As these young people must choose their first full-time job, they are required to *specify* their preferences so they may find an employer. For those who go on to graduate school or specialized education, such as pediatric nursing or advanced electrical engineering, preferences must also be specified. While some must specify an occupation, others must specify a job within an occupation. They may wish to have part-time work or summer work in the occupation of their choice. For example, a student may work as a part-time nursing assistant in a hospital so that he or she may reaffirm that the choice is appropriate.

Implementing This is the last phase prior to working. People at this point are making plans to fulfill their career objectives. They may be starting to network by meeting people who can help them get a job. Talking to a counselor in a university career-planning and placement office would be part of this phase. People may be writing résumés, having job interviews, or deciding between potential employers.

Example This example illustrates the exploration stage. Incorporated into the example is the use of the Salience Inventory, the Values Scale, the Adult Career Concerns Inventory, and the Strong Interest Inventory. The Adult Career Concerns Inventory (Super et al., 1988) gives scores for each stage and substage. The counselor will use the scores from these inventories, as well as the concepts, to think about clients' issues using a counseling model similar to that described by Super, Osborne, Walsh, Brown, and Niles (1992).

Ben is a white college junior in his second semester. His father is a stockbroker, and his mother is an airline ticket agent. He lives about 50 miles from the large city where he is enrolled in a major university as a business major. He has come to the counseling center because he is not sure whether or not to seek a business career, and if in business, he is not

Table 9-1 *Summary of Ben's Scores on Four Inventories*

Inventory	*High Scores*
The Adult Career Concerns Inventory	Crystallizing Specifying Implementing
The Salience Inventory	*Leisure* Participation Commitment Values expectations *Home and Family* Values expectations
The Values Scale	Economic rewards Advancement Prestige Risk
The Strong Interest Inventory	*Basic Interests* Athletics Sales Law and politics *Occupational Scales* Human resources director Credit manager Marketing executive

sure of the direction. In their first meeting, the counselor assigns the Adult Career Concerns Inventory, the Values Scale, the Salience Inventory, and the Strong Interest Inventory. The results, summarized in Table 9-1, show that Ben has considerable concern about the crystallization substage, the specification substage, and the implementation substage. About the other stages (establishment, maintenance, and disengagement) he has little or no concern. Regarding his scores on the Salience Inventory, Ben has high scores on leisure activities for participation, commitment, and values expectations. His scores for studying indicate moderate participation in commitment and low values expectations. Working also has moderate participation, commitment, and values expectations. The scores on the Community Service and the Home and Family scales are low to moderate, except for a high score on values expectations for home and family. On the Values Scale, Ben scores high on economic rewards, advancement, prestige, and risk. In brief, his Strong Interest Inventory reveals high interest in athletics, sales, and law and politics. He has high scores in the Occupational Scales cluster in several business occupations. He has interests that are similar to those of marketing executives, human resource directors, and credit managers. After having talked with the counselor once and having taken these inventories, Ben returns to talk about the results. Several segments of the discussion are used to illustrate a number of Super's concepts:

CL: Those were a lot of tests. I'm curious how I did.
CO: We'll go over as much as we can today, but we may not finish—in fact probably won't. [There is a lot of material to discuss and the counselor does not want to rush, as he realizes that Ben is at a critical point in his career decision making.]
CL: Well, OK. Those tests really got me thinking.
CO: What about?
CL: I really started to think about what I'm going to do. I graduate in another year, and I really haven't thought a lot about it. My friends and I talk some, but mainly we throw names around of companies and talk about who's going to have the nicest car—things like that.
CO: But you're concerned. [The counselor wonders about Ben's motivation for career counseling. However, he remembers Ben's high scores on the Adult Career Concerns Inventory, which would probably indicate that Ben is indeed concerned.]
CL: We joke about it, but sometimes it makes me nervous thinking about what happens in a year. It seems as if things will just end, and it's blank from there.
CO: Well, let's take a look at one of the inventories that you finished. [The counselor shows Ben his scores on the Adult Career Concerns Inventory.]
CL: High scores on all the exploration stages. What does that mean?
CO: You seem to be unsure of what you want to do, quite concerned about a job, and maybe wondering how to get one.
CL: Yes, all of those things, but I always thought of them as a big jumble, not as three different steps.
CO: Yes, it's hard to decide what you want to do and find a job all at once. [The counselor is pleased that Ben seems to be taking the process seriously and understands the need to take things one at a time].

Ben and the counselor go on to talk further about the results of the Adult Career Concerns Inventory and its meaning for Ben:

CO: I also wanted to talk to you about the role of work in your life.
CL: I know that I have to work hard to make a lot of money.
CO: What would you like to do with your money if you made $100,000 your first year? [Wanting to see if Ben's role values are the same as those in the Salience Inventory, the counselor wants to know in what areas Ben would participate and where his commitment is.]
CL: I'd put a down payment on a boat and a sports car and get the best stereo you ever saw. I would really like to race motorcycles, so I would get a new one. I'd find as much time as I could to mess around.
CO: You certainly want to have fun. [Leisure activities come through loud and clear in terms of participation, commitment, and values expectations. The counselor is interested in Ben's commitment to studying and working.]
CL: Yes, school is a bore. I like summertime, when I can just work and take it easy. I'm a lifeguard at a hotel pool. It's a busy hotel, but the pool isn't

very busy most times, so I get to relax, chat with people, have a good time. It's not much of a job, but the pay is OK.

CO: Pay seems important to you. [The counselor starts to explore Ben's work values.]

CL: Yes, it really is. I would like to have a nice home someday and to be able to have some free time to be with my family to do things. I'm not sure I want a family for a while. But someday I would.

CO: Sounds like you're starting to think more and more about the future. [The counselor notes that, for home and family, values expectations come out high on the Salience Inventory, while participation and commitment do not. That seems to fit with Ben's statement, as home and family are not an immediate commitment for him but may be in future years.]

Ben and the counselor continue to discuss his plans and goals. They are getting ready to talk about the Strong Interest Inventory. Wanting to put the Strong Interest Inventory in context, the counselor talks to Ben about its purpose:

CO: Let's look at your interest inventory results. It's helpful to talk about interests and careers in terms of the importance of working to you. [Not wanting to overstate the value of the Strong Interest Inventory, the counselor wants to establish a context for it.]

CL: Well, I'm curious about what it has to say.

CO: When we look at it, it may be helpful to remember that work seems to be a means to an end for you. You certainly want to get the things that work provides for you. This inventory will help you to understand how similar your interests are to those of people in different occupations.

CL: As you talk, it does sound important. I've been thinking so much about what I want to do with what I will make. I've been less concerned about what I will do.

CO: Some of your basic areas of interest seem to be in athletics and sales. [The counselor starts with the two highest scores on the Basic Interests scales.]

CL: Yes, I really like to do fun things like play tennis, basketball, volleyball, and race boats and cars.

CO: It would seem that way. The values test that you took seems to emphasize risk as well. [The counselor wants to integrate the test scores with each other and to form a clearer impression of Ben.]

CL: Sales is interesting to me. I never thought about that. I think I would like it. It's a real challenge. One summer I spent trying to sell as much as I could in an appliance store. They gave me commissions. I really did a job.

CO: You really seem to have got a lot of satisfaction from that accomplishment. [The counselor hears how important achievement is to Ben and reinforces it. At this point, the counselor is aware that Ben's values are very different from his own values. The counselor's values are more altruistic and creative, whereas Ben's are more toward achievement and economic rewards. The counselor does not want to devalue Ben just because their values are so different.]

In a counseling situation that uses four different inventories, it is impossible to give a good overview of the entire test interpretation process. However, the purpose of this illustration has been to show how the counselor can make use of Super's developmental concepts and inventories to help someone who is in the exploration stage. The issues that are important in the exploration stage are quite different from those in the establishment stage.

Establishment

The establishment stage generally ranges from the age of 25 to about 45. In general, *establishment* refers to getting established in one's work by starting in a job that is likely to mean the start of working life. In skilled, management, and professional occupations, this means work in an occupation that will probably be steady for many years. For those in semiskilled and unskilled occupations, *establishment* does not mean that a person will be established in a particular job or organization. Instead, it refers to the fact that the person will be working for much of his or her lifetime (Super et al., 1988). The substages of *stabilizing, consolidating,* and *advancing* refer to career behaviors that take place once working life has started.

Stabilizing Getting started in a job requires a minimum amount of permanence. The individual needs to know that he or she will be in this job for more than a few months. Stabilization is concerned with settling down in a job and being able to meet those job requirements that will ensure that a person can stay in the field in which he or she has started. At this point, an individual may be apprehensive about whether he or she has the skills necessary to stay with the work. As persons become more comfortable, they start to consolidate their position.

Consolidating Once a person has stabilized his or her position, often occurring in the late 20s and early 30s, consolidation can take place. The person starts to become more comfortable with her or his job or work and wishes to be known as a dependable producer, one who is competent and can be relied on by others. In this stage, individuals want bosses and coworkers to know that they can do the job well. Once they can consolidate their position and can feel secure, then they can consider advancement to higher positions.

Advancing Occurring any time in the establishment stage, but usually after stabilizing and consolidating have taken place, *advancing* refers to moving ahead into a position of more responsibility with higher pay. Particularly in business, there is a concern with advancing to positions of higher authority. To do so, individuals often plan how to get ahead and how to improve their chances of being promoted. They want their superiors to know that they do well and are capable of handling more responsibility.

Example Lucy, whose case was discussed in the two previous chapters, is now a 28-year-old physical therapist working with people who have spinal cord injuries. She lives in a large city, is unmarried, and works in a nationally known hospital on a staff with many physical therapists. Lucy has sought counseling because she has not been happy with her personal life or her work. She has recently ended a three-year relationship with a man and finds that she is lonely, having not attended to friendships when she was romantically involved. Though she had intended to go to medical school, she had been afraid that she could not finance her education, could not stay in school and study for four years after college, and needed income immediately. Now she is questioning that decision and trying to decide whether to apply to medical school. She is clear that her choice is within the field of health but is hesitant to apply to medical school. She feels frustrated in her work because she questions her supervisor's competence and feels limited by the job duties of a physical therapist. She wonders if she would be happier if she had more responsibility for patients, just like the physicians do who work with her patients.

In counseling Lucy, the counselor decides to use the Salience Inventory, the Values Scale, and the Adult Career Concerns Inventory. The counselor hopes that these instruments will help Lucy understand the importance of work in her life, the values that are important to her, and the developmental concerns that matter most to her. There are differences between Lucy's participation scores on the Salience Inventory and her commitment and values expectations scores (Table 9-2). Lucy's participation is in working, followed by leisure activities, followed by home and family. Her high scores on the Values Scales are for autonomy, lifestyle, social interaction, and achievement. The Adult Career Concerns Inventory shows that Lucy has considerable concern about crystallization and great concern about stabilizing. Other stages of development are of little or some concern to her.

Having talked about her loneliness and worries about her social isolation during the first session, Lucy brings up her career concerns with the counselor at the beginning of their second session. The counselor has just shared the results of the Salience Inventory and the Adult Career Concerns Inventory with Lucy. They are discussing the results:

CL: Work really is very important to me. I feel that I have accomplished some things just by being able to get a job in the hospital. I've shown others that I can take care of myself.

CO: Getting set and on your feet sounds important. [The counselor hears Lucy talking about stabilizing and sees the parallel between this discussion and her high score on the Stabilizing Scale.]

CL: Really, it is important to me. I think now it's even more important to me because Max and I have broken up. There were times when I thought that

Table 9-2 *Summary of Lucy's Scores on Three Inventories*

Inventory	*High Scores*
The Salience Inventory	*Working* Participation Commitment Values expectations *Leisure* Participation *Home and Family* Commitment Values expectations
The Values Scale	Autonomy Lifestyle Social interaction Achievement
The Adult Career Concerns Inventory	Crystallizing Stabilizing

we really would get married. When he continued to back off from me, and finally when I found out that he had cheated on me, that did it. It seemed then as if work was all I had.

CO: It's scary now to think that being married and having a family seems so unknown. [Being aware of the salience of home and family, the counselor is aware of how deeply Lucy is affected. That role seems to be hard for her to imagine now.]

CL: It's been so hard. I seem so much more aware of what other people are doing at work now. I don't mean just with patients, but sometimes I think about what they do when they go home. When Max and I were living together, I never thought about that.

CO: A lot more thought about you, too, and what you're going to do. [Disruption in the participation in one salient role, a relationship leading to home and family, seems to have had the effect of causing questioning of other salient roles.]

CL: Even though I really like the people I work with and still enjoy being with them, I feel more removed from them. I look at where they're going, and I look at where I'm going. I wonder if I'm going in the right direction.

CO: Sounds like we ought to talk more about medical school—you brought that up last time. [Lucy seems to want to recycle, in the sense that she wants to question her choices and return to the crystallizing stage. Further, Lucy values social interaction; her statement is confirmed by her high score on the Values Scale.]

CL: Yes, now that I'm learning a lot about physical therapists and physicians, much more than I ever knew before, I am questioning it.

CO: Sounds like you have a lot more practical experience than you got just from your internship. [The counselor hears how Lucy's world-of-work information has increased [concept discussed in the previous chapter) and how Lucy may wish to return to the question of occupational selection with new information.]

CL: I really don't want to have to depend on anyone. I want to do what I want to do.

CO: What is that? [Lucy's autonomy is apparent. She seems to have a strong sense of who she is and what she wants.]

CL: Being a physician, working with people who are badly hurt, has a great appeal to me. I think I can do it.

CO: You seem to want it but seem scared. [Understanding the wavering between the stabilizing and the crystallizing stage, the counselor sees Lucy as embarking on one career and starting to like it, but seeing another career with more potential. In some ways, a change from physical therapist to physician can be seen as advancing, rather than career change. If seen that way, it may be less traumatic. On the other hand, returning to school for several years is more than advancing.]

Using Super's instruments and concepts to help Lucy deal with her relationship and career issues provides an organizing format for the counselor. Being able to identify the life stage and the movement back and forth within it can be quite helpful in making sense of changes in a person's life. Furthermore, knowing that the role of work can change in one's life and seeing it in terms of other roles—home and family, leisure, community service, and studying—can be quite helpful. Lucy's values are very important in Lucy's decision making. Super's value concepts provide a way to label the important issues with which Lucy is struggling.

Although the establishment substages of stabilizing, consolidating, and advancing help in understanding the career issues that Lucy is faced with, problems occurring late in the establishment stage may not be addressed. Bejian and Salomone (1995) suggest that midlife stresses that occur in the early 40s are not accounted for by either the establishment stage or the maintenance stage. They suggest a sixth stage, "renewal," in which an individual confronts midlife crises, which include reexaming one's personal and career priorities, making changes based on this examination, and making different plans about the future. Their suggestions are based in part on the findings of Riverin-Simard (1988) and Williams and Savickas (1990), who found that the early 40s is a time of personal turmoil for many of the individuals they studied. Lucy may face such issues when she is more established in her career, either as a physical therapist or as a physician.

Maintenance

Individuals from about the age of 45 to 65 may be in a situation where they are not advancing but maintaining their status in their work. This can vary from individual to individual, depending upon physical abilities, company policies, personal financial situation, and motivation. The substages of holding, updating, and innovating may be found in the maintenance stage in any chronological sequence. The concepts are useful to the counselor because they help expand on the meaning of the maintenance stage.

Holding Now that some level of success has been attained, the individual is concerned with holding onto the position that he or she has. This may mean learning new things to adapt to changes that take place in the position, and being aware of activities that co-workers are involved in. In some companies, individuals may see forced early retirement or potential mass layoffs as a threat. This is enough motivation for an individual to hold his or her own.

Updating In many fields, holding one's own is not enough. For example, health and education occupations often require that workers attend continuing education programs to maintain their status in that occupation. Attendance at these programs updates workers on changes in the field. Less formal activities than continuing education seminars include attending professional meetings, visiting with colleagues or customers to see new developments in the field, and meeting people who can update one's knowledge.

Innovating Somewhat similar to updating, *innovating* refers to making progress in one's profession. It may not be enough to learn new things (updating); it may be important to make new contributions to the field. To do so, an individual might need to develop new skills as a field changes. Sometimes, there are new ways to improve one's work or to find new areas of work to learn. Innovating may sound as if it contradicts the idea of maintenance. However, in most occupations, particularly higher-level occupations, if workers stop learning new things, they will not maintain themselves but will decline and be in danger of losing their position.

Example Having knowledge of Super's stages can be useful to counselors with or without Super's inventories. In the case described next, Richard is a 57-year-old insurance salesperson. He is talking to his physician about the general fatigue that he is experiencing, along with occasional low-back pain. The physician, while not familiar with Super's instruments, is familiar with Super's life-stage theory.

CL: I seem to be tired much more than I used to be.

CO: None of the tests, as we've discussed, have shown anything to be wrong. How is your life going? [The physician decides to take the time to listen to Richard and see if she can help out. Perhaps she will make a referral to a counselor, a psychologist, or a psychiatrist, or perhaps she will be able to help Richard herself.]

CL: My twin boys are doing well in their new jobs, and my wife likes hers, so things are going well with them.

CO: But how are things going with you?

CL: At home things are fine—we have two new grandchildren, and that's great—but work is the same as it's always been.

CO: And how is that? [The physician wants to learn more about Richard's working role, as he seems content with home and family.]

CL: It's pretty drab. I have the same customers. I get some commissions for renewing their accounts. Customers refer friends to me, so I get new accounts that way. My business is pretty much established now, so I don't have to work the way I used to.

CO: Richard, the way you describe it, it doesn't sound very interesting to you. [Questioning how Richard is dealing with the maintenance stage, the physician wonders whether Richard is even holding his own in the field, let alone updating knowledge or innovating.]

CL: Yes, it is rather boring. They have seminars and I get materials all the time, but they seem like the same old stuff. I don't read half of them.

CO: What keeps you from reading them? [The physician knows the value of updating knowledge and innovating. She is hopeful that she will be able to get this across to Richard.]

CL: I don't know. There are all these people who seem brand new to the company, telling me what I ought to do and how I ought to do it. I've worked for them for 20 years.

CO: You really seem to resent their telling you what to do, almost as if you don't feel respected. [The physician wants to explore the resentment that Richard feels, believing that it may hold back his progress in his work and contribute to his overall feeling of tiredness.]

In this example, by having some idea of life stages, the physician is able to be sensitive to her patient and start to explore issues of concern. Later, she may decide to refer Richard elsewhere for counseling. For now, she has used her knowledge of adult career development and the importance of various life roles to diagnose a significant psychological issue for the client.

Disengagement

In the maintenance stage, if individuals do not update their knowledge of the field and make some effort to innovate, they are in danger of losing their job. In the previous example, Richard may be in that position. He may be starting to disengage from his work. Sometimes, the need to disengage comes from physical limitations. People in their 50s and 60s who have been involved in some kind of physical labor—for example, construction, painting, or assembly line work—may find that they are no longer able to work as long or as fast as they once were. Super (1957) originally referred to this stage as "decline" but changed his label because of its negative connotations for many people. Although people may be slowing down in their physical abilities and their ability to remember, this is also an age that is associated with wisdom. People can continue to use their mental capacities for growth and at the same time disengage from various activities. The substages of disengagement—decelerating, retirement planning, and retirement living—can be seen as tasks that older adults often, but not always, must consider.

Decelerating Slowing down one's work responsibility is what is meant by *decelerating.* For some people, this may mean finding easier ways of doing work or spending less time doing work. Others may find that it is difficult to concentrate on things for as long as they did when they were younger. Drawing away from difficult problems at work and wanting to avoid deadline pressure are signs of decelerating.

Retirement Planning Although some individuals begin their retirement planning early, almost all individuals must deal directly with retirement plans during their later years. This task includes activities such as financial planning and planning activities to do in retirement. Talking to friends, retirement counselors at work, and others will aid in this process. Some individuals may choose a new part-time job or volunteer work. In a sense, when they do this, individuals are returning to the crystallization stage and reassessing their interests, capacities (both physical and mental), and values.

Retirement Living This stage is common for people in their late 60s, who often experience changes in life roles. Leisure, home and family, and community service may become more important, whereas work will become less significant. Important aspects of retirement living are the place in which one lives, one's friends, and use of the free time that may come with retirement.

As aging populations become larger (as of 1990, over half the U.S. population was over 50), there is a greater need to address the issues of individuals facing retirement. Suggestions for counseling such individuals is given in *Retirement Counseling: A Handbook for Gerontology Practitioners* (Richardson, 1993) and in Jensen-Scott (1993). Hanisch (1994) shows that, when individuals plan their retirement, the retirement is most successful. For those retiring for health reasons, retirement is more of a problem. Similarly, Robbins, Lee, and Wan (1994) found that early retirees who adjusted well to retirement had stable and meaningful goals to enhance their quality of life.

Recycling

Super recognizes that not everyone follows these stages in the neat order outlined here. Most do not. Many reassess their career plans at various points during their lifetime. When they do this, they reenter the exploration stage, reassessing their values, interests, and capacities. On the Adult Career Concerns Inventory, Super (Super et al., 1988) uses one item to determine a person's recycling status. Because it so clearly describes the concept of recycling, the item is reprinted here:

> After working in the field for a while, many persons shift to another job for any of a variety of reasons: pay, satisfaction, opportunity for growth, shut-down, etc. When the shift is a change in field, not just working for another employer

in the same field, it is commonly called a "career change." Following are five statements which represent various stages in career change. Choose the one statement that best describes your current status.

1. I am not considering making a career change.
2. I am considering whether to make a career change.
3 I plan to make a career change and I am choosing a field to change to.
4. I have selected a new field and I am trying to get started in it.
5. I have recently made a change and I am settling down in the new field.*

The following dialogue is part of an initial interview between Matthew, a 64-year-old journalist working for a newspaper in a midsized southwestern city, and the retirement counselor who is on the staff in the newspaper's personnel office. Matthew, a Mexican American who moved to Texas at the age of 12, has been on the staff of the paper for 37 years. For 25 years, the newspaper has had a pension plan that he has participated in. Matthew's job requires him to be mobile, interviewing politicians and police officers throughout the county. In the past 15 years, Matthew has gained considerable weight, and he had a heart bypass operation 3 years ago. He is finding that he does not have the stamina that he used to have and is extremely tired at the end of the day. He has been looking forward to retirement. The counselor and Matthew have been going over the financial aspects of his retirement plan, when the counselor asks Matthew what his plans are for retirement:

CL: I've really been looking forward to relaxing and sitting around taking it easy. This job is getting to me now. My health isn't what it once was. I just want to be able to take it easy. I'm planning to work a 30-hour work week for the next nine months. My editor says that's fine and not to worry about it.

CO: And after that? [Using his knowledge of Super's life-stage theory, but not Super's inventories, the counselor recognizes that Matthew is discussing the deceleration substage of disengagement. His focus seems to be mainly on that stage and not on retirement planning or retirement living.]

CL: My home is all paid for, and my wife will be working for another few years. I'll just sit around and watch television.

CO: Does that seem enjoyable to you? [Expecting to go from an active work role to a very passive role with little activity may be unrealistic.]

CL: Well, that's not all that I'll do.

CO: And what else?

CL: Something that I've always wanted to do is work in the literacy program with adults who can't read and those who are having a hard time learning English. It really helped me when I was a boy to be able to learn English as quickly as I did. I remember, in high school, I got better grades

*Reproduced by special permission of the Publisher, Consulting Psychologists Press, Inc., Palo Alto, CA 94303, from *Adult Career Concerns Inventory,* by Donald E. Super, Albert S. Thompson, and Richard H. Lindeman. Copyright 1990 by Consulting Psychologists Press, Inc. All rights reserved. Further reproduction is prohibited without the Publisher's consent.

in English than the Anglo kids, and it wasn't even my native language. I've seen so many people suffer here because they can't read or speak English.

CO: Sounds as if you've thought about it awhile. [Moving from an active work role to an active community service role seems to be a comfortable shift.]

CL: I think about it quite a bit when I have to interview someone for an article and they can't speak well or their English is lousy. I find myself more and more giving tips to the young guys coming up in the office.

CO: You seem to like teaching. [Identifying an interest that is different from those in Matthew's current work may be helpful as Matthew and the counselor recycle to the crystallization stage. It is not a dramatic recycling, as Matthew has had some opportunity to do a little bit of teaching and has given it some thought.]

CL: Well, I never have had much opportunity to teach, but I do it informally. I try not to be obnoxious about it. Most reporters have their own style, and they don't like being told what to do. It may seem strange to you, but I'd like to do something for other Mexican Americans who have not had it as good as I have.

CO: Helping them sounds as if it will be very meaningful to you. [The values of altruism and cultural identity underlie Matthew's desire to change his role in a positive sense to community service.]

From this brief example, the utility of Super's life-stage and role salience concepts can be seen. Without them, the counselor would just be using his own intuitions as to what to look for in helping Matthew. He would not be taking advantage of the wide array of research and concept development that has been a part of the work of Super and his colleagues. It is not that Super's theory is the only theory; there are others, such as those of Levinson, Darrow, Klein, Levinson, and McKye (1978) and Erikson (1963). They have not generated as much research as Super's theory, and they are not related directly to career development. However, the use of any of the theories would probably be better than relying only on hunches.

LIFE STAGES OF WOMEN

Although Super's theory is often thought of as a theory for white middle-class males, Super has long been concerned about the career patterns of women. He proposed seven career patterns for women (Super, 1957):

1. *Stable homemaking career pattern:* Women marry shortly after they finish their education and have no significant work experience afterward.
2. *Conventional career pattern:* Women enter work after high school or college, but after marriage they cease work to enter full-time homemaking.
3. *Stable working career pattern:* After high school or college, women work continuously throughout the life span.
4. *Double-track career pattern:* This pattern characterizes those women who combine career and homemaking roles throughout their life span.

5. *Interrupted career pattern:* Women enter into work, then marriage and full-time homemaking, and later return to a career, often after children can care for themselves.
6. *Unstable career pattern:* In this pattern, women drop out of the work force, return to it, drop out, and return—repeating the cycle over again.
7. *Multiple-trial career pattern:* In such a pattern, a woman works, but never really establishes a career. She may have a number of different unrelated jobs during her lifetime. (pp. 76–78)

Super (1990) points out that the career patterns for women that he described more than 30 years ago are probably quite different now. Many changes in society have taken place to allow women to enter a much broader spectrum of careers. In research done between 1967 and 1977, Rosenfeld (1979) studied more than 5,000 women and concluded that women were far more likely to have intermittent employment than men were. In a longitudinal study, Hock, Morgan, and Hock (1985) found that, early in their marriage, women plan whether or not to work and usually follow through on trying to incorporate both self-care and care for others into a sense of identity. Trying to merge these two concerns may result in various discontinuous patterns of women's entry into the workforce.

Hughes and Galinsky (1994a) found that women with full-time employed spouses reported more psychological symptoms, less job enrichment, more household-labor and child-care burdens, and more job difficulties than did employed men. Barnett, Marshall, Raudenbush, and Brennan (1993) studied 300 white middle-class couples. Although both the men and the women found that their work experiences contributed to psychological stress, the women reported greater overall stress levels than did the men. In two other studies, Hughes and Galinsky (1994b) and Barnett, Brennan, Raudenbush, and Marshall (1994) found that psychological stress at work had an effect on marital disagreements and problems at home for both men and women. A longitudinal study of gifted women showed that many had seen few obstacles to achievement as adolescents. At age 30, many reported experience with sex discrimination, resistance to their goal achievement from family members, and role conflicts (Hollinger & Fleming, 1992). These studies suggest that career patterns for women are more discontinuous and subject to psychological stress than are career patterns for men.

Bardwick (1980) examined the typical experiences of women at various points in their adult life. It is useful to compare these observations with Super's life stages. Where Super characterizes the establishment stage as a time to stabilize oneself in a career, consolidate one's gains, and prepare to advance in the profession, Bardwick suggests that many women between the ages of 30 and 40 who have been involved in a career are concerned with not wanting to delay having children any longer. She believes that many women are concerned about balancing their professional role and their feminine role. For some women, professional success at midlife, seems to bring about not independence, but increased dependence. Whereas Super describes the maintenance stage as a time to hold one's gains and to update and innovate one's career skills, Bardwick believes that many women between the ages of 40 and 50 (the late establishment and early maintenance stages) are starting to develop more autonomy and to become more independent. This is the time when those who gave up careers so they could raise children may now return to a career. For women over 50, Bardwick sees not a time of maintenance, but of career accomplishments. For some women, their husband's retirement or death may open up more opportunities for a creative and autonomous lifestyle. Bardwick's observations of women's working patterns focus on women's concern about marriage and family and are based mainly on middle-class and upper-middle-class women. Bardwick's stages are contrasted with Super's stages to remind counselors of the importance of marriage and family to many women in their career decision making and planning.

Using Super's theory with women is made easier by the use of Super's five roles: work, community service, study, home and family, and leisure. In research for the Salience Inventory, Nevill and Super (1986) found that women in general placed a slightly higher value on family and home than on work. Super's life stages are likely to be less applicable to people for whom work is an unimportant role. Most of Super's substages are concerned with work-related activity. This suggests that the less a woman participates in work, is committed to work, and values work, the less applicable Super's life stages will be. The issue of the applicability of life-stage theory to women will probably continue to be a problem for some time. Studies by Ornstein and Isabella (1990) and Ornstein, Cron, and Slocum (1989) question the appropriateness of stage models for women. Women's values are also different from those of men. Yates (1985), discussed in Super and Nevill (1989), states that women in the military value aesthetics, personal development, working conditions, and altruism more than men do, whereas men value risks and physical prowess more than women do. Langan Fox (1991) found that women valued contact with others more than did men. Clearly, differences in men's and women's values and in their perceptions of the importance of life roles suggest that counselors need to recognize the complexity of life-span theory. The counseling examples given in this chapter all show counselors listening to the client and not trying to force life-span theory into their conceptualization of a client.

A case study that may be typical of adult women who return to college after raising a family may serve to illustrate how Super's theory can be applied. Jill is a 38-year-old white woman who is married to a truck driver. She has three teenage children in school. For the past four years, Jill has been attending classes at a local community college. She now wishes to go to a four year college but is unsure as to whether she wants a teaching curriculum or one in business. She has a slight preference for teaching but is afraid that this curriculum will be longer, as some of her credits will not transfer, and that she will have more difficulty finding a job near home. Her husband tolerates her pursuit of higher education but complains about her lack of attention to the children, because he has to spend more time with them. Jill is tired of his pressure and cannot wait until she finishes school so he will not pester her. However, she really enjoys the studying that she is doing; her view of herself as a competent individual has grown.

From the point of view of Super's life-span theory, several comments can be made. First, Jill is juggling her participation in studying and in home and family because she is committed to work as well as to home and family. She values autonomy, personal development, prestige, and achievement. From a life-stage point of view, she is recycling through the crystallization phase. Unlike students 18 years younger than she, she has greater family commitment and responsibilities. She would benefit from some help in crystallizing her abilities, interests, and values. She does not fit Bardwick's (1980) description of 30- to 40-year old women, as her children are teenagers. However, she somewhat resembles Bardwick's description of 40- to 50-year-old women. Using Super's theory may help her counselor focus on important life-role, life-stage, and value issues.

LIFE STAGES OF ADULTS OF COLOR

Researchers have been critical of the applicability of career development theory to adults of color. Smith (1983) reviews arguments of critics of career development theory who state that existing career development theories, such as Super's life-span theory, were developed from a restricted population, are based on faulty assumptions, tend to ignore social and psychological factors that affect the lives of people of color, and ignore changing economic and social situations. Articulate arguments by Osipow (1975) and Warnath (1975) question the applicability of career development theory to people of color because career theories tend not to take job market considerations and discrimination into account. For each cultural group, it can be argued that there are aspects of that culture that make the application of career theory—in this case, life-stage theory—inappropriate. A good example of this line of thinking is that of Cheatham (1990), who contrasts "Africentrism" with "Eurocentrism." Cheatham argues that African American culture differs from majority American culture in that interdependence, communalism, and concern about others in the group are valued over autonomy and competitiveness. This difference may manifest itself in the fact that African Americans are over represented in the social and behavioral sciences, including many of the helping professions. Cheatham also states that Africentrism may explain differences in African Americans' management styles and relationships with co-workers. The work of Vondracek, Lerner, and Schulenberg (1986), as described in the previous chapter, emphasizes the social and historical context of individual development that can be considered when using Super's life-stage theory. Another approach is to look at developmental issues that affect all groups that are not in the majority culture.

Use of the minority identity development model (Atkinson et al., 1989) may help in the conceptual use of Super's theory and may alleviate some of the criticisms raised here. In this discussion, the term *minority* is used rather than *people of color* because the theory of Atkinson et al. refers to differences between groups that are in the minority as opposed to those in the dominant group. For example, this theory could, with modification, be applicable in Japan where whites, blacks, and Mexicans would be in the minority. There has been very little research on the theory, yet it is included because of the balance that it provides to life-stage theory. Not being a career or age-related theory, the minority identity developmental model is less specific in its use than other models or theories described in this book. Outlined in Table 9-3, the minority identity developmental model emphasizes the attitude toward self, toward others of the same minority, toward others of different minorities, and toward the dominant culture for an individual in a minority group. Atkinson, Morten, and Sue describe five stages that individuals go through in dealing with their attitude toward self and others. In the conformity stage, minority individuals generally prefer the values of the majority culture to the values of their own culture. In Stage 2, the dissonance stage, the minority individual, through information and experience, encounters conflict and confusion between the values of his or her minority culture and those of the dominant culture. In Stage 3, the resistance and immersion stage, an individual rejects the dominant culture and embraces the minority culture. In Stage 4, the introspection stage, the minority individual begins to question his or her total acceptance of the minority culture. In Stage 5, the synergetic articulation and awareness stage, minority individuals incorporate the cultural values of both the dominant group and other minorities. They develop a desire to abolish all forms of oppression.

When discussing this model, Atkinson et al. (1989) are clear that not all minorities start in Stage 1 or finish in Stage 5. Furthermore, not all stages are experienced in the order in which they are described in Table 9-3. However, being aware that these issues can take place among minority group members at virtually any time during their lifetime can add to the use of Super's developmental theory with minority group members.

To demonstrate integrating the minority identity development model with Super's life-span theory, some examples will be given for each of Super's basic career development stages. In the exploration stage, counselors not only need to consider assessment of abilities, interests, and values, along with career information, but must also be aware of the attitudes of the individual toward self and others. For example, an individual in the conformity stage may have a self-depreciating attitude, which may make it

Table 9-3 *Summary of Minority Identity Development Model*

Stages of Minority Development Model	*Attitude toward Self*	*Attitude toward Others of the Same Minority*	*Attitude toward Others of Different Minority*	*Attitude toward Dominant Group*
Stage 1—Conformity	self-depreciating	group-depreciating	discriminatory	group-appreciating
Stage 2—Dissonance	conflict between self-depreciating and appreciating	conflict between group-depreciating and group-appreciating	conflict between dominant held views of minority hierarchy and feelings of shared experience	conflict between group-appreciating and group-depreciating
Stage 3—Resistance and immersion	self-appreciating	group-appreciating	conflict between feelings of empathy for other minority experiences and feelings of culturo-centrism	group-depreciating
Stage 4—Introspection	concern with basis of self-appreciation	concern with nature of unequivocal appreciation	concern with ethnocentric basis for judging others	concern with the basis of group depreciation
Stage 5—Synergetic articulation and awareness	self-appreciating	group-appreciating	group-appreciating	selective appreciation

From Donald R. Atkinson, George Morten, and Derald Wing Sue, *Counseling American Minorities* (3rd ed.).

difficult to appropriately assess abilities, interests, and values. Other individuals in the conformity stage may not attend to the existence of very real discrimination that may be operating in the world of work and may instead blame themselves for the problems that they encounter. Someone in the resistance and immersion stage may be unduly suspicious of the counselor's advice and information about the world of work. Also, implementing a career choice can be difficult if an individual is having to deal with employers who are in the dominant group. Having to make a place for oneself in an organization when one resists or is angry at colleagues and supervisors in the organization can be extremely difficult. Likewise, in the maintenance stage, when an individual has to update knowledge and innovate, not respecting the values of the organization with which one is working can create identity confusion. If an individual is in the dissonance stage or the resistance and immersion stage and going through Super's disengagement phase, this can be a traumatic process. One can feel quite isolated and not valued at the end of one's career. At any of Super's stages, an individual from a minority group who experiences dissonance will have more problems to contend with in terms of adjustment to his or her career and the majority culture values it supports than will a majority group member. Atkinson et al. (1989) provide a model that can add dimensionality to career issues for people of color.

In reviewing theories and studies related to racial identity development, Bowman (1993) discusses the usefulness of the Atkinson et al. (1989) model. Describing their work with African American youth between the ages of 14 and 17, D'Andrea and Daniels (1992) designed an eight-week course to promote career awareness which provided African American models from the local community as a way of developing a sense of identity. In a study of African American college students, Evans and Herr (1994) found that developing a positive racial identity was not significantly related to choosing a traditionally African American career. Applying models of racial identity to various cultural groups should help to provide more information about the career development of older adolescents and adults.

COUNSELOR ISSUES

By focusing on the comparative life-span development of the counselor and the client, we can identify potential difficulties for counselors. For example, a counselor who has just completed graduate school and is in Super's implementation substage may be confronted with a client who is planning retirement. Both the counselor and the client may worry about the gap in age. The client may feel, "How can the counselor help me? He hasn't worked; he hasn't raised a family into adulthood. How can he possibly know what it's like to retire?" A beginning counselor may share those feelings. An answer to these concerns is the counselor's ability to understand the unique situation by listening to the content and the feeling of the client. Also, by having knowledge of the context of the situation (Vondracek et al., 1986), such as retirement benefits, pension plan information, and other concrete information, the counselor can react to this criticism. Furthermore, a knowledge of the life-span issues of people in the disengagement phase is likely to make the counselor feel more comfortable.

A different type of issue may arise when the counselor is in the disengagement stage and the client is in the exploration stage. Young clients may question whether a 65-year-old counselor can help them, because the client is just at the start of his or her career. Again, the counselor's understanding of the client's knowledge of career development issues and occupational information will help to cross the age barrier. Although the counselor may be in the disengagement phase in terms of life span, that does not mean that she or he will disengage from the client in counseling. One of the indications of a good counselor is the ability to put one's own life issues aside so that one's counseling can be effective. If life-role or life-stage issues impede the counselor's listening to and helping the client, then that counselor should get counseling and consider temporarily or permanently removing himself or herself from the role of counseling.

SUMMARY

Career development issues for adults may be exceedingly complex. Commitment to, participation in, and valuing the roles of studying, working, community service, home and family, and leisure may be much more difficult than in adolescence and childhood, when the majority of the time is spent in study and leisure. Throughout the life span, the importance of roles may change, varying with the stages. When one is first exploring the type of work that he or she would enjoy and trying to choose among occupations, the career concerns are very different from when one is trying to establish oneself in a job, trying to become a dependable worker, and learning how to advance in the profession. Likewise, maintaining a position in an organization, which includes updating knowledge and innovating new processes or ideas, may create a different type of stress and conflict from when one is exploring or establishing oneself. Also, the process of disengagement or retiring from a career forces individuals to look at their life roles differently from before. At any point, individuals may wish to, or may be forced to, consider change in their career or lifestyle. This may mean recycling through previous stages. For some people, this is traumatic and may be quite difficult. The career crisis or transition that occurs is the subject of the next chapter.

References

Atkinson, D. R., Morten, G., & Sue, D. W. (1989). *Counseling American minorities: A cross-cultural perspective* (3rd. ed.). Dubuque, IA: William C. Brown.

Bardwick, J. (1980). The seasons of a woman's life. In D. McGuigan (Ed.), *Women's lives: New theory, research, and policy* (pp. 35–57). Ann Arbor: University of Michigan, Center for Continuing Education of Women.

Barnett, R. C., Brennan, R. T., Raudenbush, S. W., & Marshall, N. L. (1994). Gender and the relationship between marital-role quality and psychological distress. *Psychology of Women Quarterly, 18,* 105–127.

Barnett, R. C., Marshall, N. L., Raudenbush, S. W., & Brennan, R. T. (1993). Gender and the relationship between job experiences and psychological distress: A study of dual-earner couples. *Journal of Personality and Social Psychology, 64,* 794–806.

Bejian, D. V., & Salomone, P. R. (1995). Understanding mid-life career renewal: Implications for counseling. *Career Development Quarterly, 44,* 52–63.

Bowman, S. L. (1993). Career intervention strategies for ethnic minorities. *Career Development Quarterly, 42,* 14–25.

Cheatham, H. E. (1990). Africentricity and career development of African Americans. *Career Development Quarterly, 38,* 334–346.

Crites, J. O. (1979). *Career adjustment and development inventory.* College Park, MD: Gumpert.

D'Andrea, M., & Daniels, J. (1992). A career development program for inner-city youth. *The Career Development Quarterly, 40,* 272–280.

Duarte, M. E. (1995). Career concerns, values, and role salience in employed men. *Career Development Quarterly, 43,* 338–349.

Erikson, E. H. (1963). *Childhood and society* (2nd ed.). New York: Norton.

Evans, K. M., & Herr, E. L. (1994). The influence of racial identity and the perception of discrimination on the career aspirations of African American men and women. *Journal of Vocational Behavior, 44,* 173–184.

Gribbons, W. D., & Lohnes, P. R. (1968). *Emerging careers.* New York: Teachers College Press.

Hackbarth, J., & Mathay, G. (1991). An evaluation of two work values assessment instruments for use with hearing impaired college students. *Journal of the American Deafness and Rehabilitation Association, 24,* 88–97.

Hanisch, K. A. (1994). Reasons people retire and their relations to attitudinal and behavioral correlates in retirement. *Journal of Vocational Behavior, 45,* 1–16.

Hock, E., Morgan, K., & Hock, M. D. (1985). Employment decisions made by mothers of infants. *Psychology of Women Quarterly, 9,* 383–402.

Hollinger, C. L., & Fleming, E. S. (1992). A longitudinal examination of life choices of gifted and talented young women. *Gifted Child Quarterly, 36,* 207–212.

Hughes, D. L., & Galinsky, E. (1994a). Gender, job and family conditions, and psychological symptoms. *Psychology of Women Quarterly, 18,* 251–270.

Hughes, D. L., & Galinsky, E. (1994b). Work experiences and marital interactions: Elaborating the complexity of work. *Journal of Organizational Behavior, 15,* 423–438.

Jensen-Scott, R. L., (1993). Counseling to promote retirement adjustment. *Career Development Quarterly, 41,* 257–267.

Kanungo, R. M. (1982). *Work alienation.* New York: Praeger.

Langan Fox, J. (1991). The stability of work, self and interpersonal goals in young women and men. *European Journal of Social Psychology, 21,* 419–428.

Levinson, D. J., Darrow, C. N., Klein, E. B., Levinson, M. H., & McKye, B. (1978). *The seasons of a man's life.* New York: Knopf.

Nevill, D. D., & Super, D. E. (1986). *The Salience Inventory: Theory, application and research.* Palo Alto, CA: Consulting Psychologists Press.

Ornstein, S., Cron, W. L., & Slocum, J. W., Jr. (1989). Life stage versus career stage: A comparative test of the theories of Levinson and Super. *Journal of Organizational Behavior, 10,* 117–131.

Ornstein, S., & Isabella, L. (1990). Age vs. stage models of career attitudes of women: A partial replication and extension. *Journal of Vocational Behavior, 36,* 1–19.

Osipow, S. H. (1975). The relevance of theories of career development to special groups: Problems, needed data, and implications. In J. S. Picou & R. E. Campbell (Eds.), *Career behavior of special groups* (pp. 9–22). Columbus, OH: Merrill.

Richardson, V. E. (1993). *Retirement in counseling: A handbook for gerontology practitioners.* New York: Springer.

Riverin-Simard, D. (1988). *Phases of working life.* Montreal: Meridian Press.

Robbins, S. B., Lee, R. M., & Wan, T. T. H. (1994). Goal continuity as a mediator of early retirement adjustment: Testing a multidimensional model. *Journal of Counseling Psychology, 41,* 18–26.

Rosenfeld, R. A. (1979). Women's occupational careers: Individual and structural explanations. *Sociology of Work and Occupations, 6,* 283–311.

Smart, R. M, & Peterson, C. C. (1994). Super's stages and four-factor structure of the Adult Career Concerns Inventory in an Australian sample. *Measurement and Evaluation in Counseling and Development, 26,* 243–257.

Smith, E. J. (1983). Issues in racial minorities' career behavior. In W. B. Walsh & S. H. Osipow (Eds.), *Handbook of vocational psychology* (Vol. 1, pp. 161–222). Hillsdale, NJ: Erlbaum.

Super, D. E. (1957). *The psychology of careers.* New York: Harper & Row.

Super, D. E. (1970). *Work Values Inventory.* Boston: Houghton Mifflin.

Super, D. E. (1990). A life-span, life-space approach to career development. In D. Brown & L. Brooks (Eds.), *Career choice and development: Applying contemporary theories to practice* (2nd ed., pp. 197–261). San Francisco: Jossey-Bass.

Super, D. E., Crites, J. O., Hummel, R. C., Moser, H. P., Overstreet, P. I., & Warnath, C. F. (1957). *Vocational development: A framework for research.* New York: Teachers College Press, Columbia University.

Super, D. E., & Kidd, J. M. (1979). Vocational maturity in adulthood: Toward turning a model into a measure. *Journal of Vocational Behavior, 14,* 255–270.

Super, D. E., & Knasel, E. G. (1979). *Specifications for a measure of career adaptability in young adults.* Cambridge and Hertford, England: National Institute for Careers Education and Counseling.

Super, D. E., & Nevill, D. D. (1986). *The Salience Inventory.* Palo Alto, CA: Consulting Psychologists Press.

Super, D. E., & Nevill, D. D. (1989). *The Values Scale: Theory, research, and application.* Palo Alto, CA: Consulting Psychologists Press.

Super, D. E., Osborne, W. L., Walsh, D. J., Brown, S. D., & Niles, S. G. (1992). Developmental career assessment and counseling: The C-DAC. *Journal of Counseling and Development, 71,* 74–80.

Super, D. E., Thompson, A. S., & Lindeman, R. H. (1988). *The Adult Career Concerns Inventory.* Palo Alto, CA: Consulting Psychologists Press.

Thompson, A. S., & Lindeman, R. H. (1981). *Career Development Inventory: Vol. 1, User's manual.* Palo Alto, CA: Consulting Psychologists Press.

Vondracek, F. W., Lerner, R. M., & Schulenberg, J. E. (1986). *Career development: A life-span developmental approach.* Hillsdale, NJ: Erlbaum.

Warnath, C. F. (1975). Vocational theories: Direction to nowhere. *Personnel and Guidance Journal, 53,* 422–428.

Williams, C. P., & Savickas, M. L. (1990). Developmental tasks of career maintenance. *Journal of Vocational Behavior, 36,* 166–175.

Yates, L. (1985). *The Values Scale: Assessment of adults involved in career development.* Unpublished manuscript.

10

Adult Career Crises and Transitions

This chapter is concerned with crises and transitions in adult career development. From a stage-theory point of view, *transition* refers to movement from one stage to another. Transitions may be quite smooth, such as the transition from the establishment to the maintenance stage, provided an individual experiences relatively few abrupt changes in his or her career pattern. *Crisis* is a more negative term and refers to a situation in which a person has to develop new methods of dealing with a problem that has arisen rather suddenly. Definitions by Moos and Schaefer (1986) and Hill (1949) emphasize the suddenness and disorienting aspects of a crisis. The focus of this chapter is on career crises, disruptive situations that are likely to cause considerable consternation for the individual and may cause the person to seek counseling. Less dramatic transitions will also be covered. These crises and transitions are described in the context of Super's life-span stages.

There are several models of how individuals cope with crises or transitions. Although some will be described here, the model of Hopson and Adams (1977) will be used for conceptualizing reactions of clients to career crises and transitions. Examples will be used to identify clients in various stages of transition. Certain career crises tend to occur mainly with women and people of color. These special situations will also be examined in the context of Hopson and Adams's theory of transitions.

TYPES OF TRANSITIONS

Reviewing the literature on types of transitions, Schlossberg (1984) identifies four: anticipated, unanticipated, "chronic hassles," and events that don't happen (nonevents). Anticipated events are ones that will happen in the life span of most individuals. Examples of these would be high school graduation, marriage, starting a job, and retiring. Unanticipated transitions are those that are not expected. Examples of these would be the death of a family member or being fired or transferred. Hopson and Adams (1977) refer to anticipated crises as predictable and unanticipated crises as not predictable. "Chronic hassles" are situations such as a long commute to work, an unreasonable supervisor, concern with deadline pressures, or physical conditions. A nonevent is something that an individual wishes to happen but that never occurs. For some, this may be a promotion that does not happen or a transfer to a desired community that does not take place. A common nonevent for women is being unable to enter or leave the workforce. Some women wish to leave and spend more time with family or other pursuits but do not do so because of financial conditions. Others may wish to enter the workforce as their children grow but may hesitate to do so because of continuing responsibilities at home or lack of confidence.

Another class of transitions mentioned by Hopson and Adams (1977) is voluntary and involuntary transitions. An example of a voluntary transition would be the decision to quit one's job as an accountant and become an actor. An involuntary transition would be being fired or laid off from one's job. An anticipated transition can be involuntary. For example, being given a new sales territory may not be voluntary, but the individual may know about it for six months in advance. An unanticipated event can be voluntary. For example, making oneself available for an assignment, not knowing whether it will occur, can lead to being unsure about how such an assignment would affect one's life in the next few months. In general, crises tend to be unanticipated and involuntary. Examples would be being fired from a job, being given a radical shift in an assignment, or encountering a flood at work. These types of transitions can be sorted into useful categories.

CATEGORIES OF CAREER TRANSITIONS

In categorizing a variety of different strains on an individual's life roles, Pearlin and Leiberman (1979) and Schlossberg (1984) list common life strains on a person's career, marriage, and parenthood. The career events are classified into three areas: nonnormative events, normative role transitions, and persistent occupational problems. Normative transitions tend to be anticipated and voluntary. Situations such as starting one's first full-time job or reentering the labor market after giving birth can be predicted weeks or months in advance. Many of these examples occur in Super's exploration stage. Another normative role transition is the loss of role. This may mean movement from an occupation to retirement. In terms of Super's theory, this could be construed as the movement (in terms of retirement) from the maintenance stage into the disengagement stage. Normative transitions tend to become crises only when they are not anticipated. For example, a person who ignores impending retirement and does not plan may be shocked by the change of roles forced by retirement.

Louis (1980a, 1980b) has created five categories of normative transitions that individuals experience in work roles: entering or reentering a labor pool, taking on a different role within the same organization, moving from one organization to another, changing professions, and leaving the labor pool. A prime example of entering the labor pool is the school-to-work transition, where understanding the transition process itself is helpful. A second transition may be less formal, as individuals move within a company, changing tasks, technologies, co-workers, and/or the actual physical surroundings. The third type of transition may cause greater stress as individuals make changes to a new employer, encountering new styles of work, tasks, and co-workers. A more dramatic change occurs when one leaves one profession for another; for example, an engineer becomes an entrepreneur, a lawyer, or a farmer. The fifth type of transition is the exit: leaving for retirement, pregnancy, or a sabbatical or being laid off or fired. Using a sample of 742 U.S. Navy officers, Bruce and Scott (1994) validated the applicability of Louis's typology as a useful way of categorizing career transitions.

Events and transitions that Louis describes are likely to be experienced in nontraditional ways. Mirvis and Hall (1994) describes the "boundaryless" career, in which there may be frequent job rotations, temporary assignments, and transfers from one part of a company to another, making the experience of transitions more frequent than in the past and occurring in more configurations than those described by Louis. Such changes are likely to heighten feelings of job insecurity. More involvement with family, community, and religious organizations may reduce the tensions that result from more frequent job transitions.

To assess how well individuals believe they have made career transitions, Heppner, Multon, and Johnston (1994) developed the Career Transitions Inventory. Its five subscales measure readiness, confidence, control, perceived support, and decision independence. *Readiness* refers to how motivated an individual is to make a career transition. *Confidence* refers to an individual's sense of self-efficacy in being able to make a successful transition. *Control* refers to the degree to which individuals feel that they can make their own decisions. *Perceived support* refers to how much support individuals feel they get from family and friends. *Decision independence* refers to the extent to which individuals make the decisions based primarily on their own needs or whether or not they are considering the needs and desires of others. The Career Transition Inventory may help counselors identify significant aspects of their clients' transitions which trouble or concern them, setting the stage for discussion and exploration of these issues. These subscales would seem to apply well to Louis's five categories of normative transitions. However, nonnormative transitions create special problems.

Nonnormative career events are far more likely to become crises than normative transitions. Perhaps the most common, as well as one of the most deeply disturbing, is loss of job. Being fired or laid off is for many people a devastating experience. However, if the work role is not a salient one, it is less likely to be devastating. If a person does not value work and relies on others or savings for income, then the family, leisure, or community service role is likely to fulfill that person's needs. However, for many people during the establishment and maintenance stage, the work role is highly valued. Stability is implied by the terms *establishment* and *maintenance.* When the essence of one's career is disrupted through job termination, this stability can turn into instability. If a person is fired at the very beginning of his or her career (the exploration stage) or six months before planned retirement (the disengagement stage), the disruptions *may* be easier to handle. Other nonnormative events are promotion, transfer, or demotion to another job. Although less dramatic than termination, these changes are likely to be most powerful in the establishment and maintenance stages. When these events are unanticipated, as they often are, the experience can be traumatic, more so than both normative and persistent occupational problems.

Persistent occupational problems are career problems that persist for a long period of time, causing a cumulative effect that can lead to a transition crisis. One example is an unpleasant physical working environment. This might include working in a very hot or cold building, in cramped quarters, or in hazardous conditions. Loggers, farm workers, and chemical workers are people who may have to continually face an unpleasant working environment. Another type of career problem that may persist is pressures on the job. These pressures may take the form of work deadlines such as those that journalists must meet, or there may be pressures to produce, for example, having to increase one's sales year after year. When rewards of the job decrease—in the form of a pay decrease, a smaller commission rate, fewer vacation days, a lack of recognition for performance by superiors, or being given less interesting work tasks—worrisome problems may arise. Another significant work problem that can start out small but fester to create a very major problem is work relations with colleagues and superiors. Not being able to get along with people that one must work with daily can create an emotional strain. If it continues, a worker must decide how to change the situation. If attempts at change fail, then the worker must decide whether to live with the stress or change to another job. Although longer in duration than nonnormative events, such as getting a termination notice, these persistent problems are most significant when the work role is extremely important to the individual. Furthermore, like nonnormative transitions, these are most disruptive during the establishment and maintenance stages. How people react to persistent, nonnormative, and normative transitions is the focus of the next section (adapted from Schlossberg, 1984).

MODELS OF TRANSITIONS AND CRISES

Reaction to a crisis or a transition takes place over a period of time. The changing phases of transitions have been studied in a number of different fields. Before discussing models of transition for career concerns, it will be helpful to look at phases that occur in personal areas, so that commonalities and differences can be observed. Studying mothers of premature infants, Kaplan and Mason (1965) described four tasks that they must perform in order to have a loving relationship with their child. These tasks include being prepared for the possible loss of the child, accepting the failure to deliver a normal child, resuming the hope of a good relationship with the baby, and acknowledging the special needs of the premature baby. At the other end of the life spectrum, Kübler-Ross (1969) identified five stages encountered by individuals who become aware that they are dying. The first stage is the denial of growing awareness. The second is being angry and resenting the fact that this is happening to them. The third is bargaining, sometimes with God, for a longer life. The fourth is depression over the loss of one's own life and the loss of relationships with loved ones. The fifth phase is acceptance of the process of dying.

In their study of transition, Moos and Tsu (1976) identified two basic phases, the first directed toward dealing with and decreasing the stress that comes with the crisis, and the second directed toward attending to details of the crisis so that one can return to normal life. These observations would seem to summarize the general reaction of individuals to a crisis. However, the earlier examples of two different types of crises show that certain situations elicit different types of adaptive or maladaptive responses from individuals. A closer look at reactions of individuals to a career crisis will help to illustrate.

Studying the career transitions of 53 men whose jobs had been eliminated, Schlossberg and Leibowitz (1980) were able to categorize the process of transition in these men into five phases: disbelief, sense of betrayal, confusion, anger, and resolution. The men in the company that was studied were all subject to a planned reduction in employees. Most were surprised by this action on the part of the company and responded in disbelief. Some felt that it might not really be true or that something might happen to reinstate them in their jobs. At about the same time as the men experienced disbelief, they also felt betrayed by the company. Many felt they had been loyal to the company and the company was deserting them. Since the transition was unanticipated and involuntary, it was natural that they would experience confusion. Being surprised, they were unsure of what to do next. The company offered career assistance, which helped them mobilize their resources. Those who had difficulty resolving their confusion were angry at themselves and at the company. In fact, a sizable minority of the employees filed grievance complaints against the employer. The last phase was resolution. Three months after they had been notified of their job transition, some had been reassigned to other jobs in the company, and about half had found new jobs. Many were pleased by the eventual outcome, as some had found better jobs. In terms of Super's life-span theory, many of the men were in the maintenance stage and appeared to have a strong commitment to their role as workers. Swain (1991) applied Schlossberg's (1984) model to 10 professional athletes, who withdrew from sports and reported reactions similar to those described above.

Often, positive change and growth occur with involuntary work changes. Following 515 professionals who had been displaced involuntarily, Eby and Buch (1995) noted different reactions to this change in men and women. For the women, family flexibility in dealing with family, work, and other roles increased the chances that positive changes would occur with the involuntary change. For the men, positive growth was more likely to occur if they could avoid financial hardship and emotionally accept the job transition, as well as receive support from friends and family. Although positive growth may occur after involuntary work changes, severe reactions often take place, and individuals may seek the help of an outplacement counselor.

Outplacement counselors often have several functions (Lewis & Lewis, 1986). They help individuals deal with the shock and negative emotional impact of the negative career disruption. Also, they help individuals assess their current situation, abilities, values, and interests. From this information, they help their clients set career goals and develop strategies for a constructive job search. Depending on the clients' needs, the search may be for a job similar to the one that was lost, or it may lead to new training and education. Common skills that are taught by outplacement counselors are résumé writing, interviewing techniques, and locating job or educational opportunities. In some situations, outplacement counselors work directly for a firm or may be hired on a consulting basis by a firm. Less frequently, individuals may seek out the private services of an outplacement counselor to help them deal with involuntary transitions.

HOPSON AND ADAMS'S MODEL OF ADULT TRANSITIONS

No one model of coping with adult transitions fits every individual. One model that has been used by a number of psychologists has been that of Hopson and Adams (1977). Brammer and Abrego (1981) adopted this model in their strategies for coping with transitions. In terms of career transitions, Perosa and Perosa (1983, 1985, 1987) have found this model appropriate to the understanding of adult career crises. Hopson (1981) has slightly revised the earlier model of Hopson and Adams (1977). This revision, along with examples of its use as a conceptualization system in adult career crises and transitions, will be described in the following pages.

Figure 10-1 presents the seven stages of the model by showing the relationship of each stage or phase to mood and to time. Whether one is initially depressed or excited depends on the nature of the transition. Other phases are associated with varying degrees of depression or positive feeling. When describing each of the seven stages, we will use as a continuing example a man who has sought help from his minister because the company that he has been with for 23 years has gone bankrupt and closed its

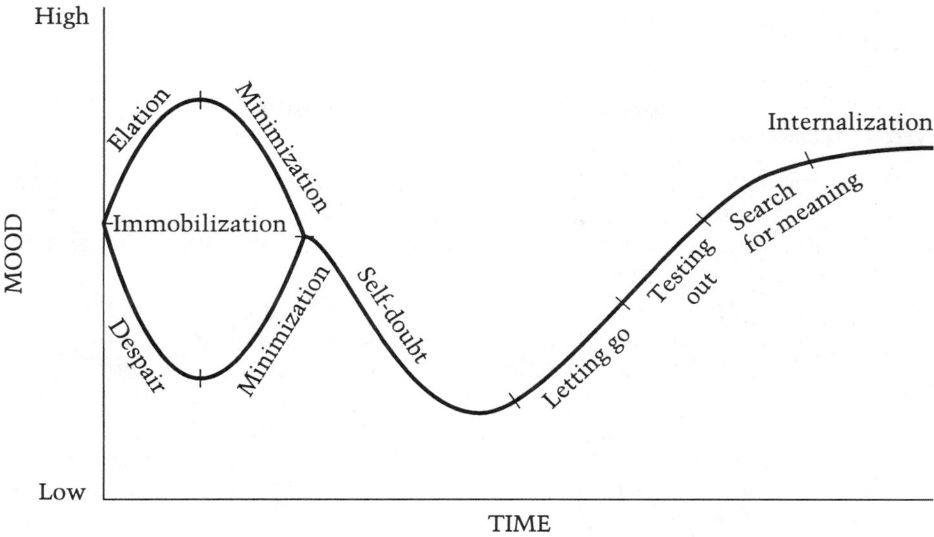

Figure 10-1 A seven-phase model of stages accompanying transition. (From *Understanding and Managing Personal Change,* by J. Adams, J. Hayes, and B. Hopson. Copyright © 1977 by Sage Publications, Inc., p. 38. Reprinted by permission.)

doors. A 55-year-old white male, John has worked hard as an inside salesman, taking orders from people around the country for bicycle parts.

Immobilization

The initial shock that occurs when one finds out that one has been fired or laid off is an example of immobilization. The person is overwhelmed, unable to make plans, perhaps even unable to respond verbally. The time period of immobilization could be a few moments or a few months. How long the period lasts depends on the nature of the event and the psychological makeup of the individual.

When John first heard from his supervisor that the company was closing in two weeks, he was speechless. He kept repeating to himself, "I can't believe it; I can't believe it." He went back to his desk at 3:30 that afternoon. For the rest of the day, he answered the phones as usual, but he was just barely able to hear the customers. His voice was hollow; he did not engage in casual talk with some customers whom he had known for many years, nor did he ask them about their inventory of bike accessories or hardware, something that he would often do. After work, he went home and sat down on the sofa. This was very uncharacteristic of him. His wife, who had come home from work earlier, was surprised by the look on his face. Had the event been a happy one, such as being given a promotion or a coveted assignment, the feeling would have been elation, rather than despair (see Figure 10-1).

Minimization

Minimization refers to the desire to make the change appear smaller than it is. Often, an individual will deny that the change is even taking place or will tell himself or herself that the event really does not matter, that things will be perfectly fine anyway.

When John returned to work the next day, things were, in a physical sense, as usual. The building was standing there; his desk was in the same place. He talked to the salespeople whose desks were near him, but before they had a chance to talk about the news, the phones started to ring. It was a very busy day, and although John's job ordinarily provided little time to talk to his co-workers, that morning he had no time at all to talk to them. At noon, half the salespeople went to lunch, while the others covered the phones. John went with them, and they talked about the closing. Most expressed surprise and said that the company was in good financial shape—that there seemed to be plenty of inventory. They could not understand why the company would be closing. A few said that perhaps they would hear in a few days that the company was going to make it after all. John's spirits were boosted; he felt a little bit better that others saw the situation the way he did. Not only was John denying the plant's closing, but so were some of his co-workers.

About seven o'clock that evening, John received a call from his minister. Knowing that his wife had called their minister during the day, John was not surprised. A portion of their conversation went like this:

CL: I was shocked like everyone else yesterday. The company had done so well for so many years, I couldn't believe it.

CO: I'm sorry to hear it. That's terrible news for you. [Although the minister has several people in his congregation who have experienced the same layoff, the minister wants to focus on John's experience, noticing how the event has immobilized him.]

CL: Well, it may not be so bad. Maybe there's a chance that the company will be able to continue and someone will buy it out.

CO: Yes, that would feel a lot better to you. That's for sure. [Knowing that a company does not give two weeks' notice to employees without being very certain, the minister is not hopeful, as John is. He recognizes the denial, as he has experienced this many times with parishioners who have lost jobs or loved ones or have had other significant losses. He knows that this is not the time to argue with John about the likelihood of the plant's reopening.]

CL: I hope it will work. It would be a terrible disaster for me if things don't work out.

CO: I know, John, you put so much of yourself into your work. [The tragedy of this crisis is dramatically clear.]

CL: I have another 12 years to go before retirement, if only the company could hold on.

CO: You feel you need the company so much. [Staying with John's feelings of desperation seems really important to the minister now.]

Self-Doubt

Many different feelings can occur at this stage. A very common one is doubting oneself and one's ability to provide for oneself and for one's dependents. Other common reactions are anxiety due to not knowing what will happen, fear of the future, sadness, and anger.

For John, the principal emotion a few days later was anger. When John realized that plans were being made to liquidate inventory, the chances of the company's continuing began to appear very small to him. When John came home that night, he called his minister. Having known the minister for 15 years, he felt very comfortable with him and had been encouraged by him to call at any time.

CL: The company never gave me a chance. After all the hours I've put in for them, I didn't get a chance to even find out what was happening. They never told me until the last minute—what a bunch of jerks they are! I can't understand how they could do such a thing.

CO: You're so angry at them. I can hear it in your voice. [John is furious, yet he is toning his language down so as not to offend the minister.]

CL: I can't understand why they would do it. Such fools! It's like they don't care about anybody who has given them service and made them rich. I'm not the only one. A lot of others have been with the company a long time. It's a rotten thing to do.

CO: It feels as if they've betrayed you after all you've done for them. [The minister just wants to stay with the anger and not challenge it. He senses that John doesn't want to hear anything else.]

Letting Go

As can be seen in Figure 10-1, the individual next starts to let go of the angry, tense, frustrated, or other feelings. This is the time when the person accepts what is really happening to him or her. The individual detaches himself or herself from the original situation and starts to look at the future.

With each passing day, it becomes clearer that the company is going to close. John starts to think about what will happen to him next. He knows that a few of the workers in the plant are being kept on to close the plant down. There is no news that anyone will buy the plant. The company is giving each person two extra weeks of severance pay, but no other assistance. The money that John has accumulated in his pension will not be affected by the closing. As he goes home on Friday night, he starts to think about the future. In the evening, he goes through the want ads in his local paper. The next day, he goes out to buy newspapers from nearby cities. He plans to look for work on Monday. At home, he starts to think about what he can do and what he is good at. From Super's life-span point of view, John now recycles from the maintenance stage to the exploration stage. Although this was an involuntary, unpredictable event, John is letting go of his angry feelings and his desperate denial of the impending plant closing. John has hobbies that he has worked on from time to time. They now become potential career directions. Also, John thinks of the church work that he has done with poor families in his city. His leisure and community service pursuits can now become career possibilities.

Testing Out

At this point individuals may develop a burst of energy, a sense of "now I can handle it." In fact, sometimes people will describe the way things should be. They may have advice for others in the same situation. In a career situation, an individual may have thoughts about how he or she is going to network [talk to other significant people in the field] and move forward.

Sunday after church services, John talks very briefly with his minister, who inquires how John is doing:

CL: Things are looking up now. I have a number of avenues that I plan to explore this week. I am going to take a couple of days off and talk to some old friends. I have some ideas about opening up an auto garage or working as a salesman for machine parts. I haven't talked to anybody yet.

CO: Nice to hear your enthusiasm, John. [It is a relief to hear that John has moved away from his preoccupation with the company's closing. Some people stay in the denial stage or are extremely angry at the company for weeks. Yet John's newfound confidence does not sound real. It may fade quickly, but it is a start.]

CL: I do hope that I'll find something. It's been such a long time since I've thought about what I might do. I guess I never thought about being in this situation. When I think of new possibilities, it isn't so bad.

CO: It's good to hear you thinking about new possibilities. It's good to see that spark. [Encouragement is given for exploring new activities that will help John move on in his search, not only for a job, but also for his own peace of mind.]

Search for Meaning

In the search-for-meaning stage, an individual seeks to understand how events are different and why. This is a cognitive process in which people try to understand not only the feelings of others, but also their own.

Having finished his work with the company and having spent a week looking for work, John is busy following leads. He has contacted auto supply stores and hardware manufacturers for job leads. He had started out looking at the possibility of opening a gas station or car repair shop. As he learned more about this option, he felt he did not have the necessary experience or capital, nor was he prepared to work in someone else's shop. This felt as if it would be a step down not only in financial reward, but also in prestige. He is more comfortable using the skills that he has developed in his 23 years of experience as a bicycle parts salesperson. As John recycles through Super's exploration stage, he reconsiders his interests, capacities, and values. This is something that he has not done for many years. As he does this, he sees his job loss as a challenge and an opportunity to improve himself. His understanding of the reasons for the company's collapse is more apparent. Not only does he have more information now about the financial situation of the company, but he is also able to be more objective and less angry in his view of the actions that have taken place in the last three weeks.

Internalization

The final phase of dealing with transitions, *internalization,* implies a change in both values and lifestyle. The individual may have developed new coping skills and has grown emotionally, spiritually, or cognitively as a result of going through a difficult crisis.

Three months after being terminated from his job, John calls his minister to tell him of the progress that he has made:

CL: It took me over two months, but I finally got a job that I think will be an improvement, a step up for me. I started working a week ago for a very large auto parts distributorship. My work will be sales, like before, but also managing some other employees. That's something that I only did informally in my old job. I really want that opportunity now. Things are looking up.

CO: Sounds very much as if they are. It's great to hear such good news from you, John.

CL: It's been a rough few months. The second month that I was out of work was pretty depressing. I started to lose confidence in my ability to get a job. I wondered who would hire an old guy like me, but I really kept going at it, even though times got discouraging. My wife was really helpful, really encouraging.

CO: The ups and downs sound pretty tough. [John sounds quite different from a few months ago. The panic, anger, and tension are gone from his voice. He seems to have been fortunate in his resolution of the crisis.]

CL: Some days, I would be really excited about possibilities. Others, I might not. But I was able to think about what I was able to do and what I couldn't. I had dreamed of owning my own business, but it took a while for me to realize that I just couldn't handle it financially, and maybe I really wasn't able to commit the energy that I think it needs.

CO: You really have done a lot of thinking about yourself and your future. [John's *search for meaning* has not been an easy one, nor has that search been one that moved steadily upward; it has been full of fits and starts.]

CL: It's been rough, but when I think where I am now, I am a lot better off than I was three months ago. I feel more sure of myself. If this were to happen to me again, I think it would be easier the next time. Things that I was so afraid of before—like losing my job and then having to get a new one—don't scare me as much. I think I know more now what I can do than I did before.

CO: You sound terrific. [Hearing John talk this way feels very good. John has *integrated* this transformation into his life. As a result, he is feeling better about himself than he did prior to the crisis. He has moved past his fears and anxieties to an excellent resolution of his transition.]

Not all crises follow Hopson and Adams's (1977) seven-phase transition model as closely as this example does. John's case was presented to illustrate the sequence of the phases. Many people's situations, as will be shown by the examples in the next sections, do not fit the model so neatly. Clearly, not everyone is able to resolve a job crisis by finding a better job. Some people facing job crises have become physically ill, committed suicide, found only temporary and inferior work, or never found work again. The advantage of Hopson and Adams's model of transition is that the counselor has an idea of what to expect. For example, if during the second phase a client denies that his job is really important, Hopson and Adams's model is useful in helping the counselor accept this, without believing the client's statement to be one that will be true for a long period of time. Rather, the counselor accepts the denial as a phase. If a client's experience does not fit Hopson and Adams's model, there is no need to attempt to force it. The career-related crises that are especially applicable to women and to people of color, which are described in the next sections, often do not fit smoothly into this model.

CAREER CRISES AFFECTING WOMEN

Three general types of career crises are far more likely to affect women than men. Women are much more likely than men to experience discrimination, to make decisions based on child-raising and family issues, and to face sexual harassment. Discrimination, when it occurs, is usually unanticipated and involuntary. The effects of discrimination are described in more detail in the example later in this section, and in Chapter 15 on sociological and economic theories of career development. The transitions out of and into the workforce or out of full-time and into part-time work are decisions that many women make at various times in their lives in consideration of children and family. In the previous chapter, Bardwick's (1980) views of child-raising and family issues at various points in a woman's life were described as they related to Super's life-span theory. Such transitions tend to be anticipated and voluntary. However, this is not always the case, and regardless of the type of transition, it can be a difficult crisis. A dramatic, unanticipated, and involuntary transition is that forced by sexual harassment. Having both severe personal and career consequences, this can be an extremely devastating experience. Betz and Fitzgerald (1987) and Fitzgerald and Ormerod (1993) describe in depth the research on discrimination, the effects of child raising on workforce participation, and sexual harassment. The relationship between career and family and the effects of sexual harassment are described in the following pages in the context of Hopson and Adams's (1977) theory.

Temporary Reentry into and Leave-Taking from the Labor Force

Women may follow a large variety of patterns in going into and out of the labor force. For many women, leaving the workforce may be relatively easy. Some may participate in maternity leave programs that allow them to reenter their position. On the other hand, others may wish to stay out for a longer period of time than their position can be held for. They may have to go through the process of job hunting all over again. For some, a career that was satisfactory prior to leaving the workforce may no longer be fulfilling. Betz and Fitzgerald (1987) discuss the coping mechanisms that women develop to manage both marriage and career. Some of these include limiting social relationships, increasing organization and delegation of home and other activities, and developing flexible jobs that allow part-time work and time at home. The greater the coping strategies, the more likely it is that few of the phases that are discussed by Hopson and Adams (1977) will be experienced. However, for some women, entry or reentry into the workforce can be traumatic. Particularly if reentry is due to divorce or the death of a husband, a woman can find herself in an uncomfortable and unfamiliar position with sole responsibility for her income and survival, as well as the survival of her family. A decision to return to school may bring about a crisis. With the possibility of increased income in the distant future, school can become a financial burden. For women deciding on a new career, new training or a return to school means returning to Super's exploration stage. When talking with a woman who is reentering the labor force, counselors may determine whether or not there are changes in self-esteem during the transition.

For example, Mary had been an elementary school teacher for seven years prior to having children but then decided to raise her family and stay at home with two young children for a six-year period. When her children were 4 and 6, she decided to return to the school system. In February, she contacted the principal of the school she had worked at and made arrangements to teach again in September. Excited about returning to work, she made arrangements for her children to go to school and attend an after-school program.

Rachel, on the other hand, had worked as a teacher for 6 years prior to raising a family of four children. After 20 years of marriage, her husband died suddenly, leaving her with few financial resources and two children in high school and two in college. She had disliked teaching and had had no plans to return to the workforce. Rachel had two crises to deal with: the death of her husband and the requirement that she return to work. Rachel's period of immobilization lasted four weeks. She was in shock over the sudden death of her husband. She did not experience a period of denial or minimization; rather, she became depressed, seeing no reason for living. Relatives helped with her children, but some grew impatient. Finally, Rachel let go of her grief somewhat and started to plan for her children. She made some attempts to get work and finally settled for a job as a grocery cashier. At this point, she had no energy to use her interests, abilities, or values. After a year as a cashier, she sought career counseling to help her decide what it was that she wished to do. A year and a half after her husband's death, she was moving back and forth between the stages of letting go and testing out, until she finally began to search for what might be most appropriate for her. These two examples illustrate the wide range of reactions possible when women reenter the labor force.

Sexual Harassment

When it occurs, depending on its nature, sexual harassment may be an unanticipated, involuntary crisis that threatens one's career and psychological health. In this section, we will define sexual harassment and discuss the different perceptions that people have of it. We will also examine who the victims are, how sexual harassment affects them, and what are stages of reacting to sexual harassment. Also, we will look at an example of dealing with sexual harassment in the workplace.

As Hotelling (1991) notes, defining sexual harassment is quite difficult, as individuals disagree on what constitutes harassment. Are sexual innuendos or sexual jokes harassment? Till (1980) described five levels of harassment, which Fitzgerald and Shullman (1985) built on in developing the Sexual Experience Questionnaire. Listed in order of severity, these levels are helpful in defining the different types of sexual harassment that women may experience.

*Level 1: Gender Harassment.*This refers to verbal remarks or nontouching behaviors that are sexist in nature. Examples would include being told suggestive stories or being required to listen to rude, sexist remarks.

Level 2: Seductive Behavior. Included here are inappropriate sexual advances. The individual may attempt to discuss a woman's sex life or may express sexual interest in the woman.

Level 3: Sexual Bribery. This refers to the request for sexual activity in return for some kind of reward. Often offered by a superior, the bribe may be a higher grade in a course, a raise in pay, or a promotion.

Level 4: Sexual Coercion. This is the opposite of sexual bribery in that an individual is coerced into sexual activity by threat of punishment. For example, if a woman is told that, if she does not engage in sexual activity, she will fail a course, lose a job, or be demoted, she is being coerced. All are potentially threatening to a woman's career.

Level 5: Sexual Assault: Such behavior includes forceful attempts to touch, grab, fondle, or kiss.

These definitions provide a useful way of viewing the different ways in which individuals perceive sexual harassment. Not surprisingly, males and females are likely to view sexual harassment quite differently (Fitzgerald & Ormerod, 1993). Men and supervisors, whether male or female, tended to blame the victim for sexual harassment more than do women co-workers or female victims. However, when sexual harassment is severe, both men and women are likely to agree that the behavior is harassment. When the behaviors are shown as being romantic or seductive, then both men and women may have difficulty determining if the activity is sexual harassment. Also, several researchers have shown that women with profeminist views are more likely to perceive behaviors as harassment (Brooks & Perot, 1991). Stockdale (1993) discusses the role of misperception theory in understanding how women's friendly behavior is sometimes perceived as sexual behavior by men, and how some types of sexual harassment can be accounted for by misperceptions. In related work, Pryor, LaVite, and Stoller (1993) found that men who have tendencies toward sexual harassment are likely to link sexuality and social dominance in their thinking. Several recent studies have added to the literature on perceptions of sexual harassment, showing that the issue is more complex than this brief review would imply.

Given the different factors influencing the differing perceptions of the definition of sexual harassment, it is difficult to determine the incidence of sexual harassment. Fitzgerald and Ormerod (1993) estimate that approximately half of the adult female population in the United States has been sexually harassed at least once while working. Not surprisingly, the most frequent types of harassment are at the least severe level. For example, Gutek (1985) conducted a telephone interview study in which 53% of the participants said that they had been sexually harassed: 15% reported harassment that included insulting looks and gestures; 20% reported insulting comments; 24% reported sexual touching; 11% believed socializing on the job was expected; and 8% believed sexual activity was expected. Other studies have reported similar results.

Given the frequency of sexual harassment, who is most likely to be harassed? Fitzgerald and Ormerod (1993) report that sexual harassment is rarely reported by males, except at the least severe level. The incidence of same-sex sexual harassment is also relatively uncommon. Regarding age, women of all ages report sexual harassment, and single women report more harassment than married women (Fitzgerald & Ormerod). Relatively little information is available regarding the differences in the incidence of harassment for women of color and homosexual women. Both groups may be harassed for their color or their sexual preference as well as for their gender. Women who have experienced sexual harassment previously are more likely to label as a form of sexual harassment behavior that they may not have classified as sexual harassment before.

A variety of studies have examined differences in the incidence of sexual harassment in different occupational groups. Gold (1987) reported that blue-collar tradeswomen were much more likely to report sexual harassment than were women who worked as secretaries, lawyers, or accountants. Baker (1989) found that female machinists reported extremely high rates of sexual harassment. Interviewing 22 African American female firefighters, Yoder and Aniakudo (1995) found that 20 reported sexual harassment; of these, 16 reported unwanted sexual touching. Researchers report that it is not the number of males working at a job site that is related to the incidence of sexual harassment, but the degree to which the work group is male-dominated.

How do victims of sexual harassment respond to the event? Fitzgerald and Ormerod (1993) summarize reactions, dividing them into two major categories: internally and externally focused strategies. Internally focused strategies include those which Hobson and Adams observed, such as minimizing a behavior or denying that it is really offensive. Other internal strategies are to put up with the harassment, to excuse the offender ("He didn't really mean it"), or to take responsibility for the incident ("I should have been wearing different clothes"). Externally focused strategies include avoiding or placating the harasser. Other approaches are more assertive, such as confronting the harasser and telling him that the behavior is unwanted. Yoder and Aniakudo (1995) reported that about half of their sample of firefighters responded to sexual harassment with aggressive verbal remarks, and that a few responded physically, such as pushing the harasser up against a wall. Other external responses include getting support from the institution, such as an appropriate supervisor, and getting social support from friends or family. Such events tend to affect other work-related attitudes, including relationships with supervisors and co-workers and general work satisfaction (Morrow, McElroy, & Phillips, 1994).

Gutek and Koss (1993) document how sexual harassment affects the careers of women as well as their physical and psychological well-being. A study by the U.S. Merit Systems Protection Board (1981) showed that over 36,000 federal employees quit their jobs or were transferred, reassigned, or fired after they reported sexual harassment. In 88 sexual harassment cases filed with the California Department of Fair Employment and Housing, half of the individuals were fired and 25% quit because of fear or frustration (Coles, 1986). Other studies show negative effects on relationships with co-workers and company loyalty. Gutek and Koss (1993) summarize studies that show that self-esteem and life satisfaction are negatively affected. Physical symptoms that were reported included stomach ailments, teeth grinding, nausea, and sleeplessness. Additionally, sexual harassment may contribute to posttraumatic stress disorder and depression (Gutek & Koss, 1993).

Sexual harassment is usually not a single event, but a series of events occurring over a period of weeks or months. Gutek and Koss describe four stages of reacting to sexual harassment that can occur over time.

Confusion and Self-Blame. Individuals may assume the responsibility for being harassed. They may be upset by their inability to stop the harassment, which may begin to worsen.

Fear and Anxiety. Fear for her career or safety may cause a woman to be afraid to drive home or to answer the phone and may affect her work performance. Her attendance at work and her ability to concentrate on her work may suffer.

Depression and Anger. When a woman recognizes that she is not responsible for the harassment, she may become less anxious and more angry. If charges are filed, the work situation may get worse, and the individual may feel despair over her progress on her job.

Disillusionment. The process of bringing charges against a harasser may be long and arduous and may not always have a successful outcome. Many organizations are not supportive of women who choose to follow through on harassment charges.

These stages bear some resemblance to those of Hopson and Adams. They differ in that they do not assume the organizational or social support of those of Hopson and Adams. As Cleveland and Kerst (1993) point out, power is an important issue in understanding sexual harassment. Women often feel powerless when harassed by a supervisor or co-worker and may feel little support from other co-workers or superiors in their organization. In the following example, the client reacts to a sexual harassment situation assertively and with power. Because she negotiates the situation well, her process of working through the incident pertains more to the optimistic model of Hopson and Adams than to the more pessimistic model of Gutek and Koss.

Roberta is a 30-year-old lawyer working in a large New York City law firm. One of five children from a poor Puerto Rican family in New York, Roberta has worked her way through college and law school with the help of scholarships that she has earned. Specializing in tax matters, Roberta has been pleased with her training and is looking forward to the opportunity to advance in this firm, which she joined six months ago. She worked for a smaller law firm for three years after graduation but felt limited. She was offered a substantial pay raise to come to her new firm. One day, as she is bending over to pick up a pencil that fell off her desk, her immediate supervisor, the head of the tax law department, pats her buttocks. She is shocked by what has happened and continues with her work, growing angrier and angrier as the day goes on. When she is leaving at the end of the day, her superior says to her, "Let me help you on with your coat." Before she has a chance to respond, he helps her with her coat, brushing his hand against her breast. She says to him coldly, "Don't do that. Get your hands away from me." He responds, "Don't complain. I didn't mean anything." Shaking as she leaves work, she goes home to her apartment, quickly calling a respected friend who is an affirmative action officer at the university that she attended as an undergraduate:

CL: I can't believe what happened today. I've got to talk to you about it. My boss, who has said hardly anything to me since I've been here, touched me twice today—on my backside and on my breast. Can you believe that?! Then the stupid jerk has the nerve to say to me, "Don't complain!" Who does he think he is?

CO: What a terrible thing! Absolutely awful. [Having dealt with situations like this before, the counselor knows this is not the time to make suggestions, although she knows methods of dealing with such situations. Recognizing that Roberta has gotten over the shock, is not minimizing what has happened, and is very angry, not depressed, she wants to listen. The fact that Roberta's reaction does not fit neatly into Hopson and Adams's theory of transition is unimportant.]

CL: I never expected that to happen. That fool—who does he think he is, that he can touch me like that!

CO: I've never heard you so angry—really, really furious. [Being aware of Roberta's anger, the counselor listens to her, knowing that, when it is time to move from this phase, Roberta will determine it.]

At the end of the 45-minute conversation, Roberta finally says, "I know I've got to do something about this. Can I call you back later tonight? I just need to sit down." The counselor agrees, and later that night, they do discuss possible actions. They talk about how to confront the supervisor, who else to talk to in the law firm, and how to proceed. By doing this, Roberta is letting go of her reaction to the situation so that she can deal with it. Being strongly committed to the role of working and being at the beginning of the establishment stage, Roberta, rather than starting to stabilize her career, now has to deal with an extremely destabilizing event. Ideally, she will be able to deal with it in such a way that her superior will be punished and his behavior will desist. However, the possibility exists that Roberta could lose her job and face a lengthy suit against her law firm. The potential ramifications of such an incident may affect not only her career mobility, but also her self-esteem. Being fired could lead to much self-questioning on her part, even though the situation was not of her making.

CAREER CRISES AFFECTING PEOPLE OF COLOR

Discrimination is well documented as a major problem for people of color in their career development. Thomas and Alderfer (1989) present a thorough review of the effect of discrimination on people of color in organizations. Discrimination is discussed in more detail in Chapter 15 in terms of the social structure of the U.S. labor market. Particularly when one is in the establishment or maintenance phase of one's career and work is important to one's self-esteem, discrimination can be quite damaging. An interesting approach to this concern was taken by Burlew and Johnson (1992), who contrasted barriers to movement toward career success among African American women. They reported that African American women in traditional occupations such as counseling and teaching experienced fewer barriers to success, such as race and gender discrimination, marital discord, and colleagues' doubt about their competence, than did African American women who were in nontraditional occupations such as law, engineering, and medicine.

Discrimination takes many forms. Overhearing a customer in a department store say "nigger" to another customer, even though it is not directed at the African American salesperson, is offensive. Being denied promotion, attractive assignments, raises, or other advantages because of racism can be devastating to an individual. When discrimination occurs, a person is likely to experience a crisis as described by Hopson and Adams. How the individual deals with that crisis will depend in some part on the situation, the supervisor, and the individual's own temperament. The model proposed by Atkinson, Morten, and Sue (1989), as outlined in Table 9-3 in the previous chapter, may describe how an individual deals with a job-related crisis caused by discrimination. For example, an individual in Atkinson et al.'s Stage 1, conformity, may blame himself or herself when faced with discrimination by a white superior, whereas someone in Stage 3, resistance and immersion, may lose self-control and respond angrily in dealing with a white superior. In Stage 5, synergetic articulation and awareness, an individual may be able to effectively confront his or her superior—and others, if need be—to remedy the discriminatory situation.

These individuals may go through Hopson and Adams's stages very differently. The person in Atkinson et al.'s Stage 1 may be stuck in Hopson and Adams's Phases 1 and 2 for some time: being shocked by the discrimination and then minimizing it—in essence, denying its importance. The person in Atkinson et al.'s Stage 3 may move quickly to Hopson and Adams's third phase of self-doubt and experience a great deal of anger. He or she may not move beyond that stage. In contrast, individuals in Stage 5 may move rather quickly through, or may skip entirely, Hopson and Adams's phases of immobilization, minimization, and self-doubt and may proceed to letting go and testing out. Ultimately, they may have a better sense of themselves for having handled the discriminatory situation positively. However, the nature of discrimination is such that, no matter how articulate and aware people of color may be, the "dominant group" may exert its power destructively.

For an example of discrimination as a crisis, let us return to Roberta. If we use Roberta as an example, the notion of "double jeopardy" can be illustrated. *Double jeopardy* refers to the fact that women of color may face occupational barriers both because they are women and because they are people of color.

Roberta was able to handle the situation with her sexist superior in a positive way. She discussed her experience with one of the law partners who had hired her. Three weeks after the incident, the supervisor left the firm. Roberta had heard rumors that similar incidents had happened to two other women in the firm. No forthright explanation was ever given of what had happened.

Roberta continued to work for the firm, being given more and more responsible tasks and being put in charge of the tax portion of large corporate accounts and for wealthy clients. When a senior member of the tax department left to join another firm, her accounts were divided among the members of the department. Two weeks after being put in charge of the tax aspect of one of the firm's largest accounts, the Doe Corporation, Roberta was told that it would be given to someone else. When she asked her new superior why that was, he became embarrassed and talked about how another member of the department had expertise that she lacked. Roberta knew that the individual mentioned did not have more expertise than she had in that matter and that the Doe Corporation had a reputation of being conservative and discriminatory.

Her immediate reaction was shock when she realized what was happening. Having experienced racism several times during her life because she was Puerto Rican, she was surprised that it would occur among people whom she believed to be philanthropic and intelligent. Having gone through the stages described by Atkinson, Morten, and Sue (1989) and having arrived at Stage 5, synergetic articulation and awareness, she did not minimize the situation, nor would she take responsibility for it by doubting herself or being depressed. She had observed hypocrisy in large corporations that stated that they had an affirmative action policy but did not act as if they did. Roberta was able to talk with her superior about different strategies for handling the situation. She talked with him about not making the switch and leaving the account in her hands. He accepted her advice and returned to a representative of the Doe Corporation to discuss it. Roberta quickly moved through many of the phases described by Hopson and Adams. She felt empowered by how she had handled the situation and by her superior's appreciation of her advice.

COUNSELOR ISSUES

Two major issues confront counselors when dealing with clients in a career crisis or transition. The first concerns the counselor's own experience with his or her own past transitions. The second concerns counseling when one is in a crisis oneself. Regarding the first, counselors need to remember that each individual experiences a crisis differently. Even though a counselor may have experienced being laid off from work at one time, the counselor may have been in a different life-span stage from the client's. Experiencing different phases of the transition and valuing different life roles would make the counselor's response different from the client's. One helpful thing that counselors can learn from their experiences with transitions is that no one can move a person through phases; a person in crisis works through phases at his or her own pace.

The second issue deals with how counselors respond when they are themselves in crisis. Crises and transformations can consume much energy and time. A counselor going through a divorce or job loss may be able to think of little else. Seeking counseling is often extremely helpful. Sometimes, that is not sufficient, and the counselor temporarily or permanently removes himself or herself from the counseling situation. It is particularly the first three phases of Hopson and Adams's model that require much self-preoccupation. The phases of letting go, testing out, search for meaning, and internalization lend themselves to less preoccupation than do the first three phases.

SUMMARY

Career crises and transitions tend to be most difficult to handle when they are unanticipated and involuntary. Further, if they are experienced at a time when work-role salience is high for an individual and that person is in the establishment and maintenance stages as described by Super, then considerable trauma may occur. Hopson and Adams (1977) offer a seven-phase model for understanding crises that can be applied to career transition. Women and people of color may experience discrimination as a type of adult life transition or crisis that white males do not experience. Further, women may encounter difficult situations in terms of reentering or leaving the world of work because of child-raising issues. Also, sexual harassment can be devastating to a woman's career development and sense of self at whatever time in the life span it occurs. Responding to a wide variety of career-related transitions is a fairly common occurrence for counselors or therapists who counsel working adults.

References

Atkinson, D. R., Morten, G., & Sue, D. W. (1989). *Counseling American minorities: A cross-cultural perspective* (3rd ed.). Dubuque, IA: William C. Brown.

Baker, N. L. (1989). *Sexual harassment and job satisfaction in traditional and non-traditional industrial occupations.* Unpublished doctoral dissertation, California School of Professional Psychology, Los Angeles.

Bardwick, J. (1980). The seasons of a woman's life. In D. McGuigan (Ed.), *Women's lives: New theory, research, and policy* (pp. 35–57). Ann Arbor: University of Michigan, Center for Continuing Education of Women.

Betz, N. E., & Fitzgerald, L. F. (1987). *The career psychology of women.* Orlando, FL: Academic Press.

Brammer, L. M., & Abrego, P. J. (1981). Intervention strategies for coping with transitions. *The Counseling Psychologist, 9*(2), 19–35.

Brooks, L., & Perot, A. (1991). Reporting sexual harassment: Exploring a predictive model. *Psychology of Women Quarterly, 15,* 31–47.

Bruce, R. A., & Scott, S. G. (1994). Varieties and commonalities of career transitions: Louis' typology revisited. *Journal of Vocational Behavior, 45,* 17–40.

Burlew, A. K., & Johnson, J. C. (1992). Role conflict and career advancement among African American women in nontraditional professions. *The Career Development Quarterly, 40,* 291–301.

Cleveland, J. N., & Kerst, M. E. (1993). Sexual harassment and perceptions of power: An un-articulated relationship. *Journal of Vocational Behavior, 42,* 49–67.

Coles, F. S. (1986). Forced to quit: Sexual harassment complaints and agency response. *Sex Roles, 14,* 81–95.

Eby, L. T., & Buch, K. (1995). Job loss as career growth: Responses to involuntary career transitions. *The Career Development Quarterly, 44,* 26–42.

Fitzgerald, L. F., & Ormerod, A. J. (1993). Breaking silence: The sexual harassment of women in academia and the workplace. In F. L. Denmark and M. A. Paludi (Eds.), *Psychology of women: A handbook of issues and theories* (pp. 553–581). Westport, CN: Greenwood.

Fitzgerald, L. F., & Shullman, S. L. (1985). *The development and validation of an objectively scored measure of sexual harassment.* Paper presented at the convention of the American Psychological Association.

Gold, Y. (1987, August). *The sexualization of the workplace: sexual harassment of pink-, white- and blue-collar workers.* Paper presented to the annual conference of the American Psychological Association, New York.

Gutek, B. (1985). *Sex and the workplace.* San Francisco: Jossey-Bass.

Gutek, B. A., & Koss, M. P. (1993). Changed women and changed organizations: Consequences of and coping with sexual harassment. *Journal of Vocational Behavior, 42,* 28–48.

Heppner, M. J., Multon, K. D., & Johnston, J. A. (1994). Assessing psychological resources during career change: Development of the Career Transitions Inventory. *Journal of Vocational Behavior, 44,* 55–74.

Hill, R. (1949). *Families under stress.* New York: Harpers.

Hopson, B. (1981). Response to papers by Schlossberg, Brammer, and Abrego. *The Counseling Psychologist, 9*(2), 36–39.

Hopson, B., & Adams, J. D. (1977). Towards an understanding of transitions: Defining some boundaries of transition. In J. Adams, J. Hayes, & B. Hopson (Eds.), *Transition: Understanding and managing personal change* (pp. 1–19). Montclair, NJ: Allenheld & Osmun.

Hotelling, K. (1991). Sexual harassment: A problem shielded by silence. *Journal of Counseling and Development, 69,* 497–501.

Kaplan, D. M., & Mason, E. A. (1965). Maternal reactions to premature birth viewed as an acute emotional disorder. In H. S. Parad (Ed.), *Crisis intervention: Selected readings* (pp. 118–128). New York: Family Service Association of America.

Kübler-Ross, E. (1969). *On death and dying.* New York: Macmillan.

Lewis, J. A., & Lewis, M. D. (1986). *Counseling programs for employees in the workplace.* Belmont, CA: Brooks Cole.

Louis, M. (1980a). Career transitions: Varieties and commonalities. *Academy of Management Review, 5,* 329–340.

Louis, M. (1980b). Surprise and sense-making: What newcomers experience in entering unfamiliar organizational settings. *Administrative Science Quarterly, 25,* 226–251.

Mirvis, P. H., & Hall, D. T. (1994). Psychological success and the boundaryless career. *Journal of Organizational Behavior, 15,* 365–380.

Moos, R. H., & Schaefer, J. A. (1986). Life transitions and crises: A conceptual overview. In R. H. Moos (Ed.), *Coping with life crises: An integrated approach* (pp. 3–28). New York: Plenum Press.

Moos, R. H., & Tsu, V. (1976). Human competence and coping: An overview. In R. H. Moos (Ed.), *Human adaptation: Coping with life crises* (pp. 3–16). Lexington, MA: Heath.

Morrow, P. C., McElroy, J. C., & Phillips, C. M. (1994). Sexual harassment behaviors and work related perceptions and attitudes. *Journal of Vocational Behavior, 45,* 295–309.

Pearlin, L. I., & Leiberman, M. A. (1979). Social sources of emotional distress. In R. Simmons (Ed.), *Research in community and mental health* (Vol 1, pp. 217–248). Greenwich, CT: JAI Press.

Perosa, S., & Perosa, L. (1983). The mid-career crisis: A description of the psychological dynamics of transition and adaptation. *Vocational Guidance Quarterly, 32,* 60–79.

Perosa, S., & Perosa, L. (1985). The mid-career crisis in relation to Super's career and Erikson's adult development theory. *International Journal of Aging and Human Development, 20*(1), 53–68.

Perosa, S., & Perosa, L. (1987). Strategies for counseling mid-career changers: A conceptual framework. *Journal of Counseling and Development, 65,* 558–561.

Pryor, J. B., LaVite, C. M., & Stoller, L. M. (1993). A social psychological analysis of sexual harassment: The period situation interaction. *Journal of Vocational Behavior, 42,* 68--83.

Schlossberg, N. K. (1984). *Counseling adults in transition.* New York: Springer.

Schlossberg, N. K., & Leibowitz, Z. B. (1980). Organizational support systems as buffers to job loss. *Journal of Vocational Behavior, 17,* 204–217.

Stockdale, M. S. (1993). The role of sexual misperceptions of women's friendliness in an emerging theory of sexual harassment. *Journal of Vocational Behavior, 42,* 84–101.

Swain, D. A. (1991). Withdrawal from sport and Schlossberg's model of transitions. *Sociology and Sport Journal, 8,* 152–160.

Thomas, D. A., & Alderfer, C. P. (1989). The influence of race on career dynamics: Theory and research on minority career experiences. In M. A. Arthur, D. T. Hall, & B. S. Lawrence (Eds.), *Handbook of career theory* (pp. 133–158). New York: Cambridge University Press.

Till, F. (1980). *Sexual harassment: A report on the sexual harassment of students.* Washington, DC: National Advisory Council on Women's Educational Programs.

U.S. Merit Systems Protection Board. (1981). *Sexual harassment of federal workers: Is it a problem?* Washington, DC: U.S. Government Printing Office.

Yoder, J. D., & Aniakudo, P. (1995). The responses of African American women firefighters to gender harassment at work. *Sex Roles, 32,* 125–137.

PART THREE

Special Focus Theories

Several theories have been developed that represent different ways of viewing the career selection process. Many of these theories have taken psychological theory and applied it to career development. In Chapter 11, psychodynamic theory is applied to career selection and adjustment by Bordin in his development of Sigmund Freud's emphasis on childhood sexuality, by Erikson through his emphasis on adolescent identity, and by Adler in his approach to the effect of early life experience and social interaction on work. Chapter 12 describes attempts to predict occupational choice from parents' child-raising styles, as well as examining the effect of attachment to parents on career decision making. Anne Roe's occupational classification system is also described. Learning theory and behavioral approaches in psychology have also had an impact on career development theory. These are described in Chapter 13 in Krumboltz's social learning theory of career development, which focuses on a systematic approach to career decision making, as well as career self-efficacy theory, which features the role of self-esteem. In Chapter 14, two different career decision-making theories are described. That of Miller-Tiedeman and Tiedeman describes the process of career decision making. In contrast, Gati's sequential elimination approach represents a way of choosing occupations based on psychological decision-making theory. Differing from psychological approaches, Chapter 15 illustrates the contribution of sociology and economic theory to the labor market and to career development issues. Each of these chapters provides important perspectives that may be useful in counseling.

11

Psychodynamic Approaches to Career Development

During the early years of the twentieth century, Sigmund Freud met, on at least a weekly basis, with students and colleagues to discuss human motivation and instinctual drives. From these meetings grew a large number of theoretical concepts that have been taken up by a wide variety of theorists to explain human behavior. Much of the interest was in early childhood development and its influence on adult behavior. These discussions included topics such as instinctual drives, aggressive behavior, and reactions to family and social factors. In this chapter, the ideas of Freud, Erikson, and Adler will be applied to career development behavior. Another important psychodynamic theorist, Carl Jung, was discussed in Chapter 5, "Myers-Briggs Type Theory," as this theory represents one aspect of Jung's work.

Sigmund Freud, who originally wanted to become a research biologist and physician, became interested in work being done with patients with symptoms of hysteria. This led to Freud's important contributions, the uncovering of childhood sexuality and later identification of psychosexual stages. As exceedingly important as these contributions were, they have had little impact on career development theory. One notable exception has been the work of Edward Bordin and his colleagues. They have investigated the relationship between career development and psychosexual stages, studying play and its role in later work behavior. The relationship between play and work is illustrated in this chapter.

Erik Erikson studied with Freud during Freud's later years. Erikson was analyzed by, and studied with, Anna Freud, who was Sigmund Freud's youngest daughter. She was particularly interested in, and wrote much about, the behavior of children. Erikson's theorizing expands on the work of Anna and Sigmund Freud, encompassing developmental stages covering the entire life span. Included in his work is an emphasis on social factors as well as instinctual drives. Erikson is perhaps best known for his work on adolescents and the identity crisis. This chapter will focus on the identity crisis as it relates to career development among adolescents.

Alfred Adler was a contemporary of Freud's who articulated his own theory of human behavior and psychotherapy. Although influenced by Freud, he was often in disagreement with Freud and gradually left Freud's group of colleagues and students. Adler's approach to human development emphasizes the social interest and the social responsibility that individuals have. He focused not on life stages, but on life themes that might characterize a person over many years. More than Freud, Adler emphasized the importance of work for individual satisfaction and social commitment. His theory offers counselors and psychotherapists suggestions for the application of Adlerian theory to career development.

There has been little work on applying psychodynamic approaches to career development, with the possible exception of work done by students of Adlerian counseling and psychotherapy. When psychodynamic approaches are used by psychologists and counselors in career development, the counselor or therapist usually has had considerable training and experience in one of the psychodynamic approaches to therapy and counseling prior to applying it to career development. Because psychodynamic theory and its application tend to be quite complex, it is rarely possible for a counselor to apply psychodynamic approaches to career development issues without a thorough training in the theory.

Although other chapters in this book show how career development theories can be used in career counseling by giving a full understanding of the theory involved, this chapter uses a different approach. Because of the complexity of the theories and the limited available information about their application, only segments of each theory are illustrated. An interested reader should consult resources that describe psychoanalytic, Eriksonian, and Adlerian theory in greater detail.

PSYCHOANALYTIC APPROACHES TO CAREER DEVELOPMENT

Freud's emphasis on childhood sexuality can be understood from his stages of childhood development. Bordin, Nachmann, and Segal (1963) have related career choice to psychosexual stages. From their work (and that of others) on childhood influences on career choice has come an emphasis on the importance of play in adult work. Play as a useful concept in career counseling will be illustrated in this section.

The Four Psychosexual Stages

Freud described four basic psychosexual stages: oral, anal, genital, and latency (Sharf, 1996). The oral stage extends from birth to about 18 months. Instinctually, infants suck and feed, using the mouth, lips, and tongue. Oral satisfaction brings about stress reduction and sleep. The anal phase begins at about the age of 18 months and lasts until about the age of 3. For the toddler in this stage, a major source of pleasure is retaining and passing feces. When adults show disgust at the child's pleasure in feces retention and play, guilt and shame may be the effect. The genital phase lasts from about age 3 to age 6. During this phase, both boys and girls become interested in pleasure that may be centered in the penis and the vagina. Curiosity about sexual differences is likely to develop. In this stage, the Oedipus complex (sexual attraction of the male child to the mother along with hostile feelings toward the father) is likely to emerge. This phase ends for the male when hostile feelings toward the father are reduced and the child identifies with the father. The Electra complex is the female counterpart to the Oedipus complex. The latency period lasts from the age of 6 until the onset of puberty. In this phase, oral, anal, and genital instinctual drives subside, and socialization with other children and adults becomes more prominent. Some research has been done to relate the degree to which the needs met in these phases affect later career choice.

During the early 1960s, several studies were done that form the basis for Bordin's initial theoretical view of the importance of early childhood development to later career choice. Using projective techniques to inquire about childhood backgrounds, Segal (1961) found differences in the reactions of accountants and creative writers in terms of their personalities and parental relations. Nachmann (1960), using biographical interviews, found differences in childhood developmental experiences among males in law, dentistry, and social work. Employing similar retrospective techniques (asking adults about their childhood), Galinsky (1962) found differences between clinical psychologists and physicists. All of these occupational groups were analyzed according to early developmental needs that influenced later career development. Information from these studies was formulated into a framework that Bordin, Nachmann, and Segal (1963) felt would predict career selection. Support for the theory was also found with engineers (Beall & Bordin, 1964); accountants (Miller, 1962; Schlesinger, 1963; Segal & Szabo, 1964); and chefs and dentists (Juni, 1981).

Although this research by Bordin and his colleagues was creative, little has been done since the mid-1960s on research relating career development to early childhood behavior in terms of psychosexual stages. The theory was criticized for not including information about significant later childhood and adolescent experiences that affect career choice. Since that time, Bordin (1990) has expanded his theory to include identity issues, as described by Erikson and discussed in the next section. For Bordin, in both the earlier and later versions of his theory, as well as for Erikson, play is an important activity that brings about joy or satisfaction. In adulthood, play is done not without effort, but with enjoyable effort. When someone says, "I enjoy my work," he or she is often referring to the components of work that seem to be fun and enjoyable, or playlike.

Play as a Theoretical Construct

To Bordin, play or the experience of joy that comes from play is sought by all individuals, at most times during their lives. Bordin understands the need to house and to feed oneself and one's family but feels that, where possible, individuals seek to derive joy from their activity (work). This desire for satisfaction or joy in one's work will lead a person to select, unconsciously, an occupation that satisfies the need for enjoyment. Play is a great part of young children's life. As children mature, play often becomes a smaller and smaller part of their school life. However, this sense of joy that comes from play will keep adolescents and adults motivated as they develop mastery in their activities.

The antithesis of play, according to psychoanalytic theory, is compulsion. *Compulsion* refers to the pressures that come from mother, father, or, less directly, teachers to do those things that the teacher or parent wishes to be done. If the child does not accede to the direct or indirect request, there is a threat of not being loved or of receiving punishment. Playing the piano because one is supposed to can become a compulsion. A compulsion to "play" the piano may persist long after the parents have forgotten about the activity. As an individual becomes older, the nature of play becomes more complex and the recognition of one's own talent becomes more important. If a child finds that he or she has limited piano-playing ability and is not making progress in that activity, what was once play may turn into a compulsion or may cease totally. Participation in athletic activities for children with limited ability often diminishes greatly. If sports are not a priority for the child's parents in the way that music or scholastic ability may be, the activity may cease and not become a compulsion. This conflict within an individual between play and compulsion is a struggle that can occur at anytime in one's life, not only in childhood.

Implications for Counseling

A topic of discussion between counselor and client that may emerge in counseling is enjoyment of an activity. Such dialogue can take place in the first session of counseling or anytime thereafter. By responding to the pleasure that the client has gained from an activity, the counselor is demonstrating that he or she understands the importance of play in work satisfaction. Such a demonstration of recognition can occur at any point in the life span of the client. The counselor may be working with a man or woman who has seven children. To acknowledge the importance of play in the life of a client does not mean that the counselor will help the client ignore family responsibilities. Rather, the counselor will help the client to integrate responsibilities (the reality principle) with work and leisure satisfaction (the pleasure principle). Often, the activity that gives joy to the individual in a later stage of life is a redefinition of an activity that gave pleasure in childhood. The following dialogue is an example of such an occurrence.

Linda is a 37-year-old married African American female with three children. She is a registered nurse, having received her degree from a state college. Currently she is working 40 hours per week as a surgical nurse in a large hospital. She has sought counseling from a career counselor at the continuing education counseling service of a large university in her city. She has become increasingly dissatisfied with nursing demands and activities. She does not look forward to going to work, nor is she enjoying meeting the demands of her patients. During her first visit with the counselor, the following discussion takes place:

CL: I've been working at the hospital for over 15 years. At first, things were new and different. Because I was brand new—right out of training—I was in awe of everyone who seemed to know what they were doing. I tried very hard to please the head nurse and to make sure that he would like my work. When the doctors would come by when I was with a patient, I would get very nervous. I was often afraid that I had done the wrong thing. I did fine. All of my evaluations were excellent. The hospital was really very busy, particularly on the weekends when I worked, and I tried very hard to make sure that I made no mistakes.

CO: You really did want your superiors to like your work. [The counselor is aware that no mention of enjoyment has been made and that the client wishes very much to please her superiors, that is, authority figures.]

CL: I really did want to please. I had struggled so hard in college to do well. I was even on the dean's list for two years. The nursing instructors often seemed scary to me, and I wanted to make sure that my work was satisfactory.

CO: For a long time pleasing others has been important to you. [Reflecting once again the importance of pleasing others, the counselor notices the absence of pleasure in Linda's description.]

CL: School and work were things for me to do to get recognition. I was in a sorority during my four years of school and really enjoyed it. I still am involved with it now. When I see some of my old friends, I can really enjoy myself and relax.

CO: It feels good to be away from the pressures of responsibility to yourself and others. [The counselor starts to feel a little more relaxed as the client relaxes and turns her focus to enjoyment.]

CL: When I am with my friends from school, people I've known almost 20 years, we can just gossip and have fun the way we did before. I remember the dances, parties, and some of the social service activities that we did together.

CO: Socializing with your friends sounds like some of the happiest times for you. [The counselor is hoping to focus more on the specific activities that the client enjoyed.]

CL: No. Those were fun times all right, but what I think I liked best were those times when I was with my father when we lived near Richmond, Virginia. My father delivered milk for a local dairy for many years. It was the best job that he could get, and he didn't feel qualified for anything else. He would often grumble when he got home, but when he got back into his garden, he was happy. He had a fair-sized plot of land, and he used to grow tomatoes, corn, cucumbers, all kinds of things. When I was little, I used to go out back and help him. At least, I used to think that I was helping him. Even when I couldn't help, he would make me think that I was helping. He would take me out back, and I'd play in that black loam, where he'd show me, with much excitement, what was coming up, what was growing, and what was ripe. When I would come home for summer vacation, even when I was doing student nursing in a hospital, I would go out in the evenings, even though they were hot, and work with him. He would tell me about new varieties of tomatoes or cauliflower that he was planting. He really liked the fact that I liked plants, too. He knew that I would listen to him and not get bored. Even when it was getting very dark, we would stay out in the backyard talking about vegetables and flowers. In elementary school and high school, I took biology a lot, and probably because of my father, I really enjoyed botany. In college, when I took biology it was botany that I liked most. I even took an elective botany course in college.

CO: What pleasure, with your father, with gardening! [The counselor is surprised that the subject has come up but is instantly attracted to the client's joy and enthusiasm about her happy times with her father.]

CL: It was fun, and I think I might have done more of it in college, but I remember a friend who is not a friend anymore, who said to me when I mentioned that I might want to learn plant science in college, "What, are you kidding? A black woman in the ag school? They'll have you picking cotton." And she started laughing. I didn't think about it much anymore.

CO: That really had an impact on your choices. [Being aware of the fragility of enjoyment, the counselor considers how to offset the discouragement of Linda's joy.]

CL: I sometimes wonder what would have happened if I had gone to the College of Agriculture and not Nursing.

CO: What do you think may have happened? [Being interested in the answer to this question, the counselor follows up and is ready to explore Linda's enjoyment. As the counselor explores, there will be an opportunity to determine whether the play that she had as a child is still active for her now, has passed, or is more related to being with her father.]

Not knowing where this enjoyment will lead, the counselor wishes to be open to follow up on this aspect of the pleasure principle. However, the counselor is very much aware of the reality principle and the importance of effort in the completion of work. The client provides joint support for her family, along with her husband. The outcome of counseling for the client may mean more work with houseplants, a garden of her own, a community garden, courses in agriculture, a master's degree or a doctorate in plant science, or a change to a career that will be very different from her current career of nursing. Wherever the change, if any, the counselor will present both joy and reality for consideration. In doing so, the counselor is developing a working alliance with the client (Meara & Patton, 1994). By working collaboratively with the client, the counselor builds an emotional bond, while also helping the client to work on specific tasks related to the goals of counseling. This emphasis on play focuses on early development as it is realized in later life. In a less direct sense, play is an important component of Erikson's stages of development.

ERIKSON'S PSYCHODYNAMIC THEORY AND IDENTITY

Erikson's theory of human development is broad, with several implications for career development. Influencing more career theorists than any other single developmental theory, Erikson's life-stage approach is frequently cited. Of particular interest are his conceptualizations about adolescent identity issues. His identity stage is the fifth of eight stages and serves as a bridge between the four stages occurring in childhood and the three stages that arise in adulthood. The focus of this section will be on the identity stage and its relationship to other stages as they affect career development.

Compared to the attraction of career development theorists to Erikson's model, the direct application of Erikson's theory to career development issues has been minimal. An effort to apply Erikson's theoretical constructs to career development has been made by Munley (1977). Some research by Munley (1975) and others (Galinsky & Fast, 1966; Powers & Griffith, 1993; Savickas, 1985; Segal & Szabo, 1964) has focused on the identity crisis. These writers have attempted to define the concept of identity and to explain it through research and case studies. Although direct application of Erikson's theory is limited, his work has had an impact on many career development theorists who are discussed in this book.

Erikson's theory is not a career development theory, but he has influenced Holland, Bordin, and Miller-Tiedeman and Tiedeman, as well as Super. For example, John Holland has used the concept of vocational identity in his theory. Holland's development of a vocational identity scale has been quite productive (see Chapter 4). Also, the developmental decision-making stages of Tiedeman and O'Hara (1963) borrow heavily from Erikson's ideas. The later work of Tiedeman and Miller-Tiedeman is also a reflection of the influence of Erikson's theory. Additionally, Bordin's (1990) revised theory of career development relies heavily on the contributions of Erikson's ego identity model. Donald Super's developmental concepts, although more directly related to the work of Buehler (1933), were also influenced by the theoretical stages of Erikson. The development of one's self-concept (Super) and a developing sense of identity (Erikson) are quite similar. How adolescents negotiate their identity crises presents a useful perspective on adolescent career development.

The Eight Stages of Ego Growth

Erikson's (1963, 1968, 1982) theory of human development proposes eight stages of ego growth. Each of these stages is identified by a "crisis." At each crisis point, the individual either makes progress in terms of growth and capacity or becomes weaker because of a failure to negotiate the stage. The individual's attitude toward self and others is a reflection of his or her ability to negotiate stages successfully. These stages depend on each other. In other words, the ability to negotiate one stage depends on the individual's success in negotiating the previous stages. Another way of looking at the stages is that they are a reflection of the interaction of the individual with his or her environment. Stages are particularly important at certain times in the life cycle. Resolution of stage crises is never complete, in that issues in resolving a stage crisis may occur at any time in a person's life. The eight crises described by Erikson (1982) are these: trust versus mistrust, autonomy versus shame and doubt, initiative versus guilt, industry versus inferiority, identity versus identity confusion, intimacy versus isolation, generativity versus stagnation, and integrity versus despair.

For Erikson, the key stage is the identity stage. Identity versus identity confusion is the stage in which individuals are moving from childhood to adulthood. This link is a particularly important one for Erikson. How an adolescent has negotiated the first four stages affects the way in which he or she will handle adolescent crises and develop as an adult.

In the following pages, each of Erikson's stages is described in the left-hand column in terms of the general issues that are a focus of the crises represented by that stage. The relationship to Freudian stages and the approximate age at which one negotiates the stage are given. Where appropriate, comments are made about the relationship of the crisis in each stage to career development issues.

Because the identity-versus-identity-confusion crisis is such an important one for the individual, Erikson has described how each of the other crises manifests itself in the identity stage (Gross, 1987). During adolescence, individuals may experience a "moratorium." This is a time when adolescents are not expected to take on adult responsibilities. Society may be indulgent of young people and permit them to act more freely than when they approach later life (Maier, 1978). It is during this time that an individual is likely to experience aspects of other stages in the guise of the identity stage. The right-hand column in the pages that follow shows how each crisis manifests itself in the identity stage. For example, trust versus mistrust emerges in the identity stage as the crisis of temporal perspective versus time confusion. Later stages also show hints of emergence in the identity stage. For example, ideological commitment versus confusion of values is a precursor to the eighth stage of Erikson's life cycle: integrity versus despair. Career implications of these crises as they emerge in the identity stage will be given.

Psychosocial Crises

1. *Trust versus mistrust:* Corresponding to Freud's oral stage, this stage takes place during the first year of life. What is important to Erikson (1982) is not so much the oral gratification of the infant as the sense of trust that develops between mother and child. If the mother is unresponsive to the child, then a feeling of mistrust may develop. This sense of trust can be applied not just to the mother, but to others as well, being important in both working and loving relationships.
2. *Autonomy versus shame:* Similar to Freud's anal stage, this occurs between the ages of 1 and 3. Erikson emphasizes psychosocial rather than psychosexual development. This is the time when the child learns to let go and to hold on, not just to bowel movements, but also to emotions and feelings. Shame and doubt may arise, not just from problems in toilet training, but from criticism by the parents. Doubt occurs when the individual cannot see or know what else is going on. Thus, doubt is in contrast to a sense of independence or autonomy.
3. *Initiative versus guilt:* Analogous to the genital stage of Freud, this period occurs around the age of 4 or 5. At this point, play is particularly important. Children take the initiative to make up games, to pretend, and to play in a variety of ways.

Crises Occurring during the Identity Stage

1. *Temporal perspective versus time confusion:* When individuals have a temporal perspective, they have trust in themselves and others that they can plan a future, and they can see themselves as being successful in the future. When there is time confusion, adolescents may feel that they need to make decisions immediately, or (the opposite) they may feel immobilized and unable to make decisions. Adolescents who do not have a temporal perspective may find it difficult to make career commitments. They are likely to move from one job to another or to see their current job only as a means to an end, for example, earning money for leisure activities.
2. *Self-certainty versus self-consciousness:* In this phase, the adolescent struggles between being self-assured and confident and being vain or apathetic. The vanity may be a mask for feelings of self-doubt or confusion. When an adolescent is feeling self-conscious, it may be difficult to choose an occupation. If a career choice takes place during this phase, the youth may feel coerced into making a choice or may feel that the choice is inappropriate. Self-certainty will lead to a feeling of direction and confidence about a career decision.
3. *Role experimentation versus role fixation:* Adolescents experiment with a variety of adult roles. They may go to extremes in doing so, for example, becoming fanatically committed to a cause. If their experimentation with roles is successful, they

Guilt occurs from the fear of doing something wrong, of being caught. This is closely related to the Oedipus and Electra complexes, in which competition for the opposite-sex parent and rivalry with the same-sex parent are felt.	During this time, the adolescent is likely to enter a moratorium, experiencing the opportunity to will develop a positive rather than a negative identity. With regard to career choice, it is at this point that they may develop a sense of ambition and purpose for their role in the world of work.
4. *Industry versus inferiority:* Between the ages of 6 and 11, as in the latency stage of Freud, the child becomes influenced not just by his or her parents, but also by other members of society. Work becomes important, particularly schoolwork. Children who are successful in their schoolwork tend to feel independent, competent, and adequate. A sense of inferiority develops when one cannot perform well in school or in other tasks. The child who has difficulty reading and is picked last for sports teams is likely to develop a feeling of inferiority. This feeling of inferiority can carry over into the workplace when the child is older, affecting competence on the job because of feelings of inadequacy.	4. *Apprenticeship versus work paralysis:* By bringing a sense of industry rather than inferiority to their work, adolescents may develop a sense of competency as they learn job-related skills in an apprenticeship situation. With a sense of inferiority, they will question their ability to work productively and may be partially or entirely paralyzed in their efforts. Without confidence, it is difficult to start and complete work tasks.
5. *Identity versus identity confusion:* A focal stage for Erikson, this occurs between the ages of about 12 and 18. Difficult to define, identity occurs when an adolescent is able to put together perceptions of himself or herself with perceptions of others. *Identity crisis and confusion* refers to uncertainty about carrying out a variety of roles. In such a situation, an adolescent may feel that he or she does not have a place, does not belong. The adolescent may not feel like an adult and may not be ready to take on adult responsibilities.	5. Same as left-hand column.

experiencing the opportunity to find himself or herself without the pressures of adult responsibilities. To concentrate on schoolwork and other work for a long period of time while in identity confusion can be very difficult, because there is no sense of belonging.

6. *Intimacy versus isolation:* To experience intimacy with others, particularly with others of the opposite sex, during young adulthood, it is important to have established a sense of identity. Then a deep relationship can develop. Regarding work, this phase refers to a commitment to the work performed, to a sense of cooperation with one's employer, enabling the individual to work well with co-workers rather than be isolated and able only to work alone.
7. *Generativity versus stagnation:* This is the longest of the stages. Occurring in middle adulthood, it can last from the ages of 25 to 65. At this point, people become parents (generativity), becoming responsible for their own children. Further, there is a demand to be productive, to provide for oneself and for one's family. In contrast, being self-absorbed leads to a feeling of stagnation, of not being able to successfully accomplish responsibilities. Regarding work tasks, being creative and productive will lead to a positive sense of self. In contrast, being overly concerned about how one is doing in one's work can lead to negative feelings and stress.
8. *Integrity versus despair: Integrity* refers to a sense of wholeness or completeness. Occurring around the age of 65 and generally associated with retire-

6. *Sexual polarization versus bisexual confusion:* A sexual orientation to the opposite sex (polarization) emerges from attraction to both sexes (bisexual confusion). Developing a sexual identity is part of developing a fuller sense of identity as a productive adult. As a full sense of identity is developed, the adolescent develops the ability to work cooperatively and loyally with others.
7. *Leadership and followership versus authority confusion:* At this point, adolescents may struggle toward developing leadership skills and rebelling against and resisting authority. With maturity comes the ability to make realistic assessments of authority figures. By appropriate leadership and followership, individuals are able to develop themselves as productive and creative working people who can deal appropriately with leadership and authority issues.
8. *Ideological commitment versus confusion of values:* Erikson believes that adolescents tend to be extremely loyal and uncompromising in their values. Gradually,

ment, this stage refers to being prepared for death, to accepting one's life, and to being content with the way one has lived. *Despair* refers to the feeling of not having done something, the feeling that "Now it's too late. I have made too many mistakes in my life." For Erikson, wisdom arises out of the struggle between integrity and despair.

they learn to incorporate the values of others into their own views. They are starting to develop wisdom, which is associated with the last of Erikson's eight crises. In adolescence, when individuals are struggling with their career choice, they are trying to identify the values that are important to them in making career decisions.

Identity Crises

From the preceding, it can be seen that each of Erikson's stages (the left-hand column) is reflected in the identity crisis by issues occurring in adolescence (the right-hand column). Although Erikson has written frequently on issues concerning the identity crisis, his work does not provide clear prescriptions for the counselor or psychotherapist. It could be said that Erikson presents an artistic rather than a scientific view of the identity crisis. Describing identity issues in the lives of clients can sometimes be difficult. One of the best ways to illustrate the importance of identity issues in a person's life is to look at the identity issues in Erikson's own life.

Identity crises are an important theme throughout Erikson's life. Before he was born in Copenhagen in 1902, his father abandoned his mother. About three years later, his Christian mother married a Jewish doctor, Theodor Homberger, who lived in Germany. Erikson found that he was considered a Christian by the Jewish community and a Jew by his Christian peers—certainly an excellent example of an identity crisis (Gross, 1987; Maier, 1978). He left high school to find himself and to develop his artistic interests. Erikson also had to decide whether to use the name of his natural or his adoptive father. This period of self-searching can be considered a "moratorium" in his life. Until the age of 25, he worked painting and carving wood. At this time, his interest in teaching and observing young children was noticed. He was invited to teach art in a small American school in Vienna. His sensitivity to children was noticed by Anna Freud, who became both his analyst and his teacher. It was during the period from 1927 through 1933 that Erikson finished his training in child psychoanalysis. Because of the development of fascism in Europe, Erikson came to the United States in 1933. Here, he taught and continued his research on human development. During the McCarthy era, the 1950s, Erikson refused to take a loyalty oath. He, like many other foreign-born professors, was urged to leave the United States. His identity as a loyal citizen was questioned. Identity issues in his own life have appeared to make him very sensitive to identity issues in the lives of others.

A Counseling Example

The following case illustrates how an identity issue may arise in counseling, creating both personal and career strains for an adolescent. Erikson's conception of stage development helps us to understand issues and difficulties that arise from a crisis at a particular point in time.

Frank is a white college sophomore who has not yet declared his major. He is attending a large university in Boston. His father is a lawyer in New York City, and his mother is vice president of a large bank. Two younger sisters are still in high school. Frank has been wondering for some time what he is going to do with his future. He is confused about his career goals and feels that he is wasting time in college because he does not know what to major in or what career to prepare for. Returning from winter vacation, he decides to talk to a counselor about his dilemma. This dialogue occurs in the first session with the counselor:

CL: My friends seem to know what they are doing—they seem to have goals, ideas. My girlfriend is premed, studies a lot, and knows where she is going.

CO: And you?

CL: I don't know. Sometimes I feel real lost. I wonder if I belong here at school. Sometimes with my courses, I just do the work, but they don't seem to matter.

CO: There's no feeling of being there, of being a part of things. [The counselor notices immediately a lack of an overall feeling of identity.]

CL: I think I used to like to do things more than I do now.

CO: What kinds of things, Frank?

CL: Well, when I first got here, I played in the marching band—trumpet. I used to like that, but it didn't seem to matter after a while, so I didn't join the band this year. The excitement of it seemed to wear off fast last year.

CO: Now things are just blah. [Again, Frank's lack of commitment seems apparent. This issue is similar to that of Erikson's first stage: trust versus mistrust.]

CL: Yeah, "blah" is a good word for it. I don't know what I'm doing, and whatever it is I'm doing, I can't seem to do it right.

CO: That statement covers a lot of territory. Let me ask you about it. What can't you do right, Frank? [Frank seems to be talking about a lack of feeling of competency, leading the counselor to think that Frank feels inferior, perhaps because of not resolving issues in the industry-versus-inferiority stage.]

CL: I did OK in high school, particularly music. I played in every band or orchestra that we had at school. I really liked the trumpet. I was always first chair, and that felt good.

CO: Something happened?

CL: Yes, I auditioned for a national competition between my junior and senior years in high school. I didn't get offered a position. At first, I was very disappointed. Then, it was after that, like nothing seemed to matter very much. I didn't care much about things after that.

CO: That seems to have been an important event for you. [The counselor hears that this disappointment is a threat to Frank's sense of identity and wonders if this alone could cause the feeling of depression that he seems to be experiencing.]

CL: Well, I guess I didn't care, and no one else seemed to care either.

CO: Go on.

CL: Well, I think that my father always thought that the music was kid stuff—fluff. You know?

CO: How did he react? [The counselor observes Frank's anger at his father, something that is not unexpected when there is a sense of a lack of identity.]

CL: It was like, "Well, so what else is new?" He has always seemed real caught up in his work. He brings work home from the office. When I was a kid I used to think that all he ever did was work.

CO: And work seemed unpleasant? [Thoughts about identification with his father and views of work occur to the counselor.]

CL: Nothing seemed fun at all. Actually, I guess fun was being at school. That always seemed funny to me because most of my friends couldn't wait to get out of school.

CO: It certainly had an effect on you. [Frank's father's commitment to work seems to be having a negative effect on Frank. He doesn't want that same feeling. Perhaps he sees that work can only be unpleasant. If so, this hampers his initiative.]

CL: It seemed that when I couldn't play the trumpet better than anybody else, I was nobody. In college, the novelty of playing in a college band lasted a while, but it wore off.

CO: Real strong feelings, Frank. [Frank has experimented with a role—Stage 3—and is hurt badly by his difficulty. He reacts in a powerful, emotional way. This type of reaction is to be expected in an identity crisis.]

Frank and the counselor spend four sessions discussing his problems. Frank is seeking a moratorium. He feels that he needs time to solve his problems. Each semester, school seems to become more futile to him. He is trying to look for meaning in his life, with school, with friends. He plans not to continue school in the fall, preferring to work so that he can continue his search for meaning in his life.

A significant effort has been devoted to studying Erikson's stages. For example, Zuschlag and Whitbourne (1994) studied three groups of college students, who were surveyed in 1967, 1977, and 1988, concluding that college seniors had more advanced emotional and cognitive development than younger students. Comparing the groups, they found that personality development in college is relatively free of changing societal pressures. Perhaps the most consistent research has been that of Marcia and colleagues. Marcia, Waterman, Matteson, Archer and Orlofsky (1993) provide a handbook for investigating Erikson's psychosocial stages, especially identity and intimacy. Marcia (1980) has modified Erikson's work so that research can be done on important stages. These stages include achievement, moratorium, foreclosure, and diffusion. Marcia's moratorium stage, similar to Erikson's concept, refers to individuals exploring possibilities but not being willing to make a commitment to a particular selection.

The interaction of moratorium with other stages raises complex questions that Stephen, Fraser, and Marcia (1992) studied. Archer (1989) provides a discussion of research on the moratorium and other stages, as well as suggestions for assisting adolescents who are experiencing identity issues. Relating Marcia's four stages to career counseling, Raskin (1989) describes hypothetical clients in each of the four stages. Marcia's (1989) contribution to the concept of identity status has been a helpful addition to Erikson's work.

A search for meaning, for identity, is important in Erikson's conception of adolescent development. The adolescent must deal not only with his or her instinctual drives, as emphasized by Sigmund Freud, but also with social issues. The adolescent develops a sense of identity separate from that of his or her parents and friends. This takes place before a feeling of intimacy with a sexual partner develops. It should also occur before commitment to an occupation—and the schooling and effort that are required for success. Erikson's emphasis on socialization issues and human growth has some resemblance to the emphasis that Alfred Adler places on the impact of society and the individual on each other.

ADLERIAN APPROACHES TO CAREER DEVELOPMENT

Adlerian psychology is distinguished by its emphasis on the individual's interaction with his or her family and society at large. Although Adler does not have a theory of career development, many of his ideas have application to career counseling and career development. Watkins (1984) adapted Adlerian theory in his formal statement of an Adlerian vocational theory. Other writers have adapted Adlerian concepts to both career assessment and career counseling. Because counselors who use Adler's theory make a distinction between counseling and psychotherapy, this distinction will be followed in this chapter. Examples will be given of how career issues can be dealt with by the use of Adlerian concepts in both counseling and psychotherapy.

Adlerian Psychology

Only a brief summary of Adlerian psychology can be given in this chapter. Mosak (1995) has written an excellent description of the psychology and psychotherapy of Alfred Adler. Another good source is the textbook *Individual Psychology* (1982) by Manaster and Corsini. With regard to Adler's own work, *Social Interest: A Challenge to Mankind* (1929/1964) is probably the best overview. In this section, Adler's constructs will be related to career development. These constructs include basic life tasks, social interests, family constellation, and lifestyle.

Basic Life Tasks Adler discussed three basic life tasks: love, social relations, and work. Freud was interested in sexuality in terms of the effect of instinctual drives on human nature, whereas Adler, acknowledging this, also examined the social aspects of sex, that is, love. He was concerned with how members of the opposite sex treat each other, both in intimate and work or social relationships. For Adler, an important construct was the interdependence of society and individuals—people relying on each other for their happiness and success. For Adler, it would be inappropriate to consider only individual needs in understanding the motivations of individuals. Social interactions directly relate to Adler's third life task: work. Work is, in most cases, a social activity, requiring interactions with patients, customers, students, superiors, colleagues, and so on. Just to survive, it is necessary to depend on the work of others. This is particularly true in a specialized economy, where few people directly produce their own food and shelter. Adler was interested in how individuals approach work and how that influences the type of work they do and the work environment in which they are employed. He saw work as a more basic and less challenging task than love and social relations, because work requires fewer interpersonal competencies.

Social Interests As can be seen from the preceding discussion, Adler emphasized the role of society in his individual psychology. He believed that individuals need to develop a view that they are part of the social enterprise, that they belong. Individuals should see themselves as contributing to the benefit of society, both in their own community and more broadly. Social interests are directly related to work. Through work, one contributes to the more productive functioning of others in the community (Watkins & Savickas, 1990). Further, work gives an individual a sense of "belongingness," a feeling that he or she matters to others. How individuals approach work and implement social interests is influenced greatly by their family relationships.

Family Constellation Adler was interested in the role and position of the child within the family. Although a number of studies have tried to relate personality type to birth order, this is a more limited concept than Adler had in mind. Birth order concerns whether the child is the firstborn, the secondborn, and so on. Adler was concerned about how the child might perceive his or her position in the family and how his or her parents and siblings might perceive the child. Such an emphasis focuses on knowing much more about the family than birth order.

An important concept arising out of the child's position within the family is encouragement versus discouragement. Discouragement can occur if the child does not feel that he or she belongs or if siblings are better at school and sports than the child. Such discouragement can lead to a feeling of inferiority, an important concept in Adler's work. This feeling can come from a subjective experience of not feeling wanted or competent. Persons with a feeling of inferiority have a sense that they are not at all what they would like to be, that they have not measured up to their ideal view of themselves. Such an attitude can easily affect one's view of work. An individual with an inferiority complex may choose to avoid difficult tasks, not to seek further education, and not to compete with others for a position. Early interactions with one's family, according to Adler, have an effect on how one accomplishes the life tasks of love, social relations, and work (Watkins & Savickas, 1990).

Lifestyle Lifestyle is the blueprint for living, the way of approaching important goals. How the lifestyle develops is a function of family constellation and early experiences within the family. One can develop a lifestyle that shows an interest in society or one that does not. Often, the lifestyle can be summarized in a word or phrase. For example, the salesperson who is always competing with colleagues and arguing with bosses may have as a lifestyle "fighting." Such a lifestyle may have developed through competitive interactions with siblings in childhood. One's lifestyle is often manifested through the choice of a career. Thus, in the preceding example, an individual chooses sales as a profession so that he or she can compete and "fight" with competitors, a continuation of childhood lifestyle. Lifestyle is reflected in the attitudes that people have toward themselves and others. It may have a dramatic effect on the way an individual lives life. A method for assessing lifestyle is to ask the client to recall early experiences. This method will be discussed more fully in a later section.

These concepts demonstrate the importance to Adler of the interaction of the child and his or her society. This summary, based on the writings of Adler (1929/1964) and the work of Mosak (1995), also shows the close relationship, in Adlerian theory, of human behavior and work. Because of this close relationship, several writers have found Adler's writings to be very influential in their development of career assessment and counseling approaches.

Goals of Adlerian Counseling and Psychotherapy

In general, those using Adler's concepts in counseling or psychotherapy try to correct mistaken ideas about the self, others, and life that arise from difficult childhood experiences in the family and, to some extent, with peers. An important goal of Adlerian counseling and psychotherapy is to decrease feelings of inferiority and replace those feelings with a sense of confidence and competence. The Adlerian counselor is often helping the client to overcome feelings of discouragement that he or she may have experienced in the family by encouraging the client and communicating care. Further, the counselor may focus on the development of social interests. This may include increased willingness to cooperate in interactions with people in the family and community and at work. The client may also be urged to change his or her lifestyle. To use the example of the salesperson, this may mean adopting a less aggressive approach when working with others in favor of a more cooperative approach, such as cooperating with peers and competing with one's own previous performance. The client and the counselor may work to achieve this without affecting the salesperson's total sales.

The general goals of Adlerian counseling are compatible with the goals of career counseling. An Adlerian counselor might help a client develop a feeling of confidence in his or her work and the ability to make a career choice. An appropriate career choice would be consistent with one's lifestyle, where possible. For example, an individual who is making a career choice, yet is dissatisfied with his or her lifestyle, may alter the lifestyle, developing more positive views toward himself or herself and others, and choose an occupation that reflects that change.

From an Adlerian point of view, the concept of lifestyle determines whether psychotherapy or counseling should be done (Dreikurs, 1961). When an individual must change his or her lifestyle, he or she requires psychotherapy. When changes can be made in behavior within the current lifestyle, then counseling takes place. In essence, counseling deals with lifestyle management; psychotherapy deals with lifestyle modification. Changing one's lifestyle requires an in-depth assessment of early family experiences. This assessment, or investigation, focuses on early recollections by the client. What the client may perceive as truth may be inaccurate assumptions or misperceptions, called *guiding fictions,* about both early and current life (Mosak, 1995). Counseling, on the other hand, may require identifying the current lifestyle and finding ways to change behavior to make that lifestyle more consistent. Career issues may require either psychotherapy or counseling, depending on whether it is necessary to change one's lifestyle.

Applying Adlerian Theory to Career Development

Some writers have applied Adlerian principles to career development. Watkins (1984) has developed theoretical constructs that make formal statements about vocational behavior in Adlerian terms. Watkins focuses on four areas: lifestyle, life tasks, family atmosphere and relationships, and early recollections. He summarizes research that, although limited, provides a view of how these four concepts of Adler's relate to career development issues. He and others have also applied these concepts to career issues that arise in counseling and psychotherapy.

Career Issues and Adlerian Psychotherapy Adlerian therapy explores the family constellation and experiences that contributed to a particular lifestyle. Adler (1931) believed that what individuals remember from their childhood strongly influences career issues in later life. In research on a small group of professional and blue-collar men, Csikszentmihalyi and Beattie (1979) found that individuals' life themes clearly related to their career development. Hafner and Fakouri (1984a, 1984b) have shown that early recollections of individuals distinguished three groups of graduate students in clinical psychology, dentistry, and law, and they made general observations about the relationship of early recollections to vocational choice. This work is supported by additional research by Hafner, Fakouri, and Etzler (1986), who studied the early recollections of engineering students. McFarland (1988) reported that early recollections discriminated the career choice of medical technologists and nurses. How to use early recollections in counseling or psychotherapy is described by McKelvie (1979). He believes that individuals can make career choices that will help them realize their lifestyles. Further, lifestyles can be understood through early recollections.

The following case illustrates the use of early recollections in psychotherapy with a career-counseling component. Sarah, a 22-year-old white female, has recently graduated from a small midwestern college. She has taken a job as a secretary in a Chicago real-estate-management firm, even though she feels that it is a dead-end job and that she does not like it. She has excellent secretarial skills and is confident of this fact. In terms of family background, her father works as an elementary school principal and her mother works as a homemaker. She has one brother two years older than she is and another brother three years younger. She has sought psychotherapy because she feels depressed and lonely. She believes that she will never accomplish anything in her lifetime and questions whether life is worth living. Additionally, she is lonely because her college friends have gone to other cities. She has a roommate and two other friends in Chicago. At this time, she is not dating.

Rather than examining the entire case, this example focuses only on the use of early recollections in assisting Sarah to explore her career and change her lifestyle. This example takes place in the second therapy session:

CL: I have just been very unhappy for a long period of time. In college there were distractions. I kept real busy, but sometimes I think I just wasn't satisfied with things. I'm sorry—I know we talked about this last time. But I guess that's what I'm focusing on now.

CO: It was helpful to talk about your unhappiness, but now I would like to focus on something else. I would like to ask you to recall your earliest memory—a recollection from when you were quite young. [The counselor at this point wishes to use an early recollection as a way of starting to gather data about Sarah's life theme.]

CL: [pause] I remember a time when I was first at school. I think it was kindergarten. I think I must have been about 5 or so. We were out in the school yard, and the school yard had a red brick wall around it. It was a large grassy area with some of the cemented part of the playground just being near the school. Anyway, I remember there was a group of maybe

10 or 15 kids playing with a ball or something in the middle of the field. Way off, in a corner under some trees, was a little girl—I guess one of my classmates, but I don't remember her as a friend. Anyway, she was standing under the tree crying or looking very sad, I'm not sure which.

CO: Can you tell me more about that little girl? [The counselor wants more information about the early recollection to build a hypothesis about a life theme.]

CL: Yes, she was a fat girl. She had on a dress fancier than what kids usually wore to school, and it didn't fit right. It was short and sloped, exaggerating her size. [Sarah gasps.] I remember how real sad I felt for her. It was like every inch of me was sad. It was funny—I never had anything like that happen to me before. I didn't cry, but the sadness overwhelmed me. That thought of her and of people like her would come back to me again.

CO: And when it would come back . . . ? [The exploration of the life theme continues.]

CL: It would overwhelm me. Sometimes it would confuse me. Sometimes I would remember that little girl. She seemed so small and all alone.

CO: And where were you standing when you saw her? [There's more effort to fill out the early recollection and to understand the client's sense of sadness.]

CL: I so much wanted to help her. I really did.

CO: And where were you standing?

CL: Oh [noticing the repeated question]. I was all alone. [Sarah cries uncontrollably for a few minutes.]

CO: So hard being all alone. [The counselor wonders about Sarah's loneliness, a sense of being excluded from the family perhaps. There is much to learn about Sarah's sense of inferiority with others.]

CL: I wanted to help her. I really did. I think after that I started to help more. I tried to help the teacher more, and I tried to help the other children with their reading. I was good at it, but I think the other kids resented it. I remember loneliness.

CO: You tried to help. [The counselor sees helping as an emergent theme.]

CL: I wanted to help, but people saw me as a boss. Maybe I was a boss. I interfered. I really wanted to interfere with that little girl. I didn't with her, but I did with others.

CO: You recall interfering with others? [The counselor wants to continue the exploration of early recollections. The theme of interfering or overhelping is now a working hypothesis for the counselor.]

This early recollection deals with a transition to a new experience as well as with a desire to help people that will emerge in an expression of career choice. Sarah seeks counseling at a time when she is experiencing a major life transition: graduation from a small college and a new job in Chicago. Her early recollection suggests that transitions are difficult for her because she feels alone, just as she felt when she was a small child. She may again be coping by noticing people who are weaker than she and who can benefit from her help. She needs to cooperate and participate, not just to help those who are weaker than she. With the counselor, she explores careers of clinical psychology and social work. They discuss whether these occupations are chosen because of wanting to feel in a position of strength regarding other people or because of an interest in helping others. As they explore this issue, both views emerge. As Sarah becomes more comfortable with herself, the need to be in a superior position diminishes. Her relationships with family and friends improve. Her choice to pursue graduate school in social work feels genuine to her.

Career Issues and Adlerian Counseling Although not well established, several methods have been used in Adlerian counseling when career issues are prominent. These techniques can be separated into assessment and counseling techniques. Regarding assessment, Klopfer (1965) mentions four methods that Adlerian counselors have found to be helpful: structured interviews, projective techniques, autobiographies, and card sorts. As Watkins and Savickas (1990) show, there are a number of creative ways to use these techniques. For example, structured interviews might include questions about life themes and life goals. Projective techniques could include the Thematic Apperception Test (TAT) or a vocational version of it (Ammons, Butler, & Herzig, 1950). Nystul (1993) has developed an instrument for analyzing life tasks, including work. Autobiographies would include responses in categories such as three used by Hahn (1963): "What I think I am like," "How other people see me," and "What I would like to be like." Card sorts use questions or activities or other stimulus materials printed on cards. Clients sort the cards into piles of "like," "dislike," or "indifferent" while talking to the counselor about their reasons for sorting in a particular manner. The material in each pile, and why it is there, is then used to examine lifestyle as a part of career choice.

Adlerian counselors use the results of assessments to help the client understand her or his life themes and goals. This typically includes stating the client's life theme to the client. In general, the goal is to help clients see themselves and their choices more clearly so that they can make better decisions (Watkins & Savickas, 1990).

Savickas's Career-Style Assessment and Counseling

A specific method for using an Adlerian approach to career issues has been suggested by Savickas (1989) and includes both assessment and counseling methods. We will use portions of his approach here as illustrations. Examples of a few assessment techniques and an excerpt from a counseling interaction will demonstrate both the assessment phase and the counseling phase.

The Assessment Phase The assessment phase begins with the career-style interview. In describing this interview, Savickas (1989) suggests that the counselor ask questions about important lifestyle issues. Each of these questions will provide the counselor with clues to the client's life goals. Examples of questions are as follows:*

Role models: "Whom did you admire when you were growing up?"
Books: "Describe your favorite book to me."
Magazines: "Which magazines do you enjoy? Tell me about one or two of them. Give me an example of an article that you particularly enjoyed."
Leisure activities: "What do you like to do in your free time?"
School subjects: "What subjects did you like best in high school?"
Mottoes: "Do you have a favorite saying or motto?"
Ambitions: "Did your parents have goals for you when you were young?"
Decisions: "How did you make the decision to attend this school?"

Questions such as these on important topics for assessing lifestyle are asked over the course of the initial career interview. Each question is explored further with more questions as a follow-up. After the interview, the counselor assesses the responses to these questions and makes hypotheses about the client's lifestyle and career goal.

An example of how a counselor may conduct an interview and make working hypotheses about the client's lifestyle as the assessment progresses is given next. In this example, only discussions about role models, an area dealing with self, and schoolwork, which deals with the environment, are reported.

Carlos is a 19-year-old college sophomore whose parents moved to Indianapolis from Argentina when he was an infant. His father is a real estate salesperson. His mother is an assistant hotel manager. Carlos has an older brother and two younger sisters. During the second year of a two-year program in general studies, Carlos seeks counseling at a community college counseling center. At the moment, he is quite unsure about what he would like to do when he finishes the year. After a brief introduction and an informal discussion with Carlos, the counselor initiates the career interview:

CO: Carlos, when you were young, whom did you admire?
CL: Well, there were baseball players that I liked. I really followed baseball. I guess the baseball player that I most admired was Roberto Clemente. He was great. I knew I wanted to be like him. He sure could hit. I can remember times when I was playing baseball, I would pretend I was like him. I'd imitate his stance, things like that.
CO: Can you think of another person whom you admired, famous or otherwise? [The counselor writes down Carlos's answer. More questions are asked to get a fuller view of models and influences in Carlos's life.]
CL: Well, I admired my father a lot.
CO: Can you name another person whom you admired? The person doesn't have to be famous and could even be fictional.

*From "Career-Style Assessment and Counseling," by M. L. Savickas. In T. Sweeney (Ed.), *Adlerian Counseling: A Practical Approach for a New Decade* (3rd ed.). Copyright © 1989 by Accelerated Development. Reprinted by Permission.

CL: Superman. Boy, he could go anywhere he wanted.

CO: Tell me what you admired about your father. [Since Carlos has already talked about admiring an athletic performer for his athletic ability, the counselor goes on to inquire about his father.]

CL: A couple of things. He always seems to know what he is doing. He seems to work hard and be in control all the time. I guess I feel real secure around him. I like that. Also, running is something he was great at. He had done this, I guess, ever since high school. I remember going to distance runs and watching him. He did real well; I was very proud of him.

CO: And Superman? [The counselor writes on her paper that Carlos admires his father's strength, the sense of security that he offers, and his athletic ability. Then she asks about the third significant figure.]

CL: When I was young, maybe 6, I really was crazy about Superman. I loved his cape. I wanted to fly around the world, leap tall buildings with a single bound. You know, that kind of stuff. Capture bad guys, save the day for poor people, things like that.

CO: Now I want to ask you about these people. How are you like Roberto Clemente, and how are you different from him? [Having obtained information about three significant role models, the counselor asks more questions that will help to identify Carlos's career style.]

CL: Well, I sure can't hit the way Roberto did. I guess I am like him in that I work hard at things. I really put in a lot of effort.

CO: And your father—how are you like him, and how are you different?

CL: Well, I think I'm a little more relaxed than he is. I don't take things quite so seriously. He is concerned about our family and taking care of us all, seeing that we can get a good education, stuff like that. But I get concerned about my brother and sisters, too. In fact, I'm that way with my girlfriend; I'm pretty protective of her.

CO: And Superman—are you super, too? [The counselor smiles as she says this.]

CL: No, I'm not super, but I guess I really would like to be. There's so much that I wish I could do if I were super.

CO: And what are some of those things? [The counselor wants to follow up on Carlos's dreams and desires.]

CL: Save the world. I guess I'm pretty idealistic. There are times at home when money is stretched pretty tight. I would like to make life easier for everyone, particularly for those who have it hard.

As the counselor gathers information, she starts to make observations about Carlos's career style and goals. This series of questions is very important in Adlerian career conceptualization, as Savickas (1989) states: "A client's model identifies a central life goal, articulates and labels the client's central concern, and reveals what the client thinks it will take to overcome that problem" (p. 300). The counselor observes Carlos's idealism, his desire to work hard and achieve great things, and to take responsibility for others. These observations will be combined with inferences made by asking similar questions about books, magazines, and leisure activities. In the next excerpt from this interview, the counselor inquires about school subjects.

Questions about school move away from a focus on oneself to a focus on work environments. The inquiry about school subjects is focused on success in terms of grades and satisfaction with school subjects, which represent a type of work environment. The emphasis in on the material studied rather than on how it was taught. By emphasizing the subject matter rather than the teaching process, the counselor is able to make inferences about potential work environments and approaches to work:

CO: Carlos, can you tell me what your favorite subjects were in high school?

CL: Sure, I really liked English. I liked typing, too. In fact, I went on to take a course in word processing after the basic typing course.

CO: What did you like about typing? [Information about client likes will help in assessing interests.]

CL: I really liked to be able to type fast, to do something that I knew I was doing well, and to do it better than the others. I was fast, I was good, and I felt good about it. It was an easy "A" for me. I really like to be able to be on top of something, like when I was typing.

CO: And word processing? [Carlos volunteers information about his interests, his motivation, and his success. The counselor continues to get more information.]

CL: It helped me type faster, better, and do more things. I liked learning little tricks you could do. I really wanted to learn all I could about that word-processing system we had in school. I guess it also made me interested in computers. I was a little nervous about them at first. I know it isn't programming or anything, but I want to take a programming course.

CO: How did you do in that course?

CL: Real well. I got "A"s throughout. Just like in English. English and the typing and word-processing courses were my best subjects in high school.

CO: What did you like about English?

CL: I learned grammar pretty well. I liked the essays that we wrote, but probably I liked writing fiction more than anything else. In fact, the more free writing that we did in the course, the more I liked it.

CO: What courses didn't you like? [Having some information about preferred work environments, the counselor now asks questions about disliked environments.]

CL: Physics. I hated physics. It was so confusing, laws and stuff. I got a "D." It was really embarrassing because it was my first "D." It was real tough. Come to think of it, I didn't do so well in math. Once stuff got so I couldn't see it clearly, it got hard.

Observations are being made by the counselor about the type of work environment that will be appropriate for Carlos. The concrete-abstract dimension seems to be emerging, as is Carlos's enjoyment of working with detail. Other questions will help to give the counselor a broad view of Carlos's career style. The counselor goes on to ask Carlos in a similar manner about favorite mottoes, ambitions, and important decisions he has made. The latter will help the counselor to form a view of Carlos's decision-making style.

After the career-style interview has been completed, the counselor makes an assessment of all of the information that has been gathered. Savickas (1989) suggests a seven-step approach, which includes the following: review interests that arise in response to questions about role models; infer the relative importance of people, things, and ideas from answers to responses about magazines and stories; and elicit more information about possible work environments from data about liked and disliked schoolwork. After this, the counselor reviews information about parental ambitions, childhood ambitions, and occupational daydreams. After reviewing all of this information, the counselor may be able to determine the client's career style. This then can be related to the presenting career-choice problem given to the counselor at the beginning of the interview. This will also help the counselor in suggesting occupations that the client may consider. Finally, the counselor can identify more occupational titles by making use of a classification system such as that of Holland or the *Dictionary of Occupational Titles.*

In the case of Carlos, the counselor is able to make hypotheses about his career style: Carlos is careful in his interactions with people and the world around him. He wants to be successful, but he wants to be secure in obtaining success. He will avoid risks, if possible. His interests seem to be in sports, writing, English, taking care of the needs of others, and reading. His career path is likely to take him into areas where he can be in control, deal with details, and feel that other people can count on him. Occupations suggested by his career style and path include editor, secretary, proofreader, bookkeeper, data entry specialist, programmer, computer operator, writer, and sports statistician. Having made this analysis, the counselor is now prepared to share this information with Carlos in career-style counseling.

Career-Style Counseling Savickas's (1989) model of Adlerian career-style counseling is structured and specific. After the career-style interview has been completed, three more sessions are required to complete counseling. The first session is a discussion of career style and path, decision-making difficulties, and interests. The second session, occurring about a week later, focuses on developing a list of occupations for further exploration. The third session may occur about a month later. It focuses on any difficulties that the individual may be having in making a choice. This model will be described in some detail here, and Carlos's experience will be used as an example.

In the *first session,* after the counselor has made an analysis of the client's career style and path, he or she shares it with the client. In doing so, the counselor gives the client the counselor's view of the client's career strengths and weaknesses. As they discuss the client's reaction to the counselor's view of the client's career style, the counselor may point out how the client's career style has been expressed in the discussion that they are having. From career style, the counselor moves to career path, the direction in which the client may be heading. Savickas uses Holland's model to help identify which career paths are likely to result in a successful and satisfactory career choice.

In Carlos's case, the counselor discusses her analysis of Carlos's career style. Carlos responds by appreciating the counselor's observations and then giving examples of word-processing techniques that he has mastered. The counselor then uses these comments to illustrate how Carlos's attention to detail and sense of responsibility and satisfaction in mastering challenging tasks are examples of his career style. From there, the counselor and Carlos talk about the direction in which Carlos is headed: his career path. They discuss decisions that Carlos needs to make in terms of setting educational and career goals. Carlos is able to state that he feels successful and satisfied when he has mastered a detailed and challenging task. This statement combines Carlos's attention to detail, sense of responsibility, and drive for mastery and success.

After the career style and path have been established, the counselor turns to assisting in problems of decision making. The client may have a private logic that is used to make decisions about careers. This private logic may have developed in childhood and may interfere with a commonsense or logical approach to decision making. On the other hand, the private logic may work very well in career decision making. An example of ineffective private logic is "If only I can graduate from college, all my worries will be over." It is the responsibility of the counselor to help the client correct these inaccurate beliefs. Savickas (1989) gives examples of several methods that Adlerian counselors have used to correct individuals' mistaken ideas about themselves or their decision making.

Carlos has approached career decision making with a rather desperate point of view. He has felt that he needs to work harder than anyone else to succeed. In his private logic, he has not differentiated his varying abilities. The counselor helps Carlos realize that some of his abilities are highly developed and may require relatively little work. For examples, the counselor discusses Carlos's skill in English and secretarial work. In contrast, Carlos's difficulties in math and physical science do require much hard work to overcome. The counselor points out that it is not necessary for Carlos to continue these activities.

Following interests can become a way of moving toward one's career goals. Interests are made of feelings, as well as meanings that are both public and private. In other words, interests may have a special meaning to a client that is different from the meaning they have to people in general. The counselor may point out that interests sometimes hold hidden meanings. The counselor then helps the client identify interests that have special and hidden meaning. From this point, the counselor is ready to move on to identify occupations that the client will explore.

At the end of the session, the counselor asks the client to think about what they have discussed, because the next session will start with reviewing the client's view of career styles, paths, and interests. A more specific homework assignment is given in which the client is asked to learn an occupational classification system, such as that of Holland, Roe, or the *Dictionary of Occupational Titles.* Using that system, the client is asked to prepare a list of occupations that he or she can discuss in the next session.

As Carlos and the counselor discuss interests, Carlos discusses his interest in learning about a spreadsheet computer program. He talks about the various capabilities of the program and his discovery of them. The counselor points out the meaning that this seems to have to Carlos: the importance of self-discovery and of feeling competent and able to figure out new tasks. This gives Carlos a feeling that he can do anything, somewhat like Superman flying through the air. The counselor then goes on to give some other examples of how Carlos has helped his younger brother to improve his basketball skills. Although a helpful behavior from his brother's point of view, for Carlos it is a way to feel capable and successful. As the counselor and Carlos discuss his interests, they begin to identify occupations that he might explore. These include editing, accounting, proofreading, journalism, bookkeeping, and secretarial work. The counselor then asks Carlos to think about what they have discussed in terms of career styles, paths, and interests, because they will discuss it in the next session. Furthermore, the counselor describes Holland's system of classifying occupations. She then asks Carlos to use Holland's *Occupations Finder* along with the *Occupational Outlook Handbook,* which she gives to him to identify occupations that they can discuss in the next session.

In the *second session,* counselors discuss the client's observations about the previous session's work. From this, they move into a discussion of occupations that the client has studied. One approach is for the counselor to ask the client to think aloud about occupations that they have talked about previously but that have not been commented on during the current counseling session. The goal of the session is to develop a short list of about six occupations for the client to explore in depth. When this has been accomplished, the counselor and client discuss ways of getting information from books, friends, and other contacts. Furthermore, they will make use of information about career decision-making strategies.

Carlos begins the second session by discussing how much work he has done during the week to investigate career plans. This activity does not surprise the counselor, as it fits in with her observations about his career style. Carlos talks about how helpful it was to review his career style and path. He gives the counselor a list of several occupations. It includes accountant, budget analyst, property manager, job analyst, and proofreader. The counselor then asks Carlos to think aloud about the occupations of sports statistician and editor. As he does so, he talks about his concern about the few positions that he believes will be available in these occupations. Next, Carlos and the counselor discuss ways to gather more information. The counselor encourages Carlos to explore other written materials as well as to ask people in several of the occupations about their own work. They then schedule an appointment for a meeting in five weeks.

It is in the *third session*, usually the last, that clients tell the counselor whether they have been successful in clarifying the alternatives and making a career choice. In some cases, clients will be pleased with their choice and their success in career decision making. Other clients will be very frustrated by their inability to choose. Still others may have made a choice, because of family pressures, that they are not pleased with. In other cases, meeting the entry requirements for the job or having a sufficient amount of money to finance the education required by the occupation may present difficulties. In these cases, the rest of the counseling session is spent in discussing career barriers and ways to overcome them. This discussion may include ways of dealing with a mother's and father's resistance to the client's choice, ways to meet entry requirements, or strategies for obtaining financial support. Possibly, another follow-up session will be required.

Profusely thanking the counselor, Carlos is delighted with his career choice: property management. Both he and the counselor see how the required attention to detail and the satisfaction in completing specific tasks are compatible with Carlos's lifestyle. After reading information in the *Occupational Outlook Handbook* about property and real estate managers, Carlos checked out books from the community college career library dealing with real estate and business occupations that combine his father's choice of real estate and his mother's choice of management. After he finished reading, he talked to the property manager of the building where his family lives. This woman was able to suggest other resources to Carlos. Then Carlos checked into degree programs in business administration. He tells the counselor that he is in the process of considering transferring most of his credits to several colleges or universities nearby that he might attend. He feels that he can continue to live at home and attend school without too much demand on his limited financial resources. Both Carlos and the counselor are pleased with Carlos's ability to analyze his career style to determine a potentially productive and satisfying career path.

The approach to career counseling just described is one of several Adlerian approaches that could be used. It is a very specific and directive approach, which is consistent with Adlerian counseling. Furthermore, it makes use of important Adlerian concepts such as lifestyle and career style, encouragement, and the use of private logic that emanates from childhood experience. The emphasis on presenting observations that the counselor has made about the client to the client is typical of Adlerian counseling.

THE ROLE OF TESTING

In general, psychodynamic theories have not included testing as in important component in their conceptualization of career selection issues. When testing has been included, often projective techniques such as the Rorschach and the TAT are used to reveal the inner dynamics of the individual's unconscious motivations. Because the application of psychoanalytic theory (Bordin's approach) and Erikson's theory to career development has been rudimentary, there has been no clear prescription for the use of tests in career counseling for these theories. Because of their emphasis on the uniqueness of the individual and his or her lifestyle, Adlerian counselors do not often use test materials. They have developed their own measures to assess lifestyle, early recollections, and family constellation. Often, the methods used are structured interviews rather than projective techniques. Savickas (1989), however, does make a link between trait and factor theory and Adlerian counseling. He shows how Adlerian counseling can be used in conjunction with interest inventories and other tests. As psychodynamic approaches to career counseling are developed, it is possible that tests and inventories will play a larger role than they do now.

THE ROLE OF OCCUPATIONAL INFORMATION

Because psychodynamic theories do not focus on career development, little can be said about the role of occupational information in career counseling based on these theories. Neither Bordin's approach nor Erikson's theories have been sufficiently developed to make a statement on the use of occupational information. Since both recognize the importance of identity issues in adolescence, it is likely that they would acknowledge the helpfulness of occupational information in making career decisions. Erikson's moratorium period is one in which an adolescent can develop information about the world (including the world of work) in his or her own idiosyncratic style.

Savickas (1989), in adapting Adler's theory to career development, is quite specific about the value of occupational information. He makes use of the occupational classification systems of other theories so that the client will have a method of identifying relevant occupations. The use of books and pamphlets is particularly important for the client in preparation for his or her second session of career counseling, when occupational prospects are discussed. Between the second and third sessions, the client may make use of more in-depth occupational information, such as talking with employers and workers in a given field. Because Adlerian counselors have developed more specific methods of career counseling than has been done for other psychodynamic theories, it is not surprising that Adlerian counselors have more to say about the use of occupational information in counseling than other psychodynamic theorists.

APPLYING THE THEORIES TO WOMEN

The three psychodynamic theories discussed in this chapter have very different views of the career development of women. Bordin's theory is not sufficiently developed to focus on issues of gender. However, Freudian theory does describe developmental differences that may have some impact on the counseling of men or women. These differences occur during the genital stage (around the age of 4). For boys, the Oedipus complex is typified by a strong unconscious attachment to the mother, with antagonism toward the father. For girls, the Electra complex refers to a repressed sexual attachment to the father. These attachments may have varying effects on later career choices. However, these effects are not explored by Bordin in terms of career development theory.

Erik Erikson has been a keen observer of American culture. He has observed the emergence of the feminist movement in the United States and has commented on its role in the development of identity among adolescent women. Furthermore, he has observed the opening of more career opportunities for women, giving them a greater opportunity to realize their needs and establish their own identity. Erikson has supported social and legal steps that have enabled the establishment of women's identity through equal career opportunities, as well as in other areas of women's lives.

A concern about equality and good relationships between the sexes was a significant aspect of Adlerian theory (Mosak, 1995) many decades before equal employment opportunities for women became accepted in the United States. Therefore, the notion of equal opportunities to further one's own lifestyle is assumed in Adlerian theory. Adler's view has been carried on by those who have applied his theory to career counseling. Often, the need to provide equal opportunities for occupational success for women is implicit rather than explicit in their writings.

APPLYING THE THEORIES TO PEOPLE OF COLOR

Because of the emphasis on the individual, psychodynamic theories have generally not focused on cultural and racial issues. Because of the limited application of Freudian theory to career issues, there is no statement from psychoanalytic theory as it relates to the career development of people of color. However, Erikson's work does have some indirect impact on this issue. When Erikson first came to the United States, he studied the child-rearing patterns of Native Americans. Furthermore, he has been an astute observer of cultural issues in the United States. Implicit in his theory is the notion that identity issues can be more complex for those whose culture is different from the majority culture.

Concern about equality in society has always been important in Adler's theory of human behavior. Savickas's career-style assessment and counseling focus on life themes, family background, and ambitions, which would seem to be applicable to clients of varied cultural backgrounds. This method allows the counselor to be sensitive to empowering aspects of an individual that the standard emphasis on interests and abilities might overlook. Because psychodynamic theories do not emphasize the career development issues or problems of people of color, it is not surprising that they provide little information on these issues.

COUNSELOR ISSUES

Neither psychoanalytic theory nor Erikson's theoretical approach addresses career development in enough detail to allow comment on counselor issues in relation to these theories. In psychoanalytic theory itself, transference and countertransference are important client-counselor relationship issues. *Transference* refers to the situation in which the patient transfers feelings toward a parent to a therapist. *Countertransference* describes the attribution of unconscious wishes of the therapist to the patient. These concepts are meaningful to the psychoanalytic therapist when dealing with personal problems. Such a therapist may find it helpful to apply them to situations involving career issues as well.

Adlerian counseling stresses a caring and encouraging relationship with the client. The directive approach of the Adlerian career counselor is one that makes use of advice and suggestion. Counselors must also deal with motivational issues when suggestions are not followed or assigned homework is not done. Because of the structure of such approaches as Savickas's, client fears or issues outside career counseling may interfere with these approaches.

SUMMARY

Psychodynamic theories are probably the most complex theories of personality, psychotherapy, and counseling. In general, little work has been done to apply them to career development. Therefore, this chapter has tried to illustrate ways in which the theories might be applied. Unlike other chapters, this chapter presents insufficient information to warrant immediate application to career clients. Readers wishing to apply any of these psychodynamic theories to their clients should consult the sources quoted in this chapter for more information. The career development approaches of Bordin, Erikson, and Adler are summarized in the following paragraphs.

Bordin has attempted to apply Freudian psychoanalytic theory to career development. In doing so, he and his colleagues have used the psychosexual stages as a conceptual framework for career choice. A major emphasis of his approach is on play and its later application to work. Since his work in the 1960s, Bordin has incorporated Erikson's ego-development and identity concepts in a broadening of his theory.

Erikson himself has not directly addressed career counseling. Munley has applied Erikson's concepts to vocational theory. However, little work has been done to extend Erikson's developmental concepts to career counseling. Because his work on identity issues is so significant, it is explained and illustrated in this chapter. Notably, Erikson's stages of development have had great influence on the theoretical work of Bordin, Super, and Tiedeman.

A more active approach to career counseling is that of Alfred Adler's students. Perhaps more research and theorizing are being doing on Adler's concepts than on the approaches of Bordin or Erikson. Adlerian concepts of lifestyle, career style, and career path have been quite helpful to counselors. However, there is no agreed-upon Adlerian approach to career counseling. One particularly creative approach, that of Savickas, is illustrated and explained in this chapter. It is likely that researchers and counselors will continue to study and develop the application of psychodynamic concepts to career counseling.

References

Adler, A. (1931). *What life should mean to you.* New York: Capricorn Books.

Adler, A. (1964). *Social interest: A challenge to mankind.* New York: Capricorn Books. (Original work published 1929)

Ammons, R. B., Butler, M. N., & Herzig, S. A. (1950). A projective test for vocational research and guidance at the college level. *Journal of Applied Psychology, 34,* 198–205.

Archer, S. L. (1989). The status of identity: Reflections on the need for intervention. *Journal of Adolescence, 12,* 345–359.

Beall, L., & Bordin, E. S. (1964). The development and personality of engineers. *Personnel and Guidance Journal, 48,* 23–32.

Bordin, E. S. (1990). Psychodynamic model of career choice and satisfaction. In D. Brown, L. Brooks, & Assoc. (Eds.), *Career choice and development: Applying contemporary theories to practice* (2nd ed., pp. 102–144). San Francisco: Jossey-Bass.

Bordin, E. S., Nachmann, B., & Segal, S. J. (1963). An articulated framework for vocational development. *Journal of Counseling Psychology, 10,* 107–116.

Buehler, C. (1933). *Der menschliche lebenslauf als psychologisches problem.* Leipzig: Hirzel.

Csikszentmihalyi, M., & Beattie, O. V. (1979). Life themes: A theoretical and empirical exploration of their origins and effects. *Journal of Humanistic Psychology, 19,* 45–63.

Dreikurs, R. (1961). The Adlerian approach to therapy. In M. I. Stein, (Ed.), *Contemporary psychotherapies* (pp. 80–94). Glencoe, IL: Free Press.

Erikson, E. H. (1963). *Childhood and society* (2nd ed.). New York: Norton.

Erikson, E. H. (1968). *Identity: Youth and crisis.* New York: Norton.

Erikson, E. H. (1982). *The life cycle completed.* New York: Norton.

Galinsky, M. D. (1962). Personality development and vocational choice of clinical psychologists and physicists. *Journal of Counseling Psychology, 13,* 89–92.

Galinsky, M. D., & Fast, I. (1966). Vocational choice as a focus of the identity search. *Journal of Counseling Psychology, 13,* 89–92.

Gross, F. L. (1987). *Introducing Erik Erikson: An invitation to his thinking.* Lanham, MD: University Press of America.

Hafner, J. L., & Fakouri, M. E. (1984a). Early recollections and vocational choice. *Individual Psychology, 40,* 54–60.

Hafner, J. L., & Fakouri, M. E. (1984b). Early recollections of individuals preparing for careers in clinical psychology, dentistry, and law. *Journal of Vocational Behavior, 24,* 236–241.

Hafner, J. L., & Fakouri, M. E., & Etzler, D. R. (1986). Early recollections of individuals preparing for careers in chemical, electrical, and mechanical engineering. *Individual Psychology, 42,* 360–366.

Hahn, M. (1963). *Psychoevaluation: Adaptation-distribution-adjustment.* New York: McGraw-Hill.

Juni, S. (1981). Career choice and quality. *Journal of Vocational Behavior, 19,* 79–83.

Klopfer, W. G. (1965). A symposium on clinical appraisal in vocational counseling. *Personnel and Guidance Journal, 43,* 867–885.

Maier, H. W. (1978). *Three theories of child development* (3rd ed.). New York: Harper & Row.

Manaster, G. L., & Corsini, R. J. (1982). *Individual psychology: Theory and practice.* Itasca, IL: F. E. Peacock.

Marcia, J. E. (1980). Identity in adolescence. In A. Adelson (Ed.), *Handbook of adolescent psychology* (pp. 159–187). New York: Wiley.

Marcia, J. E. (1989). Identity and intervention. *Journal of Adolescence, 12,* 401–410.

Marcia, J. E., Waterman, A. S., Matteson, D. R., Archer, S. L., & Orlofsky, J. (1993). *Ego identity: A handbook for psychosocial research.* New York: Springer-Verlag.

McFarland, M. (1988). Early recollections discriminate persons in two occupations: Medical technology and nursing. *Individual Psychology, 44,* 77–84.

McKelvie, W. (1979). Career counseling with early recollections. In H. A. Olsen (Ed.), *Early recollections: Their use in diagnosis and psychotherapy* (pp. 234–255). Springfield, IL: Charles C Thomas.

Meara, N. M., & Patton, M. J. (1994). Contributions of the working alliance in the practice of career counseling. *The Career Development Quarterly, 43,* 161–177.

Miller, S. (1962). Relationship of personality and occupation, setting and function. *Journal of Counseling Psychology, 9,* 115–121.

Mosak, H. H. (1995). Adlerian psychotherapy. In R. J. Corsini and D. Wedding (Eds.), *Current psychotherapies* (5th ed., pp. 51–94). Itasca, IL: F. E. Peacock.

Munley, P. H. (1975). Erik Erikson's theory of psychosocial development and vocational behavior. *Journal of Counseling Psychology, 22,* 314–319.

Munley, P. H. (1977). Erikson's theory of psychosocial development and career development. *Journal of Vocational Behavior, 10,* 261–269.

Nachmann, B. (1960). Childhood experiences and vocational choice in law, dentistry, and social work. *Journal of Counseling Psychology, 7,* 243–250.

Nystul, M. S. (1993). The Nystul Turning Point Survey: An assessment instrument to analyze Adlerian tasks of life. *Individual Psychology, 49,* 185–198.

Powers, R. L, & Griffith, J. (1993). The case of Rosie: Adlerian response. *The Career Development Quarterly, 42,* 69–75.

Raskin, P. M. (1989). Identity status research: Implications for career counseling. *Journal of Adolescence, 12,* 375–388.

Savickas, M. L. (1985). Identity in vocational development. *Journal of Vocational Behavior, 27,* 329–337.

Savickas, M. L. (1989). Career-style assessment and counseling. In T. Sweeney (Ed.), *Adlerian counseling: A practical approach for a new decade* (3rd ed., pp. 289–320). Muncie, IN: Accelerated Development.

Schlesinger, V. J. (1963). *Anal personality traits and occupational choice: A study of accountants, chemical engineers, and educational psychologists.* Unpublished doctoral dissertation, University of Michigan.

Segal, S. (1961). A psychoanalytic analysis of personality factors in vocational choice. *Journal of Counseling Psychology, 8,* 202–210.

Segal, S., & Szabo, R. (1964). Identification in two vocations: Accountants and creative writers. *Personnel and Guidance Journal, 43,* 251–255.

Sharf, R. S. (1996). *Theories of psychotherapy and counseling: Concepts and cases.* Pacific Grove, CA: Brooks/Cole.

Stephen, J., Fraser, E., & Marcia, J. E. (1992). Moratorium-achievement (Mama) cycles in lifespan and identity development. Value orientations and reasoning system correlates. *Journal of Adolescence, 15,* 283–300.

Tiedemann, D. V., & O'Hara, R. P. (1963). *Career development: Choice and adjustment.* New York: College Entrance Examination Board.

Watkins, C. E., Jr. (1984). The individual psychology of Alfred Adler: Toward an Adlerian vocational theory. *Journal of Vocational Behavior, 24,* 28–47.

Watkins, C. E., Jr., & Savickas, M. L. (1990). Psychodynamic career counseling. In W. B. Walsh & S. H. Osipow (Eds.), *Career counseling: Contemporary topics in vocational psychology* (pp. 79–116). Hillsdale, NJ: Erlbaum.

Zuschlag, M. K., & Whitbourne, S. K. (1994). Psychosocial development in three generations of college students. *Journal of Youth and Adolescence, 23,* 567–577.

12

Parental Influence Theories

Career development researchers have been interested in the questions: What impact do parents and others have on the occupational choice of children? And what impact does the child-raising experience have on the career choices and decision-making styles of children? Most theorists who have studied influences that others have on the career development of children have focused on parental influence. The impetus for the study of parental impact on career development comes from the work of Sigmund Freud and his influence on psychodynamic explanations of personal development. Although parental influence is the focus of this chapter, reference is also made to the impact on a child's development made by other family members as well as by some nonfamily members. The role of teachers, peers, and broader social influences on career choices is dealt with in the Chapter 7 discussion of Gottfredson and in the Chapter 15 discussion of studies on the effect of the work environment on the individual and of status attainment theory.

Much of this chapter is devoted to the systematic work of Anne Roe in trying to predict the occupational entry of individuals, but discussions of newer ideas from attachment theory and family therapy are also included. For over 50 years, Anne Roe investigated the influence of parental child-raising styles on individual occupational choice. In the process, she developed a widely used occupational classification system that is explained in this chapter. More recently, theories about the impact of children's attachment to their parents have also been applied to career choice. Also, family therapists have developed some concepts and practical approaches that can be applied to career counseling. These family-focused theories are the subject of this chapter.

ROE'S PERSONALITY DEVELOPMENT THEORY

Anne Roe developed a theory to predict occupational selection based on individual differences, which are biological, sociological, and psychological. More specifically, she focused on predicting occupational selection based on the psychological needs that develop from the interaction between children and their parents. She wanted to be able to show that people in certain occupations have a common background in terms of the way they were raised. To build this theory, she needed to develop an occupational classification system so that she could relate parent-child relationships to specific occupational groupings. The classification system that she developed in this process has been supported by research and has become useful to counselors, whether or not it is used in the context of her theory. Because this classification system has been used so widely and can be used for counseling conceptualization, it will be examined in some detail. Another prerequisite for Roe's theory was Maslow's hierarchy of needs. Both the hierarchy itself and its relationship to Anne Roe's theory of vocational choice will be described.

Roe's Occupational Classification System

In her book *The Psychology of Occupations* (1956), Anne Roe describes her occupational classification system in great detail. She lists the job duties and abilities required by many occupations, characterized in the 48 cells of her 8 × 6 classification system. The system has eight groups and six levels, as presented in Table 12-1. The eight groups are listed across the top of the table. The groups that adjoin each other are the closest to each other in job duties, while those that are farthest apart are least similar; this is a circular system in that Group 1 and Group 8 are similar to each other and should be regarded as adjoining. The six rows of the system represent six different levels of complexity and responsibility for each occupation. Roe's work in developing this system is described not only in *The Psychology of Occupations,* but also in Roe (1972), Roe and Klos (1972), and, more recently, Roe and Lunneborg (1990). As will be shown, this classification system has been used in the development of interest inventories and has applications to counseling.

The Eight Occupational Groups The development of the eight occupational groups represents years of careful work by Roe, followed by research validating her system. Roe (Roe & Lunneborg, 1990) describes her early work as being influenced by research on interests, some of which was done by early developers of interest inventories (Kuder, 1946; Strong, 1943). Considering this research, she selected eight groups that were suggested by many of the studies that served to identify a primary occupational characteristic. She thought of this grouping as a circle, as shown in Figure 12-1 on page 302. Lunneborg and Lunneborg (1968) demonstrate the validity of the classification of different occupations in Roe's system. Jones (1965) reaffirms Roe's order of presenting each of her eight groups. More support for Roe's system comes from six studies showing that about two-thirds of job changes occur within the same group (Roe & Lunneborg, 1990, pp. 83, 98).

Adjoining groups are the next most frequent choice of those changing occupations. A study by Knapp and Knapp (1977) showed that, when high school students changed areas of interest, they were most likely to change to a Roe category adjacent to the category of their original interest. Thus, there is support for the use of the eight groups in counseling work.

The groups are described as follows (Roe & Klos, 1972, pp. 202–203):

1. *Service:* This involves one person doing something for another person. Occupations include clinical psychologist, social worker, career counselor, nurse, waiter, and servant.
2. *Business contact:* People in this group are involved in persuading others, possibly selling products. Examples include public relations work, car sales, insurance sales, and door-to-door sales.
3. *Organization:* Management is the primary activity. It may be government on a federal, state, or local level, or it may refer to management in a privately owned company. Examples are senator, accountant, and secretary.
4. *Technology:* This category includes making, producing, maintaining, and transporting products. Included in this category are engineers, production managers, pilots, electricians, and heavy-equipment operators.
5. *Outdoor:* Protection of the environment and production of crops and forest products are included in this group. Also included is work with natural resources, such as oil and coal, as well as those found in lakes, rivers, and streams. Examples of such occupations are corporate farm manager, landscape architect, fish and game warden, miner, and lumberjack.
6. *Science:* These occupations concern the development and application of science in many areas: natural science, physical science, social science, and so on. Scientific careers include university professor, pharmacist, medical technician, and lab technician.
7. *General culture:* People in this group tend to be interested in human activity and culture. This group includes communicating and preserving culture (the humanities). Fields included are law, ministry, history, and education. Principals and teachers may be found in this group, but university science teachers would be in Group 6 and art professors in Group 8. Examples of occupations are lawyer, editor, elementary school teacher, and radio announcer.
8. *Arts and entertainment:* This group includes those who perform for the public or create. Areas include music, art, writing, and athletics. Examples of careers in this category are music conductor, museum curator, music critic, interior designer, football player, and stagehand.

Tracey and Rounds (1994) have found Meir's (1970, 1973) arranging of the eight groups to be superior to that of Roe's. They examined the relative fit using a factor analysis and suggest the arrangement described in Figure 12-2 on page 303. This statistical procedure provides a way of determining which categories are most similar to each other and thus belong next to

Table 12-1 *Roe's Classification of Occupations*

Level	*I* *Service*	*II* *Business Contact*	*III* *Organization*	*IV* *Technology*	*V* *Outdoor*	*VI* *Science*	*VII* *General Cultural*	*VIII* *Arts and Entertainment*
1	Personal therapists. Social work supervisors. Counselors.	Promoters.	U.S. president and cabinet officer. Industrial tycoon. International bankers.	Inventive geniuses. Consulting or chief engineers. Ship's commanders.	Consulting specialists.	Research scientists. University, college faculties. Medical specialists. Museum curators.	Supreme Court justices. University, college faculties. Prophets. Scholars.	Creative artists, performers (great). Teachers (university equivalent). Museum curators.
2	Social workers. Occupational therapists. Probation, truant officers (with training).	Promoters. Public relations counselors.	Certified public accountants. Business and government executives. Union officials. Brokers (average).	Applied scientists. Factory managers. Ships' officers. Engineers.	Applied scientists. Landowners and operators (large). Landscape architects.	Scientists, semi-independent. Nurses. Pharmacists. Veterinarians.	Editors. Teachers (high school and elementary).	Athletes. Art critics. Designers. Music arrangers.
3	YMCA officials. Detectives, police sergeants. Welfare workers. City inspectors.	Salesmen: auto, bond, insurance. Dealers, retail and wholesale. Confidence men.	Accountants (average). Employment managers. Owners, catering, drycleaning, and so on.	Aviators. Contractors. Foremen (DOT I). Radio operators.	County agents. Farm owners. Forest rangers. Fish, game wardens.	Technicians, medical, X-ray, museum. Weather observers. Chiropractors.	Justices of the peace. Radio announcers. Reporters. Librarians.	Ad writers Designers. Interior decorators. Showmen.

4	Barbers. Chefs. Practical nurses. Police officers.	Auctioneers. Buyers (DOT I). House canvassers. Interviewers, poll.	Cashiers, clerks, credit, express, and so on. Foremen, warehouse. Salesclerks.	Blacksmiths. Electricians. Foremen (DOT II). Mechanics (average).	Laboratory testers, dairy products, and so on. Miners. Oil well drillers.	Technical assistants.	Law clerks.	Advertising artists. Decorators, window and so on. Photographers. Racing car drivers.
5	Taxi drivers. General house workers. Waiters. City firemen.	Peddlers.	Clerks, file, stock, and so on. Notaries. Runners. Typists.	Bulldozer operators. Delivery people. Smelter workers. Truck drivers.	Gardeners. Farm tenants. Teamsters. Cowpunchers. Miners' helpers.	Veterinary hospital attendants.		Illustrators, greeting cards. Showcard writers. Stagehands.
6	Chambermaids. Hospital attendants. Elevator operators. Watchmen.		Messenger boys.	Helpers. Laborers. Wrappers. Yardmen.	Dairy hands. Farm laborers Lumberjacks.	Nontechnical helpers in scientific organizations.		

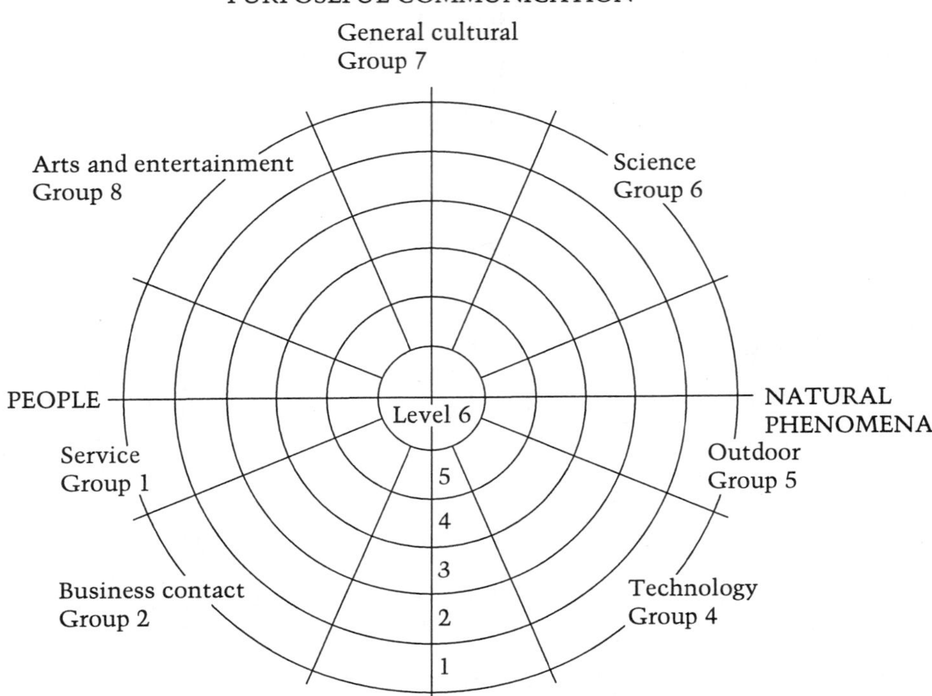

Figure 12-1 Diagram of levels and groups in Roe's classification system. (From "Early Determinants of Vocational Choice," by Anne Roe, 1957. *Journal of Counseling Psychology, 4,* pp. 212–217. Copyright 1957 by the American Psychological Association.)

each other in a circular or other arrangement. In Roe's system, the categories, as arranged, are not as similar to each other as in Meir's system. Contrast the arrangement of Roe's system in Figure 12-1 with Meir's grouping. Tracey and Rounds (1994) suggest that it would be useful for counselors to explain occupations to clients using Meir's grouping, as it is a more accurate arrangement than Roe's and would seem to update and improve on her classification system.

The Six Levels of Occupations Classification by level is based on the amount of responsibility and ability that is required by the occupation. Responsibility (Roe & Klos, 1972, p. 206) is particularly important and refers to the difficulty and complexity of decisions along with the variety

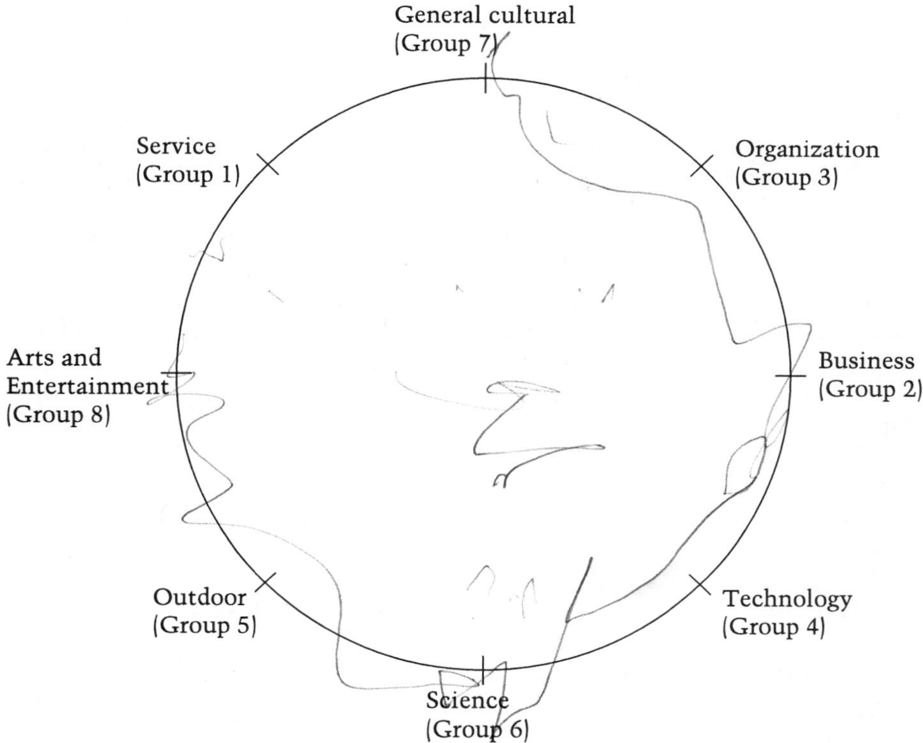

Figure 12-2 Diagram of Meir's (1970) grouping of Roe's eight groups. Roe's group numbers have been put in parentheses for comparison to Figure 12-1. The diagram is based on information from Meir (1973).

of problems that people encounter in their work. Levels of occupations can be viewed as being on a continuum, and separating occupations into such categories is often difficult. Originally, Roe developed eight levels but then condensed them into six. Figure 12-1 is useful in showing that those at the lowest levels are most similar to each other, at the center of the circle. It is easier to move from one group to another at the lower levels of occupations than at the higher levels. Because lower levels of occupations require relatively few skills, changes between groups are likely to be more frequent at lower levels than at higher levels. The six levels are described as follows (Roe & Klos, 1972, pp. 208–209):

1. *Professional and managerial 1:* Independent responsibility. This category includes those who have the highest level of responsibility within a group. Their responsibilities tend to be very important and varied. They may make policy decisions that affect many people through government, education, health, or private companies. Those in the sciences and many in

the general cultural group often have a doctorate. Others usually have a high level of education in their group.

2. *Professional and managerial 2:* Similar to Level 1 but differs in that the individual may have less independence or fewer or less important responsibilities. Often, individuals at this level have a bachelor's degree or possibly a master's degree. They may be involved in interpreting policy and making important decisions for themselves and others.

3. *Semiprofessional and small business:* Only a moderate level of responsibility for others, such as the responsibility of police sergeants for other police officers, or of retail businesspeople for their sales clerks. Often, only a high school education is required, but many people have degrees from technical schools or four-year institutions.

4. *Skilled:* Training is required, whether in the form of an apprenticeship or vocational education, at either a technical school or a high school.

5. *Semiskilled:* On-the-job training and some special schooling may be required. For example, truck drivers may receive training from their union or a special school. Taxi drivers may receive very brief training before being given assignments.

6. *Unskilled:* Little special training is required. Individuals need only to follow basic directions. No specific education is required.

Testing and Occupational Classification Roe's classification system has been helpful in interest measurement. Four interest inventories were developed through the use of Roe's classification system. Perhaps the most well known is the Career Occupational Preference System Interest Inventory. It is also known as the California Occupational Preference System (COPS; Knapp & Knapp, 1985). The COPS not only provides scores for each Roe group but also includes scales for more than one level per group. For example, science, organization, arts and entertainment, and service each have scales on two levels, and technology provides scores on three levels. The Vocational Interest Inventory (VII; Lunneborg, 1981) is a forced-choice inventory designed for high school and college students that controls for sex bias. Another inventory uses activities described in the fourth edition of the *Dictionary of Occupational Titles* (DOT). This inventory was developed for women college graduates (Lunneborg & Wilson, 1982). Meir (1975) developed two interest inventories for use in Israel. One of them contains a list of occupational titles (RAMAK). The other, Courses, contains a list of 64 college-level courses. In addition to the eight occupational groups, RAMAK provides scores on three levels: professional, semiprofessional, and skilled. These inventories can be helpful to the counselor who uses Roe's conceptual classification system by providing objective information as to the occupational groups a client may wish to consider. They may also be helpful in differentiating levels, although those inventories that do differentiate levels mainly use two or three broad levels rather than six. However, it is not necessary to use one of these inventories to use Roe's classification system in counseling.

Using Roe's Classification System in Counseling Roe's system provides a framework to make sense of a vast number of occupations. By using a classification system with a limited number of categories (eight groups and six levels), a counselor is able to organize information about occupations when talking to clients about occupational choices. Roe's system is an orderly one in that, the closer the categories are to each other, the more related the occupations are within them. Also, the levels are useful and rather easy to implement, as they are similar to educational levels and levels of responsibility. When discussing occupations, a counselor can think in terms of levels slightly above and below those that the client is mentioning. For example, if a client is considering becoming an accountant (Group 3—organization) and thinking in terms of entry-level work (Level 3), the counselor may discuss alternate career possibilities such as bookkeeper (Level 4) or certified public accountant, partnership in an accounting firm, or similar careers (Level 2). An example of a dialogue with a client about occupational information will illustrate the use of Roe's system.

George is a 17-year-old white high school senior from rural Iowa. He is talking to his high school guidance counselor about his plans for next year and about which colleges to apply to in the local area. This is his first appointment with his counselor since he talked to her in September about a year ago to select courses for his senior year.

CL: Since both my parents are farmers, that's what I know. I figured I would go to agriculture school at Iowa State. I know lots of kids who have gone this year. They're freshmen now, and they seem to like it.

CO: I'd like to hear more about your plans. [The counselor is aware that George's plans are in the outdoor (5) category, Level 3, but is not sure if this is a choice for George or if it is something that is convenient to him.]

CL: Every summer I work with my father and mother, growing, harvesting corn and soybeans. We've also got a dairy herd. It's OK; I like working with my folks.

CO: Have you done any other work? [The counselor is curious if all of George's experiences have been in the outdoor category.]

CL: No, I really haven't. Most of my time is spent either at school or with my family on the farm, or with a 4-H club.

CO: What have you done with 4-H? [Wanting to find out about the breadth of George's experience, the counselor asks about his hobby.]

CL: I have entered calves in county fairs and attended classes on judging.

CO: Other hobbies or activities that you've done? [Still looking for breadth of experience in other categories, the counselor persists.]

CL: Well, I have written up articles both for the school paper and for our 4-H newsletter, but I didn't like it very much.

CO: What is it that you didn't like? [Surprised to hear about activity from the general cultural category (8), the counselor asks for more information.]

CL: I really don't like writing or English in general. My better grades are in science, and I think I like that better. When I had biology my sophomore year, I really found that interesting.

CO: You really seemed to light up when you mentioned that. [George now has moved to the science category, and the counselor wishes to hear more about it.]

CL: I really enjoyed learning about the human body. I didn't do really well. I got a "C," but I really liked it. As you know, the teacher's good, and lots of kids like him. In fact, my grades aren't too good; I hope I can get into a college here in Iowa.

CO: Have you been disappointed in your grades? [George now is talking about possible levels, perhaps Level 3, or maybe 2.]

CL: Not too disappointed. School is really necessary, I guess. I just don't seem to care about it too much. I'm starting to think about it now a little bit more, and I think I'll do better this fall, but getting into college depends a lot on your junior year.

CO: You seem to have given some thought to your future plans. [The counselor is trying to get some idea of George's motivation as to occupational level.]

CL: Well, it's occurring to me that I might do farming all of my life, but maybe I might want to do something else.

CO: Any dreams or ideas about what that might be? [The counselor is trying to explore George's possible interest in other groups. George seems to have limited experience, mainly in Group 5, outdoors.]

To use Roe's occupational classification system as in the preceding example, it is necessary to become familiar with the six levels and eight groups. The counselor can think about clients and career information in terms of their relationship to Roe's system. The conceptualization does not have to be as concrete as the one given in this example, but being able to categorize information is useful. Using Roe's levels allows the counselor to think in terms of training, education, and individual ability. This system can be used with other theoretical systems that do not have an occupational classification system.

Maslow's Hierarchy of Needs

Central to Roe's theory of personality development and career choice is the concept of needs. Roe found that Maslow's (1954) list of needs fit her viewpoint best. Maslow's theory focuses on human needs, rather than needs derived from research on animals. These needs, involuntary or unconscious, range from the most basic to the most complex. Although Roe's theory, as will be described later, has biological and sociological underpinnings, it is the psychological motivations of individuals that are most important in her theory. These are emphasized in the later stages of Maslow's hierarchy.

The needs Maslow identified are listed in the following paragraphs in order of their strength. The physiological needs are listed first, as they must be satisfied before other needs can be met. Individuals must satisfy their physiological hunger before they can be concerned about shelter, love, or information. Although there are exceptions, in general the needs at the beginning of the list must be satisfied before the others can be satisfied. People do not need to satisfy all needs. In fact, Maslow would claim that self-actualization (the last need listed) is realized by relatively few people. The needs are described here along with their relationship to occupational choice and entry (Roe & Siegelman, 1964):

1. *Physiological needs:* These are the most basic needs, as they are required for survival. They differ from other needs in that they can be localized in the body. For example, thirst is felt in the mouth and throat. When physiological needs are not met, they become the dominating force. If you are very hungry or thirsty as you read this book, you will not be able to concentrate on the subject matter, nor will you care, until you satisfy those needs. Work provides an income used to satisfy these needs. Agriculture and hunting are a direct way of satisfying these needs.

2. *Safety needs:* These needs are met through shelter, good health, and avoidance of danger. Except in emergency, safety needs are usually met for adults. Children are more likely to be frightened by strange events than are adults. Usually, toddlers react very strongly and loudly if their safety needs are not met. For adults, during wartime and times of famine, safety and physiological needs may not be met. When these needs become predominant, the remaining needs become quite minor. From an occupational point of view, safety needs can be translated into security needs (Roe, 1956, p. 32). Some people will choose security over working with other colleagues or other benefits, as security meets safety needs more than needs for belongingness.

3. *The needs for belongingness and love:* Caring for and being cared for are the most basic needs after safety and physiological needs. Psychological problems develop in children and adults when needs for belongingness and love are not met. Sexuality is a physical need, but its expression as affection belongs in this category. In a work setting, the need for belongingness is met through relationships with one's colleagues. Occupations vary in the extent to which they offer opportunities for satisfactory coworker relationships. For many people, this is one of the most important aspects of a successful career.

4. *Esteem needs:* People need to feel important and respected by themselves and by others. One often develops self-respect by feeling respected by others. One of the main reasons for seeking counseling is low self-esteem that is not affected by positive feelings that others may have for the individual. Feeling weak and inferior to others is a common reason for entering counseling or psychotherapy. An example is people who are unemployed and therefore feel bad about themselves, perceiving themselves to be inferior to those who are working. In contrast, the respect that people receive from colleagues and superiors when they perform well does much to develop self-esteem. Self-esteem is likely to be greatest in the higher occupational levels of Roe's classification system, as there is a greater

degree of responsibility in these occupations, which brings about more self-respect and respect from others.

5. *The need for information:* People have a need for information to understand their own personal and cultural history, to understand the environment around them, and to understand themselves. Children often want to know how things work, why things are done, and what will happen next. To perform all jobs, there is a need for information. At the highest levels of Roe's classification system, people may work for years achieving an M.D. or a Ph.D. degree to acquire the information needed for a specific occupation. Most of the occupations at Levels 1 and 2 of Roe's system require that the individual master a great deal of information.

6. *The need for understanding:* We need not only to have information about our world and our career, but also to have a way to process and understand this information. Those in the higher levels of Roe's classification system must understand and interpret great amounts of information.

7. *The need for beauty:* Although this seems to be a need one can do without meeting, it is an important experience for many people. For those in the arts and entertainment field (Group 8), it is essential. Often, the need for beauty may be the most important need for creative painters, writers, and musicians.

8. *The need for self-actualization:* This is the need to be all that one can be. The more an individual is able to do, the more he or she must do. To be self-actualized, one must meet the other needs first. However, Roe differs from Maslow in that she would put self-actualization prior to the need for information, as it seems so basic to her. Work, certainly that in the higher levels as described by Roe, gives individuals an opportunity for self-actualization. For those whose abilities go beyond what is required by their occupations, self-actualization may be impeded.

Maslow's (1954) hierarchy of needs provides a platform for Roe's personality development theory. As shown here, work meets many needs, but in different ways. In general, the higher the level of occupation, the more likely it is that higher-level needs will be met. Various occupational groupings meet needs, such as those for information, beauty, and understanding, in vastly different ways. The driving force for Roe, however, was to try to understand how needs develop in children and to predict career entry from this development.

Propositions of Roe's Personality Development Theory

Roe's theory is a very broad one, based not only on Maslow's hierarchy of needs, but also on genetic and sociological factors that affect career choice. In addition, Roe tried to predict the development of interests and abilities. She also discussed the important determinants of interest. Her theory also made statements about how needs develop into motivation. Her five basic propositions are elaborated on in the following paragraphs (Roe & Lunneborg, 1990).

Limits of Genetic Inheritance People differ in their potential across a large array of characteristics. Roe believed that intelligence and temperament are more determined by heredity than are interests and attitudes.

Limits of Sociological and Economic Factors A number of limits, or restrictive factors, are beyond an individual's control, such as economic limits, race or gender, and cultural or social attitudes.

Development of Interests and Attitudes The study of the development of interests and attitudes has been an important aspect of Roe's theoretical research. Interests and attitudes were considered an excellent subject for study because Roe believed that they are relatively unaffected by genetic predisposition. The development of interests and attitudes is involuntary. Individuals don't choose parents, teachers, or many of the situations that they encounter. Even friends are chosen only to a limited degree—from the neighborhood or the classroom. Roe feels that interests and attitudes are determined by early patterns of satisfactions and frustrations. This is the most important element of Roe's theory, as it is the focus of much of her research.

Determinants of Interests Interests are determined in large part by the degree of need satisfaction. The energy that results from a partially met need may develop importance for the individual. For example, a student who wishes to satisfy his or her need for information about the human eye may develop that interest if a teacher presents material about the eye that stimulates that interest. If the student is very frustrated by the difficulty of the information or does not have the ability to grasp it, then this activity will not develop as an interest. Studying the eye is an involuntary activity. When first learning biology, the student does not say, "I choose to become interested in the study of the eye and biology." The interest develops gradually and without awareness.

Development of Needs into Motivators The more intense the needs, the more intense the need to become successful. As the need for information and understanding about the eye increases, the student will work harder to learn more about it. As he or she is rewarded for meeting this need, basic needs such as feeling loved, respected, and important may be realized. Parents may offer praise; teachers may assign high grades. In this way, needs develop into motivators.

Roe's emphasis on the development of needs and her interest in psychological factors focus her work on parent-child interaction. Being particularly interested in how the attitudes of parents frustrate or fulfill the needs of their children, Roe interviewed artists, scientists, and others to learn more about how they had been motivated by their parents. She was particularly interested in the child-raising attitudes of her subjects' parents. Much of her research was retrospective; that is, she asked adults what had happened to them as children. Retrospective research has been criticized because of the unreliability of recall over 20 or more years. Direct observation or testing of children is the preferred research method.

Roe's Model of Parent-Child Interaction

Anne Roe (1957) classified early parent-child relationships into three types, each with two subclassifications. Roe was more interested in the attitudes of parents toward their children than in the specific ways in which parents behaved toward their children. Her classification system deals with the attitude toward (or away from) the child. In this section, the predictions that Roe made about categories of occupations to be selected depending on child-raising practices will be illustrated. Research on Roe's predictions and their implications for counseling practice will be discussed. A case study dealing with career choice and style of parenting will help the reader to understand the depth and complexity of Roe's theory.

The Three Types of Parental Attitudes For Roe, parents exhibit one of the following three types of attitudes toward their children:

Concentration on the child: Roe describes two types of emotional concentration on the child. The first is overprotection. An *overprotective* parent encourages dependence in the child and restricts curiosity and exploration. An *overdemanding* parent may request perfection from the child, asking for excellent performance and setting high standards of behavior. If the child does not meet these standards, the parent may punish the child. Roe shows that it is quite possible for parents to have different styles of behavior with each of their children. For example, she states that parents of a first child may be anxious and rather overprotective but may be more relaxed with less emotional concentration on the second child.

Avoidance of the child: Roe suggests two different methods of avoidance: rejection and neglect. An *emotionally rejected* child may be criticized or punished by his or her parents and not given love and affection. A *neglected* child may be ignored for a myriad of reasons, such as parents' concern with their own problems, other children, and work.

Acceptance of the child: Parents encourage independence rather than dependence and do not ignore or reject their child, creating a relatively tension-free environment. *Casual acceptance* refers to a low-key attitude of the parent, offering a minimum of love. *Loving acceptance,* on the other hand, shows a warmer attitude of the parent toward the child, while not interfering with the child's resources by fostering dependency.

Parental Attitudes and Maslow's Hierarchy Maslow's hierarchy of needs can be used to describe, in general terms, how certain needs are met or not met, depending on parental style. In homes where there is an emotional concentration on the child, the emphasis may be on the gratification of low-level needs. Meeting the needs for belongingness, love, and esteem may be contingent on the child's conforming to the parents' wishes. Needs for information and understanding may be limited by the parents' overprotectiveness or overdemandingness. Parents who avoid the child through either emotional rejection or neglect may meet mainly physiological and safety needs. Rejecting the child, or withholding love, can have a strong negative effect in terms of children's learning to avoid interaction with others. Needs for information and understanding may develop irrespective of the parent. What provides the possibility of all the needs' being gratified is the accepting parent. Through acceptance, children are likely to feel loved and to develop an independent style that will encourage the search for information, understanding, beauty, and self-actualization. The three basic styles of parenting are shown in the second innermost ring in Figure 12-3. The subtypes of parental understanding are shown in the third ring.

Orientation toward or away from People Roe believed that the variety of parental attitudes just described bring about certain types of personalities in the child. These are outlined in the next-to-outermost ring in Figure 12-3. Roe felt that children brought up in overprotective or overdemanding homes are likely to become self-centered in that they are aware of the views of others about themselves and wish to be in a strong position in relationship to others. Children brought up in rejecting homes are likely to develop attitudes against, rather than toward, people. They may be aggressive or defensive, preferring working with data or things rather than with people. Those children brought up by accepting parents are likely not to be aggressive or defensive and are likely to be interested in people rather than data or things. Roe then related these attitudes toward people or away from people to general patterns of relating in each of the eight occupational groups.

Relationship of Parental Style to Occupational Selection Roe made predictions about the occupational selections of individuals, who she felt would develop certain attitudes toward or away from people depending on the child-raising approach of their parents. One can follow these predictions by examining Figure 12-3, moving from the outside of the circle to the inside. For example, people in Group 1, service, are likely to have a major orientation toward themselves or others. They may have been brought up in a home where they were overprotected or in one in which they felt loving acceptance from their parents. In contrast, those who select science (Group 6) may prefer things or data to people and may have been ignored or rejected by their parents. Roe recognized that each parent within a family

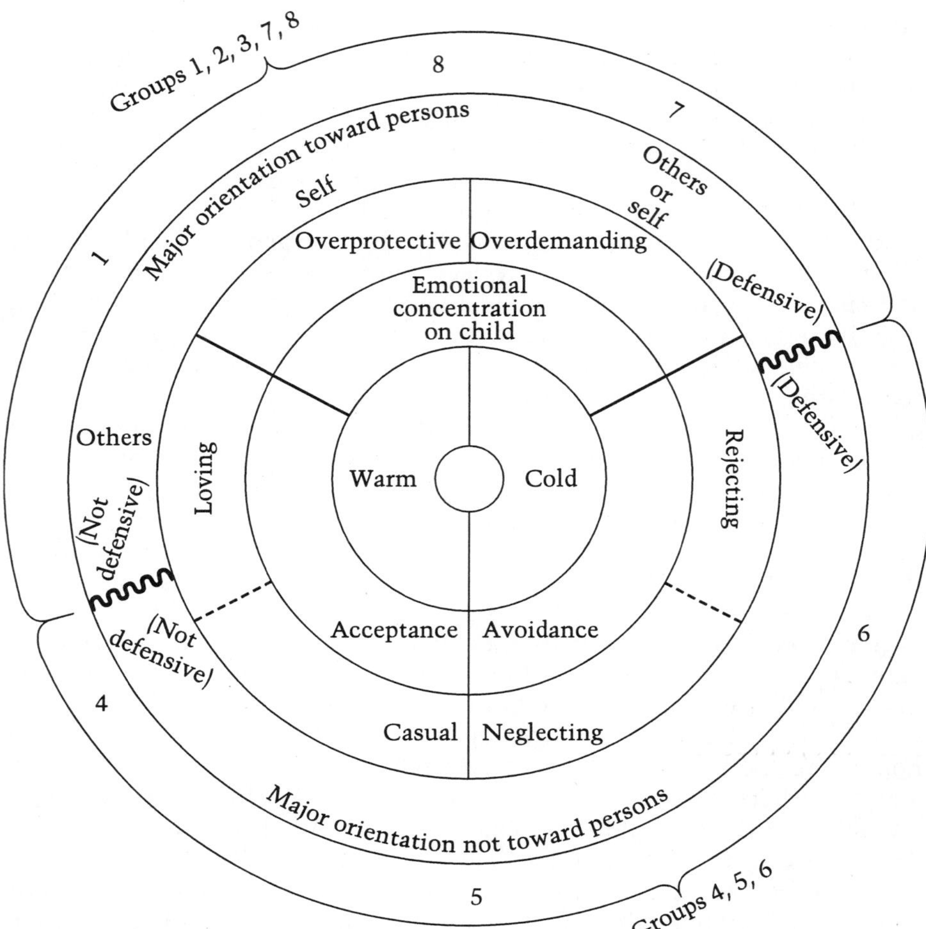

Figure 12-3 Hypothesized relations between major orientation, occupational choice, and parent-child relations. (Adapted from "Classification of Occupations," by A. Roe and D. Klos. In J. H. Whitely and A. Resnikoff (Eds.), *Vocational Development*, p. 213. Copyright © 1972 ACA. Reprinted with permission. No further reproduction authorized without written permission of the American Association for Counseling and Development.)

constellation may have a different style of parenting, and that parents may alter their styles at various times in their lives. However, she was referring to the most dominant style of child raising when she made her predictions. To do this, she developed A Parent-Child Relations Questionnaire (PCR I) based on the classification system that was described earlier (Roe & Siegelman, 1963). The questionnaire results were categorized into three basic factors: loving versus rejecting, casual versus demanding, and overt attention. These factors can be related directly to the parenting styles described earlier.

Research Support Because of the difficulty of making predictions about adult behavior from early childhood behavior and parental child-raising strategies, many complex research problems were posed by Roe's theory. Much of the research was conducted by asking people about their memories of their childhood experiences. As mentioned earlier, this retrospective data can be faulty because of selective and distant memory. Although there were many studies investigating the child-raising backgrounds of engineers, scientists, artists, ministers, homemakers, and many other occupations, the samples were quite small (Osipow, 1983). Also, the research did not deal with differences in child-raising techniques between parents or those that may have changed with time.

After reviewing the research in detail, Osipow (1983) and Roe and Lunneborg (1990) concluded that the research does not support the theory. There is no evidence that early child-raising patterns predict later occupational entry. However, both Roe and Lunneborg (1990) and Osipow (1983) did cite evidence that the work activity chosen by people within highly narrow fields of interest does reflect attitudes related to the experiences of early childhood (Roe & Lunneborg, 1990, p. 86). Thus, there is evidence that, within an occupation, people may select activities that indicate an orientation either toward or away from people. For example, a park ranger (Group 5, outdoor) who experienced little concern or attention (avoidance-neglect) from her parents may prefer activities that take her away from people, such as protecting wildlife or monitoring forests for fires or other damage. On the other hand, a park ranger who experienced love and acceptance from her parents may prefer to deal with the public through tours, assistance, or rescue operations. In summary, the research suggests a very limited application of Roe's theory in counseling. In fact, Roe (Roe & Lunneborg, 1990) is quite clear in stating that her theory was never designed for counseling application. Her work is valuable, however, because there is some limited validation as shown by the conclusions of researchers (Roe & Lunneborg, 1990), because it is a well-thought-out and tested theory, and because it provides a contrasting approach to attachment theory.

ATTACHMENT THEORY

Just as Roe has tried to make predictions based on parent-child interactions, attachment theorists have had similar intentions. Briefly, attachment theory studies the role that attachments (primarily parental) play in shaping the life of an individual (Lopez, 1995). Attachment theory grew out of object relations theory, a development of psychoanalysis (Sharf, 1996), which emphasizes the relationship that the infant has with others, particularly the mother. Bowlby (1969/1982, 1973, 1980), the most well-known attachment theorist, studied the importance of attachment, separation, and loss in human development. Unlike object relations theorists, who are interested in mother-child relationships in early childhood and their effect on psychiatric illness, some attachment theorists have studied the effect that attachment has on normal children; other attachment theorists have focused on the entire life span. Bowlby was particularly interested in how individuals' sense of being worthwhile and views of their own competence develop along with their views of others. Of great importance in this development, according to Bowlby, is the role of "attachment figures," such as the mother and the father. To study attachment, Ainsworth (Ainsworth, Blehar, Walters, & Wall, 1978) used the "strange situation" method to observe the attachment behavior of young children. This involves making unobtrusive observations of children when the mother comes and goes, when a stranger enters, and when the child is alone. From these observations, three types of responding were found: the secure pattern, the anxious-ambivalent pattern, and the avoidant pattern.

Secure Pattern. The infant responds to the caregiver easily and is able to continue exploratory behavior (an important feature for career development as described in Chapter 7). The security experienced by infants allows them to interact well with people and things in their world.

Anxious-ambivalent Pattern. Because the infant experiences the caregiver as being inconsistent, the child becomes anxious. Also, the child's view of herself or himself is one of uncertainty, as is the child's view of others. Such anxiety and uncertainty often result in decreased exploratory behavior.

Avoidant Pattern. In this pattern, the infant ignores or rejects care that is offered by an adult. Ainsworth et al. (1978) saw that such children would develop a sense of being alone in the world and of being unable to trust others.

A large amount of research has shown that these patterns are stable during the first six years of life and are different from infant moods or temperament (Lopez, 1995). Attachment patterns are less consistent in families with high stress than in those with low stress. Other researchers have modified these attachment patterns and added one or two others. Suggested by patterns of attachment is the idea that children who have a secure pattern of attachment in their first six years of life are more willing to explore relationships with others and more willing to play with objects or animals, activities leading eventually to greater familiarity with their world and the world of work. However, there is no direct evidence to support this conjecture, because, like Roe's theory, attachment theory has the very difficult task of trying to predict behavior over a long period of time. Longitudinal studies of this type have not yet been done. Also, the parental attitudes of the father, as opposed to the mother (Roe's theory), and different kinds of attachment to the mother and the father may also be significant variables.

Reviewing nonlongitudinal studies, Blustein, Prezioso, and Palladino Schultheiss (1995) have shown how attachment theory can be useful in understanding career development. Of particular importance is the relationship between attachment and exploration that is related to learning (Hazan & Shaver, 1990). Being secure, the infant, child, adolescent, and adult can more freely explore his or her world and thus develop social competence throughout life. Blustein et al. (1995) make a point that secure and close relationships are important not only in childhood, but also in late adolescence, when career exploration is a prominent activity. Suggested by their article is the idea that individuals who have secure parental relationships develop a strong sense of vocational identity and can make career decisions, in part because they have been able to explore the world of work.

Recent research adds information about the relevance of separation-attachment concepts to vocational development. O'Brien (1993) reported that attachment to the mother and emotional independence from the father were predictive of confidence in career decision making, and also, surprisingly, of career choices that were not congruent. Blustein, Walbridge, Friedlander, and Palladino (1991) found little relationship between difficulties in psychological separation and confidence in career decision making in young adults. They also found that adolescents who were closely attached to their parents, but able to act independently, were less likely than other adolescents to make early, poorly thought-out career choices. Studying college freshmen, Thomason and Winer (1994) found little relationship between career maturity and psychological separation from parents. In research investigating the behavior of employed adults, Hazan and Shaver (1990) found that securely attached workers showed better adjustment to work than did anxious-ambivalent or avoidant workers. In another study of employed adults, Hardy and Barkham (1994) reported that employers who revealed anxious-ambivalent attachments were also anxious about their performance at work and in work-related relationships. These studies suggest that the concepts of separation and attachment can add to knowledge of the career development process, but the findings are not specific enough to make concrete suggestions to counselors.

When applied to career development, attachment theory does not make specific predictions about career choices, as does Roe's theory. Because the research is limited and predictions are only partially related to career development, the suggestions for counseling application are general. Blustein et al. (1995) believe that understanding individuals' relationships with others in terms of separation and attachment is useful in working with career choice and career adjustment concerns. Particularly, discussing issues of separation from and attachment to parents that are causing problems in an adolescent's life may help individuals develop a sense of security so that they can deal with career exploration and choice issues that are causing anxiety. When working with clients who are anxious about their career choice, counselors may find it helpful to ask about current or past strains in parental relationships. For example, if her or his parents are in the process of getting a divorce or were divorced earlier, the client may feel unsure of herself or himself in deciding about how to deal with parents, siblings, and educational or career decision making. A sense of secure attachment need not be limited to family relationships. A secure relationship that develops between the client and the counselor, as well as trusting relationships between the client and his or her instructors or supervisors, may help to reduce stress in individuals who have experienced attachment difficulties in childhood or other relationships.

FAMILY SYSTEMS THERAPY

In general, family therapists and marriage counselors have paid little attention to career counseling. However, a few studies have described the effect of family relationships on career development. Of particular interest to researchers on family processes have been the enmeshed and the disengaged family (Goldenberg & Goldenberg, 1996). Basically, an enmeshed family is one in which the responsibilities in the family are unclear. For example, the mother and the father may give an eleventh-grade student different advice about choosing a career. Her younger sister may tease her about being stupid because she has no career plans. In contrast, in a disengaged family, an eleventh-grade student may be told by his father to make plans to study engineering because there are good-paying jobs in that field. The relationship between father and son is authoritarian, with the father telling the son, but not listening to him. Penick and Jepsen (1992) found that family relationships, such as enmeshment or disengagement, were stronger predictors of career development than gender, socioeconomic status, or educational achievement. In another study, Gordon (1991) found that problems in family functioning are related to the working style of employed adults, adults who experienced divorce or the loss of a family member in childhood being more likely than others to become innovative problem solvers. These types of studies are infrequent, and more research along these lines needs to be done.

One approach that family therapists use with their clients can be applied to career counseling. When working with clients who are trying to choose an occupation, it may be helpful to discuss family career patterns. McGoldrick and Gerson (1985) describe the use of the genogram as a way of drawing relationships in a family and indicating important information about them.

Okiishi (1987) describes how genograms can be used in career counseling: they encourage client self-disclosure, organize relevant information about the attitudes of the family toward work, and reveal how the work

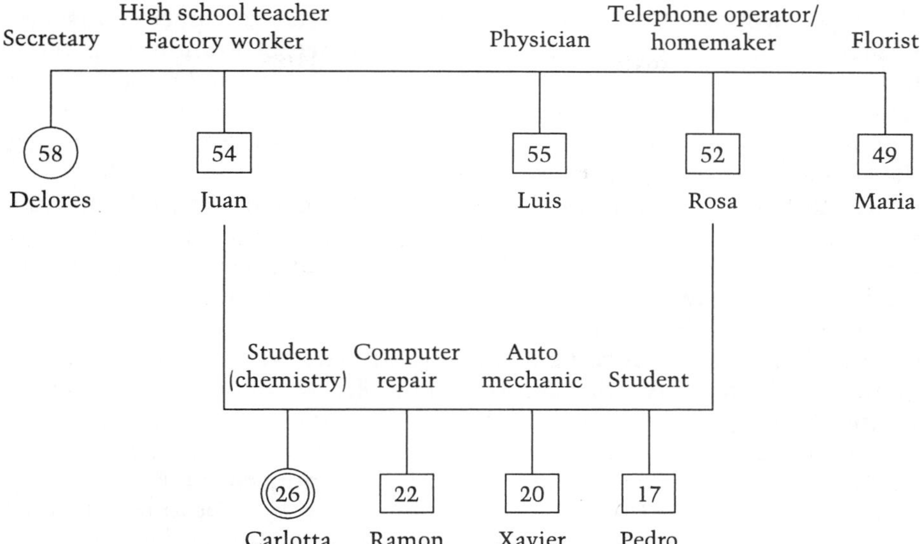

Figure 12-4 Genogram of Carlotta's family, including ages and occupations.

patterns of family members affect the client. To construct a genogram, Okiishi (1987) suggests using a large piece of newsprint or computer paper so that relevant information about the family can be listed (an abridged version is illustrated in Figure 12-4). When occupational information about the family is included, many issues of the client's view of himself or herself, others, and the work world can be explored. Counselors can find out from their clients how different family members served as role models for attitudes toward work and further education. For example, did certain relatives stereotype careers by gender, or did they especially value certain occupations such as medicine or the ministry? Did the family members have different attitudes toward obtaining more education after high school? Discussing such topics helps clients better understand the origin and the content of their own attitudes toward career decision making. The use of the genogram is illustrated in the following case.

USING PARENTAL INFLUENCE THEORIES IN COUNSELING

It is difficult to be specific in the application of parental influence theories in counseling. Although Roe's theory makes specific predictions, they have not been confirmed by research. Neither attachment theory or family systems theory has been sufficiently tested with career issues, nor has it been clearly shown how their hypotheses can be applied to career counseling. Rather, these theories emphasize the importance of examining parental influences. In the following case the counselor makes use of Roe's emphasis on parent-child interaction and on parental attitudes toward children, attachment theory's focus on closeness to and separation from parents, and the genogram in exploring these issues.

Carlotta is a 26-year-old single female whose parents were born in Cuba and emigrated to the United States when Carlotta was 5. In Cuba, Carlotta's mother had been a telephone operator and her father had been a high school teacher. Both were fluently bilingual, and Carlotta grew up speaking both English and Spanish. Carlotta is the oldest of four children, having three younger brothers, each about two years apart. Carlotta's mother was protective of Carlotta when she was young. However, as Carlotta's brothers were born, Carlotta received less and less attention. Her mother tended to neglect her except when she wanted child-care help with Carlotta's brothers. The family income after coming to the United States was quite low. Carlotta's father had to find a job in a local shoe factory. Carlotta's relationship with her father had always been warm and loving. Although it experienced some strain when they moved to the United States, the relationship essentially remained close. When Carlotta was 12, her mother was injured severely in an auto accident that considerably limited both her physical and mental functioning. At this point the relationship between Carlotta's parents deteriorated greatly. Carlotta's father was not understanding of his wife's difficulties, and they communicated little, although they lived in the same house.

Throughout her high school years, Carlotta was torn between caring for her family and pursuing school. An excellent science student, she received the praise of her biology and chemistry teachers. They supported her desire for further education. On graduation from high school, Carlotta attended a community college, where she received all "A"s. She had been working part time at a clothing store and continued to do so full time for two more years after receiving an associate's degree. She then entered a local university to complete a bachelor of science degree in chemistry. She worked for one year in a pharmaceutical laboratory as an assistant to a scientist and then returned to graduate school at a city far from home. Her intention was to receive a doctorate in chemistry and to become a professor of chemistry.

In discussing Carlotta's family, the counselor used a genogram, illustrated in Figure 12-4. Females are represented by circles, males by squares. The client is indicated by a double circle (or, if male, a double square). In this abridged version of the genogram, the occupations of Carlotta's brothers, parents, and their parents' brothers and sisters are also listed. In a larger genogram, cousins, spouses of parents' brothers and sisters, and grandparents would be included. With the genogram (Figure 12-4), the counselor had a clear approach to a discussion of the impact of Carlotta's father's changing from a high school teacher to a factory laborer, and of how his resulting dissatisfaction was played out in the family. Furthermore, the genogram was a basis for examining how her mother's career change from telephone operator to homemaker and her auto accident had affected her attitude toward herself and Carlotta. Using the genogram, the counselor was able to ascertain how Carlotta's mother (and others) had served as role models for Carlotta's career ambitions. Additionally, the counselor and Carlotta discussed the fact that her education was much more extensive than other family members (excepting her Uncle Luis, a physician). Her brother Xavier, an auto mechanic, resented her further education, and it had been a source of tension between the two of them.

When Carlotta entered counseling, she had been enrolled in a doctoral-level chemistry program for one year. She was in a panic. She was now questioning her desire to be a chemist, which she had not questioned for six years. She found the material very difficult and the professors demanding. She was questioning her ability to complete her thesis and dissertation and then continue in an extensive research program. During her first year of graduate school, Carlotta had taught a laboratory section of an undergraduate chemistry course. She had very much enjoyed teaching and was looking forward to teaching in her career. She was not sure, however, that she would be able to finish a doctoral degree. Her entire family was supportive and had become increasingly so as her brothers became older and more independent.

Her counseling dealt with several issues concerning her family relationships. Carlotta explored her relationship with her mother. She recalled times when she was 14 or 15 when she had been quite angry at her mother for not being more helpful. Now she felt some guilt about that, as she thought back to the times when her mother had been in pain from her automobile accident. She remembered very fondly good times with both parents before her adolescence. She talked of returning home occasionally on vacations and how she had played the role of peacemaker. Much of the counseling dealt with her feeling nurtured by her parents and later reversing roles to nurture both parents and brothers. In this process, she felt that her mother had withdrawn her caring from Carlotta. She recalled a profound feeling of separation from her mother when she was about 14. Perhaps as a result, helping others had become a very important role for her. It was natural for her to enjoy teaching. When she had worked in the clothing store, assisting customers in the selection of items was the part of her work that she enjoyed the most; the rest bored her. Carlotta was still fascinated by chemistry. She enjoyed her courses but was apprehensive about the coming year, when she would be working more independently with a research team. Counseling served to help her reconcile her scientific interest and her nurturing needs. It also helped to bolster her self-confidence in her ability to accomplish difficult assignments.

A follow-up contact with Carlotta ten months later revealed that she had changed the content of her research. She had changed advisers, switching to a smaller research team whose goals were more concrete and less demanding. Carlotta could see herself clearly as a chemistry teacher in a small college, where the emphasis would be on teaching and on student contact, rather than on research. She was planning to take a research assistantship the following year outside the chemistry department and in the university's program that provided help to new graduate assistants and faculty in their teaching skills.

While Roe's theory does not directly describe the occurrences in this case, the issues in the case are similar to those that concerned Roe. Parental and family relationships had an influence on Carlotta's later choices. The crisis that Carlotta faced about her future had to do with the conflict between her academic interest in chemistry and her orientation toward people and toward helping others, which had developed in her family. Furthermore, attachment theory alerts the counselor to deal with issues of Carlotta's attachment to her mother, followed by an unwanted forced separation. Although this case study may not be typical, it illustrates the relation of parent-child interactions to occupational choice. Carlotta was willing to explore the relationship between her current crisis and family issues; not all clients are willing to do so.

APPLYING THE THEORIES TO WOMEN AND PEOPLE OF COLOR

Roe (Roe & Lunneborg, 1990) was concerned that her occupational classification system did not account for women whose careers are interrupted by caring for a family. There really is no category in Roe's system for homemakers. She felt that her classification system is quite adequate for those who enter occupations and stay in the labor force.

Regarding her theory of personality development and career choice, Roe's concern about cultural background and gender is addressed in the second proposition of her theory. Roe developed a specific formula to predict career choice. Although it was not dealt with in this chapter because it has little application for counselors, the formula does show that Roe has considered cultural and gender factors quite carefully. Race is incorporated into family background as a part of her formula, and the gender of the individual has a prominent place in her formula. Because her theory relating child-raising approaches to career choice has little applicability and her research predictions were not found to hold, the theory's application to women and people of color is moot.

With regard to attachment theory, there are few, if any, gender differences reported in early childhood in attachment styles, and few differences have been found in studies relating attachment to career development (Blustein et al., 1995). Investigations on attachment have been carried out in England, Uganda, the United States, and other countries, providing a multicultural approach to this work. From a broader perspective, psychoanalytic writers such as Chodorow (1989) have discussed the impact of different social roles of men and women on child raising. However, Chodorow and other writers have provided observations that are more speculative than research that investigates attachment theory. She has not focused on career development, or on issues related to people of color.

Recently, much attention has been paid to gender and multicultural issues in family therapy, as shown by Goldenberg and Goldenberg (1996) and Sharf (1996). These authors provide an overview of how the two genders and different cultural groups vary in their child-raising strategies. Although family therapists do not focus on career development issues, their observations of the role of culture and gender in career adjustment and decision making would appear to be consistent with the research on women and people of color discussed in Chapters 7, 8, and 9.

SUMMARY

Anne Roe has contributed to career development research since the publication of her first paper (Roe & Brown, 1927). Her classification system, consisting of six levels and eight groups of occupations, is quite helpful in classifying both occupations and career choices. The occupational groups have been shown to have a meaningful relationship to each other in terms of their placement in her system. Her predictions about the effect of child-rearing practices on later occupational choice have not been borne out. However, she has pointed out the importance of meeting needs through occupational choice and has heightened counselors' awareness of the role of parenting styles in childhood development. Further insights into parental roles in career development come from attachment theory and family systems theory. This work is recent, presenting interesting questions about family influences on career choice, as well as some issues to be considered in counseling, such as discussing parental attitudes toward work and parental relationships as they affect confidence and exploration regarding career decision making.

References

Ainsworth, M. D. S., Blehar, M. C., Waters, E., & Wall, S. (1978). *Patterns of attachment: A psychological study of the strange situation.* Hillsdale, NJ: Erlbaum.

Blustein, D. L., Prezioso, M. S., & Palladino Schultheiss, D. P. (1995). Attachment theory and career development: Current status and future directions. *The Counseling Psychologist, 23,* 416–432.

Blustein, D. L., Walbridge, M. M., Friedlander, M. L., & Palladino, D. E. (1991). Contributions of psychological separation and parental attachment to the career development process. *Journal of Counseling Psychology, 38,* 39–50.

Bowlby, J. (1973). *Attachment and loss. Vol. II: Separation.* New York: Basic Books.

Bowlby, J. (1980). *Attachment and loss. Vol. III: Loss.* New York: Basic Books.
Bowlby, J. (1982). *Attachment and loss. Vol. I: Attachment.* London: Tavistock. (Original work published 1969)
Chodorow, N. J. (1989). *Feminism and psychoanalytic theory.* New Haven, CT: Yale University Press.
Goldenberg, I., & Goldenberg, H. (1996). *Family therapy: An overview* (4th ed.). Pacific Grove, CA: Brooks/Cole.
Gordon, V. Z. (1991). Successful careers and cognitive style: A follow-up study of childhood family discontinuity. *Psychological Reports, 69,* 1071–1074.
Hardy, G. E., & Barkham, M. (1994). The relationship between interpersonal attachment styles and work difficulties. *Human Relations, 47,* 263–281.
Hazan, C., & Shaver, P. R. (1990). Love and work: An attachment-theoretical perspective. *Journal of Personality and Social Psychology, 59,* 270–280.
Jones, K. J. (1965). Occupational preference and social orientation. *Personnel and Guidance Journal, 43,* 574–579.
Knapp, R. R., & Knapp, L. (1977). *Interest changes and the classification of occupations.* Unpublished manuscript.
Knapp, R. R., & Knapp, L. (1985). *California Occupational Preference System: Self-interpretation profile and guide.* San Diego: Educational and Industrial Testing Service.
Kuder, G. F. (1946). *Manual to the Kuder Preference Record.* Chicago: Science Research Associates.
Lopez, F. G. (1995). Contemporary attachment theory: An introduction with implications for counseling psychology. *The Counseling Psychologist, 23,* 395–415.
Lunneborg, P. W. (1981). *The Vocational Interest Inventory (VII) manual.* Los Angeles: Western Psychological Services.
Lunneborg, P. W., & Lunneborg, C. E. (1968). Roe's classification of occupations in predicting academic achievement. *Journal of Counseling Psychology, 15,* 8–16.
Lunneborg, P. W., & Wilson, V. M. (1982). *To work: A guide for women college graduates.* Englewood Cliffs, NJ: Prentice-Hall.
Maslow, A. H. (1954). *Motivation and personality.* New York: Harper & Row.
McGoldrick, J., & Gerson, R. (1985). *Genograms in family assessment.* New York: Norton.
Meir, E. I. (1970). Empirical test of Roe's structure of occupations and an alternative structure. *Journal of Counseling Psychology, 17,* 41–48.
Meir, E. I. (1973). The structure of occupations by interests—A small space analysis. *Journal of Vocational Behavior, 3,* 21–31.
Meir, E. I. (1975). *Manual for the RAMAK and Courses interest inventories.* Tel Aviv University, Department of Psychology.
O'Brien, K. M. (1993). *The influence of psychological separation and parental attachment on the career choices and self-efficacy beliefs of adolescent women.* Unpublished doctoral dissertation, Loyola University, Chicago.
Okiishi, R. W. (1987). The genogram as a tool in career counseling. *Journal of Counseling and Development, 66,* 139–143.
Osipow, S. H. (1983). *Theories of career development* (3rd ed.). Englewood Cliffs, NJ: Prentice-Hall.
Penick, N. I., & Jepsen, D. A. (1992). Family functioning and adolescent career development. *Career Development Quarterly, 40,* 208–222.
Roe, A. (1956). *The psychology of occupations.* New York: Wiley.

Roe, A. (1957). Early determinants of vocational choice. *Journal of Counseling Psychology, 4,* 212–217.

Roe, A. (1972). Perspectives on vocational development. In J. M. Whiteley & A. Resnikoff (Eds.), *Perspectives on vocational development* (pp. 61–82). Washington, DC: American Personnel and Guidance Association.

Roe, A., & Brown, C. F. (1927). Qualifications for dentistry: A preliminary study. *Personnel Journal, 6,* 176–181.

Roe, A., & Klos, D. (1972). Classification of occupations. In J. M. Whiteley & A. Resnikoff (Eds.), *Perspectives on vocational development* (pp. 199–221). Washington, DC: American Personnel and Guidance Association.

Roe, A., & Lunneborg, P. W. (1990). Personality development and career choice. In D. Brown, L. Brooks, & Assoc. (Eds.), *Career choice and development: Applying contemporary theories to practice* (2nd ed., pp. 68–101). San Francisco: Jossey-Bass.

Roe, A., & Siegelman, M. (1963). A Parent-Child Relations Questionnaire. *Child Development, 34,* 355–369.

Roe, A., & Siegelman, M. (1964). *The origin of interests.* Washington, DC: American Personnel and Guidance Association.

Sharf, R. S. (1996). *Theories of psychotherapy and counseling: Concepts and cases.* Pacific Grove, CA: Brooks/Cole.

Strong, E. K., Jr. (1943). *Vocational interests of men and women.* Stanford, CA: Stanford University Press.

Thomason, S. L., & Winer, J. L. (1994). Career maturity and familial independence among college freshman. *Journal of Career Development, 21,* 23–35.

Tracey, T. J., & Rounds, J. (1994). An examination of the structure of Roe's eight interest fields. *Journal of Vocational Behavior, 44,* 279–295.

13

Social Learning Theory

The study of human learning makes up a significant portion of research in theoretical, experimental, and educational psychology. Bandura (1969, 1977, 1986) has reviewed and compiled research that supports a social learning view of human behavior based on both reinforcement theory and observational learning. Bandura believes that individuals' personalities grow from their learning experiences more than from their genetic or intrapsychic processes. Bandura (1986) acknowledged the role of behavior in learning but also recognized the importance of thoughts and images in psychological functioning. He referred to the interaction of the environment, personal factors (such as memories, beliefs, preferences, and self-perceptions), and actual behavior as a *triadic reciprocal interaction system.* In this system, each of the three factors affects the other two. As shown in this chapter, Bandura valued the importance of learning by observation. Regulating these three factors is a self-system of cognitive structures and perceptions that determines individual behavior (Bandura, 1978). How individuals regulate their behavior depends on their view of how well they can deal with difficult tasks in life, a concept that Bandura (1986) refers to as *self-efficacy.* Two significant theories of career development are based on his views and are the subject of this chapter: Krumboltz's social learning theory and career self-efficacy theory.

John Krumboltz and his colleagues have developed a theory of how individuals make career decisions that emphasizes the importance of behavior (action) and cognitions (knowing or thinking) in making career decisions. It differs from most other theories in this book in that it focuses on teaching clients career decision-making techniques and helping them use these techniques effectively in selecting career alternatives. The theory also focuses on helping the counselor conceptualize issues. A general overview of this theory is presented here that considers genetic endowment, environmental conditions, learning experiences, and task approach skills. With this background, important client cognitive and behavioral skills that are needed to make career decisions are explained. Behavioral counseling skills, such as reinforcement and modeling, are important tools for the counselor. Further, there are many cognitive strategies for determining and correcting problematic beliefs about the career decision-making process that counselors are likely to find helpful. Cognitive and behavioral techniques and skills can be used by the client and the counselor in applying a systematic seven-step approach to career decision making.

Another approach, with a stronger emphasis on thinking processes than on behavioral processes, is career self-efficacy theory. Started about 15 years ago, career self-efficacy theory focuses on the strength of individuals' belief that they can successfully accomplish something. This belief in oneself has been viewed as playing a more powerful role in career choice than interests, values, or abilities. Generating many research studies that have investigated the role of self-efficacy in the career choices of women, its developers, Nancy Betz, Steven Brown, Gail Hackett, and Robert Lent, expanded the original concepts into a detailed theory of career and academic interests, choice, and performance. The cognitive concepts of self-efficacy, outcome expectation, and goal selection are significant factors in academic and career decision making. Although not emphasizing application, as does Krumboltz's social learning model, this approach gives suggestions for helping clients make academic and career choices by helping them raise the level of their belief in their own effectiveness.

Although these approaches to explaining career development vary somewhat (as will be discussed later), both rely on the writings of Albert Bandura; Krumboltz's theory uses Bandura's early work and self-efficacy theory, emphasizing his later work. More than any other theories discussed in this book, social learning approaches to career decision making are directly related to psychological research into the human learning process.

KRUMBOLTZ'S SOCIAL LEARNING THEORY

Why do people choose the occupations they do? Why do they choose one major rather than another? Why choose one college and not another college? Krumboltz's social learning theory attempts to answer these questions by examining four basic factors: genetic endowment, environmental conditions, learning experiences, and task-approach skills. Each of these factors plays an important part in the eventual selection of a specific career alternative, and all four are diagrammed in Figure 13-1. The way they interact with each other is shown here. Although many other theories of career development focus on inherited abilities and environmental events, no other theory emphasizes the importance of learning experiences and task-approach skills as social learning theory does. Each of the four components of career decision making will be described in the following paragraphs, but learning experiences and task-approach skills will receive the most attention in this section. (These are described in more detail in Mitchell and Krumboltz, 1996, and briefly in Krumboltz, 1994b.)

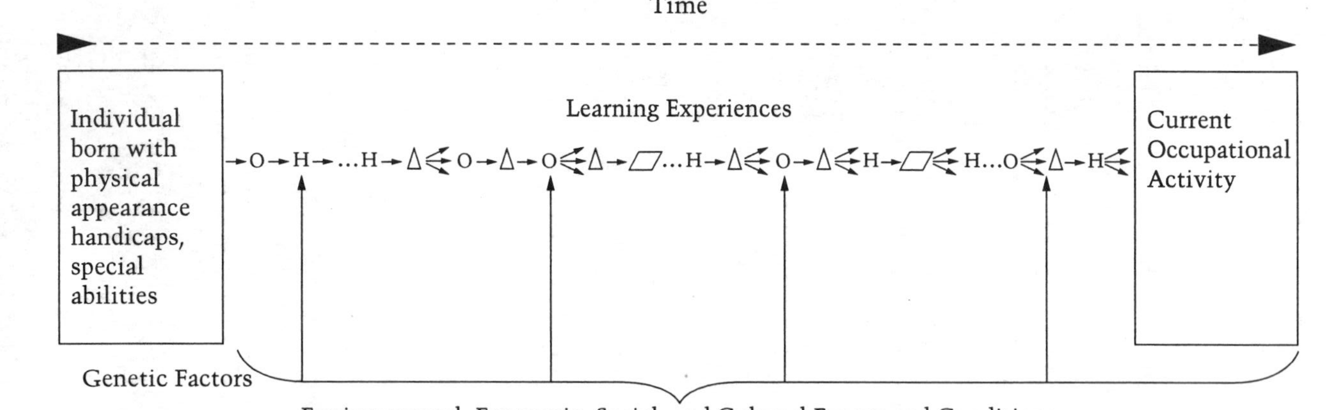

Figure 13-1 General model of factors affecting occupational selection. (From "A Social Learning Theory of Career Decision Making," by J. D. Krumboltz, p. 32. In A. M. Mitchell, G. B. Jones, & J. D. Krumboltz (eds), *Social Learning and Career Decision Making.* Copyright © 1979 by Carroll Press. Reprinted with permission.)

Genetic Endowment

Genetic endowment refers to those aspects of the individual that are inherited or innate rather than learned. These include physical appearance, such as height, hair color, and skin color; a predisposition to certain physical illnesses, and other characteristics. Additionally, some individuals are born with special abilities in the arts, music, writing, athletics, and so on. In general, the greater an individual's innate genetic abilities, the more likely he or she is to respond to learning and teaching. For example, an individual with limited musical ability (e.g., tone deafness) is unlikely to respond well to musical instruction no matter how long it is done and how well. The individual may improve but is not likely to become a skilled musician. The issue of how much of a particular ability is inherited and how much is learned is a difficult one. Social learning theory does not deal directly with this issue; rather, it focuses on learning and enhancing skills and abilities, where appropriate, as well as considering them in the career decision-making process.

Environmental Conditions and Events

A vast array of conditions affects individuals. These factors are generally outside the control of the individual. These include social, cultural, political, and economic considerations. Factors such as climate and geography also affect an individual in significant ways. Living in a polluted environment or an environment subject to earthquakes or extremely cold weather certainly has an impact on an individual's career choices. Mitchell and Krumboltz (1996) describe several conditions and events, categorized as social, educational, and occupational, that affect an individual's career decision making. Such factors may be planned or unplanned, but they are usually beyond the control of the individual.

Social Factors Changes in society have had a great effect on the available career options. For example, technological developments such as improved medicine and changes in transportation (e.g., faster cars and planes) create new jobs. The use of computers to process and store information in a wide variety of fields has also had great impact on the labor market. Abuses of technology, which lead to jobs in environmental engineering and waste management, are also important. Related to the abuse of the environment is the continuing demand for natural resources, such as oil, that require new techniques to find and remove from the earth. Social organizations, like the social security system, the GI bill program, and welfare programs, affect how people finance or seek careers and also require a staff to manage them, thus creating jobs. On another level, communities vary greatly in the occupations that they require. For example, a plains region may require ranchers and farmers, while a city requires merchants and salespeople.

Social conditions also affect the availability of and the demand for educational resources.

Educational Conditions The availability of education is influenced by both social and personal factors, for example, the degree to which a person's parents value higher education and have the ability to lend financial assistance. Related to that is the school system that an individual attends and the effect of the teachers and the resources in that system on the development of the individual's interests and abilities. Furthermore, training opportunities vary. Universities, technical schools, military service, and apprenticeship programs provide a variety of opportunities. Financial assistance also varies greatly among these institutions. The ability to get the necessary education to undertake a career is just one of several occupational considerations.

Occupational Conditions There are a number of factors affecting jobs and the job market over which individuals have little control. One of the most important is the number and nature of job opportunities. Jobs may be seasonal; limited by geographical considerations, such as logging and fishing; or may be affected by changing economic conditions. Educational requirements vary: some jobs require certification, licensure, a college degree, or other prerequisites to entry. Some jobs may require a college degree or other training when it may not really be necessary for performance of the job. Further, the salary and the prestige of jobs differ, depending on supply, demand, and cultural value. Also, labor laws or union rules may limit the number of people in a given occupation. Safety and other requirements may also affect the availability of certain occupations.

Learning Experiences

One's career preferences are a result of her or his prior learning experiences. An individual may have millions of prior learning experiences that will eventually influence his or her career decisions. Hundreds of times during a day, a schoolchild is exposed to bits of information, which he or she responds to and may feel good about, confused by, discouraged by, and so on. Because the variety of experience is so great, each individual's learning experience is different from another's. There are two basic types of learning experiences—instrumental (H) and associative (O)—that are important in career choice (see Figure 13-1).

Instrumental Learning Experiences (H) An instrumental learning experience has three components: antecedents, behaviors, and consequences. *Antecedents* refers to almost any type of condition, including genetic endowment, special abilities and skills, environmental conditions or events, and tasks or problems. People then respond to the antecedent with behaviors. The behavior may be quite obvious or it may be subtle. Likewise, the *consequences* of the behavior may be obvious or subtle. Further, the behavior may have an impact on others or it may not. Perhaps the key to understanding the instrumental learning experience is the focus on the behavior of the individual. Examples of an instrumental learning experience include taking an exam, studying for an exam, reading about an occupation, or talking to someone about his or her work. If the consequences of the behavior are positive, the individual is more likely to repeat it or similar behaviors. For example, if an individual receives an "A" on an exam, he or she is more likely to continue studying in that field and to take more courses in the same subject area than if he or she does poorly.

Associative Learning Experiences (O) When an individual pairs a situation that was previously neutral with one that is positive or negative, an associative learning experience occurs. Two types of associative learning experiences are observation and classical conditioning. Classical conditioning is an associative learning experience that occurs when an event is generalized to a category of experiences. For example, an individual who gets caught between floors for half an hour in an elevator may develop a fear of all elevators. Future uneventful elevator rides will help to change the fear, and it is likely that the individual will return to former neutral associations with elevators. Less dramatic associative learning may occur through observing others, for example, watching a mail carrier or teacher perform his or her occupation. More passive associative experiences come about through reading and hearing. Reading occupational information and hearing a discussion about occupations are frequent ways of learning occupational information. Occupational stereotypes may develop from powerful associative experiences. For example, if a child hears that "dentists like to hurt people" or "bankers want to steal your money," inaccurate information may be learned.

Task-Approach Skills

Understanding how an individual approaches a task is critical to career decision making. For the purpose of this chapter, task-approach skills include goal setting, values clarification, generating alternatives, and obtaining occupational information. Interactions among genetic endowment, environmental conditions, and learning experiences lead to skills in doing a variety of tasks. One's study skills, work habits, ways of learning, and ways of responding emotionally are a result of genetic characteristics, special abilities, environmental conditions, and instrumental and associative learning experiences. How an individual approaches a task depends on previous experience and influences the outcome of the task. For example, how an individual studies a French assignment depends on her innate ability, how she was taught French, and how much she has already learned. These factors, combined with how she prepares for the French exam, will affect the outcome (her grade). Certain task skills are particularly important in career decision making. These include setting goals, clarifying values, predicting future events, generating alternatives, and seeking occupational information. The development of these task-approach skills is a major emphasis of Krumboltz's social learning approach to career decision making.

Thoughts and beliefs arise from the four influencing factors just discussed. Thoughts and beliefs about the self and the environment arise from genetic endowment, environmental conditions, learning experiences, and task-approach skills. The ways in which individuals develop beliefs and act on them is the subject of the next section.

Client Cognitive and Behavioral Skills

How individuals apply their prior learning experience and innate abilities has a direct effect on career choice. Individuals may make observations about themselves and their environment that they will then use to make career decisions. Observations about self include observations about capacities or abilities, interests, and work values. Generalizations about the world include the world of work as well as other events outside oneself. Task-approach skills are related to the manner in which individuals approach the career decision-making process. Implicit in social learning theory is the idea that more experience provides an opportunity to make better career decisions.

Self-Observation Generalizations about Abilities People make observations about their ability to perform tasks adequately based on prior experience and information that they may have acquired about themselves. A student may observe that she is good in math but poor in music. Or she may observe that she is skillful in dealing with young children but awkward in dealing with elderly people. For many people, making accurate generalizations about their own competencies is quite difficult. People may tend to understate or overstate their abilities. Further, some students would regard a "B" as a high grade, others as a failure. Similarly, students who receive scores on the SAT or ACT that put them at the 50th percentile compared to other students may either be very disappointed or overjoyed. A person's view of his singing abilities may be quite different from the view of his audience. Thus, the accuracy of generalizations about one's own abilities is often derived from comparing one's view of one's capacities with others' view.

Self-Observation Generalizations about Interests Just as individuals make observations about what they are good at, they also generalize about what they like or do not like. If a person in a biology class did not like dissecting animals, was bored by studying anatomy, and disliked learning about plants, he may generalize that he does not like biology. Interests can be very general or very specific. For example, an individual may enjoy eighteenth-century European history but may not be as interested in other aspects of history. Interest inventories are helpful in assessing generalizations that individuals have about interests derived from learning experiences. However, interest inventories do not assess specific interests, such as an interest in eighteenth-century European history. Furthermore, interest inventories are not likely to separate an interest in chemical engineering from an interest in electrical engineering. However, they are of particular use when an individual has difficulty in identifying interests that have arisen from a large number of prior learning experiences.

Self-Observation Generalizations about Values People make judgments about the desirability of certain behaviors or events. From these judgments, they develop both personal and work values. Personal values may include a desire to be politically active or a desire to be involved in religious activity. Other personal values may include a deep love of art, music, or the natural beauty of the environment. Work values may include the desire to achieve or advance in one's profession. Other common work values include security, prestige, and high income. Some work values may be more difficult to state because they may be different from the work values that others hold. For example, a desire to persuade others by selling them a product may be more difficult to observe in oneself than the wish to help small children. Views of one's capacities, interests, and values contrast with perceptions of the world outside oneself.

Generalizations about the World As people make observations about themselves, they also make observations about the world in which they live and the people around them. Generalizations about occupations may come from both instrumental and associative learning experiences. Some generalizations may come from a great deal of actual experience. For example, a student who has worked in many retail businesses after school and during the summer may be able to make generalizations about retail sales work based on her experience. However, if her experience has not included training and management experience or exposure to managers, she may not be able to make accurate generalizations about the work of retail store managers. Some students may make generalizations based on very few associative learning experiences. For example, it is common to hear people stereotype the career of funeral director based on jokes or movies. Frequently, they have little accurate information about the job duties of a funeral director. The purpose of occupational information and experience is to provide an opportunity for people to make generalizations about the world.

Task-Approach Skills Used in Career Decision Making Often, individuals apply to career decision making the task-approach skills that they have learned in studying or working. Because career decision making requires one to make many generalizations about oneself and the world, previous task-approach skills may not be sufficient. Further, the accuracy of an individual's worldview and self-observation generalizations may need to be questioned. The accuracy of these observations may be determined by a combination of the quantity of experiences, the representativeness of the experiences, and the task-approach skills that an individual uses in evaluating these. Krumboltz and Baker (1973) outlined a sequence of seven steps used in making career decisions. A very similar approach, called DECIDES, was designed for high school students by Krumboltz and Hamel (1977). This approach is described in detail later in this section with illustrations of how counselors can use both cognitive and behavioral counseling techniques to assist clients systematically in making career decisions.

Counselor Behavioral Techniques

While many behavioral techniques have been developed by psychologists to deal with a vast variety of problems, this section will explain three procedures that follow from social learning theory and are directly related to career decision-making counseling: reinforcement, the use of role models, and the use of simulation in counseling. Reinforcement is the most important technique, with the broadest use, having an application in all phases of career decision-making counseling. In addition, the use of role models and simulation (trying out an occupation) can be particularly helpful when assisting clients in expanding their worldview generalizations.

Reinforcement Many times during the day, individuals are positively reinforced for their actions. Positive reinforcement increases the occurrence of a response. For example, a student may be thanked for helping with the breakfast dishes, taking out the trash, and doing well on a history exam. Having been rewarded (thanked), the student is more likely to continue the behavior than if the student had not been rewarded. These experiences of positive reinforcement are cumulative. As suggested earlier, they influence an individual's observations of his or her capacities, interests, and values. Mitchell and Krumboltz (1996) review a number of studies that support the importance of positive reinforcement in career decision-making activity. For example, Baird (1971) suggests that junior college students who seek additional education do so because of reinforcement for their academic work. Osipow (1972) and Mansfield (1973) demonstrate the importance of positive reinforcement in task preference. Positive reinforcement in terms of verbal praise is shown to be a valuable tool in career decision-making counseling (Krumboltz & Schroeder, 1965; Krumboltz & Thoresen, 1964; Oliver, 1975).

By reinforcing various aspects of a client's decision-making process, the counselor can assist in the accomplishment of a goal of career counseling: selecting an appropriate occupational alternative. To reinforce a client's decision-making skills, the counselor needs to be viewed as a reinforcer. In most cases, this is automatic. Clients seek out counselors for help because they value their expertise. Thus, a counselor's positive reinforcement of an activity may have greater value than that of a client's friend or acquaintance. Positive reinforcement can include expressions of approval, positive excitement, and appreciation by the counselor. A brief example will illustrate:

CL: Last week after we talked, I read about what sales managers do in the *Occupational Outlook Handbook*. It really gave me a pretty good idea. Then I went out and talked to my uncle's friend, who is a sales manager at a local paint distributorship.
CO: That's great! You really made progress in finding out about an important career possibility for you.
CL: Both the article and my uncle's friend helped me to get a better idea of the difference between being a salesperson and being a sales manager.
CO: That puts you in a better position to make an informed decision.

Both of the counselor's statements positively reinforce the client. The second statement is more subtle and less exuberant than the first. Sometimes, it is helpful for a counselor to reinforce an activity that has already been reinforced:

CL: I just got an "A" on my Latin exam.
CO: That's terrific! I know how important it was to you.
CL: It makes me feel as if I can go on to college, and to a real good one.
CO: It makes you feel good about what you can accomplish academically.

The counselor reinforces an important event for the client, even though the "A" on the Latin exam is itself reinforcing. By doing this, the counselor is assisting the client in developing accurate self-observation generalizations about her ability. Positive reinforcement can be given for both self-observation generalizations and worldview generalizations.

Role Models Through the use of role models, clients can have a valuable associative learning experience. Mitchell and Krumboltz (1990) list several studies that support the effectiveness of role models as an aid in career decision making (Almquist, 1974; Fisher, Reardon, & Burck, 1976; Pallone, Rickard, & Hurley, 1970; Thoresen, Hosford, & Krumboltz, 1970). These studies evaluate the effectiveness of peer, parental, and other role models in helping students decide among occupational alternatives.

Counselors can assist clients both by acting as role models and by providing role models for them. By describing appropriate ways to make decisions and effective decision-making strategies, counselors become role models for the client. It is likely that a client will think of the counselor's strategies in future career decision making. Furthermore, a counselor who follows a social learning framework is likely to act in an organized and decisive manner, thus providing a role model for the client. Counselors can provide other role models for clients by making available audiotapes, or possibly videotapes, of people describing their decision-making process. For group career counseling, the counselor can invite employed persons or recent graduates to discuss their career decision-making process with the group. Before doing so, the counselor should ascertain that the invited speakers will model the career decision-making process in a way consistent with social learning theory. Besides being role models for the decision-making process, individuals can also be role models for specific occupations. Audiotapes or videotapes of individuals who describe their occupation can be useful, as can referrals to job sites. There a client can watch and/or talk to a worker in a particular field.

Simulation By doing some of the tasks that an individual in a particular occupation must perform, a client can simulate a career experience. Kits designed to help high school students experience jobs were researched in several investigations (Krumboltz, 1970; Krumboltz, Baker, & Johnson, 1968; Krumboltz, Sheppard, Jones, Johnson, & Baker, 1967). The purpose of the job experience kits (Krumboltz, 1970) was to give students a chance to experience success in tasks that are common in a specific occupation. Care was taken to be certain that the initial task would not be frustrating to the client. Research done by the investigators just listed showed that students who used the job experience kits expressed more interest in that occupation than students who received written or filmed occupational information.

To some extent, job simulation is provided by high schools and vocational technical schools when they offer introductory courses to various craft and trade professions, such as carpentry, metalworking, or welding. However, often such courses do not describe an occupation to a student; rather, they just provide the student an opportunity to learn simple tasks associated with that occupation. For counselors who do not have access to job experience kits, suggestions of volunteer, part-time, or summer jobs for clients sometimes provide a simulated job experience. However, there is often the danger that an individual who seeks such work will end up doing menial tasks. For example, a student who desires to find out what it is like to be a chef could end up in a part-time job washing dishes.

Cognitive Strategies for Counseling

There is a much greater variety of cognitive than behavioral strategies for career decision-making counseling. Many of these strategies are adaptations of cognitive psychotherapeutic approaches. They will be mentioned only briefly here, as a full description is beyond the scope of this book.

Mitchell and Krumboltz (1996) describe several strategies for determining and changing inaccurate thoughts and generalizations regarding career decision making. These suggestions are concrete and are excellent illustrations of a cognitive approach to career decision making.

Some cognitive strategies that they suggest will be mentioned later in the section that explains Krumboltz and Hamel's seven-step DECIDES program for career development counseling. An interesting point that Mitchell and Krumboltz make is that, although many beliefs may be erroneous, some will be quite unimportant and not worth changing. The counselor must decide which of the client's faulty beliefs are interfering with the career decision-making process. Guidelines for assessing and changing inaccurate beliefs and generalizations are as follows:

Examine the assumptions and presuppositions of the expressed belief: Clients may often make generalizations that are inaccurate or that may inhibit them from career exploration. One example is "You have to know someone to get a job in that field." This statement can be challenged; there are other ways of getting jobs besides having a friend in the occupation. Further, there are ways to get to know people. The client's statement illustrates an inaccurate assumption.

Look for inconsistencies between words and actions: Clients may say that they realize that they need to spend time talking to people in different fields. But they may spend their time doing something else. Pointing out the difference between the behavior of a client and the intention may be helpful. In general, when clients state that they will do something, such as look at occupational information on given occupations, and then fail to follow through, there is an inconsistency between words and actions.

Test simplistic answers for inadequacies: If a client says, "I'll find a job if I only try hard enough" or "I just need to talk to a few people and I'll find a job," the client is looking at the career decision-making process from an oversimplified point of view. These types of statements contrast markedly with the systematic decision-making system suggested by Krumboltz and Hamel (1977).

Confront attempts to build an illogical consistency: Some clients may have a point of view that they want to validate, even if it doesn't fit. For example, a student may have wanted to be a dentist since the age of 6. However, she may choose to ignore the fact that her learning experiences have been quite different since that age. She needs to determine whether her self-observation generalizations of capacities, interests, and values have changed in the past ten years. A similar example is that of the client who wants to please his parents by following their direction as to the occupation that he should enter. He may have interests, capacities, and values that are inconsistent with his parents' goal that he be an engineer. He may choose to talk about the money that engineers make, their prestige, and so on, to build an illogical framework to maintain the view that engineering would be an appropriate alternative.

Identify barriers to the goal: Sometimes, clients make inaccurate self-observation generalizations about their abilities. For example, a client may say, "I can't write well enough to go to graduate school in history." The client's view of what "write well enough" means may be inaccurate. Further, the idea of writing requirements in graduate school may also be inaccurate. Or to use Krumboltz's term, the client's worldview generalization about graduate education may be lacking. Another example would be "I can't afford to go to graduate school." The client may have little information about the scholarships and teaching assistantships that may be available to graduate students.

Challenge the validity of key beliefs: Clients may have beliefs that keep them from exploring alternative occupational choices. Stereotyped and inaccurate information about occupations is found frequently among clients. Examples of such stereotypes are "Park rangers always work alone," "You need to be a genius to be a doctor," and "Engineers are no fun to be around." Mitchell and Krumboltz (1990) suggest three questions to challenge these beliefs: "How do you know this is true? What steps could you take to find out if this is true? What evidence would convince you that the opposite is true?" (p. 184).

In describing these methods for assessing and challenging inaccurate beliefs, Mitchell and Krumboltz recognize that they can be confrontive and threatening if used inappropriately. These authors emphasize the importance of a good relationship between client and counselor. The counselor would not confront these beliefs early in the first session of counseling. Mitchell and Krumboltz believe that it is essential for counselors to explain why they are uncovering beliefs and how uncovering them can be helpful to the client in career decision making. Moreover, they feel that the client should cooperate and take responsibility for discovering his or her own inaccurate beliefs.

Several cognitive theories of psychotherapy in counseling have been adapted to career decision making. Keller, Biggs, and Gysbers (1982) show how the work of Ellis, Beck, and Meichenbaum, as well as others, can be adapted to career decision making. For example, Ellis's (Ellis & Dryden, 1987) rational emotive behavior therapy stresses changing irrational beliefs to more rational ones. Using such a system, one would help a client become aware of irrational beliefs both about self and occupations that would interfere with effective career decision making. Beck (1991) is known for his development of cognitive therapy. Using a cognitive approach similar to the one that Beck uses with his patients, counselors might caution clients not to draw conclusions where evidence is lacking, not to make important career decisions based on a single incident, and not to see career events simply in extreme terms. Meichenbaum (1977) uses another cognitive approach, which, when applied to career decision making, could include planning for the next career step and reinforcing oneself, as well as instructing oneself on what to do in the process. Readers interested in these approaches might want to consult the above authors' books. These approaches offer a number of ways to work with irrational beliefs, as well as methods for using self-instruction to improve career decision-making progress.

A Systematic Seven-Step Approach to Career Decision Making

The approach to career decision making that is outlined by Krumboltz and Hamel (1977) is highly organized, detailed, and consistent with a behavioral emphasis on antecedents and consequences. The seven steps of career decision making they suggest will be illustrated by following one client through the entire process. For certain steps, there are types of problems that clients are likely to have in terms of inaccurate or unclear thoughts or beliefs. These will be integrated with the discussion of each of the steps. The acronym DECIDES can help the reader recall the concepts. Further, since the concepts are sequential in nature, it is easier to recall them than if they were unrelated. The steps are as follows: **D**efine the problem, **E**stablish an action plan, **C**larify values, **I**dentify alternatives, **D**iscover probable outcomes, **E**liminate alternatives systematically, and **S**tart action. These steps provide not just a way to conceptualize or think about a client, but also specific counselor behaviors or actions to bring about successful career decision making.

Step 1: Define the Problem The problem must be defined so that it is not only clear to both client and counselor, but also mutually agreeable (Krumboltz & Baker, 1973). Sometimes, clients are quite vague about their career decision-making problem and need some help in defining their goals. For example, "finding a career" or "finding a job that I'd like to do" is too vague. It is helpful not only to specify a goal more clearly, but also to do so within a specific time frame. For example, a clear goal would be "to identify, within two months, three occupations that are of interest and fit with my abilities." By making the goal specific, the counselor is able to modify the goal with the client's input. For example, the counselor may think that two months is not long enough and may suggest three months instead. Positive reinforcement of career decision making can be helpful to clients who feel that they may not be able to make a career choice. Some clients fail to recognize that a career choice may be possible for them. For example, some may say, "I will never be able to do what I want to do, so I may as well take any job I can get." The counselor can redefine the problem by questioning the client's beliefs. The counselor can establish an action plan that will bring about results when the problem is redefined as "listing five occupations that I might be able to do and enjoy."

Mani is a Mexican American high school junior living in Los Angeles. His father works as the doorman of a large apartment building. His mother, who has worked as a janitor, is currently unemployed. Mani has an older brother and two younger sisters. The older brother is attending a two-year program in auto mechanics. His sisters are 10 and 12 years old. Mani has come in to see his guidance counselor because he attended a job fair one evening at his high school. He felt overwhelmed and confused and was unable to select any of the occupations as being appropriate. He thought that some were unattainable, and he didn't understand the duties of many of the occupations that were presented. The following dialogue takes place near the beginning of the first counseling session with Mani:

CL: When I was at that job fair, I thought that there is so much to do, how will I ever decide?
CO: What is it that you would like to decide, Mani? [The counselor starts to assist in defining the problem.]
CL: Well, I want to have some job when I graduate.
CO: Graduate? [Mani is unclear about what he means by "graduate." Does he mean from high school, a technical school, or a college or university?]
CL: Well, I'm not sure. At least high school, but maybe I would like to go to school after that, maybe college.
CO: What kinds of decisions would you like to be able to make now? [The counselor brings the focus back to decision making.]
CL: I would like to be able to find some occupations that I can do.
CO: We can find a list of occupations that you can do and also ones that you might like. [Mani's goal, as stated, is unacceptable to the counselor. She does not want to ignore Mani's self-observed generalizations of values or interests.]
CL: Yes, I'd like to see if we can come up with a list of occupations that I'd like and maybe I could do.
CO: That sounds fine, Mani. How long a list would you like? [The counselor wants to further define tasks that she and Mani will work on.]
CL: How does seven or eight sound?
CO: That sounds good. We may even be able to narrow that list down, too. [The counselor is unsure at this point how far she and Mani will be able to go in the DECIDES process.]
CL: Yeah, that would be great if I can find a few things that I would like to do.
CO: When would you like to do that by, Mani?
CL: Gee, it's October now. How does Christmas sound?
CO: It sounds fine. [The problem is defined along with a time guideline.]

Step 2: Establish an Action Plan This phase consists of describing the entire DECIDES process. Thus, a client will be able not only to make a career decision, but also to learn a decision-making process. An action plan includes actions to be taken for each step and dates by which the actions should be completed. Most career decision makers will need to return to various portions of the action plan. Recycling through various steps is not uncommon. A written action plan provides both client and counselor with a systematic guide to actions that need to be completed in order to successfully finish the career decision-making process. One problem that can arise in this phase is that a client may not exert enough effort to make a decision. Some clients may be overwhelmed by an action plan that they develop. If so, the counselor can work with the client to make the plan manageable. If the action plan becomes overwhelming, it will defeat the purpose of career decision making. One way to provide initial positive reinforcement is to praise the client for already having defined the problem, the first step in the action plan.

Having defined the problem, the counselor now helps Mani in defining an action plan:

CO: Now that we have defined the problem, Mani, we can figure out how to find a few occupational possibilities for you.

CL: How do we do that?

CO: I want to describe a plan to you that we can follow. It will help us get to our goal. Here's a chart that we can use that describes how to make a career decision. [See Figure 13-2.] Note that the first letter of each step spells out the word *DECIDES.* That will help you remember the seven steps that we are going to follow. [The counselor follows a specific plan that she has used before.]

CL: That's OK. We've already defined the problem, so maybe we can write that in.

CO: Great. Let's do that now. [The counselor writes in the problem, which is to list seven occupations that Mani would like and can do. She also enters the day's date, since the problem is defined. Further, she is reinforcing Mani's progress in the initial steps of career decision making.]

CL: OK, and we're working on the action plan now, right?

CO: Right, you've got the idea. [The counselor writes in the day's date next to "Establish an action plan" and reinforces Mani once again.]

CL: What do we do next?

CO: Let's talk about clarifying values.

CL: What do you mean?

CO: What is important to you? What do you want to accomplish in a job?

CL: I'm not really sure. I don't have a good idea of what's important to me, but I know that I want to make money.

CO: Well, the Values Scale may help you learn more about what's important to you—your values. [The counselor writes on the sheet, "Take Values Scale; discuss values."]

CL: Yes, I'd like to do that. We can finish that real soon.

CO: I think that will take a while, Mani. Maybe we ought to give ourselves a month on that. What do you think? [The counselor uses her prior experience to set a more realistic completion date for clarifying values.]

CL: That sounds good. I guess it would take a while to do that.

CO: Let's talk a little bit about identifying alternatives. [The counselor wants to move on to the next stage so that they can complete the action plan during the session.]

CL: Well, I identified too many alternatives at the job fair; maybe that didn't work out so well.

CO: That was one way, and it was a good way, but there are other ideas. Taking an interest inventory will help you identify some alternatives that

Action Plan for ______________________ Today's Date: ______________

Step	Action	Completion Date
1. Define the problem		
2. Establish an action plan		
3. Clarify values		
4. Identify alternatives		
5. Discover probable outcomes		
6. Eliminate alternatives systematically		
7. Start action		

Figure 13-2 Form for the DECIDES process. (Adapted from *Guide to Career Decision-Making Skills,* by J. D. Krumboltz and S. A. Hamel. Copyright © 1977 by College Entrance Examination Board. Reprinted by permission.)

you might like. We may also want to have you take an ability test. That may help you find occupations that you can do. Then we can look at occupations where you have both interests and abilities. Then maybe I can direct you to specific books and pamphlets about occupations that you have interest and ability in. [The counselor first wants to positively reinforce the information seeking that Mani has already done. Then she goes on to identify steps that Mani can take in identifying alternatives.]

CL: That sounds like an awful lot to do.

CO: We'll take it one step at a time. I'll be here to help you, so it won't get to be too much. [The counselor wants to be sure that the career decision-making process itself will continue to be positively reinforcing. She wants to focus Mani's attention on each step as they go through them.]

In this way, Mani and his counselor fill out the career decision-making plan (Figure 13-2) so that they have an overview of the process of career decision making. It is likely that they will come back to this plan and revise it. Completion may be reached ahead of schedule or behind schedule. Some outcomes may be different from what either of them has anticipated. However, the process has been explained, and the ways to get to the end have been made clear.

Step 3: Clarify Values There are many ways of clarifying values inside and outside the counseling session. Within the session, the counselor can discuss values that the client has learned from previous job experience. Comparing tested values with actual experience in working can be helpful. Outside the session, the client can do several things to clarify his or her values. These may include discussing job-related values with friends and family, keeping a record of how the client spends time and money, and reading books about people whom the client admires.

Problems that clients encounter in clarifying values include drawing faulty generalizations. For example, clients may read about millionaires who have been successful and may focus on the objects they spend their money on rather than the skills they used to get to their current position. Clients may have a naive view of the process involved in the acquisition of wealth. Furthermore, they may not understand the role of values for people who have acquired wealth.

Another possible problem is comparing oneself to a single standard. A client can compare himself or herself to a very wealthy person and conclude, "I could never do that." Being alert to possible inaccurate conclusions such as this is one of the tasks of the counselor.

In the following excerpt, Mani and the counselor are discussing only one aspect of values clarification: work values learned from Mani's job delivering clothes for a dry cleaner.

CL: The first job that I ever had that really meant anything to me was this past summer when I worked for a dry cleaner. It was a small company, and I used the owner's car in the afternoon. He was pretty nervous about having me use it, but I was real careful. I was careful where I parked and how I parked and always locked the door.

CO: You really developed a sense of responsibility in your job. I bet that was helpful. [The counselor identifies a value that is reflected by Mani's work experience.]

CL: At first the owner was real worried. He seemed to look the car over each time I got back. Later, he loosened up a bit and seemed to trust me more.

CO: As the summer wore on, you became more responsible and more independent. That's great. [Reinforcing the values of responsibility and independence seems important.]

CL: I didn't make a lot of money, but I knew that. Who is going to hire a high school junior and pay him $50 an hour?

CO: You seem to understand that it takes a while to increase your salary. [The counselor is pleased that Mani's job expectations are reasonably accurate.]

CL: I know a lot about work, I guess. Mainly, I know what to watch out for. My father complains about his work all the time. He hates the tips and the "Yes, ma'am, yes sir" stuff that he does all the time. His salary doesn't change much. It stays low. He doesn't tell me exactly what, but I can guess. He keeps telling me about the value of an education, of going to college. He says, "Look at me."

CO: You seem to have learned the value of education. What would you like to do with it? [Valuing an education is rather vague; finding out about other values important to Mani seems appropriate.]

CL: I really do want to make money. If I go to college, it's for that reason. My mother works real hard. Our house is tiny. The neighborhood is lousy. Us kids are always being told we can't have this, we can't have that. I want to have this and that.

CO: Tell me more about the "this and that" that you want. [Further clarifying and specifying values will help to identify career alternatives.]

Step 4: Identify Alternatives To identify alternatives, the counselor and client need to evaluate self-observation generalizations about interests and capacities. In addition, this is the time to use books and pamphlets to learn about jobs, that is, to make accurate worldview generalizations. At this point, job experience kits can help an individual simulate a job alternative to see if it seems appropriate. In general, discussion of self-observation generalization precedes investigation of worldview generalizations. Self-observation generalizations will help an individual find books and pamphlets that will expand worldview generalizations consistent with interests and abilities. Since reading books and pamphlets takes less time than using a job experience kit, volunteering, or doing part-time work, these latter activities are usually done last. This stage of the process can be very time-consuming, as an individual may have many occupational alternatives to identify. One role of the counselor is to ascertain if the individual is learning the relevant facts about occupational alternatives. A client may be tempted to take a shortcut through this stage by jumping to conclusions about appropriate occupations.

> *CL:* I was surprised about sales as a career. I had never thought about it before, but it came up on the interest inventory that I took. I could see myself selling cars, furniture, houses—big stuff. It really would be a challenge.
>
> *CO:* Have you done any selling before? [Comparing self-observations to tested observations can be quite helpful.]
>
> *CL:* A little bit. I used to sell sub sandwiches to raise money for class trips. Stuff like that. Funny, most kids didn't like it. I thought it was fun.
>
> *CO:* The tested information seems to fit for you. [The counselor wants to make sure that Mani is not going to leave her office saying, "The test told me I should be a salesperson."]
>
> *CL:* The test also mentioned office duties. That's something I never really thought of.
>
> *CO:* Have you had any experience with that? [Again, the counselor wishes to relate tested observations to self-observations.]
>
> *CL:* No, I really haven't had any experience with it. It's hard for me to imagine.
>
> *CO:* Do you have any idea about how you could find out more?
>
> *CL:* Well, I could take the typing course. I just figured I would never do it or need it, but maybe I would. I always thought that typing would be boring.
>
> *CO:* Typing can be helpful in many jobs. You might find it a very useful skill to have. Many occupations require writing, and more and more require use of a computer, which also requires typing. [Mani seems not to know much about office skills. The counselor provides some relevant information to counter Mani's lack of knowledge.]
>
> *CL:* Well, maybe you're right. Are there a lot of jobs in business that require typing?
>
> *CO:* Quite a few. I'd like to recommend some pamphlets for you to read. [The counselor does not pretend to be a storehouse of occupational information; rather, she is prepared to refer Mani to specific sources of information that will give him more knowledge about typing in business occupations from which to make worldview generalizations.]

In this way, the counselor and the client continue to talk about Mani's interests, abilities, and potential careers. They are working toward identifying specific alternatives that Mani will be able to consider. Doing so may take several weeks. Even when this process is done, Mani may wish to continue to identify career alternatives.

Step 5: Discover Probable Outcomes Many of the tasks involved in discovering probable outcomes deal with worldview generalizations. This step focuses on the evaluation of educational and career alternatives. Using job experience kits, talking with people who work in an occupation, and visiting them at their work site can all be helpful. Furthermore, fantasizing about what it would be like to be in a specific occupation can be useful. A counselor may choose to use guided imagery to help a client imagine what it would be like to be an accountant for a day. As information about occupational alternatives is discovered, it can be compared to self-observation generalizations about interests, values, and capacities. Krumboltz and Hamel (1977) suggest a grid that compares occupational alternatives with values. This could be extended to include abilities and interests. Thus, individuals could determine if certain occupations are sufficiently interesting or fit in their ability range.

In the process of discovering probable outcomes, counselors should be careful that clients do not exaggerate the emotional impact of a specific outcome. For example, a client may say, "I just *have* to become a geneticist. There is nothing else that I could possibly consider." Or a client could state, "I could never be a doctor. Medical school would be much too hard." One role of the counselor is to explore these emotional statements to see whether their content is accurate or not. Often, the content may be inaccurate because it is based on little knowledge of the occupation and little consideration of self-observed generalizations.

CL: I really feel as if I'm learning about what's out there. I'm starting to look into several business careers. You know I was in downtown L.A., and I just walked into a real estate agency and talked to the woman there. She was real nice. She told me about what she did and a little bit about how her agency gets listings.

CO: That's great. You're really starting to get some information about a number of alternatives that might fit you. [Walking in cold to a real estate firm is not a strategy that the counselor would ordinarily recommend. However, it worked for Mani, so she will reinforce this experience rather than caution him about it and possibly dampen his enthusiasm.]

CL: I read about what real estate people do in the *Occupational Outlook Handbook.* I spoke to my boss, the guy I used to work for last summer in the dry-cleaning shop. I asked him what it was like to run a business. I never even thought of that when I worked for him. He was real nice to me. He told me a little bit about having money to start a business, different types of expenses. He asked me if I wanted to work part time again. I don't know about that, but it was nice to hear.

CO: Terrific, Mani. You're learning a lot about business through contacts that you have. Also, you are learning through some of the pamphlets that we have. [Again information-seeking behavior is being reinforced.]

CL: Wow! There really is a lot of stuff out there!

CO: You're right. It may be helpful to make a list of the occupations that you've looked into. Then you can list what values they seem to meet and also whether they are interesting and whether you think you can do them. [The counselor chooses to use a list rather than a grid as suggested by Krumboltz and Hamel. This is another way of analyzing the occupational alternatives that Mani is exploring.]

Step 6: Eliminate Alternatives Systematically Once a list of occupational alternatives has been developed, they can be compared closely so that the least appropriate alternatives can be eliminated. This may require that the client explore possible occupational alternatives in more detail. Krumboltz and Hamel (1977) suggest grouping alternatives that have similar characteristics first and then eliminating the least desirable alternatives. If individuals cannot select between two choices, Krumboltz and Hamel suggest that they continue to look for differences between the alternatives. Some occupations may be more risky to enter than others. For example, occupations in the arts are traditionally extremely competitive, whereas those in business are less so. Making predictions about the likelihood of entering a particular educational or occupational alternative is quite difficult. There is no reason for the counselor to attempt to do so.

As Krumboltz (1983) shows, there are a number of potential difficulties that clients may face in attempting to systematically eliminate alternatives. Some clients may eliminate excellent alternatives for faulty reasons. For example, a client may elect not to attempt to become a veterinarian because of the competitive nature of veterinary schools. In doing so, the client may be ignoring information about his or her own ability. Sometimes, clients choose an alternative that may not fit them for reasons that have not been well thought out. A client may state that he does not want to be a funeral director because all they do is work with dead bodies. In this case, the client has not acquired sufficient information to counter a traditional stereotype of funeral directors. Another difficulty in eliminating alternatives is in assigning too much weight to a low-probability event. An individual who chooses not to enter a health occupation because of a fear of AIDS is responding to fear rather than reality. Health occupations differ in their exposure to AIDS patients. Furthermore, knowledge about AIDS allows one to make informed decisions about how to work with AIDS patients and how to make use of occupational safeguards.

When clients have eliminated some occupational alternatives, they may find that they want to return to consider other occupations. Recycling to the previous three phases—clarifying values, identifying alternatives, and discovering probable outcomes—is not unusual. When appropriate, clients should be encouraged to return to whichever stage is necessary.

Two months after his discussion with the counselor, Mani is starting to eliminate occupational alternatives. He is on schedule in terms of the action plan that he filled out two months ago with the counselor. He has done considerable identification of alternatives and has sought much occupational information.

CL: I've come up with five occupations that I think would be good for me.

CO: What are they?

CL: Well, three sales occupations: cars, life insurance, and real estate. Also, accounting looks interesting. I think, too, that I might like being a stockbroker.

CO: I'd like to hear about some of your reasons for selecting these occupations. [The process of elimination starts with articulating some of the attractive and unattractive features of the occupations.]

CL: Well, I'm not sure I'd like to sell cars. I've talked to a lot of people and they tell me that car salespeople are sleazy.

CO: What do you think that means? [The client has picked up an occupational stereotype from others, and now it is being questioned by the counselor.]

CL: Well, I'm not sure. Maybe that they're dishonest?

CO: If you sold cars, do you think that you would be dishonest? [Personalizing the stereotype might help Mani in his thinking about being a car salesperson.]

CL: No. I don't think I would have to be dishonest. I could point out the best features of the cars and try to sell the cars based on that. I don't think I'd have to tell lies.

CO: If that's so, then that may not be an occupational alternative you have to eliminate.

CL: I guess I could do it and still feel OK about myself.

CO: What about other alternatives?

CL: Well, I was thinking about being a stockbroker. They make millions of dollars. I've been seeing them on TV—some of the ones who've been indicted, you know. They seem to make more money than people in other areas of business.

CO: How did you find out about stockbrokers? [Mani's information about stockbrokers seems to be flawed. Possibly his information has come from television only.]

CL: Well, this is one occupation I didn't get a chance to look at. I've heard a lot about it on the news.

CO: Well, Mani, you may want to go back to our career library and look it up because I don't think that your information is correct. Stockbrokers work on commission, and their salaries vary a great deal.

CL: Oh, I didn't know that. I'll look it up.

CO: Good, Mani. I think you'll find it helpful. You've learned a lot from the information seeking that you've done so far. [Rather than criticize Mani for his inaccurate information, the counselor wants to take the opportunity to positively reinforce the information seeking that he has done, as it is considerable.]

Mani and the counselor will continue to explore occupational alternatives and eliminate them. They may not be able to follow their timeline exactly, but that is all right. In this case, Mani needs to recycle to Step 5—discover probable outcomes—so that he can get more information about the occupation of stockbroker. When a sufficient number of alternatives have been eliminated, Mani will be ready to implement his career choice.

Step 7: Start Action When a choice has been made, the individual must carry through on it and start various actions leading to an occupational goal. For example, if a student decides that he wants to leave high school and get a job, he should write a résumé, get job leads, and so on. At this point, the counseling support may end, but the individual must continue job-seeking behaviors by himself or herself. Being able to return to the same decision-making procedures that were used in DECIDES will be helpful for the individual. Sometimes, individuals encounter difficulty in this process. As Krumboltz (1983) points out, people may experience anguish or anxiety over their inability to reach certain career goals. If a person applies to five colleges and is denied admission to all, he may be devastated and believe that he will be unable to enter any college. Support to counter this inaccurate belief can be helpful in encouraging the individual to apply to other colleges. Likewise, the person who is rejected by seven employers in a row may believe that no one will ever want to hire her. Knowing that the job-seeking process is a difficult one and that rejections are very common may help the individual to continue.

CL: I think I know what I want to do now.

CO: And what is that?

CL: I've decided that I want to go into sales, but I'm not sure which kind. To do that, I think that I want to go to business college, or at least to a university that has a school of business.

CO: That sounds like good thinking, Mani. [The counselor wants to reinforce Mani's decision to start action: study business. On his own, Mani can continue to use his decision-making skills to consider the probable outcomes of career alternatives.]

CL: The last few weeks, I've been thinking a lot about college. I really never had thought about it much, but I think it would really help me to have a college education to be successful in these occupations. The occupational information says that most people now have that kind of background.

CO: How do you plan to do this? [Before suggesting ways to implement the plan, it is helpful to find out what the client has considered.]

CL: I know that I need to work on my grades. I want to study harder so that I can get into college. We have no money for college, but California has such a good educational system, I think I can live at home and go to a community college. When I am in business school, then I can choose a major. I don't think I need to do that now.

CO: That's right. You seem to have given considerable thought to planning what's next.

CL: Yes, I really have. I got excited about what I can do in my life, and I don't want to mess it up by not planning.

Most career planning does not go as smoothly as the brief excerpts of Mani's progress through the DECIDES paradigm would indicate. Clients may be at different points in their career decision-making process, which may influence how they act. Perhaps more than any other theory, Krumboltz's social learning theory provides a specific guide for counselors and clients to use in career exploration. An instrument that can help counselors work through the seven steps is the Career Beliefs Inventory (Krumboltz, 1988). This instrument can assist the counselor in assessing many of the career beliefs that are potential problems for counselors and clients in the career decision-making process. The Career Beliefs Inventory contains 25 scales that measure a wide variety of beliefs, relating to such issues as experimenting with jobs, self-improvement, and learning to overcome obstacles. Krumboltz (1994a) organizes the 25 scales of the Career Beliefs Inventory into the following five categories: my current career situation, what seems necessary for my happiness, factors that influence my decisions, changes I am willing to make, and effort I am willing to initiate. Interpreting scores to clients in this sequence may help them improve their career decision-making ability. In Mani's case, the counselor has not only a method of conceptualizing client issues, but also a sequential guideline for behavioral and cognitive interventions that can be made at various points in the career decision-making process.

CAREER SELF-EFFICACY THEORY

Like Krumboltz's theory of career development, career self-efficacy theory (Lent, Brown, & Hackett, 1994; Lent & Hackett, 1987, 1994) is based on Bandura's social learning theory. Although both Krumboltz and career self-efficacy theory make use of Bandura's concepts, they emphasize different versions of his theory in their work. Both theories make use of Bandura's triadic reciprocal interaction system, focusing on the environment, personal factors, and behaviors. Both also emphasize the role of instrumental and associative learning experiences in career decision making and career development. Both also view thoughts and cognitions, which include memories, beliefs, preferences, and self-perceptions, as a part of the career decision-making and career development process.

However, they differ in several important respects. Self-efficacy theory emphasizes cognitive processes (such as self-efficacy) that moderate or regulate actions, more than does Krumboltz, who focuses on learning behaviors related to career choice and decision making. Career self-efficacy theorists have developed a model of career development that is more specific and complex than Krumboltz's (Figure 13-1), which focuses primarily on how prior learning experiences affect later learning experiences, and ultimately career choices. Career self-efficacy theorists emphasize individuals' belief system that affects their behaviors rather than concentrating on the behaviors themselves, as does Krumboltz. Although the notion of choice is clearly evident in Krumboltz's practical applications, such as the DECIDES program, it does not play as large a role in his theoretical writings as choice does for career self-efficacy theorists.

Because career self-efficacy theory is relatively recent (starting in the early 1980s), Hackett and Betz's (1981) focus has been on the development of a theory and providing research evidence to support it. Career self-efficacy theorists have paid less attention to the application of their theory than has Krumboltz. However, the theory has application for counselors, and I will illustrate some applications after describing the theory itself. First, I will examine three important cognitive concepts that regulate the career decision-making process and that are essential to career self-efficacy theory: self-efficacy, outcome expectations, and personal goals. To illustrate these concepts, we will examine Sharon's career decision-making behavior. Sharon is a 15-year-old African American who attends a large high school in San Francisco, where she is in the spring of her junior year.

Self-Efficacy

Bandura (1986) has described self-efficacy as "people's judgments of their capabilities to organize and execute courses of action required to attain designated types of performances" (p. 391). How individuals view their abilities and capacities affects academic, career, and other choices. Individuals with a low sense of self-efficacy may not persist in a difficult task, they may have thoughts that they will be unable to do the task well, and they may feel discouraged or overwhelmed by the task. Self-efficacy is a changing set of beliefs about oneself that varies, depending on the context of the situation. Some of the factors include the nature of the task, the people and surroundings that an individual has contact with, and success on similar tasks. As Lent, Brown, and Larkin (1986) have shown, there is only a moderate relationship between individuals' views of their own ability and objective measures of ability such as grades or scores on standardized exams.

Sharon is very worried about school. She doesn't like her math class and feels stupid when she's there. Although her grade for the year is "B–" so far, Sharon just believes that she can't do the algebra assignments well enough: "I never will be able to know what I'm doing in math, and the teacher seems to make it seem as if this is so easy." Some of her friends share her views, and they talk about how hard math is and how glad they will be when they are done with it. Her friends' beliefs reinforce Sharon's own sense of self-efficacy as it applies to math. There is clearly a difference between Sharon's grades in math and her sense of self-efficacy regarding math. Sharon's sense of self-efficacy about math refers to the concept of academic self-efficacy, which is different from, but related to, the concept of career self-efficacy (Lent et al., 1994). Sharon's view that she isn't very good at math is likely to affect her plans for future education and the career alternatives that she will consider.

Outcome Expectations

When individuals estimate what the probability of an outcome would be, this is referred to as *outcome expectations.* Examples are "If I play basketball, what will happen?" "If I play well what will happen?" "If I apply to Harvard University, what will happen?" and "If I ask Mrs. Brown for a reference, what will happen?" In contrast, self-efficacy beliefs are concerned with "Can I do this activity?" Examples are "How well can I play basketball?" "Can I get into Harvard?" and "Will someone evaluate my job performance effectively?" Thus, outcome expectations refer to what may happen, and self-efficacy is concerned with estimates of the ability to accomplish something. Bandura (1986) has talked about several types of outcome expectations, including the anticipation of physical, social, and self-evaluative outcomes. An example of a physical outcome expectation would be getting paid for working, a social outcome might be approval from your father for having done well at school, and a self-evaluative outcome might be being satisfied with your own performance in a class. In making judgments, individuals combine both outcome expectations ("If I do this activity, what can happen?") and self-efficacy ("Can I do this activity?"). In general, Bandura finds that self-efficacy is often more important in determining a behavior than outcome expectations. Depending on the situation, either self-efficacy or outcome expectations may be more important than other expectations. Examples from Sharon's situation will help to illustrate.

Sharon is considering the possible outcome of her next math exam. She wonders whether, if she does the homework and discusses her questions with the teacher, perhaps her math grade will be an "A" or "A–". However, her sense of self-efficacy with regard to math is low, so that she is not sure that she can do these activities, and therefore, her sense of self-efficacy may be a more powerful determinant of her eventual math performance than is her outcome expectation. Thus, it is possible that she will not do her homework or ask the teacher or other students questions, and her math performance will be poor. Another factor that may influence her performance is her goals.

Goals

Individuals do more than just respond to the events and the environment around them. They set goals that help them to organize their behavior, and to guide their actions over various periods of time. For example, a freshman in college who decides to be a lawyer must set subgoals and choose behaviors that will help her reach the goal. The reinforcement of being a lawyer will not occur for another seven years. Goals are self-motivating, and the satisfaction that comes with meeting goals, such as graduation, is highly significant. Goals, self-efficacy, and outcome expectations are related to each other and affect each other in a variety of ways.

Sharon has a goal to be a store manager. Her outcome expectation is that, if she goes to college, works part time in the mall, and enters a training program with a department store, she can reach this goal. Her self-efficacy beliefs cause her to think that she is a poor math student, will not be able to do math in high school, and therefore cannot do math in college. These beliefs will directly affect her outcome expectations and may cause her to revise her goal.

The Self-Efficacy Model of Career Choice

The career self-efficacy model of career choice is quite complex, involving interactions between self-efficacy, outcome expectations, goals, choice, outcome, and environmental factors. Related to the model of career choice are the models of interest development and performance, which are described elsewhere (Lent et al., 1994). All of these models are circular, in that concepts indirectly or directly affect each other and continue to do so throughout most of the life span. The model of self-efficacy career-choice behavior is diagrammed in Figure 13-3, and the paths of interaction among the concepts are described here.

To illustrate the self-efficacy model of career choice, it will be useful to continue our example of Sharon's academic and career concerns. The following paragraphs explain and illustrate the paths that are a part of this model. The factors that are described here are those that career self-efficacy theorists consider the most significant, but not the only ones, in career selection. The model starts out with those concepts that are key in career choice and the selection of occupations.

Self-Efficacy ——1——► Interest

Outcome Expectations ——2——► Interest

Bandura (1986) believes that interests that are likely to persist across time arise from activities that people feel they are effective in completing and in succeeding in. As individuals try out activities, such as sports, they may feel that they are not very good at them and may lose interest. Likewise, when they feel that the outcome of the activity, such as sports, will not be successful, they tend to lose interest. Sharon believes that she can't learn math well, and further, she expects that the outcome on her math exam will be poor. Both of these factors conribute to her lack of interest in math.

Interest ——3——► Goals

Individuals' interests affect their intent to do certain activities and their goals that relate to activities. Sharon has lost interest in math. She intends not to study, and she chooses other goals besides math. Because she believes that she is an excellent soprano and her expectations that she will do well are strong, based in part on being asked to be a soloist in church several times, her interest in singing (Paths 1 and 2) has grown. Therefore, her goals for singing become much stronger than those for math.

Goals ——4——► Choice Actions

The goals that individuals choose affect the actions that they take to achieve the goals. Sharon chooses to improve her singing and takes actions, such as singing lessons and more practice, to become more expert as a singer. Math becomes a relatively unimportant goal, and she spends only ten minutes a day on math homework.

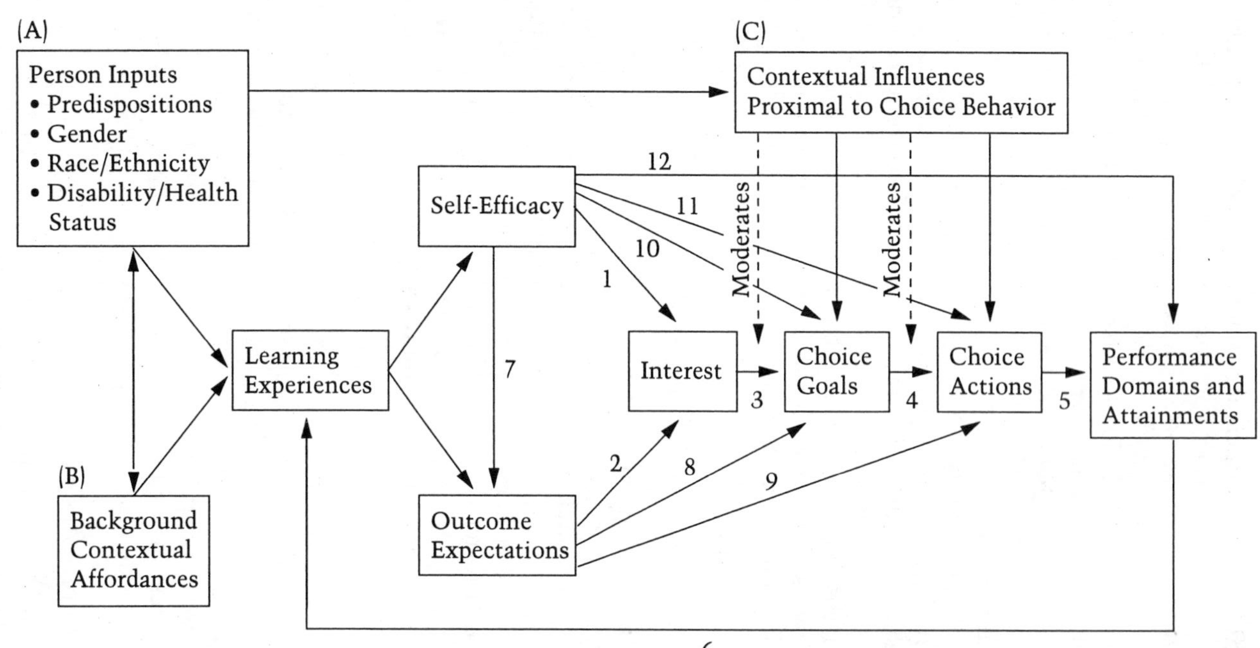

Figure 13-3 Model of person, contextual, and experiential factors affecting career-related choice behavior. (From "Toward a Unified Social Cognitive Theory of Career and Academic Interest, Choice, and Performance," by R. W. Lent, S. D. Brown, and G. Hackett, *Journal of Vocational Behavior,* 1993, vol. 45, pp. 79–122. Copyright © 1993 by Academic Press, Inc. Reprinted by Permission.)

Choice Actions ——5——► Performance Outcomes

The actions that individuals choose greatly affect the outcome of their performance. Sharon's singing improves, and her math performance decreases.

Performance Outcomes ——6——► Learning Experiences ——7——► Self-Efficacy/Outcome Expectations

The outcome of the performance that individuals experience affects their learning experiences in general, which in turn affect beliefs in self-efficacy and outcome expectations. Sharon has positive learning experiences in her chorus and as a soloist. Her beliefs about her singing ability increase, as does her expectation regarding her ability to get offers to sing. In contrast, her negative performance on math exams affects her experience of learning, and therefore, she believes that she is not a good math student (self-efficacy) and will do poorly on future math tests (outcome expectations).

Career self-efficacy theorists make clear that there are other factors that affect learning and performance. Boxes A and B in Figure 13-3 show the importance of personal and background factors. Biological predisposition, gender, race, disabilities, and other factors such as parental background have an impact. For example, Sharon has a strong, excellent voice, which contributes to her positive performance outcomes and positive learning experiences and thus to her sense of self-efficacy as a singer. With regard to math, Sharon has heard that women are not good at math (a background contextual affordance), which negatively affects her learning experience and sense of math self-effficacy.

Outcome Expectations ——8——► Goals

Outcome expectations may have a direct effect on the way individuals perceive goals. If Sharon can find no opportunities to sing professionally, this will affect her goal to be a professional singer. Although Sharon values the goal of professional singer, her expectation of a positive outcome is not great.

Self-Efficacy ——1——► Interest
Self-Efficacy ——11——► Choice Actions
Self-Efficacy ——12——► Performance Outcomes

One's belief in oneself is a major force that directly affects one's career goals, choice actions, and performance outcomes. For example, Sharon's lack of belief in her math ability not only affect her interests, her goals, and her choices related to occupations, but also her eventual occupational choice.

Contextual influences, or factors outside an individual's control, also moderate or have an impact on career choices, as seen in Box C in Figure 13-3. For example, the fact that there are few jobs for singers and Sharon has few financial resources for further singing training are likely to moderate or have an impact on her choice to be a singer.

Figure 13-3 diagrams important factors in an individual's career choice. Although self-efficacy and outcome expectations are significant factors in this process, Lent et al., (1994) do not ignore either past biological, social, or environmental influences (Box A) or current contextual factors (Box C). These authors note that, as individuals get older, it becomes more difficult to change interests, goals, and performance outcomes, as these are affected by past behaviors. This conceptualization of the choice process gives counselors a useful perspective from which to view their clients.

Counseling Example

Although there has been relatively little work on the application of career self-efficacy theory to counseling, Betz (1992) makes several suggestions that are of use to counselors. As she did in her earlier work, Betz (Hackett & Betz, 1981) focuses on counseling women. She recognizes the importance of environmental forces which affect women's beliefs about both their ability to master particular content areas, such as math and science, and their ability to enter particular career areas. Betz suggests that counselors help women understand that low self-esteem with regard to math and other areas is part of their socialization as women. Such suggestions can also be applied to people from a variety of cultures, who may be the victims of discrimination or stereotyping. Exploring how low self-esteem negatively affects the development of certain interests can be useful to clients. Observing role models in the feared area may also help to encourage the client to pursue nontraditional academic courses or actual work. Reinforcing clients' belief in their underused capabilities may be quite helpful, for example, encouraging women to persist with difficult math assignments. Sometimes, it may also be useful to reduce the anxiety that surrounds the notion of taking math or science courses. Career self-efficacy theorists recognize the negative impact of social biases and discrimination on women and people of color. Thus, they have been particularly interested in developing a theory that would explain the career choices of all people, especially women and minorities.

The following example shows how Sharon is helped with both academic and career choice issues by a counselor using career self-efficacy theory as a conceptual basis. Sharon has come to see her high school guidance counselor about picking courses for her senior year of high school. She is unsure about both her future career goals and the specific courses she will take. Furthermore, she is unsure about whether to apply to colleges.

CL: I am not sure what to take next year or what I'm going to do. Math is really getting to me. It stinks.

CO: Tell me more about math, Sharon.

CL: I just can't do it. It's getting too hard and too much boring stuff. I don't see why I should have to do it. It's a real pain.

CO: It's really frustrating. Sounds as if you try hard to do the work, but it doesn't come. [The counselor believes that Sharon is frustrated by not getting results from her work.]

CL: Well, I guess I could have tried harder to do my homework, but I guess I kind of gave up.

CO: Gave up?

CL: Yeah, I just don't think math is for me. After all, the guys in class seem to do well in it, but not the women.

CO: Sharon, you might be surprised by how many women are able to do well in science and in engineering. Many of them do very well in math. In fact, there have been a number of women who have left our school to go to college in math. [The counselor gives Sharon information that contradicts her perception of how others have done.]

CL: Well, I have done pretty well in math, but now I'm getting tired of it.

CO: Yes. I see that you've got "B"s in math. You really have done well in math before. That's great. [The counselor reinforces Sharon's math performance, hoping to influence both her math self-efficacy and outcome expectations.]

CL: Well, now, it seems that the teacher is just going too fast. I've been busy with singing, which is going great, but neither the math teacher nor I seem to have time to work on this.

CO: I'm sure that Mr. Aldo would be glad to help you with some of your algebra. Continuing with math really increases your options. You seem to have done well and liked it before. It would be great if it doesn't slip away. [The counselor is working to help Sharon boost her sense of math self-efficacy, knowing that it can affect her interest, and ultimate goals, both for academic subjects, and for her career choice.]

CL: [not convinced] Well, I could do that, but I'd really like to be a singer. Things are going great at church. I was asked to sing at a wedding, and I can't wait.

CO: The singing seems like an occupation that you like?

CL: I'd love to do it, but I just know how difficult it is. There're some people in our neighborhood who have been singing in a group for years, and they never went anywhere.

CO: Having several skills, math, music—That can really increase your options. [The counselor is well aware of the job market for singers and wants to help Sharon develop her abilities and competencies as much as possible. By doing so, Sharon can develop and broaden her goals, which will in turn give her more choices and will increase her chances of good performance. By reinforcing Sharon's interest in math, the counselor helps her to expand her career options.]

In future sessions, the counselor may help Sharon to learn more about the importance of math. If Sharon is anxious, she may show her ways to use relaxation techniques and positive self-talk to improve her confidence. The counselor may also introduce her to women who are using math in their careers. Books and pamphlets on minority mathematicians and scientists may also prove helpful. Because the counselor recognizes the negative effect of biases about math for women, she uses many techniques to help Sharon increase her sense of self-efficacy.

THE ROLE OF OCCUPATIONAL INFORMATION

Accurate occupational information is essential to the application of social learning theory. Rather than just saying that occupational information is important, Krumboltz (1970) has designed Job Experince Kits to be used to simulate occupations. Published by Science Research Associates, these kits provide exercises that are similar to tasks done by people working in the occupations. Furthermore, in research that he and his colleagues have done on career decision making, they have used occupational information seeking as a criterion for effective career planning. More than most theorists, Krumboltz has emphasized the importance of learning occupational information in the career decision-making process. Mitchell and Krumboltz (1990) cite evidence that computerized guidance systems are more effective than standard occupational information in promoting career decision making. Career self-efficacy theorists tend to focus more on explaining the career development process than on procedures for career counseling. However, Betz (1992) describes the importance of having career information that is accurate and unbiased, featuring women and people of color in nontraditional occupations. Like Krumboltz, she points out the value of role models in showing women and people of color that there are opportunities in nontraditional occupations.

THE ROLE OF TESTING

Although testing is not featured in social learning theory as it is in some other career development theories, it is still useful. Values inventories may be particularly helpful in clarifying values while using Krumboltz's DECIDES approach. Interest inventories and ability and aptitude tests may be useful in the application of both social learning theories. In the use of Krumboltz's theory, they provide information from outside the individual, so that the client can make accurate self-observation generalizations. In career self-efficacy theory, both interest and performance are important aspects of the model, and tests and inventories provide information for the client to use in making career decisions. Further, the tests give the counselor information, so that he or she may reinforce and strengthen self-efficacy beliefs and discuss outcome expectations. Since client beliefs are an integral part of Krumboltz's model, the Career Beliefs Inventory (Krumboltz, 1994a) may be of considerable help in most stages of career decision making. The Career Decision-Making Self-Efficacy Scale (Taylor & Popma, 1990) has also been used, but primarily for research purposes. It contains five-to-ten item subscales that measure career choice competencies: goal selection, gathering occupational information, problem solving, planning for the future, and accurate self-appraisal. Taylor and Betz (1983) report reliability and other information that relate this instrument to career decision making.

APPLYING SOCIAL LEARNING THEORY TO WOMEN

Mitchell and Krumboltz (1996) discuss the application of their social learning theory to women in the context of four basic components of their theory: genetic endowment and special abilities, environmental conditions and events, learning experiences, and task-approach skills. They note that, although women do not have control over their gender, they do have some (limited) control over environmental forces, and more control over their learning experiences and task-approach skills. Mitchell and Krumboltz comment on the sex stereotyping that creates traditional and nontraditional occupations for men and for women. Relatively little research has been done on Krumboltz's social learning theory as it applies to women. Almquist (1974) found that women who selected nontraditional careers were likely to have been influenced by female role models. When women were shown a videotape of other women who were being reinforced for making nontraditional career choices, the viewers of the videotape made more nontraditional career choices than did women who had not seen the videotape (Little & Roach, 1974). By calling attention to the importance of learning experiences in career decision making for women, Mitchell and Krumboltz hoped that their emphasis would alert counselors to the need to enhance opportunities for women, who have been denied these because of discrimination and other sociological factors.

Whereas career development issues for women have played a minor role in Krumboltz's social learning theory, they have been a major focus in the development of career self-efficacy theory. In their original article on career self-efficacy, Hackett and Betz (1981) proposed that career self-efficacy beliefs would play a stronger role than interests, values, or abilities in restricting women's career choices. Since this article was written, about 100 investigations have been carried out to test their propositions, as well as others that have developed as career self-efficacy theory has become increasingly systematized. Almost all of these studies have addressed self-efficacy as it relates to women's academic, career, and other choices. Because this research is so extensive, only general findings arising from the results of these studies can be presented here. Lent et al. (1994) summarize research evidence that relates to specific propositions that are a part of career self-efficacy theory. Multon, Brown, and Lent (1991) have conducted a meta-analysis of self-efficacy beliefs as they are related to academic outcomes. Also, Hackett (1995) has summarized much of the research that relates to career self-efficacy theory. The information that is presented here is drawn primarily from these sources, especially Hackett (1995).

A number of studies have examined the general topic of the relationship of self-efficacy to career-related choices (Hackett, 1995). Early research (Betz & Hackett, 1981) showed that college men's occupational self-efficacy was relatively constant across occupations, but that women scored significantly lower on occupational self-efficacy for nontraditional occupations, and significantly higher for traditionally female occupations. Other studies have shown that occupational self-efficacy predicts interest and career choice. Further, there are gender differences in occupational self-efficacy in different groups of college students for different occupational choices, job tasks, and work activities. However, gender differences in self-efficacy are usually not reported in samples that are quite similar to each other, such as high-achieving students. When tasks are particularly gender-stereotyped, differences in self-efficacy between men and women may be found. Stereotypes about how women should behave are likely to undermine women's self-esteem regarding the choice of a nontraditional career. A conclusion reached about this research is that, if women eliminate nontraditional career opportunities because of low self-efficacy beliefs, they are limiting their opportunities to find satisfying and well-paid jobs after college. Although most studies have been done on college students, research on high school students also shows gender differences in occupational self-efficacy.

Besides studying the relationship of career self-efficacy to career-related choices, researchers have found relationships between self-efficacy and the choice of a college major, career interests, and career decision-making processes. Since many women are often fearful of math or not confident in their math ability, many researchers have studied the role of math self-efficacy, showing that it is of greater importance in predicting career choice behavior than are ability and past experience. However, when women are engineering majors and presumably have confidence in their math ability, few differences are found between male and female engineering majors in levels of math self-efficacy. Other investigations have shown that the higher the level of self-efficacy beliefs, the greater the interest expressed in a specific occupational area. Although several studies have shown that both interest and self-efficacy predict the range of career options that students consider, self-efficacy has frequently been found to be a stronger predictor of academic achievement and persistence. Hackett points out that beliefs about the ability to make a career decision are only moderately related to which occupations are being considered. However, research has also shown that the more confidence individuals have in their ability to make decisions, the more likely they will be to search for occupational information.

Career self-efficacy theory is probably the most active area of current career-related investigations. Although the research has broadened since its original focus on women's lack of confidence in their academic and career choices, this still remains a major focus of research. The large number of research studies has been important in developing and confirming a model of academic interest, career choice, and career performance (Lent et al., 1994). As research has expanded in this area, more attention has been given to understanding the role of self-efficacy in individuals from diverse cultural groups.

APPLYING SOCIAL LEARNING THEORY TO PEOPLE OF COLOR

In their application of social learning theory to people of color, Mitchell and Krumboltz (1996) discuss the importance of environmental conditions. They comment that some cultures glamorize one occupation, while other cultures may favor another. Further, some cultures may value income as opposed to spirituality or educational success. Such values may reinforce certain occupations for people from different cultures. Racial discrimination is another environmental barrier to people of color, who may encounter obstructions in trying to follow through on a career choice. Although it is difficult to do so, the environment can be changed through collective action that leads to the passing of laws such as those dealing with racial discrimination and affirmative action. By emphasizing the importance of social learning and career decision making, Mitchell and Krumboltz (1990) point out that counselors can assist in developing good decision making and can help clients of color deal with discrimination that might otherwise limit their career opportunities.

Although some studies have shown the importance of role models for people of color, very little research has applied Krumboltz's social learning theory to people of color. For career self-efficacy theorists, gender differences have been the central focus. However, a number of studies have examined self-efficacy issues for people from different cultural groups. In general, the gender differences found among white Americans tend to be found in men and women in other countries (Hackett, 1995). For both male and female African American students, Post, Stewart, and Smith (1991) have found that occupational self-efficacy predicts interest in math and science occupations. Studying Native American students, Lauver and Jones (1991) found that those living on reservations were much less likely to have the opportunity to develop self-efficacy than were other students. Hackett, Betz, Casas, and Rocha-Singh (1992) found lower levels of self-efficacy for engineering careers in Mexican American students, which was due primarily to differences in academic preparation. Supporting the importance of self-efficacy for disadvantaged precollege students, Post-Kammer and Smith (1986) found that occupational self-efficacy was a better predictor of the consideration of math or science careers than were interests. These studies represent some of the efforts that have been made to apply self-efficacy theory to the academic and career choices of people of color. Hackett (1995) writes that future research should do more than note cultural differences and should focus on the effect of culture on career self-efficacy and career development.

Just as women must deal with myths about their ability that negatively affects their sense of self-efficacy, so must people of different cultures. Individuals from cultures that have been negatively stereotyped in a society may find it difficult to believe that they, as members of that culture, can achieve academically or occupationally. Furthermore, some individuals may be isolated from other members of society, as are many Native Americans who live on reservations, which limit educational and occupational information that may enhance their opportunities and enable them to develop stronger self-efficacy beliefs.

COUNSELOR ISSUES

Krumboltz views the counselor's role from a behavioral point of view. He believes it is important that the skills, interests, and values of the counselor be appropriate to the client. As Krumboltz and Baker (1973) state, "The counselor's commitment to work with the client toward the goals that they have mutually defined is highly important. It reflects the behavioral counseling viewpoint that counseling is a planned professional event in which two or more individuals contract to solve or define a problem. It emphasizes the behavioral position that one technique or counseling method is insufficient for all problem solutions" (p. 244).

In determining whether to work with a client, a counselor must decide whether the client's problem fits within the interests, competencies, and ethical standards of the counselor (Krumboltz, 1964). If counselors specialize in a type of population (for example, older adults or college students) or a specific counseling technique (such as behavioral counseling), it is important that they be certain that the needs of the client are within their areas of expertise. Furthermore, if the client has a goal that seems unethical or inappropriate to the counselor, the counselor is bound to tell the client and either not work with the client or help the client redefine his or her goal. For example, if a client says to a counselor, "I want you to guarantee me that I can get a job in business," the counselor must decline or must change the client's goal. When applying the DECIDES approach to clients, it is particularly important for counselors to listen to concerns that may not necessarily fit in with the DECIDES program. For example, if a client is grieving over the death of a parent, the counseling should be flexible enough so that the counselor will not mistake this grieving for lack of motivation to move toward a career goal. Since the concept of self-observed generalizations of abilities, interests, and values is quite broad, the counselor should be open to a discussion of experiences that may at first appear to be unrelated to career concerns.

Career self-efficacy theorists focus on cognitive processes that interact with behaviors. Self-efficacy, outcome expectations, and goals are important aspects of career self-efficacy theory. It is important that counselors be aware of their own issues or stereotypes that may interfere with helping their clients. Unrecognized biases about race and gender directly interfere with helping clients develop career self-efficacy beliefs. As counseling evolves, counselors may become aware of the differences between their clients' outcome expectations and their own view of educational and career possibilities for their clients. Similarly, as counselors help their clients to develop self-efficacy beliefs, they may find that they are developing goals for their clients different from the goals their clients develop for themselves. When they are aware of their own values and views of their clients, counselors can help clients to make their own career decisions without interfering in the decision-making process.

SUMMARY

Krumboltz's social learning theory presents a specific career decision-making model that emphasizes a behavioral orientation, with some cognitive components. The theory stresses the importance of genetic endowment, environmental conditions, learning experiences, and task-approach skills. Krumboltz and his colleagues provide both conceptualization skills and counseling techniques to help clients choose career alternatives. The behavioral counseling techniques that they suggest include reinforcement, modeling, and simulation. Their cognitive strategies include challenging and correcting inaccurate thoughts or beliefs. These techniques are used at various points throughout career decision-making counseling. A seven-step approach to decision making called DECIDES is illustrated in this chapter.

Starting with the work of Hackett and Betz (1981), who proposed that career self-efficacy plays a more important role than interests, values, and abilities in restricting women's choices, career self-efficacy theory has developed into a widely researched theory of career development. Emphasizing cognitive concepts more than behavioral ones, career self-efficacy theory has focused on the importance of self-efficacy, outcome expectations, and goals as variables in academic and career choices. As a result of a significant body of research, career self-efficacy theorists have been able to describe a detailed process of career development. Familiarity with this model can be useful for counselors in attending to and reinforcing the self-efficacy beliefs of their clients.

References

Almquist, E. M. (1974). Sex stereotypes in occupational choice: The case for college women. *Journal of Vocational Behavior, 5,* 13–21.

Baird, L. L. (1971). Cooling out and warming up in the junior college. *Measurement and Evaluation in Guidance, 4,* 160–171.

Bandura, A. (1969). *Principles of behavior modification.* New York: Holt, Rinehart & Winston.

Bandura, A. (1977). *Social learning theory.* Englewood Cliffs, NJ: Prentice-Hall.

Bandura, A. (1987). Reflections on self-efficacy. In S. Rachman (Ed.), *Advances in behaviour research and therapy* (Vol. 1, pp. 237–269). Oxford: Pergamon Press.

Bandura, A. (1986). *Social foundations of thought and action: A social cognitive theory.* Englewood Cliffs, NJ: Prentice-Hall.

Beck, A. T. (1991). Cognitive therapy: A 30-year retrospective. *American Psychologist, 46,* 368–375.

Betz, N. (1992). Counseling uses of career self-efficacy theory. *The Career Development Quarterly, 41,* 22–26.

Betz, N. E., & Hackett, G. (1981). The relationship of career-related self-efficacy expectations to perceived career options in college women and men. *Journal of Counseling, 28,* 399–410.

Ellis, A., & Dryden, W. (1987). *The practice of rational-emotive therapy.* New York: Springer.

Fisher, T. J., Reardon, R. C., & Burck, H. D. (1976). Increasing information-seeking behavior with a model-reinforced videotape. *Journal of Counseling Psychology, 23,* 234–238.

Hackett, G. (1995). Self-efficacy in career choice and development. In A. Bandura (Ed.), *Self-efficacy in changing societies* (pp. 232–258). Cambridge, England: Cambridge University Press.

Hackett, G., & Betz, N. (1981). A self-efficacy approach to the career development of women. *Journal of Vocational Behavior, 18,* 326–339.

Hackett, G., Betz, N. E., Casas, J. M., & Rocha-Singh, I. (1992). Gender, ethnicity, and social cognitive factors predicting the academic achievement of students in engineering. *Journal of Counseling Psychology, 39,* 527–538.

Keller, K. E., Biggs, D. A., & Gysbers, N. C. (1982). Career counseling from a cognitive perspective. *Personnel and Guidance Journal, 60,* 367–370.

Krumboltz, J. D. (1964). Parable of the good counselor. *Personnel and Guidance Journal, 43,* 118–124.

Krumboltz, J. D. (Ed.). (1970). *Job experience kits.* Chicago: Science Research Associates.

Krumboltz, J. D. (1979). A social learning theory of career decision making. In A. M. Mitchell, G. B. Jones, & J. D. Krumboltz (Eds.), *Social learning and career decision making* (pp. 19–49). Cranston, RI: Carroll Press.

Krumboltz, J. D. (1983). *Private rules in career decision making.* Columbus, OH: The National Center for Research in Vocational Education.

Krumboltz, J. D. (1988). *Career Beliefs Inventory.* Palo Alto, CA: Consulting Psychologists Press.

Krumboltz, J. D. (1994a). The Career Beliefs Inventory. *Journal of Counseling and Development, 72,* 424–428.

Krumboltz, J. D. (1994b). Improving career development theory from a social learning perspective. In M. L. Savickas, & R. W. Lent (Eds.), *Convergence in career development theories* (pp. 9–32). Palo Alto, CA: Consulting Psychologists Press.

Krumboltz, J. D., & Baker, R. D. (1973). Behavioral counseling for vocational decision. In H. Borow (Ed.), *Career guidance for a new age* (pp. 235–284). Boston: Houghton Mifflin.

Krumboltz, J. D., Baker, R. D., & Johnson, R. G. (1968). *Vocational problem-solving experiences for stimulating career exploration and interests: Phase II.* Washington, DC: U.S. Office of Education.

Krumboltz, J. D., & Hamel, D. A. (1977). *Guide to career decision-making skills.* New York: Educational Testing Service.

Krumboltz, J. D., & Schroeder, W. W. (1965). Promoting career planning through reinforcement and models. *Personnel and Guidance Journal, 44,* 19–26.

Krumboltz, J. D., Sheppard, L. E., Jones, G. B., Johnson, R. G., & Baker, R. D. (1967). *Vocational problem-solving experiences for stimulating career exploration and interest.* Washington, DC: U.S. Office of Education.

Krumboltz, J. D., & Thoresen, C. E. (1964). The effect of behavioral counseling in groups and individual settings on information-seeking behavior. *Journal of Counseling Psychology, 11,* 324–333.

Lauver, P. J., & Jones, R. M. (1991). Factors associated with perceived career options in American Indian, White, and Hispanic rural high school students. *Journal of Counseling Psychology, 38,* 159–166.

Lent, R. W., Brown, S. D., & Hackett, G. (1994). Toward a unified social cognitive theory of career and academic interest, choice, and performance. *Journal of Vocational Behavior, 45,* 79–122.

Lent, R. W., Brown, S. D., & Larkin, K. C. (1986). Self-efficacy in the prediction of academic performance and perceived career options. *Journal of Counseling Psychology, 33,* 165–169.

Lent, R. W., & Hackett, G. (1987). Career self-efficacy: Empirical status and future directions. *Journal of Vocational Behavior, 30,* 347–382.

Lent, R. W., & Hackett, G. (1994). Sociocognitive mechanisms of personal agency in career development: Pantheoretical prospects. In M. L. Savickas & R. W. Lent (Eds.), *Convergence in career development theories: Implications for science and practice* (pp. 77–101). Palo Alto, CA: Consulting Psychologists Press.

Little, D. M., & Roach, A. J. (1974). Videotape modeling of interest in nontraditional occupations for women. *Journal of Vocational Behavior, 5,* 133–138.

Mansfield, R. (1973). Self-esteem, self-perceived abilities, and vocational choice. *Journal of Vocational Behavior, 3,* 433–441.

Meichenbaum, D. (1977). *Cognitive behavior modification.* Morristown, NJ: General Learning Press.

Mitchell, L. K., & Krumboltz, J. D. (1990). Social learning approach to career decision making: Krumboltz's theory. In D. Brown, L. Brooks, & Assoc. (Eds.), *Career choice and development: Applying contemporary theories to practice* (2nd ed., pp. 145–196). San Francisco: Jossey-Bass.

Mitchell, L. K., & Krumboltz, J. D. (1996). Krumboltz's learning theory of career choice and counseling. In D. Brown, L. Brooks, & Assoc. (Eds.), *Career choice and development* (3rd ed., pp. 233–280). San Francisco: Jossey-Bass.

Multon, K. D., Brown, S. D., & Lent, R. W. (1991). Relation of self-efficacy beliefs to academic outcomes. A meta-analytic investigation. *Journal of Counseling Psychology, 38,* 30–38.

Oliver, L. W. (1975). The relationship of parental attitudes and parent identification to career and homemaking orientation in college women. *Journal of Vocational Behavior, 7,* 1–12.

Osipow, S. H. (1972). Success and preference: A replication and extension. *Journal of Applied Psychology, 56,* 179–180.

Pallone, N. J., Rickard, F. S., & Hurley, R. B. (1970). Key influences of occupational preference among black youth. *Journal of Counseling Psychology, 17,* 498–501.

Post, P., Stewart, M. A., & Smith, P. L. (1991). Self-efficacy, interest, and consideration of math/science and non math/science occupations among college freshmen. *Journal of Vocational Behavior, 38,* 179–186.

Post-Kammer, P., & Smith, P. I. (1986). Sex differences in math and science career self-efficacy among disadvantaged students. *Journal of Vocational Behavior, 29,* 89–101.

Taylor, K. M., & Betz, N. E. (1983). Applications of self-efficacy theory to the understanding and treatment of career indecision. *Journal of Vocational Behavior, 22,* 63–81.

Taylor, K. M., & Popma, J. (1990). An examination of the relationships among career decision-making self-efficacy, career salience, locus of control, and vocational indecision. *Journal of Vocational Behavior, 22,* 63–81.

Thoresen, C. E., Hosford, R. E., & Krumboltz, J. D. (1970). Determining effective models for counseling clients of varying competencies. *Journal of Counseling Psychology, 17,* 369–375.

14

Career Decision-Making Theory

Several career development theorists have focused their attention on career decision making. Although there are many approaches to career decision making, the models or theories can be divided into two categories: descriptive and prescriptive. Descriptive theories describe or explain the choices that an individual makes when deciding on a career or some aspect of a career. In contrast, prescriptive decision-making theories focus on an ideal approach to decision making. Descriptive theories tend to be based on studies of adolescent and adult decision making. On the other hand, prescriptive theories originate with psychological decision-making theory, which tends to be abstract and covers decision making in general, rather than dealing specifically with career decision making. In terms of their impact on career decision making, these two approaches are quite different. To illustrate this contrast, one descriptive and one prescriptive theory are presented in this chapter.

The descriptive theory presented is the individualistic perspective on career decision making of Tiedeman and Miller-Tiedeman. Their approach has been selected because of its emphasis on the complexity and uniqueness of an individual's career choice. Further, although not generating a great deal of research, their theory has generated more research than other descriptive theories. Vroom (1964) has developed an expectancy model of career decision making. Although it has prompted research, most of it has been in the area of organizational decision making (Wanous, Keon, & Latack, 1983). A somewhat similar model has been outlined by Hsu (1970), who conceives of the decision maker as a system. These models, summarized and compared in Jepsen and Dilley (1974), differ from the work of Miller-Tiedeman and Tiedeman (1990) in that they focus more on the decision itself rather than on the human qualities of the decision maker.

The prescriptive models of decision making are searches for the best way to make career decisions. They tend to emphasize a guided logical and rational approach. A typical method is the sequential elimination model. This general model of decision making was proposed by Tversky (1972) and has been adapted to the career decision-making process by Gati (1986), and Gati, Fassa, and Houminer (1995). Other prescriptive models include that of Katz (1963), who has designed a model for career decision making that focuses on the use of values. Another approach to designing a career decision-making model is that of Mitchell and Beach (1976), who emphasize the importance of the probability of an outcome and its usefulness. This is called the *subjective expected utility model.* One reason for selecting the sequential elimination approach, rather than others, as an illustration of a prescriptive decision-making theory is its ability to handle a vast array of career choices or options. In general, prescriptive career decision-making models have not been the subject of much research.

The contrast between the descriptive and prescriptive models of career decision making should become evident to the reader as the two approaches are described. The individualistic perspective on career decision making of Tiedeman and Miller-Tiedeman explains common developmental stages in decision making as well as types of career decisions. The emphasis on individuals, human values, and awareness of internal decision making is a prominent part of the work of Tiedeman and Miller-Tiedeman. It contrasts with the logical and rational approach of the sequential elimination method (Gati, 1986). This method includes the ranking of alternatives by their importance in determining the range of acceptable characteristics of occupations. These theories will be compared to each other in terms of their implications for the use of occupational information and tests. Although these theories do not speak directly to issues of women and people of color, inferences can be made from them. The implications for counseling use of these two theories are vastly different; comparisons will be made.

TIEDEMAN AND MILLER-TIEDEMAN'S INDIVIDUALISTIC PERSPECTIVE ON CAREER DECISION MAKING

To understand the approach of Tiedeman and Miller-Tiedeman to career decision making, it is necessary to understand the background from which their models evolved. In his thinking about career decision making, David Tiedeman was influenced strongly by White's (1952) individualistic approach to the study of human lives and the striving toward competence. Furthermore, Erikson's (1959) study of ego development and description of the stages of psychosocial development had an impact on Tiedeman's articulation of career decision-making stages. In addition, Tiedeman was influenced by the developmental approach to career choice as described by Super (1957) and Ginzberg, Ginsburg, Axelrad, and Herma (1951). Tiedeman's early work with Robert O'Hara shows both the influence of these theorists and a unique approach to career decision making, evident in the model of Tiedeman and O'Hara (1963). In an ambitious research project, Tiedeman applied his career decision-making paradigm to the development of a computer-assisted guidance system (Tiedeman, 1979). Tiedeman's early work is characterized by his concern about the uniqueness of the individual and the complexity of the decision-making process.

Around 1970, Anna Miller-Tiedeman joined Tiedeman and began building on his efforts in the development of her own model of career decision making. In her work, Miller-Tiedeman was influenced by the ego-development stages of Loevinger, Wessler, and Redmore (1970), the values levels of Graves (1974), and the decision strategies of Dinklage (1968), which will be described in some detail later. The emphasis of Miller-Tiedeman has been on teaching young people and adults how to live life as process, as illustrated by her work on LIFECARER® (1988, 1989), which draws widely on a vast array of disciplines, including physics and philosophy.

The approach of Tiedeman and Miller-Tiedeman is characterized by a deep respect for the individual and the individual's uniqueness and complexity. They describe their work as being "devised to deal with a person both participating in an evolving decision and becoming more conscious of his or her decision-making education" (Tiedeman & Miller-Tiedeman, 1979, p. 167). They see life decisions and career decisions as integrally related. This is demonstrated by Miller-Tiedeman's (1988, 1989) model, which she calls Life-Is-Career®. Unlike other career development theories, their view is strongly influenced by phenomenological and existential philosophical positions. This is seen in their continual focus on the humanity and individuality of the career decision maker (Tiedeman, 1992).

It is difficult to describe the models of Tiedeman and O'Hara (1963) and Miller-Tiedeman (1977, 1988, 1989) with precision. Rather than attempt this, this section will focus on the core aspects of their approach. First, Dinklage's (1968) eight types of decision making will be described to illustrate a variety of approaches to career choice and other career-related decisions. This will be followed by an explanation and illustration of Tiedeman's two major stages: anticipating and adjusting to a choice. As a framework for understanding these styles and stages, the concept of realities will be explained.

Personal and Common Realities

Reality concerns the awareness of one's career decision making (Miller-Tiedeman & Tiedeman, 1990). The question of whether a decision or act is realistic is a matter of opinion. The question is: Realistic to whom? Tiedeman and Miller-Tiedeman (1979) specify two types of reality: personal and common. *Personal reality* refers to an individual's sense of what is right. It is a feeling that the decision or direction to be taken is correct and appropriate to the decision maker. On the other hand, *common reality* is what others say the individual should do, for example, "You would be a good teacher," "You can get a better job than that," and "You can't get anywhere without a college degree." Common reality also includes the opinions of experts. The sequential elimination method described in the next section is an excellent example of common reality. It is an expert telling others the best way to make career decisions. The following discussion classifies types of individual decisions. Dinklage's categories describe eight styles of personal realities. These may become "common realities" if evaluated positively or negatively by the counselor.

Dinklage's Eight Decision-Making Strategies

Dinklage (1968) describes eight different strategies for making decisions. Four of the styles are ways of not making a decision: delaying, being fatalistic, compliant, or paralytic. The other four are styles of decision making: intuitive, impulsive, agonizing, and planful. First, the four styles of nondecision-making will be described, followed by the four decision-making styles.

Delaying: Basically, this style is one of postponement or procrastination. The individual decides that he or she will make the decision at a later time. Examples include the student who waits until the last moment to choose a major, the individual who is unhappy in a job but really does not want to think about that right now, and the student who does not know whether to go to college and finds out that he or she has delayed so long that only a few universities will accept his or her late application.

Fatalistic: This is a way of not choosing by letting others choose. The worker who decides to be passive about a problem with a supervisor at work is leaving the solution to fate (or to the supervisor). Generally, by not taking action, an individual follows the path with the fewest obstacles. For example, the individual who leaves to fate the decision about whether to go to college usually will not go to college.

Compliant: A person who complies with the plans of another lets that person make the decision for him or her. The classic example is the child whose parents want him or her to become a doctor when the child does not want to enter medicine. Sometimes, individuals are compliant because they are passive and, at other times, because they feel coerced by an authority figure.

Paralytic: When individuals are too frightened or anxious, they may feel unable to decide. Or they may feel pressure from themselves or others to make a decision but may be afraid of the consequences. Those who have had difficulty in making decisions that they were comfortable with in the past may be reluctant to make future decisions. For example, a student who has changed majors four times may be unwilling to change majors again.

All four of these decision-making styles have in common a lack of decision making. The strategies show not just one but four different ways of deciding not to decide. These are not the only ways of not making a decision, but they are common ways. In contrast, the following four decision-making styles emphasize very different approaches to the process:

Intuitive: Making a decision based on feelings rather than thoughts about what one wants to do would be intuitive. Intuitive decisions may be quite appropriate, but they can be supplemented by an analysis of one's own strengths, for example, one's abilities and interests. Certain occupational choices tend to be made on the basis of feelings. Deciding to be a minister, priest, or rabbi may be based on a spiritual feeling rather than on a cognitive decision-making process. The desire to become a stage or movie actor with full knowledge of the limited and competitive job market is an example of making a decision based on the fact that the career choice feels right.

Impulsive: An individual who does not consider many alternatives seriously is considered an impulsive decision maker. If one enters a restaurant and chooses the first item on the menu without looking at the others, this is not a disaster. However, if one chooses an occupation this way, lack of planning may create many problems.

Agonizing: Some individuals sort through information about themselves and occupations but have great difficulty making up their minds. For example, a student who knows that she wants to enter engineering but cannot decide which branch may have information from many colleges about their departments in various areas of engineering, as well as occupational information about specialties, but may have difficulty deciding among them. Thus, she may agonize over the choice for a considerable period of time.

Planful: In this approach, individuals are able to plan when making a decision. They pay attention to both their feelings and their knowledge of their abilities, interests, and values when making a career-related decision.

These categories illustrate different ways of making career decisions. There are certainly many other styles and methods. Savickas and Jarjoura (1991) have analyzed the content of the two scales of the Career Decision Scale (Certainty and Indecision) (Osipow, 1987) and have identified categories that fit somewhat with Dinklage's (perfectionistic and indecisive patterns are similar to Dinklage's category of agonizing). Other categories are more developmental and fit more with those that are described in the next section. Each individual is likely to have his or her own style and method, which will not fit any of these definitions exactly. Furthermore, clients are likely to use different styles of decision making in different career decisions. Dinklage's categories may be useful in understanding the unique decision-making style of the client. The style of decision making is quite different from the *process* of decision making. The process deals with the gradual development of and commitment to a choice, as described by

Tiedeman and O'Hara's two major stages: anticipating and adjusting to a choice. When combined with knowledge about career strategies (Dinklage), process stages provide a broad platform from which career decision making can be viewed.

Anticipating a Choice

Tiedeman and O'Hara (1963) divide the anticipating stage of decision making into four basic developmental phases: exploration, crystallization, choice, and clarification. These phases are not always sequential, nor are they age-related. Furthermore, one can be at various phases for several different career decisions at a particular point in time. In keeping with Miller-Tiedeman's concept of LIFECAREER® (1989), it is particularly important to emphasize that these phases are only a guideline. If seen that way, they become a personal reality rather than a common reality.

These phases can be guides for the counselor in understanding the decision-making process and the nature of the individual's internal cognitive and affective processes. To illustrate these phases, an example will be given of a student who is in her senior year of high school and trying to decide whether to get a job, attend college, or join the armed forces. Susan, whose parents are both Polish, is in a quandary as to what to choose. To make matters more difficult, her mother is suffering from terminal cancer, and Susan is not sure how long she will live. In this example, the counselor will help Susan to decide among her alternatives by working through the phases of exploration, crystallization, choice, and clarification. For purposes of this situation, the flow will be from each phase to the next higher phase. In other situations, progress may be made much more slowly and with less directionality than in this example.

Exploration In the exploration phase, individuals may follow leads in an unsystematic way. They may imagine themselves in different situations, try out certain behaviors, fantasize about later career goals, worry about their deepest fears, and follow avenues of choice in systematic or unsystematic ways. How they explore will reflect their own style. The counselor may help to clarify and strengthen the client's self-knowledge but does not impose a structure from outside. There is a need to take action or make a decision, but the process may not be felt clearly.

CL: Here it is December, and I don't know what to do. I graduate in May, and I don't know what to do.

CO: So many choices. [The counselor recognizes Susan's need to explore. He wants to help her to do that to the best of her ability.]

CL: It's just so hard. I don't know what to do. I've thought about school, going to college, getting a degree. I don't know how I would pay for it. I don't know what I would study. It feels so unknown. Maybe I should just get a job at home.

CO: So much pressure on you right now. You can relax a bit, and we can talk about it. [Susan seems to be paralyzed, in Dinklage's terms, by the huge responsibility that she is feeling for the decision. Categorizing in such a way helps the counselor get a sense of Susan's decision-making style at the moment.]

CL: It's just so hard to relax. I feel so bad. Every time I go home, I see my mother. Sometimes, she's had a chemotherapy treatment and she's really sick. I feel so scared then. I know I should help her. I know I should take care of her, but I should take care of myself, too.

CO: Seeing your mother sick like that—it's so hard. She's on your mind so often. [Recognizing Susan's caring and sense of responsibility for her mother, the counselor wants to help Susan explore that aspect of the decision making further.]

CL: Sometimes when I'm with her, my mind wanders. I think of her. I think of me. I've thought about me being stationed in Europe with the army. Being over there with other American soldiers. Ever since I was a little girl, I've liked to do things like march and salute. Stuff like that. My father was a policeman. When I think of him now—and he's not a policeman any longer—I think of him in his blue uniform. I was always in awe of him then. He looked so strong. Maybe that's why. But I've always enjoyed military movies, war games, all kinds of stuff like that.

CO: It seems freeing to let your imagination run like that. [Letting Susan's exploration follow her inner feelings and her imagination seems appropriate to the counselor.]

CL: Yes, I worry about my mother so. It's nice to take a break from that. It's hard, too. She's often cranky because she hurts. It's so hard for me to see her hurt. [crying] She's been so good to me.

CO: Her illness brings you back to what you have to do each day. [The counselor is aware of how difficult it is for Susan to explore when she feels such responsibility right now for her mother.]

The dialogue between counselor and client moves along this way for two more sessions. Susan moves back and forth between her responsibility for her mother and her desire to make plans. As best he can, the counselor helps Susan search within herself for the various paths that she wants to explore. He helps her to explore them and not run away from them, even though they are frightening, such as the fear of her mother's dying. Gradually, and without the counselor's immediate awareness, Susan's choices start to crystallize.

Crystallization According to Tiedeman and O'Hara (1963), "Crystallization normally represents a stabilization of thought" (p. 41). Thoughts and feelings may start to be more orderly. The advantages and disadvantages of various choices may start to emerge. Temporary choices may emerge and may be challenged and changed. Awareness of the choice may be clear, vague, or nonexistent. But more definition is found in this phase than in the exploratory phase.

At this point, Susan is in her third counseling appointment. She has been able to speak more about her fears about her mother's health with the counselor. She further explores options of working in a retail store at home, joining the army, or applying for admission to her state university.

CL: I've talked to the army recruiter in town. He was real nice to me. He was flexible about when I could enter and what I would do. He seemed to understand the situation about my mother. I guess I was kind of surprised about that, and I appreciated it.

CO: He seemed to make you feel good about yourself, as if to give you more options to do what you might want. [The counselor takes the opportunity to comment on a growing sense of self, a sense that Susan may be feeling that she can take care of herself.]

CL: I guess I want to know that I'm not stuck, that I can make different choices at different times. For a while, it felt as if I had to do one thing or the other, but I couldn't do more than one. I still don't know about school. I don't know whether I want to go to college. I really have been getting "B"s and "C"s and don't like school too much. Gosh, I don't know what I would study. Maybe English, science, math—I don't think so. I don't know.

CO: Tell me more about what you like at school. [The counselor senses Susan moving back from crystallizing some options to still exploring her likes about academic subjects. If assigning an interest inventory or values inventory will help her explore this area, then he will do so.]

CL: I like history. I like learning about different cultures, different people. I really like learning about how this country was settled. When the events seem to take place in my mind I can imagine the Revolutionary War or things like that, it's fun. I like geography, too.

CO: Can you tell me more about that? [The counselor wants Susan to continue her exploration.]

CL: I like geography because I can picture different countries. I can imagine what they would be like. I think I'd really like to travel. I'd like to travel; I'd like to help people travel. That's what I think part of the fun is about being stationed overseas. It's so different. If I were over there with the army, I'd have a free trip. I have often liked to travel with my parents. We visit relatives all over the place. I love it.

Susan continues to explore some interests while her more pressing choices are tending to crystallize in terms of what she may do in the immediate future. She is moving closer to the choice of college, the army, or home, but not an eventual career goal.

Choice As crystallization develops, a choice may occur. The person may have varying degrees of confidence about that choice. Choices vary in terms of their clarity and complexity. Sometimes, they emerge with conscious awareness, and sometimes, without.

Four weeks have passed since Susan's initial conference with the counselor. Susan is moving closer to a decision about what she plans to do in the summer.

CL: I really think that I need to be here with my mother, as long as I can. She's been getting worse. I really worry for her. I don't know how long she will live. It scares me terribly; we've been so very close. I feel as if I can join the army after that—maybe travel some. I know about possibilities for schooling. Having the army help me out—things like that. I think that might work.

CO: You seem to have things clearer in your mind. The choices seem to be falling into place. [The counselor notes how Susan has prioritized her choices in terms of time.]

CL: Yes. I've thought about it a lot. I just feel that I need so much right now to be with my mother. My father seems to need me, too; so does my younger sister. It's strange; I'm not used to that. My father was always gruff. He's such a big guy, and someone who's quiet a lot. I see him sad, crying sometimes. It's awful.

CO: I know it's really hard for you. This has been a tough time. [Susan's life and career decisions are intimately intertwined; moving back and forth from one issue to another seems natural.]

CL: It's so hard for me now. But sometimes, when I think that I can go into the army and then I can do more things that I want to do—come out and go to school, or work in a travel agency, or work for an airline—then things seem OK, but not always for long.

CO: You're really doing some thinking about the future. [The counselor is surprised to hear some career choices emerge. He is patient and feels no need to develop them at the moment.]

Clarification When individuals make a decision, they ordinarily act on it. However, they may experience doubt between the time the decision is made and when it is acted on. Time gives an opportunity to reassess the choice and to clarify the options. If the choice is questioned, the individual may return to explore, crystallize, and choose all over again. Miller-Tiedeman (1977) found that ninth-graders often leaped from exploration to choice and, depending on outcome, tended to recycle back through crystallization and clarification.

Susan continued to experience doubt about her decision. Sometimes, she felt she should just stay at home with her family and, no matter what happened with her mother, not leave them. Being with her friends and hearing about their plans would reinforce her feeling about following her inner wishes. She wanted to take a trip to visit a friend several hours away. That was a particularly meaningful experience to her as it allowed her to develop her sense of self. She could feel stronger about herself, making her own plans for the trip and spending time with her friend on an equal basis. She felt relieved not to be taking care of someone. Telling the counselor about this helped her become more aware of her goals. Taking that trip seemed to clarify her own notion of what was important to her.

The phases of anticipating a choice—exploration, crystallization, choice, and clarification—lead to the implementation of and adjustment to a choice. Once a choice has been made and is about to be acted on, the second of Tiedeman's two major stages—adjusting to a choice—begins.

Adjusting to a Choice

Acting on a choice is an important part of Tiedeman's conceptualization of decision making. He does not feel that the decision-making process is over once the choice has been made. Tiedeman and O'Hara (1963) outline three phases of adjustment: induction, reformation, and integration. These phases deal with carrying out the decision. Interaction with others is required. There may be teachers, bosses, or others whom one needs to deal with in order to carry out the decision. As an illustration of these phases, we will follow Susan in her progress through them.

Induction In this phase, a person implements his or her choice. The choice may be to go to college, take adult education courses, start a new job, or work a second part-time job. As an individual is inducted into his or her new choice, a certain amount of change will take place in response to the commitment that has been made.

Susan continued her schoolwork. When she graduated, she started to work for a pharmacy in town as a cashier and a stock clerk. She continued to discuss her plans with the army recruiter. This gave her a sense of being transitory, an awareness that her current goal (career choice) was not permanent. Throughout the summer, she had to take time off from work as her mother grew weaker. In October, her mother died, leaving Susan in shock. She felt the need to stay at home to be with her younger sister and her father. She had made friends at work who were supportive of her and who helped her in her crisis. In June of the following year, she entered the army. She had been looking forward to this experience for some time. Induction into this goal felt less transitory and more like a choice that would help her feel that she was moving in a positive direction. She felt excited, knowing that she was doing something that she had wanted to do for some time.

Reformation The introduction of a new member into a group and the reception of that individual by other members constitute reformation. Often, in this phase an individual is hesitant to join or feel a part of the group at first but may later become an advocate of the group.

For Susan, boot camp was not unexpected. She had talked to friends about basic training and was prepared. She actually enjoyed it, particularly liking the feeling of comradeship that she experienced with other members of her group. After basic training, she was assigned to the infantry. She enjoyed learning about the equipment and how to clean and operate rifles, machine guns, and such. This experience gave her a sense of belonging and excitement.

Integration In integration, the newness wears off, and the group and the individual accept each other. The excitement about the new choice may diminish and become an integral part of the individual.

As new individuals joined and left Susan's infantry group, her feeling about them and herself changed. When one of her closest friends left, she felt somewhat lonely and unsure of herself. However, when someone else entered, she enjoyed the excitement of the new discovery of this individual. After two years in the army, Susan began to give more thought to whether to reenlist, move back home, or enter college. As she did this, she reentered the exploratory phase.

As Susan went through the stages of anticipation and adjustment in her career decision-making process, her sense of self developed. She had a sense of herself not as a military person, a bereaved daughter, a friend, or a potential college student, but as a whole person. The counselor who dealt with her in the anticipation aspects of a portion of her career decision making also saw her as a whole person. He did not differentiate between career choice and other life choices. Susan was important and a valued person who developed her own career theory—a personal reality for her. The counselor helped her develop this theory but did not suggest what to do. This emphasis on the individual is consistent with the work of Tiedeman and Miller-Tiedeman. Although this discussion has focused particularly on decision-making stages and styles, they are not the only concepts that Tiedeman and Miller-Tiedeman use in their explanation of decision making.

Other Aspects of the Individualistic Perspective

Although the stages of career decision making as described by Tiedeman and O'Hara (1963) form the core of Miller-Tiedeman's model, several other influences broaden her approach. Wilson (1971) proposes four levels of learning and thinking that fit somewhat with the stages of career decision making of Tiedeman and O'Hara (1963). Wilson's levels are (1) learning about, which is congruent with the stage of anticipation of the Tiedeman and O'Hara model; (2) beginning to act; (3) carrying out; and (4) thinking about. The higher three levels of Wilson fit more closely with the three phases of the adjustment stage of Tiedeman and O'Hara: induction, reformation, and integration. Wilson focuses more on problem solving and less on decision making per se. In her work, Miller-Tiedeman also incorporates the stages of ego development as explained by Loevinger et al. (1970), who describe the evolving stages of adult responsibility and development: impulsive, self-protective, conformist, self-aware, conscientious, individualistic, autonomous, and integrated. Note the increasing amount of responsibility and self-actualization in these stages of ego development. In addition to ego development, Miller-Tiedeman also incorporates values levels as described by Graves (1974). These levels focus on how individuals respond to the world around them. Like the stages of ego development, they range from minimal to maximal levels of responsibility: reactive, traditionalistic, manipulative or exploitive, religious or sacrificial, materialistic, personalistic, and survival for all humans (deep concern for others). Graves's values focus on responsibility to others, whereas Loevinger,

Wessler and Redmore focus on responsibility to self. Integrating all of this into counseling can be difficult. The focus of this section, however, has been on those concepts most directly related to decision making. One reason for this emphasis is that the Tiedeman and O'Hara (1963) stages are the aspects of the Tiedeman and Miller-Tiedeman work that have been researched most extensively.

Research on the Individualistic Perspective

Though not a frequent object of study, the Tiedeman and O'Hara (1963) paradigm has stimulated some behavioral research. Basically, there are two types: research that tests the theory directly in terms of the accuracy of the stages of decision making and research that has studied instruments designed to measure decision-making styles.

Miller-Tiedeman and Tiedeman (1990) report two studies that bear directly on the four phases of anticipation of Tiedeman and O'Hara (1963): exploration, crystallization, choice, and clarification. Miller-Tiedeman (1977) reports that adolescent learners first make a decision; after experiencing negative consequences, return to the crystallization phase; and then go on to choose a second time. If that doesn't work, they go to the crystallization phase and then to the clarification phase before making a final choice. Thus, deciders worked on a more complex manner than predicted by Tiedeman and O'Hara (1963). In another study of adolescents, Jepsen and Grove (1981) found that rather than following the order of exploration, crystallization, choice, and clarification, the participants reversed the last two phases and choice followed clarification. Naturally, not all students respond in this way. Miller-Tiedeman (1989) points out that it is the individual style of decision making that is particularly important, not the decision-making style of a group of individuals. What is important is the personal reality of each individual, not the common reality.

In addition to research on career decision-making stages, several investigators have attempted to develop a scale to measure career decision making. Most notable is the work of Harren (1979), who developed the Assessment of Career Decision-Making. In general, research on this inventory has supported the concepts of Tiedeman and O'Hara. More recently, research has been continued by Buck and Daniels (1985) after the death of Vincent Harren in 1980. The Assessment of Career Decision-Making, as developed by Buck and Daniels, corresponds only partially to the theory of Tiedeman and O'Hara. This inventory includes scales that measure three decision-making styles: rational, intuitive, and dependent. If we compare these with the concepts described earlier by Dinklage (1968), the Dependent scale corresponds with the compliant concept; the Rational scale, with the planful concept; and the Intuitive scale, with the intuitive concept. In addition to these decision styles, Buck and Daniels measure school adjustment, consisting of three subscales (Satisfaction with School,

Involvement with Peers, and Interaction with Instructors). Also, they measure two decision-making tasks, choosing an occupation and choosing a major, on separate scales. These last scales do not correspond directly to the stages of Tiedeman and O'Hara (1963), although these scales represent critical decisions in Tiedeman and O'Hara's theory. Earlier versions of the Assessment of Career Decision-Making are more closely allied to the Tiedeman and O'Hara paradigm. Miller-Tiedeman and Tiedeman (1990) cite research on the earlier version that supports the concepts in the Tiedeman and O'Hara theory.

Much of the writing of Tiedeman and Miller-Tiedeman is at a philosophical level, partly because of their intense emphasis on the uniqueness and the perceived power of the individual. Often, their work provides a way of viewing individuals and their world rather than precise suggestions for counseling interventions. Their approach is in marked contrast to the prescriptive approach to be described next, which is concerned with the most logical way of making a career decision.

A SEQUENTIAL ELIMINATION APPROACH

Whereas some psychologists, such as Tiedeman and Miller-Tiedeman, have sought to describe the human decision-making process, other psychologists have sought to describe the best method for making various decisions. These models focus on the way the individual may be guided toward logical and rational decision making. While the decision-making process is systematic, affective and intuitive aspects may also be incorporated. Psychologists such as Simon (1955), Slovic (1975), and Tversky (1972) have described a variety of decision-making models. Others, such as Mitchell (1975) and Mitchell and Beach (1976), have applied these models to career decision making. For example, Restle (1961) has described a general decision-making model in which an individual compares the immediate situation in which he or she is involved with several ideal situations. Zeleny (1976) and Zakay and Barak (1984) have applied this model to the career decision-making process. A model known as the *expected utility model* has been adapted to career decision making by Mitchell and Beach (1976). This model considers the probability that a certain outcome will occur if a particular career decision is made. It also considers the utility or importance of certain career criteria, for example, high income, security, and leisure time. These methods and others are reviewed by Brown (1990), and some are reviewed in an earlier article by Jepsen and Dilley (1974). Rather than compare several prescriptive models of career decision making, this section will focus on one for illustration.

The sequential elimination approach is an excellent example of a rational and prescriptive approach to career decision making. Using the work of Tversky (1972), Gati (1986) and Gati et al. (1995) have described the value

Table 14-1 *The Nine Steps Involved in the Sequential Elimination Approach*

Step 1	Define and structure the decision problem
Step 2	Identify relevant aspects
Step 3	Rank aspects by importance
Step 4	Identify optimal and acceptable levels
Step 5	Eliminate occupations incompatible with preferences
Step 6	Test sensitivity to changes in preferences
Step 7	Collect additional information
Step 8	Rank alternatives by overall desirability
Step 9	Outline steps to actualize the most preferred alternative

From "Applying Decision Theory to Career Counseling Practice: The Sequential Elimination Approach," by Itamar Gati, Naomi Fassa, and Daphna Houminer (1995), *Career Development Quarterly, 43,* p. 220.

of the sequential elimination approach in career decision making. This approach is particularly suitable for situations in which an individual must choose from many alternatives (for example, which college or university to apply to, which major to choose, or which job to enter after graduation). In general, the expected utility approach may be more suitable than the sequential elimination approach in situations where an individual needs to select from just a few well-defined alternatives. An analog study (Lichtenburg, Shaffer, & Arachtingi, 1993) compares relative features of the two approaches with 101 college students.

The major purpose of the sequential elimination approach is to identity a small set of career options that are compatible with the client's preferences. This goal is achieved by a gradual step-by-step elimination of alternatives that are incompatible with the client's preferences. When using the sequential elimination approach, the counselor has a specific plan of how he or she will proceed. For this approach to work, the counselor must be aware of the progress that the counselor and the client are making as they proceed through the model. Table 14-1 summarizes the steps to be followed. These are now described in more detail, with examples, (Gati et al., 1995).

Step 1: Defining and Structuring the Decision Problem

The beginning of the career decision-making process involves the definition of the decision problem, for example, "selecting a college," "choosing an occupation," or "choosing a major." Thus, it involves a universe of potential alternatives. Many clients may need help if they have difficulty in defining their problem. Because different framing of the same problem may lead, in certain cases, to different choices, an adequate framing (that is, not too narrow nor too broad) is important. For example, for a department manager who has been offered a similar job at another business, framing the problem as "deciding between staying in the present job and accepting the offer" (without considering additional potential alternatives) may be too narrow, whereas "deciding whether to consider a transition into a new occupation" may be too broad.

Step 2: Identifying Relevant Aspects

Since the goal of counseling in this situation is to arrive at a career choice by eliminating alternatives incompatible with the individual's preferences, the counselor and the client must first identify those aspects of an occupation that are most important to the client. These aspects may include correspondence to traits of an individual, such as interests, abilities, values, and personality. They also include important job characteristics such as salary, working conditions, nature of the work, and education required. A number of aspects may be important to an individual when discussing an occupation.

Gati (1986) suggests several different ways of helping clients identify aspects of educational or occupational alternatives that are important to them. One method is to discuss directly those aspects of an occupation that are most important to an individual. Another approach (as suggested by Zakay and Barak, 1984) is to ask an individual to imagine an ideal choice, such as an ideal occupation or ideal major, and then describe it. As the individual describes the occupation, the counselor notes the characteristics that are important. For example, they might include doing work that makes one feel important or feeling the satisfaction of helping small children. Another approach, which is more complex, is to get a list of occupational alternatives from the client (if he or she can provide such a list) and then determine which aspects these alternatives have in common. For example, if a student lists as possible occupational alternatives president of a company, physician, lawyer, and pilot, the counselor may suspect that high income is important to the client. A more formal approach is Cochran's (1983) career grid. Also, if the client leaves out important aspects that the counselor thinks should be included, the counselor can inquire whether the client should consider something that the client has not thought about. In the following example, the counselor helps the client to identify the relevant aspects of a career decision. The case of Alex will be used as an illustration throughout the remaining eight steps of the sequential elimination approach.

Alex is a 25-year-old man of Japanese parentage who moved to the United States when he was an infant. On completion of high school, Alex entered a two-year program to learn how to fix and maintain business equipment such as computers and copy machines. For the past four years he has worked as a repairperson for a business equipment firm in a small city. Work that was once challenging to him is now tedious. He finds himself getting impatient with customers whom he feels are ignorant of the equipment and abuse it. Further, he wonders if he will be doing the same work forever. Neither the pay nor the job responsibilities seem to increase very much. The excerpts from the dialogue with the counselor are ones that most closely illustrate the sequential elimination approach:

CO: You've told me several things that you don't like about what you're doing. Can you tell me more about what is important to you in your career?

CL: I really would like to have something that is a challenge. Problems that I can figure out and really think about. Problems where I can spend time developing something new and better. Not just having to clean up somebody's coffee in a copy machine.

CO: Tell me some of the other things that you look for in a job, that you'd like to have now. [As Alex talks, the counselor makes notes. She writes on her pad, "design, scientific, creativity." Then she continues to solicit more aspects from Alex.]

CL: When I was a kid, I was in a car accident with my parents. My left leg was pretty much smashed up. It never really was quite right. Sometimes, I have to carry equipment upstairs. I'm always walking from place to place on my job. At the end of the day, my leg can really hurt. I think I've had enough of this. I'd like to have something where I don't have to move as much as I do now and lift heavy stuff.

CO: That sounds as if it's getting to you. Work in a less physically demanding setting sounds really important to you. [The counselor establishes that this is an important aspect for Alex to consider.]

CL: The hours aren't so important, but the lifting is.

CO: Tell me more about what you'd like to do in those hours, Alex. [The counselor notes "enjoys working" and continues to find out more about Alex's interest.]

CL: I'd like to design things, anything—a toaster, an electric chair, a coffee machine that brought you coffee in the morning—anything.

CO: Have you ever done anything like that? [The counselor writes "designing electrical equipment" and proceeds to find out about Alex's experience and abilities.]

CL: When I was a kid, I wired an electric pencil sharpener at school so that it made ringing sounds. All I got for that was trouble. I am working now on a security system for my apartment.

The counselor continues to make notes about Alex's achievements and values. This information will be used in the next step.

Step 3: Ranking Aspects by Importance

Now that the aspects regarded as relevant have been identified, they have to be ranked according to their importance. The order and manner in which the client suggests the various aspects may reflect their importance to him or her. Some aspects will stand out as being of crucial importance, and others will be less so. Some aspects may be of equal importance. In the discussion with the counselor, Alex determines that several factors are important to him. The counselor shows Alex a list of aspects that she has used to summarize his values. The list includes not having to do any lifting, creativity, electrical design, inventing, salary, prestige, and working independently.

CO: Alex, how does that list look to you?

CL: Pretty good to me. It's important to me to be well thought of [prestige]. Sometimes, I feel as if my friends are passing me by. A lot of them have college educations; so does my brother. I wonder what people think of me.

CO: That sounds really important to you. More important than anything else? [The counselor tries to determine the relative importance of each of these aspects.]

CL: Well, it's really important, almost as important as not having to do any heavy work. But to go on to a more respected field, I have to have more education. I really feel that I would need an engineering degree. The math that I had in technical school was really easy. I don't know if I can handle the math in an engineering program.

CO: I'd like to hear more about your math experience. That sounds like an important factor to you. [Not having to do any lifting may be the most important factor to Alex. Math has been introduced as a new aspect to consider.]

CL: Yes, I really need to consider my math ability. I think it's pretty good, but I haven't had much chance to try it out or use it. I did do well on the SAT math test when I took it in high school.

CO: That sounds good. Is there a reason to think that that has changed? [The counselor wants to define more clearly this new relevant aspect so that it can be ranked.]

CL: No, I really don't think so. I think I do use math some in my work, but it's fairly low-level.

CO: As we look at the list of aspects—not having to do any lifting, being creative, electrical design, inventing, salary, math ability, prestige, and working independently—which seems most important to you? [The counselor believes that not having to do any lifting is most important but wants to check that out with the client.]

CL: Picking up things and moving them, particularly heavy things. I just can't do that anymore.

CO: What's next for you in order of importance?

CL: Being creative and inventive. I guess I see them as the same thing. That's really important to me.

The counselor continues to discuss the relevant aspects with Alex. Once all aspects have been ranked, the counselor moves to considering the aspects and eliminating some occupations that do not possess the important characteristics.

Step 4: Identifying the Acceptable Range for Each Aspect

At this point, the counselor proceeds one aspect at a time, beginning with the most important aspect, until a small set of occupational alternatives has been assembled. First, the characteristic levels of the aspect under consideration are identified. For some aspects, two levels are sufficient to represent the variations (for example, night-shift work is either required or it isn't required). To simplify, the different levels of these aspects can be divided into a few categories (for example, for income: less than $30,000, $30,000–$40,000, $40,000–$60,000, and more than $60,000).

The counselor then solicits from the client the most desirable or optimal level for the aspect under consideration. In the case of Alex, "no lifting of heavy objects" may be regarded as the preferred level. For income, it is often the category that represents the highest range of income. Then, the client is encouraged to compromise (Gati, 1993) and to identify additional levels still acceptable to him or her (for example, to consider the $40,000–$60,000 level acceptable as well). Sometimes, an acceptable range may be not at one end of the continuum or the other, but somewhere in the middle. For example, the decision to have a certain amount of variety in one's work, but not too much continual change, would be an example of selecting the midrange of as aspect. In Alex's case, the decision about the most important aspect and the range is simple for him. He wants work that does not require lifting.

Step 5: Eliminating Occupations

The most important aspects are considered first, followed by the next most important aspects. If an occupation does not meet the standard that has been agreed on in the previous step, it is eliminated. The process requires that the counselor have knowledge of occupational information and the requirements of many specific jobs.

The counselor has shown Alex a list of many occupations that includes technical, scientific, and engineering occupations. As they look at the list, Alex and the counselor determine that some scientific and engineering jobs would require lifting of samples; these are eliminated. Certain geology and engineering occupations are eliminated. In some cases, these are jobs within a specific occupational title. For example, some petroleum engineering careers may be appropriate, whereas others may not. When this has been done, Alex and the counselor can proceed to the next step.

Step 6: Testing Sensitivity to Changes in Preferences

After some alternatives have been identified, it is helpful to return to Step 2 to see if certain aspects are still desirable or undesirable. For example, Alex might be asked, "Are these situations in which salary may be less important to you than security?" or "You didn't say much before about the importance of having work that you could count on, where the probability of losing your job would be very small. Are there times when security may be important to you?" This reconsideration of aspects may help Alex have more confidence in his decision-making process. He may identify new aspects (Step2) or fine-tune his ranking of aspects (Step 3).

This step is also helpful in clarifying alternatives and reexamining those that may have previously been rejected in Step 4, identifying optimal and acceptable levels. Alex might be asked to reconsider an occupation such as teaching drafting, which may have been dropped because Alex considered the salary too low. It is particularly important to reexamine alternatives if the occupation is just below the client's level of acceptability (Step 4).

Gati (1993) considers the need to compromise or at least consider compromise an important factor in Step 6. Alex could be asked if there were situations where he could do some physical work, and under what conditions his leg would not hurt him. Discussing his physical condition in some detail would help to clarify his abilities as well as his fears of possibly hurting himself further.

Step 7: Collecting Additional Information

Now that alternatives have been developed, more information is often necessary so that fully informed decisions can be made. Although printed information such as that available in the *Occupational Outlook Handbook* is useful, other sources may also be valuable. Alex may talk to civil and electrical engineers that he has met when he has repaired office equipment. Also, he may discuss admissions requirements and engineering curricula with admissions officers at nearby colleges. For information about other colleges, he may send away for college catalogs. As he gets more information about engineering occupations and the variety of places where electrical and civil engineers work, he may decide to discuss difficulties with his leg with his physician.

Step 8: Ranking Alternatives by Overall Desirability

When the list is of the right length, the client may wish to explore further the different alternatives on his or her list. Drawing on the expected utility approach, Gati (1986) suggests that it is helpful to rank the various alternatives and to compare how well the aspects of one alternative match with those of another. This process is particularly helpful when it is difficult to be precise about the acceptability of certain aspects of an occupation. Using that portion of the expected utility model that emphasizes the probability of success and/or entry into an occupation is particularly helpful, as the sequential elimination approach does not deal directly with the probability of success.

Alex decides that his first choice is an electrical engineering program. If he is not admitted to an electrical engineering program, his second choice is a liberal arts curriculum with a math major and the possibility of changing to electrical engineering later. A third alternative is a college that offers an engineering program that students can enroll in after their second year of college.

Step 9: Outlining Steps to Actualize the Most Preferred Alternative

The last stage is the planning stage for achieving the first choice. The counselor and the client discuss several actions the client can take that will increase the client's chances of realizing her or his preference. For example, Alex decides to apply to several colleges for engineering for the fall. He also enrolls in a continuing-education math course taught in the evening over the summer at a community college. Additionally, he talks to former teachers as well as his employer about serving as references for his application to college.

In our example, Alex follows a very systematic and logical approach to career decision making. He supplies the information about his preferences. The counselor supplies the format for analysis and the information about his career options. The counselor may also hope that, by following this process, Alex will learn a new and useful system for decision making in general. The counselor hopes that Alex will be able to return to this method for small as well as larger career decisions, such as the choice of educational institution or of a specific job after graduation. Thus, the counselor uses this approach not only as a way to conceptualize career decision making, but also as a method to follow in teaching the client specific career decision-making skills.

COMPARISON OF THE INDIVIDUALISTIC AND THE SEQUENTIAL ELIMINATION APPROACH

Although Tiedeman and Miller-Tiedeman as well as Gati describe decision-making approaches, their points of view are opposite. Where the individualistic approach emphasizes the growth of individuals and the need to empower them to make decisions, the sequential elimination approach emphasizes the need to guide and teach an individual about career decision making. The counselor using the sequential elimination approach is much more directive and uses more questions than the individualistic counselor. Further, the individualistic counselor is able to deal with a number of issues indirectly related to career choice, such as Susan's concern about her mother's illness. It is also possible to bring such concerns into the sequential elimination approach by framing the decision problem differently, or by viewing such a concern as an additional aspect. Susan, for example, would have to describe being close to home so that she could be with her mother as an important aspect of her career choice. Divulging such a concern may feel awkward in such a systematic, counselor-directed approach unless efforts are made to include such concerns in the decision-making process.

The philosophical differences between these two approaches yield two counseling strategies that are in marked contrast to each other. Some counselors may be attracted to the logical, systematic, and easy-to-follow style of the sequential elimination approach, and some, by the more subjective and humanistic individualistic approach. In choosing an approach to career development counseling, a counselor should determine not only the ease of use of a theory, but also its appropriateness in assisting with immediate career decision making and long-range career adjustment.

THE ROLE OF OCCUPATIONAL INFORMATION

Both approaches discussed in this chapter see the need for occupational information in career decision making. Although the individualistic approach centers on the subjective experience of individuals and their need to be sensitive to their experience, this feeling cannot occur in a vacuum. Tiedeman and Miller-Tiedeman recognize the need for individuals to incorporate the world around them (occupational information) into their own experience. On the other hand, the sequential elimination approach specifically builds occupational information into the fourth and seventh steps of the process, when the client's preferences are compared to the characteristics of the occupations, and then again when additional information is collected. To eliminate occupations whose characteristics are not within the acceptable range for a particular aspect, a counselor must know how characteristics of individuals match a variety of occupations. Knowing the characteristics of an occupation that matches the counselee's preferences, such as description, interest, abilities required, and so forth, is important to a counselor using this method. The use of an occupational classification system such as that of Roe, Holland, or the *Dictionary of Occupational Titles* can help to organize occupational information for a counselor using the sequential elimination approach.

THE ROLE OF TESTING

Although testing is compatible with both the individualistic and the sequential elimination approach, the test used and the method of interpreting tests will be different. The individualistic approach emphasizes knowledge about self and the development of self-confidence. Use of values and personality inventories would be consistent with helping clients learn more about themselves and their innermost needs. On the other hand, interest inventories and ability tests are likely to be helpful to clients using the sequential elimination approach. In both approaches, it is necessary to determine which aspects of career choice are important to clients and how important each aspect is. Further, information on work values derived from testing could be particularly useful to people using the sequential elimination approach.

The method of test interpretation is likely to be quite different for each approach. The individualistic approach emphasizes the client's assimilation of relevant information into his or her sense of self, which can then be acted on in a meaningful way, On the other hand, a counselor using the sequential elimination approach is more likely to point out to the client how her or his interests, abilities, and values fit into important aspects of the career decision-making process.

APPLYING THE THEORIES TO WOMEN AND PEOPLE OF COLOR

In general, career decision-making theories do not offer different recommendations for women or people of color. The individualistic perspective is descriptive of career choice and focuses on the needs and inner feelings of the decision maker. The four phases of anticipation of a decision and the three phases of adjusting to a decision, as described by Tiedeman and O'Hara (1963), are viewed as phases that all people can go through in decision making. Tiedeman and Miller-Tiedeman recognize that the environmental constraints on women and people of color may be different from  those on white men, but the internal decision-making processes may be similar. For example, Leong (1991) suggests that Asian Americans are more likely to use a dependent style of decision making. Martin (1991) cautions that Native Americans living on reservations may have limited occupational information that can adversely affect their career decision making. These two studies are examples of how diverse cultural backgrounds affect career decision making.

The sequential elimination approach as described by Gati (1986) recommends a specific method of career decision making. The system is based on a logical model of career decision making that can be applied to all people. However, the actual implementation of the model may be different for various groups. For example, women may rank certain aspects as more important than men. Although some research has been done on predictive decision-making methods and the sequential elimination approach (Gati & Tikotzki, 1989), there has been little emphasis on the specific application of career decision-making theories, either descriptive or predictive, to women or people of color.

COUNSELOR ISSUES

When using the individualistic approach of Tiedeman and Miller-Tiedeman, counseling may revolve around the individual's internal decision-making processes. The counselor works with the client's personal reality, being careful not to introduce the common reality from the counselor's expert knowledge of career development theory. The counselor does not want to encumber the client with "shoulds" that will interfere with the client's making the decisions that are best for him or her. Furthermore, if the counselor's own personal decision-making reality is so strong that it interferes with the client's decision making, the counselor's role is limited. For example, if a counselor is preoccupied with just starting a new job (the induction phase of the adjustment stage of the Tiedeman and O'Hara paradigm), the counselor will be more concerned about his or her performance as a counselor and may have difficulty hearing the client's career decision-making concerns.

Since the counselor's role in the sequential elimination approach is a directive one, not unlike teaching, the counselor issues are quite different from those of the individualistic perspective. Because the sequential elimination method is structured, it is important not to lose relevant information in the decision-making process. Checking with the client to make sure that elements have not been left out of the process can be helpful. While the process of using a prescriptive approach is systematic, the client plays an active role in the process, so that the counselor may need to assess the client's involvement in it. Valuable information that the client has about aspects, such as parental pressure, should be incorporated during the sequential elimination process, as it may have an important role in career decision making. This method requires counselors to take an expert role in ways that other theories do not. In this case, however, the counselor is an expert because he or she has a specific system that is likely to work to help the client decide on a future occupation. As a result, the counselor is also likely to be seen as an expert on occupational information. The system may require more familiarity with job duties, educational requirements, working conditions, and such than many other theoretical approaches.

SUMMARY

Two types of career decision-making theories have been contrasted: a descriptive and a prescriptive theory. The individualistic perspective of Tiedeman and Miller-Tiedeman includes many aspects of career decision making that individuals are likely to experience. The cornerstone of their approach is the model of decision making described by Tiedeman and O'Hara (1963), which includes four phases of anticipation of a choice and three phases of adjustment. This model, which concentrates on the inner experience of the individual and the goal of empowering the client to make a choice, is in marked contrast to the prescriptive approach. In this chapter, the sequential elimination approach was used as an example of a logical, rational, prescriptive approach to career decision making. Based on a psychological decision-making model described by Tversky (1972), the sequential elimination approach emphasizes ranking the characteristics of occupations by importance, identifying the acceptable range of these characteristics, and then eliminating the occupations that fall within this range. The chapter has been concerned with the varying implications of descriptive and prescriptive approaches to career decision-making counseling.

References

Brown, D. (1990). Models of career decision making. In D. Brown, L. Brooks, & Assoc. (Eds.), *Career choice and development: Applying contemporary theories to practice* (2nd. ed., pp. 395–421). San Francisco: Jossey-Bass.

Buck, J. N., & Daniels, M. H. (1985). *Assessment of Career Decision-Making manual.* Los Angeles: Western Psychological Services.

Cochran, L. (1983). Implicit versus explicit importance of career values in making a career decision. *Journal of Counseling Psychology, 30,* 188–193.

Dinklage, L. B. (1968). *Decision strategies of adolescents.* Unpublished doctoral dissertation: Harvard University: Cambridge.

Erikson, E. H. (1959). Identity and the life cycle. *Psychological Issues: 1* (Whole Issue).

Gati, I. (1986). Making career decisions—a sequential elimination approach. *Journal of Counseling Psychology, 33,* 408–417.

Gati, I. (1993). Career compromises. *Journal of Counseling Psychology, 40,* 416–424.

Gati, I., Fassa, N., & Houminer, D. (1995). Applying decision theory to career counseling practice: The sequential elimination approach. *Career Development Quarterly, 43,* 211–220.

Gati, I., & Tikotzki, Y. (1989). Strategies for collection and processing of occupational information in making career decisions. *Journal of Counseling Psychology, 36,* 430–439.

Ginzberg, E., Ginsburg, S. W., Axelrad, S., & Herma, J. (1951). *Occupational choice: An approach to a general theory.* New York: Columbia University Press.

Graves, C. W. (1974). Human nature prepares for a momentous leap. *Futurist, 8,* 72–85.

Harren, V. A. (1979). A model of career decision making for college students. *Journal of Vocational Behavior, 14,* 119–133.

Hsu, C. C. (1970). A conceptual model of vocational decision making. *Experimental Publication System, 8,* 270–276.

Jepsen, D. A., & Dilley, J. S. (1974). Vocational decision-making models: A review and comparative analysis. *Review of Educational Research, 44,* 331–349.

Jepsen, D. A., & Grove, W. M. (1981). Stage order and dominance in adolescent decision-making processes: An empirical test of the Tiedeman-O'Hara paradigm. *Journal of Vocational Behavior, 18,* 237–251.

Katz, M. R. (1963). *Decisions and values: A rationale for secondary school guidance.* New York: College Entrance Examination Board.

Leong, F. T. L. (1991). Career development attributes and occupational values of Asian American and White American college students. *Career Development Quarterly, 39,* 221–230.

Lichtenburg, J. W., Shaffer, M., & Arachtingi, B. M. (1993). Expected utility and sequential elimination models of career decision making. *Journal of Vocational Behavior, 42,* 237–252.

Loevinger, J., Wessler, R., & Redmore, C. (1970). *Measuring ego development* (2 vols.). San Francisco: Jossey-Bass.

Martin, W. E. (1991). Career development and American Indians living on reservations: Cross-cultural factors to consider. *Career Development Quarterly, 39,* 237–283.

Miller-Tiedeman, A. L. (1977). Structuring responsibility in adolescents: Actualizing "I" power through curriculum. In G. D. Miller (Ed.), *Developmental theory and its application in guidance programs: Systematic efforts to promote personal growth* (pp. 123–166). Minneapolis: Minnesota Department of Education.

Miller-Tiedeman, A. L. (1988). *LIFECAREER: The quantum leap into a process theory of career.* Vista, CA: Lifecareer Foundation.

Miller-Tiedeman, A. L. (1989). *How NOT to make it . . . and succeed: Life on your own terms.* Vista, CA: Lifecareer Foundation.

Miller-Tiedeman, A. L., & Tiedeman, D. V. (1990). Career decision making: An individualistic perspective. In D. Brown, L. Brooks, & Assoc. (Eds.), *Career choice and development: Applying contemporary theories to practice* (2nd ed., pp. 308–337). San Francisco: Jossey-Bass.

Mitchell, T. R., & Beach, L. R. (1976). A review of occupational preference and choice research using expectancy theory and decision theory. *Journal of Occupational Psychology, 49,* 231–248.

Mitchell, W. D. (1975). Restle's choice model: A reconceptualization for a special case. *Journal of Vocational Behavior, 6,* 315–330.

Osipow, S. H. (1987). *Career Decision Scale Manual.* Odessa, FL: Psychology Assessment Resources.

Restle, F. (1961). *Psychology of judgment and choice.* New York: Wiley.

Savickas, M. L., & Jarjoura, D. (1991). The Career Decision Scale as a type indicator. *Journal of Counseling Psychology, 38,* 85–90.

Simon, H. A. (1955). A behavioral model of rational choice. *Quarterly Journal of Economics. 49,* 99–118.

Slovic, P. (1975). Choice between equally valued alternatives. *Journal of Experimental Psychology: Human Perception and Performance, 1,* 280–387.

Super, D. E. (1957). *The psychology of careers.* New York: Harper & Row.

Tiedeman, D. V. (1979). *Career development: Designing our career machines.* Schenectady, NY: Character Research Press.

Tiedeman, D. V. (1992). Yes . . . but . . . , and . . . , so? Comments on Callanan and Greenhaus (1992). *Journal of Vocational Behavior, 41,* 232–238.

Tiedeman D. V., & Miller-Tiedeman, A. L. (1979). Choice and decision processes and career revisited. In A. M. Mitchell, G. B. Jones, & J. D. Krumboltz (Eds.), *Social learning and career decision making* (pp. 160–179). Cranston, RI: Carroll Press.

Tiedeman, D. V., & O'Hara, R. P. (1963). *Career development: Choice and adjustment.* New York: College Entrance Examination Board.

Tversky, A. (1972). Elimination by aspects: A theory of choice. *Psychology Review, 79,* 281–290.

Vroom, V. H. (1964). *Work and motivation.* New York: Wiley.

Wanous, J. P., Keon, T. L., & Latack, J. C. (1983). Expectancy theory and occupational choices: A review and test. *Organizational Behavior and Human Performance, 32,* 66–86.

White, R. W. (1952). *Lives in progress.* New York: Holt, Rinehart & Winston.

Wilson, E. H. (1971). *The development and potential testing of a system for the teaching of decision making.* Unpublished doctoral dissertation, Harvard University, Cambridge.

Zakay, D., & Barak, A. (1984). Meaning and career decision making. *Journal of Vocational Behavior, 24,* 1–14.

Zeleny, M. (1976). The attribute-dynamic model. *Management Sciences, 11,* 13–25.

15

The Labor Market: Sociological and Economic Perspectives

Counselors must not only help clients assess interests, personality, values, and abilities but also have information about occupations and the labor market. In this chapter, an overview of the labor market is given that includes the trends of growth in industries and occupations as well as information about the value of education. The fields of sociology and economics study various aspects of the labor market as well as specific occupations. This research provides insights that go beyond the compilation of data. As a result of research, some models or theories have been developed that point out inequities or obstacles in the labor market that may affect the earnings or success of different individuals. When thinking about the United States labor market (and the markets of some other countries), individuals have often held the view "Each person has an equal opportunity to succeed or fail on his or her own." Often, this assumption is oversimplified and false. A number of factors are beyond the control of individuals that may affect their eventual career choice and success. Being in the right place at the right time is a fortunate accident that may lead to exposure to a new occupation or a job offer. Losing out to another individual when applying for a job or a promotion may have a significant impact on individuals' lives. Furthermore, being taught to value an education and having consistent helpful parenting and financial support to pay for schooling occur in some people's lives, but not in others'. Discrimination because of sex or race is another variable that greatly affects individuals' career choices and financial and personal success. After describing some basic facts about the United States labor market, we will examine each of these factors as they influence how individuals deal with the labor market.

THE UNITED STATES LABOR MARKET

A labor market, basically, serves to fulfill the needs of citizens of a state, a nation, or the world. Job availability is related to the demand of individuals for food, shelter, clothing, health services, transportation, entertainment, fire and police protection, and so forth. The information about the

Table 15-1 *Employment (in Thousands) in Broad Occupational Groups, 1992 and Projected Change, 1992–2005*

Occupational Group	*1992 Employment*	*1992–2005 Percentage Change*
Total, all occupations	121,099	21.8
Executive, administrative, and managerial	12,066	25.9
Professional specialty	16,592	37.4
Technicians and related support	4,282	32.3
Marketing and sales	12,993	20.6
Administrative support, including clerical	22,349	13.7
Services	19,358	33.4
Agriculture, forestry, and fishing	3,530	3.4
Precision production, craft, and repair	13,580	13.3
Operators, fabricators, and laborers	16,349	9.5

From *Career Guide to Industries,* U.S. Department of Labor, Bureau of Labor Statistics, Washington, DC (1994), p. 5.

United States labor market in Table 15-1 describes the broad occupational groups in which individuals were employed in 1992 and their predicted growth. Employment growth is also shown in Table 15-1, with services being the group that is likely to grow the most.

Examining growth by industry, Figure 15-1 also shows that the greatest growth is in the service area. Included in this area are health, business, education, social, engineering, and other services. Over the last 75 years, there has been a marked change in the United States, with a gradual movement from manufacturing, agricultural, and mining industries to an increased demand for workers in service industries. Much of this change is due to technological efficiencies in goods-producing industries. Modernization in farming, from horse-drawn ploughs to large tractors and combines, is an example of why growth in this industry has been declining for many years and is just now starting to improve slightly. The automobile industry, with its use of robotic arms and computer technology, is another example of how technological change can slow employment growth in an industry.

Much growth in the United States to 2005 is projected to occur in occupations that do not require a college education. As Figure 15-2 shows, eight of the 10 occupations with the most projected growth require a high school education or less. Only registered nurses (second) and systems analysts (tenth) usually have a four-year bachelor's degree. Occupations such as janitor, salesperson, and cashier often have high turnover. Individuals leave them for a variety of reasons: to find a better-paying job, to return to school, to care for children, and so forth. Thus, growth reflects the need to replace these workers as well as new positions ("The American Work Force," 1993). The 30 occupations listed in Figure 15-2 represent over half of the

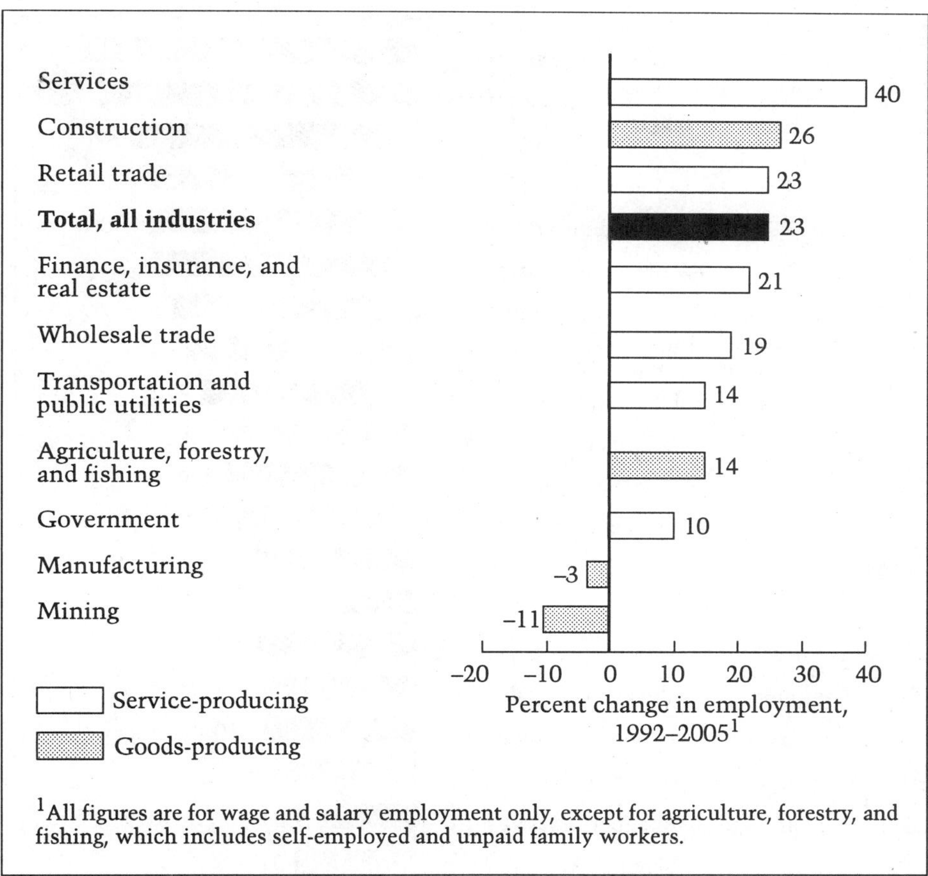

Figure 15-1. Projected growth in industries, 1992–2005. (From *Occupational Outlook Handbook,* U.S. Department of Labor, Bureau of Labor Statistics, Washington, DC, 1994, p. 14.)

projected total employment growth of occupations in the United States; the other 475 occupations surveyed by the Bureau of Labor Statistics represent the other half. Many of the jobs that are listed in Figure 15-2 have low earnings, a factor related to having high replacement needs.

Clearly, the amount of education is closely related to income. Figure 15-3 shows the vast differences in annual salary in 1992 between those without a high school education ($12,809) and those with a doctorate ($54,904) or professional degree ($74,560), such as in law or medicine. In fact, the value of an education has been growing, not declining. In 1992, the estimate of the earnings of high school graduates was 2.5 times higher than in 1975. For those with a bachelor's degree the ratio was almost 3 times higher than it was in 1975. These data emphatically point out the economic value of an education (Chart: Education,1995).

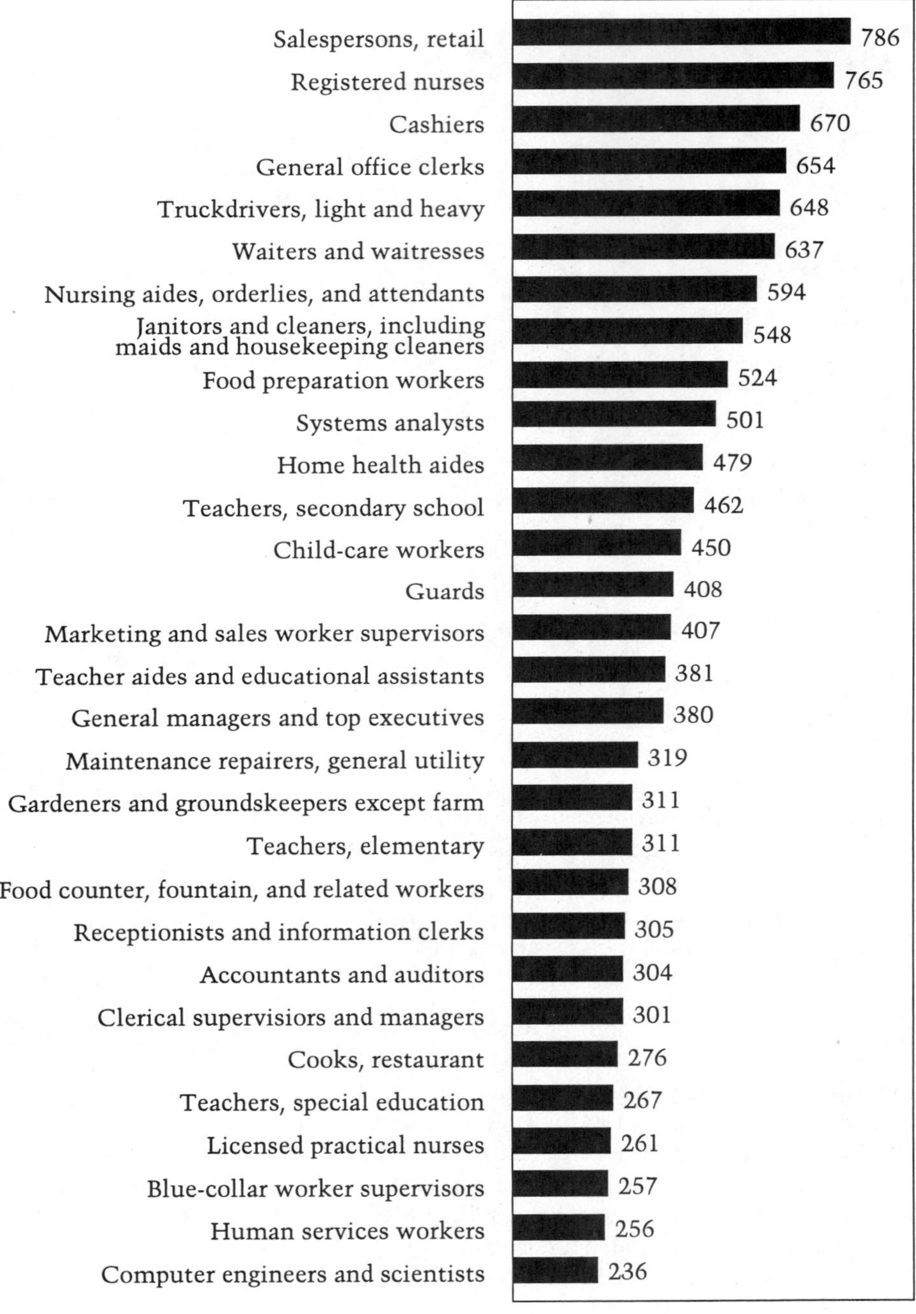

Figure 15-2 Numerical growth by occupation (in thousands), projected for 1992-2005. (From *Occupational Outlook Quarterly,* U.S. Department of Labor, Washington, DC, 1993, p. 39.)

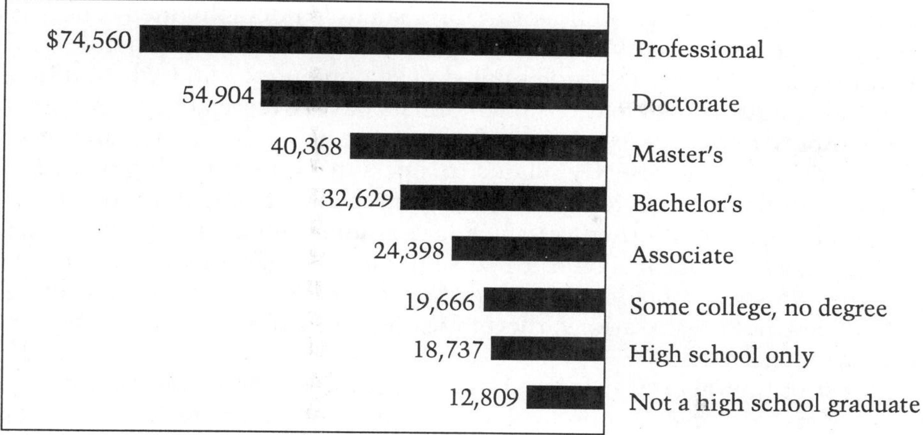

Figure 15-3 Mean annual earnings for people age 18 and over, by highest level of education, 1992. (From *Occupational Outlook Quarterly,* U.S. Department of Commerce, Bureau of the Census, Washington, DC, 1995, p. 52.)

In this brief overview of the United States labor market, only the most important features are mentioned. In general, there is considerable predicted growth for occupations that require technical skills such as systems analysts and registered nurses. However, there will also be a great need for service workers such as retail sales persons, cashiers, and clerks. Salary continues to be greatly affected by the type and amount of education that individuals have. More information on the employment of women and people of color is presented later in the chapter. More information about local labor markets can be obtained from State Occupational Information Coordinating Committees. With so much information available to counselors from so many sources, it is important to present only highly relevant information to clients, so they will not be overwhelmed by the data.

SOCIOLOGICAL AND ECONOMIC APPROACHES

Whereas psychology is primarily concerned with the study of individual behavior, sociology and economics emphasize the study of social organizations. All other chapters in this book are concerned with how individuals make career choices and decisions or adjust to career circumstances. Sociologists and economists approach the question of career choice from an entirely different perspective. Sociologists study the development, organization, and operation of human society. Economists study the production, distribution, and consumption of goods and services. More specifically, sociologists have examined family, cultural, and other social factors that predict career choice as well as variables such as unemployment and pay distributions by industry. In addition, they have studied the patterns of customs, interactions, and professional development of hundreds of different legal and illegal occupations. Economists have investigated factors such as unemployment, pay distribution by industry, job title, gender, and race, which are all factors directly related to a person's career development. For both economists and sociologists, ability, interests, values, and career decision making, among other variables, are studied when trying to predict labor market or work behavior. Because the focus of sociologists and economists is on social organizations and the focus of counselors is counseling individuals, not organizations, the application of sociological and economic theories is indirect.

Most of the theories discussed in this chapter are based on the work of sociologists. However, economists influenced the development of some of these theories, particularly when pay rates or income level has been a focus. One of the earliest theories related to career choice to be proposed by sociologists (Miller & Form, 1951) is called *accident theory.* This theory suggests that individuals make career choices based on chance opportunities, for example, applying for a job at a firm when an opening has just occurred because an employee quit. Another example would be reading a magazine article about a manufacturing process that an individual finds fascinating; the person then returns to school to develop her or his skills further.

In general, psychologists examine how the individual shapes and alters the environment through job choice or work adjustment. In contrast, several sociologists and economists have suggested ways in which the workplace changes the individual. This different frame of reference provides new insights into both the worker and the workplace.

Several theories have been the subject of a large number of research investigations. A theory that has prompted study by many sociologists is the status attainment model, which predicts the prestige level of a person's job from an individual's social (particularly family) background. The primary economic theory related to career development is human capital theory. Human capital theory suggests that individuals invest in their own education and training in order to achieve a higher-paying job with more prestige. Criticism of this model has led to the development of a dualistic theory of labor markets: primary and secondary. In the primary labor market, work is steady, organizations are large, and a prospect of promotion exists. In contrast, the secondary labor market is made up of low-paying jobs that offer little chance of advancement.

Related to status attainment and human capital theory is the study of the organizational and societal treatment of women and people of color, which critiques and elaborates on these theories. Much research has documented that women and people of color hold different types of jobs from white males, are paid less, and have less chance of advancement. Although these theories and the resulting research do not provide a method of conceptualizing career counseling, they do yield insights into the world of work that a counselor can apply in both career choice and work adjustment counseling.

ACCIDENT THEORY

Most psychological theories of career development do not consider chance an important factor because psychologists prefer to emphasize the control that an individual has in choosing among educational and occupational alternatives. However, sociologists (Caplow, 1954) have long recognized the importance of factors external to an individual that affect career choice. Writing about accident theory, Bandura (1982), a psychologist, has integrated chance encounters into a theory of social learning. Although accidents cannot be predicted, Bandura believes that the impact they have on an individual may be predicted. Furthermore, chance encounters may play a critical role in determining the course of one's life. In the United States, marriage partners rarely meet by plan; they are more likely to meet by accident—at a dance, in a supermarket, or in a classroom. Such meetings have a profound effect on the course of one's life. Also, one's encounter with an inspiring teacher, a volunteer project, or an interesting task during a summer job may clearly influence the direction of future events. How an individual deals with such events depends on her or his sense of self-efficacy, developed competencies, and task-approach skills (Bandura, 1982). Furthermore, how individuals react depends on the learning that they have acquired through modeling and reinforcement (Bandura, 1977). From another point of view, Cabral and Salomone (1990) state that a strong self-concept and a sense of internal control help an individual cope successfully with chance events. Dealing with chance encounters depends on prior experience and may be predictable, although chance encounters themselves are not predictable. The role of chance in work has been studied as it pertains to both adolescents and adults.

Much research on adolescents has been concerned with the types of work that high school students do. Adolescents often take stereotyped, common jobs: fast-food worker, gas station attendant, retail clerk, babysitter, and gardener (Osterman, 1980). As Riche, Hecker, and Burgin (1983) suggest, such employment will always be abundant. As shown in Figure 15-2 on page 394, the greatest amount of growth in adult jobs will be in relatively unskilled occupations such as driving a truck, waiting on tables, and being a cashier. High-technology and glamorous jobs may appeal to adolescents, when the reality is that the lower-level service jobs dominate the employment possibilities (Grubb, 1984). Thus, work during high school may present problems for adolescents.

Sociologists have paid particular attention to youth of low socioeconomic status. Osterman (1989) found that jobs for low socioeconomic adolescents are acquired by chance encounters, such as openings in the neighborhood. Referrals are made by friends or parents to a job that they happen to know about. The adolescents whom Osterman studied were more interested in adventure seeking, sex, and peer-group activities than in work. Osterman referred to the ages of 18 to 25, when many adolescents are not concerned with their career, as a moratorium. After this time, unemployment becomes less frequent, and the length of time on a job increases. This pattern is consistent with the findings of Kett (1982) and Richter (1994), whose reports confirm the notion of a moratorium. This is a time when conscious planning may not occur and chance factors may predominate. Whereas Osterman studied males, Werner (1989) studied both females and males. In a study in Hawaii, she found that adolescent women who did not go to college had a shorter period of moratorium than did men. Many of the women made early commitments to both work and family. Studying 2,954 white youth, Koenigsberg, Garet, and Rosenbaum (1994) found that young women with children who enter the labor force considered parenting, rather than providing financially for their family, their major responsibility, whereas young men with children reported the opposite. In many of these studies, chance was a major factor in the selection of work by both men and women.

In research on adults, the role of chance is less clear. For example, Hart, Rayner, and Christensen (1971) found that advance preparation is important for individuals who entered professional or skilled occupations. Chance played a greater role for persons entering unskilled work. In another study, Salomone and Slaney (1981) studied both male and female nonprofessional workers. They concluded that interests, needs, and skills were more important than chance in career decision making, a contrast to the findings of Hart et al. (1971). Studying women 25 years after their graduation from college, Scott and Hatalla (1990) concluded that their awareness of their abilities and interests were more important than chance factors in determining their career patterns. One implication to be drawn from the above research is that chance may play a greater role than other factors when individuals are not able to, or choose not to, consider factors such as their abilities, interests, and values.

For the counselor, chance encounters present a challenge. When an individual makes a career decision without planning or foresight, the opportunity for input by family or counselors is lost. The problem for the counselor is to identify those individuals who can profit from career counseling. In addition, Osterman (1995) stresses the importance of staying in school longer and, if possible, seeking two or more years of post-high-school education. Most of the theories that are discussed in this book provide methods of helping individuals. Super's theory of career development deals with career maturity and its relevance to adolescent career decision making (see Chapter 8, "Adolescent Career Development"). Furthermore, the career decision-making theories and the social learning theory of Krumboltz (see Chapters 13 and 14) are relevant to helping adolescent youth make career-planning decisions. Bandura (1982) emphasizes teaching communications and networking skills, which will help clients make good use of chance events. The research discussed earlier that demonstrates the impact of chance on adolescent career decision making shows the need for planning in addition to taking advantage of and creating positive opportunities.

However, some events cannot be planned. When adults encounter chance experiences that create job crises or transitions, they may find themselves in an extremely stressful situation. For example, a person may be in an automobile accident, a business may go bankrupt, or a plant may be flooded. When such an event happens, an individual may experience a career crisis. Methods for understanding and dealing with such problems are discussed in Chapter 10, "Adult Career Crises and Transitions."

THE EFFECT OF THE WORK ENVIRONMENT ON THE INDIVIDUAL

Just as an individual has an effect on his or her work—for example, producing a good performance or performing effectively—so does the work have an effect on the individual. The impact of the work on the individual has been the focus of two lines of research. Kohn and Schooler (1983) have studied the effect that work and the individual have on each other. Rosenbaum (1976, 1989) has suggested a tournament approach to understanding the impact of the organization on the individual: There are winners and losers in organizational competition for promotion. Both winners and losers are affected by the organizational environment. These two sociological approaches to career development are discussed further in the following paragraphs.

The work of Kohn and his colleagues shows that having an unchallenging job may lead to a loss of intellectual skills (Mainquist & Eichorn, 1989). Kohn and Schooler (1978) studied "substantive complexity," which they defined as "the degree to which the work requires thought and independent judgment" (p. 30). They found that the intellectual demands of a job had influenced workers' intellectual ability more than workers' ability had affected how they approached their work. In a follow-up study, Kohn and Schooler (1982) found that job conditions affect an individual's psychological functioning more than an individual's psychological functioning affects his or her job. Studies by Mortimer and Lorence (1979a, 1979b) found that autonomy at work had a positive effect on the individual's self-concept. Mortimer and Lorence used professional men, while Kohn and Schooler used a more representative sample of men. Using a sample of women, Miller, Schooler, Kohn, and Miller (1979) found results that were consistent with Kohn and Schooler's stress on the effect that the work has on the individual. The following example will illustrate the effects of work on an individual.

For four years, Pedro has worked in a factory, where he has assembled computer hardware. He has been promoted to a supervisor's job. This assignment requires that he use writing and mathematical skills that he has not used since high school graduation. As a result, his reading ability has improved. His job requires independent decision making based on reading manuals and talking to workers. At work, he must improve on skills that he has not used since high school. In a sense, the demands of Pedro's job require that he become more intelligent. He had to struggle at first to improve his math and writing skills. Not all organizations provide individuals such opportunities to develop their skills.

Some organizations make it difficult for individuals to develop skills because unknown or arbitrary rules keep individuals from advancement. The tournament system of Rosenbaum (1989) illustrates how an organizational system may affect individuals. In tournaments the best candidates are chosen for positions through a series of selective competitions. Much as in a tennis tournament, the winners advance to the next round: the losers stop competing in that tournament but may decide to enter another tournament. However, there is a significant difference between Rosenbaum's career system tournament and a tennis tournament. Rosenbaum's tournament is like a tennis tournament without rules. For example, imagine a tennis tournament where the rules for each match are different; the players don't know how many sets they will need to win a match or how many players they will have to face to win the tournament. Rosenbaum believes that individuals often do not know the organizational rules that will result in promotion or in getting a job. Early selection in a career for specific positions may determine how far and where an individual will rise on the corporate ladder. For example, failure to obtain promotion early in a career may affect an individual's entire career by limiting job promotion possibilities (Rosenbaum, 1984; Forbes, 1987). Rosenbaum (1984) also found a bias toward promoting younger employees; those over 40 are often at a marked disadvantage. These findings can be considered "rules" that employees may not know. Rosenbaum recognizes that the tournament model does not apply to all systems. For example, there are job ladders on which everyone is promoted and caste systems in which no one can be promoted. Further, there are situations such as door-to-door sales where past success is not related to future success. In general, tournaments are more likely to be found in large organizations, where there are many people competing for positions and there are a variety of career options. The tournament concept points out the impact that the environment has on the individual.

Rosenbaum (1976) has also applied his theory to the tracking of students in the educational system. As Osterman's (1989) research suggests, students who drop out of school or enter dead-end jobs are making decisions that will affect their later decisions. In a sense, they have lost in the early rounds of a tournament and will have difficulty finding tournaments that are likely to lead to high income or job satisfaction.

The research just cited suggests several factors that may interfere with individual choice. In the example below, Paul, a 35-year-old white male truck driver, is discussing his job dissatisfaction with a counselor. Paul is married, has no children, and has not completed high school. Through discussion, Paul realizes the effect that his work is having on him:

CL: I've been driving now for three years for a large trucking company. I got into it by working with my brother-in-law some. He owns his own truck, and sometimes I'd help him out by driving for him. I didn't mind it then, but it's not right for me now. I don't like it.

CO: Can you tell me more about it? [The counselor wants to learn more about Paul's response to his environmental conditions.]

CL: Well, I'm kind of confused. I was working in an auto plant for two years. Then I got laid off. I thought truck driving would be good—sitting, driving, listening to the radio. It's not that way.

CO: What way is it, Paul? [Again, the counselor wants to hear more about Paul's work environment.]

CL: Part of it's the boredom. I'm driving a trailer truck on the highway for thousands of miles. Just more and more roads. It makes me so depressed. When I get home, I'm down; I snap at my wife. She notices the difference. She says that I'm different since I took this job.

CO: That boredom is taking a toll on you. [Paul has changed because of his work. He is sad; there is a feeling of hopelessness.]

CL: It's not as if this job will go anywhere. [Smiling] Yes, I know I go everywhere all the time. That's not what I mean. I could be doing this for the rest of my life. I have no sense that I'll get anywhere. I sure didn't think about it much when I left school in the tenth grade. I had no idea I could be like this. I was pretty carefree back then.

CO: You're not carefree now.

CL: No. When I was in school, I wanted to get out of school. Now, I want to learn. I feel dumber than I ever have in my life.

The counselor notes that Paul is being deeply affected by his job environment. Paul has become upset that his intellectual functioning is not improving, and he is tense. From Kohn's point of view, he is losing intellectual capabilities because of the lack of intellectual demands of his work. Furthermore, because of Paul's education and his job choice, he is in an environment where he has, in Rosenbaum's sense, lost the tournament. To receive more training or schooling may put him into a tournament that he can win. By focusing on the effect that Paul's job has on him, the counselor can look for ways in which Paul can change, or perhaps for ways in which the job can change.

STATUS ATTAINMENT THEORY

Status attainment theory concerns issues regarding the relative role of achievement and social status in influencing occupational selection. Most research on status attainment theory has been on intergenerational change, sometimes called vertical mobility and has focused on predicting an individual's occupational role from the father's occupations. Of particular note is the early work by Blau (1956) and Blau and Duncan (1967). They, along with other researchers, found that they could predict the socioeconomic status of an individual's first job, which would then predict a current job, from the father's occupation and education. As Campbell (1983) reports, more than 500 papers were written to extend or dispute research done by Sewell, Haller, and Portes (1969) and Sewell, Haller, and Ohlendorf (1970) on status attainment theory.

As research continues on the status attainment model, it becomes more and more complex. A basic overview of status attainment theory is provided by Hotchkiss and Borow (1990) and will be followed in this discussion. Figure 15-4 outlines the path of prediction leading from variables concerning family status and cognitive functioning to the eventual prediction of occupational attainment. Family status includes the father's occupational and socioeconomic status, income, and education. Occupational status is determined by measures of prestige assessed both in the United States and throughout the world (Fredrickson, Lin, & Xing, 1992). A second group of variables measures educational performance (e.g., aptitude tests and school grades). These variables affect social-psychological processes, which include the educational and occupational aspirations of adolescents, the amount of parental and teacher encouragement to attend college, and peers' plans to attend college. These social-psychological processes then act to predict educational attainment, which is measured by the number of years of schooling. The number of years of schooling then leads to the prediction of occupational attainment measured by the status or prestige levels of the career. The statistical processes used to come to these conclusions are known as *path analysis,* a method by which variables are graphed so as to indicate their causal effect on each other (Babbie, 1973). Wilson (1989) emphasizes the influence that an adolescent's view of his or her future has on persistence in school: "Staying [in school] is the strongest known determinant of subsequent career" (p. 71).

An area that has received a considerable amount of recent attention is family influences on career choice and occupational status. Ma and Smith (1993) found that, in Taiwan, the effect of education on parental values was greater than the effect of social class for 1,210 employed married adults. Studying the educational plans of ninth-grade students, Hossler and Stage (1992) reported that parental educational expectations had a stronger influence than did the parents' level of education, student achievement, or student involvement in school activities. Examining family functioning,

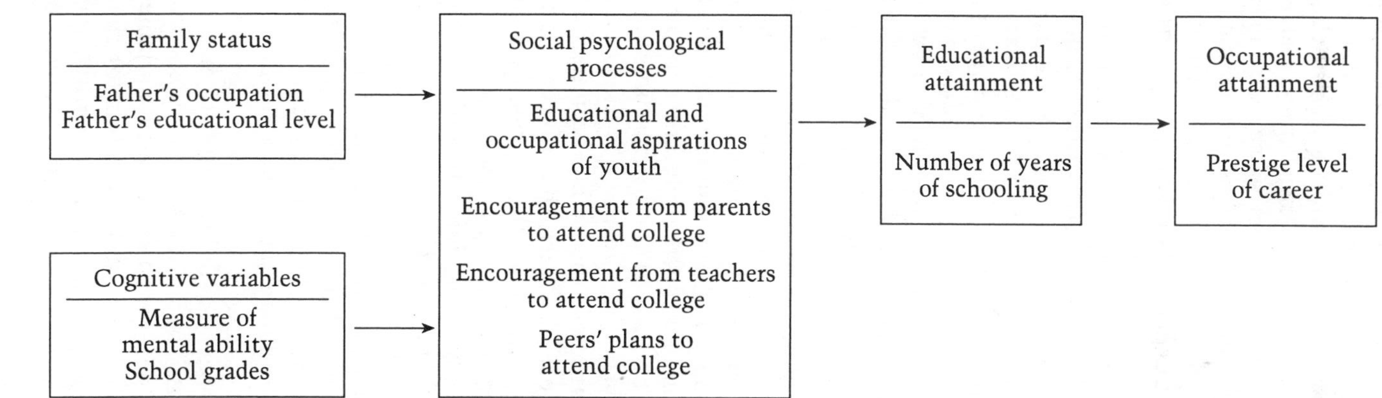

Figure 15-4 Abridged outline of an early version of the Wisconsin model of status attainment. (From "Sociological Perspectives on Work and Career Development," by L. Hotchkiss and H. Borow, in *Career Choice and Development*, 2nd ed., by D. Brown, L. Brooks, and Assoc. Copyright 1990 by Jossey-Bass, Inc. Reprinted by permission.)

Biblarz and Raftery (1993) found that divorce and separation increase the probability that individuals will be in the lowest-status jobs rather than the highest. Similarly, Li and Wotjkiewicz (1992) showed that living in a mother-only or mother-stepfather family lowers a child's socioeconomic attainment. From another point of view, Penick and Jepsen (1992) found that eleventh-graders' and their parents' perceptions of how well their family functioned predicted career choice more powerfully than the gender, socioeconomic status, and educational achievement of the student. These studies point out the influence of family expectations and functioning on the career plans and concerns of young people.

Race has also been studied as a factor in status attainment theory. Studying 76 high-level black executives, Collins (1993) reported that their high level of attainment was due to employment practices that were affected by the politics of race rather than deracialization in the labor market, suggesting that employers may have hired them because they were required to hire blacks based on corporate policy, not because the firms were fully integrated. Examining the role of high school sports participation, Sabo, Melnick, and Vanfossen (1993) found that it affected the college plans and educational expectations of white males but had little impact on the plans of black males or females. Such studies provide information about how cultural factors affect educational and occupational planning.

Even though much work has been done on the status attainment model, variables related to school performance, as well as others, still need to be researched. More recently, researchers such as Hachen (1990) have focused on the prediction of a specific job rather than occupational attainment or status. In part, because of the interest in the prediction of attainment within an organization, this research is likely to continue.

Although status attainment theory has been useful in predicting occupational attainment, it has also been the subject of criticism. Sonnenfeld (1989) states that status attainment theory has been unable to adequately explain later status changes once an individual has begun employment. He criticizes status attainment theory for failing to use recent data and for not looking at changes in occupational status within a career. Further, status attainment theory has not paid attention to changing social values that have led to less agreement on the definition of a successful career. Most important, he believes that status within a firm should be measured, rather than occupational attainment. These comments notwithstanding, status attainment theory is relevant to career decision making and work adjustment counseling.

Status attainment theory calls attention to important variables that psychological theories tend to omit. Of the theorists discussed in this book, only Gottfredson (1981) deals with sociological variables in career development theory. The variables that status attainment theory emphasizes are the importance of prestige, the status of the family, and encouragement to seek higher education. Although the United States is considered a land of equal opportunity, status attainment theory says that, in reality, one's occupational position is determined to a great extent by one's family's status (and more specifically, one's father's status). This knowledge may help a counselor who is working with a client from a low socioeconomic background think about some of the factors that are necessary for the client to attain an occupation that is much higher in status than that of his or her family. As shown previously, one of the factors related to status is lack of parental encouragement to succeed. Adolescents from a low socioeconomic background may lack parental, peer, and teacher encouragement to seek higher education (Hotchkiss & Borow, 1990). Furthermore, this background may inhibit accurate occupational aspirations.

The challenge for the counselor is to provide support and information that will help a client counter sociological processes that may interfere with making full use of her or his intellectual abilities. Status attainment theory does not say how to do this. Rather, status attainment theory underscores the importance of making special efforts to open to clients areas of the labor market that they may otherwise have considered closed. An example of a counselor dealing with an individual from a low socioeconomic background is given next.

Betty is a 15-year-old black high school sophomore, living in Chicago. Her mother is unmarried and works for a large industrial cleaning firm in the downtown section of Chicago. Betty has two younger sisters who are still in school. Her older sister is enrolled in a nursing program. Betty has been working after school for a fast-food chain. Now, as she approaches the age of 16, she is considering dropping out of school and working full time for the restaurant. In this brief excerpt, she is discussing her plans with her guidance counselor:

CL: Since I've been working at this job, I've finally been able to buy some of the clothes that I always wanted. My mother needs some of the money, too, so she takes some.

CO: Sounds as if that's made you feel useful. [The counselor comments on Betty's sense of productivity.]

CL: Yeah, feels like I'm doing something that makes sense with my life, not just sitting around in school reading stuff that seems boring.

CO: School doesn't make sense to you? [The counselor wants to challenge Betty's sweeping view of school.]

CL: Well, I guess it does. I have learned to read pretty much. I've gotten "A"s and "B"s. I thought everybody learned to read. Some of the kids I work with can barely write their names. They can hardly read the menus.

CO: Does that limit what they can do? [The counselor wants Betty to assess her own view of the relationship between schooling and advancement.]

CL: It sure does. It looks as if they'll never make more than five or six dollars an hour at that rate.

CO: How much do you think you can make at this job? [The counselor starts to examine the limitations of fast-food counter work as a full-time job.]

CL: Maybe $250 a week.

CO: That's about $12,000 a year. Does that seem like much to you?
CL: No, not really.
CO: How much would you like to earn? [The counselor is helping Betty start to think about the type of future she would like to have.]
CL: A lot more than that. My mother earns about $15,000 a year, and that's terrible.
CO: What do you think you would have to do to earn more?
CL: Everybody tells me that to earn money, you need to go to college. I could never do that.
CO: Why not? [The counselor wants to question Betty's negative assumptions about her abilities and her potential future.]
CL: We don't have any money to go to college, that's for sure.
CO: There are scholarships available. Students from this school with no support from their parents have gone on to do well in college. Something I can do to help you is to show you how you can get financial aid and to make suggestions about school. Your work is good in school—your grades show it and your teachers say it. I can help you figure out what you want to do and where you can go to school. [The counselor offers direct support and encouragement to help Betty make positive steps toward her future choices. Betty is unaware of the alternatives available to her. The counselor will help.]
CL: You think I can do this?
CO: Yes, I do. I want to show you how and help you with it.

Having a plan to follow will help Betty's counselor counter Betty's discouragement. The counselor will empower Betty to look at her options. Having established contacts with local colleges and having obtained information about financial aid, the counselor is in a position to suggest how Betty can find an alternative to a job that does not sufficiently use her abilities.

HUMAN CAPITAL THEORY

The basic idea behind human capital theory is that individuals invest in their own education and training so that they will receive increased lifetime earnings (Becker, 1964; Wachter, 1974). Career earnings are seen as a function of ability, education, and training, combined with the effort to produce effectively. Education is viewed as an investment that, when combined with appropriate job experience, will produce a desired income. Individuals (and their families) invest money in college or other training at an early point in an individual's career. This investment is realized some years later, when an individual starts to receive pay for his or her work. For example, in a study of 2,087 Columbian workers, Psacharopoulos and Velez (1992) found that education had a positive impact on individuals' earnings, even when ability was controlled for. Individual differences in preferences and abilities will produce different lifetime earnings. In human capital theory, the individual is viewed somewhat as a firm or a company: if health care and moving expenses will help improve earning power, then these, like educational expenses, can be seen as investments in one's eventual lifetime earnings.

An application of this theory to high school jobs by Stern and Nakata (1989) may help to illustrate human capital theory. Stern and Nakata found that jobs that teenagers do, which are primarily in services, sales, and labor, differ in quality. Like Greenberger and Steinberg (1986), they find that many jobs of adolescents provide immediate income but do little to develop abilities that can be used in more complex occupations. From a long-term point of view, Stern and Nakata believe that high school students will be better off after graduation if they can find jobs in high school that teach skills required in full-time occupations. They believe that schools should teach problem solving and other high-level skills that can be used after graduation. Stern and Nakata are concerned that individuals with relatively low academic abilities will choose high school jobs that will not give them an opportunity to improve their skills, and that this choice will lead to a poor long-term investment with relatively little economic payoff. Additionally, communities with a large percentage of low-skill jobs do not reward education and thus do not create incentives for students to continue or complete their education (Stallman, Johnson, Mwachofi, & Flora, 1993). Bryant (1992) shows how time spent with children can increase their eventual earnings. Also, Blaug (1985) and Bowles and Gintis (1976) believe that suitable personality traits, such as punctuality, reliability, and cooperation, along with job availability, may be more important than cognitive variables. Their writings are typical of the critics of human capital theory.

In some ways, human capital theory can be seen as an endorsement of trait and factor theory. Like trait and factor theory, human capital theory emphasizes the role of the assessment of interests and abilities in selecting an occupation. Human capital theory differs from trait and factor theory in that it emphasizes career choice as a long-term process and investment and focuses on income.

Counselors may use information culled from human capital theory to comment on an individual's choice of part-time or summer work in terms of how it will help that individual develop income over a lifetime. Furthermore, individuals who do not have sufficient income to pay for investment in the type of education they want may view immediate work as an investment. For example, an individual who wishes to become a physician but cannot pay for the education that is necessary may choose to go to college for two years, work as an emergency medical technician for two years, return to college for a year, work as a technician for two years, finish college in one year, work as a registered nurse for three years, and then go to medical school. In terms of human capital theory, this process could be viewed as a carefully planned long-term investment. However, the older an individual is when his or her education is completed, the less time there is to collect on the investment.

Human capital theory has been criticized because its goal is a monetary reward. Often, individuals have other goals, such as being elected to political office, helping others, or having leisure time. It is possible, but more difficult, to think of work as an investment that will have nonmonetary payoffs such as these. When an individual has multiple goals, such as a high income and helping others, investing in his or her abilities, preferences, and values toward this goal becomes much more complex. Thus, one of the advantages of occasionally thinking about the client in terms of human capital theory is that long-term investment is emphasized, and the individual's future development is considered. In this aspect of planning, human capital theory resembles the developmental work of Donald Super (1990).

Human capital theory assumes that the labor market is open equally to all workers. This assumption has generated much criticism and has been partially responsible for a vast amount of research demonstrating the oversimplification of human capital theory. For example, Duncan, Prus, and Sandy (1993) have shown that, although human capital theory may explain a woman's decision to work, it does not explain her occupational choice. Women who are out of the workforce for family or other reasons tend to be penalized more than males if they are working in traditionally female occupations, as they have lower starting wages (Duncan & Prus, 1992). Agreeing with these results is Kilbourne, Farkas, Beron, Weir, and England's (1994) finding that women earn less in occupations that employ a large percentage of women or that require nurturing social skills. When examining the earnings of blacks in the United States, Gyimah and Fichtenbaum (1993) found that they are paid less for the same work than whites and have fewer opportunities to obtain high-paying jobs. These observations about inequalities in the labor market will form the rationale for the rest of the chapter, including the failure of human capital theory to predict job discrimination for women and people of color. Furthermore, some research has focused on inequalities in different types of organizations. This work is related to research that is often referred to as *dual-economy theory.*

DUAL-ECONOMY THEORY

Human capital theory assumes that all individuals have an equal opportunity to compete in the labor market. Sociologists and economists have long recognized that this is not true. Disadvantaged and underprivileged groups, particularly, tend to enter different types of jobs from those who are more privileged (Berger & Piore, 1980). Dual-economy theory classifies both firms and labor markets into two groups: primary (core) and secondary (peripheral). Although originally used to describe two different types of labor markets, dualistic theory gradually evolved into a way of seeing a variety of discontinuous segments in the labor market. Originally, primary employers were seen as holding a monopolistic or oligopolistic market share, as using advanced technology, and as being nationally or internationally involved in commerce (Averitt, 1968). These large firms offered higher wages, job stability, and more chances for advancement than did those in the secondary labor market. Retail sales and fast-food businesses are examples of the secondary labor market. These jobs usually pay minimum wage or a little more, offer little chance of advancement, and have a relatively high turnover. It was hypothesized that workers who were a part of the primary labor market were not likely to move to the secondary labor market, and vice versa.

Some studies have revealed a more complex structure in the labor market than that suggested by dualistic theory. Piore and others (Berger & Piore, 1980; Doeringer & Piore, 1971; Piore, 1975, 1979; Piore & Sable, 1984) suggest three levels of the labor market. They categorize secondary work as situations that have low pay, poor working conditions, and low social status. Little security or advancement is available in these jobs, and little skill is required of the worker. Relationships with supervisors tend to be personal and informal. Members of this labor force tend to be women, adolescents, and migrants, and the turnover is frequent.

Piore and others divide the primary sector into two tiers. The lower tier of the primary sector is more substantial than the secondary market. There is more status, better working conditions, more chance for advancement, and better pay. More skill is required of the workers, and more formal training is necessary. Relationships between workers and supervisors may be informal or may be controlled by more formal union relationships. Wages are likely to be set through collective bargaining, rather than by the employer. In contrast, the upper tier of the primary market consists of managerial and professional occupations. These jobs offer higher pay, status, prestige, security, and opportunities for advancement. They require more education before employment than do jobs in the lower tier. In general, the worker has more autonomy than in the lower tier, and relationships between supervisors and workers are less important and less formal than in the lower tier.

Not all jobs fit into the primary or secondary labor markets. Piore and colleagues have stated (Berger & Piore, 1980) that craft jobs are hard to classify. They tend to fall between the upper and lower tiers of the primary sector. Although craft work may be similar to the work done by those in the lower tier, because it is often learned on the job and formal relationships between workers and supervisors exist, craftspeople tend to work independently. In that sense, their work is more like that of workers in the upper tier. Craft work includes occupations such as master plumber, electrician, and pipe fitter. One focus of research has been to discover how work is learned and how that learning is applied in each of the four strata of the job market.

How adolescents gain entry into various sectors of the labor market is explained by Osterman (1989). His research used a simple classification of primary and secondary jobs rather than the tier system proposed by Piore and others. In his study, he found that adolescents employed in the secondary labor market tended to work for small retail or contracting concerns. These firms tended to develop a reputation for hiring young people. Adolescents often heard about job openings in this sector through their friends. In contrast, jobs that were found in primary firms came more often through relatives who worked in the primary firm, than through friends.

The fact that different theorists use different numbers of sectors and different definitions of these sectors or stages is one of the criticisms of dualistic theory (Hodson & Kaufman, 1982). Other criticisms deal with the notion that data about an industry rather than data about firms have been used in research on dualistic theory. Information about industries may not take note of the various idiosyncrasies of a wide variety of organizations. Baron and Newman (1990) reviewed attempts to study segmented-labor-market theory within organizations. Recent investigations have studied the dual economy in countries outside the United States (Buffie, 1993). For example, Makarov (1994) describes a different type of dual economy in Russia, which is driven by a dual payment system, side payments in cash, and corruption.

For counselors, the value of a dualistic labor market theory is its emphasis on factors external to the client. The primary emphasis of the psychological theories that are discussed in all of the other chapters of this book is on the individual and individual choice. Dualistic theory calls attention to basic differences in broad segments of the working world. Whether the counselor thinks of the labor market in terms of two, three, four, or more sectors is not as important as the fact that counselors should be aware that there are broad differences in hiring practices, work relationships, advancement possibilities, and earnings in various categories of jobs. This information is particularly helpful to those who counsel adolescents, who are beginning their encounter with the labor market and are likely to start in the secondary labor market. This information is helpful in counseling, so that the client and the counselor can examine how to move to better (primary labor market) work situations. Counselors can help teenagers become aware that many jobs (primary) will not be available to them without more education and experience. However, experience gained on jobs will help develop personal skills such as reliability and cooperation (Blaug, 1985).

An awareness of occupational information about local employers is helpful to the counselor. Sharf (1993) stressed that counselors should have detailed knowledge about the jobs, hiring practices, pay scales, and so on of major local employers. Dual-labor-market theory provides a rationale for assessing such information. Counselors can get information that they can give to clients about wages, job stability, chances for advancement, and turnover. This information, which is useful in separating primary from secondary labor markets, will help clients understand the long-range implications of taking relatively dead-end (secondary labor market) jobs, which pay low salaries and have a rapid turnover and little chance of advancement.

WOMEN AND DISCRIMINATION IN THE WORKPLACE

Sociologists have studied the effect of gender on career outcomes. Much of this research has been in the context of status attainment theory, human capital theory, and dual-labor-market theory. Research examining the effect of gender has shown that discrimination leads to lower pay, less advancement, and occupational segregation, which results in working in occupations with lower prestige than those of men.

In describing discrimination in hiring and promotion, England and Farkas (1986) list four determinants of discrimination: taste discrimination, monopoly, error, and statistical generalization. Becker (1957) discusses *taste discrimination* as a preference not to employ members of a particular group. If employers do not hire women, fewer jobs will be available to them, and therefore, wages will be lower. The *monopoly model of discrimination* occurs when an organized group agrees to exclude another group from positions. For example, an all-male trade union's deciding not to allow women into the union is an example of the "monopoly" model of discrimination. *Error discrimination* refers to employers who do not have discriminatory taste but may underestimate the ability of women to perform the same work as men. *Statistical sex discrimination* happens when an employer applies generalizations about a group of people to an individual. England and Farkas (1986) gives this example: "If employers correctly observe that, on average, women have less mechanical knowledge than men, they may decide not to hire any women in positions requiring mechanical knowledge, screening out even those atypical ones with extensive mechanical skills" (p. 160). Whatever the form of discrimination, it acts to limit women's attainment in many ways.

To understand the employment issues of women in the workplace, it is helpful to examine unemployment data, the distribution of women in various occupations, and the salaries of women. As Table 15-2 shows, women tend to have slightly lower unemployment rates than men. Note that U.S. Bureau of Labor Statistics employment rates include only those individuals who are actively looking for work and receiving unemployment benefits. These rates exclude individuals who are able to work but are not interested in doing so and individuals who would like to work but are discouraged because they believe they will not be able to find work. Unemployment rates appear to differ markedly more by race than by sex. One reason for women's slightly lower unemployment rates is that they move in and out of the labor force more frequently than men and may be involved in family responsibilities that require them to temporarily drop out of the labor force. When they do look for work, they may accept work that men would not

Table 15-2 *Unemployment Rates in Percentages by Demographic Group, 1994*

Age	White Male	White Female	Black Male	Black Female	Hispanic Male	Hispanic Female	All
16–17	18.5	16.6	39.3	32.9	33.3	29.1	
18–19	14.7	11.8	36.5	32.5	22.5	18.1	
20–24	8.8	7.4	19.4	19.6	10.8	13.5	
25–54	4.3	3.7	9.1	8.7	7.7	9.1	
55–64	4.1	3.7	6.0	4.9	7.4	6.6	
Total	5.4	5.2	12.0	11.0	9.4	10.7	9.9

Data from U.S. Department of Labor, *Employment and Earnings* (January 1995), Table 3.

consider. Although women may have slightly lower unemployment rates than men, the types of occupations that they enter tend to pay less and to have less prestige than those that are typically male-dominated. Eccles (1995) and her colleagues find that women are less likely to enter prestigious occupations in the physical sciences or in math both because they have less confidence in their math and science abilities and because they place less subjective value on these occupational fields. As Table 15-3 illustrates, women have less than 25% of the high-paying, high-prestige professional jobs, such as engineer, physician, and lawyer, and have more than 90% of lower-paying, less-prestigious professional jobs, such as registered nurse and elementary and high school teacher. In nonprofessional occupations, women represent 98% of secretaries and 83% of maids and house cleaners. Men dominate the higher-paying nonprofessional occupations such as truck driver, mechanic, and repairer.

In general, the wages of women are between two-thirds and one-half of those of white men (see Figure 15-5). Analyzing gender-based earning inequalities, Anderson and Tomaskovic-Devey (1995) find that gender inequalities are lowest when specific rules are formulated about earnings and promotions. They find that exclusion from traditionally male and high-skill or authority jobs is part of the reason for unequal pay for women. Another issue is organizational culture, such as patriarchal views toward women, unequal promotion practices, and evaluating jobs in terms of gender. Analyzing occupational entry patterns of women in 12 industrial nations, Roos (1985) found that women from all countries had difficulty entering high-paying jobs because of their sex. Another international perspective is provided by Gunderson in *Comparable Worth and Gender Discrimination* (1994).

A detailed analysis of women's role in the labor force revealed several interesting findings. Studying the values of 7,436 full-time workers from 12

Table 15-3 *Employed Persons by Selected Occupation, Sex, Race, and Hispanic Origin, 1994*

Occupation	*Total Employed (in Thousands)*	*Percentage of Total*		
		Women	*Black*	*Hispanic*
Engineers	1,866	8.3	3.7	3.3
Physicians	628	22.3	4.2	5.2
Registered nurses	1,956	93.8	9.3	2.9
Managerial and professional	16,312	43.0	6.8	4.9
Teachers, college	838	42.5	5.0	2.9
Teachers, except college	4,330	74.9	8.9	4.3
Lawyers	821	24.6	3.3	3.1
Counseling, educational, and vocational	237	68.1	13.7	8.1
Sales occupations	14,817	49.1	7.1	6.8
Secretaries, stenographers, and typists	4,163	98.0	9.2	6.7
Food preparation workers	5,960	57.9	12.4	13.4
Nursing aides and orderlies	1,636	88.8	29.3	8.9
Janitors and cleaners	2,048	34.0	20.8	17.1
Maids and house cleaners	680	83.3	27.9	20.2
Mechanics and repairers	4,419	4.5	7.9	8.2
Truck drivers	2,815	4.5	12.4	10.7
Bus drivers	511	47.0	25.6	8.8
Garbage collectors	50	1.3	28.1	17.6

Data from U.S. Department of Labor, *Employment and Earnings* (January 1994), Table 10.

Hispanic Females	$17,760	52%
Hispanic Males	$22,859	67%
Black Females	$19,976	58%
Black Males	$24,041	70%
White Females	$22,198	65%
White Males	$34,300	100%

Figure 15-5 Earnings as a percentage of white male earnings, various demographic groups, full-time workers over 18 years old, 1990. (From U.S. Bureau of the Census, *Money Income of Households, Families, and Persons in the United States, 1990.* Series P-60, No. 174. Washington, DC: U.S. Government Printing Office, 1991, Table 31.)

different nations, Rowe and Snizek (1995) found no differences between men and women in how much they valued high income, security from being fired, free time, advancement, and a feeling of accomplishment. Rather, differences in valuing these variables depended on age, education, and occupational prestige. Studying young workers, Witkowski and Leicht (1995) report that men tend to benefit economically as they assume more family roles, but women's earnings are reduced as they assume family roles. They suggest that employers of married mothers do not value the mothers' prior work experience because they do not believe it has an impact on how long the women will continue working. This uncertainty may make employers reluctant to hire women for jobs that require administrative or other responsibilities. The authors stress the importance of family responsibilities as they affect the hiring and advancement of both men and women. Investigating the impact of societal messages on women's career development, Levine and Zimmerman (1995) found very little relationship between the occupations women aspired to and the occupations they entered. They reported that women who had selected traditional occupations as their goal had had more success than women who had selected nontraditional occupations as their goal, concluding that societal stereotypes about gender continue to affect women's career choices. Jacobs's *Gender Inequality at Work* (1995) explores these issues in greater depth.

Although discrimination against women in the labor force continues, a gradual gender desegregation of occupations has taken place since the mid-1960s. One reason is the growth in the service sector which has caused men to enter occupations that have traditionally been women's occupations, such as nursing and teaching (Lorence, 1992). However, Cotter, DeFiore, Hermsen, Kowalewski, and Vanneman (1995) suggest that women's entering traditionally male occupations will be a stronger force in occupational desegregation than men's entering traditionally female occupations. Cotter et al. also suggest several other reasons for continuing occupational desegregation: As occupations grow in the numbers needed, both men and women are likely to seek entry, thus desegregating a particular field. Equal employment legislation continues to have an impact on reducing gender discrimination, particularly in public service jobs. Also, because women are generally paid less than men, employers have an economic incentive to hire more women. As self-employment grows, gender discrimination decreases. However, women still face problems in dealing with stereotypes from customers and creditors. Thus, several economic and sociological forces point toward continued gender desegregation in the labor force.

The above description discusses discrimination from an economic and sociological, rather than from a psychological, point of view. In Chapter 7, Gottfredson's contribution to the role of sex discrimination in the career development of young children is explained. She feels that children develop an orientation to sex roles between the ages of 6 and 8 that has an important influence on their career choices for the rest of their lives. In that chapter, studies of sex-role stereotyping among children and within the educational system are discussed. In Chapter 8, the work of Betz and Fitzgerald (1987) and that of many other researchers is used to illustrate the effect of the sex-role stereotyping of adolescents in the social and educational systems. Some of the difficulties that women have in dealing with labor force expectations at various times in their adult lives are examined in Chapter 9 from the point of view of Super (1990), Bardwick (1980), and others. In explaining some of the career crises that women are likely to experience in their adult lives, Chapter 10 illustrates the potential problems of leaving and reentering the workforce, sexual harassment, and discrimination. These chapters describe the effect of sex-role stereotyping and discrimination at various stages in women's lives. In contrast, sociological and economic research demonstrates the effect of discrimination on occupational attainment and earnings.

The counselor may find it difficult to use the information about sex-role stereotyping and sex discrimination in terms of earnings and occupational attainment. Career self-efficacy theorists (Chapter 13) emphasize the importance of being attuned to women's lack of confidence in academic areas, such as math and science, and in pursuing nontraditional careers. Challenging self-limiting assumptions and reinforcing women's strengths help to increase career self-efficacy beliefs. Tittle (1982) and Fitzgerald (1986) suggest some ways of helping women with career counseling issues by examining traditional gender roles and the effects of society on these roles. Learning about the actual differences between men and women in earnings and occupational attainment may also be of value. Sometimes, counselors are in a position to influence the educational or social system in their setting. For example, high school guidance counselors may be able to identify teachers or counselors in the high school who are suggesting educational or career paths to students based on their sex. The counselors may then take action to correct this problem. Hotchkiss and Borow (1990) suggested that successful women are excellent role models for other women, as did Krumboltz (Chapter 13) in describing the importance of modeling in social learning theory.

Although the above suggestions may be helpful, even more basic in counseling women on career issues is the identification of one's own bias. Because counselors have also been raised in a society that treats men and women quite differently, they may unconsciously have developed societal values that affect their counseling. Recognizing one's sex bias without becoming upset with oneself is valuable for counselors. In the example below, a counselor uses an internal dialogue to recognize stereotyping.

Judy has been working as a secretary at the same company since she graduated from high school seven years ago. Now 25, she is married, without children, and has sought counseling because she feels limited in her job. Judy is fashionably dressed, and her appearance shows that she has spent time and effort to make herself look attractive.

CL: The people I work with are so nice to me, and it's so much fun talking with them, but I'm not sure that I like my work anymore. I'm doing the same thing each day. In fact, I'm doing more typing than I ever have before. My boss keeps giving me more and more tapes to transcribe.

CO: Can you tell me a little bit more about what is happening at work?

CL: Well, my boss is a sales manager with lots of salespeople under him. I am always busy taking calls from the salesmen and relaying messages to my boss. Then I have plenty of typing to do. I do pretty well. My boss is always telling me how well I do. He's given me pretty good pay raises. I don't get anything like the salesmen, but I guess, compared to other secretaries, I do pretty well. When the work eases up some, I certainly like it better, but maybe there is something else I'd like.

CO: What other options have you considered? [Counselor to self: "I wonder what she's complaining about? She's got a good job. She's making pretty good money. Why would she want to leave? Wait, what am I thinking? Why am I making assumptions for her? It is not my role to determine what's best for her. I am making assumptions about her role as a secretary, that it's a good one for her. Watch it!"]

CL: I'm not sure, but I've thought of being a salesperson like the men who work in our company. I think I could do that, but the company seems to hire just men.

CO: [To self: "Let me get back on track now."] We can consider a number of fields, including becoming a salesperson in your company. If there are barriers, we can look at ways to cross them. For now, let's not close any options. [The counselor is aware that before her last statement Judy has used the term *salesmen* and perhaps she sees their type of work as not being open to her.]

Because sex-role stereotyping is so pervasive in so many cultures, it is important to be alert to how such values affect the counselor. In the example above, the counselor became aware of the biases before they affected the client. Unless counselors can eliminate their own bias, their other efforts to help female clients will be limited.

PEOPLE OF COLOR AND DISCRIMINATION IN THE WORKPLACE

Just as discrimination is a barrier to occupational attainment and earnings for women, so it is for people of color. Because many studies in sociology and economics rely on large samples for their research, most work in the United States has focused on the largest minority group, African Americans. Most of the discussion in this section examines the amount and nature of discrimination against African Americans. In general, the arguments against the effectiveness of human capital theory and status attainment for women given in the previous section also apply to African Americans.

The racial discrimination that African Americans and Hispanics experience is reflected in employment and wage statistics. As Table 15-2 shows, the unemployment rate for blacks and Hispanics in 1994 was about double the rate for whites. For black and Hispanic youth, 16 to 17, and 18 to 19, the rate was extremely high—about one-third were unemployed. Not only is unemployment higher for people of color, but the types of occupations they work in differ greatly. As Table 15-3 shows, people of color tend to make up a relatively small proportion of the workers in high-skill jobs (at the top of Table 15-3) and a much larger proportion of the workers in semi-skilled and unskilled jobs (at the bottom of the table). Furthermore, the salaries of people of color tend to be from about one-half to one-third less than those of white males (Figure 15-5). Analyzing the effect of race on earnings in the United States, Ashraf (1995) notes differences within occupations and reports that blacks earn about 54% less than whites in the South but earn about a third less than whites in the rest of the country. Explaining differences in unemployment and wages has been the task of many sociologists and economists.

Many investigators have examined a variety of factors preventing people of color from attaining high-status jobs, high wages, and lower unemployment rates. Wilson, Tienda, and Wu (1995) have analyzed the racial gap in unemployment and have found that black men are more likely than white men to be unemployed because of firings and layoffs. Also, the lower average education of black men affects their unemployment rate, as there are fewer opportunities for less-educated workers. Bound and Holzer (1993) report that one reason for the high unemployment of less-educated young black men is the shift in the labor market away from manufacturing, a segment of the labor market that has traditionally employed less-educated young blacks, and to the service sector. Studying 1990 census data, Jargowsky (1994) reports that the black poor have become increasingly isolated in ghetto areas in large cities, especially in the midwestern and southwestern United States. Williams (1987) reports that black adolescents tend to move in and out of the labor force more frequently than whites; they also receive fewer job offers per time period than whites. Williams found support for the hypothesis that lower participation in the labor force results from a lack of information about jobs and other aspects of the job attainment process. Two studies (Culp & Dunson, 1986; Wallace, 1975) have found that, when black and white adolescents in the same community look for jobs, blacks experience more discrimination. Examining indirect factors that hinder the economic progress of blacks, Haggerty and Johnson (1993) report that lead poisoning and living near toxic waste sites are more frequently found for low-income people and those in minority groups. Such environmental conditions affect the health, educational attainment, and economic progress of individuals.

Discrimination is not limited to less-educated blacks. Wilson, Tienda, and Wu (1995) reported that college-educated black men had higher unemployment rates than college-educated white men, because of having difficulty entering occupations that had traditionally been closed to blacks, and because of entering occupations where the turnover is traditionally high, such as certain sales occupations.

Some writers have examined a variety of political and economic variables affecting the progress of blacks in the United States. In *Faded Dreams: The Politics and Economics of Race in America* (1994), Conroy provides a detailed political analysis of legislative and other issues that have affected black economic progress. Reviewing writings on the experience of young black men in the labor market, Skinner (1995) criticizes human capital theory, concluding that the payoff of investments in high school and college education is declining for young black men. He urges that attention be given to discrimination in housing, hiring, and job promotion, along with an effort to promote full employment and improved urban housing. Skinner also finds support for a dual labor market, with a large proportion of young black men working for service employers (in the secondary labor market) in large urban cities. Piore (1979) uses the dual-labor-market theory to explain differences in the participation of black and white youth in the labor market. His view is summarized by Osterman (1989):

> The first generation of black migrants from South to North accepted poor quality, secondary Northern jobs because their frame of reference was conditions in the rural South. From this perspective the Northern jobs were not so bad, and in any case, many of these migrants expected to return south. However, many of them remained in the North, and their children found themselves expected to accept the same secondary work. The children's frame of reference was the

> North. In this context, and with sensitivities heightened by the Civil Rights Movement, the jobs were not acceptable. The consequence was either outright rejection of the work or behavior patterns that rendered them an undesirable labor force. (p. 239)

Ogbu (1989, 1992, 1993) has found that black children's orientation to society is unlike that of white children. Furthermore, he has differentiated the cultural orientation of minority children who are of immigrant origins, and those, like blacks, who are an involuntary minority group, having been brought to the United States as slaves. He believes that black children's view is a product of the collective experience of black people in the workforce, both currently and in the past. Furthermore, he feels that this heritage applies to middle-class blacks as well as to lower-class blacks. This sociological observation is different from the usual explanation for lack of participation in the labor market, which is that blacks receive education that is inferior to that of whites (Smith, 1981).

Another view expressed by Ogbu (1989, 1992, 1993) is that the experience of black Americans, as an involuntary minority group, in looking for work has led them to believe that getting ahead is important. However, this belief has not led to concentration on academic work or academic effort. He believes that blacks perceive a job ceiling (being denied entrance to high-paying jobs). This perception in turn has led to a negative perception of the value of education. He believes that black youths perceive school learning as a threat to their sense of identity and security, rather than as an opportunity for advancement. His research suggests a sense of disenfranchisement and a distrust of white Americans. He reports somewhat similar observations on Mexican Americans. Werner (1989) studied minority groups in Hawaii and suggested that the views of native Hawaiians, whom she considered similar to a castelike minority, had attitudes similar to the blacks of Ogbu's (1989) study (a captive minority group). Filipino and Japanese youth had attitudes that were more like those of the voluntary immigrants in Ogbu's study. However, Butcher (1994) compared the pay and employment of recent black immigrants to the United States with that of African Americans. She found that, when there were wage differences, they were due to the selection process of immigration rather than to cultural differences. With the exception of this last study, these findings help to explain differing attitudes of people of color to job entry.

As stated by Hotchkiss and Borow (1990, 1996), blacks may already have high educational expectations. The issue is how to help blacks (and other people of color) to realize their goals. They suggest that strengthening work-related attitudes and information is helpful. Furthermore, they suggest using community, school, and parental resources to help adolescents of color develop attitudes that will be effective in the labor market. The challenge to counselors is great because people of color are, in general, less likely than whites to have access to counseling resources.

Just as there are stereotyped attitudes in the United States toward women, so is there prejudice toward people of color. It is difficult for people, counselors included, not to be exposed to and incorporate prejudices and discrimination. It is important for counselors to recognize and cope with any of their own attitudes that will prevent effective counseling of people of color. Sometimes, reactions are visceral rather than conscious, as the following example shows.

Brian is a black freshman at a large midwestern university. He has been recruited on an athletic scholarship to play football. He is a large man—6 feet, 3 inches, weighing 260 pounds. Like many other freshmen, he has found the transition from high school to college difficult. His football coach, sensing that Brian is unsure about his major and his course performance, recommends counseling. This dialogue starts with the beginning of the counseling interview:

CO: How can I help you, Brian?

CL: Coach sent me here because he knows that I might be headed for some trouble.

CO: Can you tell me more about this? [Since walking with Brian from the waiting room, the counselor has been aware of a feeling right in the middle of the stomach. There is a sense of fear, but there seems to be no reason for it. Brian is pleasant and friendly. The counselor becomes aware that the fear is not due to Brian; rather, it comes from old feelings of prejudice based on skin color and body size. Being aware of these feelings reduces the counselor's physical sense of anxiety. The counselor starts to relax and focus away from old feelings and toward Brian.]

CL: I received a "D" in math and a "D" in science, and I'm worried.

CO: It feels really bad for you to get those grades now. I want to see what I can do to help you. [As the counselor's upper body moves slightly toward Brian, so does the counselor's attention. The counselor is now genuinely interested in Brian, and personal distractions have diminished.]

Not all counselors become aware of their feelings so quickly; some never become aware of them. If the counselor is to continue to feel tension or negative feelings toward the client because of prejudice, the effectiveness of counseling will be greatly diminished. If the counselor believes that blacks are better in some professions than in others, the counselor will be doing a disservice to clients. Feelings and beliefs of prejudice are likely to undermine counseling, no matter what else the counselor does.

In addition to identifying their own prejudice, counselors often need to help their clients deal with the discrimination that they encounter in the job application process or in the workplace. Familiarity with affirmative action guidelines and legal procedures that address grievances is helpful. However, a counselor may find assertiveness techniques useful, so that legal action is not necessary. Examples of dealing with discrimination are given in Chapter 10.

SUMMARY

Unlike the others in this book, this chapter has focused on the labor market and the influence of social and economic factors on the individual's career development. Different sociological and economic theoretical positions provide different views of the labor market. Accident theory suggests the importance of factors that occur by chance, over which the individual has little control. Some sociologists have studied how the environment affects the individual, an approach quite dissimilar to that of psychologists, who are concerned with individuals' making choices and influencing their environment. An area much studied by sociologists is status attainment theory, which emphasizes the importance of parental and aspirational variables in occupational attainment. A theory developed by economists, human capital theory views individuals as investing in themselves, their education, and training, to increase their lifetime earnings. The theory of dual labor markets opposes human capital theory, suggesting that there are core and peripheral labor markets that provide different pay rates, opportunities for advancement, and working conditions. The study of discrimination, which has been well documented for both women and people of color, also addresses the oversimplification of human capital theory. Each theory, as well as research on the discrimination against women and people of color, provides insights that counselors may use in their work.

References

The American work force: 1992–2005. (1993). *Occupational Outlook Quarterly, 37,* 4–44.

Anderson, C. D., & Tomaskovic-Devey, D. (1995). Patriarchal pressures: An exploration of organizational processes that exacerbate and erode gender earnings inequality. *Work and Occupations, 22,* 328–356.

Ashraf, J. (1995). The effect of race on earnings in the United States. *Applied Economics Letters, 2,* 72–75.

Averitt, R. T. (1968). *The dual economy: The dynamics of American industry structure.* New York: Norton.

Babbie, E. R. (1973). *The practice of social research.* Belmont, CA: Wadsworth.

Bandura, A. (1977). Self-efficacy: Toward a unifying theory of behavioral change. *Psychological Review, 84,* 191–215.

Bandura, A. (1982). The psychology of chance encounters and life paths. *American Psychologist, 37,* 747–755.

Bardwick, J. (1980). The seasons of a woman's life. In D. McGuigan (Ed.), *Women's lives: New theory, research, and policy.* Ann Arbor: University of Michigan Center for Continuing Education of Women.

Baron, J. N., & Newman, A. E. (1990). For what it's worth: Organizations, occupations, and the value of work done by women and non-whites. *American Sociological Review, 55,* 155–175.

Becker, G. S. (1957). *The economics of discrimination.* Chicago: University of Chicago Press.

Becker, G. (1964). *Human capital.* New York: Columbia University Press.

Berger, G. S., & Piore, M. J. (1980). *Dualism and discontinuity in industrial societies.* New York: Cambridge University Press.

Betz, N. E., & Fitzgerald, L. F. (1987). *The career psychology of women.* Orlando, FL: Academic Press.

Biblarz, T. J., & Raftery, A. E. (1993). The effects of family disruption on social mobility. *American Sociological Review, 58,* 97–109.

Blau, P. M. (1956). Social mobility and interpersonal relations. *American Sociological Review, 21,* 290–295.

Blau, P. M., & Duncan, O. D. (1967). *The American occupational structure.* New York: Wiley.

Blaug, M. (1985). Where are we now in the economics of education? *Economics of Education Review, 4,* 17–28.

Bound, J., & Holzer, H. J. (1993). Industrial shifts, skills levels, and the labor market for white and black males. *Review of Economics and Statistics, 75,* 387–396.

Bowles, S., & Gintis, H. (1976). *Schooling in capitalist America.* New York: Basic Books.

Bryant, W. K. (1992). Human capital, time use, and other family behavior. *Journal of Family and Economic Issues, 113,* 395–405.

Buffie, E. F. (1993). Direct foreign investment, crowding out, and underemployment in the dualistic economy. *Oxford Economic Papers, 45,* 639–667.

Butcher, K. F. (1994). Black immigrants in the United States: A comparison with native blacks and other immigrants. *Industrial and Labor Relations Review, 47,* 265–284.

Cabral, A. C., & Salomone, P. R. (1990). Chance and careers: Normative versus contextual development. *The Career Development Quarterly, 39,* 5–17.

Campbell, R. T. (1983). Status attainment research: End of the beginning or beginning of the end? *Sociology of Education, 56,* 47–62.

Caplow, T. (1954). *The sociology of work.* Minneapolis: University of Minnesota Press.

Chart: Education. It pays for the rest of your life. (1995). *Occupational Outlook Quarterly, 39,* 52.

Collins, S. M. (1993). Blacks on the bubble: The vulnerability of black executives in white corporations. *Sociological Quarterly, 34,* 429–447.

Conroy, M. (1994). *Faded dreams: The politics and economics of race in America.* New York: Cambridge University Press.

Cotter, D. A., DeFiore, J., Hermsen, J. M., Kowalewski, B. M., & Vanneman, R. (1995). Occupational gender desegregation in the 1980s. *Work and Occupations, 22,* 3–21.

Culp, J., & Dunson, B. (1986). Brothers of a different color: A preliminary look at employer treatment of White and Black youth. In R. Freeman & H. Holzer (Eds.), *The Black youth employment crisis* (pp. 233–260). Chicago: University of Chicago Press.

Doeringer, P. B., & Piore, M. J. (1971). *Internal labor markets and manpower analysis.* Lexington, MA: D. C. Heath.

Duncan, K. C., & Prus, M. J. (1992). Starting wages of women in female and male occupations: A test of the human capital explanation of occupational sex segregation. *Social Science Journal, 29,* 479–493.

Duncan, K. C., Prus, M. J., & Sandy, J. G. (1993). Marital status, children and women's labor market choices. *Journal of Socio-Economics, 22,* 277–288.

Eccles, J. S. (1995). Understanding women's educational and occupational choices. *Psychology of Women Quarterly, 18,* 585–609.

England, P., & Farkas, G. (1986). *Household, employment, and gender: A social, economic, and demographic view.* New York: Aldine.

Fitzgerald, L. F. (1986). Career counseling women: Principles, procedures and problems. In Z. B. Leibowitz & H. D. Lea (Eds.), *Adult career development: Concepts, issues, and practices* (pp. 17–131). Cranston, RI: Carroll Press.

Forbes, J. B. (1987). Early intraorganizational mobility: Patterns and influences. *Academy of Management Journal, 30,* 110–125.

Fredrickson, R. H., Lin, J. G., & Xing, S. (1992). Social status ranking of occupations in the People's Republic of China, Taiwan, and the United States. *The Career Development Quarterly, 40,* 351–360.

Gottfredson, L. S. (1981). Circumscription and compromise: A developmental theory of occupational aspirations. *Journal of Counseling Psychology, 28,* 545–579.

Gottfredson, L. S. (1996). Gottfredson's theory of circumscription and compromise. In D. Brown, L. Brooks, & Assoc. (Eds.), *Career choice and development* (3rd ed., pp. 179–232). San Francisco: Jossey-Bass.

Greenberger, E., & Steinberg, L. D. (1986). *When teenagers work.* New York: Basic Books.

Grubb, W. N. (1984). The bandwagon once more: Vocational preparation for high-tech occupations. *Harvard Educational Review, 54,* 429–451.

Gunderson, M. (1994). *Comparable worth and gender discrimination.* Geneva: International Labour Office.

Gyimah, B. K., & Fichtenbaum, R. (1993). Black-white wage differential: The relative importance of human capital and labor market structure. *Review of Black Political Economy, 21,* 19–52.

Hachen, D. S. (1990). Three models of job mobility in labor markets. *Work and Occupations, 17,* 320–354.

Haggerty, M., & Johnson, C. (1995). The hidden barriers of occupational segregation. *Journal of Economic Issues, 29,* 211–223.

Hart, D. H., Rayner, R., & Christensen, E. R. (1971). Planning, preparation and chance in occupational entry. *Journal of Vocational Behavior, 1,* 279–285.

Hodson, R., & Kaufman, R. L. (1982). Economic dualism: A critical review. *American Sociological Review, 47,* 727–739.

Hossler, D., & Stage, F. K. (1992). Family and high school experience influences on the postsecondary educational plans of ninth-grade students. *American Educational Research Journal, 29,* 425–451.

Hotchkiss, L., & Borow, H. (1990). Sociological perspectives on work and career development. In D. Brown, L. Brooks, & Assoc. (Eds.), *Career choice and development* (2nd ed., pp. 262–307). San Francisco: Jossey-Bass.

Hotchkiss, L., & Borow, H. (1996). Sociological perspectives on work and career development. In D. Brown, L. Brooks, & Assoc. (Eds.), *Career choice and development* (3rd ed., pp. 281–334). San Francisco: Jossey-Bass.

Jacobs, J. A. (Ed.). (1995). *Gender inequality at work.* Thousand Oaks, CA: Sage.

Jargowsky, P. A. (1994). Ghetto poverty of blacks in the 1980s. *Journal of Policy Analysis and Management, 13,* 288–310.

Kett, J. (1982). The adolescence of vocational education. In H. Kanton & D. Tyack (Eds.), *Work, youth, and schooling: Historical perspectives on vocationalism in American education* (pp. 79–109). Stanford, CA: Stanford University Press.

Kilbourne, B. S., Farkas, G., Beron, K., Weir, D., & England, P. (1994). Return to skill, compensating differentials, and gender bias: Effects of occupational characteristics on the wages of white women and men. *American Journal of Sociology, 100,* 689–719.

Koenigsberg, J., Garet, M. S., & Rosenbaum, J. E. (1994). The effect of family on the job exits of young adults: A competing risk model. *Work and Occupations, 21,* 33–63.

Kohn, M., & Schooler, C. (1978). The reciprocal effects of the substantive complexity of work and intellectual flexibility: A longitudinal assessment. *American Journal of Sociology, 84,* 24–52.

Kohn, M. L., & Schooler, C. (1982). Reciprocal effects of job conditions and personality. *American Journal of Sociology, 87,* 1257–1286.

Kohn, M. L., & Schooler, C. (1983). *Work and personality.* Norwood, NJ: Ablex.

Levine, P. B., & Zimmerman, D. J. (1995). A comparison of the sex-type of occupational aspirations and subsequent achievement. *Work and Occupations, 22,* 73–84.

Li, J. H., & Wotjkiewicz, R. A. (1992). A new look at the effects of family structure on status attainment. *Social Science Quarterly, 73,* 581–595.

Lorence, J. (1992). Service sector growth and metropolitan occupational sex segregation. *Work and Occupations, 19,* 128–156.

Ma, L. C., & Smith, K. B. (1993). Education, social class, and parental values in Taiwan. *Journal of Social Psychology, 133,* 579–580.

Mainquist, S., & Eichorn, D. (1989). Competence in work settings. In D. Stern & D. Eichorn (Eds.), *Adolescence and work* (pp. 327–367). Hillsdale, NJ: Erlbaum.

Makarov, V. L. (1994). Dual economy in Russia today. *Economic Review, 45,* 117–125.

Miller, D. C., & Form, W. H. (1951). *Industrial sociology.* New York: Harper & Row.

Miller, J., Schooler, C., Kohn, M. L., & Miller, K. A. (1979). Women and work: The psychological effects of occupational conditions. *American Journal of Sociology, 85,* 156–166.

Mortimer, J., & Lorence, J. (1979a). Occupational experience and the self-concept: A longitudinal study. *Social Psychology Quarterly, 42,* 307–323.

Mortimer, J., & Lorence, J. (1979b). Work experience and occupational value socialization: A longitudinal study. *American Journal of Sociology, 84,* 1361–1385.

Ogbu, J. (1989). Cultural boundaries and minority youth orientation toward work preparation. In D. Stern & D. Eichorn, *Adolescence and work* (pp. 101–140). Hillsdale, NJ: Erlbaum.

Ogbu, J. (1992). Adaptation to minority status and impact on school success. *Theory into Practice, 31,* 287–295.

Ogbu, J. (1993). Differences in cultural frame of reference. *International Journal of Behavioral Development, 16,* 483–506.

Osterman, P. (1980). *Getting started: The youth labor market.* Cambridge: MIT Press.

Osterman, P. (1989). The job market for adolescents. In D. Stern & D. Eichorn (Eds.), *Adolescence and work* (pp. 235–256). Hillsdale, NJ: Erlbaum.

Osterman, P. (1995). The youth labor market: Skill deficiencies and public policy. In A. Howard (Ed.), *The changing nature of work* (pp. 223–237). San Francisco: Jossey-Bass.

Penick, N. I., & Jepsen, D. A. (1992). Family functioning and adolescent career development. *The Career Development Quarterly, 40,* 208–222.

Piore, M. J. (1975). Notes for a theory of labor market stratification. In R. L. Edwards, M. Riech, & D. M. Gordon (Eds.), *Labor market segmentation* (pp. 125–150). Lexington, MA: Heath.

Piore, M. J. (1979). *Birds of passage: Migrant labor and industrial societies.* New York: Cambridge University Press.

Piore, M. J., & Sable, C. F. (1984). *The second industrial divide: Possibilities for prosperity.* New York: Basic Books.

Psacharopoulos, G., & Velez, E. (1992). Schooling, ability, and earnings in Columbia, 1988. *Economic Development and Cultural Change, 40,* 629–643.

Riche, R., Hecker, D., & Burgin, J. (1983). High technology today and tomorrow: A small slice of the employment pie. *Monthly Labor Review, 106,* 50–58.

Richter, R. (1994). Post-adolescence as a new phase in the family cycle? *Innovation, 7,* 63–68.

Roos, P. A. (1985). *Gender and work: A comparative analysis of industrial societies.* Albany: State University of New York Press.

Rosenbaum, J. E. (1976). *Making equality: The hidden curriculum of high school tracking.* New York: Wiley-Interscience.

Rosenbaum, J. E. (1984). *Career mobility in a corporate hierarchy.* New York: Academic Press.

Rosenbaum, J. E. (1989). Organization career systems and employee misperceptions. In M. B. Arthur, D. T. Hall, & B. S. Lawrence (Eds.), *Handbook of career theory* (pp. 329–353). New York: Cambridge University Press.

Rowe, R., & Snizek, W. E. (1995). Gender differences in work values: Perpetuating the myth. *Work and Occupations, 22,* 215–229.

Sabo, D., Melnick, M. J., & Vanfossen, B. E. (1993). High school athletic participation and postsecondary educational and occupational mobility: A focus on race and gender. *Sociology of Sport Journal, 10,* 44–56.

Salomone, P. R., & Slaney, R. B. (1981). The influence of chance and contingency factors on the vocational choice process of nonprofessional workers. *Journal of Vocational Behavior, 19,* 25–35.

Scott, J., & Hatalla, J. (1990). The influence of chance and contingency factors on career patterns of college-educated women. *The Career Development Quarterly, 39,* 18–30.

Sewell, W. H., Haller, A. O., & Ohlendorf, G. W. (1970). The educational and early occupational attainment process: Replication and revision. *American Sociological Review, 35,* 1014–1027.

Sewell, W. H., Haller, A. O., & Portes, A. (1969). The educational and early occupational attainment process. *American Sociological Review, 34,* 82–92.

Sharf, R. S. (1993). *Occupational outlook overview.* Pacific Grove, CA: Brooks/Cole.

Skinner, C. (1995). Urban labor markets and young black men: A literature review. *Journal of Economic Issues, 29,* 47–65.

Smith, E. J. (1981). The black female adolescent: A review of the educational, career, and psychological literature. *Psychology of Women Quarterly, 6,* 261–288.

Sonnenfeld, J. A. (1989). Career system profiles and strategic staffing. In M. B. Arthur, D. T. Hall, & B. S. Lawrence (Eds.), *Handbook of career theory* (pp. 202–224). New York: Cambridge University Press.

Stallman, J. I., Johnson, T. G., Mwachofi, A., & Flora, J. L. (1993). Labor market incentives to stay in school. *Journal of Agriculture and Applied Economics, 25,* 82–94.

Stern, D., & Nakata, Y. F. (1989). Characteristics of high school students' paid work, and employment experience after graduation. In D. Stern & D. Eichorn (Eds.), *Adolescence and work* (pp. 189–233). Hillsdale, NJ: Erlbaum.

Super, D. E. (1990). A life-span, life-space approach to career development. In D. Brown, L. Brooks, & Assoc. (Eds.), *Career choice and development* (2nd ed., pp. 197–261). San Francisco: Jossey-Bass.

Tittle, C. K. (1982). Career counseling in contemporary U.S. high schools: An addendum to Rehberg and Hotchkiss. *Educational Researcher, 11,* 12–18.

Wachter, M. L. (1974). Primary and secondary labor markets: A critique of the dual approach. *Brookings Papers on Economic Activity, 3,* 637–693.

Wallace, P. (1975). *Pathways into work.* Lexington, MA: D. C. Heath.

Werner, E. E. (1989). Adolescents and work: A longitudinal perspective on gender and cultural variability. In D. Stern & D. Eichorn (Eds.), *Adolescence and work* (pp. 159–187). Hillsdale, NJ: Erlbaum.

Williams, D. R. (1987). *Labor force participation of black and white youth.* Ann Arbor, MI: UMI Research Press.

Wilson, A. B. (1989). Dreams and aspirations in the status attainment model. In D. Stern & D. Eichorn (Eds.), *Adolescence and work* (pp. 49–73). Hillsdale, NJ: Erlbaum.

Wilson, F. D., Tienda, M., & Wu, L. (1995). Race and unemployment: Labor market experiences of black and white men, 1968–1988. *Work and Occupations, 22,* 245–270.

Witkowski, K. M., & Leicht, K. T. (1995). The effects of gender segregation, labor force participation, and family roles on the earnings of young adult workers. *Work and Occupations, 22,* 48–72.

PART FOUR

Theoretical Integration

Counselors rarely use one theoretical orientation to career development without at least making some use of other theories. Being able to combine theories when working with a client may make a counselor more flexible in meeting a wide range of client needs. These needs may include career choice, work adjustment, and placement counseling as well as others. Some theories meet the needs of certain types of clients more than do others; for example, some are better than others for adolescent clients. It is the purpose of Chapter 16 to describe the many ways that theories can be used in combination.

16

Theories in Combination

The previous chapters have each explained how a particular theory or theories can be used in counseling. These chapters have looked at theories in isolation. However, it is possible to combine theories to fit both one's theoretical counseling orientation and the work setting. Much of this chapter concerns the appropriateness of different combinations of career development theories for individuals in specific age ranges.

Throughout this book, the focus has been on using career development theory in individual counseling. This focus has been used to illustrate the application of theory. However, counselors are often in situations where there is not sufficient time for individual counseling or where other methods may seem more appropriate. This chapter addresses those situations. Noncounseling uses of career development theory, such as in administering self-help and computer materials, will be described. Some counselors work with career groups, either by choice or because career groups are an efficient way of providing career services to large numbers of clients. Career group counseling will be discussed.

Two special applications of theory have not yet been addressed. The first is using career development theory when career counseling issues are not the presenting problem. The second concerns the implication of career development theory for job search or placement strategies. Since most of this book has focused on career choice and work adjustment, it is fitting to also include information about implications for job search strategies. Although most career development theories have not addressed this issue directly, giving job search assistance is a very important role for many counselors.

Topics that have been covered throughout this book have included the roles of testing and occupational information, the career development of women and people of color, and the counselor issues raised by specific theories. For each of these topics, comparisons will be made among theories.

COMBINING THEORIES

To discuss how theories can be used with each other in counseling, it will be helpful to categorize them into three groups: trait and factor theory, life-span theory, and career decision-making theories. The trait and factor theories include general trait and factor theory (Chapter 2), Lofquist and Dawis's work adjustment theory (Chapter 3), Holland's typology (Chapter 4), and Myers-Briggs type theory (Chapter 5). With regard to life-span theory, the focus will be mainly on the work of Super (Chapters 6–9), but will also include that of Gottfredson (Chapter 7), Atkinson, Morten, and Sue (Chapter 9), and Hopson and Adams's theory of transitions (Chapter 10). The career decision-making theories include Krumboltz's social learning theory (Chapter 13) and the individualistic perspective of Tiedeman and Miller-Tiedeman as well as the sequential elimination approach of Gati (Chapter 14). Four types of theories that do not fit neatly into any of these categories are those of psychodynamic theory (Chapter 11), parental influence theories (Chapter 12), career self-efficacy theory (Chapter 13), and the sociological and economic theories of career development (Chapter 15). There are very different reasons for not including these theories in this section on combining theories. Unless a counselor is trained in psychodynamic counseling, psychodynamic theory may be difficult to use in career counseling. The major contributions of psychodynamic theory to career development are the emphasis on play versus compulsivity, the emphasis on identity in career selection, and the Adlerian focus on the family and social aspects of career choice. Regarding parental theories of personality development, only some evidence has been found to support their hypotheses. Thus, it may be inappropriate to use them in discussions of counseling conceptualization. However, Roe's eight occupational groupings have been found useful by counselors and test developers alike. They are discussed further in the section on occupational information. Applications of career self-efficacy theory have not been well developed, but its emphasis on increasing self-esteem in counseling is useful. Sociological and economic theories of career development provide informative insights into the labor market, especially for counseling women and people of color. However, because of their emphasis on the working environment rather than the individual, they are limited in providing an overall conceptualization of career counseling. Because these theories do have much to offer, they will be alluded to in later sections of this chapter.

Combining Life-Span Theory with Trait and Factor and Career Decision-Making Theories

Because it encompasses the entire life span, Super's life-span theory has received considerable attention. Super's theory is compatible with theories such as trait and factor and career decision-making theories. Such theories focus on career choice or work adjustment at a particular point in time. Therefore, it is helpful to examine which trait and factor theories and career decision-making theories are most useful at which stage in the life span. Such an approach is compatible with Super's (1990) suggestions for counseling, which incorporate Holland's model as well as trait and factor approaches. Figure 16-1 examines seven theories in terms of their appropriateness for different age groups according to Super's life stages. The solid line shows when, in an individual's lifetime, the theory is likely to be most useful. The dotted line shows when it is likely to be helpful, but not as pertinent. In the following pages we will discuss the applicability of non-life-span theories to life-span theories in relation to childhood, early adolescence, late adolescence and adulthood, and adult career transitions.

Childhood The developmental models of Ginzberg, Ginsburg, Alexrad, and Herma (1951), Super (1990), and Gottfredson (1996) provide information about the career development of children. Trait and factor and career decision-making theorists have little to say about this period. Ginzberg and his colleagues emphasize the development of interests, capacities, and values. Gottfredson's focus on orientation to size and power, sex roles, social class variables, and self-awareness provides an interesting insight into the development of career choice. Super's (1990) emphasis on the development of curiosity, exploration, and information leading to the development of interests, an accurate time perspective, and a self-concept is yet another helpful view of the career development process of children. Since career selection and work adjustment are inappropriate at this age, developmental life-span theories provide useful information for the counselor that is not provided by trait and factor and career decision-making theories.

Early Adolescence At this point, the convergence of life-span theory and other theories becomes murky. The work of Crites (1978) and Super (1990) emphasizes the importance of career maturity, which is desirable before career selection takes place. Super's concepts of career planning, which include career exploration, decision making, world-of-work information, and knowledge of preferred occupation, focus on the readiness of the individual. According to developmental theorists such as Super, it is at the point of vocational readiness (or some approximation thereof) that trait and factor and career decision-making theories are useful. For trait and factor theorists, with the possible exception of Holland, readiness for self-assessment is not a focus. For Tiedeman and Miller-Tiedeman, who have devised developmental models of career decision making, readiness would be more of a concern than for either Gati (1986) or Krumboltz (Mitchell & Krumboltz, 1990), who do not incorporate developmental concepts in their approaches. The age group that is the focus of concern for the concept of readiness for career selection is adolescence from the eighth grade through the twelfth grade. The Career Development Inventory (Super et al., 1971; Thompson & Lindeman, 1981) was developed to determine maturity and readiness to explore careers. Often, trait and factor and career decision-making theories are used with this age group without measures of readiness. Whether students who may be only partially ready to explore career

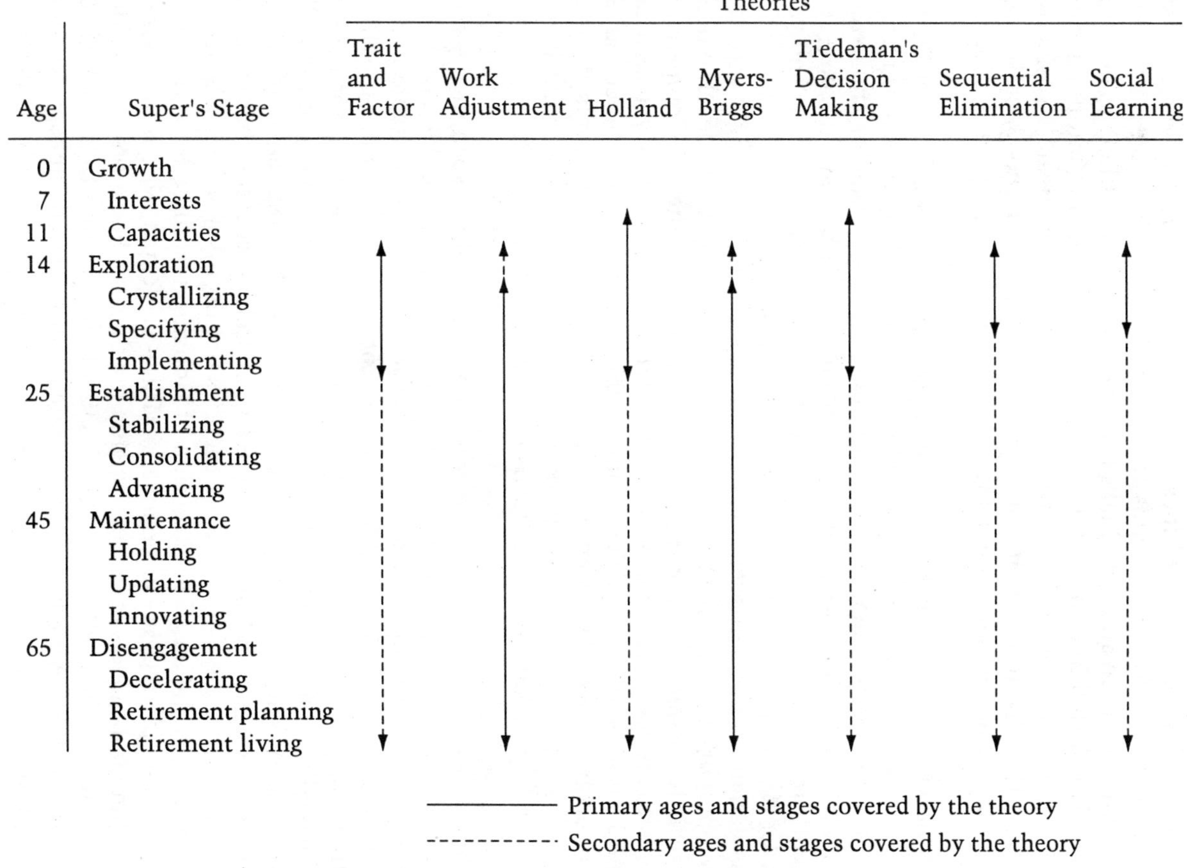

Figure 16-1 How various career development theories relate to Super's life-span stages.

alternatives can benefit from trait and factor theory or career decision-making approaches is unknown.

Late Adolescence and Adulthood In high school and college, counseling for career choice is common. With regard to trait and factor theories, some counselors use a variety of tests measuring interests, abilities, personality, and/or values that follow the general trait and factor model. Others find the six personalities and environments of Holland to be quite useful. Because the concepts of the Myers-Briggs theory are rather complex, that theory is rarely used with high school students. The work adjustment theory of Lofquist and Dawis can be used with high school students but rarely is. To benefit from the use of work adjustment theory, the client should have experience and knowledge of work-related values and needs. Most high school students have had limited work experience. In terms of decision-making theories, most are applicable to high school students, as well as college students. Krumboltz's social learning theory, which emphasizes faulty beliefs, may be particularly appropriate for high school students, who may have many misconceptions about career selection. His view of correcting inaccurate information in order to make career decisions is somewhat similar to Super's notion of having accurate occupational knowledge and information about career decision making.

Adult Career Development Super's stages of adult career development as described in Figure 16-1 provide a way to view trait and factor and decision-making theories. The stage of exploration, which includes the substages of crystallizing, specifying, and implementing, is the stage in which trait and factor and decision-making theories are most likely to be used. However, Super's concept of recycling would suggest that exploring one's career can occur at almost any age. Certainly, general trait and factor theory, as well as the theories of Holland and Myers-Briggs, can be useful in career selection, as work adjustment theory can be. The decision-making theories of Gati, Krumboltz, and Tiedeman and Tiedeman-Miller fit Super's exploration phase. Also, the anticipating stage of Tiedeman's theory is somewhat similar to the crystallizing substage of Super's exploration stage. The adjusting stage of Tiedeman is in many ways comparable to the specifying and implementing substages of exploration (Super, 1990). Likewise, the elimination of occupational alternatives that occurs in both Krumboltz's social learning theory and Gati's sequential elimination approach is similar to the specifying substage of exploration (Super, 1990). The major difference is that Super focuses on continual development of occupational growth, as do Miller-Tiedeman and Tiedeman (1990), whereas Krumboltz and Gati are more concerned with the decision-making process itself.

In the establishment, maintenance, and disengagement stages, work adjustment is an important issue. Although Holland's theory and general trait and factor theory may address this issue, the work adjustment theory of Lofquist and Dawis and the Myers-Briggs typology are specifically concerned with ways of helping individuals adjust to work concerns. Work adjustment theory does this by attending to the congruence between the needs, values, and abilities of the client, on the one hand, and the reinforcers offered by the job, on the other. Myers-Briggs type theory examines work adjustment by attending to the judging and perceiving patterns of the client in comparison to those of his or her colleagues and other aspects of the work environment. These approaches are appropriate to retirement issues as well as problems that arise at work. The decision-making theorists provide a model that is helpful not only in career choice, but in decision making in general as well. Therefore, the approaches of Gati, Krumboltz, and Tiedeman and Miller-Tiedeman contain elements that can be used at any phase of the career development process, such as when a worker experiences conflicts with his or her superior and must decide how to resolve them.

Also related to the establishment, maintenance, and disengagement stages is the approach to crises and transitions proposed by Hopson and Adams (1977). They recognize that problems arising from being fired or laid off, sexual harassment, and other crises can be very serious for an individual. This appears to be particularly true for those individuals who see their role as worker as being very important, and who are in the establishment or maintenance stages as described by Super. Hopson and Adams suggest that individuals react to crises in this sequence: shock and immobilization, minimization and denial, self-doubt, letting go, testing options, searching for meaning, and integration. For some counselors, it may be helpful to look at issues such as job loss from the point of view of Hopson and Adams's transition theory, work adjustment theory, and the perceiving and judging style of the Myers-Briggs typology. For example, whether an individual deals more in the inner world or the outer world (introversion-extraversion) and senses or intuits may be related to how he or she deals with the initial shock of job termination and the minimization phase. Often, several different theoretical points of view will add to the counselor's understanding of a career crisis.

Combining Trait and Factor Theories

Can a counselor use more than one trait and factor theory without being confused or possibly confusing the client? Briefly, the answer is yes. A lengthier answer can be arrived at by examining Table 16-1. Each trait and factor theory emphasizes certain traits and factors more than others. For example, general trait and factor theory allows the counselor to emphasize aptitudes, interests, values, and personality in any way that he or she wishes to do so. Many tests and inventories are available in each of these categories (Table 16-1 provides a sample of some of these). It is up to the counselor to emphasize those tests and inventories that seem most appropriate. Holland's system emphasizes use of either the Self-Directed Search or the Vocational Preference Inventory, measures of interests and self-estimates of competencies. Work adjustment theory stresses measurement of aptitudes and values with the General Aptitude Test Battery and the Minnesota Importance Questionnaire. For career selection purposes, the Myers-Briggs typology is an incomplete trait and factor theory, focusing on personality measurement. Because these theories emphasize different traits, it is quite possible to use them in combination.

For example, using Holland's Self-Directed Search with the Myers-Briggs Type Indicator provides information about work personality as measured by interests and self-estimated competencies (Self-Directed Search) and perceiving and judging style (the Myers-Briggs Type Indicator). Similarly, either or both of these theories could be used with the work adjustment theory. As more theories are used, the addition of more concepts may create confusion for both client and counselor. In general, however, there seems to be little overlap in the approaches of general trait and factor theory, Holland's theory, work adjustment theory, and the Myers-Briggs typology.

Combining Career Decision-Making Theories

Unlike trait and factor theories, which tend to differ from each other because they measure different characteristics of individuals, career decision-making theories tend to describe the same process. Therefore, it is unlikely that a counselor would wish to use more than one career decision-making theory in counseling. Krumboltz's social learning theory uses a specific seven-stage process, DECIDES, which requires behavioral and cognitive interventions from the counselor. The sequential elimination approach of Gati is somewhat similar to that of Krumboltz, but focuses on an ideal model of career decision making and the gradual elimination of occupational alternatives. In contrast, the individualistic perspective of Tiedeman and Miller-Tiedeman emphasizes the subjective experience of the client and the recycling of career decision-making stages. Stages of exploration, crystallization, choice, and clarification are guidelines rather than prescriptions for the counselor to follow. Likewise, the stages of induction, reformation, and integration are ways of implementing and adjusting to a choice. These are not the only theories of career decision making. Many others are mentioned in Chapter 14, "Career Decision-Making Theory." Furthermore, the Myers-Briggs typology can be seen as a theory of career decision making because it focuses on making perceptions about events and then judging or deciding about those events. However, it does not offer specific steps as the other theories do. If a counselor does decide to use a career decision-making theory in counseling, it is important that the theory fit the counselor's orientation as well as the client population.

Table 16-1 *Tests and Inventories Associated with Specific Career Development Theories*

	Test Type					
Theory	*Aptitude*	*Interest*	*Values*	*Personality*	*Decision-Making*	*Maturity and Development*
Trait and factor theory*	Scholastic Assessment Test	Kuder Preference Record	Study of Values	California Psychological Inventory		
	Differential Appti-tude Tests	Strong Interest Inventory	Values Scale	Sixteen Personality Factor Questionnaire		
	General Aptitude Test Battery	California Occupational Preference Survey				
	Armed Services Vocational Aptitude Battery					
Holland's typology		Self-Directed Search				
		Vocational Preference Inventory				

Myers-Briggs typology			Myers-Briggs Type Indicator		
Work adjustment theory	General Aptitude Test Battery	Minnesota Importance Questionnaire			
Super's life-span theory		Values Scale Salience Inventory			Career Development Inventory Adult Career Concerns Inventory
Krumboltz's social learning theory				Career Beliefs Inventory	

*Trait and factor theory can make use of many tests and inventories. Examples are presented here.

The Counselor's Choice

Each of the theories described in the preceding pages has been supported by varying amounts of research. In general, these theories are clear and concise. For the counselor, they offer a tested approach to understanding and helping clients with career problems. Whether a counselor uses one theory or several in the conceptualization of client issues is a personal decision. There is no information to suggest the most appropriate number of theories to use.

NONCOUNSELING APPLICATIONS OF THEORIES

Practical considerations, such as a large caseload and little time available for career counseling, often require counselors to look for other methods besides individual counseling to help their clientele with issues of career selection. Some noncounseling interventions can serve as a way of identifying those individuals who might profit from further counseling. In some cases, noncounseling materials are offered as the only career selection aid. Three noncounseling applications of theories are described here: screening methods, paper-and-pencil materials, and computerized guidance systems.

Screening Methods

Some theorists have developed tests or inventories that screen for the clients who will benefit most from counseling. Another use of screening is to separate clients into groups by test score so that appropriate counseling interventions can be offered. An excellent example of a screening instrument is Super's Career Development Inventory (Super et al., 1971). For example, depending on how a student scores on this instrument, he or she can be referred either to counseling for career choice or to information that will increase the level of his or her vocational maturity, so that he or she can then be assigned to a career selection intervention. Holland's Self-Directed Search can be used in a similar manner. Those students who are not able to arrive at a series of acceptable career alternatives through the Self-Directed Search can be scheduled for individual or group career counseling. Although many other inventories and tests are not normally used in this manner, it may be possible to do so.

Paper-and-Pencil Materials

Most theories do not offer materials designed to be used in lieu of counseling. Holland's Self-Directed Search is a notable exception. Holland (1992) believes that help in selecting an occupation can be provided through easy-to-use inventories and supplemental materials, so that, in many cases, counseling will be unnecessary. The Self-Directed Search is designed so that individuals can score the inventory themselves as well as interpret it. Professionals should not be necessary, except in situations where the results of the Self-Directed Search are confusing or incomplete. In addition, Holland developed *The Occupations Finder*, which lists hundreds of careers sorted by Holland three-letter codes. Thus, a student can look up in *The Occupations Finder* the three-letter code that he or she received on the Self-Directed Search and locate careers that exactly, or nearly, match that code. Also, Holland (1985) has written an easy-to-read eight-page booklet called *You and Your Career* that advises students how to understand the Holland six-type system and how to make career decisions. Many educational systems have used these instruments to provide career assistance to their students. Counselors wishing to use these materials need to consider the cost effectiveness of these relatively inexpensive materials and the merits of a system that does not stress a counseling approach to career selection.

Computerized Guidance Systems

Since the early 1970s, computer-assisted guidance systems have become an integral part of career counseling. Although these systems are designed to be used as an adjunct to counseling, they are occasionally used similarly to Holland's Self-Directed Search. For example, a computerized guidance system can be assigned to individuals so that they may select appropriate careers. If this method is not sufficient for an individual, then counseling may be offered. These instruments have been reviewed by a number of authors (Harris-Bowlsbey, 1984; Rayman, 1990). Two systems are particularly well known and have been highly developed: DISCOVER and SIGI PLUS. Both systems follow the trait and factor method in that they help individuals assess their abilities, interests, and values. Then, the systems provide occupational and educational information for the people using the system. A match is made between the self-assessment of the individual and occupational information. Clients then go on to select the occupations that would fit them best. SIGI PLUS emphasizes the values aspect of self-assessment, whereas DISCOVER uses some portions of Super's developmental life-span theory in its approach.

These descriptions do not do justice to the sophisticated interactive nature of these programs. Both are available for many computers and have large databases of occupational information. Their self-assessment sections are, in many ways, similar to paper-and-pencil assessments of interests, self-estimated competencies, and values. Other computer systems are also available. Evaluating SIGI PLUS and DISCOVER, Peterson, Ryan-Jones, Sampson, and Reardon (1994) found no practical differences in effectiveness between the systems. Studying SIGI PLUS, Lenz, Reardon, and Sampson (1993) reported that, as students' scores on Holland's Enterprising and Social categories increased, their rating of SIGI PLUS's contribution to their own knowledge of self and of occupations decreased, a finding suggesting that students responded differently to SIGI PLUS depending on their personality type. Rayman's (1990) review of DISCOVER and SIGI PLUS, as well as of the role of computers in career counseling, describes, in depth, the issues and systems mentioned above.

SPECIAL COUNSELING ISSUES

A number of counseling issues have implications for career development theories. One important concern is group counseling. Sometimes because of preference, and often because of limited time, counselors choose to use career group counseling rather than individual counseling. Most of the theories that have been discussed in this book lend themselves to the group approach. Another issue that arises is career counseling as a related concern. Some counselors work in a setting where they deal with personal or family problems to which career issues are related. For example, they may rarely do counseling for career choice and more often do work adjustment counseling as a part of other issues. Selecting a career development theory to use in that case may be different than if one's chief responsibility is career counseling. Another issue that occasionally faces counselors is changing the career development theories that one uses when one changes work setting. For example, if a counselor changes from a job in which he or she has worked with children to one in which he or she is working with adults, the career development theory that the counselor uses may be different in the two settings. Another duty of counselors is placement and job search counseling. The theories that have been discussed in this book have implications for helping people locate a job once they have decided about the career that they wish to pursue. Although these issues do not apply to all counselors, they do arise for many.

Group Career Counseling

The concepts and materials that career development theorists provide for counselors can be applied in most group settings. In his review of career group counseling, Kivlighan (1990) found that most studies of career groups revealed that a primary purpose was imparting information to clients. Other purposes included helping clients in self-understanding and in learning about others. Some features of group counseling that are not available in individual counseling are motivation from peers, an opportunity to learn from the experience of peers, and the opportunity to help and be helped by people who are in a similar situation. Also groups can be designed for specific populations, such as those with disabilities (Zunker, 1994), community-college students (Zagora & Cramer, 1994), and displaced homemakers (McAllister & Ponterotto, 1992). Herr and Cramer (1996) make similar recommendations. They find that role-playing certain situations and using a board game such as the Life Career Game, in which people can play different roles, are excellent group-career-counseling techniques. Whether the goal of career group counseling is career selection or work adjustment, career groups can fulfill many of the functions of individual career counseling.

Trait and factor theory can be adapted rather easily to a group counseling format. If using general trait and factor theory, the counselor must select the tests and inventories that will be used for the group. Interpretation of tests can be done in a group, with the counselor suggesting meanings of the test results, and other group members adding input. Similarly, the materials developed by Holland can be used in a group setting. Because they are particularly easy to understand, they can be used with clients with a wide range of ages and abilities. The Myers-Briggs Type Indicator is used widely in group settings, with both career and other issues or in structured exercises (Tieger & Barron-Tieger, 1992). In discussion, group members can give feedback to each other about their views of the person's type. Discussion of the kind of work setting that would fit a particular individual's type is often quite instructive. Although Lofquist and Dawis's work adjustment theory is often thought of in terms of individual vocational rehabilitation counseling, it, too, can be used in career groups. Administering the General Aptitude Test Battery and the Minnesota Importance Questionnaire for discussion and interpretation in a group may be quite conducive to exploration. However, the counselor needs to be prepared to make suggestions to the group as to which occupations would match their abilities and values.

Developmental theory can be used in several different ways in group counseling. With adolescents, career maturity issues, which include career planning, career exploration, and finding out about the world of work, can be a focus. Further, Super's (1990) rainbow enables adolescents to examine where they have been and what they might expect in the future. Looking behind and looking ahead can also apply to adults. Adults who are contemplating making career changes or are experiencing work adjustment problems may find it helpful to examine the importance of various roles in their life, such as worker, leisurite, citizen, and student. Looking at life roles in the context of the stages of exploration, establishment, maintenance, and disengagement can help clients see how they compare to other members of the group in terms of the similarity and the dissimilarity of their life situations, a process that will give them a sense of understanding about their life situation. Super's theory also supplies a context for understanding career crises such as firings and layoffs.

Career decision-making theory can be applied readily to the group process. In fact, Krumboltz and Hamel's *Guide to Career Decision-Making Skills* (1977) is designed for high school career groups. These materials use the DECIDES approach, which is described in Krumboltz's social learning theory (Chapter 13). The structured approach of the sequential elimination method can also be used in a group format, as can many other prescriptive models of career decision making. The less structured approach of Miller-Tiedeman (1989), which focuses on the human qualities of the decision maker, lends itself to a more process-oriented and affectively oriented career decision-making group.

Career Counseling as a Related Issue

For counselors who do career counseling infrequently or have clients who present work adjustment problems, certain theories may be particularly appropriate. In terms of trait and factor theories, the Myers-Briggs typology and Lofquist and Dawis's work adjustment theory may be particularly helpful. The former emphasizes perceiving and judging styles, whereas the latter emphasizes abilities and work-related values that directly correspond to job issues. These theories may provide useful insights into work adjustment difficulties, such as problems with colleagues or superiors and difficulties with job requirements. Another theory that is particularly helpful for working with career issues when they are a related concern is that of Super. By assessing how important the work role is in comparison to that of student, citizen, leisurite, and family member, the counselor can put career issues into a useful perspective. The career stages of Super also provide a way of understanding the kinds of work-related problems that adults experience. For children, Super's and Gottfredson's developmental theories can be particularly valuable, since they can be used to examine exploratory and sex-role behavior that other theories do not (see Figure 16-1 for a comparison).

Changing Work Settings

The ages and ability levels of the clients may determine the type of theory that the counselor chooses. For example, if a high school guidance counselor who has used Super's concepts of vocational maturity along with Holland's typology moves to a junior college setting, in which he or she is dealing with returning adult students, his or her choice of theory may change. The counselor may wish to use Myers-Briggs typological theory in addition to Holland's theory or may wish to replace Holland's theory with the work adjustment theory of Lofquist and Dawis. In general, counselors may be less likely to change their theory of counseling and/or psychotherapy when they move from one work setting to another, than to modify the career development theory that they use.

Placement Counseling

Most career development theorists have been more concerned with career selection and career adjustment than they have been with issues of finding a job. However, many authors have written job search books to help individuals find employment. Most notable of these is *What Color Is Your Parachute?* (Bolles, 1996). This book, which is updated each year, is designed for adult job hunters and career changers. It deals with issues such as finding out about the labor market, where jobs are, how to get leads, writing résumés, and conducting oneself during job interviews. Many writers, such as Bolles, emphasizes the importance of developing a network of people who can help in the job search. However, most advice is practical and not related to theory.

One exception is the work of Azrin and Besalel (1980), who have developed the concept of the "job club." This approach is based on the behavioral principle of positive reinforcement. Focusing on professionals who had lost jobs, Azrin developed a structured approach so that members of the job club could reinforce each other's progress in job seeking. The effectiveness of this approach has been shown by Mann and Svorai (1994) with young adults with modest cognitive impairments, with unemployed older workers (Rife & Belcher, 1994), and in a workfare setting (Stidham & Remley, 1992). The action-oriented approach of Azrin to getting a job once one has lost a job contrasts with the approach of Hopson and Adams (1977), which emphasizes understanding the stages of a crisis. Although these approaches are very different, they are not incompatible. Hopson and Adams provide a way of understanding a crisis that may help in knowing when is the best time to implement an action-oriented program such as that of Azrin.

The focus of Azrin is on looking for work when one has experienced a job crisis. The career development theories discussed in this book offer a way of viewing both crisis and more normal transitions that occur when individuals graduate from high school or college and then look for work.

One approach to finding a job can be extrapolated from Holland's theory. Often, people who are looking for work are encouraged to sell themselves to employers, to develop a network of contacts that can help them find a job, and to be assertive in their job search. This type of behavior is most similar to that of the Enterprising individual, who often enjoys persuading others and selling. The assertive approach recommended by many job search strategists may be more difficult for Realistic, Conventional, and Investigative types to employ. A counselor, when assisting a client in the job search process, may wish to consider his or her client's Holland type and how that person can develop an appropriate job search strategy.

Using the Myers-Briggs typology, individuals who deal with the outer world (extraversion) may be more comfortable in using assertive job search strategies than those who deal with the inner world (introversion). Similarly, those individuals who take a sensing approach to finding information about job openings may have a very different style from those who take an intuiting approach. For example, those who acquire information about the job market based on intuition may exaggerate the difficulties that they are facing.

Super's concept of role salience can be helpful in career placement counseling. Clients vary as to how much they value the worker role in contrast to that of student, leisurite, citizen, or homemaker. This notion of role provides an opportunity to put the entire context of the job search into perspective. The stage theory of Super also provides a broader context within which to view job search strategies. The job search process itself fits within the specifying and implementing substages of the exploration stage.

Career decision-making theory offers yet another perspective on job search strategies. The adjustment stage of Tiedeman and O'Hara (1963) provides an interesting subjective view of the job search process. The first substage, induction, highlights the importance of change in an individual's life and the uncertainty surrounding the change that occurs during the job search process. Reformation concerns not the job-hunting process, but the initial reaction to the job once one has been hired. This phase deals with adjustment to work and to new colleagues. Finally, the integration substage describes moving away from the newness of a job to other aspects in one's life and other career possibilities.

In contrast to the individualistic perspective of Tiedeman and Miller-Tiedeman is the DECIDES approach of Krumboltz. The final stage, starting action, involves actually starting to look for work. Since the job-hunting process is often seen by an individual as a process of many rejections, the cognitive and behavioral approach of Krumboltz can be useful. Reinforcing the job search process itself, rather than its outcome, is an important part of the starting-action phase. Because individuals may be discouraged as they start to look for work, attending to inaccurate beliefs and correcting them is part of the role of the counselor using social learning theory. These perspectives and those of other career development theorists offer an interesting approach to the job search process that is different from the pragmatic approach of most job search books.

TEST USE IN THEORIES

Career development theories vary as to the importance of tests in the conceptualization of client career problems. In general, trait and factor theories rely more heavily on test use than does life-span theory, which in turn uses tests more than career decision-making theories. A comparison of test use is provided in Table 16-1, listing the trait, factor, or characteristic measured for theories described in this book.

Part of the success of trait and factor theory relies on the ability of test developers to accurately measure traits and factors such as aptitudes, interests, values, and personality. General trait and factor theory requires that career counselors select tests that are reliable and valid. Matching the measured traits and factors of a client with characteristics of a job is the essence of applying trait and factor theory. Holland's typological theory also measures traits and factors but categorizes them into six types that are then matched with environmental types. There are several inventories, such as the Strong Interest Inventory, that provide scores for the six types. In addition, Holland's Vocational Preference Inventory and Self-Directed Search are designed to provide scores for the six types so that matching can occur with occupational environments. The Myers-Briggs Type Indicator gives information to the counselor about the personality type of the client. Those counselors who use the Myers-Briggs type theory in their work rely heavily on the Myers-Briggs Type Indicator to assess personality style. Perhaps the most precise use of testing occurs in work adjustment theory. Client scores on the General Aptitude Test Battery and the Minnesota Importance Questionnaire are matched with the ability patterns and needs and values reinforcer patterns of over 1,700 occupations. It is fair to conclude that, without accurate measurement of traits and factors, there would be no trait and factor theory.

For life-span theory, testing serves the purpose of identifying important developmental issues that individuals must face. Super's Career Development Inventory assesses the developmental phase of career maturity. Super's Adult Career Concerns Inventory assesses the extent to which adults are concerned about issues relating to the exploration, establishment, maintenance, or disengagement stage, or to any of the substages. In general, inventories that measure developmental tasks or stages are less precise than those that measure traits and factors. The reason is that life-span issues are broader and less predictable than measurements of aptitudes or interests. However, such instruments can still be useful in conceptualizing career concerns.

Career decision-making theory focuses on the process of selecting occupations. Although testing is often a part of this process, it is a secondary focus, whereas for trait and factor theory it is a primary focus. The subjective approach of Tiedeman and Miller-Tiedeman in their individualistic perspective is more concerned with the client's internal experience of decision-making issues than with more objective methods of measuring the process. The Assessment of Career Decision-Making Scale (Buck & Daniels, 1985) measures some of the concepts of Tiedeman and O'Hara's (1963) theory of decision making. However, this instrument is quite different from the approach taken by Miller-Tiedeman (1988, 1989) in her work on LIFECAREER®. In contrast, Gati's (1986) sequential elimination method can make use of testing in identifying important aspects of occupations and ranking them prior to eliminating occupations whose characteristics do not seem appropriate to the individual. For Krumboltz, values inventories can help individuals in the process of clarifying values. Aptitude tests and interest inventories can help in identifying alternatives and in discovering probable outcomes of these alternatives. In addition, the Career Beliefs

Inventory provides assistance in assessing inaccurate beliefs that clients may have that interfere with the career decision-making process. Thus, for career decision-making theories, as well as for other theories of career development, the purpose of the theory and the role of testing are highly related.

OCCUPATIONAL CLASSIFICATION SYSTEMS AND CAREER DEVELOPMENT THEORIES

The development of classification systems for occupations has been associated with trait and factor theory because occupations must be classified so that they can be matched with measured traits and factors of individuals. The focus of various classification systems differs widely. For comparison, Table 16-2 lists the groupings used in three classification systems (Roe's, the *Dictionary of Occupational Titles,* and the *Guide for Occupational Exploration*) and cross-classifies them by Holland's system. This provides an opportunity to see how the four systems relate to each other. Roe's eight groupings are somewhat similar to those of Holland, with some overlap. The 12 categories of the *Guide for Occupational Exploration* represent a more detailed categorization system than Holland's. The 17,000 occupations listed in the *Dictionary of Occupational Titles* have as their primary classification the eight categories listed in Table 16-2. The predominance of Realistic occupations in this first level of the *Dictionary of Occupational Titles* categorization is indicative of the large number of Realistic occupations in the definitions. The *Dictionary of Holland Occupational Codes* provides a Holland code identification for each of the occupations listed in the *Dictionary of Occupational Titles.* How career development theories make use of classification systems is the subject of this section.

As previously stated, classification systems are essential for use in trait and factor theory. Those counselors who use a general trait and factor theory can choose from classification systems that fit the tests and inventories they wish to use in counseling. For Holland's theory, it is essential to use his classification system. Although Roe's personality system may not be viewed as a trait and factor theory, the part of the theory that describes the classification system does fit with trait and factor theory. The California Occupational Preference Inventory, for example, uses Roe's classification system, as do several other inventories. On the other hand, work adjustment theory categorizes occupations according to the system of the *Dictionary of Occupational Titles.* In general, the theories or tests that counselors select are likely to dictate the classification system that the counselor will use.

For life-span theory, classification systems become important when career selections are to be made. When that occurs, life-span theorists

Table 16-2 *Comparison of Holland's Classification System to Three Other Systems**

Roe's Groups	*Dictionary of Occupational Titles*	*Guide for Occupational Exploration*
Service (S, R)	Professional, technical, and managerial occupations (A, E, I, S)	Artistic (A)
Business contact (E)	Clerical and sales occupations (C, E)	Scientific (I, R)
Organizations (E, C)	Service occupations (S, R)	Plants and animals (I, R)
Technology (R, I)	Agricultural, fishery, forestry, and related occupations (R)	Protective (S, R)
Outdoor (R, I)	Processing occupations (R)	Mechanical (I, R)
Science (I, R)	Machine trades occupations (R)	Industrial (R)
General cultural (A)	Benchwork occupations (R)	Business detail (E)
Arts and entertainment (A)	Structural work occupations (R)	Selling (E)
	Miscellaneous occupations	Accommodating (S, E, R)
		Humanitarian (S)
		Leading-influencing (E)
		Physical-performance (A)

*Letters in parentheses represent the Holland code that roughly corresponds to the occupational grouping: (R) Realistic, (I) Investigative, (A) Artistic, (S) Social, (E) Enterprising, and (C) Conventional.

incorporate developmental concepts as well as trait and factor theory. Therefore, life-span theorists are likely to make use of classification systems in the same way as trait and factor theorists.

For career decision-making theorists, the selection of tests and inventories, which may be a secondary part of counseling, will determine the occupational classification system to be used. The classification of occupations is not a major emphasis of career decision-making theorists.

HOW THEORIES APPLY TO CAREER DEVELOPMENT ISSUES OF WOMEN

Much of the information about the career development of women has come from life-span theory rather than from trait and factor or career decision-making theory. It is life-span theory that draws attention to sex-role issues that affect career development in childhood, adolescence, and adulthood. Knowledge of sex-role stereotyping and sex-role issues of women in various stages of their lives can help in work adjustment and career selection. In contrast, the information available from trait and factor and career decsion-making theories about gender differences is minimal. However, the recent research on career self-efficacy theory as it affects women is a notable exception.

With regard to trait and factor theory, some research shows differences in the interests and abilities of men and women. It is often difficult to separate learned from genetic characteristics. For example, if women do more poorly than men in math, is that poor performance due to a lack of innate ability or to socialization that women should not be as good in math as men are? Research reviewed in Part Two suggests that it is the latter. Similarly, in Holland's typology, women predominate in the Social and Artistic areas. This is a reflection of socialization rather than misclassification in using Holland's system. This information should not be used to suggest that women whose personalities are Realistic or Investigative are in some way aberrant and should be considering other occupations. There are some differences between the scores of men and women on the Minnesota Importance Questionnaire, which is an important component of work adjustment theory. Lofquist and Dawis suggest that it is the individual's needs that are important, not those of women or men in general. A similar conclusion can be reached about the Myers-Briggs typology. Although women tend to predominate in the feeling category and men in the thinking category (Myers, 1962), this fact may have few implications for individual counseling. The fact that men and women in general may differ on various traits and factors cannot be generalized to the individual client, who may have interests, aptitudes, and personality patterns that are atypical of those of other women.

With regard to career decision-making theories, there are some findings useful in the counseling of women. In his social learning theory, Krumboltz emphasizes the importance of role models for women. He points out that, although groups such as women may have limited control over environmental conditions, there are ways through collective action that cultural biases such as sex discrimination can be changed. Another social learning theory, career self-efficacy theory, investigates how environmental factors affect the way women learn about their academic and career competencies in the process of making career choices. The descriptive approach of Tiedeman and Miller-Tiedeman and the prescriptive approach of Gati focus on the

decision-making process rather than emphasize issues of sex role. That is not to say that these theorists consider sex-role stereotyping unimportant.

Examining the life-span development of women was a major focus of the chapters in Part Two. Gottfredson's attention to the impact of sex role on career choice at ages 6 to 8 has been instrumental in emphasizing that the career choices that men and women make in their adolescence and adulthood are different. Gottfredson's theories of circumscription and compromise are useful in highlighting these differences. Betz and Fitzgerald (1987) discuss the impact of the educational system on sex-role stereotyping of adolescent women. In adulthood, the career development of women is often more varied than that of men, with family and child-care considerations leading to varied patterns of leaving and reentering the labor force. In addition to these concerns, women are far more likely than men to face sexual harassment issues in the workplace. Knowledge of these issues can help counselors provide an enlightened approach to working with women who have career choice or work adjustment problems.

HOW THEORIES APPLY TO CAREER DEVELOPMENT ISSUES OF PEOPLE OF COLOR

In general, there has been much less research on the career development of people of color than on that of women. One reason is that there are a large number of cultural groups. In the United States, much research has focused on differences between African Americans and whites. Trait and factor theory, as well as career decision-making theory, has provided relatively little information about varying characteristics of people of color. One difficulty in interpreting the research in trait and factor theory is that it is important not to apply generalizations about the interests, aptitudes, and personalities of a group to an individual client. Social learning theory emphasizes environmental influences on self-efficacy and the importance of role models who have the same cultural background as the client. Other career decision-making theories do not focus on cultural background.

Perhaps the life-span perspective has the most to say about issues affecting people of color. In general, children of color may be prevented from, or may have limited access to, exploratory activities that help them acquire information that leads to career maturity. Smith (1983) suggests that high aspirations of adolescents of color are often thwarted because of limited access to educational and occupational opportunities. Research discussed in Chapter 15 suggests that adolescents of color are more likely to find jobs in the secondary labor market and to encounter job discrimination. Negative attitudes toward work can be the result of a historical pattern of experiencing discrimination from one generation to another. The work of Vondracek and his colleagues emphasizes the importance for counselors of being aware not only of the individual's development but also of the context of the individual's historical and social situation. The minority identity development model of Atkinson, Morten, and Sue (1989) can be helpful to counselors in understanding how people of color may react to a variety of work situations. Their model suggests that people of color may start in a stage of conformity and move through dissonance, resistance, emergence, and introspection to a stage of synergetic articulation and awareness. This theory is useful in understanding how minorities relate to their own group as well as to the majority group. Although not a model of career development, it has direct applicability to issues of job selection and work adjustment.

The need for counselors to attend to issues of women and people of color in career development is highlighted by the research of sociologists and economists. They document, over and over again, that women and people of color receive less pay than white men for equal work and are often denied access to jobs that are likely to lead to advancement and higher pay. The sociological and economic theories of career development draw conclusions about broad groups from their studies of large numbers of people. However, for the individual counselor, their research is a reminder to look for attitudes within oneself that may hinder the career development of a client who is female or of another ethnic group.

COUNSELOR ISSUES

Career development theories not only provide a means of conceptualizing the client's concerns but also suggest a perspective on client-counselor issues. From a trait and factor point of view, it is often helpful to look at the traits and factors of the client and compare them to those of the counselor. In a life-span perspective, a contrast between the counselor's life stage and that of the client can be helpful in counseling situations. With regard to decision-making theories, being aware of the contrast between the decision-making style and progress of the client and that of the counselor can be instructive.

Trait and Factor Theories

In general, when using trait and factor theory, it is helpful for the counselor to be aware that the abilities, aptitudes, personality, values, and interests of the client are likely to be very different from those of the counselor. Appreciating a wide range of interests, abilities, and values can be helpful to the counselor in working with many problems.

From the point of view of Holland's typology, the less congruent the counselor's type is with the client's type, the more likely it is that the counselor will have to deal with a value conflict. For example, a counselor who

is primarily Social in orientation may not enjoy organizing and working with numbers as does a person who is Conventional.

With regard to the Myers-Briggs typological theory, researchers (Yeakley, 1983) point out the importance of using a communication style that is similar to that of the client. For example, if the counselor's primary way of perceiving is through sensing and the client's way of perceiving is through intuiting, each will be looking at events from a different point of view. It is important for the counselor to adapt to or understand the client's communication style.

Lofquist and Dawis, in their theory of work adjustment, view the client and the counselor as serving as environments for each other. As environments, they reinforce each other and meet each other's needs in different ways. Being aware of both his or her own needs and those of the client can help the counselor in offering appropriate reinforcers for the client. For example, if the client has a need for responsibility, it may be helpful for the counselor to let the client act independently and make little acknowledgment of the counseling process in order to achieve a satisfactory result. This may mean sacrificing the counselor's own altruistic needs. Although trait and factor theory is generally not thought of as encompassing approaches that have an impact on the client-counselor relationship, it is clear that all of these theories can be viewed in this manner.

Life-Span Theories

Life-span theory draws attention to the different roles and stages of the client and the counselor. For example, a 65-year-old person who is counseling a 15-year-old is working with someone whose interests, exploratory behavior, and self-concept are at relatively early stages. For the counselor, focusing on the client's issues and not on his or her own will cross the large generational gap. Similarly, counselors often work with clients in crises. Knowing that each individual in each crisis is different will help the counselor to refrain from applying his or her own experience with a crisis to that of the client. Also, being aware of sex-role issues when the client is of the other sex can help the counselor focus on the needs and issues of the client. For example, being aware of a client's early experiences with sex bias in school may affect how the counselor assists the client with career selection issues.

Career Decision-Making Theories

Implications of career decision-making theories for counselors vary. Krumboltz and Baker (1973) point out that counselors using social learning theory should be careful that their counseling skills match the needs of the client. Further, they believe it is important for client and counselor to have mutually agreeable goals. If a counselor is expert in working with a specific type of client but chooses to work with a very different type of client, that behavior may be unethical. A counselor who uses the individualistic perspective of Tiedeman and Miller-Tiedeman needs to be clear about the subjective experience of career decision making of the client, which may be vastly different from that of the counselor. Appreciating the client's unique individuality is one of the main goals of the individualistic perspective on career decision making. In contrast, the prescriptive approach, as exemplified by the sequential elimination method, may be so structured that the counselor needs to be certain that the structure does not preclude discussion of matters affecting career choice that do not fit into it.

Sociological and Economic Approaches

The implications of sociological and economic perspectives on career choice are quite different from those of the psychological approaches. Sociological and economic research on career development factors points out the many inequalities that exist for people of color and women as they deal with the labor market. Rather than assume that these apply to each client, the counselor can use this information as background from which to evaluate the client's individual issues. Further, the research of sociologists and economists into race and gender issues can serve as a guide to evaluating one's own values and prejudices.

CONCLUSION

The theories that have been discussed in this book provide useful approaches to problems of career choice and work adjustment. In many cases, the theorists and many of their colleagues have spent 20, 30, or more years developing, evaluating, and refining their theories. Through research and evaluation, they have modified and strengthened their work, at the same time providing new and better tests and inventories for counselors to use. In addition, new theorists have developed perspectives and insights into the career-development-choice process that provide new ways for counselors to view their clients. The continuing research into and the development of revised and new theories is evidence that career development theory will continue to offer new and better tools and ideas for counselors to use. Implicit in the work of these theorists and researchers is the importance that they attribute to careers and career problems. They have great respect for the role of the counselor, whose work can significantly improve the client's satisfaction with his or her life.

References

Atkinson, D. R., Morten, G., & Sue, D. W. (1989). *Counseling American minorities: A cross cultural perspective* (3rd ed.). Dubuque, IA: W. C. Brown.

Azrin, N. H., & Besalel, V. A. (1980). *Job club counselor's manual: A behavioral approach to vocational counseling.* Baltimore: University Park Press.

Betz, N. E., & Fitzgerald, L. F. (1987). *The career psychology of women.* Orlando, FL: Academic Press.

Bolles, R. N. (1996). *What color is your parachute?* (26th ed.). San Francisco: Ten Speed Press.

Buck, J. N., & Daniels, M. H. (1985). *Assessment of career-decision making manual.* Los Angeles: Western Psychological Services.

Crites, J. O. (1978). *Theory and research handbook for the career maturity inventory.* Monterey, CA: CTB, McGraw-Hill.

Gati, I. (1986). Making career decisions—A sequential elimination approach. *Journal of Counseling Psychology, 33,* 408–417.

Ginzberg, E., Ginsburg, S. W., Axelrad, S., & Herma, J. (1951). *Occupational choice: An approach to a general theory.* New York: Columbia University Press.

Gottfredson, L. S. (1996). A theory of circumscription and compromise. In D. Brown, L. Brooks & Assoc. (Eds.), *Career choice and development: Applying contemporary theories to practice* (3rd ed.). San Francisco: Jossey-Bass.

Harris-Bowlsbey, J. (1984). The computer and career development. *Journal of Counseling and Development, 63,* 145–148.

Herr, E. L., & Cramer, S. H. (1996). *Career guidance through the life span* (5th ed.). New York: Harper Collins.

Holland, J. L. (1985). *You and your career.* Odessa, FL: Psychological Assessment Resources.

Holland, J. L. (1992). *Making vocational choices: A theory of vocational personalities and work environments.* Odessa, FL: Psychological Assessment Resources.

Hopson, B., & Adams, J. D. (1977). Towards an understanding of transitions: Defining some boundaries of transition. In J. Adams, J. Hayes, & B. Hopson (Eds.), *Transition: Understanding and managing personal change.* Montclair, NJ: Allenheld & Osmun.

Kivlighan, D. M. (1990). Career group therapy. *The Counseling Psychologist, 18,* 64–79.

Krumboltz, J. D., & Baker, R. D. (1973). Behavioral counseling for vocational decision. In H. Borow (Ed.), *Career guidance for a new age* (pp. 235–284). Boston: Houghton Mifflin.

Krumboltz, J. D., & Hamel, D. A. (1977). *Guide to career decision-making skills.* New York: Educational Testing Service.

Lenz, J. G., Reardon, C., & Sampson, J. P. (1993). Holland's theory and effective use of computer assisted career guidance systems. *Journal of Career Development, 19,* 245–253.

Mann, W. C., & Svorai, S. B. (1994). COMPETE: A model for vocational evaluation, training, employment, and community for integration for persons with cognitive impairments. *American Journal of Occupational Therapy, 48,* 446–451.

McAllister, S., & Ponterotto, J. G. (1992). A career group program for displaced homemakers. *Journal for Specialists in Group Work, 17,* 29–36.

Miller-Tiedeman, A. L. (1988). *LIFECAREER: The quantum leap into a process of career.* Vista, CA: Lifecareer Foundation.

Miller-Tiedeman, A. L. (1989). *How to NOT make it . . . and succeed: The truth about your LIFECAREER.* Vista, CA: Lifecareer Foundation.

Miller-Tiedeman, A. L., & Tiedeman, D. V. (1990). Career decision-making: An individualistic perspective: In D. Brown, L. Brooks, & Assoc. (Eds.), *Career choice and development* (2nd ed., pp. 308–377). San Francisco: Jossey-Bass.

Mitchell, L. K., & Krumboltz, J. D. (1990). Social learning approach to career decision making: Krumboltz's theory. In D. Brown, L. Brooks, & Assoc. (Eds.), *Career choice and development* (2nd ed, pp. 308–337). San Francisco: Jossey-Bass.

Myers, I. B. (1962). *Manual: The Myers Briggs Type Indicator.* Princeton, NJ: Educational Testing Service.

Peterson, G. W., Ryan-Jones, R. E., Sampson, J. P., & Reardon, R. C. (1994). A comparison of the effectiveness of three computer assisted career guidance systems: DISCOVER, SIGI, and SIGI PLUS. *Computers in Human Behavior, 1,* 189–198.

Rayman, J. R. (1990). Computers and career counseling. In W. B. Walsh & S. H. Osipow (Eds.), *Career counseling: Contemporary topics in vocational psychology* (pp. 225–262). Hillsdale, NJ: Erlbaum.

Rife, J. C., & Belcher, J. R. (1994). Assisting unemployed older workers to become reemployed: An experimental evaluation. *Research on Social Work Practice, 4,* 3–13.

Smith, E. J. (1983). Issues in racial minorities; career behavior. In W. B. Walsh & S. H. Osipow (Eds.), *Handbook of vocational psychology* (Vol. 1, pp. 161–222). Hillsdale, NJ: Erlbaum.

Stidham, H. H., & Remley, T. P., Jr. (1992). Job club methodology applied in a workfare setting. *Journal of Employment Counseling, 29,* 69–76.

Super, D. E. (1990). A life-span, life-space approach to career development. In D. Brown, L. Brooks, & Assoc. (Eds.), *Career choice and development* (2nd ed., pp. 197–261). San Francisco: Jossey-Bass.

Super, D. E., Bohn, M. J., Forrest, D. J., Jordaan, J. P., Lindeman, R. H., & Thompson, A. S. (1971). *Career Development Inventory.* New York: Teachers College, Columbia University.

Thompson, A. S., & Lindeman, R. H. (1981). *Career Development Inventory, Vol. 1: User's manual.* Palo Alto, CA: Consulting Psychologists Press.

Tiedeman, D. V., & O'Hara, R. P. (1963). *Career development: Choice and adjustment.* New York: College Entrance Examination Board.

Tieger, P. D., & Barron-Tieger, B. (1992). *Do what you are: Discover the perfect career for you through the secrets of personality type.* Boston: Little, Brown.

Yeakley, F. R. (1983). Implications of communication style research for psychological type theory. *Research in Psychological Type, 6,* 5–23.

Zagora, M. A., & Cramer, S. H. (1994). The effects of vocational identity status on outcomes of a career decision-making intervention for community college students. *Journal of College Student Development, 35,* 239–247.

Zunker, V. G. (1994). *Career counseling: Applied concepts of life planning* (4th ed.). Pacific Grove, CA: Brooks/Cole.

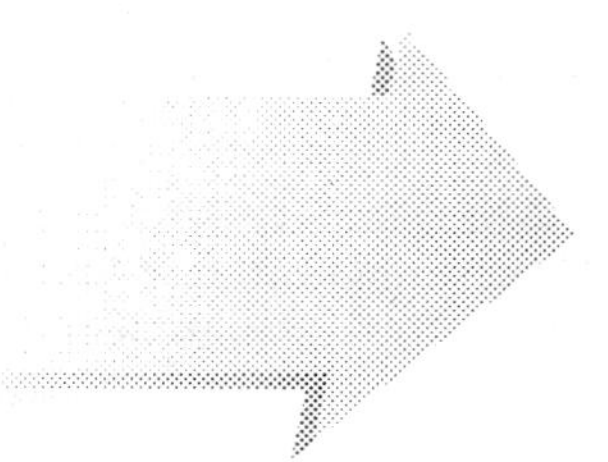

Appendix: Tests and Their Publishers

Test or Inventory	*Publisher or Distributor*
ACT Assessment Program: Academic Tests	American College Testing Program
Adult Career Concerns Inventory	Consulting Psychologists Press
Armed Services Vocational Aptitude Battery	U.S. Military Entrance Processing Command
Assessment of Career Decision Making	Western Psychological Services
California Occupational Preference Survey	Educational and Industrial Testing Service
California Psychological Inventory	Consulting Psychologists Press
Career Beliefs Inventory	Consulting Psychologists Press
Career Decision Scale	Psychological Assessment Resources
Career Development Inventory	Consulting Psychologists Press
Career Maturity Inventory	Chronicle Guidance Publications
Differential Aptitude Tests	Psychological Corporation
General Aptitude Test Battery	U.S. Employment Service
Job Experience Kits	Science Research Associates
Kuder Preference Record	Science Research Associates
Minnesota Importance Questionnaire	Vocational Psychology Research
Minnesota Job Description Questionnaire	Vocational Psychology Research
Minnesota Multiphasic Personality Inventory	National Computer Systems
Minnesota Satisfaction Questionnaire	Vocational Psychology Research
Minnesota Satisfactoriness Scales	Vocational Psychology Research
Myers-Briggs Type Indicator	Consulting Psychologists Press
Rorschach	Psychological Assessment Resources
Salience Inventory	Consulting Psychologists Press
Scholastic Assessment Test	Educational Testing Service
Self-Directed Search	Psychological Assessment Resources
Sixteen Personality Factor Questionnaire	Institute for Personality and Ability Testing
Strong Interest Inventory	Consulting Psychologists Press
Study of Values	Houghton Mifflin
Thematic Apperception Test	Harvard University Press

Values Scale	Consulting Psychologists Press
Vocational Interest Inventory	Western Psychological Services
Vocational Preference Inventory	Psychological Assessment Resources

Publishers' Addresses

American College Testing Program, P.O. Box 168, Iowa City, IA 52243

Chronicle Guidance Publications, P.O. Box 1190, Moravia, NY 13118-1190

Consulting Psychologists Press, 3803 East Bayshore Road, Palo Alto, CA 94303

Educational and Industrial Testing Service, P.O. Box 7234, San Diego, CA 92107

Educational Testing Service, P.O. Box 6736, Princeton, NJ 08541-6736

Harvard University Press, 79 Garden Street, Cambridge, MA 02138

Houghton Mifflin Company, One Beacon Street, Boston, MA 02108

Institute for Personality and Ability Testing, P.O. Box 188, Champaign, IL 61820-0188

National Computer Systems, P.O. Box 1416, Minneapolis, MN 55440

Psychological Assessment Resources, P.O. Box 998, Odessa, FL 33556

Psychological Corporation, 555 Academic Court, San Antonio, TX 78204-2498

Science Research Associates, 155 North Wacker Drive, Chicago, IL 60606

U.S. Employment Service, Division of Program Planning and Operations, Employment and Training Administration, U.S. Department of Labor, 601 D Street N.W., Washington, DC 20213

U.S. Military Entrance Processing Command, Testing Directorate, 2500 Green Bay Road, North Chicago, IL 60064

Vocational Psychology Research, Department of Psychology, University of Minnesota, 75 East River Road, Minneapolis, MN 55455

Western Psychological Services, 12031 Wilshire Boulevard, Los Angeles, CA 90025

Name Index

Subject Index

TO THE OWNER OF THIS BOOK:

I hope that you have found *Applying Career Development Theory to Counseling,* Second Edition, useful. So that this book can be improved in a future edition, would you take the time to complete this sheet and return it? Thank you.

School and address: ______________________________

Department: ______________________________

Instructor's name: ______________________________

1. What I like most about this book is: ______________________________

____

____

2. What I like least about this book is: ______________________________

____

____

3. My general reaction to this book is: ______________________________

____

4. The name of the course in which I used this book is: ______________________________

____

5. Were all of the chapters of the book assigned for you to read? ______________________________

If not, which ones weren't? ______________________________

6. In the space below, or on a separate sheet of paper, please write specific suggestions for improving this book and anything else you'd care to share about your experience in using the book.

____

____

____

____

Optional:

Your name: ______________________ Date: ______________________

May Brooks/Cole quote you, either in promotion for *Applying Career Development Theory to Counseling,* Second Edition, or in future publishing ventures?

Yes: __________ No: __________

Sincerely,

Richard S. Sharf

FOLD HERE

NO POSTAGE NECESSARY IF MAILED IN THE UNITED STATES

BUSINESS REPLY MAIL

FIRST CLASS PERMIT NO. 358 PACIFIC GROVE, CA

POSTAGE WILL BE PAID BY ADDRESSEE

ATT: *Richard S. Sharf*

Brooks/Cole Publishing Company
511 Forest Lodge Road
Pacific Grove, California 93950-9968

FOLD HERE